THE
CHILD in
JEWISH
HISTORY

THE CHILD in JEWISH HISTORY

JOHN COOPER

JASON ARONSON INC.
Northvale, New Jersey
London

This book was set in 11 pt. Souvenir by Alpha Graphics of Pittsfield, New Hampshire.

Permissions for excerpted materials are listed in the Credits section at the back of the book.

10 9 8 7 6 5 4 3 2 1

Library of Congress Cataloging-in-Publication Data

Cooper, John, 1935–
    The child in Jewish History / John Cooper.
        p.   cm.
    Includes bibliographical references and index.
    ISBN 1-56821-956-3 (alk. paper)
        1. Jewish religious education of children—History.   2. Child
    rearing—Religious aspects—Judaism—History.   3. Jewish children—
    History.   I. Title.
    BM103.C65   1996
    305.23'089'924—dc20   96-9603
                                                             CIP

Manufactured in the United States of America. Jason Aronson Inc. offers books and cassettes. For information and catalog write to Jason Aronson Inc., 230 Livingston Street, Northvale, New Jersey 07647.

To Judy
and our children
Flower and Zaki
with Love

Contents

Acknowledgments

I would like to thank Professor Samuel Kottek for reading through the first four chapters of my book, and saving me from a number of pitfalls. I am further indebted to him for permitting me to use his translation of passages from *Sefer Hasidim* relating to the upbringing of children. I should also like to acknowledge the help of Rose Bennett, Professor Eoin Bourke, Arieh Handler, Chaim Klein, the late Rabbi Dr. S. B. Leperer, Ethel Levine, Professor Steven Lowenstein, Professor Ivan G. Marcus, Carole Malkin, Nilda Maxwell, Chaya Melamed, Rabbi Samuel Rodrigues-Pereira, Aubrey Silverstone, Dr. Norman Solomon, and Judith Vandervelde. In addition, I would like to thank Fred Worms for his assistance and Marc Herman of the Maccabi Union for allowing me to utilise Micah Gold's two reports on Jewish youth. I am also grateful to Professor David Caesarani, Dr. George Eisen and Rabbi Dr. Jacob J. Schacter for permitting me to use material from their doctoral theses, and to Rabbi Dr. Schacter for allowing me to quote his translation of several autobiographical passages of Rabbi Jacob Emden. My brother, Rabbi Dr. Martin Cooper, has been a constant source of encouragement and help, obtaining material for me which I could not find elsewhere.

If there are any errors of fact or judgement in the book, these faults are mine alone.

My sincere thanks to Ezra Kahn, the librarian of Jews' College, London, and his assistants. Also Dr. Piet van Boxel and Roy Segal, the librarians of Leo Baeck College, all of whom took such trouble to answer my inquiries, along with the staffs of the British Library, the H. U. C. Library in Jerusalem, the Jewish National Library, the Yad Izhak Ben-Zvi, and Rickie Burman, Carol Siegel, and Debbie Seedburgh of The Jewish Museum, London. To Rickie Burman and Carol Siegel I am grateful for permission to quote from the Jewish Museum's transcripts of oral history interviews.

My deep gratitude to Arthur Kurzweil for supporting this project, which is a venture into new territory for Jewish historians, and special thanks to the editors Tony Rubin and Suzanne Davidson for the care which they have lavished on the manuscript.

My wife Judy and children, Flower and Zaki, have provided a loving and stimulating environment while I was carrying out the research and writing of this book. The completed volume is a token of my thanks.

Foreword

The gifted curator of a recent exhibition on "Jews and Medicine" at the Tel Aviv Museum of the Jewish Diaspora inserted as a motto to her essay published in the catalogue (entitled "Why Medicine")[1] the old humorous tale: A Jewish mother is walking down the street with her two young boys. A passerby asks her how old they are. "The doctor is three," the mother answers, "and the lawyer is two years old."

Being myself both a medical historian and a pediatrician, I can readily attest that the centrality of child-rearing in Jewish lore has always been, and remains, undisputed. This was already expressed by the Psalmist: "Your wife shall be like a fruitful wine in the recesses of your house; your children like olive plants around your table . . . And you shall see your children's children, and peace upon Israel" [Psalm 128: 3–6].

The Jewish people is generally addressed in the Bible as "the Children of Israel," originally a reference to the twelve sons of Jacob/Israel, who became the Twelve Tribes from which the people ultimately developed.

---

1. Natalia Berger: "Why Medicine?" In *Jews and Medicine; Religion, Culture, Science.* Tel Aviv: Museum of the Jewish Diaspora, 1995, pp. 13–31.

Among the numerous terms used in Hebrew for children, one is probably the most descriptive and true to life: *Na'ar* (fem. *na'arah*). Most lexicographers derive it from the root *na'er*: To stir, to shake, to move. Indeed, movement is a characteristic feature of the child, and was in ancient times a characterization of life. As in Greek (*paîs*) and in Latin (*puēr*), the Hebrew *na'ar* was also used to designate a servant, a page. I have once remarked[2] that the apparent antinomy between an etymology implying agitation and effervescence, and a sense of obedience and submission, may be particularly appropriate and complementary when describing children.

It is stated in the Bible, on the one hand: "You are the children of the Lord your God" [Deut. 14:1]. On the other hand, we read: For to me the children of Israel are servants: they are my servants . . . I am the Lord your God" [Levit. 25: 55]. Children and servants, loving and obedient: the way children should react toward their Father.

"The Child in Jewish History," or perhaps one could have entitled this research "The Child in Jewish Lore." John Cooper has indeed produced a thorough study on the way in which children were reared and educated in ancient Israel and in the talmudic age. He has extended his research to the Middle Ages, the Early Modern period, and well into modern times, particularly in Britain and in America.

Since William M. Feldman (1880–1939), no comprehensive study has been published, to our knowledge, on childhood in Jewish sources.[3] We feel that we could aptly apply to the work of John Cooper what Sir James Crichton-Browne (1840–1938) wrote in his brief introduction to Feldman's book:

"[Cooper]'s book on the Jewish Child is a work of unique scholarship, of deep scientific insight, of perfect lucidity, and of great literary charm" [p. xxiii].

And quoting again from the Psalmist:

> . . . Children are a heritage of the Lord
> And the fruit of the womb is a reward.
>   [Psalm 127: 3]

---

2. Cf. my essay "On Children and Childhood in Ancient Jewish Sources (A study in philological anthropology)". *Koroth* 9 (1987) 5–6, pp. 452*–471*. This quote on p. 456*.

3. W. M. Feldman: *The Jewish Child; Its History, Folklore, Biology & Sociology.* London: Baillière, Tindall & Cox, 1917.

Rewarding as well is the fruit of Cooper's research.

Samuel S. Kottek, M.D.
The Harry Friedenwald Chair of Medical History
The Hebrew University-Hadassah Medical School
Jerusalem

Introduction

The publication by the French historian Philippe Ariès of *Centuries of Childhood* in Britain and America in 1962, followed by a volume of essays edited by Lloyd deMause in 1974, started a new genre: the history of childhood. In particular Ariès constructed a totally new model of this history, based on the assumption that there was little caring interaction between parents and their offspring until the sixteenth century or later, that the concepts of childhood and adolescence did not exist before the Early Modern period, and that until then the death of young children was received with callous indifference by their parents because it was so frequent. According to Ariès, prior to the Enlightenment children were treated as "little adults." Even adolescence was a recent invention. "The first typical adolescent of modern times was Wagner's *Siegfried*; the music . . . expressed for the first time that combination of (provisional) purity, physical strength, naturism, spontaneity and *joie de vivre* which was to make the adolescent the hero of our twentieth century, the century of adolescence." In the key essay in the collection *The History of Childhood* (1974), which Lloyd deMause wrote, he maintained that the child was subjected to dan-

1

gerous projections by adults until the eighteenth century and was treated with cruelty. He was swaddled, sent to a wet nurse far from home, often purged with enemas, regularly whipped, and sometimes abandoned. Since the works of Ariès and Lloyd deMause appeared, their assumptions have been vigorously debated and frequently overturned by other historians, but nevertheless their ideas are still stimulating and must be taken into consideration when outlining an alternative approach.[1]

This volume sets out to adumbrate some tentative answers to the issues raised by Ariès and Lloyd deMause for the history of Jewish childhood; and to construct a history around some of the themes first selected by them, such as breast-feeding by mothers as opposed to wet-nursing, swaddling and its disappearance, the attitudes toward the death of children, infanticide and the abandonment of children, punishment in the home and school, and so on. To explore this subject is not to ignore some of the pioneering researches in this field by Jewish historians, namely, Leopold Löw's *Die Lebensalter in Der Jüdischen Literatur* (1875), William Feldman's *The Jewish Child: Its History, Folklore, Biology & Sociology* (1917), and Regina Lilientalowa's *Dziecko Zydowskie* (1927). If Löw's study was utilized by Solomon Schechter (1850–1915) in a well-known essay and by Israel Abrahams in his classic *Jewish Life in the Middle Ages* (1896), it is too antiquated to be a reliable historical guide, but it contains useful material. Again, Feldman's coverage of the talmudic source material is still worth attention, although he scarcely dealt with the Middle Ages, and what he had to say on East European Jewry was scrappy, considering that he was a doctor ministering to the needs of the immigrant Jews in London in the early part of this century. Despite the fact that unfortunately I did not have access to Regina Lilientalow's volume, which is in Polish, I have looked at some of her research that appeared in German. To these studies should perhaps be added Hayyim Schauss's in *The Lifetime of a Jew* (1950), which is an engrossing historical survey of the life cycle, devoting considerable space to the evolution of the circumcision ceremony and the bar mitzvah.[2]

---

1. Philippe Ariès, *Centuries of Childhood* (Harmondsworth: Penguin Books, 1979), of which the original French edition was published in 1960. Lloyd deMause, *The History of Childhood* (London: Souvenir Press, 1976), of which the first American edition was published in 1974.

2. Leopold Löw, *Die Lebensalter in Der Jüdischen Literatur* (Szegedin, 1875). William Feldman, *The Jewish Child: Its History, Folklore, Biology, and Sociology*

Among the more recent historians of aspects of Jewish childhood are Professors Ivan G. Marcus on rituals of medieval childhood, particularly the ceremony of initiation into a heder, Ephraim Kanarfogel on medieval Jewish education and childrearing practices, and Samuel Kottek on child care in the Bible and Talmud as well as the *Sefer Ḥasidim*. All these historians have been influenced by the new approach to childhood history initiated by Ariès and deMause and the ongoing debate provoked by them. Moreover, it is also necessary to take into account the wide-ranging studies of Abraham Stahl on the traditional attitudes toward the death of young children in Oriental Jewish communities and the disappearance of swaddling in societies undergoing the modernization process.[3]

We open our account with a chapter on the biblical period, and we try to restore the lost world of childhood in ancient Israel by reconstructing the structure of the joint family in the villages and showing how the harsh agricultural conditions resulted in these units being headed by a patriarch who was a strict disciplinarian, yet someone who possessed nurturant qualities. At the same time, Israelite society was more egalitarian than that

(London: Balliere, Tindall and Cox, 1917). Regina Lilientalowa, *Dziecko Zydowskie* (Cracow: 1927). Regina Liliental, *"Das Kind bei den Juden,"* *" Mitteilungen zur Judischen Volkskunde* 25, no. 1 (1908) : 1–24 and 26, no. 2 (1908) : 41–55.

3. Ivan G. Marcus, *Piety and Society: The Jewish Pietists of Medieval Germany* (Leiden: E. J. Brill, 1981). Ivan G. Marcus, "Jewish Schools in Medieval Europe," *Melton Journal* 21 (Winter 1987). Ivan G. Marcus, *Rituals of Childhood: Jewish Acculturation in Medieval Europe* (Yale University Press, 1996). Ephraim Kanarfogel, "Attitudes Toward Childhood and Children in Medieval Jewish Society," in *Approaches to Judaism in Medieval Times*, ed. David R. Blumenthal (Chico, Calif.: Scholars Press, 1985), vol. 2., pp. 1–34. Ephraim Kanarfogel, *Jewish Education and Society in the High Middle Ages* (Detroit: Wayne State University Press, 1992). Samuel Kottek, "Care of Children in the Bible and Talmud," *Koroth* 7, no. 5–6 (1977) : 427–436. Samuel Kottek, "On Children and Childhood in Ancient Jewish Sources," *Koroth* 9, no. 5–6 (1987) : 452–471. Samuel Kottek, "Childhood in Medieval Jewry as Depicted in *Sefer Hasidim* (12th–13th Century) : Medical, Psychological and Educational Aspects," *Koroth* 8, no. 9–10 (August 1984) : 376–395. Abraham Stahl, "Children and Childhood in the View of the Traditional Jewish-Oriental Family," *Journal of Comparative Family Studies* 9 (1978) : 347–354. Abraham Stahl, "Parents' Attitudes towards the Death of Infants in the Traditional Jewish-Oriental Family," *Journal of Comparative Family Studies* 22, no. 1 (Spring 1991) : 75–83. Abraham Stahl, "Swaddling: Its Disappearance as an Illustration of the Process of Cultural Change," *Koroth* 8, no. 7–8 (August 1983) : 285–298. Abraham Stahl, *Family and Child-rearing in Oriental Jewry: Sources, References, Comparisons* (Hebrew) (Jerusalem: Academon, 1993).

of surrounding nations, and mothers had a more respected role in the upbringing of their children. To our surprise, there was no national network of primary schools functioning in ancient Israel; instruction in the essential articles of faith and in religious traditions was imparted by a father to his sons. Other topics considered in this chapter include the institution of circumcision, the socialization of the child, the campaign against child sacrifice, and debt-bondage.

As there is more detailed evidence for the talmudic age, we devote two chapters to the period 1 C.E. to 500 C.E. While the extended family became attenuated after the destruction of the Temple, the ideal became the loving, monogamous, nuclear family based on the Roman model, even if ties to kin remained strong. We try to show how the Jewish family, which resembled the Roman family in certain respects, differed in other ways from the pagan world. Apart from upper-class families, wet-nursing was rejected by the bulk of Jewry, who believed in the importance of the close bonding of mother and child. The Jews, who were one of the first peoples to detest child sacrifice, now extended this ban to include infanticide and abortion. Homosexuality, particularly the seduction of youths, came under renewed interdict by Philo and the rabbis, thereby distinguishing Judaism from pagan Hellenistic culture. At the same time, the Jews borrowed one of the key institutions of the Graeco-Roman world, the school, and utilized it as a means of instilling their own values in the classroom, thereby preserving Jewish culture. We also examine a number of other subjects, including whether or not parents were emotionally closer to their children in the talmudic age, the attitudes toward the death of young children, and how harsh punishment was in these early schools.

Next we investigate infancy, childhood, and adolescence during the Middle Ages. We turn first to the tribulations of childbirth and compare the religious and magical means devised by Jews and Christians to protect the parturient mother and the special vigil over the child on the eve of circumcision and before baptism. We discuss the initiation of the child into the heder in a rite of passage that was more important than the bar mitzvah ceremony during the medieval period, and the critical role of the Jewish elementary school. Among the other topics covered in this section are the slaughter of children by their parents during the Crusades to prevent their enforced conversion, wet-nursing, medieval childrearing practices as expounded in the *Sefer Hasidim*, the attitude toward the death of young children, and the development of the bar mitzvah ceremony. Even so, in medieval Germany there was still a certain anger and awkwardness in the relationship between parents and children, which the Jews shared with their neighbors.

When we reach the early modern period, we are on firmer ground for understanding infancy and childhood because of the illuminating autobiographical material. Of these authors, Glückel's memoirs are in some respects the most revealing, particularly when she deals with childbirth. In this chapter, we consider child care and education, focusing on the moral and ethical guides addressed to parents and the degree to which there may have been some abandonment of adolescent children. While the family in the seventeenth and early eighteenth centuries was still dominated by an authoritarian father who was a stern disciplinarian, we discuss whether or not the new, more permissive world for children created in the later eighteenth century may have embraced Jewish children as well. We earlier explored the subject of the continued kidnapping of Jewish children and their surreptitious baptism, a theme first outlined when we dealt with the medieval period. To end the chapter, we turn our attention to the swelling numbers and growing impact of Jewish youth and the various measures devised to contain their boisterousness.

We now move on to Eastern Europe, where we examine childhood and traditional learning in the heder and house of study. We show how the parents were idealized but were remote from their children, how fathers were strict disciplinarians yet were frightened to display their aggressive tendencies because of the anti-Semitic environment, and how parents left most of the corporal punishment of their offspring to teachers. Nonetheless, the heder was an effective educational agency that stimulated the imagination of children and was sufficiently flexible in design to allow considerable opportunity for play. Finally, we describe higher talmudic education in the house of study and in the new institution, the yeshiva, and the difficulties students encountered in maintaining themselves, which may have left them receptive to the new ideas circulating in the outside world.

In the last three chapters, we discuss the modernization of Jewish youth in Germany, Britain, and the United States after the disintegration of the traditional system of education. We examine the reasons for the low infant mortality rates among Jewish families, which was a unique feature of Jewish childhood, and the new childrearing practices of second- and third-generation parents that enhanced their children's learning abilities. We summarize the research on the Jews' insistence on prolonged education, which resulted in their extraordinary social mobility, and show how the Jews followed similar paths in Austria and Germany as well as Britain and the United States. Instead of meekly accepting anti-Semitic rebuffs like their parents, the youths who revolted in Central and Eastern Europe before the First World War were molded into a tougher generation of Jewish adolescents, and the process continued in Britain and the United States between the two World Wars. Here we turn our gaze on street life, the sporting activities of Jewish youngsters, and the youth organizations. If upper-class Jewish children frequently were taken away from their Jewish roots, they were soon followed by children brought up in suburban Britain and America who had received a scant Jewish education.

Originally I had planned to devote separate chapters to children growing up on the kibbutz, as this topic features in many anthologies of the sociology of the family, and to the often harsh experiences of Jewish children incarcerated in an orphanage. While dealing with orphans, I had also intended to cover what happened to such children after the First and Second World Wars and the struggle waged to unite Jewish orphans with their relatives after 1945. For reasons of space these chapters had to be jettisoned, and only a few remarks can be devoted to these matters in the Conclusion.

1

Children in Ancient Israel

INTRODUCTION: THE FAMILY

Lloyd deMause complained after reading over two thousand references to children in the Bible, "You find lots on child sacrifice, on stoning children, on beating them, on their strict obedience, on their love for their parents, and on their role as carriers of the family name, but not a single one that reveals any empathy with their needs." So, too, Simone Weil was outraged by certain biblical stories, in particular the rather humorless tale about a band of small urchins who mocked Elisha by calling him "bald head," for which they were punished when forty-two of them were mauled by bears (2 Kings 2:23–24). Nonetheless, the modern critical evaluation of biblical sources has gone too far; and it is only by carefully re-examining these sources with the assistance of insights gained from archaeology and anthropology that it may be possible to reconstruct a plausible account of childhood in biblical times.[1]

---

1. Lloyd deMause, *The History of Childhood* (London: Souvenir Press, 1976), pp. 16 and 17 (hereafter cited as deMause, *Childhood*). Simone Petrement, *Simone Weil* (New York: Schocken Books, 1988), p. 346.

7

To understand the position of children in the society of ancient Israel, we must first widen our focus by delineating the family system in which they grew up. In a seminal article published in 1985, Lawrence E. Stager demonstrated that the typical family system of the common people in the villages in ancient Israel was the joint family, with two or three houses each containing a single related nuclear family built next door to each other and sharing a common compound or courtyard. For example, when certain Danites seized some cultic objects belonging to Micah, they were pursued and arrested by the "men who were in the houses comprising the household of Micah" (Judg. 18:22). It could be suggested that the family organization of the elite from the time of the Patriarchs until the last kings of Judah had similar features in that a series of multiple households under the control of different wives, who were sometimes related, were united through their attachment to a single male head, just as a single male head presided over the village joint family. After 1200 B.C.E., Israelite villages in the Hill Country flourished and numbered between a hundred and a hundred and fifty inhabitants in each settlement.

The typical joint family within the village comprised the father and mother, unwed children, married sons and their wives and children as potential members. However, because life expectancy in ancient Israel was no higher than forty years and because of the frequent onslaught of infectious disease, fewer than 30 percent of these families spanned more than two generations. Accordingly, children were often disciplined by their aunts and uncles, but more rarely had a patriarchal grandfather to look up to as a role model. In ancient Greece only 5 percent of the population lived to the age of seventy, and in Israel the proportion reaching this age must have been similar. The joint family was governed by the grandfather, if he was living, but otherwise by the eldest male, and two or three households would be linked together as an economic unit, farming the ancestral estate and sharing an open courtyard, where the women from the related nuclear familes utilized the hand-mills and mortars for grinding corn, baked bread in the ovens located there, and cooked; but sometimes there were cooking facilities on the ground floor of the individual houses.[2]

---

2. Lawrence E. Stager, "The Archaeology of the Family in Ancient Israel, *Bulletin of the American Schools of Oriental Research* 260 (1985): 1–36 (hereafter cited as Stager). S. D. Goitein, *A Mediterranean Society: The Individual* (Berkeley and Los Angeles: University of California Press, 1988), Vol. 5, p. 127. Carol Meyers, *Discovering Eve: Ancient Israelite Women in Context* (New York: Oxford University Press, 1991), p. 144 (hereafter cited as Meyers, *Eve*).

Each nuclear family lived in a rectilinear building or pillared house of two stories, consisting of two to four rooms. While the central room on the ground floor served as a kitchen containing the hearth and ovens, and the rooms at the side of the house were utilized as stables for domestic animals such as sheep and goats, the rooms on the second floor served as a dining room, sleeping quarters, and recreation room. Clusters of two or three of these houses with a shared courtyard were the living quarters of the extended family or *bet ab*.[3]

The average joint family unit in the villages in ancient Israel consisted of some twelve to fourteen members. The men and women of the family pooled their resources and worked the ancestral plots of land as one unit. By intensive labor, these family units cleared the land of scrub and trees and introduced terracing to the hillsides, allowing the Israelites to create fertile fields, orchards, gardens, and vineyards, while the scarcity of water led to the construction of cisterns to hoard this precious commodity during the summer dry season. The need to sow grain at the beginning of the rainy season, the critical importance of harvesting the crops within a matter of days or weeks of their ripening and the sudden torrential downpour of rain in the late spring, and the fact that the individual farmers had to have an exact knowledge of the local climatic and soil conditions in their particular section of the highlands of Palestine—all these factors meant that the patriarchal head of the household acting in concert with other heads of extended families had to be vested with great authority in charting the agricultural strategy for each joint family and mobilizing their labor accordingly.[4]

However, historians now believe that only the cooperation of the whole village community, the *mispaḥah*, not just the extended family, could have mobilized sufficient labor in the mature village system for the construction and regular maintenance of the network of terraces. Again, the peak periods of agricultural activity during the staggered sowing season, when draft animals were in heavy demand for plowing, and at harvest time also encouraged the mobilization of the wider village community. All the village institutions were being stretched to cope with the land hunger of a rapidly rising population.[5]

---

3. Stager, pp. 11–17 and 22–23.

4. Meyers, *Eve*, pp. 54–63 and 185 and 186.

5. F. S. Frick, "Ecology, Agriculture and Patterns of Settlement," in *The World of Ancient Israel: Sociological, Anthropological and Political Perspectives*, ed. R. E. Clements (Cambridge: Cambridge University Press, 1989), pp. 67–93.

Hence the precariousness of survival in harsh agricultural conditions led to the emphasis on patriarchal authority and strict discipline throughout the family, which necessarily affected the children. The authority of the head of the household was bolstered by his possession of the household gods, the teraphim, which he utilized to conduct the family ritual in the earlier ages. Hence these families stressed the importance of matrimonial alliances between cousins and the institution of levirate marriage to keep the ancestral plots of land within the joint family. Under the law of the levirate, when brothers lived together and one of them died, it was customary for the surviving brother to marry the widow, if there was no heir, and any son born to them was regarded as the son and heir of the deceased brother (Deut. 25:5–10). The rite of circumcision, as we shall see, was practised in part to encourage fertility and the birth of children, particularly male heirs to inherit the ancestral farm, so that they could carry out the necessary funeral and memorial rites for their ancestors, who were buried on it.[6]

BIRTH

As in many traditional societies, only female family members and friends were supposed to be present when a woman went into labor (1 Sam. 4:20). The father had to absent himself and await such tidings as "A child is born to you, a son" from a messenger (Jer. 20:15). For the actual birth the woman kneeled or crouched between two stones as in ancient Egypt or on the ground to enable the midwife to assist at the birth of the infant. The child was allowed to rest on the ground or floor at birth to draw strength from his native soil and the blessings of his deceased ancestors. In the ancient world, childbearing was fraught with danger and the mortality rate for pregnant women was high. While Carol Meyers noted that the life expectancy for a man was about forty years, that for a woman was closer

---

6. Ktziah Spanier, "Rachel's Theft of the Teraphim: Her Struggle for Family Primacy," *Vetus Testamentum* 42, no. 3 (July 1992): 404–411. Raphael Patai, *Golden River to Golden Road* (Philadelphia: University of Pennsylvania Press, 1967), pp. 135–176. Raphael Patai, *Family, Love and the Bible* (London: MacGibbon and Kee, 1960), pp. 82–88 (hereafter cited as Patai, *Family*). Herbert Chanan Brichto, "Kin, Cult, Land and Afterlife—A Biblical Complex," *HUC Annual* 44 (1973): 1–54 but particularly 11, 23, and 50 (hereafter cited as Brichto).

to thirty mainly because of the heavy maternal death rate, but both these figures may be overoptimistic estimates. According to Aline Rousselle, between 5 and 10 percent of women in the ancient world died at the end of their pregnancy or shortly after the child was delivered. However, if 20 percent of all married women in Florence in the fifteenth century died in childbirth, it is possible that the previously cited estimate of Aline Rousselle is overcautious and far too low; and we should bear this in mind when considering the situation in ancient Israel.[7]

Angel's study of skeletal remains for ancient Greece shows an average of 4.3 births per woman; but in ancient Israel it has been suggested by Meyers that only two children in each family survived into adult life. Although the death of children in ancient Israel was taken for granted by contemporaries and rarely discussed in the biblical texts, the abundance of tombs of infants discovered by archaeologists enables us to gauge the heavy infant mortality rates prevailing in ancient Israel. In one burial cave at Meiron in Palestine, the remains in which have been dated from the first century B.C.E. to the fourth century C.E., 35 percent of the individuals were children who had died below the age of five years, while the evidence from tombs indicates that nearly half the population did not survive the age of eighteen years. In contrast, in the sixteenth and seventeenth centuries in rural England between a quarter and a third of the children of peers and peasants died below the age of fifteen years. This is an additional means of checking the accuracy of the even heavier infant mortality rates in ancient Israel.[8]

7. Patai, *Family*, p. 166. Samuel Radbill, "La Pediatrie Dans La Bible," *Rev. de la hist. de la méd. héb.* 65 (October 1964), p. 146 (herafter cited as Radbill, *Paediatrics*). Meyers, *Eve*, pp. 112 and 113. Aline Rousselle, "Body Politics in Ancient Rome," in *A History of Women: From Ancient Goddesses to Christian Saints*, ed. Pauline Schmitt Pantel (Cambridge, Mass.: Harvard University Press, 1992), vol. 1, p. 298. Shulamith Shahar, *Childhood in the Middle Ages* (London: Routledge, 1992), p. 35 (hereafter cited as Shahar, *Childhood*).

8. Sarah B. Pomeroy, *Goddesses, Whores, Wives and Slaves: Women in Classical Antiquity* (New York: Schocken Books, 1975), p. 68. Rene Voeltzel, "*L'Enfant Chez Les Hebreux*" in *L'Enfant 1. Antiquite—Afrique—Asie*, in *Recueils de la Societe Jean Bodin* (Brussels 1975), pp. 135 and 136 (hereafter cited as Voeltzel). Meyers, *Eve*, p. 112. Eric M. Meyers, James F. Strange, and Carol Meyers, *Meiron Excavation Project* (Cambridge, Mass.: American Schools of Oriental Research, 1981), Vol. 3, pp. 110 and 111. Lawrence Stone, *The Family, Sex and Marriage in England 1500–1800* (Harmondsworth: Penguin Books, 1979), pp. 55 and 56.

Nonetheless, the evidence of the Bible shows that there was a definite rise in the population in ancient Israel, particularly among the upper class; and this feature of large families among the elite and small families among the poor was a regular population pattern in both the ancient world and pre-modern Europe. David was the youngest of eight sons, while his three eldest brothers were old enough to be fighting in Saul's army (1 Sam. 17:12–15). David himself had six sons born to him in Hebron by different wives, quite apart from Solomon, who was born later (2 Sam. 3:2–5). Further, Lawrence Stager estimated that the population of the Hill Country increased from 40, 000 to 80, 000 inhabitants from Iron Age I (1200–930 B.C.E.) to Iron Age II (930–586 B.C.E.).[9]

There is an interesting passage in Ezekiel, couched in negative form, which if read carefully reveals the standard procedure in ancient Israel for treating a newly born baby at birth: ". . . when you were born, your navel-string was not tied, you were not bathed in water ready for the rubbing, you were not salted as you should have been nor wrapped in swaddling clothes" (Ezek. 16:4). Each of these procedures not only had prophylactic motives but was vested with ritual significance; and Raphael Patai has shown how they were still adhered to in Arab lands throughout the Middle East until recent decades.[10]

Starting with the severing of the navel cord, the cutting and tying of the navel cord of the infant symbolized the formal acceptance of the newly born babe into its family and usually took place in a special ceremony held among the Arabs some twelve hours after the birth of a child. In Egypt different songs were sung at the ceremony for boys and girls. His family rhapsodized a boy with these lines:

Who supports his father,
Except him who descends from his loins,
May your legs be fit for the stirrup,
And your mouth for an answer.

So too, it was stated in the Talmud that "We tie up the navel string. R. Jose said: We cut [it] too; and we bury the after-birth, so that the infant may be kept warm. R. Simeon b. Gamliel said: Princesses hide [it] in bowls of oil, wealthy women in wool fleeces, and poor women in soft rags"

---

9. Stager, p. 25.
10. Patai, *Family*, p. 169.

(Shabbat 129b). If the child was rejected—and there are hints in the Ezekiel text, part of which we have quoted in the preceding paragraph, that daughters sometimes were rejected by their parents in ancient Israel—then there may have been a degree of female infanticide at this time, just as the Arabs prior to the emergence of Islam and sometimes even later subjected girls on occasion to infanticide by burying them in the earth. In the ancient world and in modern India, males outnumbered females in the population, because boys were better fed and treated, and we would surmise that this was equally the case in ancient Israel, particularly as there may have been a degree of female infanticide.[11]

Often the Arabs did not wash a child until the third, seventh, or fortieth day of its life, and songs were sung to protect the children from evil spirits, demonstrating that the washing was not done merely for hygienic reasons. The ceremony was marked by a feast for the women, perhaps as a way of thanking the females who had assisted the midwife at the birth of the child. Possibly similar ceremonies existed in ancient Israel.

Both the Talmud and St. Jerome confirm that newly born babies were still salted by Jews in the first centuries of the Common Era; and it was a practice recommended by the physicians Galen (130–200 C.E.) and Soranus of Ephesus. Recently the historian R. Étienne asserted that the salting of babies was undertaken to eliminate mucus. Salt because of its antiseptic preventive qualities also came to be the symbol for vitality and long life. However, Theodor Gaster has pointed out that the Arabs protected their children from evil by placing salt in their hands on the seventh day after birth, while the next day the midwife or women from the family scattered salt about the house, exclaiming, "salt in every envious eye"; and Catholics at baptism placed salt on an infant's lips to exorcise the devil, confirming that the salting of babies was not undertaken merely for hygienic purposes.[12]

---

11. Patai, *Family*, pp. 168 and 169. Radbill, *Paediatrics*, *Rev. d' hist. de la méd. héb.* 66 (December 1964), p. 170 for a contrary view on female infanticide.

12. John Boswell, *The Kindness of Strangers: The Abandonment of Children in Western Europe from Late Antiquity to the Renaissance* (New York: Pantheon Books, 1988), p. 146. Robert Étienne, "Ancient Medical Conscience and the Life of Children," *Journal of Psychohistory* 4, no. 2 (Fall 1976): 144 and 145. Radbill, *Paediatrics*, p. 146. Theodor H. Gaster, *Myth Legend and Custom in the Old Testament*, Vol. 2 (New York: Harper and Row, 1975), pp. 618 and 619.

CIRCUMCISION

While circumcision was in general terms an operation performed on males to remove the foreskin of the penis, there was no detailed technical description of the surgical aspects of circumcision in the Bible. We therefore turn to delineating the different social functions of this ceremony, as it possessed various levels of meaning. When Abraham was ninety-nine years old and his son Ishmael was thirteen, all the men of Abraham's household were circumcised (Gen. 17:24–27). Later Isaac was circumcised eight days after birth in accordance with an earlier instruction, and the necessity of circumcising all Israelite males on the eighth day after birth was emphasized in Leviticus 12:3, a significant shift of the time of circumcision to infancy instead of the usual tribal initiation rite at puberty. Nonetheless, the antiquity of the custom among the Israelites was attested by the fact that the operation was carried out by using flint knives, although later, knives of metal were used (Exod. 4:25 and Josh. 5:2–3).

While the practice of circumcision was widespread in the ancient cultures of the Middle East, particularly among the Egyptians and certain Mesopotamian peoples, the Israelite initiation rite gave it a new emphasis by stressing that it was a physical mark of the binding covenant between God and Abraham and his descendants: "This is my covenant, which ye shall keep, between Me and you and thy seed after thee: every male among you shall be circumcised" (Gen. 17:10). "What is more logical and appropriate," commented Gerda Lerner, "than to use as the leading symbol of the covenant the organ which produces this 'seed' and which 'plants' it in the female womb?"[13]

The practice of circumcision in many societies was originally a tribal initiation rite connected with the marriage of the eligible adolescent males. Among certain African tribes and the Bedouin today this is still the case, while according to de Vaux, circumcision among the ancient Egyptians was probably an operation carried out at puberty, when marriages were arranged. According to Patai, among the peasant farmers of Palestine "a young man at the circumcision ceremony gets a bride whom he marries almost at once." It is possible that similar circumstances prevailed in ancient Israel, as the story of the Shechemites being circumcised at the behest of Jacob's sons before they would agree to the marriage of the local ruler's

---

13. Gerda Lerner, *The Creation of Patriarchy* (New York: Oxford University Press, 1986), p. 192.

son to their sister Dinah seems to point to (Gen. 34:13–14). Again, when Zipporah circumcised Moses' son, she cried out, "Surely, a bridegroom of the blood art thou to me" (Exod. 4:25), a strange choice of phrase that seems to echo this connection between circumcision and eligibility for marriage.[14]

Howard Eilberg-Schwartz in *The Savage in Judaism* (1990) asserted that the ritual of circumcision in ancient Israel could be illuminated by a comparison with the themes common in the African tribal rites of circumcision, such as fertility, procreation, and intergenerational continuity between males. Van Gennep commented that the ceremony accompanying the rite of circumcision in Israel could be regarded as initiation into "social puberty." According to Eilberg-Schwartz, "Circumcision is a symbol that God will make Abraham fruitful and multiply." Further, the removal of excess skin from the male sexual organ unfurled the penis for its reproductive function. Just as the biblical narrative often associated circumcision and fruit trees, so the cutting off of excess skin and the pruning of young fruit trees symbolically and actually increased the desired yield of fruit and the human population. So, too, Herbert Chanan Brichto pointed out that the Bible often focused on the symbolism of persons as trees and their descendants as fruit.[15]

Circumcision was also a social process linking different generations of men in a blood brotherhood, from which women were excluded. The cut of circumcision, particularly from the time of the Babylonian Exile, but even earlier at the time of the conflict with the Philistines (Judg. 14:3 and 1 Sam. 18:25–27), showed how the lineages of the Jews were set apart from those of other people and the rite of circumcision created a bridge between Jewish men of different generations. According to Eilberg-Schwartz, male circumcision on the eighth day after birth was a "postpartum ritual" separating the male infant from "the impurity of his mother," thus enabling the male child to join the purity of the brotherhood of men.[16]

---

14. Roland de Vaux, *Ancient Israel: Its Life and Institutions* (London: Darton, Longman and Todd, 1976), p. 47 (hereafter cited as Vaux, *Ancient Israel*). Patai, *Family*, pp. 181 and 182.

15. Howard Eilberg-Schwartz, *The Savage in Judaism: An Anthropology of Israelite Religion and Ancient Judaism* (Bloomington and Indianapolis: Indiana University Press, 1990), pp. 144 and 148 (hereafter cited as *Savage in Judaism*).

16. *Savage in Judaism*, pp. 162, 163, 171, 174, and 175. Voeltzel, p. 146. W. O. E. Osterley and Theodore H. Robinson, *Hebrew Religion: Its Origins and Developments* (London: S. P. C. K. 1937), p. 286.

BREAST-FEEDING

Because of the high infant mortality rates existing in the ancient world, Philippe Ariès and some of his followers concluded that parental affection for young children was something that had originated in the seventeenth or eighteenth centuries. It was argued that in the past, on account of the probable short life span of an infant, it was not worthwhile for parents to invest much emotional capital in their children and that ties of love were consequently slender. However, Shulamith Shahar, the Israeli historian of medieval childhood, quoted a study showing that in Guatemala, Indian infants were caringly nurtured by their mothers despite the high infant mortality rates, thereby proving the fallacy of this argument.[17]

So, too, the biblical narrative is rich in maternal imagery in general and imagery of God as a loving, nursing mother, which when read with attention gives us an insight into the accepted social attitudes and values in child care in ancient Israel. Moses complained, "How have I displeased the Lord that I am burdened with the care of this whole people? Am I their mother? Have I brought them into the world, and am I called upon to carry them in my bosom, like a nurse with her babies, to the land promised by thee on oath to their fathers?" (Num. 11:11–12). On the other hand, this passage should be contrasted with some sentences in Deuteronomy, where the Lord is depicted as the loving mother of Israel:

As an eagle that stirreth up her nest,
Hovereth over her young,
Spreadeth abroad her wings, taketh them,
Beareth them on her pinions,
The Lord alone led him [Israel]. (Deut. 32:11–12)

These biblical images of God's maternal love for Israel and Zion, Jerusalem, reach their culmination in Isaiah:

But Zion says,
"The Lord has forsaken me; my God has forgotten me."
Can a woman forget the infant
at her breast,
or a loving mother the child of
her womb?" (Isa. 49:14–15)

---

17. Shahar, *Childhood*, p. 2.

Both this passage and the following passage we shall quote from Isaiah stress the importance of the maternal bonding of the mother and child in ancient Israel, when a child was breast-fed for up to three or four years. Isaiah exclaimed, "Rejoice ye with Jerusalem . . . that ye may suck, and be satisfied with the breasts of her consolations; that ye may drink deeply of the abundance of her glory. For thus saith the Lord: Behold, I will extend . . . the wealth of the nations to her like an overflowing stream, And ye shall suck thereof; and ye shall be borne upon the side, And shall be dandled upon the knees. As one whom your mother comforteth, so will I comfort you . . ." (Isa. 66:10–13).

Patai has suggested that Samuel must have been a child of three or four when he started to serve in the sanctuary at Shilo with Eli the priest, and no longer an infant. So, too, Isaiah assumed that the weaned child was old enough to understand a message of the Lord, which supports the conclusion that the child was old enough to speak and be taught what the Lord required of him. The clearest evidence of the length of breast-feeding was in the Second Book of Maccabees, where a mother pleaded with her son, "I carried you nine months in the womb, suckled you three years, reared you and brought you up to your present age" (2 Macc. 7:27). In the biblical period only the children of royal and upper-class families were suckled by wet nurses, such as Rebecca's nurse Deborah (Gen. 24:59 and 35:8) and Saul's grandson Mephibosheth, who was accidentally dropped by his nurse and left lame. Greek and Roman sources also show that children were weaned at the age of two or three years. Among Arab peasants in Palestine, whereas girls were nursed for a limit of two years, boys were breast-fed for three or four years and sometimes longer, and it is possible that similar customs existed in ancient Israel.[18]

The sucking infant, the yoneq, was a distinctive and important category in ancient Israel (Lam. 4:4 and Jer. 44:7), distinguished both from the weaned child and children in general. Literary images of the nursing child were such a recurring theme in the Bible that they must have triggered a response in their audience. If Moses only reluctantly identified himself with a maternal role, the prophet Isaiah more positively endorsed such images. In terms of psycho-history we would assert that not only did the long in-

---

18. Phyllis Trible, "Depatriarchalizing in Biblical Interpretation," in *The Jewish Woman: New Perspectives*, ed. Elizabeth Koltun (New York: Schocken Books, 1976), pp. 218–221. Patai, *Family*, pp. 173–175. Voeltzel, p. 139. DeMause, *Childhood*, p. 36.

tensely satisfying periods of breast-feeding in ancient Israel boost the adult males' sense of worth and implant in them a more robust feeling of self-confidence and unending optimism; but men also identified themselves sufficiently strongly with their mothers to develop nurturant capabilities and roles. When they brought up their own children, the men displayed this maternal side of their personality, and on a national scale a few outstanding individuals preached a prophetic and optimistic message of a resurgent Jewish state.

SOCIALIZATION AND EDUCATION

Even if children in ancient Israel spent more time with their mothers than their fathers in their early years, both parents actively shared in the task of socializing and educating their children. Carol Meyers, in her brilliant reconstruction of the family life of the pioneering Israelite peasant farmers, perhaps exaggerated the social influence of women and glamorized their roles; her model was in short far too egalitarian. We would picture the communal compound of the joint family as the hub of social activity in ancient Israel, with the womenfolk of the extended family engaged for long periods of time each day in the grinding of grain and the baking of loaves of barley bread and generally in the processing and more rarely in the cooking of food. To appreciate the tedious amount of time spent by Israelite women in grinding grain for their daily bread, we should note that a traveler to the Sudan observed that a slave girl working with a saddle-stone mill had to toil from morning to evening to extract sufficient flour to feed eight persons. No doubt the Israelite women chatted as they worked, while their young children played nearby and at times helped their mothers in the preparation of food.[19]

Fathers frequently assisted their wives in the upbringing of their children in ancient Israel. They used to transport infants by cradling them in their arms (Num. 11:12), or shared the task of carrying bigger children on their shoulders (Isa. 49:22) or on the side of their bodies (Isa. 66:12). A passage in Hosea wonderfully depicts how involved fathers were in helping toddlers to take their first steps: "When Israel was a boy, I loved him. . . . It was I who taught Ephraim to walk, I who had taken them in my

---

19. Meyers, *Eve*, p. 151. Naum Jasny, "The Daily Bread of the Ancient Greeks and Romans," *Osiris* 9 (1950): 235.

arms; but they did not know that I harnessed them in leading-strings and led them with bonds of love—that I had lifted them like a little child to my cheek, that I had bent down and fed them" (Hos. 11:1–4). As the child grew older, the parents' love for him deepened. When King Jeroboam's son fell ill, he sent his wife in disguise to consult the blind and aged prophet Ahijah to ascertain the fate of the child (1 Kings 14:1–18).

We have confirmation that boys and girls played in the streets of villages and the thoroughfares of Jerusalem (Jer. 6:11 and Zech. 8:5). Children imitated adults by staging mock weddings and funerals in the street. Matthew denounced his generation for being "like children sitting in the market-place and shouting at each other, 'We piped for you and you would not dance.' 'We wept and wailed, and you would not mourn'" (Matt. 11:16–17). Archaeologists have uncovered whistles, earthenware rattles, small human figures, and models of animals with which children played. Children also enjoyed various board games. Dr. Irving Finkel has traced the game of "Asha," which survived among the Jewish community of Cochin until recent times, back to a game played in Mesopotamia in 2600 B.C.E. The Royal Game of Ur was played on a board with twenty squares, the contestants each had five pieces that they moved around a track, and there were advantages and penalties for landing on different squares. During excavations at the Israelite town of Gezer the archaeologist R. A. S. Macalister found a number of board games, including one that was similar to the modern game of "Halma."[20]

Whereas the older boys followed their fathers into the fields to learn the techniques and skills of the farmer (2 Kings 4:18), we would suggest on the basis of the model of the later Arab peasant family that the girls as they grew up stayed with their mothers in the house and family compound, unless they went out as a group. Gradually a range of household chores devolved on them, starting with the task of looking after younger siblings. Girls were taught to be subservient; they learned to obey their mothers and elder sisters, to serve their fathers and brothers. In the evening the

---

20. E. W. Heaton, *Everyday Life in Old Testament Times* (London: B. T. Batsford, 1957), p. 80. R. A. Stewart Macalister, *The Excavations at Gezer*, Vol. 2. (London: John Murray, 1912), pp. 299–306. Morris Silver, *Prophets and Markets: The Political Economy of Ancient Israel* (Boston: Kluwer Nijhoff, 1983), pp. 87–89. T. A. Holland, "A Study of Palestinian Iron Age Baked Clay Figurines with Special Reference to Jerusalem," *Levant* 9 (1977): 121–155. Despite criticism that some of these figurines may have been cultic objects, the consensus seems to be that a large percentage of them were toys.

young women ventured out in a group to draw water from the local well, an onerous task with little prestige attached to it (Gen. 24:11). Bands of boys freely roamed the village streets (Jer. 6:11). Not so the older girls and young maidens, who either assisted their mothers in grinding grain and baking (2 Sam. 13:8) or in spinning and weaving to make the family's clothes; or kept together when they were harvesting in the fields, just as Ruth kept close to Boaz's maidens, gleaning with them until the end of the barley and wheat harvests (Ruth 2:22 and 23). Carol Meyers speculated that Israelite women, and we would add adolescents, probably contributed to hoeing and weeding and labored in the vegetable gardens, vineyards, and orchards. Despite the number of female prophets in ancient Israel and the important role played by wise women, despite the emphasis on the female figure of Wisdom throughout the Bible, it is likely that the family structure was authoritarian. Yet Israelite mothers were respected as equals of their husbands by their children, they were not as downtrodden as the later Arab women, and it might be best to designate the ancient Israelite family as a form of modified patriarchy.[21]

According to Hyam Maccoby, the dynamics of the Israelite family evolved because of a "truce" established between fathers and sons "at a cost of sexual renunciation." Further, "the symbolic castration of circumcision releases the Jews from the fate of Oedipus." Reconciliation between fathers and sons created a social space in which women could enhance their own roles and social status. In turn, sons could identify with the creative aspects of the personalities of both parents, with the feminine attributes of softness and wisdom (Greek *sophia* and Hebrew *hokma*) and with the striving of heroes like Moses and David.[22]

H. G. Wells praised "the Jewish religion, because it was a literature-sustained religion, [which] led to the first efforts to provide elementary

---

21. Raphael Patai, *Golden River to Golden Road* (Philadelphia: University of Pennsylvania Press, 1967), pp. 97 and 98. Meyers, *Eve*, pp. 90–92, 105, 106, and 146.

22. Hyam Maccoby, "Freud and Moses," *Midstream* 26, no. 2 (February 1980): 14, 15. E. Wellisch, *Isaac and Oedipus: The Sacrifice of Isaac: The Akedah* (London: Routledge and Kegan Paul, 1954), pp. 87–88. As Abraham prepared to sacrifice Isaac, the progress of his knife was arrested when he thought of Sarah. Finally, God called him, and as soon as Abraham realized he did not have to sacrifice his son, a new love for Isaac welled up in him and became the central core of his religion, thereby increasing his capacity for object love. In other words, Abraham's love for Isaac was now mutual and less narcissistic than before.

instruction for all children of the community." W. F. Albright had already pointed out that the simplicity of the Hebrew language as compared with the complex languages of surrounding nations produced widespread literacy in ancient Israel. However, James L. Crenshaw, after a thorough analysis of the evidence, concluded that most parents in Israel under the monarchy educated their children in their own homes, adding that there was a dearth of evidence for the existence of royal schools. Nonetheless, the marked increase in the number of Hebrew inscriptions that have been found dating from the eighth century B.C.E. onwards led André Lemaire to conclude that there must have been systematic teaching and schools at least in the royal fortresses, for example at Kadesh Barnea and Kuntilat-Ajrud and in certain villages. If schools existed then in ancient Israel, they would have resembled Koranic schools held in a room in a teacher's house or in the corner of a public place, which would have left no clear archaeological trace. It is unlikely, though, that there was a widespread school system among Jews prior to the Hellenistic era, when a nationwide network of scribes began to function in the towns and villages. Here was a group from whom the teaching profession was widely recruited.[23]

"Attend, my son, to your father's instruction and do not reject the teaching of your mother . . ." (Prov. 1:8). A similar refrain was repeated throughout the book of Proverbs. However, the weight of the evidence in the Bible showed that fathers increasingly assumed the role of teachers of their children in ancient Israel, expounding the commandments in the Torah (Deut. 6:4–9) and the history of their people, particularly the Exodus from Egypt (Ex. 12:26–27 and Deut. 6:20–25) to their children.

> Listen, my sons, to a father's instruction, consider attentively how to gain understanding; for it is sound learning I give you; so do not forsake my teaching. I too have been a father's son, tender in years, my mother's only child. He taught me and said to me: hold fast to my words with all your heart, keep my command-

---

23. *The Pentateuch and Haftorahs,* ed. J. H. Hertz (London: Soncino Press, 1947), p. 818. James L. Crenshaw, "Education in Ancient Israel, " *Journal of Biblical Literature* 104, no. 4 (December 1985): 601–615. André Lemaire, "Sagesse et Ecoles," *Vetus Testamentum* 34, no. 3 (1984): 270–281. Zvee Zahavy, "Political and Social Dimensions in the Formation of Early Jewish Prayer: The Case of the Shema." *Proceedings of the 10th World Congress of Jewish Studies,* Jerusalem, August 16–24, 1989 (Jerusalem: The World Union of Jewish Studies, 1990), Division C, Vol. 1, *Jewish Thought and Literature,* pp. 33–40.

ments and you will have life. . . . The first thing is to acquire wisdom; gain understanding though it cost you all you have. Do not forsake her, and she will keep you
safe, love her, and she will guard you; cherish her, and she will lift you high; if only
you embrace her, she will bring you honor. (Prov. 4:1–8)

In the ancient world, both in Sumer and Egypt, physical chastisement
of pupils was closely associated with education, and who better to administer physical correction than the father: "And know ye this day; for I speak
not with your children that have not seen the chastisement of the Lord . . ."
(Deut. 11:2). During this period children, by means of moral and religious
exhortation and corporal punishment, were encouraged to conform to their
father's wishes and those of the extended family, by sacrificing their spirit
of independence. Yet a balance was achieved. There was no mere sinking
into a family-centered society, children made a subtle identification with
the nurturant mother, and fathers were often emotionally warm and demon-
strative, all of which fostered a spirit of communal endeavor when the
children became adults.[24]

Scholars have argued that the book of Proverbs had a didactic structure and probably served as a textbook for pupils in an educational establishment. In this Wisdom literature the world was viewed as based on the
principle of "retributive justice," under which what a person contributed
to his family and community was repaid. In certain respects the book of
Proverbs was similar in purpose to the manuals of etiquette and good
manners of the Renaissance and the eighteenth century, which assisted
people to become gentlemen and women by exercising self-control and
being guided by the wisdom of their parents and elders; but the Bible did
not present a uniform series of ideal types of men or women. Moses slew
the Egyptian taskmaster in anger and struck the rock when the water would
not flow. He unleashed aggression in various circumstances, whereas the
genteel types portrayed in the Wisdom literature seem to be too cool, too
self-possessed and somewhat emasculated through a parental regime with
too rigid a discipline. This indicates that the styles of bringing up children
varied in different periods in ancient Israel and probably also among the
different social classes, although at times the Wisdom literature might be
discussing ideal types of behavior for sages rather than real life situations

---

24. *The Interpreter's Dictionary of the Bible*, s.v. Education O. T., Vol. E–J (Nash-
ville and New York: Abingdon Press, 1962), pp. 27–34, particularly p. 28. Patai, *Family*, p. 192.

of the peasant farmers. Moreover, aggression within the family was diffused by permitting a degree of sibling rivalry.[25]

Throughout the book of Proverbs the message was that learning had
to be reinforced by physical coercion. The father depicted in Proverbs seems
both remote and punitive: "A wise man heareth his father's instruction:
but a scorner heareth not rebuke. . . . He that spareth his rod hateth his
son but he that loveth him chasteneth him betimes" (Prov. 13:1 and 24).
"Foolishness is bound in the heart of a child; but the rod of correction
shall drive it far from him" (Prov. 22:15). "Withhold not correction from
the child: for if thou beateth him with the rod, he shall not die. Thou . . .
shall deliver his soul from the nether world. Hear thou, my son, and be
wise, and guide thine heart in the way. Be not among winebibbers: among
riotous eaters of flesh: for the drunkard and the glutton shall come to
poverty. . . . Hearken unto thy father, that begat thee, and despise
not thy mother when she is old" (Prov. 23:12-22). "Chastise thy son
while there is hope for him, but be careful not to flog him to death" (Prov.
19:18). Much the same stern line on discipline was enunciated in the
second-century tract of Ben Sirah (Ecclesiasticus 30:1-12).

On the other hand, the Torah proclaimed that whoever struck his
father or mother should be put to death (Ex. 21:15); likewise if anyone
cursed his parents, he could face the death penalty as a punishment (Ex.
21:17), although the Talmud doubted whether these penalties were ever
exacted. Article 195 of the code of Hammurabi decreed that if a son struck
his father, his hand should be cut off. In contrast, the Torah regarded the
offense of hitting a parent as more heinous and deserving of greater punishment, and was less narrowly patriarchal in outlook, as offenses against
a mother were viewed as equally grave and culpable. The peasant family
was a more important and more egalitarian institution in ancient Israel than
in Mesopotamia, while the Israelite mothers probably had a more crucial
role to play in the socialization of their children. According to Joseph
Fleishman, the aim of the law against striking parents was to protect aged
parents from being humiliated and beaten by an unscrupulous child who
wished to drive them off the ancestral estate. He believed that two verses
in Proverbs described the social ills this law was seeking to address. Prov-

---

25. James G. Williams, "Proverbs and Ecclesiastes," in *The Literary Guide to the
Bible*, ed. Robert Alter and Frank Kermode (London: Fontana Press, 1989), pp. 263–
282.

erbs 19:26 condemns "a son who causes shame and disgrace, plunders his father, puts his mother to flight." Proverbs 28:24 denounces a son "who robs his father and mother and says, it is no offense . . . [as] a companion to vandals."[26]

The second offense in Exodus 21:17 of cursing (mekallel) a parent was the opposite of honoring (kbd) one's father and mother. The Torah forbade a person to revile his parents, thereby humiliating them and refusing to recognize their authority and legal rights. Possibly the law was analogous in part to other Near Eastern law codes that protected a widow from the machinations of unscrupulous heirs. Thus Proverbs 30:17 warns that "the eye that mocks a father and disdains the homage due to a mother, the ravens of the brook will gouge it out, young eagles will devour it." If a son did not listen to his parents, after they gave him a warning to mend his conduct, they were to accuse him in front of the elders of the town, saying "'This son of ours is disobedient and out of control; he will not obey us, he is a wastrel and drunkard.' Then all the men of the town shall stone him to death . . ." (Deut. 21:18–21). Fleishman declared that this passage restricted the application of the law of cursing parents previously outlined in Exodus.[27]

The authority of both parents over their children was enshrined in the Ten Commandments, the fifth one of which enjoined children to "Honor your father and mother that you may long endure on the Land that the Lord your God is giving you" (Ex. 20:12). The thrust of this verse was, according to Herbert Chanan Brichto, that for children to feel security of tenure on the sacred ancestral land they not only had to show deference to their parents in their lifetime but had to continue to respect their parents' memory after their death. Proverbs 20:20 stated that "whoever shows disrespect (curses) for his father and mother, his lamp [a symbol for a line of descendants] will be extinguished in utter darkness," that is, his line will come to an end. Although parents depended on children for the performance of memorial rites for a felicitous condition in the afterlife, their

26. Joseph Fleishman, "Offences against Parents Punishable by Death," *The Jewish Law Annual*, Vol. 10, Institute of Jewish Law (Boston University School of Law) (Philadelphia and Reading: Harwood Academic Publishers, 1992), pp. 7–17 (hereafter cited as Fleishman, *Offences against Parents*).

27. Fleishman, *Offences against Parents*, pp. 17–37.

continued well-being was also contingent on how well they had inculcated their progeny with the moral norms of the Torah (Deut. 11:18–21).[28]

Sometimes a father favored his youngest son, stirring intense family rivalry and tension with the other sons, who felt slighted: "Now Israel [Jacob] loved Joseph more than all his children, because he was the son of his old age; and he made for him a coat of many colors. And when his brethren saw that their father loved him more than all his brethren, they hated him . . ." (Gen. 37:4). Under biblical law the eldest son was expected to receive a double portion of his father's estate on the death of his father (Deut. 21:17). Further, it was decreed in Deuteronomy 25:15–17 that if a man had two wives, and that if both had borne sons but the younger son was the child of the favorite wife, the father in disposing of his estate was not to deprive his eldest son of his birthright; yet popular custom, Roland de Vaux remarked, often overrode the law.[29]

During the biblical period, there was no clear-cut division between childhood and adolescence, and the different stages of childhood tended to be somewhat blurred and confused, thus supporting the contention of Philippe Ariès about the lack of clear-cut demarcations of the stages of childhood in the past. Yeled was the usual biblical term for an infant, being mentioned some 85 times in the Bible. According to the medieval biblical exegete Abraham Ibn Ezra, in Daniel 1:4 yeled referred to a child of fifteen. An even more common biblical term was na'ar (boy), which occurred some 225 times, yet in Jeremiah 1:6 an infant who was too young to speak was called a na'ar. When Joseph was seventeen years old, he was also described in Genesis 37:2 as a na'ar; again, Joshua at the age of fifty-six years in Exodus 33:11 was still called a na'ar. Both Ibn Ezra and Nachmanides agreed that na'ar could sometimes mean a servant as well as a child, someone who submitted to the authority of the paterfamilias without demur. Nachmanides remarked that the terms yeled and na'ar were often interchangeable in the Scriptures.[30]

Nonetheless, a clear distinction was drawn in the Bible between persons over twenty years of age, who were classified as adults, and (for males)

---

28. Brichto, pp. 30–34.

29. Vaux, *Ancient Israel*, p. 42.

30. Samuel S. Kottek, "On Children and Childhood in Ancient Jewish Sources," *Koroth* 9, nos. 5–6 (1987): 452–471.

as potential soldiers, and those under that age, who were regarded as children and adolescents. What is unique about the biblical narratives is that the Israelites were reconstituted as a nation in the wilderness with the discarding and gradual extinction of the adult generation and with emphasis placed on the new generation of children to promote the birth of the nation (Num. 14:28–31).

THE PROBLEM OF CHILD SACRIFICE

We must now turn our attention to the problem of whether or not there was child sacrifice in ancient Israel, and if so, the extent of such sacrifice. Second, was it a popular cult or was it confined to royal circles? Until 1935 there was a consensus among scholars that the biblical Molech was a god to whom children were sacrificed, but Otto Eissfeldt then put forward the hypothesis that this word when referred to in the Bible was a technical term for a type of child sacrifice like the Punic or Carthaginian term *mlk*. De Vaux, who supported Eissfeldt's basic position, later maintained that an animal was increasingly substituted for the human victim. Eissfeldt further claimed that as a result of the Deuteronomic reform under Josiah (639–609 B.C.E.) the term Molech had been freshly interpreted as a divine name because child sacrifice had previously been a legitimate feature of the Israelite cult, particularly the sacrifice of the firstborn child. According to Eissfeldt, child sacrifice was allowed in Israel but rarely practiced from the time of the Patriarchs until the reign of Josiah, and he surmised that the Deuteronomic reformers banned child sacrifice altogether in Israel. Other scholars declared that the Molech cult did not involve human sacrifice but was merely a symbolic passing through the fire by the supposed victims. Summing up the state of research in 1968, W. F. Albright contended that "there are probably few competent scholars who now believe that a god Molech is intended in any biblical passages referring to human sacrifice."[31]

Recently George Heider (1985) and John Day (1989) have refuted Eissfeld's theory and shown that the Syro-Palestinian god Malik or Molech

---

31. John Day, *Molech, A God of Human Sacrifice in the Old Testament* (Cambridge: Cambridge University Press, 1989), p. 82 (hereafter cited as Day, *Molech*). George C. Heider, *The Cult of Molek: A Reassessment* (Sheffield: JSOT Press, 1985), pp. 35–38, 51, 56, 57, and 64 (hereafter cited as Heider, *Molek*).

was widely worshiped in the ancient Near East. In Akkadian sources the deity known as Malik was equated with the underworld god Nergal. So, too, in the Bible a connection was posited between Molech and the underworld: "You journeyed to Molech with oil and multiplied your perfumes, you sent envoys far off, and sent down even to Sheol" (Isa. 57:9). Heider asserted that the sustained biblical polemic directed against the Canaanites as the source of Molech worship and the Syro-Palestinian origins of the god both suggested that the Israelites borrowed the Molech cult from their Canaanite neighbors. In criticism of this position, Marc Brettler declared that the real culprits were the Arameans, a Western Semitic people with whose deity Adad-Milki Molech may possibly have been connected. After the conquest of Samaria by the Assyrians in 722 B.C.E., foreign tribes were settled there, among whom were the Sepharvites, who originated from Hamath in Syria. ". . . the Sepharvites burnt their children as offerings to Adad-Milki and Anammelech, the gods of the Sepharvim" (2 Kings 17:31). According to Heider, there was yet a third possibility, namely that the Molech cult was of Phoenician origin, having been adopted by Solomon, who was influenced by Hiram, King of Tyre; the god of Tyre, Melqart, could be a counterpart of Molech, thus establishing a clear link between the cult as practiced in the Punic colonies in North Africa and Molech worship in ancient Israel.[32]

A. R. W. Green, surveying child sacrifice in the ancient Near East, in 1975 wrote,

> That these sacrifices indeed were customary at Carthage, Constantine, Sousse, Sardinia, Sicily, and other Punic sites has been well attested by classical and Roman writers, and the many urn-burials of children and pointed stelae at sacred sites. The combined evidence from the Roman and classical authors, the stelae, and the remains uncovered at these sacred precincts yields a description of Molek sacrifices. They were almost always linked to Kronos-Saturnus (Baal-Hammon). The Phoenicians would vow their children to Kronos, on whose bronze statue, with extended arms over a bronze brazier, the children were placed and burnt. The victim then fell from the extended arms of the idol into a prepared pit [*Tophet*], a number of which have been uncovered at the previously discussed sites.[33]

---

32. Heider, *Molek*, pp. 401 and 404. Day, *Molech*, p. 84. Marc Brettler, Review of Day, *Molech*, *AJS Review* 7, no. 1 (Spring 1982): 98–100.

33. Alberto Ravinell Whitney Green, *The Role of Human Sacrifice in the Ancient Near East* (Missoula, Mont.: Scholars Press), pp. 182–184 (hereafter cited as Green, *Human Sacrifice*).

The Punic archaeological evidence corroborated the literary evidence in the Bible for a cult of child sacrifice, the only weak link in the chain being the paucity of archaeological evidence in the Phoenician homeland, for which a number of reasons have been adduced. The most significant parallels were the sacrifice of children by fire to a god within a sacred precinct. The fact that the archaeological evidence from the Punic colonies dated from the inception of these settlements made it likely that the colonists had carried the cult with them from their original home. Green stated that "the reasons for such sacrifices are said to be national emergencies which are brought about by wars, drought, and plagues . . ."; but Stager voiced the possibility that in Carthage the elite may have utilized child sacrifice as a means of limiting the size of families, thus enabling a few heirs to inherit large estates. He disputed the view that the earlier the period in time, the more likely it was that the victims were animals rather than children. After examining the ratio of human to animal bones from urns in different strata in Carthage, his conclusion was that children were sacrificed on a larger scale in a later age.[34]

Moreover, the literary evidence points to the continuance of child sacrifice in Syria into the second and third centuries C.E. Children were hurled to death from the temple of Atargatis, while in the second century a child was sacrificed in front of Trajan, possibly by the emperor himself. Elagabalus, who was Syrian born and emperor in Rome 218–222 C.E., tried in vain to introduce the eastern custom of sacrificing noble children.[35]

The Torah railed against child sacrifice, warning Israelites, "Do not dedicate any of your offspring to Molech . . ." (Lev. 18:21). Again the warning was repeated in a different form in Deuteronomy: "Let no one be found among you who makes his son and daughter pass through fire . . ." (Deut. 18:10). Abraham appeared at first not to question the divine call to sacrifice his son Isaac, which seems to indicate that the narrative relates to a period when such notions were almost universally accepted. Here the later bizarre and somewhat inconclusive story of Jephtah sadly having to sacrifice his daughter to celebrate his victory in battle also comes to mind (Judges chapter 11). Abraham was ordered to go to the "land of Moriah," a place name of great antiquity, of which the exact geographical location

---

34. Green, *Human Sacrifice*, pp. 183 and 184. Heider, *Molek*, pp. 200, 201, 202, and 203.

35. Aline Rousselle, *Porneia on Desire and the Body in Antiquity* (Oxford: Blackwell, 1993), pp. 124, 127, and 128.

has been lost, but which was later identified in Chronicles with Jerusalem (2 Chron. 3:1). Under certain kings of Judah, there was a cult of child sacrifice associated with Jerusalem, although we do not know if the cult was of ancient foundation there. Possibly it went back to pagan times; interestingly enough, Abraham had a friendly relationship with Melchizedek, King of Salem, an early name for Jerusalem. Moreover, the story of the binding of Isaac, the *Akedah*, in Genesis highlights the use of fire in the sacrifice, which again brings it into line with the later biblical narratives of the cult of Molech (Gen. 22:6), while Abraham was also ordered by God to go to a hallowed place (a sacred precinct?) for the sacrifice.[36]

The focus of the Molech cult in the Kingdom of Judah was the *Tophet* in the valley of Hinnom outside Jerusalem. The sacrifices were carried out in the *Tophet*, which in the cognate terms in Syriac and Aramaic meant fireplace, oven, or furnace. Heider further stated that the cult was well established by the time of King Ahaz (743–727 B.C.E.) and was practiced in Jerusalem, apart from the reigns of Josiah (639–609 B.C.E.) and Hezekiah (727–698 B.C.E.), until the fall of the city in 587/6 B.C.E.; it may even have been revived for a time after the return of the Jews from the Babylonian Exile. Despite the prophets' denunciation of child sacrifice, there is the implication in their writings that certain sections of the population believed that they were carrying out God's will. According to Jeremiah, whose prophetic writings have been dated between 627 and 585 B.C.E., "they built the high places to Baal in the valley of the son of Hinnom, to offer up their sons and daughters to Molech, though I did not command them, nor did it enter my mind, that they should do this abomination, to cause Judah to sin" (Jer. 32:35). So, too, Ezekiel attacked those who had "defiled my sanctuary on the same day and profaned my Sabbaths. For when they slaughtered their children in sacrifice to the idols, on the same day they came into my sanctuary to profane it" (Ezek. 23:38–39). As many of the biblical passages associated with Molech worship refer to children in general or sons and daughters, it is clear that this cult was not merely linked to the slaughter of the first born.[37]

---

36. Nahum M. Sarna, *Understanding Genesis: The Heritage of Biblical Israel* (New York: Schocken Books, 1972), pp. 158, 159, 160, and 161–163.

37. Heider, *Molek*, p. 408. Day, *Molech*, pp. 65–69. Baruch A. Levine, *The JPS Torah Commentary: Leviticus* (Philadelphia: Jewish Publication Society, 1989), pp. 258–260 (hereafter cited as Levine, *Leviticus*).

Whereas the prophets indicate that the cult of Molech was popular, the location of the cult outside Jerusalem may indicate that the Molech cult in Judah was specially concerned with the ancestors of the royal house, just as the evidence from Mari and Ugarit suggest that this was a royal cult. Heider discerned a clear connection between the cult and dealings with the dead as a means of divination, examples of this being King Saul's consultation with the witch of Endor and King Asa (908–867 B.C.E.), who sought help and the cure of his sickness from his ancestors, the Rephaim. Isaiah also accused the rulers of Jerusalem of making a covenant with death or Sheol to avert a national catastrophe. The Israelites could have been performing rites to care for their own ancestors, who were buried on the ancestral farm holding, and who in turn were concerned with ensuring the continued fertility of their progeny. Isaiah condemned those "who sit in the tombs, and in secret places pass the night; who eat swine's flesh, and broth of unclean things is [in] their vessels" (Isa. 63:4). These activities were connected with a cult of the dead, in which the participants slept in rock-cut tombs to receive a revelation through a dream and ate swine's flesh in a ritual feast devoted to a chthonic deity, one who belonged to the earth or the underworld.[38]

On the other hand, it is possible that the cult of Molech, which was once confined to the royal houses of Israel and Judah and the aristocratic elite, became increasingly broadly based and popular with time; and that to a degree it was deliberately utilized as a means of family limitation to prevent the disintegration of large estates and the division of the peasant's ancestral holding into too many small parcels of land, as population pressure grew.

DEBT-BONDAGE

At the beginning of this chapter, we proposed a simple model of the peasant farming community in ancient Israel based on a number of related and separate nuclear families living in households grouped together to form an extended family and cooperating in the tilling of the ancestral holding; but by the time of the Israelite and Judean monarchy and the postexilic community under Nehemiah in the late fifth century B.C.E. this model was no longer relevant.

---

38. Heider, *Molek*, pp. 389, 390, 399, and 406–408. Day, *Molech*, p. 58.

There was a deepening differentiation of class divisions in the rural areas with the emergence of a landlord class, known as mighty men of wealth (*gibbore ha-ḥayil*), who plowed large estates with teams of oxen and the help of landless laborers and slaves. Such an estate was that of Saul, whose steward Ziba supervised the twenty household slaves and other hired and indentured laborers when they plowed the fields of their master. In the Northern Kingdom the large estates were concentrated in Samaria, while in Judah the powerful landowners were less dominant and were often promoted by the monarchs from among their supporters. For the ambitious youths, *ne'arim*, from the landowning class, there were opportunities for advancement in the priesthood, the army, and the royal bureaucracy.[39]

In times of general famine and localized bad harvests or family misfortune, peasants fell into distress and sold themselves and their children into indentured servitude, a process known as debt-bondage. In the Northern Kingdom, probably because of the abundance of latifundia, there was much rural poverty. A story was told concerning Elisha, a contemporary of King Ahab (871–852 B.C.E.), who assisted the widow of a member of the prophetic order when she was under great financial pressure from creditors. After a creditor seized her "two boys as his slaves," Elisha produced enough oil for her to "redeem" her sons and still left enough over for her to live on what remained (2 Kings 4:1–7). So, too, the prophet Amos, who preached in the Northern Kingdom in the reign of Jeroboam II (782–743 B.C.E.), in a series of scathing and somewhat enigmatic remarks attacked wealthy individuals who "sell the righteous for silver and the needy for a pair of shoes; that pant after the dust of the earth on the head of the poor . . ." (Amos 2:6 and 7). In every seventh year, these rural debts were cancelled and the indentured servants were supposedly freed (Deut. 25:12), although there is a vigorous debate among historians as to whether these proclamations, such as the release decreed by King Zedekiah (Jer. 34), were merely acts of propaganda or were actually implemented.[40]

---

39. Hanoch Reviv, "Social Structure of Ancient Israel," in *History until 1880* (Jerusalem: Keter Books, 1973), pp. 75–77. Louis Wallis, *God and the Social Process* (Chicago: University of Chicago Press, 1933), pp. 104, 106, 142, and 143.

40. M. I. Finley, "Debt-bondage and the Problem of Slavery," in *Economy and Society in Ancient Greece* (Harmondsworth: Penguin Books, 1983), pp. 162 and 163 (hereafter cited as Finley, *Debt-bondage*). Bernard S. Jackson, "Biblical Laws of Slavery: A Comparative Approach," in *Slavery and Other Forms of Unfree Labour*, ed. Leonie Archer (London: Routledge, 1988), pp. 86–101.

In the ancient world, an impoverished father sometimes sold his daughter into an affluent family in the hope that she would be married to the master of the house or his son. Exodus 21:7–11 attempted to protect the rights of a slave girl who was sold as a wife or concubine by stipulating that she was to be released if her master failed to fulfill his contractual obligations toward her. A pre-exilic tomb inscription of a royal steward indicated that he had arranged for his amah or slave girl from such a marriage to be buried next to him.[41]

Some slaves were captured in battle, as was stated in Leviticus: ". . . it is from the nations round about you that you may acquire male and female slaves. You may also buy them from among the children of aliens resident among you . . ." (Lev. 25:44). However, if the master sought the services of a female debt slave for the performance of household or nonsexual labor, he was permitted to allow her to work for him for only six years, after which he had to release her (Deut. 21:12–18). Again, Israelites were warned not to treat a fellow countryman as a slave, but he was to remain as a "bound or hired laborer" until his release in the Jubilee year (Lev. 25:39–40). If it is thought that this biblical passage in Leviticus is contradicted by the laws outlined in Exodus 21:2–6 and Deuteronomy 15:12–18, Gregory Chirichigno, after a careful analysis of the Near Eastern law codes, argued that this was not the case. He asserted that the seven-year release applied only in situations in which a debtor was forced to sell a member of his family to pay a debt; and that the fifty-year release applied in situations where persons were compelled to sell themselves and the patrimonial land or who were merely constrained to sell such family land.[42]

Under Nehemiah in the late fifth century B.C.E. these trends were accentuated:

> There came a time, when the common people, both men and women, raised a great outcry against their fellow Jews. Some complained that they were giving their sons and daughters as pledges for food and to keep themselves alive, some also there were that said, we have mortgaged our lands, vineyards and houses, that we might buy corn, because of the dearth. . . . We have borrowed money from the king's tribute, and that upon our lands and vineyards. Yet now our flesh is as the

---

41. Nahum M. Sarna, The *JPS Torah Commentary: Exodus* (Philadephia: Jewish Publication Society, 1991), p. 120. Gregory C. Chirichigno, *Debt-Slavery in Israel and the Ancient Near East* (Sheffield: JSOT Press, 1993), p. 254 (hereafter cited as Chirichigno, *Debt-Slavery*).
42. Levine, *Leviticus*, pp. 170 and 171. Chirichigno, *Debt-Slavery*, pp. 281 and 300.

flesh of our brethren, our children as their children: and lo, we bring into bondage our sons and daughters to be servants, and some of our daughters were brought into bondage already; neither is it in our power to redeem them . . . (Neh. 5:1–5).

Nehemiah upbraided the nobles and rulers of the people, urging them to "restore . . . to them, even this day, their lands, their vineyards, their oliveyards, and their houses, and also the hundredth part of the money, and of the corn, the wine and the oil, that ye exact of them" (Neh. 5:11). He also asserted that while the Jewish aristocracy had redeemed fellow Jews indentured to Gentiles, they still left their fellow Jews in thrall to other Jews (Neh. 5:8). By an ingenious plan Nehemiah, the Persian governor of Judea, out of "fear of the Lord" proclaimed a year of release, so that indentures and financial claims were cancelled and land was restored to its original owners; and the Jewish aristocracy had to swear that they would implement these measures swiftly. However, according to Ephraim Urbach, debt-bondage continued unabated among the Jews despite Nehemiah's reforms, for the next three centuries until the Hasmoneans' foreign conquests glutted the market with slaves. In contrast to Palestinian practice among the Jewish community of Elephantine in Egypt, creditors were denied the remedy of seizing children or cattle in contracts where the debtor defaulted.[43]

---

43. Finley, Debt-bondage, p. 163. E. E. Urbach, The Laws Regarding Slavery As a Source for Social History of the Period of the Second Temple, the Mishnah and Talmud (Jerusalem, 1964), pp. 1–41. Elias J. Bickerman, The Jews in the Greek Age (Cambridge, Mass.: Harvard University Press, 1988), pp. 42, 156, and 158.

2

Children in the Talmudic Age: Infancy and the Family

INFANTICIDE AND ABORTION

While the Torah and the prophets denounced the murder of children in unequivocal terms—"Shall I give the fruit of my body for the sin of my soul?" (Mic. 6: 7)—they were silent on the question of infanticide. During the Hellenistic and Roman eras, the Jews were faced with the challenge of an ideology that espoused the swift extinction of the lives of infants who were deemed to be physically weak or who were superfluous because they happened to be female. Responding to this challenge, Judaism clearly defined its views on this issue and insisted that it was a religious duty for Jews to rear all their children. Although one historian has attributed this novel idea to Egyptian influence or more specifically to the ideas of Alexandrian philosophy, it is more likely that it drew its inspiration from the existing pro-life and child protection ideology universally current in Jewish circles both in Palestine and Egypt in the first century B.C.E.[1]

---

1. John Boswell, *The Kindness of Strangers: The Abandonment of Children in Western Europe from Late Antiquity to the Renaissance* (New York: Pantheon Books, 1988), p. 149 (hereafter cited as Boswell, *Abandonment*).

35

It is true that Diodorus Siculus declared that native Egyptians did not expose their children like the Greeks. Not only did "they [the Egyptians] raise all their offspring," but parents who slew their children were punished. Moreover, Greeks and Romans in Egypt often left their unwanted babies on manure heaps, from where they were rescued by native Egyptians who adopted them and sometimes gave them "copro" names, referring to their origin, such as "Kopreus," to indicate that they were found abandoned on a dungheap. However, even if there is a dispute among historians as to whether exposure of infants started in Egypt in the Hellenistic or Roman periods, it is clear that with the advent of Roman rule, native Egyptian ideological constraints against infanticide crumbled.[2]

According to Mark Golden, the historian of ancient Greek childhood, "Now, it is likely (though not beyond reasonable doubt) that the exposure of newborns, especially newborn girls, was widespread and even common at Athens." Moreover, the comic Greek poet Posidippus summarized the prevailing attitudes when he remarked that "everyone, even a poor man raises a son; everyone, even a rich man, exposes a daughter." As a result, the older Greek cities started to have a shrinking population, a fact noted by the second century B.C.E. historian Polybius. If there was no hope of providing a sufficient dowry for a daughter, she was exposed by the Greeks at birth. In a well-known letter to his pregnant wife in 1 B.C.E., Hilarian wrote: "I ask and beg you to take good care of our baby son, and as soon as I receive payment I will send it up to you. If you are delivered of a child [before I return home], if it is a boy keep it, if it is a girl discard it."[3]

Further, during excavations in the Palestinian city of Ashkelon, the remains of almost a hundred infants were found in a Roman-Byzantine sewer connected to a bathhouse. After examining the bone size and dental development of these infants, experts at the Hebrew University concluded that these infants, who were probably mainly females, were killed by being callously thrown into a drain shortly after their birth. However, after studying

2. Lawrence E. Stager, "Infanticide at Ashkelon," *Biblical Archaeology Review* 17, no. 4 (1991): 47 (hereafter cited as Stager, "Infanticide"). Sarah B. Pomeroy, *Women in Hellenistic Egypt from Alexander to Cleopatra* (New York: Schocken Books, 1984), pp. 138–139 (hereafter cited as Pomeroy, *Hellenistic Women*).

3. Mark Golden, *Children and Childhood in Classical Athens* (Baltimore: Johns Hopkins University Press, 1993), p. 87 (hereafter cited as Golden, *Athenian Childhood*). Pomeroy, *Hellenistic Women*, p. 136. Stager, "Infanticide," p. 47.

comparative evidence on infanticide assembled by anthropologists and historians for pre-industrial Europe, Golden claimed that the key factor affecting attitudes to child care in such societies was whether or not a child was really wanted; and that in ancient Greece infanticide "coexisted with care and affection for children" whose survival was desired.[4]

The first indication of the new attitude among Jews is to be found in the comments of Hecataeus of Abdera (c. 300 B.C.E.), a Graeco-Egyptian writer, who declared that Moses "required those who dwelt in the land to rear their children, and since offspring could be cared for at little cost, the Jews were from the start a populous nation."[5]

Later the Jewish philosopher Philo of Alexandria (c. 30 B.C.E.–40 C.E.) eloquently expounded the new norms and castigated those who slaughtered their own infants.

> If the guardians of the children cut them off from these blessings, if at their very birth they deny them all share in them, they must rest assured that they are breaking the laws of Nature and stand self-condemned on the gravest of charges, love of pleasure, hatred of men, murder and, the worst abomination of all, murder of their own children. For they are pleasure-lovers when they mate, not to procreate children and perpetuate the race, but like pigs and goats in quest of the enjoyment which such intercourse gives. . . . For no one is so foolish as to suppose that those who have treated dishonourably their own flesh and blood will deal honourably with strangers. As to the charges of murder in general and murder of their own children in particular the clearest proofs of their truth is supplied by the parents. Some of them do the deed with their own hands; with monstrous cruelty and barbarity they stifle and throttle the first breath which the infants draw or throw them into a river or into the depths of the sea, after attaching some heavy substance to make them sink more quickly under its weight. Others take them to be exposed in some desert place, hoping, they themselves say, that they may be saved, but leaving them in actual truth to suffer the most distressing fate. For all the beasts that feed on human flesh visit the spot and feast unhindered on the infants, a fine banquet provided by their sole guardians, those who above all should keep them safe, their fathers and mothers. Carnivorous birds, too, come flying down and gobble up the fragments . . .[6]

---

4. Stager, "Infanticide," p. 47. Golden, *Athenian Childhood*, p. 87.

5. Menachem Stern, ed., *Greek and Latin Authors on Jews and Judaism: From Herodotus to Plutarch* ed. (Jerusalem: Israel Academy of Sciences and Humanities, 1974). Vol. 1., pp. 29 and 34.

6. Philo, *The Special Laws*, trans. F. H. Colson. Loeb Classical Library (Cambridge, Mass.: Harvard University Press, 1950), Vol. 7 (3:112–115) pp. 547 and 549 (hereafter cited as Philo, *Special Laws*).

Philo, in the Special Laws, following the Stoic philosophers, condemned sexual activity if it was for pleasure and not for the procreation of children, but the reasoning behind his criticism of the consequences of unbridled passion, the birth of unwanted infants who were killed, was new: "So Moses, then, as I have said, implicitly and indirectly forbade the exposure of children, when he pronounced the sentence of death against those who cause the miscarriage of mothers in cases where the foetus is fully formed. . . ." To reach this conclusion, Philo reiterated the views of the translators of the Greek version of the Bible, which was produced in Alexandria in the third century B.C.E. and known as the Septuagint, in his understanding of Exodus 21:22 and 23: ". . . if [there be] no form [yet, to the fetus], he shall be fined. . . . But if [there be] form, then shalt thou give life for life." This interpretation was achieved by translating the Hebrew word *ason* as "form," instead of by its plain meaning of "harm." However, if according to Samuel Belkin this translation was also known to Jews in Palestine, Philo's interpretation had a possible basis in Mishnaic law or halakhah. Belkin drew attention to a parallel rabbinic ruling that if a woman who had been condemned to death by a court was already seated on a birthstool, her execution was postponed until the child was born because she was carrying a fully formed fetus (Arakhin 1:4).[7]

Philo continued,

And therefore infanticide undoubtedly is murder, since the displeasure of the law is not concerned with ages but with a breach of faith to the race. Though indeed, if age had to be taken into consideration, infanticide to my mind gives a greater cause for indignation, for in the case of adults quarrels and differences supply any number of reasonable pretexts, but with mere babes, who have passed into the light and the life of human kind, not even a false charge can be brought against such absolute innocence.[8]

---

7. David Biale, *Eros and the Jews: From Biblical Israel to Contemporary America* (New York: Basic Books, 1992), pp. 37–39 (hereafter cited as Biale, *Eros and Jews*). Peter Brown, *The Body and Society* (London: Faber and Faber, 1990), p. 21. Philo, *Special Laws*, p. 449. David M. Feldman, *Marital Relations, Birth Control, and Abortion in Jewish Law* (New York: Schocken Books, 1975), p. 257. Samuel Belkin, *Philo and Oral Law: The Philonic Interpretation of Biblical Law in Relation to Palestinian Halakah* (New York: Johnson Reprint Corporation, 1968), pp. 132–135 (hereafter cited as Belkin, *Philo*).

8. Philo, *Special Laws* (3:118–119), p. 551.

In his book *On Virtues* Philo advanced a fresh argument against infanticide by stating that just as the Torah showed mercy to newly born animals, so humans should be merciful to their newly born offspring.

> Can you not see that our all-excellent lawgiver was at pains to insure that even in the case of irrational animals, the offspring should not be separated from their mother so long as it is being suckled? Still more for your sake, good sirs, was that order given, that if nature does not, instruction may teach you the duty of family love. . . . So desirous is he to sow in diverse forms the seeds of gentleness and moderation in their minds, that he lays down another enactment of the same nature as the preceding. He forbids them to sacrifice the mother and its offspring on the same day. . . .[9]

Similar views against the exposure of infants and abortion were shared by the Jews in Palestine because the underlying philosophy was the same in both areas. The Jewish historian Josephus (37–105 C.E.), in his tract "Against Apion," declared that "the Law, moreover, enjoins us to bring up all our offspring, and forbids women to cause abortion of what is begotten, or to destroy it afterward; and if any woman appears to have done so, she will be a murderer of her child, by destroying a living creature, and diminishing human kind; and if any one, therefore, proceeds to such fornification, or murder, he cannot be clean" (2:25). Yet this approach to infanticide was not merely confined to those with a knowledge of Greek philosophy like Philo and Josephus but was part of the concern of the rabbis. In the Tosefta, the earliest commentary on the Mishnah, it was held that one should not employ a pagan midwife, as she might kill a newly born child (Tosefta Avodah Zarah 3:3). Again, the rabbis in the Talmud proclaimed that "one desecrates the Sabbath for the sake of a baby of one day, but not for the sake of the dead body of David, King of Israel" (Shabbat 151b). From another relatively early source, the Roman historian Tacitus (c. 55–115 C.E.), there is supporting evidence of the Palestinian Jews' opposition to infanticide: "They take thought to increase their numbers; for they regard it as a crime to kill any late-born [unwanted] child, and they believe that the souls of those who are killed in battle or by the executioner are immortal: hence comes their passion for begetting children, and their scorn of death" (Histories 5:5). No wonder that the Church

---

9. Philo: *On Virtues*, trans. F. H. Colson. Loeb Classical Library (Cambridge, Mass.: Harvard University Press, 1960), Vol 8 (133–134) p. 245.

Father Jerome could complain in the fourth century that the Jews were breeding like vermin.[10]

Despite the strictures of Philo and the rabbis against the exposure of infants, there was nonetheless a problem of abandoned infants in Palestinian cities and other places where Jews dwelt. Even so, it was probably of smaller dimensions than elsewhere. The prophet Jeremiah asserted that "for even a doe in the field gave birth and departed, for there was no grass" (Jer. 14:5), hinting that mothers at the time of the destruction of the First Temple abandoned children whom they could not feed. The Mishnah referred to ten genealogical classes who returned to Judaea from the Babylonian Exile, among whom were *asufi*, defined as those "who were picked up from the street and knows neither his father nor his mother" (Kiddushin 4:2).

In another portion of the Mishnah, the legal position surrounding foundlings was set out. "If he [a Jew] found an abandoned child in a city, and most of the people were gentiles, it may be deemed as a gentile child; if most of them were Israelites, it may be deemed an Israelitish child; if they were equal, it may be deemed an Israelitish child. R. Judah says: It should be determined by which are more wont to abandon children" (Makhshirin 2:7). Obviously R. Judah was arguing in the latter instance that it was now unusual for Jews to abandon infants, so that the foundling should not be regarded as a Jewish child. Was this a relatively new idea in the first two centuries C.E. and was it only now that Jewish attitudes to the exposure of children were crystallizing?

When the Babylonian Talmud dealt with the problem it decided that "if [the inhabitants of the town are] half to half [the child is] an Israelite . . ." (Ketubot 15b), which may indicate that the problem of abandoned children worsened over the centuries. During times of war and famine, Jewish infants were sometimes orphaned because their parents had been killed or had died from hunger or disease; Elijah, while "searching for those who were languishing with hunger in Jerusalem . . . found a child faint with hunger lying upon a dunghill" (Sanhedrin 63b); and the Talmud also mentioned "[children thrown away] on account of poverty [literally hunger] . . ." (Kiddushin 73a). Moreover, the Babylonian Talmud discussed in consid-

10. *The Works of Favius Josephus*, trans. William Whinston (London: William Milner, 1866), p. 657. Menachem Stern, ed., *Greek and Latin Authors on Jews and Judaism: From Tacitus to Simplicius* (Jerusalem: Israel Academy of Sciences and Humanities, 1980), Vol. 2, p. 26, Vol. 1, p. 33.

erable detail the definition of which children were to be classified as foundlings, which may indicate that this was a live and important issue in
Babylonia. "If he [the foundling] is found circumcised, he is not [forbidden
in marriage to the higher genealogical classes concerned with purity of
descent] on account of the law of foundling. If his limbs are set, he is not
[forbidden] as a foundling. If he has been massaged with oil, fully powdered, has beads hung on him, wears a tablet [with an inscription] or an
amulet, he is not considered a foundling. If he is suspended on a palm
tree, if a wild beast can reach him, he is [forbidden] as a foundling; if not,
he is not considered as a foundling. . . . [If found in] a synagogue near a
town where many congregate, it is not a foundling; otherwise, it is." Further, "Amemar said: [If found in] a pit of date stones, he is considered a
foundling; in the swift current of a river, he is not a foundling [parents
would not place him in a location where boats regularly plied, if he was
unfit]; in shallow water, he is a foundling; in the side passages off public
thoroughfares, he is not a foundling; in a public thoroughfare, he is a foundling [as it is dangerous to leave a child there]. Said Raba: But in famine
years he is not considered a foundling" (Kiddushin 73a).

We are also told that "on the day that Abraham weaned his son Isaac,
he made a great banquet, and all the peoples of the world derided him
saying, 'Have you seen that old man and woman, who brought a foundling from the street and now claim him as their son!'" (Baba Metzia 87a).
In the Tanna De-be Eliyahu, "R. Jose said: Once I was walking in the great
city of Rome where I saw the emperor riding a horse. . . . The emperor
happened to see a Jewish infant girl, smitten with boils, who had been
cast on a dung heap." No doubt there was a social reality underlying these
legendary tales, but the literary stories are relatively sparse and there is no
archaeological record of the mass murder of infants by Jews. It is doubtful
whether the abandonment of children in Jewish circles ever reached anything like the scale that it attained among the pagans, particularly the Greeks
and the Romans. In fact, Jewish law made it easy for parents to reclaim
their own abandoned children, once the immediate crisis caused by a famine was over.[11]

We have seen that when he examined the issue of abortion Philo, following the translation of the biblical text in the Septuagint, drew a distinction between killing a fetus that was not properly formed and one that had

---

11. *Tanna Debe Eliyyahu: The Lore of the School of Elijah*, trans. William G.
Braude and Israel J. Kapstein (Philadelphia: Jewish Publication Society, 1981), p. 464.

a distinctive shape, which he concluded was akin to murder. This was a different interpretation from the plain meaning of the Hebrew text of the Bible, which declared that ". . . if men strive together, and hurt a woman with child, so that her fruit depart, and yet no harm follow, he shall surely be fined, according as the woman's husband shall lay upon him; and he shall pay as the judges determine [perhaps according to the degree of the woman's pregnancy]. But that if any harm follow [to the woman], then thou shalt give life for life" (Exod. 21:22 and 23). Philo declared,

> If a man comes to blows with a pregnant woman and strikes her on the belly and she miscarries, then, if the result of the miscarriage is unshaped and undeveloped, he must be fined both for the outrage and for obstructing the artist Nature in her creative work of bringing into life the fairest of living creatures, man. But, if the offspring is already shaped and all the limbs have their proper qualities and places in the system, he must die, for that which answers to this description is a human being, which he has destroyed in the laboratory of Nature who judges that the hour has not yet come for bringing it out into the light, like a statue lying in a studio requiring nothing more than to be conveyed outside and released from confinement.[12]

Summing up his close scrutiny of the sources, Samuel Belkin stated: "All the sources which we have discussed show that Philo's statement has its background in Tannaitic Halakah, although it is possible that the later Tannaitic Halakah was·more lenient with a man who killed a foetus than with one who killed a child already born." We see an expression of this later viewpoint in a passage in Josephus: "He that kicks a woman with child so that she miscarries, let him pay a fine in money as the judges shall determine, as having diminished the population by the destruction of what was in her womb, and let money also be given to the woman's husband by him" (Antiquities 4, 8, 33). Elsewhere in "Against Apion" we have seen that Josephus maintained in a fashion similar to Philo that abortion could be a capital offense: "Weyl and Frankel understand Josephus' words to imply legal prosecution and punishment for abortion," declared Belkin. "Aptowitzer thinks, however, that the 'matter under consideration is only of moral valuation.'"[13]

---

12. Belkin, *Philo*, p. 130. Philo, *Special Laws* (3: 108–109), p. 545.

13. Belkin, *Philo*, p. 136. Samuel Belkin, "The Alexandrian Source for Contra Apionem, " *Jewish Quarterly Review* 27 (1936–37): 7 (hereafter cited as Belkin, "Alexandrian Source"). V. Aptowitzer, "Notes on Jewish Criminal Law," *Jewish Quarterly Review* 15 (1924): 111.

Through the Judeo-Christians these Jewish rulings against infanticide and abortion entered the mainstream of Christian thought, as they were elaborated by the Church Fathers. The *Sibylline Oracles*, a work mainly composed by Jews in Egypt during the reign of the Emperor Hadrian before 130 C.E. but also containing Christian elements, proclaimed: "Rear your own offspring and do not kill it" (interestingly enough this admonition against infanticide was couched in the feminine form). So, too, the *Didache*, a Christian work with strong Jewish elements dating from the first half of the second century C.E., condemned both infanticide and abortion in a similar manner to Philo and Josephus and warned: "Thou shalt not murder, thou shalt not commit adultery, thou shalt not corrupt youths, thou shalt not commit fornification, thou shalt not steal, thou shalt not play the sorcerer, thou shalt not use witchcraft, thou shalt not slay a child by abortion, neither put to death one that is born." Further, the *Didache* castigated "Child-murderers, who go the way of death, who slay God's image in the womb."[14]

Under Jewish intellectual stimulus early Christianity rejected both the exposure of children and abortion. Recent research by John M. Riddle has established that the Greek doctors of the Roman period recommended abortifacients derived from plant substances that were much more effective and safer than has hitherto been thought to be the case; and that these doctors' prescriptions were based on widely used folk remedies. In a petition to the emperor Marcus Aurelius (161–180 C.E.), the Christian philosopher Athenagoras claimed that Christians "call women who take medications to induce abortions murderers" and "forbid the exposure of a child, because it is the same as killing a child."[15]

Moreover, the Church Father Tertullian wrote in his *Apology* in 198 C.E. that pagans slaughtered infants "either by drowning, or by exposing them to the cold or death from hunger or the dogs. . . . But we are not

---

14. *The Old Testament Pseudepigrapha*, ed. James H. Charlesworth (London: Darton, Longman, and Todd, 1983), Sibylline Oracles chapter 3:765, p. 379. *The Teaching of the Twelve Apostles [Didache]*, ed. C. Taylor (Cambridge: Deighton Bell, 1886), Chapter 2, p. 123. Utta Ranke-Heinemann, *Eunuchs for the Kingdom of Heaven: The Catholic Church and Sexuality* (Harmondsworth: Penguin Books, 1991), p. 69 (hereafter cited as Ranke-Heinemann, *Catholic Sexual Attitudes*). Boswell, *Abandonment*, p. 149.

15. Ranke-Heinemann, *Catholic Sexual Attitudes*, pp. 66–68. John M. Riddle, *Contraception and Abortion from the Ancient World to the Renaissance* (Boston: Harvard University Press, 1993).

permitted, since murder has been prohibited to us once and for all, even to destroy . . . the fetus in the womb. It makes no difference whether one destroys a life that has already been born or one that is in the process of birth." Another Church Father, Ambrose, who died in 397 c.e., stated that "the poor expose their children, the rich kill the fruit of their own bodies in the womb lest their property be divided up, and they destroy their own children in the womb with murderous potions." We can now appreciate that later Christian apologists repeated Jewish philosophical arguments against abortion and infanticide with which we are now familiar. No doubt swayed by these new Jewish and Christian ideals, the Roman state in 374 c.e. branded infanticide as murder, while a fourth-century Christian compilation, the Apostolic Constitutions, following Philo's rationale condemned the killing of a fetus that was in a perfectly formed shape.[16]

CHILDBIRTH AND INFANCY

The Talmud declared that "at five one [a boy] is ready to study the Bible . . . at eighteen [the groom is ready] for the wedding." Elsewhere there was a tradition that God waited patiently for a man to marry before he was twenty, but became angry if he remained a bachelor after that age. On the other hand, inscriptions on Jewish tombstones show that girls married between the ages of twelve and eighteen years with the average age for marriage for girls probably being fifteen. In Rome the surviving records tell us that two girls married at twelve, two at fifteen, one at fifteen or sixteen, and one a year or two later. Nonetheless, it has been noted that rabbinic discussions stated that girls were betrothed at twelve years, followed by marriage and cohabitation a year later, but this does not seem to have accorded with common practice. On the whole, Jewish girls married later than pagans, with less chance of death at childbirth, as their physiques were more fully developed.

Epitaphs on tombstones frequently stressed the theme of the premature death of the deceased, instead of marriage, which in the natural order of events was their due, a pervasive theme of regret that the Jews shared with the Greeks and Romans on their own memorials. One such inscription contained the wording "Look at my tombstone, passer-by, weep as

16. Ranke-Heinemann, *Catholic Sexual Attitudes*, pp. 68–69.

you gaze; beat five times with your hands for a five-year-old. For early and without marriage I live in my tomb."

Whereas the Scriptures understood the words "be fruitful and multiply" as a blessing, rabbinic law made procreation into a divine commandment, perhaps modeling itself on the legislation of the Roman emperor Augustus obliging men to marry and have children. According to Jeremy Cohen, the rabbis not only believed in the divine election of the Jewish people at Sinai when God revealed the Torah to them, "but the covenant and election bespoken by God's blessing of the first parents [in Genesis 1:28] was now exclusively theirs as well," so that it was now the duty of Jews to procreate and to produce large families. As the aim of marriage was the perpetuation of the family through the birth of children, barren women were regarded as objects of pity; and many midrashim dwell on the theme of how God would make them fruitful, by emphasizing the motif of "Sing, O barren one" (Isa. 54:1) and its connection with the seven barren wives who eventually became the joyous mothers of children.[17]

The blocking of a window to prevent the admission of demons who wanted to suck the newborn baby's blood, the tying of a piece of iron to the mother's bed, and the leaving of a meal on a table for magical spirits to feast on, all these were pagan practices forbidden by the sages at childbirth. In Palestine women used to put on a small stone amulet, called the "stone of preservation," which was replaced by a bagel in later centuries, to protect themselves against miscarriages. Again, the sages ruled that to allay her anxiety it was permissible to place a cup of water before a woman in confinement and to tie a hen to her. When a woman went into labor, she was settled by a midwife onto the birthing chair, which had a seat with

---

17. S. Safrai and M. Stern, ed., *The Jewish People in the First Century: Historical Geography, Political History, Social, Cultural, and Religious Life and Institutions* (Assen: Van Gorcum, 1976), Vol. 2, p. 755 (hereafter cited as Safrai and Stern). Pieter W. Van Der Horst, *Ancient Jewish Epitaphs: An Introductory Survey of a Millenium of Jewish Funeral Epigraphy (300 B.C.E.–700 C.E.)* (Kampen, the Netherlands: Kok Pharos Publishing House, 1991), pp. 46, 48, and 104 (hereafter cited as Van Der Horst). Harry Joshua Leon, *The Jews of Ancient Rome* (Philadelphia: Jewish Publication Society, 1960), pp. 230–231 (hereafter cited as Leon, *Jews of Rome*). Robert Gordis, "'Be Fruitful and Multiply'—Biography of a Mitzvah," *Midstream* 28, no. 7 (Aug./ Sep. 1982): 21–29. Jeremy Cohen, *Be Fertile and Increase: Fill the Earth and Master It: The Ancient and Medieval Career of a Biblical Text* (Ithaca, N.Y.: Cornell University Press, 1989), pp. 126 and 158–165. Mary Callaway, *Sing, O Barren One: A Study in Comparative Midrash* (Atlanta: Scholars Press, 1986), pp. 116–139.

a crescent-shaped cavity and a handle for the woman to grip while strain-
ing, but the midwife was seated below the laboring woman to simplify the
task of delivering the infant.[18]

Childbirth was still difficult in the Roman and Babylonian worlds, in spite
of the new medical techniques that were being devised. A poignant re-
minder of this was the recent discovery in Jerusalem of a fourth century
C.E. skeleton of a girl aged about fourteen with the remains of a forty-week-
old fetus and traces of a substance initially believed to be cannabis, which
was often given by a midwife to the mother to inhale to assist the process
of childbirth. Later the author of the archaeological report expressed some
doubt as to whether or not he had clearly identified what was used. Midwives possessed considerable obstetrical skills. "If a fetus died inside its
mother, the midwife who by means of intra-uterine manipulation touched
the fetus inside the womb becomes impure for seven days" (Yevamot 103a).
If necessary, cesarean sections were performed by surgeons. "If a woman
dies in labor on the Sabbath-day, one must fetch a knife," Samuel the
physician declared, "open her abdomen, and extract the child" (Arakhin
7a); but despite William Feldman's assertions to the contrary, it is doubtful whether such operations were carried out successfully on a living woman
in this period. In critical situations the fetus was removed by morcellation
by means of a hooked knife and traction hook to save the life of the mother.
The midrash mentioned that "some children are liable to be born lame or
blind or cripples, or require the amputation of a limb so that they come
out safely" (Exodus Rabbah 1:15). Again, it is doubtful whether infants
survived a severe amputation.[19]

There was also a widespread belief among the rabbis, shared with the
Greeks and Romans, that a seven-month-old baby had a better chance of

---

18. Safrai and Stern, pp. 764–766. Aline Rousselle, "Body Politics in Ancient Rome,"
in *A History of Women in the West: From Ancient Goddesses to Christian Saints*,
ed. Pauline Schmitt Pantel (Cambridge, Mass.: Belknap Press of Harvard University, 1992),
p. 300 (hereafter cited as Rousselle, "Body Politics"). Ralph Jackson, *Doctors and Diseases in the Roman Empire* (London: British Museum Publications, 1988), pp. 96–99
(hereafter cited as Jackson, *Doctors*).

19. "Remains Found of an Ancient Dope Smoker," *The Independent*, 20 May 1993.
W. M. Feldman, *The Jewish Child: Its History, Folklore, Biology, and Sociology* (Lon-
don: Balliere, Tindall, and Cox, 1917), pp. 157 and 160 (hereafter cited as Feldman,
Jewish Child). Jackson, *Doctors*, pp. 104–106. Suessman Muntner, "Medicine in Ancient
Israel," in Fred Rosner, *Medicine in the Bible and the Talmud* (New York: Ktav Publishing
House, 1977), p. 16.

survival at birth than one at eight months—all of them believed that some fetuses were fully developed at seven months and ready to be born, whereas other fetuses were not mature enough for birth until nine months; thus birth at eight months could be hazardous. What underlay this mistaken hypothesis was an explanation of why certain premature babies survived while others who outwardly seemed more hardy and viable died.[20]

Despite the various palliative medical measures outlined above, we have seen that Aline Rousselle estimated that in Rome at least 5 to 10 percent of mothers perished in childbirth or in its ensuing complications. The evidence from the tombstones seems to suggest that a lower natal mortality rate prevailed among Jews, as Jewish girls married later than pagans and Christians, so that fewer tended to die prematurely at childbirth because of an underdeveloped physique. Leviticus Rabbah 27:7 touched on the frequency of death among the women in childbirth, exclaiming "Me'afa' [a thing of nought] means from the hundred cries which a woman utters when she sits on the birthstool, when it is a case of ninety-nine chances of death and one of life." So, too, the tombstone of the young Jewess Arsinoe in Egypt entreated wayfarers to weep for her, as "I was bereaved of my mother when I was a little girl, and when the flower of my youth made me ready for a bridegroom, my father married me to Phabeis, and Fate brought me to the end of my life in bearing my firstborn child." The Mishnah warned that women died in childbirth on account of their failure to observe the kindling of the Sabbath lights, negligence in the separation of the offering of dough when baking bread, and through failure to adhere to the laws of menstrual purity (Shabbat 2:6).[21]

The Talmud declared that there was a psychic influence on the mother of the child at the moment of conception. R. Eliezer had an ascetic attitude toward sex, agreeing with the Stoics and Philo that sexual intercourse

---

20. Abraham Wasserstein, "Normal and Abnormal Gestation Periods in Humans: A Survey of Ancient Opinion (Greek, Roman, and Rabbinic)," *Koroth* 9, no. 1–2 (Fall 1985): 221–229.

21. Rousselle, "Body Politics," p. 298. B. Blumenkranz, "*Quelques notations démographiques sur les Juifs de Rome des premiers siècles*" in *Studia Patristica*, ed. F. L. Cross (Berlin: Akademie-Verlag, 1961), pp. 344 and 345. Van Der Horst, p. 150. William Horbury and David Noy, *Jewish Inscriptions of Graeco-Roman Egypt* (Cambridge: Cambridge University Press, 1992), pp. 37, 38, 159, 174, and 182–184. Inscription numbers 23, 106, 33, 85, and 99 recording death of women in childbirth (hereafter cited as Horbury and Noy, *Egyptian Jewish Inscriptions*).

was legitimate only for the procreation of children and taking the view that the sexual act should be brief and hurried. "They asked Imma Shalom [Mother of Peace] the wife of Rabbi Eliezer, 'Why do you have such beautiful children?' She said to them, 'He does not have intercourse with me at the beginning of the night, nor at the end of the night, but at midnight, and when he has intercourse with me, he unveils an inch and veils it again, and appears as if he was driven by a demon'" (Nedarim 20a–20b), probably meaning that he does it quickly as if a demon was compelling him. Moreover, a Babylonian sage, R. Johanan b. Dahabai, declared that "people are born lame because they [that is their parents] overturned their table [that is, had intercourse in a nonmissionary position]; dumb, because they converse during intercourse; blind, because they look at 'that place'" (Nedarim 20a). The other sages, however, rejected his ruling. It was also reported that "R. Johanan [who was famous for his beauty] was accustomed to go and sit at the gates of the bathing place. He said: When the daughters of Israel come up from bathing they look at me and they have children as handsome as I am" (Berakhot 20a); this was because they allegedly retained his image in their minds when they went home and conceived.[22]

Male sons and heirs were regarded as being particularly important, yet it was unlikely that they were better fed and treated than daughters. From an analysis of tombstone inscriptions Peter Van der Horst estimated that for the period 300 B.C.E. to 700 C.E. the average age for death for Jewish men was 28.4 years, while for women it was 27 years; but for pagans there was approximately a five-year difference between the sexes for life expectancy, which seems to indicate a wider disparity in the quality of the food and material comforts enjoyed by men and women in the Gentile world. Perhaps the welcome given to all children at birth was an attitude that persisted among the Jews. Nonetheless, the chief reason for their higher life expectancy was the fact that Jewish women married later, when they were more physically robust and mature and more able to cope with the strains of childbirth.

"Without both male and female children the world could not exist," proclaimed the Talmud, "but blessed is he whose children are male and woe to him whose children are female" (Bava Batra 16b). While it is true

_____

22. Daniel Boyarin, *Carnal Israel: Reading Sex in Talmudic Culture* (Berkeley and Los Angeles: University of California Press, 1993), pp. 47 and 48 (hereafter cited as Boyarin, *Carnal Israel*). Biale, *Eros and Jews*, pp. 50, 51, and 249.

that families rejoiced at the birth of a daughter, the greatest joy was reserved for the birth of a son. "Even though the infant issues from the womb of its mother filthy and soiled, full of secretions and blood, all embrace and kiss it, more especially if it is a male" (Leviticus Rabbah 27:7). So, too, R. Isaac citing R. Ammi further stated: "When a male comes into this world his provision comes with him. . . . A female has nothing with her, [the Hebrew for] female [nekevah] implying 'she comes with nothing' [nekiyyah ba'ah]" (Niddah 31b). "A girl is for her father a vain treasure," proclaimed the Talmud, "because of his fears for her, he does not sleep at night. As long as she is young, from fear that she be seduced; when a maiden, from fear lest she become a harlot; when of age, lest she remain unmarried; if married, from fear that she have no children; when older, lest she be addicted to sorcery" (Sanhedrin 100b); yet other talmudic sages had a more positive evaluation of girls.[23]

After the birth of a son, guests gathered every night for a week prior to the circumcision to protect the child. Whereas in Palestine there was unrestrained rejoicing and feasting on the occasion of the circumcision of a son, the Egyptian Jews, particularly in Alexandria, treated the occasion as one of sobriety, as they were concerned that too much revelry and feasting could degenerate into pagan licentiousness; in the same way, steps were taken to ensure that the excesses of a Roman banquet were not duplicated in the Seder service. In Palestine "old," strong wine was drunk at the circumcision feast. "My father, Abayah, was one of the notable men of his generation, and at my circumcision he invited all the notables of Jerusalem, including R. Eliezer and R. Joshua. And when they had eaten and drunk, they sang some ordinary songs and others alphabetical acrostics" (Midrash Rabbah Ruth 6:4). It appears that Philo criticized the Alexandrian Jews for celebrating the rite in a pagan fashion, a criticism echoed in Josephus. "For come, if you please," asserted Philo, "and contemplate with me the much celebrated festivities of men . . . among barbarians and Greek nations . . . the following are the most remarkable and celebrated points: security, relaxation, truce, drunkenness, revelling, luxury, amusements, music at the door, banquets throughout the night, unseemly pleasures, wedding feasts during the day . . . wakefulness during the night for the indulgence of immoderate appetites . . ." According to Josephus, "Nay, indeed, the Law does not permit us to make festivals at the birth of

---

23. Van Der Horst, pp. 73–76. Safrai and Stern, p. 750.

our children and thereby afford occasion of drinking to excess, but it ordains that the very beginning of our education should be immediately directed to sobriety." By the first or second century C.E. it was the custom to name sons at the circumcision ceremony.[24]

During the talmudic age, circumcision was performed by specially qualified Jewish physicians, although women were allowed to perform the operation if no one else was available. At the same time, circumcision came to include "the tearing of the genital mucus membrane and laying bare the glans" (peri'ah) in addition to the cutting of the foreskin, and oral suction was applied to the wound by the mohel (circumciser) to stop the bleeding (Shabbat 133b and Mishnah Shabbat 19:2–6).

What was the meaning given to the rite of circumcision in this age? First and foremost, circumcision was a marker setting Jewish males apart from others in the Graeco-Roman world, a point emphasized by Tacitus, who declared, "They adopted circumcision to distinguish themselves from other peoples by this difference. Those who are converted to their ways follow the same practice . . ." Second, Philo and certain rabbis interpreted the rite as being designed to curb sexual desire. Philo asserted that "for since among all passions that of intercourse between man and woman is greatest, the lawgivers have commended that that instrument which serves this intercourse, be mutilated, pointing out, that these powerful passions must be bridled, and thinking not only this, but all passions would be controlled through this one."[25]

By the second century C.E. the sages in Palestine and later in Babylonia recognized that hemophilia could be transmitted genetically through the female line. "For it was taught: If she circumcised her first child and he died [as a result of bleeding from the operation], and a second one also died [similarly], she must not circumcise her third child" (Yevamot 64b).

24. Safrai and Stern, p. 767. Belkin, "Alexandrian Source," pp. 19–21.

25. Joseph Gutmann, The Jewish Life Cycle (Leiden: E. J. Brill, 1987), p. 4. Nissan Rubin, The Beginning of Life: Rites of Birth, Circumcision, and Redemption of the First-Born in the Talmud and Midrash (Hebrew) (Israel: Hakkibutz Hameuchad, 1995), p. 120. Feldman, Jewish Child, p. 207. Biale, Eros and Jews, p. 48. Michael Signer, "To See Ourselves as Others See Us: Circumcision in Pagan Antiquity and the Christian Middle Ages," in Berit Mila in the Reform Context, ed. Lewis M. Barth (New York: Berit Mila Board of Reform Judaism, 1990), pp. 118 and 119 (hereafter cited as Barth, Berit Mila). Lloyd deMause, "The Evolution of Childhood," in The History of Childhood, ed. Lloyd deMause (London: Souvenir Press, 1974), p. 24 (hereafter cited as deMause, Childhood).

Although Maimonides believed that the operation on the third child could be postponed until the child grew up and he became vigorous, the Mishnah appears to indicate that certain priests remained uncircumcised throughout their lives because their two elder brothers had died as infants (Yevamot 8:1); this is supported by the fact that these priests were not allowed to eat the heave offering.[26]

In 174 B.C.E. Jason persuaded the Greek ruler of Judaea to transfer the high priesthood to him, in return for which greater sums of money would be paid as tribute to Antiochus. As part of the process of Hellenization, the city of Jerusalem gained recognition as a Greek polis, while a gymnasium and an ephebate, a center for training military conscripts and for further education, were established. Overwhelmed with a desire to come to an accommodation with Hellenistic culture, sometimes tinged with a degree of self-hatred, many young Jews had a cosmetic operation performed on themselves to disguise the signs of circumcision, thereby avoiding the mockery of the Greeks who frequented the public baths and wrestling schools. Finally, Antiochus issued an edict banning the rite of circumcision, which was repealed only by the revolt of the Maccabees in 167 C.E.

Again, after the destruction of the Temple in 70 C.E., the morale of the Jews ebbed and the Mishnah referred to those who "violated the Covenant," while the Apocryphal Book of Baruch stated, "That I have seen many of Thy people who have forsaken Thy covenant, and thrown off the yoke of Thy religion." Suetonius related that "in the days of Domitian [Emperor 81–96] the collection of the Jewish tax was carried out with especial severity. . . . I myself remember a scene from my youth, when the Procurator, surrounded by a host of his assistants, subjected an old man of about 90 to a physical examination, in order to determine whether or not he was circumcised."

In 131 C.E., the emperor Hadrian issued a decree, not directed against Jews alone, making circumcision illegal, one of the factors that precipitated the Bar Kokhba Revolt in the following year. For these reasons, once again the practice of disguising the signs of circumcision became widespread among the Jews, as testified by a statement in the Tosefta: "Many who had obliterated their sign of the Covenant were circumcised in the days of Bar Koziba." Because of this reluctance to become circumcised, the rabbis modified the operation by ruling that the glans penis was to be

---

26. Fred Rosner, *Medicine in the Bible and the Talmud* (New York: Ktav Publishing House, 1977), pp. 43, 44, and 47. Feldman, *Jewish Child*, p. 206.

laid bare during the operation to ensure that the signs of circumcision could not be concealed in the future.[27]

At the same time, the rabbis developed arguments in the fifth century to counter the beliefs of the Graeco-Roman world that circumcision resulted in the mutilation of the body. Rather, the rabbis in various midrashim held that circumcision, by removing a slight blemish, contributed to the perfection of the body. "R. Judah said: In the case of a fig, its only defect is its stalk. Remove it and blemish ceases. Thus, the Holy One Blessed be He said to Abraham, "Your only defect is this foreskin. Remove it and the blemish is cancelled. 'Walk before Me and be perfect'" (Genesis Rabbah 17:1). For the opposite reason, Paul abandoned the rite of circumcision as an essential prerequisite for conversion to Christianity when he aimed his missionary efforts at the pagan Graeco-Roman world.[28]

All infants were swaddled, that is, their limbs were bound in bandages for a period of approximately two months in ancient Rome, according to Soranus, an eminent physician active in Rome between 98 and 138 C.E., thereby slowing down their heartbeat and rendering them extremely docile and sleepy. To understand the practice of swaddling more clearly, we shall quote in full the description of Soranus, although of course there were variations in the techniques of swaddling in different parts of the Mediterranean:

> But this method of bandaging is hard to endure and cruel, [referring to the method adopted by the Thessalians]. Rather one must mold every part according to its natural shape, [and] if something has been twisted during the time of delivery, one must correct it and bring it into its natural shape. . . . The midwife should put the newborn down gently on her lap which has been covered entirely with wool or with a piece of cloth so that the infant may not cool down when laid bare while every part is swaddled. Then she must take soft woolen bandages which are clean and not too worn out, some of them three fingers in breadth, others four fingers. . . .
>
> The midwife then should take the end of the bandage, put it over its hand and, winding it round, carry it over the extended fingers; then over the middle of the

27. Emil Schurer, *The History of the Jewish People in the Age of Jesus Christ*, ed. Geza Vermes, Fergus Millar, and Matthew Black (Edinburgh: A. & C. Black, 1973), Vol. 1., pp. 148, 149, 155, and 538–540 (hereafter cited as Schurer, *Revised*). Gedaliah Alon, *The Jews in their Land in the Talmudic Age* (Jerusalem: Magnes Press, 1980), Vol. 1, pp. 75 and 76. Vol. 2 (1984), p. 659 (hereafter cited as Alon, *Jews in the Talmudic Age*).

28. Lewis M. Barth, "Berit Mila in Midrash and Agada," pp. 104–112, and Michael Signer, pp. 113–122 in Barth, *Berit Mila*.

hand, the forearm and the upper arm, slightly compressing the parts at the wrist but keeping the rest of the armpit loose. Having also swaddled the other arm in the same manner, she should then wrap one of the broader bandages circularly around the thorax [the part of the body between the neck and abdomen], exerting an even pressure when swaddling males, but in females binding the parts at the breast more tightly, yet keeping the region of the loins loose, for in women this form is more becoming. After this one must swaddle each leg separately, for to join them naked and bind them up together is apt to produce ulceration; for the juxtaposition of bodies which are as yet soft makes them quickly burn with inflammation. The midwife must wind the bandage to the very tips of the toes, keep the region of the thighs and the calves loose, but tighten the parts at the knees and their hollows as well as the instep and the ankles, so that the ends of the feet be broadened but their middle might be contracted. Afterwards she should lay the arms along the sides and the feet one against the other, and with a broad bandage she should wrap up the whole infant circularly from the thorax to the feet; since if the hands are put inside the wrapping, they become accustomed to extension . . . however, by wrapping up the little hands just at first, they are prevented from becoming twisted by inordinate movements. Also, putting the fingers to the eyes often causes impaired vision.[29]

The swaddling of infants was practiced in both Judaea and Babylonia, probably for a similar length of time. "Or straighten an infant's limb," Rabbah b. Bar Hanah said in R. Johanan's name: "To swaddle an infant on the Sabbath is permitted. But we learnt: you may not straighten—There it refers to the spinal vertebrae, which appears as building [a form of work which was forbidden on the Sabbath]" (Shabbat 147b). Manipulation of the spinal column was practiced by holding the infant's ankles tightly for the vertebrae to stretch and for the spinal column to become more flexible: "Hillel answered the question 'Why are the heads of the Babylonians round?' by saying, 'because they have no skilful midwives' who could stretch the heads."[30]

Swaddling has been denounced by doctors and child historians as a cruel and unnecessary procedure and it is interesting to note that the strictures of Dr. Julius Preuss in his *Biblisch-Talmudische Medizin* (1911) against swaddling were as severe as those of Lloyd deMause in 1974. It should be

29. DeMause, *Childhood*, pp. 37 and 38. *Soranus' Gynaecology*, trans. Owsei Temkin (Baltimore: Johns Hopkins University Press, 1956), pp. 84–86 (hereafter cited as Soranus).

30. Julius Preuss, *Biblical and Talmudic Medicine,* trans. Fred Rosner (New York: Hebrew Publishing Company, 1983), p. 403 (hereafter cited as Preuss, *Talmudic Medicine*).

stressed that it lasted for a relatively short period of time during infancy in the ancient world and that the hips of infant girls in Rome were left unbound to encourage the growth of a large pelvis, which would become important later in life for them during childbirth; and it is likely that these more tolerant practices as regards infant girls spread to Judaea. Moreover, there is no evidence to suggest that Jewish infants were left to "stew in" their "own excrement" because their swaddling bands were changed infrequently. Such neglect, Soranus averred, could cause a "child's stomach to become weak and it [could] lie awake on account of itching or suffer some ulceration subsequently," but among Jews the overwhelming majority of the children were cared for by their own mothers, not by wet nurses, which made such neglect less likely to occur. Again, Galen (129– 199 c.e.), the eminent physician, opposed tight swaddling bands that caused babies discomfort.

Indeed, Ruth Benedict declared that the impact of the practice of swaddling could vary between cultures, depending on the intention of the mother when she swaddled her child. Moreover, Abraham Stahl suggested that swaddling was the initial step in socializing infants in societies with an authoritarian family structure, as we would argue Judaea was in the talmudic age: "Parents . . . foster passivity in their children: they do not encourage the development of intellectual curiosity, the asking of questions, the manipulation of objects. . . . Tight swaddling clothes may be seen as the first symbolic step, in leading toward passivity."[31]

Among the duties of a wife enumerated in the Mishnah, which she was obliged to perform for her husband, was the suckling of their child, in addition to which she had to grind the grain, bake the bread, do his washing, cook, make his bed, and work (Ketubot 5:5). If she brought her husband two female slaves on her marriage, she was allowed to hand the baby over to one of the slave girls for her to breast-feed. Most of the tannaitic sources prescribed a period of two years for the nursing to continue, but

31. DeMause, Childhood, pp. 37–38. Preuss, Talmudic Medicine, p. 403. Rousselle, "Body Politics," p. 299. Keith R. Bradley, "Wet-nursing at Rome: A Study in Social Relations," in The Family in Ancient Rome, ed. Beryl Rawson (London: Routledge, 1992), p. 219. Soranus, pp. 93 and 94. Martha Wolfenstein, "Social Variants in Moral Training of Children," in Childhood in Contemporary Cultures, ed. Margaret Mead and Martha Wolfenstein (Chicago: University of Chicago Press, 1964), p. 366. Geoffrey Gorer, The People of Great Russia: A Psychological Study (London: Cresset Press, 1959), pp. 197–226. Abraham Stahl, "Swaddling: Its Disappearance as an Illustration of the Process of Cultural Change," Koroth 8, no. 7–8 (August 1983): 297 and 298.

a variant tradition stipulated that the child could be suckled for a shorter period of eighteen months, as a widow who was still nursing her child was not permitted to remarry for eighteen months in case this interfered with her ability to go on producing milk. Likewise in a Jewish contract from Egypt of 18 B.C.E. embodying the standard conditions, the wet nurse's term of employment was fixed at eighteen months:

> Theodote agrees [with Marcus] that she will for 18 months . . . bring up and suckle in her own house in the city with her own milk pure and uncontaminated the foundling slave baby Tyche which Marcus has entrusted to her, receiving from him as payment for her milk and care [payment for the first nine months of] 8 drachmai of silver besides olive-oil . . . providing her monthly care honestly and taking fitting thought for the child, not damaging her milk, not lying with a man, not conceiving, not taking another child to suckle . . . Theodote shall bring the child to Marcus for inspection each month.

Nevertheless one rabbinic authority maintained that children could be breast-fed for four or five years, although this no doubt was unusual. Because of the commonly held belief that breast milk was formed from menstrual blood, which would not flow during pregnancy, ancient authorities advised against employing menstruating or pregnant women as wet nurses, as their milk would be spoiled.[32]

If a wife in Palestine was breast-feeding her own child, her husband was obliged to lessen her work and increase her maintenance (Ketubot 5:9). In Babylonia, if a woman was given a small allowance for board, she nevertheless was obliged to eat a great quantity of her own food in order to maintain a healthy supply of milk (Ketubot 60b). Babies were left in a cradle during the day in Palestine, but not in Babylonia, where they were tended on the mothers' laps (Oholot 12:4 and Avot de R. Nathan Chapter 29).

In contrast, in Roman upper-class families, the young infants were shortly after birth handed over to a wet nurse, who was responsible for supervising the education of the child with the assistance of a "pedagogue," usually a male slave, until puberty. Childhood in Rome was different from the modern West, where mothers are involved in the early years of their children's upbringing. Again, unlike Judaea and Babylonia, there was no special bonding between mother and child. Festus, when describing sec-

---

32. Safrai and Stern, p. 768. *Corpus Papyrorum Judaicarum*, ed. Victor A. Tcherikover and Alexander Fuchs (Cambridge, Mass.: Harvard University Press, 1960), Vol. 2, pp. 17–19. Valerie Fildes, *Wet Nursing: A History from Antiquity to the Present* (Oxford: Basil Blackwell, 1988), pp. 5–9 (hereafter cited as Fildes, *Wet Nursing*).

ond century Rome, declared that certain columns in the vegetable market were called the Lactaria "because it was there they brought children who had to be nourished with milk [by wet nurses, who plied for hire]." In upper-class families in Rome, infants were nursed at home mostly by slaves or hired help, but they were not boarded with families in the country, the only exception being foundlings who were nursed elsewhere. Under Roman influence, authorities in Palestine permitted the use of heathen slave girls as wet nurses unconditionally, although the Mishnah asserted that such wet nurses were to suckle the baby in the child's father's house (Avodah Zarah 2:1).[33]

Whereas the House of Shammai, which reflected the viewpoint of the upper class in Palestine, stated that women who vowed not to suckle their child must pull the breast out of its mouth, the House of Hillel, which was more sympathetic to the plebeian viewpoint, asserted that a husband could compel his wife to breast-feed their child (J. Ketubot 5:6 and Ketubot 59b). To resist the cultural penetration of Roman values in childrearing, the sages encouraged mothers to suckle their own children instead of relying on pagan wet nurses: "Our mother Sarah was extremely modest. Said Abraham to her: 'This is not a time for modesty, but uncover your breasts so that all may know that the Holy One, blessed be He, had begun to perform miracles.' She uncovered her breasts and milk gushed forth as from two fountains, and noble ladies came and had their children suckled by her, saying, 'We do not merit that our children should be suckled with the milk of the righteous woman'" (Genesis Rabbah 53:9). In the version of this story recounted in the Babylonian Talmud, each visiting lady brought her own child with her, "but not the wet nurse" (Baba Metzia 87a). Sarah was held out as a role model and, in an ironic reversal of roles, she suckled the children of noble ladies, the type of women who now wanted slave girls to breast-feed their children.

R. Achai claimed that he who purchased grain in the market was like a suckling whose mother was dead and who was brought to a wet nurse

---

33. Paul Veyne, "The Roman Empire," in *A History of Private Life: From Pagan Rome to Byzantium*, ed. Paul Veyne (Cambridge, Mass.: Belknap Press of Harvard University, 1987), p. 14 (hereafter cited as Veyne, *Private Life*). George D. Sussman, *Selling Mother's Milk: The Wet-Nursing Business in France 1715–1914* (Urbana and Chicago: University of Illinois Press, 1982), p. 3. Fildes, *Wet Nursing*, pp. 12–14 and 18.

to suck without being satisfied; but he who grew his own grain was like a suckling who throve on the breasts of his mother, showing that there were sages who appreciated that the child's mental and physical well-being depended on a close contact with its mother. So, too, R. Meir condemned the employment of heathen wet nurses, ostensibly on grounds that they could harm the child. Outside Palestine, Rome, and Egypt, it was doubtful whether the Roman habits of widespread wet-nursing were followed by more than a fraction of the Jewish elite.[34]

In Babylonia it was thought to be advisable that while a woman was nursing a child she should not eat any of the following items, which were believed to be injurious to the quality of the milk that she was producing: "For instance cuscuta [a plant used for brewing beer], lichen, small fishes and earth. Abaye said: Even pumpkins and quinces. R. Papa said: Even a palm's heart and unripe dates. R. Ashi said: Even *kamak* [curdled milk] and fish-hash. Some of these cause the flow of milk to stop while others cause the milk to become turbid" (Ketubot 60b). Similarly Soranus advised wet nurses "to forgo leek and onions, garlic, preserved meat or fish, radish, pulse, and all preserved food . . . and most vegetables . . . ; and meat of sheep and oxen, and this especially if roasted . . ." If an infant's mother had died, he was suckled by a hired nurse or a rota of neighboring mothers; sometimes women milked the milk from their breasts into a cup or bowl to feed the child or gave it milk to drink in an animal's horn; and if a mother fell pregnant, she fed her baby on cow's milk and eggs.[35]

In the tractate Eruvin there was an interesting discussion by the rabbis of when the dependency of a child on his mother comes to an end, which perhaps explains why boys were sent to school at six or seven; it also shows the crucial role of women in a child's early upbringing: "R. Simeon b. Lakish explained: Any child who, when awakening, does not cry . . . 'Mother!' Is this imaginable? Do not bigger children also cry mother? Rather say: Any child who, when he wakes, does not persistently cry mother [can no longer be classified as dependent]. And what [is the age of such a child]? About four or five! R. Joshua son of R. Idi replied . . . even a child of the age of six prefers his mother's company" (Eruvin 82a).

---

34. Preuss, *Talmudic Medicine*, p. 406. Feldman, *Jewish Child*, p. 406.

35. Soranus, pp. 98 and 99. Samuel Krauss, *Talmudische Archaologie* (Hildesheim: Georg Olms, 1966), Vol. 2, pp. 9 and 10. Feldman, *Jewish Child*, p. 180.

THE STRUCTURE OF THE JEWISH FAMILY

In order to understand what was happening to Jewish children during the talmudic age, it is necessary to hazard a hypothesis as to the changing structure of the family within which they grew to adulthood. Ze'ev Safrai claimed that whereas the extended family was common during the Second Temple period, in the time of the Mishnah and under the amoraim to a lesser degree the nuclear family predominated. If it is fairly certain that the joint family of the biblical age had started to disintegrate, was it replaced by the extended family in a modified form or by the Roman style of nuclear family? Let us examine the evidence. Raphael Patai stressed the importance of marriage between cousins among the Israelites and their descendants as a means of preserving family property as well as enhancing the strength of kinship ties. Tobias, the hero of the fourth century B.C.E. Book of Tobit, not only married his uncle's daughter but inherited his wife's family farm, as his spouse had no brothers (Tob. 6:9 and 7:2, 10–12). Again, the apocalyptic Book of Jubilees, written in the second century B.C.E., stated that the early saints married their cousins (Book of Jubilees 4:15, 16, 20, 27, 28, and 33). Prior to the Maccabean revolt in 167 B.C.E., the historian Shimon Applebaum has identified a group of hereditary peasant lessees on royal lands, independent peasant proprietors elsewhere, and the estates of large landowners, probably broken up by the followers of Judah Maccabee. During the time of the amoraim, R. Hiyya mentioned that brothers remained partners, presumably for working joint property, for up to three generations. When we turn to the neighboring Egyptian Jewish community, it appears that in Shlomo Goitein's words, marriage "between first cousins was extremely common in Geniza [medieval] times." Thus it is likely that some vestiges of the extended family, and in particular cousin marriages, did continue to subsist among the Jewish peasantry in the intervening period in Roman Palestine. It is difficult to believe that members of the same family did not continue to reside in proximity to each other in towns and villages, as this was still the case in the Early Modern era throughout the Middle East.[36]

------

36. Ze'ev Safrai, "Family Structure During the Period of the Mishnah and Talmud," (Hebrew) *Milet* 1 (1983): 129–156. Safrai cautiously argued that the extended family re-emerged under the amoraim. Raphael Patai, *Family, Love, and the Bible* (London: MacGibbon and Kee, 1960), p. 24, Shimon Applebaum, *Judaea in Hellenistic and Roman Times* (Leiden: E. J. Brill, 1989), pp. 37 and 38. Louis Finkelstein, *The Phari-*

Among the aristocracy, and in particular the Herodian royal family and priestly families, uncle–niece marriage was commonly practiced, so that marriages between close kin seemed to mirror the custom prevailing among the peasantry. The Tosefta to Kiddushin 1:4 proclaimed that "a man should not marry until his sister's daughter grows up or until he finds a girl from a family with his own standards." There were some six examples of uncle–niece marriage recorded within the family of Herod. For instance, Herod married both the daughter of his own brother and that of his sister. Again, Josephus also noted instances of uncle-niece marriage among the priestly family of the Tobiads. In the geneological records kept in the Temple before it was destroyed, the families of the patrician class in Jerusalem were depicted as those into which members of the priestly class might freely marry, but marriage to close relatives was more prevalent. Moreover, Louis Finkelstein contrasted the urbane Jerusalem patrician class with the country gentry, who were characterized as spending a lifetime "in the unstimulating companionship of subjected wives, intimidated children and brutalized slaves."[37]

A long tradition of scholarship has established that the rabbinic polemic in favor of uncle–niece marriage was framed to combat the condemnation of such marriages by sectarians, such as the Zadokite community, as incestuous; and that such polemic had a strong theoretical motivation, as uncle–niece marriages were not common among the rabbis. Within the ranks of the rabbis, Eliezer b. Hyrcanus married his sister's daughter against his will (Avot de R. Nathan 16:32a), but he was according to one source of priestly stock. Other cases of such marriages were those involving the brother of R. Gamaliel (Yevamot 15b) and R. Ha-Gelili (Genesis Rabbah 17:3). Here it is interesting to note that the brother of R. Gamaliel was connected with the house of Hillel, one of the few Jewish families still owning huge tracts of land in Roman Palestine, so that uncle–niece marriage may have been used as a device to prevent the disintegration of such large estates. Earlier the old ruling class had disappeared, as influential aristocratic

sees: The Sociological Background of their Faith (Philadelphia: Jewish Publication Society, 1946), Vol. 2, p. 652 (hereafter cited as Finkelstein, Pharisees). S. D. Goitein, A Mediterranean Society: The Family (Berkeley and Los Angeles: University of California Press, 1978), Vol. 3, p. 27 (hereafter cited as Goitein, Family).

37. Goitein, Family, p. 433. Chaim Rabin, Qumran Studies (Oxford: Oxford University Press, 1957), p. 91 (hereafter cited as Rabin, Qumran Studies). Finkelstein, Pharisees, Vol. 2, p. 652 and Vol. 1, p. 18.

families in Judaea had been decimated by Herod before his death in 4 B.C.E. The family of Josephus was one of the few Jewish families to retain their estates. While Roman emperors owned large estates in the Jordan valley, most of the latifundia were situated outside the Jewish areas.[38]

How big were the aristocratic Jewish families? Whereas the House of Shammai stipulated the necessity for two sons to fulfill the duty of procreation, the House of Hillel stated that a son or daughter would suffice. The House of Shammai was regarded as reflecting the upper-class view of society. There is a divergent tradition in Genesis Rabbah from the third century C.E. ascribing to Shammai the position that a person was obligated to produce two sons and two daughters, a figure that may have been close to the usual standard then prevailing in upper-class households. In contrast, if a freeborn Roman woman desired to be released from guardianship, she had to produce three children. We have some evidence from Josephus that high priestly families often exceeded the peasant norm of two children per family. In 70 C.E. three of the sons of Matthias b. Boethus were executed for treason. Moreover, three sons of the high priest Ishmael fled to the Roman lines, as did the four sons of another Matthias. Ananus b. Sethi was high priest for nine years and had five sons, all of whom succeeded him in the position. We also have a tombstone from Alexandria, probably from the late Roman period, in which Samuel thanks the Lord for his nine children. Another tombstone from Rome commemorates Veriana, the mother of five children, but a number of the Roman Jewish monumental inscriptions refer to three children, which may well have been the number of children in better-off families. Such households in Palestine were swollen in size by up to four slaves and other retainers, although slaves were not employed in tilling the fields, nor were they present in large numbers in the home: "Who is a man of wealth?" R. Tarfon asked with pardonable exaggeration. "He who possesses a hundred fields and a hundred slaves."[39]

38. Rabin, *Qumran Studies*, p. 92. Geza Vermes, *The Dead Sea Scrolls in English* (Harmondsworth: Penguin Books, 1968), p. 36 (hereafter cited as Vermes, *Dead Sea Scrolls*). S. Lowy, "The Extent of Jewish Polygamy in Talmudic Times," *Journal of Jewish Studies* 9 (1958): 137. Martin Goodman, *The Ruling Class of Judaea: The Origins of the Jewish Revolt Against Rome* (Cambridge: Cambridge University Press, 1987), p. 38 (hereafter cited as Goodman, *Jewish Revolt*). M. Avi-Yonah, *The Jews of Palestine: A Political History from the Bar Kokhba War to the Arab Conquest* (Oxford: Basil Blackwell, 1976), p. 21.

39. Cohen, *Be Fertile*, pp. 126–129. Goodman, *Jewish Revolt*, pp. 44 and 210. Horbury and Noy, *Egyptian Jewish Inscriptions*, pp. 216 and 217. Leon, *Jews of Rome*,

During the first and perhaps even into the second century of the Common Era, many small peasant proprietors survived. But from the early third century onwards, ancestral Jewish land holdings were sold and large areas of land were engrossed by powerful non-Jewish landlords, who replaced the independent peasant proprietors with various kinds of tenancies. Wide tracts of land also fell out of cultivation. It was not only the depradations of the Romans that undermined the Judaean peasantry, but the recurrent bad harvests that plunged families into debt when their savings and resources were so slender.[40]

Gedaliah Alon assigned a tradition reported in the Jerusalem Talmud to the period following the destruction of the Temple in 70 C.E., although this is contested by other authorities: "When someone would sell an inherited property, his relatives would bring jugs and fill them up with parched corn and nuts and break them before the children, and the children would collect the parched corn and nuts and say, 'Mr. So-and-so has been cut off from the inherited property'" (J. Ketubot 2:10). Summing up, Daniel Sperber declared, "This ancient custom, which was in practice until the destruction of the Second Temple (70 C.E.) and was well known to the Tanna'im, demonstrates the strong family attachment to their holding. Its sale outside the family circle was seen as a grave affront to the family's dignity and pride." Even in tannaitic times, the peasant proprietors tried to keep the ancestral holding intact by retaining the "joint holding by brothers" (Bava Batra 9:4); and two brothers who were grandsons of Judah, the brother of Jesus, were reported by Eusebius as living on the family farm in Galilee in the reign of the emperor Domitian (81–96 C.E.). Martin Goodman's skepticism about "the extended family sticking together in this period" seems to be too sweeping a generalization.[41]

However, from the second century C.E., the ruling of Abba Saul gained increasing support in Palestine, namely that a man no longer had to marry his deceased brother's wife, but had to release her in the ḥalitza (unshoeing)

---

p. 231. Martin Goodman, *State and Society in Roman Galilee A. D. 132–212* (Totowa, N.J.: Rowman Allanheld, 1983), p. 37 (hereafter cited as Goodman, *Roman Galilee*). Finkelstein, *Pharisees*, Vol. 1, p. 14.

40. Daniel Sperber, *Roman Palestine: 200–400, The Land* (Ramat-Gan: Bar Ilan University, 1978), pp. 3–6 (hereafter cited as Sperber, *Roman Palestine*). Martin Goodman, "The First Jewish Revolt: Social Conflict and the Problem of Debt," *Journal of Jewish Studies* 33 (1982): 417–427.

41. Alon, *Jews in the Talmudic Age*, Vol. 1, pp. 155 and 156. Goodman, *Roman Galilee*, p. 36. Sperber, *Roman Palestine*, p. 174.

ceremony. For as families ceased to own the ancestral holding, there seemed to be no compelling economic reason for the younger brother to marry the childless widow of his dead elder brother. It could, however, be argued that where kinship ties were very strong, they were not much diminished when peasants in Palestine became tenant farmers or migrated en masse to the towns. Even the institution of the merging of households (the *eruv*) with common meals eaten on the Sabbath by plebeians may have been easy to organize in the first instance, as the families sharing the same court may have been related. On the other hand, the Babylonian rabbis decreed that the levirate obligation took precedence over the unshoeing ceremony because the rural family's attachment to the soil persisted here for many centuries longer than in Palestine, thereby allowing archaic forms of family organization to survive. It was not until 787 C.E. that a geonic ordinance permitted a widow to enforce her marriage portion on some property other than real estate or creditors to seize an orphan's chattels instead of land in Babylonia, as it was only from the fifth century onwards that Jewish ownership of land in Babylonia started to decline.[42]

Under the impact of Roman law and civilization, the old extended Jewish family of biblical times atrophied in Palestine. The big commercial tombs of the First Temple prior to 586 B.C.E. of the Judaean aristocracy were replaced in the first century C.E. by small family tomb complexes with places reserved for the immediate nuclear family. According to Martin Goodman, a man turned to his nuclear family and to his neighbors for assistance or to borrow farm equipment rather than to his wider extended family.[43]

Nonetheless, we believe that, particularly in rural areas, a man's neighbors were more often than not still part of his kin group and not strangers—the extended family was transformed into a looser form of organization. We have already cited one passage from the Jerusalem Talmud to this effect; there is also a parallel passage (J. Ketubot 2:10), perhaps relating to priestly families but possibly of wider significance, which supplies us with an early version of the charivari, a well-known European institution that regulated marital behavior. Even more pertinent as far as the importance of kin is concerned is the following passage in the Mishnah,

---

42. Z. W. Falk, *Jewish Matrimonial Law in the Middle Ages* (Oxford: Oxford University Press, 1966), pp. 9 and 10. Sperber, *Roman Palestine*, pp. 182 and 183.

43. Goodman, *Jewish Revolt*, pp. 68 and 69. Goodman, *Roman Galilee*, pp. 36 and 37.

which is supported by the comments in the Jerusalem Talmud: "This measure applies to the priests, Levites, and Israelites [concerning the Poorman's tithe]. If he wants to save [for his own poor kinsfolk] he takes away half and gives half [to the poor that come to him]" (Pe'ah 8:6). Lawrence Stone, in criticizing Alan Macfarlane's approach to the pre-Modern English nuclear family, made some observations applicable to the Jewish family in the talmudic age: ". . . household residence tells us nothing whatever about emotional relationships. Thus court records reveal continuous ties to parents, siblings, uncles and other relatives outside the household." Elsewhere, in traditional French society, "a network of marriages, kinship, friendships and feuds enclosed these villages," Fernand Braudel claimed, despite the ban by the medieval Church on the marriage of cousins.[44]

Again, having been influenced by Roman law and civilization and the exhortations of the Church Fathers, the rabbis increasingly supported monogamy in Palestine, whereas in Babylonia there was considerable sympathy for the polygamist position. Under Roman rule, Jewish families in Palestine became monogamous, even borrowing the ring worn by the wife as a symbol of her married status from the Romans, but the power of the male head of the family—the paterfamilias—was less than total in the Jewish family. Yigael Yadin, however, pointed out that in Palestine the Temple Scroll strongly condemned polygamy: "He shall not take in addition to her (the first wife) another wife, for she alone shall be with him all the days of her life. But if she dies, he shall marry another." The Damascus Rule (IV–V), another sectarian document, went further, castigating those who took "a second wife while the first is alive" as committing the sin of "fornification." So too, a Palestinian midrashic commentary declared, "If Adam was intended to be polygamous God would have given him ten wives, not one"; and a Palestinian sage, R. Ami, remarked that "he who takes a second wife should release the first and pay her ketubah" (Yevamot 65a).[45]

44. Martine Segalen, Love and Power in the Peasant Family (Oxford: Basil Blackwell, 1983), pp. 43–47. Lawrence Stone's review of Alan Macfarlane's Marriage and Love in England in the Times Literary Supplement, 16 May 1986. Fernand Braudel, The Identity of France: History and Environment (London: Fontance Press, 1989). Vol. I, p. 118 (hereafter cited as Braudel, Identity of France).

45. Geza Vermes, "Sectarian Matrimonial Halakhah in the Damascus Rule," in Studies in Jewish Legal History: Essays in Honour of David Daube, ed. Bernard S. Jackson (London: Jewish Chronicle Publications, 1974), pp. 197–202. Vermes, Dead Sea Scrolls,

What, however, was the character of married life during the talmudic age? From tomb inscriptions in Rome we have thirteen instances of the span of married life, which ranged in length from fifteen months to thirty-four years, but on the whole it was much shorter than the duration of married life today: fifteen years together was then considered a long time. If the previous analysis of the average life span for Jewish men and women in the Roman Empire is correct, this would tend to suggest an approximation of lifestyles for Jewish couples and more egalitarianism in food consumption and material comforts than among pagans, and a more discerning attitude in encouraging the later marriage of Jewish girls. In a survey of 165 epitaphs of married Christian women, it was found that 35 had died at fifteen years or less, the majority from the accidents of childbirth. Again, the fact that in Egypt Jewish husbands alone remarked in tombstone inscriptions on the fact that their wives had died in childbirth could be because they had a more caring attitude toward their wives. Nonetheless, although women could freely visit their parents in Palestine, participate in festivities, attend the house of mourning, and undertake charitable work, shopping in the market was usually done by their husbands and the family structure was at best a modified form of patriarchy.[46]

While the old Roman moral code insisted that marriage was designed for the harmonious running of the household and the procreation of children, not for companionship, mutual affection, and sexual pleasure, the increasing adoption of monogamy under Roman influence also forced a redefinition of the purpose of marriage among Jews in Palestine and Italy. Within Rome much importance was attached to domestic comfort and conjugal love and friendship by the first century B.C.E., and by 100 C.E. such attitudes were commonplace throughout the Roman Empire. Yet the old ways of thinking sometimes persisted in times of population crisis after the destruction of the Temple, as can be seen in R. Joshua's remark: "Wed a wife in thy youth and wed a wife in thine old age. Beget children in thy youth and beget children in thine old age. Say not, 'I shall not wed a wife.'

---

p. 36. Isaiah M. Gafni, "The Institution of Marriage in Rabbinic Times," in *The Jewish Family: Metaphor and Memory*, ed. David Kraemer (New York: Oxford University Press, 1989), pp. 22 and 23.

46. Leon, *Jews of Rome*, p. 231. Suzanne Dixon, *The Roman Mother* (London: Routledge, 1990), p. 31 (hereafter cited as Dixon, *Roman Mother*). Blumenkranz, *Jews of Rome*, pp. 344 and 345. Horbury and Noy, *Egyptian Jewish Inscriptions*, p. 184. Safrai and Stern, pp. 762 and 763.

On the contrary, wed a wife and beget sons and daughters, and add fruitfulness and increase the world. 'For thou knowest not' if both will survive in thy hand . . ." Certain rabbis praised Noah and Moses, whom they depicted as refraining from sexual intercourse, while according to David Biale they and some other rabbis had a pessimistic and ambivalent attitude toward sexuality, although we should not make the error of assuming that the negative ideals of a section of the rabbinic elite were shared in this respect by the masses. On the other hand, glimmerings of the new attitudes are already discernible in the uxorious message of the prophet Hosea.[47]

Again we turn to the midrash for enlightenment as to the new attitudes on marriage in Palestine following the destruction of the Temple in 70 C.E. The Palestinian discourse on sexuality of the first C.E. was close in approach to that of the Stoics, in which sex was an "irritating and necessary part of human existence" for procreation; but the later Palestinian position and the even more positive response of the Babylonian sages was that sexual companionship was a gift of God for the "pleasure and well-being of humans." A childless woman from Sidon, who was faced with being divorced by her husband because she had failed to become pregnant after ten years of marriage, "got him too drunk [at a farewell feast]. When his sensibility returned to him, he said, 'My daughter, choose any precious object of mine that is in the house, and take it with you when you go to your father's house.' What did she do? When he was asleep, she told her manservants and maidservants and said to them, 'Pick him up in the bed, and take him to father's house' . . . At midnight he woke up. . . . He said, 'What am I doing in your father's house?' . . . She said to him, 'Did you not say to me this very evening, any precious which you have in your house, take and go to your father's house? There is no object which is more precious to me than you' . . . ." (Song of Songs Rabbah 1:31). In rabbinic practice, sexual relations were permitted during pregnancy and following menopause, when the object of intercourse was not procreation of children, whereas Philo prohibited intercourse with an infertile woman. According to the Talmud, "The unmarried person lives without joy, without blessing, and without good" (Yevamot 62b).[48]

---

47. Veyne, *Private Life*, pp. 37 and 40. Dixon, *Roman Mother*, p. 2. Judah Goldin, *Studies in Midrash and Related Literature*, ed. Barry Eichler and Jeffrey H. Tigay (Philadelphia: Jewish Publication Society, 1988), pp. 114 and 115. Biale, *Eros and the Jews*, pp. 34 and 35.

48. Boyarin, *Carnal Israel*, pp. 47–57.

Within marriage, there was a new emphasis placed on harmony between husband and wife, which also ultimately involved their children and
familial affection generally. Indeed, the rabbis elaborated on a theme first
expressed in Ecclesiastes on what a bane a bad wife was: "Rather when
one is humble and his wife is humble, and his sons and members of his
household are humble. . . . But when he is arrogant, they all cause harm.
. . . When he comes back home, [if his family are humble] he finds peace
within it. Everyone whose wife is quarrelsome leaves home uneasy" (Avot
de R. Nathan Chapter 14). In Babylonia, where the sages increasingly
favored sexual satisfaction within marriage rather than deferring to the Stoic
and ascetic ideals that were sweeping the Roman world, there were also
numerous statements in support of pleasing one's wife: "Our masters
taught: He who loves his wife as his own person, who honors her more
than his own person, who directs his sons and daughters on to the right
path, and marries them off at puberty—of him, Scripture says, 'And thou
shalt know that thy tent is in peace' (Job 5:24)" (Yevamot 62b). Or take
these statements that may be folk sayings and closer to everyday life:
"People say if your wife is short, bend down and whisper to her" [to solicit
her counsel]; and "A man should always be careful about wronging his
wife. Since her tears come quickly, punishment for wronging her is quick
to come" (Bava Metzia 59a). Unlike the Roman elite, as depicted by Keith
Bradley, Jewish families may have been severed by the death of a spouse
but escaped from the blight of a rapid succession of divorces and what
was tantamount to serial marriage. "When a man's first wife dies during
his lifetime, it is as though the Temple had been destroyed in his lifetime.
When a man's wife dies in his lifetime the world becomes dark for him"
(Sanhedrin 22a).[49]

Above all, the new ideals in marriage are most apparent in the Jewish
community in Rome. In the Greek memorial inscriptions phrases denot-

---

49. Keith R. Bradley, *Discovering the Roman Family: Studies in Roman Social
History* (New York: Oxford University Press, 1991), pp. 126–139. See p. 139. "Stated
differently, the high incidence of remarriage in upper-class Roman society—which was,
on the one hand, a natural sequel of the absence of any realistic idea that marriage was
a permanently binding love bond to one partner, and which led, on the other hand, to a
lack of clustering among descendants—helped to create the prospect of a profoundly
unsettled beginning to life for the offspring of the elite." *The Book of Legends Sefer
Ha-Aggadah: Legends from the Talmud and Midrash*, ed. Haim Nachman Bialik and
Yehoshua Hana Ravnitzky and trans. William G. Braude (New York: Schocken Books,
1992), pp. 621 and 622.

ing affection for one's spouse, such as "beloved," "sweet," "sweetest," and "devoted to her husband" were common. Latin inscriptions extolled the virtues of the deceased in similar terms, using the adjectives "sweetest" (*dulcissimus*) and "dearest" (*carissimus*) frequently and supplying evidence that the Jews were internalizing the new matrimonial values as well. Occasionally these epitaphs were longer and more revealing. "You lived a good life with your husband. I am grateful to you for your thoughtfulness and your soul"; or the wife Lucilla, who was remembered as "the glory of Sophronius, a woman highly praised." Flavia Maria erected a tombstone in memory of her "incomparable" and "most sweet husband" of 38, with whom she "lived 16 years without any complaint." Most eloquent of all was this husband's tribute to his wife:

> Here lies Regina, covered by this tomb, which, to reveal his love, her husband raised. A score of years plus one, four months, and eight Days more she spent in wedlock by his side. Again she'll live, again see the light . . . Thy life so chaste, thy love of all thy people, Observance of our Law, and faithfulness Unto our marriage bond, which thou didst strive Ever to glorify. For all these deeds Thy future bliss is certain. In this faith Thy sorrowing husband finds his only comfort.[50]

Having dealt with this subject at some length because the emotional tone of the relationship between husband and wife in turn set the pattern for the relations between parents and children, we now turn to the question of the size of the family of the Jewish peasant proprietor. Ben David, on the basis of a comparison with the Arab cultivators of Palestine in 1909–1923, claimed that the ancient Jewish holding was seven hectares (one hectare = 2.471 acres) in area, with enough resources to support a family of six to nine persons. By way of comparison, wealthy peasants in eighteenth-century France owned, according to one "over-generous" estimate 10 hectares of land or as many as 20 hectares. However, if the source quoted above referring to a joint holding in Galilee during the reign of Domitian (81–96 C.E.) is to be believed, it was only some 4.78 hectares in size, while it was shared by two families. Thus a survey that showed farms of 2.5 hectares in Western Samaria for the peasant proprietors was not only near the norm in the first two centuries of the Common Era but fits in well with the one known example of a peasant farm in Galilee. Other evidence from the Mishnah and the Bar Kokhba land contracts show that some holdings were fragmentary, no more than .3 or .1 hectares in size,

---

50. Leon, *Jews of Rome*, pp. 127–129, 132, 133, 248, and 249.

although a number of these plots of land must have been a component in a multiple holding. No doubt there was a stratum of affluent peasant proprietors in Galilee and elsewhere, veritable "kulaks," who possessed estates of more than 7 hectares and sometimes considerably in excess of that size, and who employed both the ordinary smallholders and landless laborers for the harvest and grape-picking, as such arrangements were common in all agrarian communities. It was from the ranks of such upper-class peasant or "yeoman" families that the bandit chief with a wife and seven children, who bargained with Herod, probably emerged.[51]

Magen Broshi, when discussing the diet in Palestine during the Roman period, estimated that a housewife would have to undertake three hours of milling to prepare enough flour daily to feed a family of five or six persons, which seems a more reasonable conjecture for the size of a Jewish peasant family than Ben David's; even so, we believe that this is still too high a figure. From the Mishnah it appears that the House of Hillel proposed that a person fulfilled the duty of procreation by producing a son or daughter, whereas the House of Shammai stipulated that it could be two sons. This would give us a minimum size of four or five persons per peasant family, which was probably close to the norm; and a table cited by Lawrence Stager suggested that if life expectancy was forty years, a nuclear family that reproduced itself at a moderate rate would number 4.6 or 5.4 persons, but we know that life expectancy in Roman Palestine was approximately thirty years for a male, giving us even smaller households than those supplied by the previous table. Apart from this, it is doubtful whether landless laborers or the farms of many of the fragmented smallholdings could sustain households numbering four persons.[52]

From the Mishnah and the sources quoted in the Talmud as well as comparative evidence from other agrarian societies, we would construct a model of rural society in Palestine in the talmudic era with a thin layer of

51. Gildas Hamel, *Poverty and Charity in Roman Palestine, First Three Centuries C.E.* (Berkeley and Los Angeles: University of California Press, 1990), p. 134 (hereafter cited as Hamel, *Poverty*). Goodman, *Roman Galilee*, p. 35. Braudel, *Identity of France*, Vol. I, p. 74. Safrai and Stern, p. 657. Brent D. Shaw, "Tyrants, Bandits, and Kings: Personal Power in Josephus," *Journal of Jewish Studies* 44, no. 2 (Autumn 1993): 186.

52. Magen Broshi, "The Diet of Palestine in the Roman Period—Introductory Notes," *The Israel Museum Journal* 5 (Spring 1986): 44. Lawrence Stager, "The Archaeology of the Family in Ancient Israel," *Bulletin of the American Schools of Oriental Research* (1985): 21.

wealthy peasants and landowners, and struggling below them a mass of smallholders with farms of various sizes and landless laborers, both of whom assisted their more affluent compatriots. A laborer or smallholder in Palestine during the talmudic era would be hired by a farmer to help gather in the harvest of figs "on condition that I and my family may eat of them" or "that my son may eat of them instead of my receiving a wage" (Maaserot 2:7). Moreover, "Laborers may eat the topmost grapes of the [vine-]rows, but must not parch them at the fire!—There it [the prohibition] is on account of loss of time but our problem arises when he has his wife or children with him; what then? . . . [the laborer] may not parch [the crops] at the fire and eat, nor warm them in the earth, nor crush them on a rock; but he may crush them between his hands and eat them" (Bava Metzia 89b). As Gildas Hamel noted, "One must imagine children following their father and receiving from him part of his food, which constituted much of his salary." Nonetheless, the Tosefta warned that "[the worker] may not hunger and extenuate himself by providing his children with his foods, on account of the fraud it causes to the owner's work." Field hands and their families were in a constant state of undernourishment, prompting them to eat their bread with brine to increase their ability to consume greater quantities of fruit. During the harvest and fruit-picking season, it was customary for wives to assist their husbands or to obtain employment with their husbands as fruitpickers.[53]

If the households of the elite and the affluent peasants contained many children, the mass of peasantry or the urban poor must have struggled to maintain two children; and it is doubtful whether landless laborers and beggars could have brought up more than one or two children, without the help of the new charitable institutions that came into being as a result of the changes in the structure of the family in Palestine. As the material quality of life must have varied considerably in different types of houses, so the life experiences of children being reared in these households must have diverged from one another: the children of the landless laborers probably suffered from malnutrition at times. Further, the lack of means of the poorer sections of the population, the *am ha-aretz*, meant that the religious instruction of their children was restricted, and it is doubtful whether

53. Hamel, *Poverty*, pp. 37 and 38. J. Duncan and M. Derrett, "Workers in the Vineyard: A Parable of Jesus," in *Studies in Jewish Legal History: Essays in Honour of David Daube*, ed. Bernard S. Jackson (London: Jewish Chronicle Publications, 1974), pp. 64–91.

the children of the urban and rural poor attended the newly created network of elementary schools in large numbers. On the other hand, the new emotional quality of married life among the more affluent sections of society and the wealthier peasants engendered a slightly less authoritarian way of raising children and the establishment of a more loving and trusting relationship between parents and children.

3

Children in the Talmudic Age: Childhood and Adolescence

EARLY CHILDHOOD

All the evidence we have suggests that there were warm emotional ties between parents and children among Jews in the talmudic age. Unlike the Roman father, who had the right to raise his child from the earth where the midwife had left it after birth, thereby formally recognizing the infant as his child and not exposing or abandoning it, Jewish parents accepted every newborn child.[1]

Childhood was evaluated positively in rabbinic literature, and was spoken of as a "crown of roses" in contrast to the "crown of willow-rods [heavy to bear]" of old age. One Rabbi lamented, "Alas! it goes never to return" (Shabbat 152a). Again, in the midrash to Ecclesiastes Rabbah "R. Samuel b. Isaac taught . . . the seven 'vanities' mentioned in Ecclesiastes correspond to the seven worlds that a man beholds. At age one he is like a king, seated in a litter while all hug and kiss him. At two and three he is like a pig, sticking his hands in the gutters" (Ecclesiastes Rabbah 1: 2).

---

1. Veyne, *Private Life*, Vol. 1., p. 9.

The latter sentence refers factually to a young infant crawling on all fours, creeping into places where he should not go and becoming dirty very quickly, and to a toddler beginning to explore his home and its surroundings. The passage from the midrash continued, "at ten he [the child] skips like a kid . . .", a happy picture of the child playing. According to the evaluation of the rabbis, children were the most important social group in society for perpetuating the study of the Torah and the continuity of the Jewish people; and in the ancient world, it is difficult to find any other nation among whom children were so admired and highly rated as the Jews. "R. Judah said: Come and see how beloved are children by the Holy One, blessed be He. The Sanhedrin was exiled, but Shechinah [the divine presence] did not go into exile with them. The priestly watches were exiled, but the Shechinah did not go into exile with them. When, however, children were exiled, the Shechinah went into exile with them" (Lamentations Rabbah 1: 32).[2]

Instead of the biblical terms "child," "youth," or "son," which could create emotional distance between parents and children, Nathan Morris argued that the Talmud used warmer phrases, such as "suckling" or "the little one," although another educational historian, Eliezer Ebner, doubted whether there was a more lenient attitude toward children in the talmudic age, as the Bible contained a related word for suckling (yoneq). During the talmudic age, a little boy and girl were respectively called tinok and tinoket, which came to mean both suckling and child; and these emotionally warmer terms of endearment survived into later childhood and sometimes into adulthood, which was something new. For instance, R. Zadok referred to a young priest he was acquainted with, who officiated in the Temple, as tinok. In addition, the Talmud called schoolchildren tinokot shel beth rabban (the children of their master's house). By dwelling on this term, parents tried to recapture the closeness of the relationship between mother and child at infancy, which was a model for the warm family attachments formed later in life.[3]

2. Nathan Morris, The Jewish School: An Introduction to the History of Jewish Education (London: Eyre and Spottiswoode, 1937), p. 221 (hereafter cited as Morris, Education). David Kraemer, "Images of Childhood and Adolescence in Talmudic Literature" in The Jewish Family: Metaphor and Memory, ed. David Kraemer (New York: Oxford University Press, 1989), pp. 65–80 (hereafter cited as Kraemer, Jewish Family).

3. Morris, Education, p. 221. Eliezer Ebner, Elementary Education in Ancient Israel During the Tannaitic Period (10–220 C.E.) (New York: Bloch Publishing Company,

While the Romans delighted in the playfulness of children and writers occasionally remarked on their innocence, thus approaching Jewish ideals, they placed their emphasis, according to Suzanne Dixon, "on relations with the adult child, in contrast with the modern cultural emphasis on the parents and the very young child." Moreover, they praised children for acting like adults. So, too, the Greeks in the Classical age had no fond memories of childhood; it was a privilege of the gods for those who were particularly favored to pass through childhood quickly. In Mark Golden's words, "Children were regarded as physically weak, morally incompetent, mentally incapable." However, children in rabbinic literature were also categorized as being frivolous and irresponsible, being tempted by gifts and money (Bava Batra 156a); and the tannaim, the rabbinic teachers in the period of the Mishnah, believed that "children can commit actions, but they have no thoughts." Nonetheless, the sages were of the opinion that "their [the children's] breath is free from sin," which was a much more positive and reassuring evaluation of the worth of childhood than that of the Greeks and Romans. Equally positive was R. Hama b. Abba's appraisal of children: "Until thirteen years, the son is punished for the sin of the father, from now on, each one dies for his own sins." Even where children were compared to the evil inclination, the sexual urge, David Kraemer asserted that their sexuality was never regarded as "evil or tempting."[4]

However, Shlomo Goitein argued that "despite many warm words about children in talmudic literature, childhood in general was regarded as a state of imperfection; to occupy oneself with such lowly creatures as minors was almost degradation." For "'the impulses of man are evil from childhood,' or, as our sages said, the evil impulse exists in man's heart from childhood" (Ecclesiastes Rabbah 4:13). Such an attitude toward childhood was not an integral part of the worldview of the old civilizations of the

---

1956), p. 30 (hereafter cited as Ebner, *Education*). Samuel S. Kottek, "On Children and Childhood in Ancient Jewish Sources," *Koroth* 9, no. 5–6 (Spring 1987): 461 (hereafter cited as Kottek, *Childhood*).

4. Suzanne Dixon, *The Roman Family* (Baltimore: Johns Hopkins University Press, 1992), p. 119 (hereafter cited as Dixon, *Roman Family*). Mark Golden, *Children and Childhood in Classical Athens* (Baltimore: Johns Hopkins University Press, 1993), pp. 5 and 6 (hereafter cited as Golden, *Athenian Childhood*). Kraemer, *Jewish Family*, pp. 68 and 69. Israel Lebendiger, "The Minor in Jewish Law" in *Studies in Jewish Jurisprudence*, ed. Edward Gershfield (New York: Hermon Press 1971), p. 102 (hereafter cited as Lebendiger, *Jewish Law*).

Middle East, but was, according to Goitein, inherited from Hellenistic culture. Again, there are echoes of these Greek notions in the earlier strata of rabbinic thought, such as the saying attributed to R. Dosa: "Morning sleep, and midday wine, and children's talk, and attending the houses of assembly of the ignorant put a man out of the world" (Ethics of the Fathers 3:14). Nevertheless, in late antiquity and the Middle Ages, even if the Jewish family still had an authoritarian structure, the relations between parents and children were less stiff and significantly warmer; and it may be doubted whether the Greek ideals of childhood had permeated rabbinic thought, as Greek institutions and certain concepts were eagerly absorbed by the Jews without their necessarily endorsing every Greek value. While the old Jewish values of honor, service, and reverence toward parents were not discarded, these were gradually being replaced by the concept of love and mutual affection, which did not lapse on the children's marriage. "Until a man takes a wife, he directs his love toward his parents. Once he marries, he directs his love toward his wife . . ." (Pirke de R. Eliezer, chapter 32, and see also Gen. 2:24). There was also a talmudic dictum that once a man had children he directed all his love toward them, forgetting his feeling for his parents.[5]

Peter Van der Horst asserted "that Jews shared with pagans both the fate of a short life expectancy—the average length of life having been perhaps about 30 years or even less—and the fate of a high infant and child mortality, probably not half of those born reaching adulthood." In excavations carried out at Meiron in northern Israel, archaeologists noted that "the remains of 197 individuals were identified [from one burial cave, which were dated from the first century B.C.E. to the fourth century C.E.], of whom 95, nearly 50%, had died before reaching the age of 18. Within this age range, the highest mortality occurred within the first five years of life (70% of all childhood and adolescent deaths)." Harry Joshua Leon

5. S. D. Goitein, *A Mediterranean Society: The Community* (Berkeley and Los Angeles: University of California Press, 1971), Vol. 2, p. 174 (hereafter cited as Goitein, *Community*). S. D. Goitein, "Jewish Education in Yemen," in *Between Past and Future: Essays and Studies on Aspects of Immigrant Absorption in Israel*, ed. Carl Frankenstein (Jerusalem: The Henrietta Szold Foundation for Child and Youth Welfare, 1953), pp. 113 and 114. Gerald Blidstein, *Honor Thy Father and Mother: Filial Responsibility in Jewish Law and Ethics* (New York: Ktav Publishing House, 1975), pp. 37–59 (hereafter cited as Blidstein, *Honor*).

remarked on a similar phenomenon in the Roman catacombs, declaring that "the visitor to the Jewish catacombs . . . will be impressed by the large number of small loculi, apparently the graves of children, unmarked by any epitaph . . ."[6]

We shall now briefly focus on examples of surviving Jewish epitaphs, the first one of which is from the Egyptian town of Leontopolis: "Teuphilion son of Abition, untimely dead, excellent one, friend of all, farewell. About 5 years old." Among the finest of the laments for a child in funeral inscriptions is one from Rome: "Would I, who reared you, Justus, my child, were able to place you in a golden coffin. Now, O Lord, (vouchsafe) in thy righteous judgment that Justus, a peerless child, may sleep in peace. Here I lie, Justus, aged 4 years, 8 months, sweet to my foster father, Theodotus, the foster father, to his most sweet child." Another touching inscription from Rome was worded "Here lies Probus, a child who lived 2 years and one month, 3 days. He loved his father, loved his mother. In peace you sleep." Although the Jewish epitaphs for young children from Egypt are on the whole terser and less revealing than those from Rome, we have literary evidence from the Fourth Book of Maccabees, written in Alexandria in the century before the destruction of the Temple in 70 c.e., of children's affection for their parents, which must in some measure have been reciprocated. The Alexandrian author related the story of the martyrdom of Hannah and her seven sons, who "loved their mother so that they obeyed her till their death, and observed the commandment [of honoring their mother and father] . . . O sublime quality, love of parents and fondness of parents." As Gerald Blidstein commented, the biblical concept of honoring one's parents was slowly transmuted into the idea of loving them, an unfreezing of emotional attitudes and social hierarchies. Yet some degree of ambivalence remained in a family structure best described as diluted authoritarianism, for enforced reverence for parents sometimes engendered hatred; parents were still deeply uncertain of their children's

---

6. Pieter W. Van Der Horst, *Ancient Jewish Epitaphs: An Introductory Survey of a Millenium of Jewish Funeral Epigraphy (300 B.C.E.–700 C.E.)* (Kampen, the Netherlands: Kok Pharos Publishing House, 1991), p. 84 (hereafter cited as Van Der Horst). Eric M. Meyers, James F. Strange, and Carol Meyers, *Meiron Excavation Project* (Cambridge, Mass: American Schools of Oriental Research, 1981), Vol. 3, p. 110. Harry Joshua Leon, *The Jews of Ancient Rome* (Philadelphia: Jewish Publication Society, 1960), p. 230 (hereafter cited as Leon, *Jews of Rome*).

abiding affection, as on marriage they might direct all their love toward their spouses or would only care about their own children.[7]

In fact, Jewish inscriptions on tombs tended to pay more attention to the deaths of young children than did pagans. "This can be seen most clearly in Africa," asserted Van der Horst, "where the underrepresentation of children in pagan epitaphs is very striking, whereas from the almost 300 Jewish age indications from Africa including Egypt some 55 are of children of under 10 years. In Rome we see something similar: almost 25% of the Jews whose age is mentioned had died between birth and 5 years of age [in some 36 instances]. We cannot but conclude that apparently Jews did not fully conform to the pagan practice of denying very young children stones with epitaphs. Whether we can also conclude from this, as Bernard Blumenkrantz does, "that Jews had greater parental love for their children than pagans . . . is uncertain." Despite this qualification, Van der Horst concedes that this "has something to do with Jewish beliefs and values." We have already drawn attention to the higher life expectancy figure for Jewish women as compared with pagans and Christians because Jews looked askance at the marriage of young adolescent girls, at least in Rome. We would conclude that there was more equality in the treatment of sexes among the Jews, marked principally by the care and consideration for young girls.[8]

Among the Romans, not only were the majority of children who died young not commemorated by funeral monuments, but excessive grief by parents was viewed as distasteful. Lawrence Stone has argued that parents in the past limited their psychological involvement with young children, whose chances of survival were poor, to preserve their own mental equanimity. Hence the Romans shielded themselves from direct involvement with their infant children by a battery of wet nurses, pedagogues, and other slave helpers. Apart from some upper-class Jewish families in Egypt, Rome, and Palestine, there was much interaction between parents and young children among the Jews, and the more interaction, the higher the emotional attachments became; and the greater the outpouring of grief

---

7. William Horbury and David Noy, *Jewish Inscriptions of Graeco-Roman Egypt* (Cambridge: Cambridge University Press, 1992), p. 180. Leon, *Jews of Rome*, pp. 287 and 317. Blidstein, *Honor*, pp. 33 and 34.

8. Van Der Horst, p. 81. B. Blumenkranz, "*Quelques notations demographiques sur les Juifs de Rome des premiers siecles*," ed. F. L. Cross, *Studia Patristica* (Berlin: Akademie-Verlag, 1961), Vol. 4, Part 2, pp. 341–347.

among the Jews and the psychological need to commemorate such a loss by the erection of a monument.[9]

According to Thomas Wiedemann, in the classical period children had been excluded from civic life, but in late antiquity "Jews and Christians responded to [the high infant mortality rates] by giving not just the youngest child, but even the child in the womb, the same right to a place within the religious community as any adult." Hence the sages declared that if a child died from an accident after thirty days or even earlier, "he may be considered by his father and mother and all his kinsfolk as a full bridegroom," and be buried with rites appropriate to an adult. Yet the concern of the bereaved parents did not end here, but continued, as they were anxious about their child's fate in the afterlife. Some rabbis believed that children were entitled to benefit from resurrection from the moment of conception; other sages thought that such entitlement accrued only when the children were able to talk. The rabbis consequently developed a new doctrine, according to Saul Lieberman, by claiming "that the Lord himself teaches Torah to the babies [who died in their infancy]" or to children who failed to attain the age of thirteen years and one day. According to another version, "the angel Metatron teaches them. . . . The *Midrash Othiyyoth de R. 'Akiba* states that the angel gathers all the souls of the embryos that died in their mother's wombs, of the sucklings who died on the breasts of their mothers, and of the school children who died [during their study] of the five books of the Pentateuch. He arranges them into separate classes and teaches them Torah, wisdom (i.e., *Halacha*), *Haggada*, etc.," an early indication that children were sometimes graded into different classes.[10]

Moreover, Lieberman suggested that "some Babylonian rabbis link the resurrection of boys to their circumcision [corresponding to the insistence of the early Christians on the necessity of infant baptism, when children were gravely ill] . . . Rav Naḥshon Gaon [ninth century C.E.] reports the custom of circumcising a dead baby on the tomb and giving him a name etc." In late antiquity "R. Eleazar said . . . There are three kinds of tears

9. Lawrence Stone, *The Family, Sex, and Marriage in England 1500–1800* (Harmondsworth: Penguin Books, 1979), p. 57. Dixon, *Roman Family*, pp. 99, 100, 104, and 131. Suzanne Dixon, *The Roman Mother* (London: Routledge, 1990), pp. 24 and 25 (hereafter cited as Dixon, *Roman Mother*).

10. Thomas Wiedemann, *Adults and Children in the Roman Empire* (London: Routledge, 1989), pp. 188 and 204 (hereafter cited as Wiedemann, *Roman Children*). Saul Lieberman, *Texts and Studies* (New York: Ktav Publishing House, 1974), pp. 262–267 (hereafter cited as Lieberman, *Texts*).

which are harmful: tears caused by smoke, weeping [through grief and straining] in a privy, but [tears that result from the death] of a grown-up child are worst of all. It is related of a woman that she had a grown-up son who died, and she wept over him at night until her eyelashes fell out" (Lamentations Rabbah 2:15).[11]

Despite the fact that the discipline of children was still harsh in the talmudic age and that corporal punishment was common, there was more of an attempt by parents in late antiquity to identify with the needs and aspirations of the growing child; and to discipline children in a more even-handed manner, so that children were "repelled with the left hand and attracted with the right" (Sotah 47a; Sanhedrin 107b). This means that discipline should not only be instilled in the child by stern methods, but that the child's good intentions should be reinforced by positive means, such as clear expressions of love and sensible gifts. The rabbis saw a parallel between children and the evil inclination, sexual passion, which both had to be allowed a certain measure of free rein and to flourish and to be controlled rather than repressed." Again, in a midrash from the Mekhilta, which may date back to tannaitic times, "Rabbi says: It is revealed and known . . . that a man honors his mother more than his father because she sways him with persuasive words" (Mekhilta Bahodesh 8). In an early medieval midrash, there was an embellishment of a talmudic story about a heathen called Dama ben Netinah, who was renowned for his filial piety: "When the slipper [with which his mother was hitting him] fell from her hand, he reached forward and returned it to her; he only said: 'Enough mother,'" but another midrash claimed that she was mentally disturbed. If this was the case and the mother was striking a grown-up, the story sounds fanciful and cannot be used to support the contention that mothers used harsh disciplinary methods against children during the talmudic age, while in addition the embroidery to the tale was devised in the medieval period. In the loose extended family, discipline and love were also supplied by a group of alternative mothers and uncles.[12]

Partly because of the long periods of breast-feeding and the close bonding between mothers and infants, and partly because of the development of a strong maternal side in Jewish fathers in the prophetic age, there was intensive interaction between Jewish parents and their young children in

---

11. Lieberman, *Texts*, p. 265.
12. Blidstein, *Honor*, pp. 43 and 44.

late antiquity. A midrash possibly composed in the third century C.E. but more likely, according to William Braude, in late antiquity or the Medieval period stated that "once it happened that a man who made out his will specified: My son shall inherit nothing at all of mine until he acts the fool. R. Jose bar Judah and Rabbi went to R. Joshua ben Karha to get an opinion about this provision. When they found him in the field, they saw he was crawling on his hands and knees, that a reed was sticking out of his mouth, and that he was being pulled along by his child. . . . When they asked him about the provision in the will, he began to laugh, and said to them . . . 'For a man to enjoy his children, he must fool around with them'" (Midrash on Psalms 92:13). In the Talmud another sage, Rabbah, in an anecdote from Babylonia again dating from the fourth century or later, bought "clay vessels in a damaged condition for his children who would break them" (Yoma 78b). In contrast, there was emotional distance between Roman fathers and their sons, who addressed them in the chilling phrase of "sir" and who were succoured by wet nurses and male pedagogues up to the age of puberty.

In the Mishnah and Talmud there were references to a number of toys, including balls stuffed with rags, toy wagons or go-carts, and "the chair of the little one," which were universal throughout the Mediterranean area in this age, as boys playing with such carts and children playing with balls are depicted in Greek and Roman funeral monuments and on vases. One sad Jewish epitaph from the Egyptian city of Leontopolis commented, "My parents suffer likewise for the son who pleased them, and my friends look for their comrade and companion." Ball games were played by boys and adolescents by throwing or rolling the ball to each other, or the ball was hurled with force against a wall. According to Joshua Schwartz, girls mostly tossed a ball to each other, playing a game of catch; another pastime popular with them was fivestones, played very much like the modern game with knucklebones or *astragaloi*, which were caught on the back of their hands.[13]

---

13. Morris, *Education*, p. 221. Golden, *Athenian Childhood*, p. 72. Veyne, *Private Life*, p. 16. Sussman Muntner, "Physical Training in the Talmud and Bible," *Koroth* 9, no. 11–12 (1991): 863 (hereafter cited as Muntner, *Physical Training*). Lesley Beaumont, "Child's Play in Ancient Athens," *History Today* (August 1994): 30–35. Lecture of Professor Joshua Schwartz on "Aspects of Leisure-Time Activities in Jewish Society During the Second Temple, Mishnah and Talmud Periods" on 9 January 1995. Joshua Schwartz, "A Child's Wagon," (Hebrew) *Tarbiz* 63, no. 3 (Apr.–June 1994): 375–392.

With such a supportive and emotionally warm and secure upbringing, the Jewish children under the later Roman Empire emerged as mischievous and self-confident, if not a trifle cheeky. Children teased cats and tied the tails of sheep together. A story was told "about a man who was standing in the synagogue praying, and his son was standing at his side. As the congregation was responding 'halleluja!' the boy was shouting frivolous words. He did this repeatedly. When the people remonstrated, the father pleaded: 'What can I do? He is only a child. Let him have his fun.'" Again, when some "ass-drivers complained to Rabbi Simeon bar Yohai that his son Eleazar . . . played some pranks at their expense, he reprimanded them and told them that they were to blame, for they had insulted the youngster by calling him a glutton." A midrash composed between 640 and 900 C.E. well illustrates the attitude of the children: "One of the men of Sepphoris [a town in Galilee] once had occasion to celebrate the circumcision of his son," and among his visitors was R. Simeon b. Halafta.

> When they [the visitors] arrived at the city-gate they heard the sound of some children standing and playing in front of a house. On beholding R. Simeon . . . , who was a distinguished-looking and handsome man, they exclaimed, "You will not move from here until you dance a little for us." He said to them, "You cannot have this from me because I am an old man." He railed at them but they were not frightened or cowed. He lifted up his face and saw the house about to over-turn [on the children]; so he said to them, "Repeat after me what I say to you. Go and tell the owner of the house that if he is asleep, he should wake up, because the beginning of a sin is sweet but its end is bitter." At the sound of their voices the owner of the house awakened and he came out and fell before the rabbi's feet, saying, "My master, I beg of you not to pay attention to their words because they are young and foolish." (Ecclesiastes Rabbah 3:2)[14]

When this story is compared with the horrendous Elisha episode in the Bible and the conduct expected of young males in Roman elite families, the contrast is clear-cut. Fathers looked on approvingly at the bawdy and impudent remarks of their young sons in ancient Rome, whereas the rabbis tried to curb the overboisterous behavior of young children and direct it to socially approved lines, so that it harmonized with and reinforced the humane values of Jewish society. On the other hand, the Christians drew on the Bible for their ideas on corporal punishment and disciplining children, but because this was combined with the fear engendered by harsh

---

14. Morris, *Education*, p. 224.

notions of hell that pervaded family life, Christian parents tended to be stricter disciplinarians.[15]

Philo, in contrast, asserted that "a father and mother are in fact gods . . ." (*The Decalogue*, sec. 120), "divine because they have brought others to birth and have raised not being into being" (*Special Laws* 2:225), sentiments far removed from rabbinic beliefs; and closer to Aristotle, who declared that "one should honor one's parents as one does the gods," and close, too, to the ideas of the Stoics. "Honor, therefore, he [the lawgiver] says, next to God thy father and mother" (*Special Laws* 2:235), argued Philo. He also claimed that "fathers have the right to upbraid their children and admonish them severely and if they do not submit to threats conveyed in words to beat and degrade them and put them in bonds. And further if in the face of this they continue to rebel . . . the law permits the parents to extend the punishment to death, though here it requires more than the father alone or the mother alone" (*Special Laws* 2:223). Further, Philo asserted that "parents have not only been given . . . the power of a master corresponding to the two primary forms under which servants are owned, one when they are home-bred, the other when they are purchased. For parents pay out a sum many times the value of a slave on their children, and for them to nurses, tutors, and teachers, apart from the cost of their clothes, food, and superintendence in sickness and health from their earliest years until they are full grown" (*Special Laws* 2:233). Parents also had to provide their children with a Greek-style education in schools and the gymnasium, after which their sons could study philosophy to attain the "good life."[16]

Critics of Philo have noted that he followed Greek thought by depersonalizing God, whereas the rabbis, following biblical imagery and metaphor, saw God as their father, someone with whom there could be a close relationship. Behind Philo's ideology, there may be an indication of the values of upper-class Jewish families in Alexandria, with children attended by wet nurses and slave pedagogues, so that the relations between the children and their parents were "cool" and distant. Hence parents were constructed by Philo in the Greek image of the depersonalized god. He

---

15. Philip Greven, *Spare the Child: The Religious Roots of Punishment and the Psychological Impact of Physical Abuse* (New York: Vintage Books, 1992), pp. 52–66.

16. Blidstein, *Honor*, pp. 6 and 7. Philo, *The Decalogue*, trans. F. H. Colson. Loeb Classical Library (Cambridge, Mass.: Harvard University Press, 1950), Vol. 7, p. 67.

also tended to exaggerate the father's authority, where the Bible stressed the equality of both parents, and he may have been influenced by the Roman doctrine of *patria potestas*. Gerald Blidstein remarked that the legal system in the later Roman Empire curbed the father's powers and elevated the status of the mother, perhaps due to the absorption of biblical and Jewish ideals by the Church, which in turn influenced the Roman legal system. Philo explained that the lawgiver "omitted any mention of love for parents because it is learned and taught by instinct and requires no injunction, but did enjoin fear for the sake of those who are in the habit of neglecting their duty." Moreover, the rabbis, unlike Philo, would never have regarded children as being comparable to servants or slaves in their relationship with their parents.[17]

THE JEWISH SCHOOL

The study of the Torah was cultivated to teach both children and adults the right modes of religious conduct and social action; it was also a form of worship that brought the Jewish people closer to God. To lead the good life, it was necessary to live by the ideals of *Torah uMitzvot* (Torah and commandments) or *Torah uMa'asim Tovim* (Torah and good deeds). "No one is really a free man," declared Nathan Morris, "unless he is engaged in the study of the Torah which is reminiscent of the Greek ideal of contemplative knowledge."[18]

According to Philo and Josephus, these ideals were imbibed at infancy: "Even before any instruction in the holy laws and unwritten customs, they are taught, so to speak, from their swaddling-clothes by parents, teachers, and educators to believe in one God, the one Father and Creator of the world" (Philo, *Legat.* 16: 115). Philo thereby linked the containment and security of the swaddled infant with the watchful presence of the parents, in this case the father and then beyond the earthly father, God. Moreover, Josephus stated that the Torah "also commands us to bring

---

17. Blidstein, *Honor*, pp. 8, 31–35, 38, and 175–176. Veyne, *Private Life*, pp. 14–17. Dixon, *Roman Family*, pp. 160 and 161.

18. S. Safrai, "Education and the Study of the Torah" in *The Jewish People in the First Century: Historical Geography, Political History, Social, Cultural & Religious Life and Institutions*, ed. S. Safrai and M. Stern (Assen: Van Gorcum, 1976), Vol. 2, pp. 945–969, particularly p. 945 (hereafter cited as Safrai). Ebner, *Education*, p. 24.

those children up in learning and to exercise them in the laws, and to make them acquainted with the acts of their predecessors, in order to [obtain] their imitation of them, and that they may be nourished up in the laws from their infancy, and might neither transgress them, nor yet have any pretence for their ignorance of them (*Contra Apion* 2:26). Again, images conjured up from infancy, but this time more compatible with the laws being equated with the nourishment flowing from the mother's breasts. A talmudic passage said exactly this: "With whom do you find the cream of the Torah? With him who spits out upon it the milk which he has sucked from the breasts of his mother" (Berakhot 63b). Josephus added elsewhere: "Since we acquire them [the laws] from our earliest consciousness, we have them as it were engraved on our souls" (*Contra Apion* 2:18).[19]

As the survival of the Jewish people was contingent on following a Torah-centered way of life, schoolchildren were invested with enormous prestige and they became during the talmudic age the most important and vital social group in Jewish society. We have already quoted the midrash about the divine presence following only the children into exile, but there were other positive statements, such as "schoolchildren may not be made to neglect their studies even for the building of the Temple" and "the world endures only for the sake of the breath of schoolchildren [as they memorized and preserved the sacred texts]" (Shabbat 119b). Another talmudic source asked, "What does God do in the fourth quarter [of the day]? He sits and instructs the schoolchildren . . ." (Avodah Zarah 3b]. In a midrash of R. Abba b. Kahana, a third-century sage, all the heathens assembled before the Cynic philosopher, Abnomos of Gedara, who was a friend of R. Meir, and asked him when was the best time to destroy the Jews. "'Go round to their synagogues and schools,' he replied, 'and if you can find their children with voices uplifted you cannot subjugate them; if not, you can . . .'" (Genesis Rabbah 65:20). Further, "R. Issachar said: If a child read Moshe as Mushe, Aharon as Aharu, Efron as Efran, God says, 'His babbling (*liglugo*) is beloved to me' . . . The Rabbis said: Even if a child skips the Name of God many times he comes to no harm; what is more the Lord declares: 'And his omission (*dilugo*) is beloved to Me'" (Canticles Rabbah 2:4). Moreover, "R. Huna b. R. Aḥa said: When children leave their school a *Bath Kol* [heavenly voice] goes forth and says to them, 'Go

---

19. Emil Schurer, *The History of the Jewish People in the Age of Jesus Christ*, ed. Geza Vermes, Fergus Millar, and Matthew Black (Edinburgh: T. & T. Clark, 1986), Vol. 2, pp. 417 and 418 (hereafter cited as Schurer, *Revised*).

thy way, eat thy bread with joy, the breath of your mouth has been accepted by Me like the sweet savor [of incense]'" (Ecclesiastes Rabbah 9:7).

Saul Lieberman pointed out that the "procedure of consulting the verses casually uttered by children in the synagogue was the most frequent among the Rabbis"; it was a way of inquiring of *Bath Kol*, the heavenly voice, when they wanted an answer to a problem that exercised them. In the pagan classical world children were similarly consulted, but here it was because they were regarded as being marginal, as not properly belonging to the civic or human community, that they could mediate between the divine and human worlds.[20]

A peculiar consequence of this new ideology and reverence for children among Jews was that even children who had died were already so meritorious that they could rescue their sinful fathers from a fate worse than death, that of staying in hell. "R. Judah says: 'It refers to children who are buried early in life through the sins of their fathers in this world. Hereinafter they will range themselves with the band of the righteous, while their fathers will be ranged with the band of the wicked . . . which means they returned from the descent to Gehinnom [hell] and were rescued through the merit of the children. Therefore every man is under an obligation to teach his son Torah that he may rescue him from Gehinnom'" (Ecclesiastes Rabbah 6:1).

A tradition embodied in the Jerusalem Talmud that Simeon ben Shetah, who was president of the Sanhedrin during the reigns of Alexander Jannaeus and Salome (103–76 B.C.E.), decreed "that children [*tinokot*] should go to school (*bet sefer*)" (Jerusalem Ketubot 32c) appears to be legendary and misleading. More to the point perhaps is the tradition transmitted in the Babylonian talmud by Rav, a sage who lived in Palestine for many years. "Rabbi Judah said in the name of Rabbi: Truly it may be remembered to this man's credit! Joshua ben Gamla is his name. Had he not lived, the Torah would have been forgotten in Israel. For at first, whoever had a father was taught the Torah by him; whoever had none, did not learn the Torah. . . . Afterwards it was ordained that teachers of boys should be appointed in Jerusalem . . . But only whoever had a father was sent to school by him; whoever had none, did not go. Then it was ordained that

---

20. Saul Lieberman, *Hellenism in Jewish Palestine: Studies in Literary Transmission Beliefs and Manners of Palestine in the 1st Century B.C.E.–4th Century C.E.* (New York: Jewish Theological Seminary of America, 1950), pp. 194–199 (hereafter cited as Lieberman, *Hellenism*). Wiedemann, *Roman Children*, pp. 185 and 186.

teachers should be appointed in every province, and that boys of sixteen and seventeen be sent to them. But he whose teacher was angry with him ran away [a typically rebellious and uncowed youth of the period], until Joshua ben Gamla came and decreed that teachers be appointed in every province and every town, and children aged six or seven be brought to them" (Bava Batra 21a).[21]

From the evidence of the Mishnah, it is clear that there was a fairly extensive, if incomplete, network of schools operating in Palestine by the second century C.E. Therefore, it might be plausible to suggest that Joshua ben Gamla, the High Priest in 63–65 C.E., took steps to construct a national system of schools in Palestine by building on the pioneering efforts of others or the expulsion of the Romans and the direct rule of the Sanhedrin (66–67 C.E.) may have resulted in revolutionary innovations in elementary education. On the other hand, Nathan Morris pointed out that Joshua ben Gamla was not presented by Josephus or in other places in the Talmud as a scholarly person or one of integrity, so that his role in school reform has been grossly exaggerated. It is more likely that his or the Sanhedrin's efforts were confined to the establishment of some model elementary schools in Jerusalem. Earlier, the Jewish aristocratic leadership in Jerusalem may perhaps have drawn on the example of the Greek elementary school in the city that Herod went to, and in which (according to Martin Hengel) their own sons "were probably instructed." The priests in Jerusalem also admired the Greek gymnasium in Alexandria attended by the Jewish upper class until 41 C.E. It should be added that the families of the Jewish elites in the two cities were interrelated. With the destruction of the Temple in 70 C.E. and the Bar Kokhba revolt in 132 C.E., the movement for setting up a national system of Jewish elementary schools no doubt gained unprecedented momentum, as the Jewish rabbinic leadership devised new means of countering the onslaughts of Graeco-Roman civilization by adopting the institutions of the enemy—the Greek elementary school. In this movement, according to William Chomsky, R. Judah ha-Nasi (second century C.E.) was a prime participant, although Moses Aberbach maintained that universal education for boys in Palestine was only introduced by his grandson R. Judah II in the middle of the third century C.E., as there were still localities without a single teacher.[22]

21. Schurer, Revised, p. 418.

22. Schurer, Revised, p. 418. Nathan Morris, A History of Jewish Education: From the Earliest Times to the End of the Talmudic Period (Jerusalem: Rubin Mass, 1977), Vol. 1, pp. 69–75. William Chomsky, "Adumbrations of Modern Educational Ideas in

In Palestine, elementary schools were situated in the prayer halls of synagogues or in nearby rooms; in smaller towns the hazzan, the synagogue attendant, either taught in the school or assisted other teachers, particularly the local scribes. In Babylonia, teachers often held schools in the courtyards of their homes, sometimes becoming involved in a dispute with their neighbors because the lessons were loud and noisy. So crucial was the Torah education of schoolchildren that everyone who encouraged it was amply rewarded. R. Tanhum, son of R. Abba, declared that ". . . if one who has no children pays fees to Bible and Mishnah teachers . . . if one who has no children circumcises those of other people or prepare books and lends them to others—of such a one, the Holy One, blessed be He says . . . 'I must repay him by giving him wealth and children who will read the books'" (Numbers Rabbah 14:2). Children were usually taken to school by their mothers, as a midrash informs us that a mother washes the faces of her sons, "so that they would go before the teacher. And at the sixth hour, noon, she would stand and receive her sons who returned from school." Further proof that mothers took their children to school was the ruling that bachelors could not teach in elementary school because there was a greater risk of some impropriety occurring.[23]

In contrast, among Roman elite families, slaves brought some of the clothes for the young pupil to wear and also handed him water to wash, after which he left the bedroom, in the words of one autobiographical fragment, ". . . with my tutor (*paidagogos*) and my nurse to greet my father and mother. I greet them both and kiss them both . . . I go to find my writing kit and my exercise book and give them to my slave. . . . Followed by my tutor, I go out of the house and set off to school." We are in a different world from the Jewish one. Here there is no close contact between mother and child and here coaching is done by the slave tutor, not by an interested father. Relations between the child and his parents in the Roman household seem to be correct and dutiful but cold, as they are filtered through a host of intermediaries.[24]

Rabbinic Literature," *Gratz College Annual* (1972), pp. 25 and 26. Moses Aberbach, "The Development of the Jewish Elementary School System During the Talmudic Age," in *Studies in Jewish Education*, ed. Janet Aviad (Jerusalem: Magnes Press, 1988), Vol. 3, pp. 269 and 299 (hereafter cited as Aberbach, *Education*). Martin Hengel, *Judaism and Hellenism* (London: SCM Press Ltd, 1974), Vol. 1, pp. 76 and 77.

23. Safrai, pp. 953 and 954. Ebner, p. 53.

24. Keith Hopkins, "Everyday Life for the Roman Schoolboy," *History Today* (October 1993), pp. 26 and 27 (hereafter cited as Hopkins, *Roman Schoolboy*).

Children attended the elementary school (*bet sefer*) from the age of five, six, or seven until they were twelve or thirteen years old, although the *Ethics of the Fathers* claimed that they had to stay at this school only until they were ten. Rav said, "Before the age of six do not accept pupils; from that age you can accept them and stuff them like an ox" (Bava Batra 21a). Jewish schools in Palestine first concentrated on developing the reading skills of their pupils by teaching them the letters of the alphabet and then making them learn syllables in every possible combination, in the manner of Hellenistic schools. In the Greek schools the easiest syllables were tried first, "and these apparently were not simply pronounced according to their sound but by the name of each individual letter first, and then as joined together—thus beta-alpha-ba; beta-ei-be; beta-eta-be . . ." In Jewish schools, the teachers wrote the letters on a wax board with a stylus, after which the pupils would recite them. Support for the view that the Jews borrowed their method of teaching the alphabet from the Hellenistic schools comes from Egypt in the Middle Ages, where examples of children's exercise books with the letters of the alphabet and their combinations have been recovered from the Cairo Geniza. Judah Goldin went further, claiming that Jewish boys, like their counterparts in Hellenistic schools, were taught aphorisms consisting of the pithy sayings of the great sages and stories extolling the exemplary conduct of these rabbis, the equivalent of the Greek heroes, on which to model their own behavior. Having mastered selected elementary texts written on small scrolls, the pupils graduated to reading from the Torah itself.[25]

Above all, the elementary school taught children to read the complete text of the Torah and the prophets and to translate them, starting with the book of Leviticus. R. Assi explained, "Why do young children commence with the book of Leviticus and not Genesis? Surely it is because young children are pure, and the sacrifices are pure; so let the pure come and engage in the study of the pure" (Leviticus Rabbah 7:3). The children sat on the ground or in rows on benches, chanting the lessons and repeating the exact reading of the biblical text after hearing it rendered by their teacher, as the development of a retentive memory was of supreme impor-

---

25. Safrai, pp. 950 and 952. Judah Goldin, "Several Sidelights of a Torah Education in Tannaite and Early Amoraic Times," in *Studies in Midrash and Related Literature* (Philadelphia: Jewish Publication Society, 1988), pp. 201–213 (hereafter cited as Goldin, *Education*). H. I. Marrou, *A History of Education in Antiquity* (New York: Mentor Books, 1964), pp. 211 and 212 (hereafter cited as Marrou, *Education*).

tance when the Hebrew text of the Scriptures had not as yet been furnished with vowel signs. For example, "R. Ḥiyya b. Abba said: I was passing the Babylonian synagogue of Sepphoris, when I heard children sitting
and reciting the verse, And Abraham journeyed from thence . . ." It was
common practice to stop a child in the street and ask him what verse he
had learned at school on that day, although it is likely that he had been
taught more than one verse. In St. Jerome's time in the fourth century,
people were impressed by the ability of some Jews "to recite all the [183]
generations from Adam to Zerubbabel with such accuracy and facility, as
if they were simply giving their names." According to Shlomo Goitein,
"the pupil wasted most of his time memorizing," but this is unfair if applied to a culture without the printed book, as the unvocalized text of the
Torah could not be recited again accurately unless it was committed to
memory. It is now argued by some scholars that the Hebrew text was first
vocalized by teachers to assist their pupils in learning to read, and in any
case in an oral culture where the aim was communicating with others there
was no such thing as silent reading. To facilitate the pupil's task of memorizing the texts of the Torah, a system of cantillation was devised by teachers
at an early date, perhaps modeled on the Greek way poetry was recited
with melody.[26]

Sometimes fathers went over school lessons with their sons. ". . .
R. Ḥiyya b. Abba did not taste meat before revising [the previous day's
lesson] with the child and adding [another verse]" (Kiddushin 30a); more
occasionally grandfathers, who were few in numbers in the ancient world,
similarly assisted their grandsons. School was held daily, apart from festivals, but on Friday night boys would chant the Torah reading for the Sabbath with their teachers or by themselves. On the Sabbath the pupils did
not learn anything fresh, but reviewed their past week's lessons. From the
third century onwards, children were allowed home from school earlier at
10 A.M. between the Seventeenth of Tammuz and the Ninth of Ab (July to
August), when the sun was at its hottest.[27]

During the first two centuries of the Common Era, the synagogue was
a community house where the central feature of the service was the reading of the Torah and where homiletic discourses were delivered; it was
only later that prayer became an important component of the service. The

---

    26. Schurer, *Revised*, p. 419. Safrai, pp. 950–954. Goldin, *Education*, pp. 206
and 207. Morris, *Education*, pp. 136 and 141–143. Marrou, *Education*, p. 214.
    27. Safrai, p. 954. Ebner, *Education*, pp. 71 and 72.

principal purpose of teaching in schools was to prepare boys to read a portion from the Torah or to act as a translator of the text, which was a relatively easy task in Palestine. The triennial cycle of reading the Law was well within the compass of a child, who had no more than five or six verses alloted to him on the Sabbath: "A minor may read or may translate the Torah . . ." (Megillah 4:6). If children had only one verse of the Torah reading to translate into Aramaic—the everyday language of the period— at the time, they usually recited two to three verses of the prophets together in translation.[28]

We must now turn our attention to the degree to which children were taught prayers at home and in the school. As the liturgy was still in a state of flux and synagogue prayers did not become a central feature of the service until the third century, it is doubtful whether fathers began to teach their sons the *Shema* before the end of the first century. Minors were exempted from reciting the *Shema* and from putting on tefillin, but they were expected to say the *Amidah* and the grace after meals (Berakhot 3:3). According to Tzvee Zahavy, the *Shema* contained the themes of the unity and love of God, the Exodus, and the centrality of Torah study, all themes beloved of the scribal party, many of whom were teachers who may have promoted them in the new schools after the destruction of the Temple. In Tosefta Hagigah 1:2 it was suggested that a child should be taught to perform the various mitzvot (commandments) as soon as he could carry them out. Thus "[a minor who] knows how to shake, is liable as to *lulav*, [who] knows how to wrap [around a garment] is liable to fringes; [who] knows how to speak, his father instructs him [in] . . . *Shema*, and Torah and the holy tongue [Hebrew] . . . ; [who] is able to eat . . . an olive's amount of roasted meat, they slaughter the passover sacrifice for him." From being a celebration of the paschal sacrifice, the rabbinic Seder at Passover became "a banquet for Torah study." The Mishnah adopted the biblical idea of the parent instructing his child about the Passover ritual and used it for its own purposes, by inventing questions about dipping twice, and the eating of matzah and roasted meat. In opposition to the scribal class, the rabbis and particularly the patriachate sponsored the *Amidah*, the Eighteen Benedictions, with its motifs of the Temple, Jerusalem, and emphasis on the house of David to consolidate their own claims to leadership of the

---

28. Dan Urman, "The House of Assembly and the House of Study: Are They One and the Same?" *Journal of Jewish Studies* 44, no. 2 (Autumn 1993): 239–241 (hereafter cited as Urman, *House of Study*). Ebner, *Education*, p. 80.

Jewish people. We can see how the liturgy was first formulated and studied by school pupils in the third century from a comment in the Babylonian
Talmud, when it was said that the song at the Red Sea was recited in the
same fashion as "the minor who reads the *Hallel* in the *Bet haSefer* and
the others repeat after him every sentence."[29]

Boys put on tefillin and were called up to read a portion of the Torah
before they reached thirteen during the talmudic age, so that as yet the
age for the attainment of a majority in civil law and for participating in
religious ceremonies did not coincide. It is questionable whether the practice of fathers teaching their children the *Shema* became general before
the third century C.E. There was no special religious ceremony to mark
the attainment of puberty by boys during the talmudic era and early Middle
Ages; the bar mitzvah ceremony did not evolve before the fourteenth century, according to one authority.[30]

Nathan Morris observed that no educational reformer had decided to
limit the size of classes to twenty-five pupils per teacher until the fourth
century C.E., thereby confirming Philippe Ariès' theory about the inchoate
organization of ancient and medieval schools: "Raba further said: The
number of pupils to be assigned to each teacher is twenty-five. If there are
fifty, we appoint two teachers. If there are forty, we appoint an assistant,
at the expense of the town" (Bava Batra 21a). Morris wrote, "Since there
was no idea of the technique of class teaching in those times, we hear at
no attempt at classification. Children from the age of six, or even younger,
up to probably the age of thirteen, were taught in the same school and the
same class."[31]

Secular subjects, such as mathematics, Greek, gymnastics, and instrumental music were not part of the curriculum of the Jewish elementary
schools. It is even doubtful whether the pupils were taught to write, as
this was a special skill reserved for the educated elite and scribes. Eliezer
Ebner, after quoting the Tosefta, which spoke of "the minor who holds

---

29. Zvee Zahavy, "Political and Social Dimensions in the Formation of Early Jewish
Prayer: The Case of the Shema," *Proceedings of the Tenth World Congress in Jewish
Studies*, August 16–24, 1989 (Jerusalem: World Union of Jewish Studies, 1990), Divi-
sion C, Vol. 1, pp. 33–40. Baruch M. Bokser, *The Origins of the Seder: The Passover
Rite and Early Rabbinic Judaism* (Berkeley and Los Angeles: University of California
Press, 1984), pp. 40–41 and 68 and 69.

30. Lebendiger, *Jewish Law*, pp. 102–106.

31. Morris, *Education*, p. 168.

the *Kalamus* (pen-rod) and the grown-up leads his hand and he writes," concluded that the rudiments of writing may have been taught in some schools during the tannaitic period, but that calligraphy as practiced in Greek schools was not taught. Nor was it customary for girls to be enrolled at school—although a minority of sages ruled that they should be taught the Torah, and the daughters of R. Abbahu learned Greek.[32]

Was the discipline in the Jewish home and school as severe as in their Hellenistic and Roman equivalents? Were Jewish fathers and teachers brutal floggers? In the second century B.C.E. Ben Sirah, following the author of Proverbs, recommended that "a man who loves his son will whip him often so that when he grows up he may be a joy to him" (Ecclesiasticus 2:2). The Hebrew word for instruction, *musar*, also had the meaning of chastisement but was translated into Greek by the compilers of the Septuagint solely by a word meaning punishment. Not only was the *hazzan* the official of the court who administered corporal punishment on its behalf, but he often served as a schoolmaster and it is probable that he was a strict disciplinarian in the classroom. When we recall Philo's attitude toward punishment, Jewish views on discipline seem to resemble those of their pagan neighbors in first or second century Egypt. In a school exercise a pupil from Roman Egypt had copied a line penned by his teacher: "Work hard boy, or you will be thrashed," while another father had pleaded with his son's teacher, "Beat him; because ever since he left his father he has had no other beatings and he likes getting a few; his back has got accustomed to them and needs its daily dose." Augustine wrote that "I was sent to school in order to read. I was too young to understand what the purpose of the whole thing was, and nevertheless if I was idle in my studies, I was flogged . . ." Even certain rabbis boasted about the "goodly blows" which they had received from teachers as a stimulus to their later scholarship. So, too, the Mishnah laid down that a father or teacher who administered a harsh flogging to a child from which he died were not to be held liable for the minor's death (Makkot 2:2).[33]

While the rod of the Bible was replaced by the strap in the talmudic age, it is likely that Jewish teachers utilized several varieties of strap, like their secular counterparts, including the equivalents of the Hellenistic oxtail strap. Culprits were "bent over a post" by the teachers, after which they

---

32. Safrai, pp. 954 and 957. Ebner, *Education*, pp. 82 and 83.
33. Marrou, *Education*, p. 221. Safrai, p. 942. Hopkins, *Roman Schoolboy*, p. 27. Wiedemann, *Roman Children*, p. 165. Morris, p. 175.

were lashed across the shoulders with a strap: "The case is like that of a child who misbehaved and was beaten with a strap," commented the Midrash; "Whenever people wanted to frighten him they used to remind him of the strap with which he had been beaten" (Numbers Rabbah 16:18). In Palestine, in contrast to Roman Egypt, pupils may have been intimidated psychologically but were not administered with a daily dose of the strap. In the Babylonian version of this tale about the strap, it was stated, "Who becomes apprehensive? He who is accustomed to be daily punished" (Sukkah 29a). It is difficult to tell whether or not this is merely a literary embellishment or reflects the greater degree of violence in Babylonian society as compared with Palestine. A teacher in fifth-century Babylonia punished his pupils so excessively that he was dismissed from his post, but he was reinstated because no teacher who was so thorough could be found to replace him. Such cases were probably exceptional and, after all, the teacher was dismissed for a time. Again, the Talmud related two cautionary tales of children who killed themselves rather than face the brutal punishment threatened by their fathers, but these incidents may have been admonitory stories rather than real-life happenings. However, because of *verbal* overreaction by fathers, the sages warned that "one must not threaten a child, but either flog him immediately or keep silent and say nothing about it" (Semahot 2:4–6).[34]

From the third century C.E. onwards in Palestine and Babylonia, the rabbis favored the reduction of corporal punishment and the disciplining of teachers, even dismissing them from their teaching positions in schools: "Rav [third century] also said . . . : When you punish a pupil, only hit him with a shoe latchet. The attentive one will read; and if one is inattentive, put him next to a diligent one" (Bava Batra 21a). R. Isaac declared that children should be taught "with patience and sensitivity." Many masters supported softer techniques to gain their pupils' interest, as one teacher explained to Rav: "I also have a fish pond, and the boy who is unwilling to learn, I bribe with these and coax him until he comes and learns" (Taanit 24a).[35]

Summing up, it could be argued that discipline in the home and school, although sometimes harsh, was less brutal in Palestine and Babylonia than in Greece and Rome, which were coarsened by endemic slavery; and the important role alloted to slaves in the education and upbringing of children. To differentiate themselves from slaves, whom they both loved and

---

34. Ebner, *Education*, p. 36. Morris, *Education*, pp. 173–176.
35. Kraemer, *Jewish Family*, p. 69. Safrai, p. 955.

despised, Athenians were extremely violent to slaves when they grew up and the violence tended to be arbitrary. In fact, just as the link between slavery and violence has been frequently noted in American scholarship dealing with the old Southern states, so the slave societies of ancient Greece and Rome were suffused with brutality. Traumatized by the violence inflicted on them by their masters, the slaves exacted their revenge by frequently thrashing their master's children with added vigor. What the rabbis advocated instead was selective punishment: "Then why 'He that spareth his rod hateth his son'? To teach you that anyone who refrains from chastising his son causes him to fall into evil ways and thus comes to hate him. . . . But a father who chastises his son causes the son to have additional love for him and he honors him . . ." (Exodus Rabbah 1:1). While the Babylonian Talmud incidentally mentioned the possibility of a father striking his son with a strong blow and debated, perhaps academically, whether or not it was compulsory for fathers and masters to continue to chasten a child who was already learned, there were social curbs on a father beating a grown-up son (Moed Katan 17a). Moreover, Judaism also had a less developed doctrine of hell than early Christianity, another factor pointing to the lesser level of punishment and violence in Jewish society.[36]

Unlike the Hellenistic schools, which catered to a small elite in the cities and discriminated against the bulk of the rural population, the Jewish elementary school became universal. After the destruction of the Temple in 70 c.e., the new Greek-style schools spread slowly in Palestine at the end of the first century and throughout the second century, leaving large sections of the population outside the educational system; in Babylonia, where the elementary schools were based on the Palestinian model, progress was even slower. Many scholars have documented the contemptuous remarks uttered by the sages during this period against the *amei ha-aretz*, mostly rural inhabitants but also including some city merchants in this period, who were ignorant of the Torah. In our previous chapter we have touched on rural poverty and its disastrous consequences for elementary schooling, which was only overcome by making free provision for the children of the poor. Even so, not all finished a course of six or seven years schooling and absenteeism must have been high at harvest periods: "Our Rabbis taught: Who is an *am ha-aretz*? Anyone who does not recite the *Shema* evening and morning. . . . Anyone who has sons and does not bring them up to the study of the Torah" (Berakhot 47b). During the first

---

36. Golden, *Childhood*, pp. 155–163.

two centuries the houses of study, unlike the Jewish elementary schools, may have deliberately excluded sections of the population, particularly the more nationalistic elements, and given a privileged position to the sons of sages. Only from the third century to the fifth century onwards with the continuing spread of the elementary schools among the *amei ha-aretz* were these social divisions healed.[37]

At the same time, Jewish girls, unlike the daughters of citizens living in the Hellenistic cities, were excluded from the elementary schools, although their fathers may sometimes have taught them Torah and other advanced studies. Shoshana Pantel Zolty has pointed out that the best evidence for this is in a passage from the Tosefta: "The *zav* and the *zavah* and the *niddah* and the *yoledet* (women in various stages of impurity) are permitted to read all of the Scriptures and to study *Mishnah, Midrash, Halakhot,* and *Aggadot*" (Tosefta: Berakhot 2:12). As the Mishnah forbade women to be teachers of children (Kiddushin 4:13), Zolty has argued that women may have sometimes studied the Torah; we would add that they were now being squeezed out of the system. However, the key to the exclusion of women from the formal educational system was not so much the ruling that women were not obligated to perform all time-bound positive commandments as the enforcement of a ban on them from reading a portion of the Torah in the synagogue. Hence there was no need for them to attend elementary school, when the primary purpose of the school was to teach children to read from the Torah; yet there must be a lingering suspicion that Jewish girls in cities with a Hellenistic cultural background may occasionally have attended elementary schools.[38]

Having been taught the Bible at school from the age of six, for some five years, the boys were then encouraged to study the Mishnah, the oral Law, until the age of twelve or thirteen years, when the majority of them left school for good: "As it usually occurs, one thousand people study the Bible, but only one hundred complete it. One hundred study the Mishnah,

---

37. Aharon Oppenheimer, *The 'Am Ha-Aretz': A Study in the Social History of the Jewish People in the Hellenistic-Roman Period* (Leiden: E. J. Brill, 1977), pp. 171–175. Shmuel Safrai, "Elementary Education, Its Religious and Social Significance in the Talmudic Period," in *Jewish Society Through the Ages,* ed. H. H. Ben-Sasson and S. Ettinger (London: Vallentine Mitchell, 1971), pp. 166–168. Urman, *House of Study,* pp. 242 and 248. Marrou, *Education,* p. 148.

38. Shoshana Pantel Zolty, *"And All Your Children Shall Be Learned": Women and the Study of the Torah in Jewish Law and History* (Northvale, N.J.: Jason Aronson, 1993), pp. 114–116. Safrai, p. 955. Sotah 3:4. Megillah 23a.

but only ten complete it. Ten study the Talmud, but only one reaches the degree of rabbinical ordination" (Leviticus Rabbah 2:1). Unless pupils came from wealthy families or were gifted and determined, they did not proceed at the age of twelve or thirteen years to a house of study (*bet midrash*) to sit at the feet of teachers and learn with adults. It has recently been argued by Dan Urman that these *batei midrash* were specially built structures, designed to be used as schoolhouses for secondary and further education. Following the great expansion of the elementary school system, there was a flood of ambitious pupils clamoring for admission to the elitist houses of study, from which many were excluded by doorkeepers demanding payment of fees. A view attributed to the school of Shammai that students should be taught only if they were "wise, modest, of good family and wealthy" seems to date from this period. There was a struggle to make these secondary schools more democratic and universal, during which the doorkeepers were finally removed, perhaps in the time of Rabban Gamaliel of Yavneh (c. 80–120 C.E.) but more likely later. After a number of years spent at such schoolhouses, the youths could go on to become disciples of one of the great sages. Again, if the youth belonged to one of the elite families, he could be taught Greek by a private tutor because he would have dealings with the imperial bureaucracy and governors or with the Greek-speaking merchants. There was a rabbinic prohibition against the study of Greek wisdom until one was a mature adult, and there was a rabbinic ban on teaching Greek during the War with Quietus in 117 C.E. Nevertheless, the bulk of the population hovered on the brink of subsistence in Palestine and the majority of youths at the age of twelve were taught a trade by their fathers and did not proceed to any form of secondary education. The Talmud declared that the father who failed in this obligation of training his son in a craft was teaching him brigandage (Kiddushin 82a).[39]

THE LEGAL STATUS OF CHILDREN

In the biblical age children were placed under the authority (*potestas*) of their father, the patriarchal family head, until they married. If he died, they were released from his control before marriage. Children were often classed

---

39. Safrai, pp. 953 and 959. Ebner, *Education*, pp. 70 and 84–86. Lieberman, *Hellenism*, pp. 100–113. Urman, *House of Study*, pp. 242–257. Aberbach, *Education*, p. 295.

with the proselyte, slave, widow, and orphan in biblical law. During this period, the minor was vested with slender property rights that enabled him to establish his own private fund (*segullah*). Because of the limited legal rights of children in the biblical age, there was no term for a minor in biblical law, but when a youth attained the age of twenty years certain additional rights and responsibilities devolved on him, such as the duty of serving in the army.[40]

Moreover, a person in Roman law remained under the *potestas* of his father, however old he himself was, so long as his father survived. Under Roman law the male head, the paterfamilias, had the power of life and death over his children, mostly exercised in deciding whether or not they would be permitted to survive after birth; and authority to administer property on their behalf whatever their age, to punish them corporally or to sell them into slavery, and to conclude and terminate marriages for them. Beryl Rawson argued that the father's power was somewhat limited in reality by a son setting up his own household, although even here he might be dependent on his father's allowance. Paul Veyne pointed out that in a pre-industrial society such as Rome the heavy mortality rate removed most fathers at a relatively early age, thereby giving their sons their freedom. In addition, under the Roman emperors and the Christian era, not only were the father's rights further restricted, but in Egypt the Roman concept of *patria potestas* was so whittled down that it amounted to little more than guardianship. Thus sons could later dispute an unwelcome choice of marriage partner and the father's right to disrupt harmonious marriages was relinquished, while adult children could keep their earnings, particularly if they were derived from military service.[41]

In contrast, the rabbis fixed the age when children attained their majority and were said to have legal capacity for certain acts as twelve years for a girl and thirteen years for a boy, when they were called *gedolim*; they were liberated from the control of their father. A girl under twelve was known as a *ketana* (small girl), between twelve and twelve and a half years

40. Boaz Cohen, *Jewish and Roman Law: A Comparative Study* (New York: Jewish Theological Seminary of America, 1966), Vol. 1, p. 214 (hereafter cited as Cohen, *Roman Law*).

41. Cohen, *Roman Law*, p. 215. Dixon, *Roman Mother*, pp. 26–28. Beryl Rawson, "The Roman Family," in *The Family in Ancient Rome*, ed. Beryl Rawson (London: Routledge, 1992), p. 14, and W. K. Lacey, "Patria Potestas," in the same volume, pp. 121–144. Blidstein, *Honor*, pp. 32, 36, 175–176.

she was known as a *na'ara*, but once she had reached twelve and a half years she was designated a *bogeret* (*beger* = age of majority). A child with legal capacity was designated a *gadol*, but the equivalent in Roman law, *puberes* (grown-up person), sometimes lacked such capacity; a child who was under age in Jewish law was called a *katan*, corresponding to the *impubes* (under the age of puberty) in Roman law. According to talmudic law, if there was a dispute as to whether or not a boy had reached puberty, it was settled by examining him and looking for physical signs, such as the growth of two hairs (Berakhot 47b). Whereas, similar to the Talmud, Justinian remarked that whether or not a person was judged to be pubescent depended both on one's age and physical development, in Roman law girls reaching twelve years and boys fourteen years were still judged to be minors who did not attain their majority in the legal sense until they were twenty-five.[42]

Nonetheless, the preceding remarks on the age of majority in Jewish law need some qualification. Raba asserted that a minor could keep a gift for himself if he were sufficiently intelligent to throw away a pebble but keep a nut that was given to him. The Talmud also questioned whether or not the purchase or sale of chattels by children (*pa'utot*) was valid. To this, R. Judah replied that he understood that the children had to be six or seven years of age to give or acquire a good title to chattels, R. Kahana said seven or eight, while a third source claimed that the children had to be nine or ten.[43]

According to the Mishnah, "A man may remain alone with his mother or with his daughter; and he may sleep with them with bodies touching. But if they are become of age, she must sleep in her clothes and he in his" (Kiddushin 4:12). The Talmud carried the debate further as to the definition of the age, R. Ada stating, "For a girl, nine years and a day; for a boy, twelve years and a day. Others state: for a girl, twelve years and a day; for a boy, thirteen years and a day. . . . Rafram b. Papa said in R. Hisda's name: This was taught only of one [a girl] who is not shy of standing nude before him [her father]; but if she is shy of standing nude before him, it is forbidden [for them to sleep in bodily contact]. What is the reason? Temptation stirs her" (Kiddushin 81b). There seems to have been some confusion in rabbinic thought as to the age when childhood sexuality began and

---

42. Cohen, *Roman Law*, pp. 214–216. Kottek, *Childhood*, p. 453. Lebendiger, *Jewish Law*, pp. 99–102.

43. Cohen, *Roman Law*, pp. 227 and 237.

the age when breaches of the sexual code were morally significant for the individual, almost tantamount to a denial of early childhood sexuality.[44]

In rabbinic law, minor sons and daughters remained under the father's control until their marriage. "The father has control over his daughter as touching her betrothal . . . ; and he has the right to aught found by her and to the work of her hands . . . ; but he has not the use of her property during her lifetime" (Ketubot 4:4). So too, a minor son's property remained under his father's control, so that "What is found by a man's minor son or daughter . . . belong to him" (Bava Metzia 1:5); and Ze'ev Falk suggested that a minor son's earnings as well as those of a daughter under the age of twelve and a half years belonged to their father. While sons inherited their father's property, daughters on their father's death were entitled to maintenance until they married. Later it was ruled that "the sons inherit and the daughters receive maintenance and support" (Tosefta Ketubot 6:1), meaning that the sons had to give their sister a dowry out of the estate, if their father was no longer alive to do so. In contrast to Roman law, where even adults could be adopted by wealthy testators as children and heirs, there was no such mechanism in Jewish law for the adoption of children, even when the institution of levirate marriage, which was used as an alternative, was slipping into decay.[45]

In addition, the father had the authority to give away his minor daughter in marriage. Despite the fact that this was a right also assumed by her mother and brothers, if her father was dead, the rabbis introduced the institution of *Mi'un* to curtail this right. Under the legal loophole that was created, the minor female orphan possessed the right to repudiate the marriage contracted for her by her mother and brothers.[46]

Under the legal system still prevailing in Palestine in the first century C.E., a father was not obliged to maintain his children, as there would always be members of the extended family ready to exert pressure on a neglectful father to fulfill his duties or to feed a hungry child, if he failed to do so. R. Eleazar b. Azaria (active 80–120 C.E.), who came from an aristocratic

---

44. Kraemer, *Childhood*, p. 68.

45. Ze'ev W. Falk, *Introduction to Jewish Law of the Second Commonwealth* (Leiden: E. J. Brill, 1978), Part 2, pp. 323, 324, and 336 (hereafter cited as Falk, *Family Law*). Alfredo Mordechai Rabello, "On *Patria Potestas* in Roman and Jewish Law," *Dine Israel: An Annual of Jewish Law and Israeli Family Law* 5 (1974): 129.

46. Lebendiger, pp. 152–159.

family with multiple kinship ties, was thus of the opinion that a father was not under a legal obligation to maintain his children. With the destruction of the Jewish community in the series of revolts against Rome culminating in the Bar Kokhba rebellion in 132 C.E. and with the disintegration of the tightly-knit extended Jewish family in Palestine, a new situation arose and the law had to be recast to offer greater protection to children. So, too, the extended family system having decayed in Palestine (particularly in the larger cities), kinsmen could no longer be relied on to protect young orphans who had inherited substantial estates; following the Greek example and terminology, guardians called *epitropos*, who were not related to the minor, were appointed. R. Eleazar b. R. Simon (active 165–200 C.E.) indicated the desperation of the economic situation in Palestine at the beginning of the third century C.E., commenting that "it is easier for a man to grow myriads of olives in Galilee than to rear one child in Eretz Israel" (Genesis Rabbah 20:6).[47]

Having assembled at the Galilean town of Usha after 140 C.E., the sages now decreed that a man was obliged by law to feed his children and not to rely on handouts from charity funds. Among the Palestinian amoraim who fully accepted the Usha legislation on this point, were Resh Lakish, R. Judah b. Ḥananiah, and Ulla. Earlier R. Meir and R. Judah, who were among the leaders at Usha, declared that there was an obligation on fathers to maintain children under the general laws of charity, but that it was a commandment exceptionally incumbent on them to maintain small children. R. Yoḥanan b. Berokah, of the third generation of tannaim, had ruled that there was a full legal obligation on fathers to maintain their daughters. So, too, Ulpian, a Roman lawyer in the latter half of the second century C.E. at about the time of the Usha decree, mentioned the Emperor Pius, who reigned 135–167, issuing orders enforcing the obligation of maintenance on fathers; and held that ". . . even where the children are not in [the] power [of their father] they must be supported by their parents and they, on the other hand, must support their parents." As yet, it is unclear whether the Roman and Palestinian legislation on the maintenance of children was responding to the same social pressures or whether the rabbis were influenced by the new concepts devised by Roman lawyers. Again, R. Yoḥanan affirmed that a minor's transactions were legal, although this was contrary

---

47. Falk, *Family Law*, pp. 326 and 327.

to biblical law, because under the new disturbed social conditions he might be obliged to support himself.[48]

On the other hand, in Babylonia, where archaic family structures persisted among the Jews for much longer and where the impact of Roman legislation was negligible, the sages did not accept the validity of the Usha regulation, merely exerting moral pressure on recalcitrant fathers. Only toward the end of the amoraic period in Babylonia did the sages decide that if a father was a person of means he could be compelled to support his children under the pressure of the law.[49]

In the biblical age, a man was empowered to sell both his son and daughter as security for his debts. During the talmudic age, the rabbis curtailed these rights, and the power to sell sons lapsed, while restrictions were placed on the right to sell a daughter. It was decided that "a man may sell his daughter but a woman may not sell her daughter . . ." (Sotah 3:8). Elsewhere it was stated that "she that is a minor [less than twelve years old] is subject to the right of sale; and no fine is incurred through her [by her violater or seducer] but through a *na'ara* [a girl aged between twelve and twelve and a half years] a fine is incurred and she is not subject to the right of sale. If she is past her girlhood, she is [as a *bogeret*] not subject to the right of sale, nor can a fine be incurred through her" (Ketubot 3:8).[50]

Nonetheless, Ephraim Urbach believed that in the period between Nehemiah and the Maccabean age, peasant smallholders impoverished by bad harvests and debt continued to offer their sons and daughters for sale. From information contained in the Zeno papyrus, it appears that there was a thriving trade in the export of Jewish slaves into Egypt in the third century B.C.E. According to the Mishnah, "If someone sells himself and his sons as slaves to Gentiles one does not ransom him, but one does ransom the sons after their father's death" (Gittin 4:8). A midrashic comment demonstrates that until the destruction of the Second Temple, the kin of the family that had fallen into debt in Palestine still regarded it as their

---

48. Gedaliah Alon, *The Jews in their Land in the Talmudic Age* (Jerusalem: Magnes Press, 1984), Vol. 2, pp. 574 and 661 (hereafter cited as Alon, *Talmudic Age*). Elimelech Westreich, "A Father's Obligation to Maintain His Children in Talmudic Law," *The Jewish Law Annual* 10 (1992): 177–212 (hereafter cited as Westreich, *Maintenance of Children*).

49. Westreich, *Maintenance of Children*, pp. 201–210.

50. Falk, *Family Law*, p. 323.

duty to try and redeem those family members who had fallen into debt bondage, or to keep them in their own service, thus indicating that the extended kinship network was still intact: "And if he be not redeemed 'by these' . . . R. Yose the Galilean says that 'by these', i. e., his own kin, must manumit him, but others not being his kin may retain him in their service. R. Akiva says that 'by these' means that these, his own kin, may retain him in their own service, but others not being of his kin must manumit him" (Sifra Behar 9).[51]

So, too, the evidence from the Talmud appears to confirm that the sale of daughters remained more common than that of sons. Daughters were low priority as useful members of the family unit, sometimes lower than that of the family investment in chattels and land: "A man is not free to sell his daughter," the sages warned, "put the proceeds into his purse and use them for the purchase of a beast, household effects, or slaves, for the rearing of sheep or goats, or even to invest in business, unless he is poor (and devoid of capital); but if he does so, the sale is nevertheless valid" (Tosefta Arakhin 5:7). R. Yose b. Ḥanina stated that the sale of a daughter could come next after selling one's house to raise capital but before lending money on interest. Further, R. Yose Ha-Kohen and R. Zekhariah spoke of an infant girl prior to the destruction of the Second Temple deposited as a pledge in Ashkelon, in whom her family had "disclaimed all interest" (Eduyyot 8:2). After the wars of 66–64 C.E. and the Bar Kokhba revolt of 132–135 C.E. against the Romans, many Jews including children were sold as slaves in Palestine; in the third century C.E. the soldiers of the Roman occupying power seized Jewish children as sureties who could be sold into slavery if their parents failed to pay all the taxes that were levied.[52]

YOUTH

At twelve or thirteen years, a youth left elementary school when he either started working on the family farm or as a hired laborer, or was apprenticed by his father to some master in a suitable craft or was taught the

---

51. E. E. Urbach, *The Laws Regarding Slavery As a Source for Social History of the Period of the Second Temple, the Mishna and Talmud* (Jerusalem, 1964), pp. 13–16 (hereafter cited as Urbach, *Laws of Slavery*).

52. Urbach, *Laws of Slavery*, pp. 17 and 18. Alon, *Talmudic Age*, Vol. 1, p. 31.

secrets of a skilled trade by his own father. Usually the term of apprenticeship was for five years, but it could vary from anything between six years and six months. A baker told one mother in Caesarea, who brought her son to him, "Let him stay with me five years and I shall teach him to make 500 sorts of goods baked out of white flour; if he stays with me for another five years, he will be able to bake 1,000 sorts" (Lamentations Rabbah 3:6).[53]

"Rabbi said . . . happy is he who sees his parents in a superior craft, and woe to him who sees his parents in a mean craft. The world cannot exist without a perfume-maker and without a tanner—happy is he whose craft is that of a perfume-maker, and woe to him who is a tanner by trade" (Kiddushin 82a). Rabbi Meir contended that "a man should always teach his son a cleanly craft, and let him pray to him to whom riches and possessions belong, for there is no craft wherein there is not both poverty and wealth; for poverty comes not from a man's craft . . . but all is according to his merit" (Kiddushin 4:14). Certain occupations were despised by the rabbis. Abba Gorion of Zaidan declared that "a man should not teach his son to be an ass-driver or a camel-driver, or a barber or a sailor, or a herdsman or a shopkeeper, for their craft is the craft of robbers." Even less complimentary remarks were made about doctors and butchers, the latter trade being a target for intellectuals from talmudic times until the East European era because of the bovine brawn of butchers often coupled with considerable wealth. "R. Judah says . . . the best among physicians is destined for Gehinnom [hell], and the most seemly of butchers is a partner of Amalek" (Kiddushin 4:14). Again, the sages taught that trades associated with frequent contact with female customers should be avoided, yet it is doubtful whether these adverse comments had much impact on choice of occupation, as skilled trades were preferred to agriculture because there was less chance of unemployment."He whose business is with women has a bad character. For example, goldsmiths, carders, handmill sharpeners, pedlars, wool-dressers, hairdressers, laundrymen, blood-letters, bath attendants, and tanners" (Kiddushin 82a).

Unless the juveniles came from a wealthy family, they had little time to

53. Mark Wischnitzer, A History of Jewish Crafts and Guilds (New York: Jonathan David, 1965), p. 35. Keith R. Bradley, Discovering the Roman Family: Studies in Roman Social History (New York: Oxford University Press, 1991), pp. 107, 108, and 111 (hereafter cited as Bradley, Roman Family).

engage in carefree pleasures; the span of youth was short for agricultural-
ists and working-class teenagers, subject as they were to a life of toil and
drudgery enlivened by the Sabbath and festive occasions, and adolescent
freedom was heavily curtailed. Usually the hours of labor of an apprentice
were long and tedious, "from sunrise to sunset." If a girl had reached fifteen, she was probably married and soon afterward she was already bearing children and busy looking after them, while a youth at eighteen or twenty
was ready for the bridal chamber. "At twenty he is like a neighing horse,
adorning himself and seeking a wife. Having married, he is like an ass [that
is, a beast of burden]" (Eccles. Rabbah 12:1).[54]

Briefly during their teenage years, some of the youths from affluent
families rebelled, dandified their appearance, appeared somewhat effemi-
nate, and sought the attention of the more easy-going maidens; sometimes the sexual boundaries may have been blurred, as the following
midrashic passages have similarities to Philo's denunciations of homosexuals. Despite the sages' assertion to R. Judah that "Israel are not suspected
of either pederasty and bestiality . . . ," it is possible that there may have
been occasional homosexual overtures. The delineation of Joseph in the
midrash was a portrait of a narcissistic youth. "Joseph, being seventeen
years old. . . . It means, however, that he behaved like a boy, pencilling
his eyes, curling his hair, and lifting his heel" (Midrash Rabbah 84:7). Also
note a similar comment in an earlier midrash. "R. Ami said: The Tempter
does not walk at the side [of the street] but in the broad highway, and when
he sees a person rolling his eyes, smoothing his hair [in self-satisfaction],
and lifting his heel [in pride], he exclaims, 'This man belongs to me!' . . .
R. Abin said: If one indulges his evil bent in youth, it will eventually rule
over him in his old age" (Genesis Rabbah 22:6). There was much rabbinic
anxiety over rebellious youths not acquiring steady working habits and
learning a necessary craft skill, thereby conditioning them to leading a life
of dissipation and riotous living, which must have reflected wider parental
concerns. "R. Nehorai said: In the generation in which the son of David
comes, the young will insult their elders, old men and women alike who
will be made to wait upon the young . . ." At the same time, the rabbis
whittled down the parents' right enshrined in biblical law to demand the
death penalty for a rebellious son, thus undermining their power through

---

54. Bradley, *Roman Family*, p. 110.

loss of this deterrent and thereby increasing their anxiety of an incipient generational rebellion.[55]

Although gymnastics was not part of the curriculum of the Jewish elementary school nor one of the components of higher education, it would be wrong to conclude from this, like the author of the article in the *Encyclopaedia Judaica*, that the Jews in the talmudic age had "a negative and antipathetic attitude toward sport." A father had the duty of bringing up his son to be strong and well-built in body (Eduyyot 2:9). In talmudic parlance, "The divine majesty dwells in a well-shaped man" (Bekhorot 64a); and Tacitus, who was a hostile critic of the Jews, conceded that "their bodies are strong, able to cope with hardships." Fathers were expected to teach their sons swimming, as their lives "may depend on it" (Kiddushin 30b), but even among the Greeks swimming was regarded as an everyday skill, not as a competitive sport for professionals. The Talmud advised that "one who wishes to stay healthy and prevent intestinal disorders should go swimming in summer and winter" (Gittin 70a). Therapeutic exercises were also discussed in the commentary of R. Hananel, who stated that "you raise your arm in front, and at the back, do knee-bends until you get warmed up and perspire. It serves as a healing-cure." Again, "You must not run on the Sabbath for the sake of exercise, but you may walk in an ordinary way the entire day" (Tosefta Shabbat 16:22). Boys and adolescents enthusiastically played a variety of ball games, but as yet team games with a ball were unknown both to the Greeks and the Jews. So too, the Talmud recommended vigorous exercise for those who wanted to digest a heavy meal. "When our wise men have finished eating and drinking they used to sing, to play games and dance."[56]

Herod, who reigned from 37 B.C.E. to 4 C.E., erected stadiums at Caesarea, Sebaste, Tiberias, Jericho, and elsewhere; and introduced a Palestinian Olympiad with competitions in boxing, archery, athletics, and other sports every five years. An inscription found in Aphrodias dating from the reign of Marcus Aurelius (Roman Emperor 161–180 C.E.) included the names

---

55. *Tanna Debe Eliyyahu: The Lore of the School of Elijah*, trans. William G. Braude and Israel J. Kapstein (Philadelphia: Jewish Publication Society, 1981), p. 479. Mordechai Frishtik, "Physical Violence by Parents Against Their Children in Jewish History and Jewish Law," *The Jewish Law Annual* 10 (1992): 93–94. Emiel Eyben, *Restless Youth in Ancient Rome* (London: Routledge, 1993), pp. 256–258.

56. *Encyclopaedia Judaica* (Jerusalem: Keter Books, 1981), Vol. 15, Col. 291. Article on Sports. Muntner, *Physical Training*, pp. 860–865. Marrou, *Education*, p. 168.

of victors from Palestinian cities. A Jewish contingent at the Tyre games held concurrently with the 152nd Olympic games in Greece brought the customary gifts for Hercules only on condition that they were devoted to a nonidolatrous cause. Children from the families of the Jewish elite in Jerusalem, Alexandria, and Asia Minor attended Greek secondary schools and participated in the ephebia until the early imperial age, where they took part in athletic contests and sometimes acquired skills in Greek culture and philosophy. According to Philo, Claudius warned the Jews of Alexandria that they "should not strive in gymnasiarchic and cosmetic games." If these examples referred to the pinnacles of sporting endeavour by Jews in Palestine and the Diaspora, there must have been a much wider local network of gymnasiums and stadiums available for Jewish athletes to train in from adolescence.[57]

Here in these Greek schools children from upper-class Jewish families not only perfected their athletic skills in the gymnasium but trained their minds "by means of letters and arithmetic and geometry and music . . ." Philo, in an autobiographical passage, asserted that "when first I was incited by the goads of philosophy to desire her I consorted with one of her handmaids, Grammar, and all that I begat by her, writing, reading, and study of the writings of the poets, I dedicated to her mistress. And again I kept company with another, namely Geometry, and was charmed with her beauty, for she showed symmetry and proportion in every part. . . . Again my ardor moved me to keep company with a third; rich in rhythm, harmony, and melody was she, and her name was Music, and from her I begat diatonics, chromatics, and enharmonics, conjunct and disjunct melodies, conforming with the consonance of the fourth, fifth, or octave intervals."[58]

Traces of the imbibing of Greek values as regards physical exercise and prowess by members of the Jewish elite in Palestine can be found in the Mishnah and Talmud. The first example relates to a running competition in the Temple between young priests. "Originally whosoever (of the priestly family the turn of which fell on that day) desired to remove (the ashes from) the altar, did so. If there were many, they would run and mount the ramp (of the altar) and he that came first within four cubits (of the altar) obtained

---

57. *Encyclopaedia Judaica*, Vol. 15, Cols. 291 and 292. Muntner, *Physical Training*, p. 863.

58. Alan Mendelson, *Secular Education in Philo of Alexandria* (Cincinnati: Hebrew Union College Press, 1982), pp. 25 and 26.

the privilege . . ." (Yoma 23a). Second, in the Mishnah, it was stated that on the Sabbath "they [wrestlers] may oil and massage their stomach, but not exercise (the body) and not scrape. They may not go down to the . . . [wrestling ground to exercise in the mud] and may not use artificial emetics" (Shabbat 22:6). Saul Lieberman pointed out the remarkably detailed knowledge of wrestling practices and explained that wrestlers used "to oil themselves, to grapple and trip each other and wallow in the clay." Further, "Thus, Seneca calls the wrestlers, whose knowledge consists of oil and mud, 'contemptible vomitors,' vomiting being closely associated with the oil of the body and the exercises in mud—just as in our Mishnah."[59]

While there was a considerable groundswell of opinion among Jews in favor of participating in sports and athletic exercise, both Philo and the rabbis unanimously condemned such other Greek values as nudity and every manifestation of homosexuality, basing themselves on a biblical injunction. "If a man lies with a male as one lies with a woman, the two of them have done an abhorrent thing, they shall be put to death . . . (Lev. 20:13). According to the Greek worldview, it was wholesome for a boy at puberty to take a slightly older member of the citizen elite as a homosexual lover, whom he could look up to as an admirable model for acquiring the expected modes of adult behavior and attitude. Among the Greeks, homosexuality was an institution that marked the "transition between boyhood and manhood." Within the Roman empire the general Hellenization of culture and the longer periods of military service abroad required of males both significantly increased the level of pederasty at all levels of society. To protect vulnerable adolescent male citizens in Rome from the unwelcome solicitations of predatory male homosexual lovers, the Scantinian Law was a valuable defense against male homosexual rape, even if it did little to safeguard young male slaves from abuse; but the Romans regarded homosexuality less as a moral crime and more as the degradation of a free citizen.[60]

---

59. Raphael Patai, *Man and Temple in Ancient Jewish Myth and Ritual* (London: Thomas Nelson and Sons, 1947), pp. 38, 39, and 73–76. Saul Lieberman, *Greek in Jewish Palestine: Studies in the Life and Manners of Jewish Palestine in the 11th–14th Centuries* (New York: The Jewish Theological Seminary of America, 1942), pp. 92–97.

60. Golden, *Athenian Childhood*, pp. 58–61. Michael Gray-Fow, "Pederasty, the Scantinian Law, and the Roman Army," *Journal of Psychohistory* 13, no. 4 (Spring 1986): 448–460. (hereafter cited as Gray-Fow).

To Philo, homosexuality was the antithesis of Judaism, replacing the duty of procreation and fertility by sterility and corrupting youths when they needed the protection of society. Philo declared,

> In former days the very mention of it was a disgrace, but now it is a matter for boasting not only to the active but to the passive partners, who habituate themselves to endure the disease of effemination, let both body and soul run to waste, and leave no ember of their male sex nature to smoulder. Mark how conspicuously they braid and adorn the hair of their heads, and how they scrub and paint their faces with cosmetics and pigments and the like, and smother themselves with fragrant unguents. . . . He [the homosexual lover] pursues an unnatural pleasure and does his best to render cities desolate and uninhabited by destroying the means of procreation. . . . The reason is, I think, to be found in the prizes awarded in many nations to licentiousness and effeminacy. Certainly you may see these hybrids of men and women continually strutting about through the thick of the market, heading the processions at the feasts . . . leading the mysteries and initiations. . . . (*Special Laws* 3:37–42)

In passing, the parallels between the earlier midrashic passages we have quoted and the description of the appearance of the youthful homosexuals in Philo should be noted. As far as the luxurious banquets were concerned, among the amenities offered to the guests were "grown lads newly bearded with the down just blooming on their cheeks, recently pets of pederasts, elaborately dressed up for the heavier services, a proof of the opulence of the hosts . . ." (*Contemplative Life* 52).

Philo further asserted that "men mounted males without respect for the sex nature which the active partner shares with the passive; and so when they tried to beget children they were discovered to be incapable of any but a sterile seed. . . . Then, as little by little they accustomed those who were by their nature men to submit to play the part of women, they saddled them with the formidable curse of a female disease. For not only did they emasculate their bodies by luxury and voluptuousness but they worked a further degeneration in their souls and, as far as in them lay, were corrupting the whole of mankind" (*On Abraham* 135–136). So many times did Philo discuss the dangers of homosexuality, particularly for youths, that there must be a suspicion that this was not just an abstract philosophical problem but a core issue that concerned upper-class Alexandrian Jewish society.

The rabbis were anxious to keep Jewish children apart from older Gentile children, who were above the age of nine years and one day, and away from the company of slaves, who were believed to be licentious, to ensure that they did not pick up homosexual practices. The *Sibylline Oracles* admonished, "Avoid adultery and indiscriminate intercourse with males . . ." Further, "male will have intercourse with male and they will set up boys in houses of ill-fame . . ." Upright persons ". . . do not engage in impious intercourse with male children, as do Phoenicians, Egyptians, and Romans, spacious Greeks and many nations of others, Persians and Galatians and all Asia, transgressing the holy law of immortal God . . ." Similarly the early Christian work the *Didache* warned that "thou shall not corrupt youths." However, to return to rabbinic thought in this matter, "Rab said: Pederasty with a child below nine years of age is not deemed as pederasty with a child above that [age] . . . Rab maintains that only he who is able to engage in sexual intercourse may as the passive subject of pederasty throw guilt [upon the active offender] . . ." (Sanhedrin 54b). Nonetheless, so successful was the rabbinic campaign against homosexuality that it remained a fringe problem in the talmudic age. Christianity adopted Judaism's abhorrence of homosexuality, particularly the seduction of adolescents, and as soon as Christianity came to power within the Roman Empire from 325 C.E. onwards, it became a moral crime; so much so that in 390 C.E. passive homosexuals could be punished by being burnt alive.[61]

The institution of universal education by late antiquity and the supreme importance vested in schoolchildren by Jews both helped to a certain extent to differentiate children from infants and children from adolescents in the talmudic age. So too, the growth of apprenticeship in towns in the Roman era sharpened the divide between childhood and adolescence. Yet the various Hebrew terms for children remained interchangeable during the Middle Ages and the distinction between the different stages of childhood was still somewhat hazy at times during the talmudic age. A girl after puberty was classified as an adult, but because it was then common for girls to be

---

61. Philo, *On the Contemplative Life*, trans. F. H. Colson. Loeb Classical Library (Cambridge, Mass.: Harvard University Press, 1941), Vol. 9, p. 143. Philo, *On Abraham*, trans. F. H. Colson. Loeb Classical Library (Cambridge, Mass.: Harvard University Press, 1935), Vol. 6, p. 71. *The Old Testament Pseudepigraphia*, ed. James H. Charlesworth (London: Darton, Longman and Todd, 1983), Vol. 1. *Sibylline Oracles*, pp. 366 and 375. C. Taylor, *The Teaching of the Twelve Apostles [Didache]* (Cambridge: Deighton Bell and Co.), p. 123. Uta Ranke-Heinemann, *Eunuchs for the Kingdom of Heaven: The Catholic Church and Sexuality* (Harmondsworth: Penguin Books, 1991), pp. 322 and 323. Gray-Fow, p. 456.

betrothed at fifteen she, unlike her brothers, hardly had the opportunity to explore during adolescence. While the five-year term of apprenticeship for youths in the cities created some limited social space for them to mature and grow psychologically, even if their leisure time was restricted, the same opportunities were lacking for boys in rural areas, where childhood was prolonged. Again, the legal, religious, and sexual definitions of childhood and maturity were often distinctive in this period and did not coalesce easily with the educational distinctions to form neat categories and stages of development.[62]

We have assembled evidence from literary sources and the inscriptions on funeral monuments to show that the new Roman ideals of conjugal love spread across the empire and outside into Babylonia, thus producing a family atmosphere more conducive to a relaxation of parental controls and the employment of a slightly more permissive approach in the upbringing of children. In turn, the attachment between parents and young children among Jews became increasingly strong and emotionally warm in the talmudic age, almost certainly stronger than in the pagan world. Moreover, in late antiquity and in the early Middle Ages there was an increased softening of attitudes among Jews as regards the rearing and disciplining of children in Babylonia and Palestine, perhaps in a conscious attempt to reject Greek and Roman values, just as Daniel Boyarin has suggested that the Babylonian sages formulated their views on sexuality by spurning Greek values. On the other hand, despite the Jews' ideological rejection of infanticide and homosexuality and partly with the aim of protecting adolescents, children were still sold by their parents into debt slavery until 70 C.E., when Jewish political power collapsed and parents themselves were sold into slavery in large numbers. Even so, Jews continued to abandon infants in cases of poverty and political crisis, although the problem remained small and never attained the levels of pagan societies.

C. John Somerville asserted that "when people organize for social change . . . it is never long before they recognize that the rising generation will be crucial to their enterprise. Special efforts will be made to secure their loyalty. . . . One would expect the evidence of interest in children to bunch up around social movements." Further, he suggested that the

---

62. Ephraim Kanarfogel, *Jewish Education and Society in the High Middle Ages* (Detroit: Wayne State University Press, 1992), p. 137, n. 30.

Puritans' interest in children was based on instrumental motives for their own survival rather than psychological reasons, and that while these instrumental motives were not disinterested, they led "to increased understanding of the child's needs and greater definition of the notion of childhood." We would argue that rabbinic Judaism was one of the first religious reform movements, which would help explain the focus of the Pharisees on childhood and the innovations introduced by them.[63]

---

63. C. John Somerville, "English Puritans and Children: A Social-Cultural Explanation," *Journal of Psychohistory* 6, no. 1 (Summer 1978): 113 and 114.

4

Children in the Middle Ages: Infancy and Early Childhood

INTRODUCTION: THE FAMILY

Whereas in the early Middle Ages the Jewish population of Europe was concentrated on the Mediterranean coast, by 1500 the bulk of the population had shifted and was living in Central and Eastern Europe. The Jewish population grew slowly from 450,000 in 1300 to 600,000 in 1490. In the past it was thought that Jewish familes in Western Europe during the Middle Ages were large, couples "with fewer than three children" being the exception. However, a closer scrutiny of the sources by Kenneth Stow has yielded a new picture. Examining a memorial list of Jewish victims of the Crusaders in the Rhineland city of Mainz for 1096, Stow estimated that 34 families had one child and 42 two children, making a total of 118 out of the 216 children belonging to the community. Out of the remaining families 20 were childless and 26 had three or more children. Since 44 of the 122 families were one-parent families, the average medieval Rhineland Jewish family was small, consisting of 3.39 persons, because so many children died shortly after birth or before five years of age.

V. D. Lipman, writing about the Jewish family in medieval Norwich, reached the same conclusion, arguing that there were three families with five children, one possibly with six, but that most families had two or three children. Similarly, tradesmen in an English village in Kent in the seventeenth century had households numbering on average 3.9 persons, while those of laborers were smaller, averaging 3.2 persons, and those of the poor 2.1 persons. Only the wealthier Jewish households tended to be bigger, such as banking families at Florence in 1427, who with retainers numbered nine or ten persons.[1]

So, too, the average Jewish family in medieval Egypt was usually small, including one or two sons among its members, whereas daughters were often not listed. Nonetheless, the affluent families of judges, doctors, government officials, and merchants were sometimes bigger, having on occasion between four and six sons as members; yet no family exceeded a natural limit of seven sons in the medieval period, so that the wish for a newly born baby to become "a brother of seven or eight [brothers]" remained unfulfilled. Unlike the West European Jewish family pattern, marriage between first cousins was common among Jews living in the Islamic world and the earlier European Jews dwelling in the Mediterranean world, such as Ahimaaz ben Patiel of Capua in Southern Italy, who in the eleventh century married his daughter Cassia to his nephew. So, too, Judah Asheri (died 1349), who was born in Germany but settled in Spain, remarked that "one of the good methods which I desired for maintaining the family record was the marriage of my sons to members of my father's house. . . . Furthermore, the women of our family have grown accustomed to the ways of students, and the love of the Torah has entered their hearts, so that they are a help to their husbands in their scholarly pursuits. Moreover, they are not used to extravagant expenditure; they do not demand luxuries, the provision of which disturbs a man from his

---

1. B. Blumenkranz, "Germany 843–1096," in Cecil Roth, *The Dark Ages: Jews in Christian Europe 711–1096*, ed. Cecil Roth (London: W. H. Allen, 1966), p. 165 (hereafter cited as Roth, *Dark Ages*). Kenneth R. Stow, "The Jewish Family in the High Middle Ages: Form and Function," *American Historical Review* (1987): 1088, 1090, and 1091. V. D. Lipman, *The Jews of Medieval Norwich* (London: Jewish Historical Society of England, 1967), pp. 46 and 47. Jean-Louis Flandrin, *Families in Former Times: Kinship, Household and Sexuality* (Cambridge: Cambridge University Press, 1979), pp. 56 and 57 (hereafter cited as Flandrin, *Families*).

study. Then again, children for the most part resemble the mother's family." As Cecil Roth pointed out, the average size of the medieval family among the wealthy Jewish elite, even when they had relatively large families, did not approach the size of the bourgeois Jewish family in the nineteenth century.[2]

CHILDBIRTH

Demographers have demonstrated that about 10 percent of mothers died in the Middle Ages as a consequence of childbirth, although the numbers could have been even higher in urban areas. Again we should remember that it has been calculated that prior to 1800, 11 percent of all fertile women among the European ruling families died in childbirth, while in Switzerland in 1800 the death rate among mothers was 1 or 1.5 per hundred births. If the average female gave birth to some six children during her lifetime, this meant that there was still an 8 percent chance of her dying in childbirth. Figures for death in childbirth for Florence in 1424, 1425, and 1430 suggest that some 20 percent of married women died in childbirth. If Jewish population was heavily concentrated in urban areas in both Western Europe and the Middle East during the Middle Ages, it may have been the case that the death rate of Jewish women in childbirth was inclined at times to reach the higher levels of Florence, even though we do not possess any exact figures for Jewish maternal mortality in this period. Yet evidence from the medieval Jewish cemetery in York suggests a contrary hypothesis, namely that death rates for Jewish mothers were lower than their Christian neighbors. Whereas at St. Helen-on-the-Walls 56 percent of the adult females had died by the age of thirty-five compared with 36 percent of the males, in the medieval Jewish burial ground at Jewbury in York the difference between the male and female death rates for this age group were not significant, although it was a prime period for childbearing. When we recall that the evidence from the epitaphs in the Jewish cata-

---

2. Goitein, *Family*, pp. 237–240. Roth, *Dark Ages*, p. 252. Israel Abrahams, *Hebrew Ethical Wills* (Philadelphia: Jewish Publication Society, 1948), Part 2, pp. 184 and 185 (hereafter cited as Abrahams, *Ethical Wills*). Cecil Roth, *Gleanings: Essays in Jewish History, Letters, and Art* (New York: Hermon Press, 1967), pp. 22–24.

combs in Rome point in the same direction, it appears that the findings from an examination of the skeletal remains recovered from the Jewish cemetery at York may be something more than a freak result.[3]

We do, however, have indirect evidence from the writings of the Tosafists, medieval rabbinic commentators from France, of quite heavy maternal mortality rates, as they dealt extensively with the question of the return of a dowry in the case of the premature death of a young wife in childbirth. R. Jacob Tam (died 1171) decreed that the dowry was to be returned to the wife's family if she died without issue during the first year of marriage. In the Rhine valley, it was the custom to wait for two years, and if no children were born, half the dowry was returned to the wife's father in the event of her death. From the medieval Arab lands, we have the evidence of a number of wills made by pregnant women who feared that they would not survive the birth of a child.[4]

When a woman went into labor in Europe during the Middle Ages, she was assisted by a number of other women, including a midwife, who rotated the fetus in cases of difficulty until it was in the natural birth position. Sometimes among the upper classes, the services of a male doctor were called upon, if the birth was complicated and the midwife could no longer cope. Should the woman die in childbirth, a cesarean section was undertaken on some occasions to try to save the life of her child. Nevertheless, one rabbi declared that "in our days [fifteenth and sixteenth centuries] no operation is performed to remove the child from a woman who died during labor. . . . We are no longer skilled in ascertaining the death of a woman while the child is still alive. Maybe she is only unconscious and the operation would cause her death." There was a custom among Jews in Egypt during the sixteenth century when a woman died during labor to beat her

---

3. Flandrin, *Families*, p. 217. Edward Shorter, *Women's Bodies: A Social History of Women's Encounter with Health, Ill-Health, and Medicine* (New Brunswick, N.J.: Transaction Publishers, 1991), pp. 47 and 98–100 (hereafter cited as Shorter, *Women's Bodies*). Shulamith Shahar, *Childhood in the Middle Ages* (London: Routledge, 1992), p. 35 (hereafter cited as Shahar, *Medieval Childhood*). J. M. Lilley, G. Stroud, D. R. Brothwell, and M. H. Williamson, *The Jewish Burial Ground at Jewbury York* (York: York Archaeological Trust, 1994), pp. 434 and 435.

4. Louis Rabinowitz, *The Social Life of the Jews of Northern France in the 12th and 14th Centuries as Reflected in the Rabbinical Literature of the Period* (London: Edward Goldston, 1938), p. 144 and 258 (hereafter cited as Rabinowitz, *Social Life*). Goitein, *Family*, p. 232.

on the abdomen with brooms to ensure that the fetus died. This practice was prohibited by R. David ibn Abi Zimra.[5]

The heavy maternal death rates in childbirth in traditional society coupled with the high infant mortality rates in the first days after birth and particularly during the infant's first year engendered a deep-seated anxiety in families at times of childbirth and surrounding the circumcision ceremony. To assuage these fears, a host of folk customs and superstitions evolved in Western Europe and the Eastern Mediterranean. The Jews shared these with their Christian and Muslim neighbors and were afforded a certain degree of psychological comfort and reassurance. The objective of these measures was to repel or thwart the malign influence of demons or evil spirits, which were thought to imperil the life of the parturient mother and her newborn child. Raphael Patai has discussed in exhaustive detail the magical palliatives adopted by Jewish women in childbirth in both Europe and the Islamic lands over the course of centuries, but there is still the need for a survey that concentrates on one region at a time by showing a cluster of such practices. What we mean is the need for a survey using Weber's concept of the ideal type, as the plethora of practices over millennia and vastly different regions tends to be confusing. Among Jews in early modern Germany and Alsace the wearing of amulets of mineral and vegetable origin, the introduction of an object of iron into the delivery room, the display of the husband's trousers or some article of clothing belonging to him, and the tying of amulets to the woman in the childbed made from snakeskin—all were practices commonly utilized by Jews and by their Christian neighbors in France and Germany in the seventeenth and eighteenth centuries.[6]

Amulets of mineral, vegetable, or animal origin were widely used in the Middle Ages, sometimes being handed down by middle-class Jewish fami-

---

5. Ron Barkai, "A Medieval Hebrew Treatise on Obstetrics," *Medical History* 33 (1989): 100–108 (hereafter cited as Barkai, *Obstetrics*). H. J. Zimmels, *Magicians, Theologians, and Doctors* (London: Edward Goldston, 1952), p. 69 (hereafter cited as Zimmels, *Magicians and Doctors*).

6. Raphael Patai, "Jewish Birth Customs," in *On Jewish Folklore* (Detroit: Wayne State University Press, 1983), pp. 337–443 but especially pp. 369–382. Herman Pollack, *Jewish Folkways in Germanic Lands 1648–1806* (Cambridge, Mass.: M. I. T. Press, 1971), pp. 16 and 17 (hereafter cited as Pollack, *Folkways*). Jacques Gélis, *History of Childbirth: Fertility, Pregnancy and Birth in Early Modern Europe* (Oxford: Polity Press, 1991), pp. 115–119, 145, and 148 (hereafter cited as Gélis, *Childbirth*).

lies from generation to generation as valuable heirlooms. As soon as the
first birth pains were felt, these amulets were attached to expectant mothers. They were quickly removed once the baby was born because it was
felt that leaving the amulets in place for too long was unlucky owing to
their potency and that hemorrhaging might result. Prior to the start of the
actual birth process, the amulet was usually draped around the mother's
neck to keep the baby high in the womb, but once the labor pains commenced the amulet was either placed on the abdomen of the parturient
mother or tied to her left thigh.[7]

Among amulets the eagle-stone, which was a smaller, loose stone within
a larger stone, was particularly popular in early modern France, enjoying
a wide circulation during the Middle Ages, although it had first appeared
in Jewish circles in the talmudic age. As far as Southern Europe was concerned, Maimonides declared in his treatise on the Sabbath that "a woman
may go out wearing a preserving stone—or its counterweight which has
been weighed accurately for medical use. Not only a woman already pregnant may wear such a stone, but any other woman also may do so as a
preventive of miscarriage in the event of pregnancy." One writer claimed
that "this stone [the eagle-stone] is pierced through the middle, and is round,
about as large and heavy as a medium-sized egg, glassy in appearance,
and is to be found in the fields . . ." By analogy, the rattling of the smaller
stone within the larger eagle-stone was meant to reassure the parturient
mother that she would have an easy labor and that her child would be
born without any complications. Not only were there references to this
stone by the medieval French and German rabbinic authorities, but belief
in its efficacy lingered on among German Gentiles until the nineteenth
century. Again, in the *Sefer Gematriot*, a fourteenth-century work from
Northern Europe, the value of the ruby was explained. "Its use is to prevent the woman who wears it from suffering a miscarriage. It is also good
for women who suffer excessively in childbirth, and, consumed with food
and drink [in a powdered form], it is good for fertility."[8]

---

7. Gélis, *Childbirth*, pp. 117 and 118. R. Ibn Adret of Barcelona (1235–1310) set
out the conditions under which amulets could be written on the Sabbath for women who
were in labor. See Abraham A. Neuman, *The Jews in Spain: Their Social, Political,
and Cultural Life During the Middle Ages* (New York: Octagon Books, 1980), Vol. 2,
p. 109 (hereafter cited as Neuman, *Jews in Spain*).

8. Gélis, *Childbirth*, pp. 115 and 116. Shahar, *Medieval Childhood*, pp. 36 and
269 note 16. Fred Rosner, *Medicine in the Mishneh Torah of Maimonides* (New York:

So, too, a fourteenth-century Jewish medical manual probably written in Spain in line with Christian and Muslim authorities recommended that a plant known as agrimony be tied to an expectant mother's thigh with its roots pointing upwards, as the plant was invested with the power of attraction; it was believed that placing it near the woman's genitalia could assist in the rapid expulsion of the fetus. However, so powerful was the attractive force of agrimony that the author cautioned against leaving it in position after the infant's birth, for this could result in a prolapsed uterus. In seventeenth-century Poland R. Eliyahu Baal Shem from the town of Chelm advised that for a woman who has difficulty in labor, "Take *belzen zamen* [*belzen* (?) seeds] and tie them in a piece of linen cloth, and tie it to her right thigh, and she will deliver it quickly." Further, as an alternative remedy, "Put on her belly, that is on her body and not on the shirt, and also under her right and left armpits, a powder made of *hopfen* [hops], and she will deliver with the help of God, blessed be he." If these techniques were tried in medieval Spain and seventeenth-century Poland, it is obvious that their use was widespread throughout Europe and whatever remedies had traveled eastward to Poland must have been utilized beforehand in Germany.[9]

Other rites that Jews and Christians shared in eighteenth-century France and Germany were the use of iron as a repellant to protect the parturient woman and the newly born baby and the custom of drawing a magic circle around the childbed. A legend that surfaced in the talmudic era in a Palestinian Aramaic text depicted a fiend called Sideros (iron, in Greek) who killed infants but who was so successfully pursued by helpers of the mother that they extracted a promise from him to spare the infants whenever their names were recited. The original names of the helpers were Swny, Swswny, and Snygly, whom it was claimed in the Greek version of the tale were the woman's brothers, and these became the three names associated with the magical circle; sometimes the helper was solely identified with Elijah. Although the name of the evil being *Werzelya* (Aramaic *Parzela* and

Ktav Publishing House, 1984), p. 282 (hereafter cited as Rosner, *Maimonides*). J. Horace Nunemaker, "Obstetrical and Urinary Remedies of Thirteenth Century Spain," *Bulletin of the History of Medicine* 15 (1944): 162, 163, and 168–169. M. Gudemann, *Geschichte Des Erziehungswesens Und Der Cultur Der Aberlandischen Juden* (Vienna, 1880), Vol. 1, p. 214 (hereafter cited as Gudemann). Joshua Trachtenberg, *Jewish Magic and Superstition: A Study in Folk Religion* (New York: Atheneum, 1975), pp. 133, 134, 137, and 295 note 3 (hereafter cited as Trachtenberg, *Magic*).

9. Barkai, p. 111. Patai, *Jewish Folklore*, pp. 344 and 373.

Hebrew *Barzel* for iron) occurred in an old Ethiopic version of the story, this was forgotten later when the name of the female demon Lilith (Sumerian *lil* meaning air) was substituted in later Jewish legend. Around 1000 C.E., a work entitled *The Alphabet of Ben Sira* first suggested the utterance of the names of the three helpers, who were now identified as angels, as a means of combating the depravations of Lilith. Joshua Trachtenberg pointed out that iron, which was a product of civilization, was regarded as being very effective against the demons of preliterate, premetal society.[10]

In an eighteenth-century German version of the story printed on an amulet, based in turn on a late medieval or modern formulation from an area where Spanish was spoken, it was recounted that Elijah, having met Lilith on the road, questioned her as to where she was going. She replied: "I am going to the house of X daughter of Y, the woman in childbirth, to kill her and take away her son, to drink his blood, to suck the marrow of his bones and to eat his flesh." In return for being exempted from banishment by Elijah, Lilith promised him to spare that woman and her son when her various names were recited, while these amulets also carried the names of the three guardian angels: Sanvi, Sansanvi, and Semangelaf. A popular medieval amulet invoking these angels' assistance against Lilith was printed in the *Sefer Raziel* in Amsterdam in 1701, although the work itself was compiled in Northern Europe in the thirteenth century. According to R. Elijah Levita, amulets to ward off Lilith were popular in Germany in the sixteenth century. In Alsace during the second half of the nineteenth century, printed amulets called *Scheimestafeln* bearing representations of a lion or parrot with Psalm 121 and the names of the three angels were still hung on the walls of the birth chamber.[11]

Nonetheless, as we have seen, iron was the favorite antidemonic device to counter Lilith and her predecessors, and in seventeenth-century Germany it was the custom among Jews in Frankfurt for a woman to carry a knife during the last days of her pregnancy when she was alone at home.

10. Joseph Naveh and Shaul Shaked, *Amulets and Magic Bowls: Aramaic Incantations of Late Antiquity* (Jerusalem: Magnes Press, 1987), pp. 105–121 (hereafter cited as Naveh and Shaked, *Amulets*). Gershom Scholem, *Kabbalah* (New York: New American Library, 1974), pp. 356–361. Joseph Dan, "Samael, Lilith, and the Concept of Evil," *AJS Review* (1980): 17–40 (hereafter cited as Dan, *Samael and Lilith*).

11. Naveh and Shaked, *Amulets*, pp. 118 and 119, and 121. Trachtenberg, *Magic*: see frontispiece and pp. 169 and 315. Freddy Raphael, "*Rites de naissance et medecine populaire dans le judaisme rural d'Alsace,*" *Revue de la Societe d'ethnographie francaise* 1, no. 3–4 (1971): 83–86 (hereafter cited as Raphael, *Rites of Birth*).

In 1715 Schudt reported that in this town so long as a woman was in childbed an old woman brandished a rusty sword and made a circuit of the room with it each night, while reciting an incantation. These knives bore an inscription from Exodus 22:17, "Thou shalt not suffer a sorceress to live," a verse that was also carried by the pictorial amulets. The knife known as a *krasmesser*, or in Alsatian Yiddish as *kreismesser*, either took its name from an acrostic on the Hebrew phrase *kra satan* (destroy satan) or described the magic circles (*kreis*) made around the woman. In nineteenth-century Poland, iron was also used to protect women at childbirth with the claim that the Hebrew for iron, *barzel*, represented the initial letters of the names of the patriarchs' wives, Bilha, Rachel, Zilpa, and Leah. In the Lower Rhine region, a woman recalled that at the beginning of this century, a dagger was left at the top of her mother's bed during childbirth and that her grandmother performed a circuit with it every evening.[12]

According to Hayim b. Bezalel (died 1588), in the days prior to the delivery of a child, a circle was drawn on the floor around the lying-in bed and the names of the guardian angels—Sanvi, Sansavi, Semangelaf, Adam, and Eve—were chalked on the walls or door of the room with the inscription "Barring Lilith." Another source stated that "it is a widespread custom among us Ashkenazim to make a circle around the walls of the room in which the woman in childbirth lies, with neter [nitre] or embers, and to write on every wall, 'Adam, Eve, Out Lilith.'" In mid-nineteenth-century Alsace, village Jews, like their Christian neighbors, still drew protective circles around women in childbirth. The folklorist Angelo Rappoport reported in 1937 that "the practice of drawing circles with chalk on the wall still prevails in Poland, and it was once widely spread in Germany."[13]

During the Middle Ages, Jewish and Christian women in Germany wore a piece of cloth taken from their husband's trousers, jacket, or belt to endow them with additional strength during a difficult labor; and once the child was born, they placed the trousers on or in the bed to prevent strong

---

12. Pollack, *Folkways*, pp. 16 and 212. Raphael, *Rites of Birth*, pp. 86–88.

13. Trachtenberg, *Magic*, p. 169. Pollack, *Folkways*, p. 18. Patai, *Jewish Folklore*, pp. 411 and 412. Angelo S. Rappoport, *The Folklore of the Jews* (London: Soncino Press, 1937), p. 94. The practice of drawing protective circles for women in childbirth persisted in Alsace throughout the nineteenth century. See Paula Hyman, "Village Jews and City Jews in Alsace," in *Assimilation and Community: The Jews in Nineteenth Century Europe*, ed. Jonathan Frankel and Steven J. Zipperstein (Cambridge: Cambridge University Press, 1992), p. 116.

afterpangs. Alternatively, among Catholics in eighteenth-century France, a wife wore her husband's hat or trousers in the hope that the womb would recognize the smell of its progenitor and expel the fetus, and a similar form of logic may have prevailed among Jews in the Middle Ages. David Tevle Ashkenazi of Moravia (died 1734) advised that a virgin should encircle a parturient woman three times, on each occasion touching the mother's abdomen; following this a snakeskin, which had obvious phallic symbolism, was placed on her abdomen. In the mid-nineteenth century in the Jura area of France, "when a young woman feels the first pangs of childbirth, a young virgin is immediately called in, sits by the mother's bed and holds her hand until the moment of delivery." Here the logic was that the proximity of opposites, virgin and pregnant mother, attract the birth of the fetus. Outside Europe in places such as the Turkish empire, women who went into labor, including Jewish women, often wore a belt of human skin stripped from the corpses of fallen soldiers to increase their strength; perhaps the use of the snakeskin in Europe was a partial substitute for this.[14]

The *Sefer Ḥasidim*, a thirteenth-century compilation from the Rhineland, recommended that "if a woman was lying on the bed of sickness [during childbirth], people in the room should utter prayers of mercy for her and the well-being of the child."[15]

Mireille Laget observed that "the men and women of the seventeenth and eighteenth centuries experienced childbirth as a phenomenon over which they had no control." According to this early modern peasant worldview, which also influenced Jewish circles, "men and women, animals and vegetables, all obeyed great laws of germination and putrefaction, by which everything that died was to be born again, and there was no real separation perceived between human beings and the earth from which they sprang . . . men and women thought analogically, saw all the objects and entities of the natural world as being like something else, so that a plant or a root shaped like part of the human body must necessarily correspond to and provide a cure for any ill it might suffer . . ." In one of the rural areas of England between the sixteenth and eighteenth centuries, it has been estimated that deaths from hemorrhage and puerperal

---

14. Gudemann, Vol. 1, p. 214. Gélis, *Childbirth*, pp. 145, 146, and 148. Pollack, *Folkways*, p. 17. Patai, *Jewish Folklore*, pp. 376 and 428 note 341. Zimmels, *Magicians and Doctors*, p. 136.

15. *Sefer Ḥasidim* (Warsaw: Lewin-Epsztein, n.d.), p. 121, Number 487.

sepsis may have accounted for 25 maternal deaths for every 1,000 children who were baptized. We can now see why there was a proliferation of amulets in Jewish households at childbirth and how the system of magic that regulated them was based on a theory of correspondences or "signatures" between plants and animals. Thus it was dangerous to upset the natural rhythm of the universe by intervening and performing operations at childbirth.[16]

If the maternal death rate in the West European capital cities declined at the end of the eighteenth century, it was because doctors and midwives were more skilled and competent, while a greater range of maneuvers to engage the fetus in a favorable birth position were available. Since the seventeenth century forceps were used by doctors in England and Holland, but in the following century in France obstetricians were still encountering opposition from doctors and midwives. Although there were a number of recorded cases in France of women surviving cesarean operations in the eighteenth century, it was not until the end of the century that the techniques were sufficiently perfected for them to be performed more extensively, even if the danger of rapid infection remained. After 1847, Ignaz Semmelweis, in the leading Viennese maternity hospital, made his students wash in chloride of lime before carrying out internal examinations of female patients, but maternal mortality started to decline only in the 1870s with Joseph Lister's discovery of antisepsis in 1867. Despite variations over the years, the maternal mortality rate in England and Wales between 1855 and 1934 averaged 4.6 per 1,000 live births, persistently refusing to decline. In sum, the medical advances of the nineteenth and twentieth centuries only slowly led to the elimination of generalized infection and hemorrhaging at childbirth, thus in the second half of this century drastically reducing maternal mortality.[17]

---

16. Mireille Laget, "Childbirth in the Seventeenth- and Eighteenth-Century France: Obstetrical Practices and Collective Attitudes," in *Medicine and Society in France: Selections from the Annales*, ed. Robert Forster and Orest Ranum (Baltimore: Johns Hopkins University Press, 1980), pp. 171 and 172 (hereafter cited as Laget, *Obstetrics*). Review of Jacques Gélis' *History of Childbirth* by Caroline Steedman in *Social History of Medicine* 5, no. 2 (August 1992): 344. Gélis, *Childbirth*, pp. 5, 6, and 8. Ralph Jackson, *Doctors and Diseases in the Roman Empire* (London: British Museum Publications, 1988), p. 106.

17. Shorter, *Women's Bodies*, pp. 47, 99, 100, and 101. Laget, *Obstetrics*, pp. 170 and 171. Lara V. Marks, *Model Mothers: Jewish Mothers and Maternity Provision in East London 1870–1939* (Oxford: Clarendon Press, 1994), pp. 87–91.

Many of these advances took until after the Second World War to filter through to the traditional Jewish communities of Eastern Europe and the Middle East, so that the use of amulets took a long time to fall out of fashion; yet in France the effectiveness of amulets had been questioned by some doctors from the end of the seventeenth century. On the other hand, even the traditional Jewish community in Alsace was still using iron knives to repel evil spirits in the lying-in room at the beginning of the century, along with printed amulets pinned to the curtains of the birth chamber. So too, William Feldman noted that prior to the First World War, "Even in the Jewish quarter in [the East End] of London certain amulets are used to protect the mother and child from their special fiend Lilith, Adam's first wife . . ." Within the Jewish community in Poland all the multifarious traditional practices to safeguard a woman at childbirth persisted through the interwar period (1918–1939), including the amulets with Psalm 121, purchased from the *heder* teacher. These amulets, pasted up in the mother's room, contained the phrase "Israel's guardian never slumbers, never sleeps." If the *mohel's* (circumciser's) iron knife was placed under the mother's pillow the night before the circumcision in pre–World War II Poland as a means of ensuring the safety of the infant, such customs had become meaningless in postwar America. One *mohel* declared that he no longer followed the custom "'because I have lost too many knives that way', [to which] the father answered, 'Oh, don't worry. We still have the knife you left for the last baby.'" With the failure of the maternal mortality rates to recede until the 1940s even in countries with the most advanced medical facilities, and with anxiety levels still so steep, we can now understand why almost everywhere in Eastern Europe and the Middle East the magical protective practices surrounding childbirth were so entrenched and took so long to dismantle.[18]

Moreover, in Turkey the Spanish Jewish community was still extensively using amulets together with other measures to protect the mother and the newborn infant in the 1920s and 1930s. Special care was taken to decorate a four-poster bed for childbirth, every effort being made to ensure that the color red appeared in the bedding, as this was thought to embody

---

18. W. M. Feldman, *The Jewish Child: Its History, Folklore, Biology & Sociology* (London: Balliere, Tindall and Cox, 1917), p. 167. Raphael, *Rites of Birth*, pp. 86–88. Paula E. Hyman, *The Emancipation of the Jews in Alsace: Acculturation and Tradition in the Nineteenth Century* (New Haven: Yale University Press, 1991), p. 72 (hereafter cited as Hyman, *Alsace*). Henry C. Romberg, *Bris Milah* (New York: Feldheim, 1982), pp. 49 and 50.

amuletic significance. After childbirth the new Sephardi mothers wore on their heads an amuletic kerchief known as a *tocadór de parida* with God's name embroidered on it plus the names of the three angels, Sanvi, Sansavi, and Semangelof; sometimes the embroidery included the expression "beyond Lilith"; in addition, gold and diamond jewelry covered the upper portion of their faces, thereby concealing them from the evil eye. So too, Michael Weingarten, who observed a Yemenite community in Israel, declared that "one particularly common form is the amulet to protect the newborn baby from evil spirits, especially that of Lilith. . . . I have seen this used in almost every crib in Rosh Haayin, though some more modern families have substituted a copy of the Hebrew Bible at the foot of the crib."[19]

THE EVE OF CIRCUMCISION AND
THE CIRCUMCISION CEREMONY

In the Middle Ages, a ceremony known as the "watch night," *Wachnacht*, in Southern Germany and the *veglia* in Italy was observed to protect the baby boy from a fatal assault by demons on the night or nights preceding his circumcision. In the European version of *The Alphabet of Ben Sira*, Lilith told the angels, who had been instructed to persuade her to return to Adam: "I know I was created for the sole purpose of making babies ill from the day of their birth until the eighth day when I have permission [to harm them], and after eight days I have no permission. And if it is female, [I have such permission] for twelve days." As early as the eleventh century, R. Eliezer ben Isaac the Great had warned: "Do not leave an infant boy in his cradle alone in the house by day or night, nor pass thou the night alone in any abode. For under such circumstances, Lilith seizes man or child in her fatal embrace."[20]

---

19. Russo-Katz, "Childbirth," in *Sephardi Jews in the Ottoman Empire: Aspects of Material Culture*, ed. Esther Juhasz (Jerusalem: Israel Museum, 1990), pp. 254–270 but especially pp. 260–262 on the many different kinds of amulets, only a few of which we could cover in the text (hereafter cited as Russo-Katz, *Sephardi Childbirth*). Michael A. Weingarten, *Changing Heath and Changing Culture: The Yemenite Jews in Israel* (Westport, Conn.: Praeger, 1992), p. 111.

20. Elliott Horowitz, "The Eve of Circumcision: A Chapter in the History of Jewish Nightlife," *Journal of Social History* 23, no. 1 (1989): 46 (hereafter cited as Horowitz, *Watch Night*). Dan, *Samael and Lilith*, pp. 20–22. Abrahams, *Ethical Wills*, Part 1, 1926, p. 48.

Recently Elliot Horowitz has made a superb study of the "watch night," and we have drawn heavily on his findings in the next few paragraphs. In the Zohar, a mystical tract written in thirteenth-century Spain, there was an allusion to menfolk staying awake all night on the eve of a circumcision to study the Torah. Rabbi Aaron of Lunel, a town in Provence with a culture similar to that of Spanish Jewry, added a few decades afterwards that "in some places the members of the mother's household remain awake for the first seven nights after her giving birth to a boy or girl . . . and on the eighth night (i. e., the eve of the eighth day) this is practiced everywhere with singing and dancing." Not only was fruit distributed to guests on the night before the circumcision, but "in one place it is customary to recite liturgical poems (piyyutim) on the eighth day." We also know from the records of the Inquisition that the Marranos celebrated a ceremony known as hadas, in which female relatives and friends assembled in the mother's room on the night before the circumcision "singing and dancing to the accompaniment of cymbals and feasting to their hearts' content" on fruit. Increasingly, however, Marranos completely abandoned the circumcision rite, as this was too obvious an indicator of the family's Jewish affiliation. So, too, Rabbi Joseph Colon, in a responsum from Italy, mentioned the custom of meeting in the mother's room on the eve of the circumcision to feast on fruit, a symbol of fertility. During its migration to Italy the religious content of the festival, which was originally pronounced in Spain and Provence, seems to have dwindled, with an emphasis placed on the eating of fruit as a symbol of fertility.[21]

We can see this more clearly in sources from Western and Eastern Europe in the fifteenth and sixteenth centuries, when the "watch night" was regarded as an antidemonic ceremony with a focus on staying awake all night, while most of the religious elements were jettisoned. We have a report from a priest who observed the ceremony on the night before the circumcision in fifteenth-century Vienna: ". . . friends gather in the home of the mother . . . they 'watch' ['sit up': wachen] the entire night, so that Satan should not come and kill the child, and Lilith, the mother of Satan, should not strangle him." Again, R. Moses b. Abraham Mat, a Galician rabbi, wrote in 1584 that the celebrants kept awake all night "because Satan seeks to prevent the child from [fulfilling] the commandment of circumcision . . ." A non-Jewish Swiss lexicographer, Johannes Buxtorf,

---

21. Horowitz, Watch Night, pp. 47, 48, and 62 note 18.

described the eve of circumcision festivities in 1603 as one of "jollity and facetious merriment."[22]

Having lasted the entire night, the festival was a combination of card playing, dice throwing, singing and storytelling, drinking and serving special delicacies, and the minimal recital of prayers. Reports from the sixteenth century and early seventeenth century spoke of dancing for seven nights and gambling in the week before the circumcision. Despite attempts to suppress the popular aspects of the *veglia* in Italy, R. Tranquilo Corcos in 1727 admitted that many of its old features survived in Rome: "For the father gathers together friends and relatives . . . and with a joyous heart they partake of delicacies. They drink fine wine from elegant vessels . . . and instead of reciting prayers of praise and thanksgiving to God, all sing lusty songs with their faces ablaze. They engage in vain and ridiculous activities, young and old, women and children. Some dance, young men and maidens together, mouthing obscenities and devising sins in their hearts . . ." The apostate Paolo Sebastiano Medici, in his book on Jewish customs published in 1736, reported that while the eve of circumcision festivities opened with a stimulating address by the rabbi, the celebrations continued with music, dancing, eating, drinking, and revelling and that some guests stayed the whole night to protect the infant from the attentions of Lilith. For Germany, Johann Schudt, writing in the early eighteenth century about the "watch night" celebrations, claimed that besides a few of the more pious individuals praying, the rest of the guests amused themselves throughout the entire night, eating, drinking, and gambling. To a certain extent the "watch night" or *veglia* was a woman's festival in Europe with certain activities, such as dancing and possibly gambling being confined to women, as the festival became increasingly sacralized for the men.[23]

Among the Spanish Jews in the Turkish Empire, however, the night before the circumcision, known as *viola*, from the old Castilian *vispera*, eve, survived as a joyous occasion with a mixture of religious devotion and secular merriment until the twentieth century. If a mother had lost a succession of babies, her infant son was dressed before the circumcision in a garment made from the material intended for his grandmother's shroud, as this augured well for a future long life. At the *viola* in Salonika the rabbi delivered a short sermon, concluding with the *Kaddish*. Then a children's

22. Horowitz, *Watch Night*, pp. 47, 48, 62 note 22, and 63 note 23. Pollack, *Folkways*, pp. 19–22.
23. Horowitz, *Watch Night*, pp. 49, 50, 55 and 56.

choir, accompanied by a Turkish style orchestra, sang songs in Hebrew and ballads in Ladino with an emphasis on the subject of birth. Afterwards there was a party for friends of the family at which many kinds of sweet delicacies and drinks were served, sometimes lasting until the early hours of the morning. During the mid-nineteenth century, R. Palaggi tried in vain to promote all-night Torah study as the essential core of the vigil and to curb the festivities, confessing that he "was also very distressed about the small number of our people, who, when they held a *leil shemira* [night of vigil], hire musicians and singers, and spend the night drinking wine, playing instruments . . . and engaging in other such frivolities." We can see how the watch night ceremony in the Eastern Mediterranean remained a potential source of tension, as it also embraced the values of the counterculture, too much drinking and the risk of slipping into bawdy song.[24]

A similar situation prevailed among the Sephardim on the island of Rhodes until the Second World War. Either the father and a few close relatives sat up studying all night as they watched over the child, or the guarding was entrusted to one or two women. "It was a continuous party in the house of the new mother with beautiful songs and musicians," one celebrant recalled. Other measures taken to protect the sleeping infant before the circumcision were the hanging of a sword in his room, a display of lights to blind any evil spirits, and the attachment of a branch of rue sprinkled with *alhavaka* (gold leaf) to the baby's pillow as a symbol of good luck. If the child was circumcised in the synagogue, the godmother and baby together with guests marched through the Jewish quarter accompanied on their way by musicians.[25]

During the seventeenth and eighteenth centuries the ceremony of *yidishkerts* (to judaize by the *kerts* circumcision candle) was commonly adhered to by Jews in Southern Germany between the Rhone Valley and Furth. Whereas Gentile French parents in Early Modern France were especially vigilant before their unnamed infant's baptism, by keeping a solicitous watch over the baby, by burning a candle (often the Candlemas candle) and by leaving a metal object close to their child to deter harmful spirits, Jews in

---

24. Michael Molho, *Usos Y Costumbres De Los Sefardies de Salonica* (Madrid-Barcelona: Instituto Arias Montano, 1950), pp. 62–64. Michael Molho, "Birth and Childhood among the Jews of Salonica," *Edoth* 2, no. 3–4 (Apr.–July 1947): 260. Russo-Katz, *Sephardi Childbirth*, pp. 261, 262, and 269 note 38.

25. Isaac Jack Lévy, *Jewish Rhodes: A Lost Culture* (Berkeley: Judah L. Magnes Museum, 1989), p. 45. Rebecca Amato Levy, *I Remember Rhodes* (New York: Sepher-Hermon, 1987), pp. 11 and 12 (hereafter cited as Rebecca Levy, *Rhodes*).

Southern Germany utilized the same practices to protect their infant son before the circumcision ceremony, particularly by burning candles—a parallel already alluded to by Moritz Gudemann, a pioneer in Jewish studies, in 1888. There were also similarities with the practices of the Spanish Jews, as we have outlined above.[26]

From the time of the Talmud, it was noted that "carrying a torch at night is as good as having a companion (to keep the demons away) . . ." Although the custom may be traced to at least the twelfth century in Germany, when Eleazar ben Judah, the Rokeach (1160–1238), related that female friends of his mother assembled after she had given birth and lit an oil lamp, the first mention of candles burning during the "watch night" ceremony was by the Maharil a couple of centuries later. According to R. Jacob ben Moses Molin, the Maharil (1335–1427), the practice was already established in the Rhineland in the fourteenth century, when twelve candles were lit in the synagogue (where the circumcision now took place) to signify the twelve tribes of Israel, with the addition of one big candle. Moreover, in North Africa in the sixteenth century, a traveler noted that "they circumcise indifferently at home or the Synagogue. Though for the greater parade, the wealthier Jews seldom neglect to carry their children to the Synagogue"; and in Fez the infant was carried there in a procession with "several boys whereof one carries a torch of twelve lights, denoting the twelve tribes of Israel; another brings a dish of sand, another the circumcising instrument, oil, and soft linen rags." Similarly in Venice, students from the yeshiva participated in the mid-seventeenth century in a torchlight procession for a wealthy communal figure prior to the *veglia*. At the same time that the torches were thought to guard the sleeping infant from attacks by demons, they symbolized with overtones of class dominance the magnificence and munificence of the child's wealthy parents.[27]

To revert to the Middle Ages, Jewish polemic in the thirteenth century *Sefer Nizzahon Vetus* avowed against Paul in his Letter to the Romans, which questioned the necessity for circumcision, that ". . . Abraham was

---

26. Pollack, *Folkways*, pp. 18 and 19. Gélis, *Childbirth*, pp. 195 and 196. Gudemann, Vol. 3, pp. 103–104. Horowitz, *Watch Night*, p. 61 note 12. Joseph Gutmann, *The Jewish Life Cycle* (Leiden: E. J. Brill, 1987), pp. 4 and 5.

27. Trachtenberg, p. 172. Pollack, *Folkways*, p. 19. Hayyim Schauss, *The Lifetime of a Jew* (New York: Union of American Hebrew Congregations, 1967), pp. 41 and 42 (hereafter cited as Schauss, *Lifetime*). Abraham Cohen, *An Anglo-Jewish Scrapbook 1600–1840: The Jew Through English Eyes* (London: M. L. Cailingold, 1943), p. 291 (hereafter cited as Cohen, *Scrapbook*). Horowitz, *Watch Night*, p. 65 note 45.

ninety-nine years old when he was circumcised. . . . One may ask why God did not command him to be circumcised at an earlier age. The answer is that he waited so that the people of the world would see and learn from Abraham who, although an old man, did not balk at circumcision." Again, the Zohar asserted that once Abraham was circumcised, the letter H was added to his name, thereby connecting him with *Hesed*, divine loving-kindness, and *Shekhinah*, the divine presence. Hence "Rabbi Simeon said: A man who has a son is linked to the *Shekhinah* . . . and the child that is circumcised is linked to the *Shekhinah*, who is a door to all the celestial crowns, a door that is linked to the holy name." Further, "The blood that comes from the child [at circumcision] is preserved before the Holy One, blessed be He. . . . It is because of this blood that the world is perfumed with Love . . . [through the tempering of divine judgment]."[28]

In Babylonia under the Geonim, the circumcision ceremony was reformulated. Not only was the synagogue now often the preferred venue for the celebration of the rite, instead of the home, but there was a new officiant who had a key role in the ceremony, the *sandek* (godfather). He was mentioned for the first time in late midrashim and in the writings of the Geonim, who also stated that it was necessary to provide two chairs or a double-seated chair at the ceremony: one for Elijah, who protected the infant at this dangerous time, the other for the *sandek*, who held the child while the *mohel* carried out the operation. Pleas were added in a prayer for the recovery of the mother and for the health of the baby, and some persons named the child at this propitious time. After the blessing on wine was recited, the cup was passed to the mother, who drank some of its contents to enable her to regain her strength following the ordeal of childbirth. It has been argued by Daniel Sperber that the prayer for the well-being of the mother and child was in Old Aramaic and amuletic in character, attesting to its antiquity and possible origin in Eretz Israel. When R. Meir of Rothenburg in the thirteenth century banned women from entering the synagogue during the circumcision ceremony, the prayer became obsolete and women could no longer drink the wine, nor were they henceforth allowed to perform the role of *sandek*. Hence other per-

---

28. Michael Signer, "To See Ourselves as Others See Us: Circumcision in Pagan Antiquity and the Christian Middle Ages," in *Berit Mila in the Reform Context*, ed. Lewis M. Barth (New York: Berit Mila Board of Reform Judaism, 1990), pp. 122–124. Isaiah Tishby, *The Wisdom of the Zohar*, trans. David Goldstein (Oxford: Oxford University Press, 1989), Vol. 3, pp. 1180 and 1181, Zohar III 13b–14a.

sons had to drink the wine, such as the infant's father, the *mohel*, and the beadle.[29]

There was a good description of the circumcision ceremony in the *Machzor Vitry* in the twelfth century. The godfather prepared a banquet on the eve of circumcision, which may indicate that the custom of the "watch night" was already in existence. "On the eighth day, they rise betimes and go to the synagogue to pray . . . and they kindle lights . . . and two thrones are set up, and covered with a sheet or any other adornment. One is for Elijah . . . and the other for the godfather who sits upon it, the child on his knees . . ." In parenthesis it should be remarked that the custom of the Geonim of holding the circumcision ceremony in the synagogue, instead of the parents' home as was the case in the talmudic age, was adhered to in medieval France.

The account in the *Machzor Vitry* continued,

> The child is washed in warm water, and robed in sumptuous garments, a linen sheet and mantle and an ornamental hat on his head, as on his wedding day, and he is borne in triumph to the Synagogue, after [the] service, and the congregation rise before him and say, 'Blessed be He that cometh,' and he who brings him responds, 'In the name of the Lord.' The father thereupon takes him and recites the blessing . . . and hands him over to the godfather, who sits on the throne and holds him on his lap, and the Mohel comes and performs the ceremony, sucking out the blood with his lips. A few drops of wine are given to the child, and then the bandages are placed over it, well smeared with olive oil, and then the herbs [to ease the pain], and a large bandage placed over it. The Mohel then recites the customary blessings, and the mother is also given to drink of the wine.

After the circumcision was concluded, the father of the baby boy arranged a ceremonial banquet, just as he had earlier arranged a sumptuous banquet on the Sabbath before the circumcision known as *Shabbat Zakhor*.[30]

For another description of a circumcision ceremony we turn to an English traveler's account of what he had witnessed in sixteenth-century Prague:

> At the door [of the synagogue], the women not permitted to enter, delivered the child to the father, who carried it to the altar, and then there was a general offer-

29. Nissan Rubin, *The Beginning of Life: Rites of Birth, Circumcision and Redemption of the First-born in the Talmud and Midrash* (Hebrew) (Israel: Hakkibutz Hameuchad, 1995), pp. 120 and 121. Daniel Sperber, "On the Drinking of Wine during the Circumcision," (Hebrew) *Milet* 1 (1983).

30. Schauss, *Lifetime*, p. 309 note 48. Rabinowitz, *Social Life*, pp. 190 and 191. Pollack, *Folkways*, p. 20.

ing made with great emulation who should carry the box of powder, who the salt, who the knife, as in England we offer who shall have the bride's gloves. [There were bids for the privilege which went to the highest bidders, but the money collected went to charity.] Then the child's linen clothes being opened, the Rabbi cut off his prepuce, and . . . did with his mouth suck the blood of his privy part, and after drawing and spitting out of much blood, sprinkled a red powder upon the wound. . . . Then the prepuce or foreskin was taken out, and put into a box of salt to be buried after it in the churchyards. The father held the child all this time in his arms, and together with the godfather testified that it was the seed of Abraham, and so gave the name to it.[31]

In an account of the customs of the Worms community compiled by Yuspa Shammash in the seventeenth century, he wrote that the most respected ladies in the congregation of the synagogue escorted the baby boy from his home to the synagogue, where the wife of the *sandek* (Byzantine Greek *syndikos*, meaning godfather) handed him to her husband to hold during the ceremony. Sometimes a gentleman known as the *kvater* (Yiddish for assistant or godfather but also meaning boon companion or gossip, from the German *gevatter*, godfather) carried the child from his home to the synagogue, where he entrusted him to the *sandek*. Sometimes the latter held the child on his knees throughout the ceremony while seated on a chair, a second vacant armchair being left to honor the prophet Elijah, the designated protector of the infant; sometimes the *sandek* occupied one or two seats on the special Elijah's chair, the other seat being reserved for the guardian of the young infants. In the course of the seventeenth and eighteenth centuries, the circumcision ceremony ceased to be a public spectacle and was once again celebrated in Europe within the confines of the home, perhaps as family life became more private.[32]

In essence the medieval circumcision ceremony could be interpreted as a rite of male bonding, an initiation into a blood brotherhood, in which the *mohel* sucked blood from the infant's circumcision wound, which was considered to be of medical importance, and in return gave him some drops

---

31. Cohen, *Scrapbook*, pp. 290 and 291.

32. Pollack, *Folkways*, pp. 22, 23, 24, and 215 note 52. Daniel J. Lasker, "Transubstantiation, Elijah's Chair, Plato, and the Jewish-Christian Debate," *Revue des Études Juives* 143 (Jan.–June 1984). Ruth Jacoby, "The Small Elijah Chair," *Jewish Art* 18 (1992): 70–77. In Oriental Jewish communities, where everyone sat on the floor and the *sandek* on a cushion, a small symbolic chair was provided for Elijah. In the West, where everyone was accustomed to sitting on chairs, he had to be provided with a big chair.

of wine (blood) to drink. According to tradition the circumciser sipped a few drops of wine into his mouth, sucked the wound, and then spat out the wine; and then once again while reciting the blessing naming the child, he moistened the baby's lips with wine. This was in contrast to the pubertal initiation rites at adolescence practiced by the ancient Greeks and various tribal societies, in which mature males indulged in homosexual practices with young adolescents. Pederastic sex was at the core of Hellenistic culture and the areas to which it spread in the Near East, thereby later influencing some Jews in medieval Spain and the Middle East.[33]

During the nineteenth century and early part of this century, Jews discarded the custom of the *mohel* (circumciser) sucking the blood, some three times according to Montaigne (1553–1592), from the infant's circumcision wound and then spitting it out. In Poland during the seventeenth century the *mohel* swallowed some wine, swilling it with the blood drawn from the wound in his mouth before spitting it into a receptacle. Swayed by the belief in Western Europe that this practice resulted in the spread of syphilis, tuberculosis, and diphtheria, this long-standing practice was replaced by more hygienic methods, such as suction through a tapered glass tube, the preferred technique of the orthodox German Jewish communities, or the application of a swab. In the talmudic age and into the medieval period, wounds inflicted by implements of iron were regarded as causing inflammation (Hullin 77a), for which the only recognized method of treatment was the sucking of the poison from the wound, a procedure followed by the *mohel* in the circumcision ceremony. David ben Aryeh, a seventeenth-century Polish rabbi, interpreted the *mohel's* act as one charged with kabbalistic significance, as by sucking the blood the *mohel* drew evil out of the child. Sucking the infant's blood, a practice known as *metsitsa*, was banned by The Reform Jewish Supreme Ecclesiastical Authority in Germany in 1856 and the community council in Berlin in 1888. To circumvent the ban, R. Cahn of Fulda developed the glass tube for use in circumcision. According to Dr. Asher Asher, writing in London in 1873, the abolition of this practice of *metsitsa* in Paris in 1844 (and in the rest of France by the 1850s), Vienna, Wurtemburg, and Belgium was not found to retard the healing process, despite talmudic comments to the contrary, but the original practice persisted in

---

33. Eva C. Keuls, *The Reign of the Phallus: Sexual Politics in Ancient Athens* (Berkeley and Los Angeles: University of California Press, 1993), pp. 274–299. Preuss, *Talmudic Medicine*, p. 243.

Eastern Europe and is still in use in Israel and among the ultra-Orthodox today.[34]

So, too, the boy's banquet, the *knabenschmause*, held at the parents' home on the night before the circumcision, was abolished in many places in Northern Germany by the start of the nineteenth century or drastically reduced in scale. Reformers were concerned with not upsetting the recovery of the mother convalescing after childbirth. In Dessau only a small breakfast was allowed after the circumcision, to which ten relatives were invited. During the nineteenth century the circumcision ceremony became a more intimate, private family event in Europe, although among the Sephardim of Turkey and Rhodes, where the loose extended family network survived prior to the Second World War, the occasion of the circumcision remained a public, communal affair.[35]

Moreover, the *Machzor Vitry* mentioned another early medieval ceremony, the first cradling of the child after the circumcision, only vestiges of which have survived. The baby boy, having been dressed in all the finery he had previously worn, was put in a cradle before a quorum of ten adult males. A copy of the Pentateuch was placed on him, while the men present said in unison, "May this child fulfill what is written in this book!" Then a quill pen and a bottle of ink having been placed in the child's hand, the company exclaimed that the infant boy should grow up to be a scribe and write a Torah scroll with his own hand. After this, a verse was quoted from the Torah, promising the child a life of abundance. Later in Eastern Europe sugar, raisins, cakes, and coins were tossed in the cradle before the infant was placed in it, thereby repeating the message, if not the ritual, of the medieval ceremony.[36]

---

34. Robert Bonfil, *Jewish Life in Renaissance Italy* (Berkeley and Los Angeles: University of California Press, 1994), pp. 251 and 252 (hereafter cited as Bonfil, *Renaissance Jews*). Nigel Allan, "A Polish Rabbi's Circumcision Manual," *Medical History* 33 (1989): 253. Cohen, *Scrapbook*, p. 290. Asher Asher, *The Rite of Jewish Circumcision* (London Philip Vallentine, 1873), pp. 26 and 27. Mordechai Breuer, *Modernity Within Tradition: The Social History of Orthodox Jewry in Imperial Germany* (New York: Columbia University Press, 1992), pp. 257–260. Max Grunwald, *Vienna* (Philadelphia: Jewish Publication Society, 1936), p. 376. Phyllis Cohen Albert, *The Modernization of French Jewry* (Hanover, N.H.: Brandeis University Press, 1977), pp. 219 and 220. Harry C. Romberg, *Bris Milah* (New York: Feldheim Publishers, 1982), pp. 57 and 58. *Brit Milah Newsletter* 6, no. 1 (13 May 1994): 10 and 11.

35. Leopold Löw, *Die Lebensalter in Der Jüdischen Literatur* (Szegedin, 1875), pp. 91 and 92.

36. Schauss, *Lifetime*, pp. 79 and 80.

Since at least the fifteenth century and possibly earlier, rabbinic authorities in Southern Germany and Alsace had remarked on the *hollekreisch* ceremony, which was held on the fourth Sabbath after a child's birth, when he or she was given a second forename for secular use. Children from the village who were under the age of thirteen formed a protective circle and gathered around the infant sleeping in the cradle, which the older boys or girls lifted three times, at the same time asking the child's father in a chant what the child's name was to be. When he told them, they repeated the name three times in a rhymed verse. For boys a Pentateuch and prayer shawl were also placed in the cradle. All the children were treated to a bag of sweets and an assortment of exotic fruit. Possibly the *hollekreisch* ceremony represented a fusion between pagan ideology and Jewish practices mentioned in the *Machzor Vitry*, but in its present form it was probably a late medieval innovation discussed in the writings of R. Moses Mintz. Although the rite was abandoned in some large towns at an early date, the country towns and villages clung tenaciously to it; so much so that it disappeared in certain towns in Southern Germany and the rural parts of Alsace only at the outbreak of World War II.[37]

Whereas a Hebrew name was bestowed on a boy at the circumcision ceremony, in seventeenth century Italy mothers usually visited the synagogue one month after they had given birth, when the infant girl was blessed and given a name, first approved of by her father. Similarly throughout Turkey and the Balkans an infant daughter was given a name at a ceremony known as *fadas* (old Spanish for godmother) between seven and thirty days after birth. The baby was brought in on a silk pillow by a young virgin dressed as a bride. Throughout the ceremony the infant, adorned in jewelry supplied by other members of the family to symbolize future good fortune, was held by the rabbi in the presence of at least ten men. A tray of rice and sweets was prepared, symbols of fertility and happiness, in which ten candles were inserted. After they were lit by female relatives of the infant, the rabbi recited a prayer and named the infant. Yet despite this beautiful ceremony, the attitude of Sephardim toward infant daughters was ambivalent because they were regarded as a drain on the family's economic

---

37. Pollack, *Folkways*, pp. 27 and 28. Schauss, *Lifetime*, pp. 44–46. Jacob Picard, "Childhood in the Village," *Leo Baeck Institute Year Book* IV (1959), p. 280. Hyman, *Alsace*, p. 72. Marion A. Kaplan, *The Making of the Jewish Middle Class: Women, Family, and Identity in Imperial Germany* (New York: Oxford University Press, 1991), pp. 80, 257 and 258 note 114. Raphael, *Rites of Birth*, pp. 88–90.

resources. It was necessary for nineteenth-century rabbis to deliver sermons in which they castigated popular attitudes.[38]

A piece of the swaddling bands in which the baby boy had been wrapped for the circumcision ceremony, known to Jews in Germany as a *wimpel*, was later embroidered or painted for use as a binder for the Torah scroll and was usually brought by the child to the synagogue when he was aged three and toilet-trained. Attested to in Germany from the fifteenth century, the custom of fashioning a Torah binder from swaddling clothes spread into eastern France, northern Italy, Bohemia, and Moravia and as far afield as the Sephardi communities of Salonika and Izmir. What was put on the *wimpel* was the infant's name and date of birth together with the prayer recited at the circumcision ceremony, which mentioned that the boy might grow up to a life of Torah study, marriage, and good deeds. The binder was illustrated with scenes depicting these themes. Not only was the binder presented to the synagogue on the boy's first visit there after birth, but it was the custom to utilize the same binder on the occasion of his bar mitzvah; thus symbolically the young male child was bound to the Law from birth.[39]

Jewish society in medieval Northwestern Europe invented many new institutions to succor and encourage infants and growing children—the elaborate procedures and rituals to protect the mother and infant at childbirth and circumcision, the *wimpel* made out of swaddling clothes, the *hollekreisch* secular naming ceremony, the Torah initiation ceremony into school, and the bar mitzvah ceremony. Some but not all of these institutions were duplicated among the Sephardi and Oriental Jewish communities in the Middle East and North Africa. What this inventiveness does indicate was a burgeoning love and concern for the welfare of children, probably more intense than that of the talmudic age, and increasing in intensity in the early modern period.[40]

---

38. Bonfil, *Renaissance Jews*, pp. 247 and 148. Rebecca Levy, *Rhodes*, pp. 12 and 13. Helen Hill, "*Simchat Bat* Gives Fairer Start to Fairer Sex," *Jewish Chronicle* 5 August 1994. Russo-Katz, *Sephardi Childbirth*, pp. 257 and 268 note 16.

39. Patricia Hidiroglou, "*Langes De Circoncision Historiés En France,*" *Revue des Études Juives* 143 (Jan.–June 1984): 113–134. Russo-Katz, *Sephardi Childbirth*, p. 256. Ruth Gay, *The Jews of Germany: A Historical Portrait* (New Haven: Yale University Press, 1992), p. 48. *Ashkenaz: The German Jewish Heritage*, ed. Gertrude Hirschler (New York: Yeshiva University Museum, 1988), p. 198.

40. Solomon B. Freehof, "Ceremonial Creativity among the Ashkenazim," *The Jewish Quarterly Review*, Seventy-Fifth Anniversary Volume (1967): 210–223.

WET-NURSING

R. Menaḥem b. Aron Ibn Zeraḥ (born in France c. 1310) declared that "the newborn child must be anointed with astringents . . . because the child is soft. His skin must be toughened so that it will not be damaged easily by external agents. Also, he must be swaddled . . . so that his limbs will not be crooked." In medieval France Jewish children were bathed in milk as well as being annointed with oil; and during the Middle Ages regular bathing for children with hot or tepid water sometimes two or three times daily was much more popular than it was in the eighteenth century.[41]

Jewish sources including Maimonides frequently attest to the practice of swaddling babies. Baḥya Ibn Paquda believed that God would do his best for man just "as the mother takes passionate care of her child, cleaning and washing him and unbinding him (=swaddling)"; but fathers may have assisted in the day-to-day care of their infant children as well. In his ethical will composed about 1190 C.E., R. Judah Ibn Tibbon mentioned that "Thou knowest, my son, how I swaddled thee and brought thee up, how I led thee in the paths of wisdom and virtue. I fed and clothed thee . . ." Among the lower classes and in the homes of wet nurses in medieval Christian Europe, it was likely that swaddling clothes were not changed frequently, which could lead to sores and irritation for the baby, but among the highly motivated and cultured Jewish communities of medieval France and Germany it was probable that higher standards of personal hygiene and infant care prevailed on the whole. The English "Midwives Book" (1671) when dealing with swaddling recommended that a mother should "Shift the child's clouts often, for the Piss and Dung." Nevertheless, if an infant was swaddled, sometimes the hands, sometimes the torso, and sometimes the lower body were left free, while in England by the seventeenth century a baby had its outer layer of swaddling bands removed after one to three months and replaced by an outer coat, so that the pernicious effects attributable to swaddling should not be exaggerated. Stephen Wilson suggested that "in the environment of Early Modern Europe, swaddling kept babies warm and out of harm's way as no other

---

41. Ephraim Kanarfogel, "Attitudes toward Childhood and Children in Medieval Jewish Society," in *Approaches to Judaism in Medieval Times*, ed. David R. Blumenthal (Chico, Calif.: Scholars Press, 1985), pp. 23 and 24 (hereafter cited as Kanarfogel, *Childhood*). Rabinowitz, *Social Life*, p. 233. Shahar, *Medieval Childhood*, p. 83.

procedure . . ." Indeed, certain psychologists were convinced that the warmth and stability provided by swaddling was beneficial psychologically to the infant.[42]

Wet-nursing was widely utilized by the West European aristocracy and upper bourgeoisie in the towns from the eleventh century; by the late Middle Ages, there is evidence from the Northern Italian towns that even small merchants and artisans sent their children to wet nurses in the country-side to be suckled. So too, in medieval middle-class Jewish households in France, Germany, Spain, and Italy, Christian wet nurses suckled Jewish infants in their employers' homes, where they were closely supervised, but their presence sometimes caused dissension within the house. We are informed by the *Sefer Ḥasidim*, a composite work principally written by Judah He-Hasid, who died in 1217, and Eleazar of Worms (1176–1238), of a town in Germany where a number of Jews had been converted. "And there were also wet-nurses and servants who used to eat within the (Jew-ish) houses unclean (forbidden) food. As a consequence little children also ate (such food) and even grown-ups could not avoid using polluted ves-sels. Therefore Jews were urged to leave that town" (*Sefer Ḥasidim* Bologna edition 480). In another Jewish household in Germany, despite the fact that two Christian wet nurses were always quarrelling, the head of the family was wary of sacking them, as he stated that so long as they feared each other they would not rob him. His friends rebuked him, ex-plaining that they were concerned that one of the wet nurses could cause the death of his child while being supervised by the other, something for which he would be blamed (*Sefer Ḥasidim* Bologna edition 672). From the evidence contained in the *Sefer Ḥasidim*, it appears that the pres-ence of Christian wet nurses was pervasive in the homes of the richer Jewish families in the medieval Rhineland provinces. According to the *Sefer Ha-*

---

42. Kanarfogel, *Childhood*, p. 24. Patai, *Jewish Folklore*, p. 402. Abrahams, *Ethical Wills*, Part 1, p. 57. Rabinowitz, *Social Life*, p. 233. Shahar, *Medieval Childhood*, pp. 86 and 87. Stephen Wilson, "The Myth of Motherhood a Myth: The Historical View of European Childrearing," *Social History* 9, no. 2 (1984): 194 and 195 (hereafter cited as Wilson, *Myth of Motherhood*). Tana de Zulueta, "Indian Cradle that Shocks Cam-bridge," *Sunday Times*, 16 July 1978. "Chisholm discovered that Navajos [American Indians] use their cradleboards very much as westerners use cradles. Though in the first three months Navajo babies spend up to 18 hours a day on the cradleboard, they spend less and less time as they grow older. . . . The [Navajo] mothers confirmed what the labo-ratory experiments had shown, that swaddling itself helps put the baby to sleep."

Pardes, even needy Jews sometimes employed Christian women to suckle their infants.[43]

Nonetheless, despite various papal and ecclesiastical edicts against Jews employing Christian wet nurses, they continued to work for Jewish masters and it is doubtful whether these multifarious decrees were implemented successfully against the Jews at a local level. Phillip II of France refused to enforce the decision of the Third Lateran Council of 1179 against the employment by Jews of Christian servants, including nurses, so that Pope Innocent III vainly appealed to French ecclesiastical authorities in 1205 to compel observance of this ban. He complained that during Easter, when "the Christian women who are nurses for the children of Jews, take in the body and blood of Jesus Christ [at communion], the Jews make these women pour their milk into the latrine for three days before they again give suck to the children." What lay behind this diatribe was the belief already enunciated by Aristotle that menstrual blood rose to the breasts and became converted into milk, a viewpoint supported by Galen and medieval writers in the Islamic world, including Maimonides. Yehiel of Paris, in his disputation with Nicholas Donin in 1240, asked, "Do we then apply the Talmud to Christians . . . go into the Jewish streets and see the business on Christian festivals. Every day we sell them animals, we have partnership transactions with them, we give our children to them to nurse, we teach them Hebrew." In spite of later edicts in France forbidding Christian wet nurses to seek employment with Jews, the practice continued unabated and in 1781 a girl was censured in Carpentras in Southern France for carrying a bucket of water into a Jewish house where she was nursing a child.[44]

---

43. Valerie Fildes, *Wet Nursing: A History from Antiquity to the Present* (Oxford: Basil Blackwell, 1988), p. 34 (hereafter cited as Fildes, *Wet Nursing*). Shahar, *Medieval Childhood*, pp. 58 and 279 note 30. Christine Klapisch-Zuber, *Women, Family and Ritual in Renaissance Italy* (Chicago: University of Chicago Press, 1985), pp. 133 and 134. S. Simonsohn, *History of the Jews in the Duchy of Mantua* (Jerusalem: Kiryath Sepher, 1977), pp. 159 and 160 (hereafter cited as Simonsohn, *Mantua*). Samuel Kottek, "Childhood in Medieval Jewry as Depicted in *Sefer Hasidim* (12th–13th century): Medical, Psychological and Educational Aspects," *Koroth* 8, no. 9–10 (August 1984): 381 (hereafter cited as Kottek, *Childhood Among the Pietists*).

44. Salo Wittmayer Baron, *A Social and Religious History of the Jews* (New York: Columbia University Press, 1957), Vol. 4, pp. 61, 62, 68, 69, and 269 (hereafter cited as Baron, *Social History of the Jews*). Solomon Grayzel, *The Church and the Jews in the 13th Century: A Study of their Relations during the Years 1198–1254 based on*

We encounter the same limitations in ecclesiastical power in Germany, Poland, and Spain, when bishops tried to prevent Christian wet nurses offering their services to Jewish families. Frederick II in Germany renewed the privilege of Worms to cover the whole of German Jewry in 1236, stating that Jews were to freely employ Christian servants, maids, and nurses. "Let neither bishop nor any cleric controvert that." Earlier Pope Gregory IX in 1233 reprimanded the German bishops for permitting Jews to employ Christian servants, whom they circumcised, and nurses "with whom they committed enormous" sins. To jump forward in time, we find that in eighteenth-century Hamburg, unmarried mothers or perhaps exprostitutes acted as wet nurses in Jewish households, where they had their illegitimate offspring living with them. An anonymous memorandum from Poland dated at 1267 but probably originating in a later period attacked Jews, claiming that "they hire Christian women to nurse their children whom they force to cohabit with them . . ." Unlike the situation in Renaissance Italy and later France, where the boarding-out of children with wet nurses was common, the Gentiles in medieval Spain hired a wet nurse who was expected to breast-feed the infant in its parents' home for three years for a small annual wage. The Cortes of Vallodid in 1258 prohibited Christians from feeding Jewish infants, followed by an edict in Jerez in 1268. Yet despite decrees from lay and ecclesiastical authorities, Spanish Christian nurses continued to suckle Jewish infants through the fourteenth and even into the fifteenth century. In addition, we know from a responsum of R. Adret (1235–1310) that Jews in Spain sometimes sent their infants to Jewish wet nurses who resided in another city.[45]

---

the Papal Letters and the Conciliar Decrees of the Period (New York: Hermon Press, 1966), pp. 114 and 115. Rabinowitz, Social Life, p. 90. Marianne Calmann, The Carriere of Carpentras (Oxford: Oxford University Press, 1984), p. 214.

45. Baron, Social History of the Jews, Vol. 4, pp. 68 and 69 and Vol. 9 (1965), pp. 26 and 252 note 26. Jacob R. Marcus, Communal Sick-Care in the German Ghetto (Cincinnati: Hebrew Union College Press, 1978), p. 184. Baron, Social History of the Jews, Vol. 10 (1965), p. 34. Fildes, Wet Nursing, pp. 39 and 40. Heath Dillard, Daughters of the Reconquest: Women in Castilian Town Society 1100–1300 (Cambridge: Cambridge University Press, 1984), p. 156 (hereafter cited as Dillard, Daughters of the Reconquest). Neuman, Jews in Spain, Vol. 2, p. 208. Yitzhak Baer, A History of the Jews in Spain (Philadelphia: Jewish Publication Society, 1978), Vol. 1, p. 318. Simonsohn, Mantua, pp. 159 and 160. The Church in Italy gave Christian nurses permission to suckle Jewish children, so long as these activities were confined to the ghetto area.

In medieval Egypt most Jewish mothers breast-fed their children in their own homes for two years, this time span being in accordance with the advice of the contemporary Jewish and Muslim physicians. In contrast, in eighteenth-century Aleppo we find a greater use of wet nurses by the Jewish community, a practice that was either a survival from the Hellenistic age or a usage imported by the European merchant community. Alex Russell claimed that "the female married domestics, among the Jews at Aleppo, continue in service till they have children of their own, and are very often employed as nurses in the families of their former masters. The Jewish women more frequently call in the aid of a wet nurse, than the Christians of equal rank, and seldom continue to suckle their child, especially if a male, after they are assured of being pregnant; but, where no impediment intervenes, the child is kept at the breast eighteen or twenty months. They appeared to be more prolific than either the Turkish or the Christian women, but a larger proportion of their children, as far as I could judge, died in infancy." Unless it was true that fewer Jewish babies were handled and nursed by their own mothers or at least closely supervised by them, when a wet nurse was employed, than in the Muslim and Christian communities, this last observation of Russell appears to contradict the finding of low infant mortality rates among Jews elsewhere and is, therefore, questionable.[46]

Christian and Muslim authorities, whether medical or religious, like the Greek and Roman doctors and moralists had an ambivalent attitude toward the breast-feeding of infants, recommending at one and the same time that mothers should nurse their own children and hire wet nurses. In this they were followed by a number of Jewish scholars, although Gersonides was of the opinion that Jewish mothers should suckle their own children. Again, R. Menahem Ibn Zerah suggested that the nursing of an infant by its own mother was preferable, as the fetus had been nourished by its mother's menstrual blood while still in the womb. As Maimonides aptly put it, basing himself on the medical theory of the ancient world: "Milk of the mother is the proper nutrition for the newborn infant, because its composition is the same as the blood from which he was created." Moreover, R. Menahem devoted a section in his writings to the qualities parents should be seeking when selecting a nurse for their child, thus echoing

---

46. Goitein, *Family*, pp. 233 and 255. Alexander Russell, *The Natural History of Aleppo* (London: Ward, Lock, and Bowden, 1794), Vol. 2, p. 83.

the general ambivalent attitude toward breast-feeding by the mother. He also adopted the advice of medical authorities from the ancient world that the nurse should not have intercourse with her partner for the period of time, usually two years, but in Spain it could sometimes be as long as four years, for which she had contracted to feed an infant, because there was a belief that having sexual relations spoiled the quality of her milk. However, breaking with earlier talmudic formulations the Be'er Hetev, a seventeenth-century Polish luminary, stipulated that fathers were obligated to provide a wet nurse with sufficient means to buy adequate provisions for herself and the infant she was nursing.[47]

The preceding analysis seems to indicate that wet-nursing was quite common among middle-class Jewish families in medieval Europe, although not as widespread as among their Christian neighbors, but not on a comparable scale among similar Jewish households in the Middle East until much later. By the early modern period, poorer Jewish families in Europe were also employing wet nurses. Because of kashrut, Jewish dietary regulations, Jewish families were loath to farm their infant out to a Gentile wet nurse in the country, but insisted on the wet nurses contracting to stay in the homes of their Jewish employers, where their activities could be carefully monitored. When Jewish mothers from wealthy families avoided breast-feeding by availing themselves of the services of a wet nurse, they quickly became fertile once again, and families in such circles tended to be larger. Among the poor, Jewish mothers tended to nurse the children themselves and as a consequence were less fertile, producing fewer children. If a child was reared in a household containing both its own mother and a wet nurse, the child's emotional and physical needs were split between two different persons, thereby possibly producing a similar adult pattern of behavior, in which physical and emotional needs were shared between a wife and a mistress. Perhaps this could partially account for the sexual behavior of the Spanish Jews, who often divided their affection between a wife and a concubine, or for the proliferation of divorce

---

47. Shahar, *Medieval Childhood*, pp. 55–57. Avner Gil'adi, *Children of Islam: Concepts of Childhood in Medieval Muslim Society* (London: Macmillan, 1992), p. 24 (hereafter cited as Gil'adi, *Muslim Childhood*). Kanarfogel, *Childhood*, pp. 17, 18, and 23. Fildes, *Wet Nursing*, p. 18. Dillard, *Daughters of the Reconquest*, p. 156. Julius Preuss, *Biblical and Talmudic Medicine*, trans. Fred Rosner (New York: Hebrew Publishing Company, 1983), pp. 404 and 409. Rosner, *Maimonides*, p. 175.

and serial marriage among many fifteenth-century Southern German Jewish communities.[48]

Whereas classical and medieval European childrearing manuals suggested that babies should be fed on demand when they cried, Muslim doctors advocated restricting breast-feeding to two or three sessions a day. Muslim physicians believed that crying was beneficial for children. This was also a view espoused by Bahya Ben Joseph Ibn Paquda, a Jewish philosopher from eleventh or twelfth century Spain, who exclaimed, "How wonderful is the matter of crying! According to the best of physicians, crying is beneficial to the baby, because he has some humidity in his brain which would cause him great harm were it left there, but crying dissolves this humidity and the baby is saved from its bad effect." It could be argued that feeding on demand in Western Europe encouraged the growth of a more relaxed and slightly freer personality, whereas the rigid feeding schedules favored by Muslim pediatricians fostered the evolution of a more inflexible and more authoritarian personality in Muslim states. Jews, of course, shared these character traits with their Gentile neighbors.[49]

"If a child is crying and you order the nurse to sing him a lullaby," proclaimed the *Sefer Ḥasidim*, "and she chooses to sing a heathen song (i.e., a song of non-Jewish worship), this should be prohibited, even if you do not hear it yourself, but only the child—and even if the child is already asleep and the singing is intended only to prevent him from waking up again. On the other hand, it is also prohibited to use verses (of the Pentateuch) for the same purpose" (*Sefer Ḥasidim* Parma edition 346). For Spain there is the evidence of a fourteenth-century guide entitled *Zeda la-derekh*, which more positively recommended that mothers should sing to their babies to encourage contentment. Since there was a tradition of a sympathetic response to a baby crying in medieval Western Europe, it is likely that Jews like their Christian neighbors soothed the howls of a baby with a lullaby, although the lines of these songs have been lost. If there

---

48. Yom Tov Assis, "Sexual Behaviour in Medieval Hispano-Jewish Society," in *Essays in Honour of Chimen Abramsky*, ed. Ada Rapoport-Albert and Steven J. Zipperstein (London: Peter Halban, 1988), pp. 25–59.

49. Shahar, *Medieval Childhood*, p. 78. Gil`adi, *Muslim Childhood*, p. 25. Bahya Ben Joseph Ibn Paquda, *The Book of Direction to the Duties of the Heart*, trans. Menahem Mansoor (London: Routledge & Kegan Paul, 1973), p. 163.

was a dearth of such songs, how else can one explain a deluge of Yiddish lullabies in the nineteenth century? Surely they were drawing on older sources.[50]

CHILDREARING: THEORETICAL ORIENTATIONS

During the Middle Ages there was a common ambivalent attitude toward children among Jews, Christians, and Muslims, who shared both a Hellenistic and biblical heritage. According to the Christian viewpoint influenced by Augustine, the capacity to reason had not been activated in childhood, the infant was born in sin, and was motivated by anger, aggressiveness, and jealousy. So too, Avner Gil'adi in his study of childhood in medieval Islamic society, following the general orientation of Shlomo Goitein, pointed out that Al-Ghazali (1058–1111) regarded childhood as a "passage" leading to the "parlor" of adulthood, characterizing it as a "time of weakness and vulnerability of spirit, ignorance and absence of intellectual grasp, of a lack of willpower and control by lower powers of the spirit." Yet the roots of these ideas were possibly to be found in biblical thought but certainly in rabbinic doctrine, perhaps because these concepts were part of a wider eastern Mediterranean intellectual armory.[51]

We shall focus first on the negative aspects of this tradition. In Genesis 8:21 it was stated that "the imagination of man's heart is evil from his youth," while in Deuteronomy 1:39 the Israelites were told that their children, who "in that day had no knowledge between good and evil" would enter the promised land. In an early midrash it was stated that "Antoninus asked our Teacher: 'When is the evil urge placed in man?' 'As soon as he

---

50. Kottek, *Childhood Among Medieval Pietists*, pp. 381 and 382. Schauss, *Lifetime*, p. 80. Kenneth R. Stow, "The Jewish Family in the Rhineland in the High Middle Ages: Form and Function," *American Historical Review* 92 (1987): 1102.

51. Shahar, *Medieval Childhood*, p. 14. Gil'adi, *Muslim Childhood*, p. 47. S. D. Goitein, "Jewish Education in Yemen as an Archetype of Traditional Jewish Education," in *Between Past and Future: Essays and Studies on Aspects of Immigrant Absorption in Israel*, ed. C. Frankenstein (Jerusalem: Henrietta Szold Foundation for Child and Youth Welfare, 1953), pp. 113 and 114. Abraham Stahl, "Children and Childhood in the View of the Traditional Jewish-Oriental Family," *Journal of Comparative Family Studies* 9, no. 3 (Autumn 1978): 351 and 352 (hereafter cited as Stahl, *Children and Childhood*).

is formed [in embryo],' he replied. 'If so,' he objected, 'he would dig through the womb and emerge; rather it is when he emerges [from the womb].' Rabbi agreed with him . . ." (Genesis Rabbah 34:10). Basing himself on this ancient midrashic explanation, Rashi (1040–1105), the supreme medieval commentator, voiced the opinion that "from the time [the embryo] bestirs itself to come out from the belly of its mother, there is placed in it the evil inclination," all of which approached close to the Christian doctrine of original sin. To conclude this overview of Rashi's thinking on this topic, dealing with Ecclesiastes 4:13, which claimed that "better is a poor and wise child than an old and foolish king," Rashi expressed the opinion that the good inclination came to a person at thirteen years of age, but that he remained poor because the limbs of his body struggled to reject this control. Persuaded by the arguments of both Aristotle and the rabbis, Maimonides (1135–1204) concurred, declaring that our sages "also say that the evil inclination we receive at our birth; for 'at the door sin croucheth' (Gen. 4:7), as it is distinctly said in the Law, 'And the imagination of the heart of man is evil from his youth' (Gen. 8:21). The good inclination, however, comes when the mind is developed."[52]

Nachmanides (1194–1270) offered a similar explanation of Genesis 8:21, although he also proffered alternative ways of looking at this verse by remarking that it could mean "on account of his youth" or "in his youth," thereby watering down the theory of incipient evil or original sin. Since the generation of the flood, the Italian exegete Sforno (c. 1470 or 1475–1550) asserted, the evil inclination was to be found in men from birth, whereas before they already had the necessary intellectual illumination during their youth to suppress their baser desires. All the time, though, as we approach the modern era we witness the gradual abandonment of the rabbinic view that man is inherently evil from birth until we encounter the exegesis of the postenlightenment neo-orthodox thinker R. Samson Raphael Hirsch (1808–1888), whose thought glowed with optimism about man's potentialities. With regard to Genesis 8:21, he proclaimed that "neither good nor bad impressions cling very fast to them [youths], human nature is still in its natural state with them, not yet cloaked with hypocrisy,

52. *The Pentateuch and Rashi's Commentary: Genesis*, trans. R. Abraham Ben Isaiah and R. Benjamin Sharfman (Brooklyn: S. S. & R. Publishing, 1949), Chapter 8:21. Charles B. Chavel, *Encyclopedia of Torah Thoughts* (New York: Shilo Publishing House, 1980), p. 302. Moses Maimonides, *The Guide of the Perplexed* (New York: Dover Publications, 1956), pp. 298 and 299, Book III, chapter 22.

easily shakes off both good and bad impressions. . . . Woe unto them that take the average child and adolescent nature to be evil!"[53]

At the same time, the three monotheistic religions shared a common more optimistic view of childhood, based on the biblical concepts of holiness and purity as contrasted with the profane and the impure, childhood innocence as contrasted with narrow adult self-seeking. Similarly in late Greek literature there were occasional passages that highlighted "the special 'purity' of children, purity that comes of their being 'unsullied' by the world of the body, making them beloved of the gods . . ." As far as Judaism was concerned, there were the words of Psalms 8:3, "Out of the mouths of babes and sucklings hast thou ordained strength." More interesting still is the midrashic gloss put on this verse that dates from the early medieval period. When the Torah was given to the children of Israel, they offered God adult sureties as a guarantee that they would continue to live by the Law; yet all these adult sureties were rejected as unsuitable. Hence, "When the people of Israel asked: 'Who are those not in debt to Thee?' God answered: 'Infants.' Whereupon the people of Israel brought sucklings at their mothers' breasts, and pregnant women whose wombs became transparent as glass so that the embryos could see God and speak with Him. And the Holy One, blessed be He, asked the sucklings and the embryos: 'Will you be sureties for your fathers, so that if I give them the Torah they will live by it, but that if they do not, you will be forfeited because of them?' They replied: 'Yes.'" Here we have the natural social order inverted and a wonderful description of the power of childhood innocence. Nor was this all. We have already touched on the generally roseate view of childhood formulated by the sages in the talmudic age, which made the survival of the Jewish people hinge on the flourishing of the Jewish elementary school system, thereby investing children and childhood with enormous prestige. According to R. Isaac b. Yedayah, who lived in thirteenth-century Provence, God taught all schoolchildren, not just those who died prematurely, by endowing them with innate attributes that enabled them eventually to acquire knowledge and perfection. The help of fathers and teachers would not have sufficed without this divine gift. Likewise Moses ibn Tibbon, commenting

---

53. Charles B. Chavel, *Ramban (Nachmanides) Commentary on the Torah: Genesis* (New York: Shilo Publishing House, 1971), pp. 131 and 132. *Sforno: Commentary on the Torah: Bereishis/ Sh'mos*, trans. R. Raphael Pelcovitz (Brooklyn: Mesorah Publications, 1987), p. 50. *The Pentateuch of Samson Raphael Hirsch: Genesis*, trans. Isaac Levy (London, 1959), pp. 166 and 167.

on the same talmudic phrase that "God sits and teaches schoolchildren" (Avodah Zarah 3b), suggested that the teaching of children meant the regeneration of the Jewish people by training the younger generation to replace their elders.[54]

Medieval Christians not only believed in the purity and innocence of childhood and the generosity of children, but they also had a belief in the efficacy of the prayer of children and their unblinking vision, uncluttered by adult preconceptions. Some Christian physicians elaborated Galen's view that "the normal child is good in every way, and requires no correction of manners; what is needed is prevention of corrupting influences . . . from bad habits, in eating and drinking, in exercise, in shows, and in what they hear . . ." Again, the medieval Muslims endorsed the view that the child's soul was pure and that the innocence with which the child was imbued made it possible to encourage the growth of his good qualities. Al-Ghazali suggested that "if he is made accustomed to good and is so taught, he will grow up in goodness; he will win happiness in this world and the next, and his parents and teachers will have a share in his reward . . ."[55]

ATTITUDES TOWARD THE DEATH OF CHILDREN

While in England it was estimated that 200 to 300 out of every 1,000 infants died under the age of five years in the sixteenth and seventeenth centuries, Lebrun, in a study of eighteenth-century France, found that only 574 of every 1,000 children reached the age of five years; and that the great preponderance of infant mortality was concentrated in the first year after birth, 280 children dying before approaching their first birthday. Moreover, it has been calculated that in more recent times half the Jewish children born in Yemen failed to reach the age of five, which accords well

---

54. Shahar, *Medieval Childhood*, pp. 17, 100, and 101. George Boas, *The Cult of Childhood* (London: Warburg Institute, 1966), p. 15. *The Midrash on Psalms*, trans. William G. Braude (New Haven: Yale University Press, 1959), Vol. 1, pp. 124–126. Marc Saperstein, *Decoding the Rabbis: A Thirteenth Century Commentary on the Aggadah* (Cambridge, Mass.: Harvard University Press, 1980), pp. 32 and 225 note 47.

55. Luke Demaitre, "The Idea of Childhood and Child Care in the Medical Writings of the Middle Ages," *Journal of Psychohistory* 4, no. 1 (Spring 1977): 481 (hereafter cited as Demaitre, *Medical Writings*). Shahar, p. 16. Gil'adi, *Muslim Childhood*, p. 51.

with Lebrun's estimate for France. Michele Savonarola, a fifteenth-century physician from Padua, declared that many infants under the age of two succumbed to certain diseases that were not fatal to older children. Both European and Arab doctors distinguished the first phase of childhood as stretching from birth to dentition or to two years, when children began talking. Despite the primitive nature of medieval pediatric techniques, there was some degree of success. Paolo Bagellardo boasted of curing a Hebrew child with an abdominal swelling; and Judah Asheri, having been struck down with a serious eye infection as a child, looked back with gratitude to the treatment of "a Jewess, a skilled oculist . . . she treated me for about two months, and then died" before completing her work.[56]

Philippe Ariès, the great French historian of childhood, first put forward the hypothesis in 1960 that "in medieval society the idea of childhood did not exist," that during the Middle Ages people disapproved of coddling or making a fuss over the antics of little children and that there was no close supervision of the child's moral development until the Jesuits reformed elementary education at the end of the sixteenth century, when they tried to instil reason and encourage the child to control his own behavior. Further, as the young child had according to Montaigne "neither mental activities nor recognizable bodily shape," parents showed a callous indifference to the death of young children prior to the sixteenth century. All these conclusions have either been contested or greatly modified by subsequent historical research, without any clear-cut synthesis emerging to replace them.[57]

To help clarify the feelings aroused by the death of young infants during the Middle Ages, we shall focus on a recent anthropological study of the attitudes toward the early demise of young children in Brazil by Nancy Scheper-Hughes, entitled *Death Without Weeping*. Whereas some anthropologists were firmly of the opinion that women had deep feelings about the death of their infants, which they learned to suppress, Scheper-Hughes, a medically trained anthropologist, after studying the reactions of mothers

---

56. Shahar, *Medieval Childhood*, p. 35. Stahl, *Children and Childhood*, p. 349. Demaitre, *Medical Writings*, pp. 465, 466, and 478. Abrahams, *Ethical Wills*, Part 2, pp. 165 and 166.

57. Philippe Ariès, *Centuries of Childhood* (Harmondsworth: Penguin Books, 1979), pp. 36, 38, 39, 112–118, and 127–129. Kanarfogel, *Childhood*, p. 36. Ephraim Kanarfogel, *Jewish Education and Society in the High Middle Ages* (Detroit: Wayne State University Press, 1992), p. 137 note 28.

in a Brazilian shantytown concluded that poor women were conditioned not to grieve over the death of their infants. In north-eastern Brazil as the child grew older, the mother's attitude changed to one of positive concern. One informant, when speaking about her three-year-old son to another anthropologist, remarked, "If he died as a baby it would be OK, but now that he is getting big, Ave Maria! If he died now I would be very upset." Yet children who died within a year of birth were considered so pure and so free of sin that they were known as "little angels" and it was assumed that they would go straight up to heaven. Again, when Scheper-Hughes returned red-eyed with a dead infant after failing to save its life in the local hospital, the child's mother greeted her incredulously, turning to her neighbors and saying, "Tsk! tsk! Poor thing! Funny isn't she?" The baby was buried in a simple cardboard coffin, accompanied by a procession of jostling and playful children. "As the procession was about to leave, . . . [Scheper-Hughes] asked whether a prayer would be recited. 'It's only a baby,' one of the women scolded . . ." Mothers in the Brazilian slums sometimes contributed to their children's deaths by their passive neglect. One such mother confessed that "I was sick all the way through the pregnancy and her infancy. I didn't pay any attention to her . . . with all that I have to attend to, I didn't fuss. . . . I didn't boil her water . . . I wasn't vigilant against flies and mosquitoes . . . In the end Julieta died because . . . she herself never took hold. . . . She decided to die."[58]

With the insights gained from this anthropological study, it may be easier to evaluate the Jewish attitude toward the death of infants during the Middle Ages, to decide whether it was taken for granted or was considered to be emotionally draining for parents. Among the feudal nobility and some of the wealthy urban burghers, young children were brought up by a battery of wet nurses and servants before being dispatched to the homes of others to complete their education and training, so that parents were somewhat insulated from the death of their children. Jews, on the contrary, nearly always had their children living at home, even where the family had hired wet nurses; and even when the wife, such as the spouse of R. Judah ibn Tibbon, came from a distinguished and educated family, she often brought up a child "without a man or woman to help her." Judah Asheri, a wealthy communal rabbi who died in Spain in 1394, declared that "God in His

58. Nancy Scheper-Hughes, *Death Without Weeping: The Violence of Everyday Life in Brazil* (Berkeley and Los Angeles: University of California Press, 1992), and a review by Daniel Gross in the *Times Literary Supplement*, 1 July 1994.

mercy gave me five sons, and I considered myself through them as a live man among my people and brethren. But for my sins there was taken the one, 'the middle bar' [his third son], on which I thought my house was founded. . . . I call heaven and earth to witness that I deserve this and double from God, for I know that His judgments are right. . . . I found consolation in the knowledge that my son was not punished by heaven for any sin of his, for he spent his days, which were few, in the eternal Law." Judah Asheri seems to have had a special mark of affection for this son, who was probably over six years of age, although he accepted his death as divinely decreed with perfect faith, yet it seems he was troubled by a diffuse feeling of guilt.[59]

Great sensitivity was shown in Germany by medieval pietists, *hasidim*, to couples who had prematurely lost their children. The *Sefer Ḥasidim* cautioned people against bringing their son or daughter on a visit to the home of parents who had recently lost a child, leaving them childless (*Sefer Ḥasidim* Bologna 640). Further, "There were in a town many childless people. Therefore, a father told his boy not to come to him during the prayer to kiss him, so that they [the childless] should not feel unhappy" (*Sefer Ḥasidim* Bologna 639). Fathers often prayed while carrying small children, such as a medieval Rhineland scholar who used to pray with a small child on his lap or shoulder, whom he would remove when reciting the *Shema*. Doubtless strong emotional bonds developed between fathers and toddlers in well-established religious families to the extent that the passing of such infants would have caused their parents great anguish. This would be in contrast to the situation prevailing in those Jewish families just hovering on the breadline, in which poverty deadened feelings of grief when infants died.[60]

Until boys were placed in the hands of a religious teacher at the age of five or six, all children remained principally in the charge and care of their mothers, whose degree of pain and distress at the death of a young child can only be guessed at, as most of the history of medieval Jewish motherhood in Europe was never recorded. Clearly all mothers, whatever their social class, felt such losses deeply, once the child had passed the age of three, with an ascending scale of grief, according to Maimonides, as the child

---

59. Shahar, *Medieval Childhood*, pp. 116 and 117. Abrahams, *Ethical Wills*, Part 1, p. 78 and Part 2, p. 168.

60. Kottek, *Childhood Among the Medieval Pietists*, pp. 379 and 380. Kanarfogel, *Childhood*, p. 8.

grew older: ". . . the parents of a child that is just born take lightly matters concerning it, for up to that time the imaginative form that compels the parents to love it is not yet consolidated. For this imaginative form increases through habitual contact and grows with the growth of the child. . . . For the love of the father and of the mother for the child when it has just been born is not like their love for it when it is one year old, and their love for it when it is one year old is not like their love when it is six years old."[61]

Echoing sentiments in the Midrash, the *Sefer Ḥasidim* claimed that parents were deeply affected by the premature death of children, so that their teeth became loose, their eyes weak, and their strength ebbed. Moreover, the *Sefer Ḥasidim* recommended that if a family had a succession of children who died, they should move to another town, where the change of environment would perhaps lift their psychological malaise. If newborn children continued to die, parents were advised to wear an amulet for solace and to protect infants born to them in the future (*Sefer Ḥasidim* Bologna 247). On the other hand, the willingness with which certain Ashkenazi fathers slaughtered their own children at the time of the Crusades rather than see them converted shows both awesome faith and at the same time betrays disturbing manifestations of hidden hostility to their own kin; this is a subject that we shall return to in the next chapter.[62]

However, in the course of the Crusades Jewish children were often murdered by Gentile brigands. The outpouring of grief by R. Eleazar ben Judah of Worms at the death of his wife and daughters went deep, but his mourning for his eldest daughter, who was almost a young woman, seems more poignant than his remarks about his younger daughter. This is in line with Maimonides' previous dictum about an ascending scale of grief on the death of older children, with whom there had been more sustained interaction and consequently greater emotional involvement.

> Let me tell the story of my eldest daughter, Bellet: She was thirteen years old, and as chaste as a bride. She had learnt all the prayers and songs from her mother, who was modest and kind, sweet and wise. The girl took after her beautiful mother and every night she would make my bed and take off my shoes. She did her housework quickly, and always spoke the truth. She worshipped her Maker, she weaved and sewed and embroidered . . . , she was filled with reverence and pure love for her Creator. For the sake of Heaven, she sat down by me to hear my teaching . . .

---

61. Moses Maimonides, *The Guide of the Perplexed*, trans. Shlomo Pines (Chicago: University of Chicago Press, 1963), Book III, chapter 69, p. 610.

62. Kottek, *Childhood Among the Medieval Pietists*, p. 379.

When describing his younger daughter Hannah, R. Eleazar was more concise:

> . . . every day she would recite the first portion of the *Shema*. She was six years old, and she knew to weave and sew and embroider and to delight me with her singing.[63]

Among the families of impoverished scholars and possibly among the Jewish poor in general, there may have been an ambivalent attitude toward the death of infants under the age of three, compounded by guilt at their neglect of their own children that had contributed to these infants dying at a tender age. "One scholar used to say: I have fathered a son and girl (having thus fulfilled the obligation of begetting children), but my wife is again pregnant and I am poor, how shall I manage to raise another child? Now the teacher said to him: when the child is born, the Lord has provided for him milk in his mother's breasts, therefore be not anxious. Nevertheless the scholar continued to lament. Then a boy was born, and fell ill after some time. The father asked the Rabbi to pray for his recovery. But the teacher rebuked him (for being so inconsistent) and the child died" (*Sefer Hasidim* Bologna 520). When another young scholar mentioned in the course of a discussion that he would rather his wife did not conceive than that the child failed to survive, his teacher intervened, remarking that the death of a child could save parents from death and suffering (*Sefer Hasidim* Bologna 501). Both these tales can be interpreted as showing an indifferent attitude toward the survival of young children. In the first story the young scholar announced that he did not want another child, as he would be unable to ensure that the child was properly fed, a depressed attitude that he probably shared with his wife, who in all likelihood inadequately fed and neglected the baby. Indeed, the *Sefer Hasidim* denounced fathers who were too proud to apply to charitable funds, thereby exposing their children to starvation (*Sefer Hasidim* Bologna 1040). Even more reprehensible were fathers who sought charity but then neglected their own children. "He is prone to indulge in drink, but his children lack nourishment. He may even patronize a harlot or pocket dishonest gain" (*Sefer Hasidim* Parma 855).[64]

---

63. T. Carmi, *The Penguin Book of Hebrew Verse* (Harmondsworth: Penguin Books, 1982), pp. 387 and 388.

64. Kottek, *Childhood Among the Medieval Pietists*, pp. 379 and 380. Abraham Kronbach, "Social Thinking in the *Sefer Hasidim*," *H.U.C. Annual* 22 (1949): 37, 71,

We would contend that a minority of Jewish parents within the traditional Islamic world were also hard pressed by the dire poverty in which they lived, thus generating defeatist and passive attitudes. They had to be cajoled by rabbinic authorities to have faith and to strive for a living rather than allow their children to succumb to hunger, as witnessed by a folktale recounted by R. Nissim ben Jacob Ibn Shahin: "The sages tell the story of a poor man who had several children and a wife.·. . . His wife said to him, 'Cousin, arise and go to the market place—perchance you will find something there to sustain us, else we shall perish of hunger.' He replied, 'Sister, where shall I turn? . . . I have no relative to whom I might go . . . nor do I have a friend. I have no one but God Most High.' Whereat she desisted from him, but . . . the children's hunger grew so fierce that they wept and screamed . . ." Even if the story contained some hyperbole, it nevertheless accurately reflected the real social conditions in eleventh-century North Africa.[65]

Following outbreaks of plague and particularly the Black Death of the fourteenth century, Muslim authors composed a new genre of consolation treatises for parents who had lost a child, encouraging them to have faith and show steadfastness (*sabr*) in such situations like certain model parents. In a *hadith*, a report of a saying or action of Muhammad, it was narrated that the wife of Abu Talham refused to tell her husband that their son had died until she had conceived again on the following night; as a reward for her steadfastness she later gave birth to a son plus eight other children. When his wife informed Abu Talham of the death of their first child, she used a parable, possibly taken from a Jewish source: "Your son was a loan borrowed from God, may he be blessed and exalted, and God has taken his soul . . ." Moreover, in two Muslim consolation treatises of the fourteenth and fifteenth centuries, Muhammad praised a steadfast Jewish woman who, while preparing a feast for her husband's guests, had to cope with the death of their two young sons who fell down a well and died; but she concealed the news from her husband so as not to disrupt the festivities and covered up their bodies in another room. Again, she

---

and 75. *Sefer Ḥasidim*, Bologna, 1027. If a wealthy, stingy man became poor, it was reasonable not to show graciousness toward his children, a somewhat harsh way of thinking by modern standards.

65. Nissim ben Jacob Ibn Shahin, *An Elegant Composition Concerning Relief After Adversity*, trans. William M. Brinner (New Haven: Yale University Press, 1977), pp. 90 and 91 (hereafter cited as Brinner, *Relief After Adversity*).

had intercourse with her husband, and after conceiving anew, the boys at her call came running out of the room, restored to life, because of her deep faith. "Glory be to God! They were both dead, and God quickened them as a reward for my steadfastness." Avner Gil'adi has argued that many elements in the well-known tale in Midrash Proverbs of Beruryah hiding the death of their two sons on the Sabbath from her husband, R. Meir, may be derived from this latter *hadith* report, although in the rabbinic version the boys failed to come back to life.[66]

During the course of the plagues and the Black Death in the Middle East, a high percentage of the victims were newly born babies and children; and with the rapid onset of the plague, all the children in one family could suddenly be wiped out. Running through the Muslim and Jewish consolation treatises were the motifs of steadfast faith, when it was tested most harshly by the premature death of children, and at the same time a denial of the significance of the deaths of these children or alternatively a denial that the children had in fact died. In an elaboration of the *hadith* report about a Muslim couple, one author declared, "This woman showed steadfastness, accepted [the death of her son], acted deliberately, and prepared for herself a reward for her patience [in the hereafter]. Therefore God replaced her lost child with a better one." By disparaging a young child of unproven abilities and whose personality had hardly developed, the author sought somewhat disingenuously to console bereaved parents, but no doubt this was a universal attitude at the time. Again, the well-known consolation tract of R. Nissim ben Jacob Ibn Shahin (born about 990 C.E.) from the North African city of Kairouan and the oral Jewish folktales from the Middle East, which likewise sometimes drew on the *hadith* reports as a source, denied that the two boys had died. According to R. Nissim, "When the evening came, the wall was cleared from over the two boys [after the Sabbath], and they were found alive and were taken to their parents . . . [who] asked them, 'What was it that saved you?' The boys replied, 'The wooden beam of the wall formed a roof over us and made a brace between us and the stones of the earth . . .' They then thanked God Most High for their safe escape and for his great kindness to them. Moreover the reward

---

66. Avner Gil'adi, "*Sabr* (Steadfastness) of Bereaved Parents: A Motif in Medieval Muslim Consolation Treatises and Some Parallels in Jewish Writings," *Jewish Quarterly Review* 809, no. 1–2 (July–October 1989): 37–40, 43, 44, 45, and 46 (hereafter cited as Gil'adi, *Bereaved Parents*).

for their steadfastness and the recompense for their firm confidence in Him remained reserved for them in the hereafter."[67]

Abraham Stahl's researches among Oriental Jewish families has increased our understanding of the attitudes shown to the death of children in traditional society in Europe and throughout the Middle East and North Africa, where such attitudes persisted into the twentieth century. Often in Oriental Jewish families only two or three children survived from as many as the ten or fifteen children who were actually born. Neighbors consoled a mother who mourned the death of her infant by telling her that she would bear more children, as her social status was dependent on her fecundity and ability to keep on producing children. A Tunisian Jewish woman reprimanded her son for attempting to travel 400 kilometers to take her grandchild to Tunis, where there were modern medical facilities, by objecting: "What is the matter? . . . This baby will go and another will take its place." However, if a child was seriously ill, most parents were not passive but sought the assistance of local folk healers and rabbinic prayer to save the life of the child. Here we have the repetition of the two themes prevalent in the medieval consolation literature, the belief that the bereaved parents would be granted the blessing of more children and a mechanism for defense of the ego (Anna Freud), a denial that the dead children were important in their own right and a feeling that they were easily replaceable by other, more worthy children. In a Tunisian Jewish memoir it was recalled that "any child's death brought great grief, but since it occurred so frequently it seemed inevitable and it was accepted as the will of God."[68]

To summarize our argument so far, the death of an infant under the age of one or two years in traditional society in both Europe and the Islamic lands was universally accepted by Jews as being God's will or as a punish-

67. Michael Dols, *The Black Death in the Middle East* (Princeton, N.J.: Princeton University Press, 1977), pp. 178, 181, and 186. Avner Gil'adi, "Concepts of Childhood and Attitudes Towards Children in Medieval Islam . . . with Special Reference to Reactions to Infant and Child Mortality," *Journal of the Economic and Social History of the Orient*, Part 2 (June 1989), p. 138 (hereafter cited as Gil`adi, *Childhood*). Gil'adi, *Bereaved Parents*, pp. 41, 46, and 47. Brinner, *Relief After Adversity*, pp. 90 and 91.

68. Abraham Stahl, "Parents' Attitudes toward the Death of Infants in the Traditional Jewish-Oriental Family," *Journal of Comparative Family Studies* 22, no. 1 (Spring 1991): 76, 77, 78, 79, and 80 (hereafter cited as Stahl, *Parents' Attitudes*). Stahl, *Children and Childhood*, pp. 348 and 349.

ment for the parents' sins. Rahma, a lady from Iraq speaking of her own experiences, commented: "A girl was born, too early. She was very small. . . . After three days she died. It was difficult, but it was from Heaven. . . . People said: 'Kapparah' [i.e., atonement, meaning that the child's death was to be regarded as an expiation for the parents' sins]. You will give birth to others . . ." Such views were espoused equally by the rabbinic elite and the masses, both in Europe and throughout the Middle East and North Africa. Because of the belief that sometimes the deaths of children were caused by the evil eye, there was on occasion a social dimension to the ideology: the demise of these infants was attributed to the malevolence of close kin or neighbors in a tightly knit society that seethed with tensions and hidden resentments. So too, both in Europe and in the Middle East, there was a minority of parents who neglected their offspring and who were to a certain extent responsible for their early death; and another minority group of parents possibly among the medieval Ashkenazim but certainly among the Oriental Jews, particularly women, who by rejecting the prevailing social norms were inconsolable at the death of a young child.[69]

Stahl stated that six women out of a sample of thirty Oriental Jewish women expressed great sorrow when they spoke about the deaths of their infant children. Naomi from Iraq voiced her opinion with tears in her eyes, denying that people took such deaths "in their stride," and asserting to the contrary, "No, it caused much pain." Hannah from Persia claimed that whereas her family accepted the death of her baby, "she wept for a whole year, behaviour which seemed not only strange, but even dangerous. For should not one accept the lot decreed to him by higher powers? Finally it appeared necessary to have recourse to magic. A neighbour woman told her to take the baby's clothes and burn them." A Moroccan woman interviewed by someone else remarked that "eight children of mine died. . . . Those who passed away were one week old, one month, one year; one dies the eve of his circumcision. . . . Those who departed—it is as if they killed me."[70]

What was missing from Stahl's sample were the comments of male respondents, but this can be supplemented by *hadith* reports and Muslim consolation literature, which showed that fathers were often prone to weeping at an infant's death or were distraught at the sight of their son's

---

69. Stahl, *Parents' Attitudes*, pp. 79 and 80.
70. Stahl, *Parents' Attitudes*, pp. 78–80.

toys or refrained from eating and drinking. A Muslim doctor of the ninth or tenth century C.E. commented that "the loss of a beloved child . . . can release such sadness and dejection that melancholy is the result." It is surely plausible to suggest that the reactions of Jewish fathers in the Arab lands, when bereaved of an infant or a favorite child, were similar, but it is clear that there was general sadness at the passing of an older child. On a visit to Egypt in 1888, Elkan Adler noticed a five-hundred-year-old inscription in a synagogue commemorating "David Solomon, who was snatched away while of tender years; the spirit of the Lord brought him to rest. May the Lord comfort the heart of our brother, the princely Joshua, son of our Rabbi and Teacher . . ."[71]

Funeral rites for infants in medieval societies were often perfunctory, in keeping with the resigned acceptance of such deaths among both Christians and Jews. So long as the baby lived, particularly if it was a boy, complicated rituals were devised to protect him both at birth and through the circumcision ceremony, which bespeaks considerable emotional investment. Under Jewish law, a child who died after attaining the age of thirty days had to be mourned for seven days. Yet a thirteenth-century Italian rabbi confessed that "among us, the custom is not to keep mourning rites for children less than one year old, and I do not know the reason for this custom." In Southern France and medieval Spain, there was a custom of not mourning for a firstborn male child, who was regarded as consecrated to God. Meiri explained that in some places, this was extended to not observing any mourning for a firstborn boy who had died under the age of thirteen; elsewhere such young men were not mourned unless they reached the age of twenty. In the Atlas mountains in Morocco, there were short mourning rites for young children because so many of them died. So, too, "among the Sephardic Jews in Jerusalem at the beginning of the century the gravedigger took the little corpse [of a small child] and brought it by himself to the cemetery, the parents were not present . . ."[72]

Likewise, when an infant died in Oriental Jewish families the same family name was bestowed on a brother or sister, so that the name should be handed down to the next generation and not disappear into oblivion. Among the Ashkenazim, if a baby died, the next child to be born would

71. Gil'adi, *Childhood*, pp. 143–145. Elkan Adler, *Jews in Many Lands* (London: Macmillan, 1905), pp. 30 and 31.

72. Stahl, *Children and Childhood*, p. 350. Stahl, *Parents' Attitudes*, p. 77. Kanarfogel, *Childhood*, p. 27.

be given the same name preceded by the name of Chaim. Stephen Wilson criticized the view that parents were indifferent in such situations, arguing that bestowing the same name on successive children was partly because names were frequently attached to "roles within the family (and hence even to particular pieces of property) . . ." and partly because these names may have invoked the protection of particular saints. On the other hand, parents and particularly mothers were often solicitous over the welfare of dead infant boys, circumcising them from the ninth century C.E. onwards to ensure that they would gain the benefit of resurrection. During late antiquity and the Dark Ages, the Church had started baptizing infants as soon as possible after birth, instead of as adults, to safeguard their chance of salvation, a process that quickened in the eleventh century. Swayed by similar notions with regard to circumcision, the Jews during the Middle Ages attached increasing importance to circumcising dead infants, possibly borrowing from the Christians the idea that circumcision represented, in the words of one fourteenth-century Spanish Kabbalist, the seal of salvation.[73]

---

73. Stahl, *Parents' Attitudes*, p. 77. Abraham Stahl, *Family and Child-rearing in Oriental Jewry: Sources, References, Comparisons* (Hebrew) (Jerusalem: Academon, 1993), p. 366. Schauss, *Lifetime*, pp. 47 and 48. Wilson, *Myth of Motherhood*, pp. 183 and 184. Saul Lieberman, "After Life in Rabbinic Literature," in *Texts and Studies* (New York: Ktav Publishing House, 1974), pp. 525–527. Peter Cramer, *Baptism and Change in the Early Middle Ages c. 200–c. 1150* (Cambridge: Cambridge University Press, 1994). Mary Martin McLaughlin, "Survivors and Surrogates: Children and Parents from the Ninth to the Thirteenth Centuries," in *The History of Childhood*, ed. Lloyd deMause (London: Souvenir Press, 1974), p. 142 note 15.

5

Children in the Middle Ages: Childhood and Adolescence

CHILDREARING: PRACTICAL CONSIDERATIONS

Although cradles were mentioned in both secular and Jewish sources from the eleventh century in Europe, the medieval cradle, unlike its ancient counterpart, could be rocked, which was also an inducement for a mother to lull a fretful baby to sleep with a lullaby; all this bespeaks a growing devotion of the mother to her infant child. Within Christian society in Europe from the twelfth century onwards, there was the growth of the cult of the virgin, the ideal mother: "Lo, brethren, let us try to understand the affection of this good Mother . . . the tenderness with which she beholds the Infant in her arms, sees him hang on her breast, hears him cry as children do at the little hurts of his body; and hastens to forestall all evils which may happen to him . . ." So too, there was not only a new, more gentle image of Jesus the Child abroad instead of God the Father, the stern judge of mankind, but Jesus was now endowed with maternal qualities; and Ivan Marcus has argued that the new sense of childhood that pervades the *Sefer Ḥasidim* may be articulating the concerns about children also felt by the

surrounding Christian society. On the other hand, it could equally plausi-
bly be suggested that the nurturant qualities of fathers was a pervasive theme
in Jewish biblical thought and later literature and that the wider European
Christian society was merely catching up with the Jewish minority in this
respect. Despite the fact that our sources are sparse as to the role of the
medieval Jewish mother, we may safely infer that she looked after her sons
until they were five and her daughters until they were grown up; and that
in Western Europe from the twelfth century onwards, she shared in the
heightened awareness of the infant's needs, imbued as she was with a
deeper sense of maternal love and responsibility.[1]

To enable them to walk, children were placed in a go-cart and helped
by their parents. A fifteenth-century illustration from Germany shows a
mother and perhaps somewhat surprisingly his grandfather assisting a little
boy in taking his first steps, although the aid could possibly be coming
from an elderly father. Indeed, the Jewish philosopher Ibn Paquda, like
his fellow Spanish countryman R. Judah Ibn Tibbon, emphasized that both
parents should participate in the care of the young child, demonstrating
that the twelfth-century Christian stress on men's maternal qualities was a
concept already widely appreciated by Jews. "Then the body grows stronger and the baby starts to discern colors and hear voices," declared Ibn
Paquda, "while God puts mercy and compassion into the hearts of his
parents so that his upbringing is easy for them, even to the point that his
food and drink are more important to them than their own. And all the
trouble and the pain of his care, like washing, cleaning and fondling him,
guarding him against misfortune even against his will, all seem to them

---

1. Shulamith Shahar, *Childhood in the Middle Ages* (London: Routledge, 1992),
p. 89 (hereafter cited as Shahar, *Medieval Childhood*). Israel Abrahams, *Hebrew Ethical Wills* (Philadelphia: Jewish Publication Society, 1926), Vol. 1, p. 48 (hereafter cited
as Abrahams, *Ethical Wills*). R. W. Southern, *The Making of the Middle Ages* (London: Arrow Books, 1959), pp. 247–249. Norman F. Cantor, *Inventing the Middle Ages:
The Lives, Works, and Ideas of the Great Medievalists of the Twentieth Century*
(Cambridge: Lutterworth Press, 1992), pp. 355 and 364. Caroline Walker Bynum, *Jesus
as Mother: Studies in the Spirituality of the High Middle Ages* (Berkeley and Los
Angeles: University of California Press, 1992), pp. 110–166. Mary Martin McLaughlin,
"Survivors and Surrogates," in *The History of Childhood*, ed. Lloyd deMause (London:
Souvenir Press, 1974), p. 133 (hereafter cited as McLaughlin, *Survivors*). Ivan G. Marcus,
"Jewish Learning in the Middle Ages," *Melton Journal* (Autumn 1992): 23 (hereafter
cited as Marcus, *Jewish Learning*). Thérèse and Mendel Metzger, *Jewish Life in the
Middle Ages* (London: Alpine Fine Arts Collection, 1985), pp. 203 and 204 (hereafter
cited as Metzger, *Jewish Life*).

only a trifle. When he passes from infancy to childhood his parents do not come to dislike him nor do they grow weary of his many demands and his lack of comprehension of all their trouble in feeding him and cleaning after him. On the contrary, their love and concern for him grow until they reach their peak when he learns to talk in an orderly and reasonable way . . ."[2]

Further, R. Isaac b. Yedayah, who flourished in thirteenth-century Provence, believed that fathers were so indulgent to toddlers that they themselves could easily slip into baby talk and that their love for an infant could be more intense than that for an older child; but that it was nevertheless the duty of a father to correct unweaned children in order to teach them the difference between right and wrong. We must also recall R. Eleazar's tribute to his two young daughters who were murdered by the Crusaders, a sympathetic portrait of the ties that bound father and daughter together, even if sometimes the relationship was overformal and hierarchical. In the last couple of paragraphs, we have then a number of instances of Jewish fathers actively involved in their children's upbringing and to a degree empathizing with their needs.[3]

Toilet training was not invested with such a crucial role in molding the personality of the child during the Middle Ages as it was in Western Europe from the eighteenth century onwards, nor did it commence at such an early age. It is likely that in the medieval period the young child's garments were loose fitting and open like this description of children's clothing in a village in modern China: "Up to the age of six all children wear trousers open behind," Jan Myrdal recalled. "There is no flap or fall arrangement, but the actual fork of the trousers is hemmed on both sides . . . so that when the child sits or squats, this gapes, forming a large opening through

---

2. Israel Abrahams, *Jewish Life in the Middle Ages* (London: Edward Goldston, 1932), p. 142 (hereafter cited as Abrahams, *Jewish Life*). Metzger, *Jewish Life*, p. 204. Abrahams, *Ethical Wills*, Vol. 1, p. 57. Bahaya Ben Joseph Ibn Paquda, *The Book of Directions of Duties of the Heart*, trans. Menahem Mansoor (London: Routledge and Kegan Paul, 1992), pp. 162 and 163 (hereafter cited as Paquda, *Duties of the Heart*).

3. Ephraim Kanarfogel, "Attitudes Toward Childhood and Children in Medieval Jewish Society," in *Approaches to Judaism in Medieval Times*, ed. David Blumenthal (Chico, Calif.: Scholars Press, 1985), Vol. 2, pp. 4 and 22 (hereafter cited as Kanarfogel, *Childhood*). For the general Christian background in Southern France, which parallels Jewish developments, see Linda M. Paterson, *The World of the Troubadors: Medieval Occitan Society, c. 1100–c. 1300* (Cambridge: Cambridge University Press, 1993), p. 281. "Adults calm babies crying, and talk to them in tender and intimate language. Small children are assumed to have a natural appeal and vulnerability."

which the child can relieve itself. People reckon that a child ought to be 'house-trained' by the time it is eighteen months and able to walk properly; by three, it should be able to keep itself dry, and by six it is considered to have sufficient control of its bladder to wear trousers with the seam sewn up."[4]

From the tales recounted in the *Sefer Ḥasidim*, it appears that the arrangements for the toilet training of children in Europe were similar. On one occasion, a father was sitting at a table where he was studying a religious text and his small child entered the room, where he accidentally defecated or urinated on the floor. If this happened, the *Sefer Ḥasidim* advised the father to cover up his sacred books and to spread some earth on the floor before removing the mess or washing the urine off the floor. On no account, the *Sefer Ḥasidim* admonished, was the child to be punished if he did not comprehend the consequence of his actions, as this could result in his harming himself by retaining his feces and urine for too long a time (*Sefer Ḥasidim* Bologna 919). Again, the *Sefer Ḥasidim* recommended that "towards evening, a man should not take a child on to his lap, lest the child dirty his [father's] clothes, [this is not satisfactory because] they will not be as clean as before. Also while the father looks for water, the time for praying the *Minḥah* [afternoon] service may pass. . . . In addition, it is possible that when the father tries to put the child down, the child will cry. The father will be most concerned with the child and not with giving honor to his Creator" (*Sefer Ḥasidim* Parma 432). What these stories illustrate was the relaxed regime during the Middle Ages in toilet training and the loose-fitting clothing worn by young children, in which accidents were inevitable, but they also point to the father's involvement in the child's upbringing, his closeness to the young infant, and his emotional alertness to the child's needs.[5]

Children were toilet trained in medieval society by watching and imitating their older brothers or fathers, just as in preliterate societies small children were led into the bushes by a big brother and learned bowel con-

---

4. Lloyd deMause, "The Evolution of Childhood," in *The History of Childhood*, ed. Lloyd deMause (London: Souvenir Press, 1974), p. 40. Jan Myrdal, *Report from a Chinese Village* (Harmondsworth: Penguin Books, 1967), p. 56.

5. S. Kottek, "Childhood in Medieval Jewry as Depicted in *Sefer Hasidim* (12th–13th Century): Medical, Psychological, and Educational Aspects," *Koroth* 8, no. 9–10 (August 1984): 386 and 387 (hereafter cited as Kottek, *Childhood in Sefer Hasidim*). Kanarfogel, *Childhood*, p. 7.

trol by imitating him. Among the wealthier classes in medieval London, children were first trained by seating them on chamber pots, while we would surmise that similar conditions prevailed on the Continent in the more affluent Jewish families. People were freer about their bodily functions in medieval society, and the *Sefer Hasidim* cautioned fathers against studying a sacred text in the outhouse when they went to relieve themselves; rather they should take one of their children with them and chat to them, and if they were reluctant to do this because this could become too much of a habit for the child, they could as a last resort pore over their household accounts! (*Sefer Hasidim* Bologna 954). If one prominent medieval rabbi wore his tefillin in the privy, as it was alleged, to afford some protection in a place supposed to be infested with demons, we can guess that these dark and smelly latrines could have been a terrifying place at times for a child to visit at night. Under the medieval regime, where tight anal control from an early age was not insisted on, parents did not demand such high standards of cleanliness and orderliness from their children as was later to be the case. Thus, "If someone brings his children to the house of a friend and the children, as is customary at that age, are unclean around their nose, he should wipe away the filth. . . . But if a friend comes to his . . . house and is disgusted by the aspect of the children, the father is not at fault, because this is how the children normally look" (*Sefer Hasidim* Bologna 641).[6]

It has been suggested by Thérèse and Mendel Metzger that from the surviving iconography of Jewish children during the Middle Ages young girls appeared close to their mothers or under someone else's control. Girls were also trained from an early age to be assiduous in carrying out household tasks, such as cleaning, sewing and weaving, embroidery, making beds, and assisting in the kitchen.[7]

In contrast, boys had much more license for roaming on the streets and playing boisterous games, such as mounting the *steckenpferd*, a hobbyhorse on which the rider jumped while brandishing a whip. In

---

6. Erik H. Erikson, *Childhood and Society* (Harmondsworth: Penguin Books, 1965), p. 75. Barbara A. Hanawalt, *Growing Up in Medieval London: The Experience of Childhood History* (New York: Oxford University Press, 1993), p. 28 (hereafter cited as Hanawalt, *Medieval London*). Kottek, *Childhood in Sefer Hasidim*, pp. 386 and 388. Joshua Trachtenberg, *Jewish Magic and Superstition: A Study in Folk Religion* (New York: Atheneum, 1975), p. 145 (hereafter cited as Trachtenberg, *Jewish Magic*).

7. Metzger, *Jewish Life*, pp. 203 and 204.

medieval France, however, children of both sexes played ball games on the festivals, and in Italy such games were even permitted on the Sabbath, particularly tennis, one early version of which could be played with the hand. Another medieval game that children loved was blindman's bluff, but boys must have found more enjoyable the rough-and-tumble of a game in which each side tried to capture the other side's representatives. Quieter games were played by children with nuts and apples in a number of different versions, by rolling these fruits against a similar object belonging to an opponent, and victory was awarded to the player who first struck an article belonging to his opponent. Jews participated in athletic contests in Augsburg in 1470, including foot races, the broad jump, and putting the shot. In Rome in 1466 Pope Paul II inaugurated the carnival in a new form, which included four races on foot, among them a competition for Jewish runners under twenty over a course almost a mile long. With the passage of time, the Jewish athletes became targets for the crowd to mock until this spectacle was abolished in 1688. Jews were not always the victims in these intercommunal contests. In Venice in 1571 when a Christian porter with two assistants carried bread in an annual procession through the Ghetto after Passover, both he and the bread were pelted with mud and stones and tarred by brushes dipped in dirt by a waiting crowd, mostly consisting of Jewish children.[8]

Pietists in Germany were insistent that their children should not play with other Jewish children because they thought there was a risk that they could succumb to moral dangers and acquire the discordant and, to them, degenerate values of the larger Jewish society. "A [pietist] said to his son:

---

8. Metzger, *Jewish Life*, p. 209. Abrahams, *Jewish Life*, pp. 403, 405, and 406. Louis Rabinowitz, *The Social Life of the Jews of Northern France in the 12th–14th Centuries as Reflected in the Rabbinical Literature of the Period* (London: Edward Goldston, 1938), pp. 225–227 (hereafter cited as Rabinowitz, *Social Life of French Jews*). Arthur Hanak, *Physical Education of Jews in the Middle Ages and Early Modern Times* (Tel Aviv: Maccabi World Union, 1987), pp. 15–41. Although the *Shulchan Aruch* forbade ball playing on the Sabbath and festivals, certain authorities including Maimonides allowed it on private land with a firm surface and a hard ball. Medieval Jews also indulged in wrestling, and swimming was more popular among them than among Gentiles. Jacob R. Marcus, *The Rise and Destiny of the German Jew* (Cincinnati: Union of American Hebrew Congregations, 1934), p. 238. Hermann Vogelstein, *Rome* (Philadelphia: Jewish Publication Society, 1940), pp. 231–233. Cecil Roth, *The History of the Jews in Italy* (Philadelphia: Jewish Publication Society, 1946), pp. 396 and 387. Brian Pullan, *The Jews of Europe and the Inquisition of Venice 1550–1670* (Oxford: Basil Blackwell, 1983), pp. 163 and 164.

Why have you taken up with violent boys . . . ? He replied: I have used my wits to attract them to Torah study. For when I saw that they wanted to gamble, I taught them to play a game with biblical verses. The first person says a verse which ends with the letter alef [A], and so on, through the alphabet. Whoever cannot think of the next verse is the loser. Look what I have done: They are (still playing but are also) studying Torah . . . his father replied: You wanted to attract them (to Torah) but you have ensnared yourself. You have taught them Torah, all right, but to fool around with it . . ."[9]

Again, Jewish fathers in medieval Egypt who were traveling away from home on business wrote to their wives and relatives complaining about "letting the boy miss the school and play in the streets." A father who was head of a yeshiva grieved for his six-year-old son who had died, praising him for never playing on the streets or at home and sharing whatever food he had, "whether he had plenty or little," with the poor, and for asking intelligent questions in his studies; but such a lifestyle approached close to that of the German pietists and it was doubtful whether the families of ordinary Jews in Egypt or elsewhere brought up their children in such a strict way.[10]

Parental discipline in medieval Germany was not always firm, and fathers could on some occasions adopt a laissez-faire attitude and on others act capriciously. According to Israel Abrahams, medieval Jewish literature "contain[s] frequent laments that the children were allowed too much licence at table, in synagogue, and in the presence of their elders generally." A father, we are informed by the *Sefer Ḥasidim*, permitted his young child to climb onto the table where he usually placed his religious books and at which he ate. While clambering off the table, the child injured his foot by stepping on a knife, which the father admitted was his fault for failing to remove the religious texts from the table (*Sefer Ḥasidim* Bologna 920). On another occasion, "a Sage entered a house and heard a four-year-old child call his father 'son-of-a-bitch' [literally 'son of a prostitute'], and the

9. Ivan G. Marcus, *Piety and Society: The Jewish Pietists of Medieval Germany* (Leiden: E. J. Brill, 1981), p. 95 (hereafter cited as Marcus, *Pietists*).

10. S. D. Goitein, *A Mediterranean Society: The Community* (Berkeley and Los Angeles: University of California Press, 1971), Vol. 2, p. 174 (hereafter cited as Goitein, *Community*. S. D. Goitein, *A Mediterranean Society: The Family* (Berkeley and Los Angeles: University of California Press, 1978), Vol. 3, p. 234 (hereafter cited as Goitein, *Family*).

father beat him for that. Afterwards the child desecrated the Sabbath, but the father did not react. So the Sage said: Why did you react when the child said what he said? If he did not even know what a whore is, why do you care? And even if he does understand what he says, it is an outrage to himself as well as to you; moreover, if he is capable of understanding you should have prevented him from desecrating the Sabbath" (*Sefer Ḥasidim* Bologna 864). Unless punishment had an educative purpose, the sage warned that it was useless, and in addition punishment needed to adhere to fixed principles. By being inconsistent at times in their punishment of their young sons and by being punitive, medieval Jewish fathers and teachers encouraged the growth of a new generation of authoritarian adults.[11]

During the Middle Ages, when an individual was in contact mainly with a small number of persons who expected him to behave in an approved way, the chief means of sanction to enforce the correct mode of conduct was to shame this individual, if he deviated from these prescribed paths in his actions. "Think now of the trait of shame, which is peculiar to man," Ibn Paquda asserted. "How great is its power and how immense its uses and advantages! Were it not for shame, nobody would welcome a guest or fulfill a promise or take care of any needs or perform good works or avoid evil in anything. Even many of the commandments of the Law are obeyed only out of shame, for most people would not truly respect their parents, were it not for shame, not to speak of respecting others. They would not return a thing entrusted to them nor refrain from any foul deed. Whoever does anything mentioned above does it only after discarding the cover of shame . . ."[12]

Later during the Renaissance and Reformation, parental values were internalized by children and they felt guilty if they departed from these norms, but nevertheless the medieval pietists in Germany and pious Jews in the Islamic world were experimenting with a lifestyle of inward reflection on the minutiae of daily living that was a halfway house to incorporat-

---

11. Abrahams, *Jewish Life*, p. 142. Kottek, *Childhood in Sefer Hasidim*, pp. 386 and 387. Robert A. Levine, "The Internalization of Political Values in Stateless Societies," in *Personalities and Culture,* ed. Robert Hunter (Garden City, N.Y.: Natural History Press, 1967), pp. 199 and 200.

12. Paquda, *Duties of the Heart*, p. 165. David Riesman, *The Lonely Crowd: A Study of the Changing American Character* (New Haven: Yale University Press, 1955), p. 25 (hereafter cited as Riesman, *Lonely Crowd*).

ing guilt as a feature of human motivation. If the medieval schoolman Abelard discerned the value of an act in the inner intention of an individual, and not in the outer deed, Robert Chazan found similar thought processes among twelfth-century Jews, even among children. "It is not enough to die for the unity of the Divine Name; one must articulate a full awareness of the sacrifice to be made and then undertake it with a full heart. Even children are enjoined to give their full assent to their own demise. Thus, Isaac ben David the *parnas* . . . asked his children: 'Do you wish that I sacrifice you to our God?'" Another respect in which the notion of guilt started to be instilled in young children during the Middle Ages was by teaching them about paradise and hell, about reward and punishment, at an age when they accepted everything that they were taught uncritically. It was in the late twelfth century and the early thirteenth century that the idea of individual judgment after death gained a new significance.[13]

What was the extent of discipline in the Jewish home and school during the Middle Ages? The view of Rav, a third-century Babylonian sage, that the pupil should be struck with a small strap was confirmed by Maimonides and appeared afresh in the standard law codes, in the *Tur* and the *Shulchan Aruch*, but was this the reality? Israel Abrahams put forward the somewhat contradictory propositions that in the home, "discipline was severe and corporal punishment habitual," but that in school, "it was not severe." Bearing in mind the accounts in nineteenth-century memoirs and other evidence of sadistic heder teachers and brutal discipline, it was unlikely that the punishment meted out by the masters in the elementary school during the Middle Ages was mild, although as we have seen in Germany, fathers could adopt at times in the home a surprisingly permissive and relaxed attitude. Moreover, a father in medieval Egypt wrote to the teacher of his two sons to ensure that they were not spanked for arriving late in school, as there were valid reasons for this, with the implication that this was the usual punishment inflicted for such an offense. A widow with a small son had a clause written into her marriage contract in which her future husband promised that "he will feed and clothe this orphan and teach him a craft. He will be to him like the children borne to him by

---

13. Riesman, *Lonely Crowd*, pp. 14 and 15. Robert Chazan, *European Jewry in the First Crusade* (Berkeley and Los Angeles: University of California Press, 1987), pp. 134 and 135 (hereafter cited as Chazan, *First Crusade*). Jacques Le Goff, *The Birth of Purgatory* (London: Scholar Press, 1984), p. 370. Kottek, *Childhood in Sefer Hasidim*, p. 387.

the bride, he will not turn him out, or beat, or humiliate him with words."
When a father made a journey to Egypt, he left his son with relations in
Damascus who reported that "he is happy and gay in the company of our
children. He goes to school with them, dresses like them, and plays with
them. He is not a stranger. Everyone loves him. They all sleep on one
mattress. She [the writer's wife] shows him love more than she does to
her own children." All these examples indicate that, despite being beaten
from time to time both at home and probably more frequently at school,
the average Jewish child was well treated by his parents by the standards
of the age.[14]

As far as school was concerned, the comment of the medieval *Machzor
Vitry* may well have been true when describing the initiation of a Jewish
pupil into his studies: "And when they start to teach him, they at first
encourage him and in the end the strap is used on his back." In medieval
Europe it was commonly believed that failure by a parent or teacher to
beat a child could result in his sinking into sloth and evil ways and endan-
gering his soul. This point of view was also encapsulated in Rashi's mode
of thinking. Witness his comment on Proverbs 3:12: "Just like a father
whose only wish is to do good to his son and so he soothes and appeases
him [i. e., speaks words of kindness and affection] after he hit him with the
rod . . ." The attitude of the *Sefer Hasidim* to corporal punishment was
equivocal. On the one hand, it warned parents not to "entrust your son[s]
to irascible teachers, who will slap them or punish them exceedingly"; on
the other hand, foster parents were advised to admonish and slap orphans
as they would their own children, while the rearing of children was compared to that of a dog that had to be beaten to make him a faithful companion. Again, Maimonides confirmed the opinion of the Mishnah that a
father, and a teacher in the course of his duties, who hit a boy were exempted from punishment should this unintentionally cause the child's death,
a point of view supported by R. Adret (1235–1310). Violence was endemic in any case throughout the European feudal world and the medieval Islamic lands, where Maimonides suggested that a rebellious wife, who
was often no more than a child, could be forced by her husband to obey

14. Elliott Horowitz, "The Way We Were: Jewish Life in the Middle Ages," *Jewish
History* 1, no. 1 (Spring 1986): 81 (hereafter cited as Horowitz, *The Way We Were*).
Abrahams, *Jewish Life*, pp. 142 and 37. Goitein, *Family*, 234.

him by whipping her; the Jewish communities were not immune from these brutal influences.[15]

Having said all this about the rigorous mode of punishment in elementary schools, there was evidence from Egypt that teachers were sometimes careful to leave the matter of punishment to parents, fearing that any harshness on their part could lead to the withdrawal of the pupil from the school, and Jewish teachers in early modern Europe voiced the same concerns. Both the illustrations from the fourteenth century Spanish Sarajevo Haggadah and the Coburg Pentateuch show heder teachers with whips, the emblem of their office. A classroom wall chart published in Ferrara in 1590, however, showed a teacher actually flogging his pupil. R. Joseph of Arles in the early sixteenth century threatened his yeshiva students with a whip, while in the same century the author of the *Brandt-spiegel* advised teachers to strike pupils with rods of varying sizes according to the pupil's age and always to have a whip at hand. When Jonah Gerondi's (died 1263) *Sefer Ha-Yirah* was reworked in a Yiddish version in 1583, there was an incidental remark in it that he who had studied the Torah in his youth "That his teacher struck him, He should not complain." Elliott Horowitz has argued that this evidence supports Ariès' contention that references to corporal punishment were rare until the end of the fourteenth century, whereas in the sixteenth century pupils of all ages were whipped for a greater range of offenses. Lawrence Stone suggested that "conditions were extremely brutal in the sixteenth- and seventeenth-century home and school, but that the deterioration from the late medieval period may be exaggerated by the differences in the amount and nature of the evidence." In contrast, Steven Ozment concluded for sixteenth-century Europe that moderate corporal punishment was a regular feature at both home and school, especially between the ages of six and twelve, but that harsh

---

15. Simha Assaf, *Mekorot le-Toldot ha-Hinukh be-Yisrael* [Sources for the History of Jewish Education] (Tel Aviv: Dvir, 1954), Vol. 1, pp. 2 and 119 (hereafter cited as Assaf, *Sources*). Shahar, *Childhood*, p. 173. Hayim Halevy Donin, *To Raise a Jewish Child* (New York: Basic Books, 1977), p. 67. Kottek, *Childhood in Sefer Hasidim*, p. 389. Shoshana Matzner-Bekerman, *The Jewish Child: Halakhic Perspectives* (New York: Ktav, 1984), p. 135. Mordechai Frishtik, "Physical Violence by Parents against their Children in Jewish History and Jewish Law," *Jewish Law Annual* 10 (1992): 82 and 83. Avraham Grossman, "Medieval Rabbinic Views on Wife Beating 800–1300," *Jewish History* 5, no. 1 (Spring 1991): 53–62.

and arbitrary punishment was looked at askance and that brutality was condemned. Much the same can be said about the role of discipline in medieval Jewish family life, although there were occasions when the impoverished and frustrated village teachers on short-term contracts found it difficult to abide by these ideals and acted in a cruel fashion.[16]

In medieval Northern Europe a Jewish apologist boasted about the superiority of Jewish family life and their perfectionism in rearing children:

> Whether old or young, Jews study the Torah and teach their children from infancy to read books, attend houses of prayer, abstain from profanities, but to speak in a clean language, and be careful about taking oaths. They also watch their daughters lest they become licentious and run around with rather than stay away from men; thus there is no apparent promiscuity among them. Nor do they break through walls to steal, or hold up travelers on the roads. But you profane your speech and swear by the name of God, His . . . entire body, even his genitals, and your daughters are licentious, some living in houses of prostitution; many of you are thieves and robbers. Indeed, the Jews are pious, take pity on their brethren lest they beg from door to door; they bring the poor to their houses and give them food and drink. They also give away a portion of their wealth so that they [the poor] may marry off their daughters or ransom captives. They also properly observe their Sabbaths and holidays.

So, too, the Franciscan Berthold von Regensburg (c. 1200–1272) "on several occasions . . . praises Jews for being more scrupulous in their religious observance than most Christians, especially with regard to holy days, prayer, honoring one's parents, and sexual abstinence during a wife's menstrual period." At its best, Jewish family life undoubtedly lived up to this idealized portrait, but there were sectors in both Europe and the Islamic lands where this sketch was not completely true: there was prostitution in certain Jewish communities, and the pietists in Germany were influenced by Christian notions of celibacy and uneasy over sexuality and having too

---

16. Goitein, *Community*, p. 182. Isidore Fishman, *The History of Jewish Education in Central Europe: From the End of the Sixteenth to the End of the Eighteenth Century* (London: Edward Goldston, 1944), p. 83 (hereafter cited as Fishman, *Jewish Education*). Israel Zinberg, *A History of Jewish Literature: Old Yiddish Literature from Its Origins to the Haskalah Period* (New York: Ktav, 1975), Vol. 7, p. 145. Horowitz, *The Way We Were*, pp. 80–82. Lawrence Stone, "The Rise of the Nuclear Family in Early Modern England: The Patriarchal Stage." in *The Family in History*, ed. Charles E. Rosenberg (Philadelphia: University of Pennsylvania Press, 1975), p. 37. Steven Ozment, *When Fathers Ruled: Family Life in Reformation Europe* (Cambridge, Mass.: Harvard University Press, 1983), pp. 135–149.

close a relationship with their own wives; there were also impoverished Jews whose children were poorly educated and ignorant.[17]

THE INITIATION CEREMONY INTO THE HEDER

At the age of five or six a boy in Northern France and Germany was initiated into his Hebrew studies in an intricate ceremony that had already been fully developed by the end of the eleventh century. The ceremony re-enacted in symbolic form the giving of the Torah on Mount Sinai, so that it was staged at Shavuot (Pentecost), the traditional anniversary on which the bestowing of the Torah on the Jewish people was celebrated. According to another source, the ceremony sometimes took place in the month of Nisan during the spring, when the weather was "neither hot nor cold." The ceremony, which was a rite of passage marking the induction of the Jewish boy into the cultural domain of his people, was more important to these medieval Ashkenazi communities than the Jewish confirmation rites, the bar mitzvah service, which was elaborated only later; and was distinctive from the rite of circumcision, where there was more emphasis placed on the physical bonding and where the baby was the passive recipient of cultural values.

We have three accounts of this initiation ceremony in the *Machzor Vitry*, the *Sefer Ha-Rokeach*, and the *Sefer Assufot*, all of which agree on the essential details. We shall commence our survey with a description of the ceremony contained in the *Machzor Vitry*, which was compiled by Simcha of Vitry (died c. 1105): "When a man introduces his son to the study of the Torah, they write the letters of the Hebrew alphabet for him on a slate; and they wash him and dress him in clean clothes. Three cakes made of fine flour and honey are kneaded for him by a virgin; and they boil for him three eggs and they bring him apples and other varieties of fruit. They invite a scholarly and important person to conduct him to the school. He covers him with his coat and leads him to the synagogue. They feed the boy on the cakes of honey, eggs and fruit; and the letters of the alphabet

17. Salo Baron, *A Social and Religious History of the Jews* (New York: Columbia University Press, 1965), Vol. 9, pp. 128. Jeremy Cohen, *The Friars and the Jews: The Evolution of Medieval Anti-Judaism* (Ithaca, N.Y.: Cornell University Press, 1983), p. 231. Judith R. Baskin, "From Separation to Displacement: The Problem of Women in *Sefer Ḥasidim*," *AJS Review* 19, no. 1 (1994): 1–18.

are read to him. After that the letters [on the slate] are covered with honey and they tell him to lick; and they return him to his mother so concealed. . . . He begins his study with Leviticus; and they train him to sway with his body as he studies."[18]

What was the purpose of the ceremony? It was to incorporate the child symbolically into the ranks of the Jewish people by making him imagine he was standing with his ancestors at the foot of Mount Sinai to receive the Torah: "It was as though they brought him to Mount Sinai," the account in the *Machzor Vitry* remarked. Thus the parents purified their children for this occasion by washing them and clothing them in clean garments following the instructions outlined in Exodus 19:3. The young boy was covered with a cloak, not a prayer shawl, on his way to the synagogue or his teacher's house, as was clearly shown in an early fourteenth-century illustration, partly for reasons of modesty and partly to protect him from the evil eye. From a Hamburg manuscript dated 1317, we learn that the child was brought to the synagogue by a respected member of the community under his cloak in order to conceal him from a dog (an omen of death), a pig (an unclean animal contrasted with the pure child), and in some texts from the gaze of a non-Jew (the outsider, who was excluded from the holy community). This was based on the text in Exodus 34:3: "And no man shall come up with thee [Moses], neither let any man be seen throughout all the mount; neither let the flock nor herds feed before that mount"; and the fact that Moses sent away his Gentile father-in-law Jethro before the granting of the Torah. The separation of the child from the rest of his people and from the gaze of outsiders, by concealing him under a cloak, was a typical and crucial first step in an important rite of passage, which this ceremony was. Additional emphasis was placed on the concept of purity by ensuring that a virgin prepared the honey cakes, that white and sweet-tasting chicken's eggs were hard-boiled as part of the ritual meal, and that the pure child was inaugurated into the study of the Torah by learning about the sacred sacrificial code contained in Leviticus, the pure dealing with the pure. During the second phase of the rite of passage, the threshold or liminal phase, the neophyte was symbolically reborn by partaking of a hard-boiled egg, a symbol of rebirth.[19]

---

18. Assaf, *Sources*, pp. 2 and 3. *Machzor Vitry*, ed. S. Hurwitz (Nuremberg: I. Bulka, 1923), pp. 628–630.

19. Assaf, *Sources*, pp. 2 and 3. Naftali Zvi Roth, "The Torah Education of Children at Pentecost," (Hebrew) *Yeda-'Am* 11, no. 30 (Autumn 1965): 9–12. Metzger, *Jewish*

According to the *Sefer Ha-Rokeach* of R. Eleazar Judah ben Kalonymos of Worms (1160–1238), the child was placed on the teacher's lap together with a slate on which the alphabet was written backwards and forwards. Also a few biblical verses were inscribed on the slate, including the words "Moses commanded us the Torah, an inheritance of the congregation of Jacob" (Deut. 33:4), and the opening words of Leviticus, "And the Lord called unto Moses, and spoke unto him out of the tent of meeting, saying," (Lev. 1:1), and "May the Torah be my occupation," the last taken from a children's prayer. The teacher then recited the letters of the alphabet, which the child repeated after him. The alphabet was again chanted by the teacher but this time backwards, to be followed by the child's repetition of the individual letters. Honey was smeared over the letters on the slate, which the child licked off with his tongue in order to ingest all the letters of the alphabet and the message to make the study of the Torah his lifelong vocation, so that these concepts were completely absorbed by him. During this liminal phase of the ceremony the boy submitted to an ordeal, thus being humiliated and being rendered passive so as to be fashioned anew and endowed with fresh powers, particularly those of a retentive memory.[20]

Next the boy was handed one of the honey cakes, on which was written verses from Isaiah 50:4–5: "The Lord God has given me the tongue of a teacher and skill to console the weary with a word in the morning; he sharpened my hearing that I might listen like one who is taught. The Lord God opened my ears and I did not disobey or turn back in defiance." Finally, the boy was given a hard-boiled egg with a verse from Ezekiel (3:3): "Son of man, swallow this scroll I give you and fill yourself full. So I ate it, and it tasted as sweet as honey." The *Sefer Assufot* added some verses from Psalm 119 to the inscriptions on the egg, including the words "From all my teachers have I learned wisdom" and "How sweet are Thy words unto my taste! Yea, sweeter than honey to my mouth!" All the verses on the cake and egg were read aloud by the teacher and pronounced after him by his new pupil, who then ate the cake, the egg, and the fruit. Various sources inform us that the pupil was then conducted to the bank of a river by the teacher or to a pool stocked with fish, because the Torah was lik-

---

Life, p. 210. Trachtenberg, *Jewish Magic*, pp. 162 and 211. Victor W. Turner, "Betwixt and Between: The Liminal Period in Rites de Passage," in *The Proceedings of the American Ethnological Society: Symposium on New Approaches to the Study of Religion* (Seattle: University of Washington Press, 1964), pp. 4–20.

20. Assaf, *Sources*, pp. 3 and 4.

ened to water. "As water rests not in the elevated places, but flows downward and gathers in the lowlands, so the Torah resides only with the humble and modest, not with the proud and presumptuous." In the evening the celebrations were concluded when the boy's parents gave a party for him.[21]

According to Ivan Marcus, this childhood initiation ceremony was modeled on a Jewish magical rite for memory retention associated with an angel called the "Prince of the Torah," which had been delineated in ancient mystical writings, the *Heikhalot* literature. In the opinion of Gershom Scholem this supernatural figure went back to the fourth century C.E. and was charged with distributing knowledge of the Torah among men; his magical powers had an affinity to the doctrines of Hermeticism. This concept of the "Prince of the Torah" was brought by Jewish immigrants from Palestine to Italy and thence to the medieval Rhineland communities and Northern France. Here the adult memory rite was adapted to the use of children to enable them to learn texts from the Torah by heart. Vestiges of similar practices have been reported in Jewish communities in the Mediterranean area. In seventeenth-century North Africa they prepared a breakfast consisting of sweet food for children who were attending school for the first time, while in the Balkans when a new pupil went to school his mother distributed fritters.[22]

In traditional societies, food or drink were used as instruments to impart knowledge of the letters of the alphabet and revered texts to young boys and more mature students and as essential aids to memory. As Diane Roskies pointed out, "education, reading instruction included, is analogous to ingestion." From the time of the geonim, it was believed that "'all the scholars of Israel and their pupils used' to eat cakes and eggs so inscribed

---

21. Assaf, *Sources*, pp. 3 and 4. Louis Ginzberg, *Students, Scholars and Saints* Philadelphia: Jewish Publication Society, 1928), pp. 19–21. S. E. Stern, "Ceremony of Induction of Children to Education by R. Efraim of Bonn and from the *Sefer Assufot*," (Hebrew) *Zefunot* 1 (1988): 15–21.

22. Ivan G. Marcus, "Jewish Schools in Medieval Europe," *Melton Journal* 21 (Winter 1987): 5 (hereafter cited as Marcus, *Jewish Schools*). Gershom Scholem, *Jewish Gnosticism, Merkabah Mysticism, and Talmudic Tradition* (New York: Jewish Theological Seminary, 1960), p. 12. Moshe Idel, *Kabbalah New Perspectives* (New Haven: Yale University Press, 1988), pp. 168 and 360 note 91. Herbert C. Dobrinsky, *A Treasury of Sephardic Laws and Customs* (New York: Ktav, 1986), p. 141. Diane Roskies, "Alphabet Instruction in the East European Heder: Some Comparative and Historical Notes," *Yivo Annual of Jewish Social Science* 17 (1978): 25 (hereafter cited as Roskies, *Alphabet Instruction*).

[with biblical verses], 'and therefore they are successful.'" In ancient Greece the alphabet was written with chalk on the inside of a bowl into which wine was poured for the children to drink so as to absorb the letters of the alphabet into their systems. There were many analogous practices reported in medieval Jewish sources, in which incantations and love potions were written on scraps of paper and soaked in wine or water, after which the resulting concoction was swallowed. During the 1930s in Kurdistan when Jewish parents had a backward child, they still consulted a sage who wrote "the names of certain angels on paper or on an egg, washes the ink off, and gives the water to the child to drink." Much importance was attached to the recitation of potent magical names. R. Judah the Pious (d. 1217) wrote some of these magical names in the sand, which a favorite pupil licked up, thereby instantly gaining his teacher's mystical knowledge. Similarly an incantation contained in the *Siddur Amram* (c. 860), which was recited at the end of the Sabbath, also had a prominent place in the initiation ceremony for children joining a heder. "I conjure you, Poteh (or Purah), prince of forgetting, to remove my stupidity from me and to throw it on to the hills and high places, by the holy name of Armas, Arimas, Armimas, Ansis, Yael, Petahel." To this formula the *Sefer Assufot* added the repetition some ten times of the names of the angels of destruction, Negef, Segef, and Agaf. By reciting this prayer it was hoped that Poteh, the demon of forgetfulness, would be obliterated and the memory strengthened.[23]

In addition, the child ate honey cakes and eggs with biblical texts as a means of opening the mind (*Sefer Ha-Rokeach*) or "because doing this is good for developing the mind" (*Sefer Assufot*), thereby facilitating the learning process and making it easy for the child to memorize large sections of the Torah. Literally, the medieval expression for mind was the heart, which was believed to be the seat of memory; hence record = re + *cor*, Latin for heart. This ability to store vast quantities of knowledge in the memory was vital in medieval society, which was primarily an oral culture; even reading chiefly meant reading aloud. In the *Sefer Raziel*, a thirteenth-century compilation drawing on geonic material, there were many such

---

23. Roskies, *Alphabet Instruction*, pp. 26 and 27. Trachtenberg, *Jewish Magic*, pp. 102, 122, and 123. Moritz Gudemann, *Geschichte des Erziehungwesens und der Cultur der abendlandischen Juden* (Vienna, 1880), Vol. 1, p. 53. Erich Brauer, *The Jews of Kurdistan* (Detroit: Wayne State University Press, 1993), p. 246. Bernard Heller, "*Le Nom Divin de Vingt-Deux Lettres*," *Revue des Études Juives* 55 (1908): 69–74. Bernard Heller, *Revue des Études Juives* 57 (1909): 107 and 108.

magical recipes for making cakes that were used for multifarious purposes, with the divine names inscribed on their surface. In England, hornbook molds for baking gingerbread were popular from the fourteenth to the nineteenth century, producing a chart of Latin letters impressed on the cake. Children were given one letter of the alphabet to eat and identify at a time. Knowledge, in Diane Roskies' phrase, had to be "swallowed." Whereas certain foods such as honey and the hearts or brains of animals were favored in the folk tradition, as they were thought to stimulate memory, the Jews in Eastern Europe believed that cakes made from dough remnants clogged the brain and should be avoided by schoolboys. Honey was commonly utilized as a metaphor for learning in medieval Hebrew poetry. It was thus no coincidence that the medieval Jews utilized honey cakes, which were closely related to gingerbread hornbook cakes, for their initiation ceremonies at school.[24]

Belief in the efficacy of magic was widespread in medieval Europe. "Jews knew of men who had no shadows, of evil spirits lurking in caverns, they feared the evil-eye, believed in witches and ghouls who devoured children, trusted to spells and incantations," Israel Abrahams conceded. Even R. Meir of Rothenburg approved of children wearing amulets around their necks to ward off the evil eye, so long as they had been designed by experts. Nevertheless, the critical stance of the pietists helped in part to undermine confidence in such views about magic. R. Eleazar mentioned that his teacher Judah the Pious "did not want children to be fed the cake because biblical verses are written on it. It is not proper to excrete (biblical verses)," although he disagreed with his mentor about this; and R. Meir of Rothenburg proclaimed that an "erasure on a Sabbath or holiday is biblically prohibited only because such erasure produces space for further writing . . . , while eating the cakes has no such effect. Rabbinically, however, even the form of erasure brought about by eating is prohibited; but we pay no attention

---

24. Assaf, *Sources*, p. 4. Marcus, *Pietists*, p. 113. Marshall McLuhan, *The Gutenberg Galaxy* (London: Routledge and Kegan Paul, 1967), pp. 82–84. Trachtenberg, *Jewish Magic*, pp. 122, 123, and 297 note 23. Roskies, *Alphabet Instruction*, pp. 26–28. Andrew W. Tuer, *History of the Horn-Book* (London: Leadenhall Press, 1896), 2 vol. Marvin I. Herzog, *The Yiddish Language in Northern Poland: Its Geography and History* (Bloomington: Indiana University Press, 1965), pp. 30 and 47. John Cooper, *Eat and Be Satisfied: A Social History of Jewish Food* (Northvale, N.J.: Jason Aronson, 1993), pp. 117 and 118.

to children who eat such cake, since the Court is not enjoined to restrain children from eating forbidden food."[25]

More provocatively, Ivan Marcus in *Rituals of Childhood* (1996) asserted that certain features of the *heder* initiation ceremony internalized and parodied motifs from medieval Christian culture, creating a counterritual which challenged the claims of the majority faith. The Jewish teacher with the new pupil on his lap during the initiation ceremony was modelled on the Christian image of the Madonna nursing her child, but the Jewish child was being fed Torah foods. When the Jewish schoolboy ate cakes of honey during the schooling rite, he was ingesting the words of the Torah as manna. This was a Jewish polemic, which insisted that the Torah was the bread of life, not Jesus, by ritualizing the eating of cakes during the initiation ceremony in the "form of the eucharistic loaf." Medieval Christians understood the eucharist rite "as a child sacrifice in which one eats Christ as a small boy." According to rabbinic doctrine, a pure child who studied the Torah was likened to a sacrifice offered on behalf of the Jewish community in the Temple, and by continuing to learn, the child, and not the Christian saviour Jesus, could secure redemption for his people.

By the sixteenth century, the custom of initiating a Jewish child into school at Shavuot had become extinct in Southern Germany. R. David b. Isaac of Fulda (c. 1540–1607), who was born in Friedberg, admitted that "had I known of the rite [against forgetfulness and to open the heart] while my children were still young, I would have employed this remedy for them. However, I was unaware of it until I recently received it, when I discovered it in a very old text." Elsewhere the ceremony survived in a truncated form. It appears from the testimony of R. Zevi Aaron Kaidanover of Vilna, who died in Frankfurt-on-Main in 1701, that the pupil's father or mother still concealed him under a coat when he was first escorted to the heder. Other features of the ceremony that were retained were the recitation of the alphabet forwards and backwards both by the teacher and then by the pupil; having accomplished this, the child still licked honey off letters of the alphabet inscribed on a slate. Parents were now advised by R. Kaidanover to fast on their son's first day at school and to

---

25. Abrahams, *Jewish Life*, p. 391. Irving A. Agus, *R. Meir of Rothenburg* (New York: Ktav, 1970), pp. 209 and 210. Marcus, *Pietists*, pp. 113 and 114. Irving A. Agus, *Rabbi Meir of Rothenburg* (Philadelphia: Dropsie College, 1947), Vol. 1, p. 192.

hold a festive meal to which the poor should be invited and to distribute charity.[26]

In the early seventeenth century, R. Moses Henochs of Prague noted in his work the *Brandtspeigel* (Burning Mirror) that before a new pupil was taken to the heder on this occasion, his father offered him a wafer dipped in honey, adding the following blessing: "May it please the Almighty that just as these wafers are sweet so may the words of the Torah be sweet to thee and like honey upon the tongue." When the child commenced his studies, the teacher threw fruit on the floor as an inducement for him to learn, exclaiming that "an angel has thrown them down for you in order that you may study with zest," although the names of specific angels were no longer recited and the ceremony against forgetfulness was omitted; the latter appears to be a foreshadowing of nineteenth-century practice in Eastern Europe. Almost alone, R. Jacob Emden (1698–1776), who was brought up in Altona in Northern Germany, quoted the customs referred to in the *Sefer Ha-Rokeach* in full; but then went on to complain that some of these practices, such as eating the cakes with scriptural verses, had been abandoned and that the inner, spiritual meaning of the ceremony had been lost.[27]

In Eastern Europe, a boy was taken to the heder for his first lesson on any day his parents deemed appropriate and no longer on Shavuot. Here the ceremony was renamed *alef-vayzn*, showing the letter *alef*, the first letter of the Hebrew alphabet, to the child. In the nineteenth and early twentieth century, the child was sometimes carried to school wrapped in a prayer shawl or with a tefillin bag thrown over his head, a survival of the custom of concealing the pure child from the eyes of unlucky or impure persons and animals. Although late nineteenth-century heder memoirs do not refer to the baking of special cakes and the boiling of eggs with inscriptions for the first lesson, they do reveal that children were given alphabet biscuits and almonds engraved with Hebrew letters to munch, while in some places honey was still spread over letters of the alphabet on a slate. When the young boy participated in his first lesson, his father or the teacher stood

---

26. Eric Zimmer, "R. David b. Isaac of Fulda: The Trials and Tribulations of a Sixteenth Century Rabbi," *Jewish Social Studies* 45, no. 3–4 (1983): 223 and 230 note 49. Fishman, *Jewish Education*, p. 76. Assaf, *Sources*, p. 163.

27. Fishman, *Jewish Education*, p. 76. Assaf, *Sources*, pp. 58 and 59. Jacob Emden, *Migdal Oz* (Zhitomir, 1874), p. 32, section dealing with the bringing of the pupil to the teacher's house.

behind him and showered sweets or a coin on to him, as happened to my uncle in pre–World War I London. The teacher then explained to the rapt pupil that "an angel threw this down so that you will want to study." In some communities, however, new pupils were handed a glass of water in which yeast for baking hallah had been dissolved, with the symbolic message that in the same way the knowledge of the Torah would rise in the child. In place of cakes and eggs with magically potent inscriptions, parents now substituted simple gifts of sweets and coins to make the child associate the learning process with something pleasant.[28]

With the decline of magic in the seventeenth century and with the diminution of the need to memorize sacred texts because of the later abundance of printed books and primers, the magical ceremony against forgetfulness and to open the child's mind to the learning process started to disappear in the Early Modern period. By the nineteenth century the heder initiation ceremony had become somewhat trivialized, so that with the abandonment of the old heder system after the First World War, the last vestiges of the ceremony vanished among the Ashkenazim, apart from the Hasidim, who preserved certain traditions.[29]

THE ELEMENTARY SCHOOL

Whereas the more numerous Spanish Jews in the Middle Ages managed to support some communal schools, the smaller Jewish communities of Northern Europe, particularly those of France and Germany, relied on private contracts made between parents and teachers. Wealthy Jewish fathers sometimes hired teachers for poor children, as the *Sefer Ḥasidim* referred to a father who punished his son by ordering him to "fast or donate money to poor people who have nothing with which to hire tutors for their sons." In medieval Egypt and other countries in the Islamic heartland, the community maintained schools for the poor and orphans, while

---

28. Roskies, *Alphabet Instruction*, pp. 24–27. Yekhiel Shtern, "A Kheyder in Tyszowie (Tishevits)," in *East European Jews in Two Worlds: Studies from the Yivo Annual*, ed. Deborah Dash Moore (Evanston, Ill.: Northwestern University Press, 1990), p. 54.

29. Stanley Jeyaraja Tambiah, *Magic, Science, Religion, and the Scope of Rationality* (Cambridge: Cambridge University Press, 1990), pp. 18–31. Roskies, *Alphabet Instruction*, pp. 22, 48, and 49.

in later centuries these indigent pupils attended ordinary schools, at which their tuition fees were paid by the community. Even in medieval Spain the majority of parents made their own arrangements for the hiring of elementary teachers for their children, but charitable and later communal funds were made available to pay the tuition fees of poor pupils, whose numbers had been decreasing in the early fifteenth century because of the prohibitive cost of attending school, and to supplement teachers' incomes. Most medieval Jewish elementary schools had such a small enrollment of pupils that they did not assume any institutional form, the majority being conducted in the teacher's own home, nor were permanent buildings a prominent feature of West European schools until the Renaissance and Reformation.[30]

In a source from twelfth-century France, a father instructed his son's tutor to teach him the letters of the Hebrew alphabet in the first month of his studies, the vowels during the second month, and combinations of letters with vowels to form words during the third month. After this, he was to teach him the Pentateuch, starting with the opening verses of Leviticus.[31]

The aim of the medieval schools was to prepare a Jewish boy to participate fully in the synagogue service, just as Christian elementary schools prepared pupils to read the psalter and other church service books or song schools instructed choristers on how to sing hymns that were often learned by heart. Likewise, Muslim boys in the Islamic lands were taught to memorize the Koran. Adults in medieval Egypt often learned a Torah portion by heart, as the text in the scroll contained no vowels or musical notes. Incidentally, teachers between the seventh and eighth centuries experimented with vowel systems to improve their pupils' reading fluency, and ultimately the Tiberian system was chosen, as Hebrew ceased to be a language spoken in the home. Parents were proud of their sons when they were able to chant the weekly Torah portion alloted to their father or to render a simultaneous Aramaic translation of the reading, verse by verse. A business letter

---

30. Marcus, *Jewish Learning*, p. 23. Ephraim Kanarfogel, *Jewish Education and Society in the High Middle Ages* (Detroit: Wayne State University Press, 1992), pp. 20, 21, and 124 note 28 (hereafter cited as Kanarfogel, *Jewish Education*). Goitein, *Community*, pp. 183 and 186. Abraham A. Neuman, *The Jews in Spain: Their Social, Political, and Cultural Life During the Middle Ages* (New York: Octagon Books, 1980), Vol. 2, pp. 65–67 (hereafter cited as Neuman, *Jews in Spain*). Jo Ann Hoeppner Moran, *The Growth of English Schooling 1340–1548* (Princeton, N.J.: Princeton University Press, 1985), p. 14 (hereafter cited as Moran, *English Schooling*).

31. Marcus, *Jewish Schools*, p. 5.

from Cairo to a merchant in India applauded his son: "Your boy Faraj now reads the Targum [the Aramaic translation of the Pentateuch] accompanying the lections—as I guaranteed you he would." Each week the teacher would write three or four verses from the weekly portion of the Torah reading on a slate, gradually increasing this to whole chapters that the pupils learned to translate into the vernacular. Between eight and ten years, a boy was taught the prophets and the hagiographa. In addition, certain parts of the synagogue liturgy were reserved for boys to recite. At the age of ten, boys started to study the Mishnah and then a minority of the pupils went on to the Talmud at thirteen years.[32]

Among the documents surviving in the Cairo Genizah are children's exercise books and teaching aids that illuminate the pedagogic methods utilized in medieval primary schools. Pupils were assisted in mastering Hebrew by coloring enlarged letters of the alphabet drawn in outline by the teachers. Teachers also sketched these letters in black ink, around which the pupil drew a fresh outline of the letter in a glowing color. On the covers of the exercise books were drawings, such as eight intertwined snakes with the heads of fish or birds or a seven-branched candelabrum—all these teaching methods and pictorial illustrations helped to break the tedium of rote learning. Every pupil also had wooden boards to practice writing in order to recognize the Hebrew letters, but as soon as this knowledge had been acquired, writing lessons were dropped and most pupils could merely pen their signatures in a clumsy fashion.[33]

The Greeks perfected the art of memory, passing on their technique of the trained memory to the Romans, which was of supreme importance before the proliferation of the printed book and even after its advent, as texts from books were still memorized in the age of Erasmus (1466–1536). So too, the medieval Jews used all manner of mnemonic devices to help a pupil to retain what he had learned at school, in addition to employing magical techniques for boosting memory, which we have already discussed. But much of the history of memory-perfecting exercises in Jewish elementary schools remains to be written. Some of the pupils undoubtedly wore

32. Goitein, *Community*, pp. 174, 175, and 177. Moran, *English Schooling*, pp. 40, 53, 54, and 60. Edward William Lane, *An Account of the Manners and Customs of the Modern Egyptians* (written 1833–1835) (London: Ward, Lock and Bowden, n.d.), pp. 48–50 (hereafter cited as Lane, *Modern Egyptians*). William Chomsky, "Jewish Education in the Medieval Period," *Gratz College Annual* (1975): 45 (hereafter cited as Chomsky, *Medieval Jewish Education*). Abrahams, *Jewish Life*, pp. 375 and 376.

33. Goitein, *Community*, pp. 178 and 179.

special amulets and possibly a few may have taken drugs to stimulate the learning process. Of course, the principal reason for this was the shortage of books, which the pupils diligently learned to read from all directions, even upside down. The standard practice was to have the same lesson repeated three or four times, after which the pupil was supposed to study it again at home. If a pupil could not remember a lesson, he was advised "to review it forty times" to make certain that he had imbibed it. "Always repeat, if possible going back to the beginning of the tractate," counseled R. Judah ben Asher. "Our sages . . . have said . . . 'He who repeats his chapter a hundred times cannot be compared to him who repeats it a hundred and one times.'" In addition, as an aid to memory, a pupil was urged to employ all his senses, his eyes and his ears, to chant and to move his body as he studied. According to William Chomsky, one fifteenth-century grammarian, Profiat Duran, believed that "singing and multiple body-activity . . . excites 'natural warmth' (i.e., the emotions), stimulates understanding and concentration, and underpins memory and retention. This . . . is the reason for the practice of bodily swinging and swaying in vogue among 'Torah students' . . ." Similarly in Egypt, "All [the young Muslims] who are learning to read," remarked Edward William Lane in 1842, "recite, or chant their lessons aloud, at the same time rocking their heads or bodies incessantly backwards and forwards; which practice is observed by almost all persons reciting the Kur-an; being thought to assist the memory. The noise may be imagined." Magical techniques, drugs, and rhythmic chanting supported by body movement may have relaxed the pupils, thereby increasing their receptiveness to the lesson being taught to an optimum level.[34]

---

34. Frances Yates, *The Art of Memory* (London: Pimlico, 1992), pp. 11, 12, 18, 63, and 64. See Moran, *English Schooling*, p. 36. "Even with the greater accessibility of books, however, memorization, often enhanced by the use of interrogatories, remained fundamental to late medieval and early Renaissance learning." Israel Abrahams, *Hebrew Ethical Wills* (Philadelphia: Jewish Publication Society, 1926), Vol. 2, p. 172 (hereafter cited as Abrahams, *Ethical Wills*, Vol. 2). Norman Roth, "'Deal Gently with the Young Man': Love of Boys in Medieval Hebrew Poetry of Spain," *Speculum* 57, no. 1 (1982): 20. "As is evident from a variety of sources, knowledge of the Hebrew Bible by heart was far from uncommon, and not only among the highly educated. . . . Even in the late fourteenth century, for example, Isaac b. Sheshet, Rabbi of Saragossa received a query about Song of Songs 1: 2, 'for your love is better than wine.' Every schoolchild knows the passage, he was told; why then was it necessary for Rabbi Akiva to be questioned about its meaning in the Talmud (Avodah Zara 29b)?" Ibn Al-Jazzār on Forgetfulness and its Treatment, ed. and trans. Gerrit Bos. (Royal Asiatic Society: London, 1995).

What did the curriculum of these Jewish schools consist of? The Spanish Jewish community placed great emphasis on the study of the Bible, Hebrew grammar, and the law codes, whereas the educated elite progressed to the study of the Mishnah and Talmud as well as scientific and philosophical subjects. In the Ashkenazi community, among the learned families the focus was more and more on the study of the Talmud, which, according to R. Tam, encompassed many salient passages from the Bible and the whole Mishnah. R. Judah ben Asher, who emigrated to Spain from Germany, advised his sons to "appoint regular periods for studying the Bible with grammar and commentary. As in my childhood I did not study it—for in Germany they had not the custom—I have not been able to teach it here." Only a small percentage of the pupils in Jewish elementary schools in Europe and the Islamic lands were taught to write as well as to read, writing being reserved in medieval Egypt for those who wished to become merchants, doctors, and rabbis or government officials. A ruling of Hay Gaon, who died in 1038, stated that "it is permitted to teach Arabic calligraphy and arithmetic in the synagogue together with the Sacred Law," but the evidence from medieval Egypt shows that arithmetic was scarcely taught at the elementary level.[35]

Parents were instructed by the *Sefer Ḥasidim* that "if you see that he [your son] is doing well in the study of the Bible but not in the Talmud, do not compel him to learn Talmud, but if he proceeds successfully in Talmudic studies, do not force him to learn the Bible . . ." (*Sefer Ḥasidim* Bologna 308). During the Middle Ages, as was pointed out by Philippe Ariès, classes were not graded according to age or the standard reached by the pupil, a point considered by the *Sefer Ḥasidim*. "If a teacher becomes aware of the fact that some of the children are far more intelligent than others, so that it is not to their benefit to study with the others, he should not refrain from saying so. He should tell the fathers of bright pupils that these need a special teacher, even if this means for himself a financial loss" (*Sefer Ḥasidim* Bologna 308). Frequently, though, in medieval Egypt teachers were helped by relatives or employees who served as assistant teachers, thus meeting the needs of pupils at different levels.[36]

---

35. Rabinowitz, *Social Life of French Jews*, p. 216. Marcus, *Jewuish Schools*, p. 5. Abrahams, *Ethical Wills*, Vol. 2, p. 174. Goitein, *Community*, pp. 177–179.

36. Kottek, *Childhood in Sefer Ḥasidim*, pp. 387 and 388. Goitein, *Community*, p. 186.

A student of Abelard (1079–1142) had this encomium for the medieval Jewish school: "If the Christians educate their sons, they do so not
for God, but for gain, in order that the one brother, if he be a clerk, may
help his father and mother and his other brothers. They say a clerk will
have no heirs. . . . But the Jews, out of zeal for God and love of the law,
put as many sons as they have to letters, that each may understand God's
law. . . . A Jew, however poor, if he had ten sons would put them all to
letters . . . and not only his sons but his daughters."[37]

But how true was this statement? Dealing first with women, the *Sefer
Ḥasidim* asserted that bachelors should not coach girls; rather it was better for a "father to teach his daughter or his wife," and within the pietist
families in Germany there was a high standard of religious education.
Eleazar of Mainz, a fourteenth-century pietist, urged his children that "even
if compelled to solicit from others the money to pay a teacher, they must
not let the young, of both sexes, go without instruction in the Torah." A
father mourning his grown-up daughter in Egypt remembered coaching
her as a little girl: "Would I could listen to you again while I taught you the
Bible or quested you in its knowledge by heart . . .", but here in the Middle
East women sometimes assisted their fathers and husbands as teachers in
elementary schools and there were a few references to girls attending such
schools. Girls from rabbinical and prosperous families were often taught
to write, as witnessed by one of Rashi's daughters, who recorded a responsum that was dictated by him, and the tale of a pietist who decided to
teach his daughters to write. "If they do not know how to write, they will
be forced to request men to write their receipts for pledges when they
lend money. They will be alone with those men who write for them and
they may sin . . ." If only a small minority of Jewish men had acquired
writing skills, we can be certain that the percentage of women who could
wield a pen was even less than this. Yet it is likely that most Ashkenazi
women were outside the formal educational system during the Middle Ages,
as they had to follow prayer leaders in the synagogue because of their poor
reading skills, even if they were taught the major prayers and blessings,
the laws of the Sabbath, kashrut, and the appropriate modes of marital
conduct and general behavior. It was suggested for two orphan girls in
medieval Egypt that they should be taught such feminine skills as embroi-

---

37. Robert Chazan, *Medieval Jewry in Northern France: A Political and Social
History* (Baltimore: Johns Hopkins University Press, 1974), p. 52.

dery and that a private tutor should be hired, "so that they should not grow up like wild animals and not even know 'Hear Israel,'" the *Shema*.[38]

Despite all the efforts invested in the education of Jewish boys, there was still an illiterate minority in Europe; possibly in the Middle East Jewish religious instruction was more universal among males. Haim Soloveitchik observed that many of the words explained in *le Glossaire de Bale* were very simple, which indicated that there were a large number of individuals in Europe who had only a most elementary knowledge of Hebrew in the thirteenth century. In medieval France there were men who were unable to read or make the appropriate responses to prayers, while in Spain similar conditions prevailed. Solomon Freehof claimed that neglect of important religious customs was rife in medieval France, Germany, and Spain, quoting among others Joseph Bechor Shor, who denounced those Jews who neglected to wear tefillin (phylacteries) or affix mezuzot to their houses. It has been estimated after careful research that the lay reading rate in the dioceses of York in Northern England was 15 percent in 1530, giving a 20–25 percent male literacy rate; we would conclude in all probability that in the then contemporary world a majority of Jewish males could read and that in some communities reading may have been an almost universal skill.[39]

THE BAR MITZVAH AND APPRENTICESHIP

Just as the ceremony of infant baptism was devised by the Church in rivalry to the Jewish rite of circumcision, so the bar mitzvah ceremony evolved in medieval Germany in competition with the Church, which now offered

38. Judith R. Baskin, "Jewish Women in the Middle Ages," in *Jewish Women in Historical Perspective*, ed. Judith R. Baskin (Detroit: Wayne State University Press, 1991), p. 104. Judith R. Baskin, "From Separation to Displacement: The Problem of Women in *Sefer Ḥasidim*," *AJS Review* 19, no. 1 (1994): 6 and 7. Abrahams, *Ethical Wills*, Vol. 2, p. 210. Goitein, *Community*, pp. 183–185. Shoshana Pantel Zolty, *"And All Your Children Shall be Learned"* (Northvale, N.J.: Jason Aronson, 1993), p. 177.

39. Shaul Stampfer, "*Heder* Study, Knowledge of Torah, and the Maintenance of Social Stratification in Traditional East European Jewish Society," in *Studies in Jewish Education*, ed. Janet Aviad (Jerusalem: Magnes Press, 1988), Vol. 3, p. 272. Rabinowitz, *Social Life of French Jews*, pp. 220. Neuman, *Jews in Spain*, Vol. 2, p. 64. Solomon Freehof, "Home Rituals and the Spanish Synagogue," in *Studies and Essays in Honor of Abraham A. Neuman*, ed. Meir Ben-Horin, Bernard D. Weinryb, and Solomon Zeitlin (Leiden: E. J. Brill, 1962), pp. 216 and 217. Moran, *English Schooling*, pp. 223–225.

a confirmation rite to young children or to adolescents. Originally the rite of baptism, which can be traced to Matthew 3:13–16 and was essentially a Jewish purification ritual, was administered only to adults who wished to join the Christian community and seek the means of salvation within it. St. Augustine (354–430) supported the doctrine that infants should be baptized at birth because human nature was so flawed that baptism was a fundamental requirement for salvation. Bishops in fifth-century Gaul and eighth-century C.E. Germany were unable to visit all the parts of their diocese to baptize the infants, so that they left this task to their priests and later "confirmed" that this task had been effectively carried out. Gradually the interval between confirmation and baptism was extended to a few years, after which it was agreed that infants could no longer be confirmed. During the fourteenth and fifteenth centuries the confirmation of infants became rare on the Continent. The Council of Cologne in 1280 decreed that not only was seven to be the age for confirmation but that some candidates could be confirmed when they were ten years or older. Indeed, certain experts in canon law held that confirmation could not be administered to a child under twelve years of age. So in practice a unified initiation rite split into two, baptism and confirmation, of which the Jewish equivalents were circumcision and the bar mitzvah ceremony.[40]

Moreover, Ivan Marcus has argued in the *Rituals of Childhood*, just as monasteries from the twelfth century onwards refused to accept boys until they had reached the age of twelve or fourteen, so Jewish authorities in medieval Europe postponed the age of religious majority to thirteen. In both instances, the child was not permitted to take on religious obligations until he was mature enough to consent to them.

The midrash mentioned that when a boy reached the age of thirteen, his father was no longer responsible for his education, and it contained the phrase "Blessed be He, who has rid me of this responsibility" (Genesis Rabbah 63:10). Yet there was no evidence that there was a formal coming-of-age ceremony in the talmudic period as there was during the Middle Ages. R. Moses Isserles (c. 1525–1572) in his commentary on the Tur declared that the "Maharil [1355–1427] has written in the name of

---

40. Peter Cramer, *Baptism and Change in the Early Middle Ages c. 200–c. 1150* (Cambridge: Cambridge University Press, 1993). J. D. C. Fisher, *Christian Initiation: Baptism in the Medieval West: A Study of the Disintegration of the Primitive Rite of Initiation* (London: S. P. C. K., 1965), pp. 120, 123, and 140. Joseph Gutmann, *The Jewish Life Cycle* (Leiden: E. J. Brill, 1987), p. 10.

Mordecai [mid-thirteenth century] that when a man's son is bar mitzvah, he must pronounce the blessing, 'Praised be Thou, who hast rid me of the responsibility,' etc." (Orach Hayyim 225). When the Maharil's son celebrated his bar mitzvah and was called up to the reading of the Torah on the Sabbath, he recited the blessing about being relieved of responsibility for his son's misdemeanors, as the lad had come of age. The Maharil also had the custom of "bless[ing] every boy who was bar mitzvah." Aaron Ha-Cohen of Lunel (early fourteenth century), like Mordecai a rabbi from Southern France, also referred to the blessing recited by a father when divesting himself of responsibility for his son when the boy reached thirteen. Thus it was clear that the bar mitzvah ceremony had begun to evolve among the Jews in Southern France and Germany in the thirteenth or fourteenth centuries, albeit in a limited form. The principal emphasis was on the father thanking God for allowing his son to grow up and become an adult who could be called to account for his own actions. That was why Arnaldo Momigliano's attempt to push back the origins of such a ceremony in Cologne to 1120 by means of analyzing a convert's memoirs is not convincing, for he purported to find traces of a banquet, the passing of gifts, and possibly a bar mitzvah speech in this autobiographical tract, all elements that developed much later.[41]

The Christian Hebraist Johannes Buxtorf, writing in the early seventeenth century, gave an account of the bar mitzvah ceremony similar to that of R. Isserles.

> At thirteen years of age he [a boy] is called Bar Mitzvah, the son of the commandments, which he is bound to keep and observe all the commandments, in number six hundred and thirteen . . . his father calls ten Jews unto him, and in their presence witnesseth, that his son has come to full age, and being instructed in the commandments, hath learned the manner and custom of the Zizim and Tephillin . . . as also the form of blessing and his daily prayers . . . the Father saith a certain short prayer, in which chiefly he gives God thanks, that he hath delivered and unburdened him of the punishment due unto his son for his sin; further entreating him, that his son by the help of the Divine Grace, may for many days remain safe and without danger, and be industrious in good works.

---

41. Solomon B. Freehof, "Ceremonial Creativity Among the Ashkenazim," in *The Seventy-Fifth Anniversary Volume of the Jewish Quarterly Review* (1967), ed. Abraham A. Neuman and Solomon Zeitlin, pp. 219–221 (hereafter cited as Freehof, *Ceremonial Creativity*). Arnaldo Momigliano, "A Medieval Jewish Autobiography," in *History and Imagination: Essays in Honour of H. R. Trevor-Roper*, ed. Hugh Lloyd-Jones, Valerie Pearl, and Blair Worden (London: Duckworth, 1981), pp. 30–36.

So too, the Italian rabbi Leon Modena, writing in 1614 and 1615, clarified what Buxtorf said, adding "some call him [a boy over the age of bar mitzvah] . . . *Bar de minian*; that is to say, one that is of age to do any business, and may make One, in the number of Ten, that are required to be present at any of their Publick acts of Devotion. And whatever Contracts he makes, they are of force . . . in a word, both in Spirituall, and Temporal Affaires, he is absolute Lord and Master of Himself." However, it was not until the fifteenth century that the term bar mitzvah was used to connote the occasion of a youth assuming both spiritual and legal obligations (*Sefer Ziyyoni* to Gen. 1:5).[42]

Steps were taken in medieval Europe to withdraw permission for boys under thirteen to wear tefillin and to prevent them from being called up to the reading of the Law. From the twelfth century onwards, objections began to be voiced in Germany and Poland to minors putting on tefillin until it was ruled in the sixteenth century by R. Moses Isserles that boys should wait until thirteen years and a day before donning tefillin, a custom that was subsequently modified a century later in the *Magen Avraham* of R. Abraham Gumbiner (d. 1683), by stipulating that boys could practice wearing tefillin two or three months before their bar mitzvah.[43]

Again, from the thirteenth century onwards the right of minors to be called up to the reading of the Torah, which had existed since the time of the Mishnah, was gradually curtailed in Europe, perhaps in case they put adults to shame. Whereas in the twelfth century congregants in Palestine, the Balkans, and Italy could still read their portions from the Torah themselves, without the need of assistance, the precentor in thirteenth-century Germany and Bohemia took over this function, as many laymen were no longer sufficiently familiar with the text; and soon this also became the practice in France and Spain. Thus it became important for bar mitzvah

---

42. Johannes Buxtorfius, *The Jewish Synagogue* (London, 1663), pp. 69 and 70. *Encyclopaedia Judaica*, article on the "Bar Mitzvah, Bat Mitzvah," (Jerusalem: Keter Publishing House, 1971), Vol. 4, Col. 243. Leon Modena, *The History of the Rites, Customes, and Manner of Life of the Present Jews throughout the World* (London, 1650), p. 214 (hereafter cited as Modena, *Rites*).

43. Leopold Löw, *Die Lebensalter in Der Jüdischen Literatur* (Szegedin: Sigmund Burger's Wwe, 1875), p. 211 (hereafter cited as Löw, *Lebensalter*). R. Abraham Isaac Sperling, *Reasons for Jewish Customs and Traditions* (New York: Bloch, 1968), p. 27. Hayyim Schauss, *The Lifetime of a Jew Throughout the Ages of Jewish History* (New York: Union of American Hebrew Congregations, 1967), p. 115 (hereafter cited as Schauss, *Lifetime*).

boys to display their ability to read from the Torah scroll themselves on the Sabbath after they had turned thirteen and one day, and by the sixteenth century this had become obligatory among the Ashkenazim. In the seventeenth century Yuspa Shammash of Worms declared that while only bar mitzvah boys with a pleasant voice were permitted to conduct the service on this occasion, all the boys were required to read a portion from the Torah on the Sabbath. Similarly in 1738 Abraham Mears could write that in England "when Boys arrive in their thirteenth Year, they are for the first time called up to the Law that is read on the Altar in their Synagogue on the Sabbath-Day, and read a Chapter or more in the Law themselves, and when the prayers are over, the Boy's Father or Mother, or next nearest relation, gives a Treat to all the other Boys that were his School-Fellows . . . and some of those Boys Fathers . . ."[44]

Whereas in the Middle Ages the main focus of the bar mitzvah ceremony was on the father divesting himself of responsibility, during the early modern period in Europe there was a change of emphasis, a shift of attention to the boy that could perhaps be paralleled in Luther's devising of the study period before an adolescent youth could be confirmed. The obligatory call up to the Torah on the Sabbath of the bar mitzvah, the lavish party given in honor of the boy, and the talmudic discourse delivered by the youth, all focused the minds of family and friends on the new recruit to adult ranks as never before.

R. Solomon Luria (1510–1573) in Poland, when speaking of the "Bar Mitzvah party which Ashkenazim have," stated that it could not be a *seudah shel mitzvah*, a religious banquet, unless a halachic discourse was given. By the seventeenth century, so lavish were the bar mitzvah parties in scale that communal regulations were passed in an endeavor to restrict the munificence of the entertainment. In Poland the Council of the Four Lands decreed in 1659 that no more than ten strangers could be invited to a bar mitzvah feast, although it was necessary that one of the guests should be a poor man. In Worms in the seventeenth century, the bar mitzvah boy

---

44. Löw, *Lebensalter*, pp. 211 and 212. Schauss, *Lifetime*, p. 115. Ismar Elbogen, *Jewish Liturgy: A Comprehensive History*, trans. Raymond P. Scheindling (Philadelphia: Jewish Publication Society, 1993), p. 140. Assaf, *Sources*, p. 120. Herman Pollack, *Jewish Folkways in Germanic Lands 1648–1806* (Cambridge, Mass.: M.I.T. Press, 1971), p. 60 (hereafter cited as Pollack, *Folkways*). Gamaliel Ben Pedahzur [Abraham Mears], *The Book of Religion, Ceremonies, and Prayers of the Jews* (London, 1738), p. 30.

"dressed in new garments," delivered a *derashah*, a talmudic discourse, after the meal on Saturday afternoon, and followed up by reciting grace. In Germany in the eighteenth century, sumptuary laws were introduced to prevent the bar mitzvah boy wearing a wig on this occasion in an adult fashion, an indication that new distinctions were being drawn between adolescence and adulthood. In Ancona in Italy, a communal *pragmatica* ordained in 1766 that a festive banquet could not be arranged for anyone outside the immediate family on the occasion of a bar mitzvah, but that callers at the house might be supplied with coffee and sweetmeats; a similar set of communal regulations from Rome dated 1702 did not discuss the bar mitzvah ceremony, alerting us to the fact that it had probably not as yet arrived there.[45]

Even so, the medieval traditions of children participating like adults in the Sabbath and festival services lingered to a certain extent in Europe and to a greater degree throughout the Oriental Jewish communities in the Middle East. In early seventeenth-century Italy, Leon Modena remarked that on the Sabbath the lesson from the Prophets "is read by some Child, for the most part, to exercise him in Reading the Scripture," and occasionally the lesson was read by a precocious child little more than a toddler. In fact, the Bevis Marks synagogue in London has preserved an eighteenth-century mahogany stool for children to stand on while chanting the *Haftorah*, the lesson from the Prophets. In Russia, Shmarya Levin (1867–1935) declared that "the Synagogue ceremonies of the Bar Mitzvah held no terrors for me. At the age of seven I had already been called up to the pulpit for the reading of the week's section of the Prophets"; much the same was said by my own teacher, who hailed from Lithuania.[46]

From the Ashkenazi communities in Northern Italy, the custom of the bar mitzvah ceremony traveled southward, where it was slowly adopted by the Spanish Sephardim; yet the ceremony had made so little impact on

45. Freehof, *Ceremonial Creativity*, p. 220. Cecil Roth, "Bar Mitzvah—Its History and Its Association," in *Bar Mitzvah*, ed. Abraham I. Katsh (New York: Shengold, 1955), p. 20 (hereafter cited as Roth, *Bar Mitzvah*). Pollack, *Folkways*, p. 34. Assaf, *Sources*, p. 120. Isaac Rivkind, *Le-Ot u-le-Zikkaron: Bar Mitzvah: A Study in Cultural History* (New York, 1942), pp. 49–59. Hermann Vogelstein, *Rome* (Philadelphia: Jewish Publication Society, 1940), pp. 381–392.

46. Modena, *Rites*, p. 114. Robert Bonfil, *Jewish Life in Renaissance Italy* (Berkeley and Los Angeles: University of California Press, 1994), pp. 130 and 131. Roth, *Bar Mitzvah*, p. 21. Shmarya Levin, *Childhood in Exile* (London: George Routledge and Sons, 1935), p. 269.

the Sephardim in London that in the second half of the nineteenth century the Haham Benjamin Artom composed a special prayer for the occasion. Nonetheless, the bar mitzvah ceremony was unknown to the traditional Jewish communities in the Middle East and North Africa until the modern era. In a Sephardi community from Rhodes, which settled in Seattle, the institution of the bar mitzvah service on the Sabbath did not take place until the 1930s. In Shiraz in Iran the ceremony had little significance, as boys were called up to the Torah at the age of seven or eight, while there was no special party to mark the coming of age. What was stressed instead was the first occasion on which boys donned their tefillin, for which they often waited until fifteen or sixteen. So too, in Yemen, where there was no fixed age for wearing tefillin or being called up to the Torah, there was no special celebration of the Bar Mitzvah. Here Jewish lads sometimes put on tefillin at eight or nine, sometimes they waited until they were thirteen or fourteen. Just as in the talmudic age, small boys in Yemen were entitled "to read in the Torah and translate [that is, read the Aramaic translation]" (Meg. 4:6) or to intone the lesson from the Prophets (Meg. 4:5).[47]

In India in the Baghdadi community, "A boy can read *maftir* at any age, eight, nine or ten; as soon as he is able to read from the Torah, he is called up in synagogue and the first occasion is known as his *maftir*. This is a very great day and is usually celebrated with a party at home. In those days, people did not give presents for *maftir* or *barmitzva* (1920s). The parents would give the child a new suit or . . . (tallis)." Many of the Oriental Jewish communities stressed the donning of tefillin for the first time on a weekday, sometimes later celebrated with musical entertainment, as the chief characteristic of the bar mitzvah rather than the calling up to the Torah on the Sabbath, as practiced by the Ashkenazim. "On the morning of my *barmitzva*," recalled a respondent from Calcutta, "I was not allowed to eat. My father and my master made me wear my *tephellin*. My grandfather was present. I read my prayers and took off the *tephellin* and then

---

47. Freehof, p. 219. Marc D. Angel, "The American Experience of a Sephardic Synagogue," in *The American Synagogue: A Sanctuary Transformed*, ed. Jack Wertheimer (Hanover, N.H.: Brandeis University Press, 1995), p. 162. Laurence D. Loeb, *Outcaste: Jewish Life in Southern Iran* (New York: Gordon and Breach, 1977), pp. 199 and 202. S. D. Goitein, "Jewish Education in Yemen as an Archetype of Traditional Jewish Education," in *Between Past and Future: Essays and Studies on Aspects of Immigrant Absorption in Israel*, ed. Carl Frankenstein (Jerusalem: Henrietta Szold Foundation for Child and Youth Welfare, 1953), p. 115.

was allowed to eat." We would suggest that without the example of the Christian confirmation service, there was no stimulus for a bar mitzvah ceremony to develop as an important rite of passage at adolescence throughout the Muslim lands; rather there was a low-key function that was held during the week.[48]

We would conclude that the evolution of the bar mitzvah ceremony in part corroborated the cogency of Philippe Ariès' contention about the medieval blurring of the boundaries between childhood and adult status and the tendency to encourage precocious adult behavior by young children because in traditional society the years of childhood tended to be compressed. This was not altogether surprising when the average adult life span was so short. During the Middle Ages the term *adolescentia* for a few writers meant that period of life extending from birth to the age of twenty-five or thirty, but for most authorities the term was employed to define young adulthood, a period lasting from fourteen to twenty-eight years. This medieval definition did not correspond to the modern word *adolescence*. Despite the absence of a youth culture during the Middle Ages, Barbara Hanawalt questioned the argument of those historians who contend that adolescence did not exist then, declaring that there were other indicators of the phenomenon. If the dividing line between childhood and adolescence started to be defined more clearly in Western Europe from the late Middle Ages by the institution of the bar mitzvah and more sharply still from the sixteenth century, in the Middle East and to a lesser extent in Eastern Europe the ambiguous status of childhood persisted into the modern age.[49]

Another factor that helped to underscore the distinction between childhood and adolescence during the Middle Ages was the growth of apprenticeship. Although a small stratum of youths went on to study in yeshiva, the majority of Jewish adolescents were taught a trade by their father or were sent away from home to be apprenticed under a contract to a master craftsman. In Europe boys were usually apprenticed between the ages of eleven or twelve, but youths could be apprenticed at any age up to twenty.

---

48. Flower Elias and Judith Elias Cooper, *The Jews of Calcutta: The Autobiography of A Community, 1798–1972* (Calcutta: Jewish Association of Calcutta, 1974), pp. 132–134.

49. James A. Schultz, "Medieval Adolescence: The Claims of History and the Silence of German Narrative," *Speculum* 66 (1991): 519–539. Hanawalt, *Medieval London*, pp. 7–13.

If the standard length of the term of such a contract was five years, it could also be shorter. A contract from Catalonia in Spain dated 1386 made between a Jewish youth and a tailor provided that the master would feed, clothe, and teach him the trade, while the youngster would faithfully serve him for one year; in addition to the contract being signed before a notary, both parties took an oath on the Torah to uphold it. In Rome an apprenticeship contract dated 1544 and written in Hebrew stipulated that the tailoring contract was to be for three years, that the master was to board and lodge the boy, while his mother was to clothe him. In an apprenticeship contract from Fustat in Egypt dated 1027, a father hired his son to a weaver for a monthly wage of 15 dirhems for a limited period of four months, after which he was to receive the regular wage of a worker; both the father and son signed the contract with the master, which appears to indicate that the lad was over thirteen years of age. Merchants, particularly the overseas traders, sent their sons to relatives or business colleagues to learn the necessary skills; and parents sometimes came to an arrangement with a merchant to teach their children arithmetic and writing.[50]

Not all the relationships between the apprentices and their masters were always happy. Rabbi Solomon Ibn Adret in Spain decided in one instance that where a boy was discontented with his master, he could break the contract of apprenticeship, provided that he was acting as an independent person in talmudic law. A merchant in Palermo in Italy wrote an anxious letter to a relative in Old Cairo about his own son, who was living there with him: "Do not leave Joseph without your secure guidance. . . . Do not let him go around with [hole in the manuscript] . . . He is with you. My son is your son. My pride is your pride. . . . You know the boy. This is his first travel abroad . . ."[51]

Moreover, there was evidence in medieval Jewish society of generational conflict between elders and youth both in Egypt and Southern France, where R. Isaac penned some bitter words. Modest women sometimes "give birth to unworthy sons, who speak shamefully to their mother and do not refrain from spitting in their father's face . . ." In the medieval Middle East, youths and men in their twenties joined forces against the respectable, well-

50. Shahar, *Medieval Childhood*, pp. 227–229 and 231–237. Mark Wischnitzer, *A History of Jewish Crafts and Guilds* (New York: Jonathan David, 1965), pp. 112 and 144 (hereafter cited as Wischnitzer, *Crafts*). Goitein, *Family*, p. 237. Goitein, *Community*, pp. 177 and 191–192.

51. Wischnitzer, *Crafts*, p. 112. Goitein, *Family*, pp. 62, and 191–192.

established citizens in conflicts within the Jewish community. Marriage thus marked only a partial departure from the ranks of adolescence. Although sixteen for a girl and eighteen for a boy was considered a proper age to marry, it was still thought meritorious to conclude a marriage for daughters at thirteen or fourteen and for boys a couple of years later. In medieval Egypt and elsewhere, families were not eager to employ orphan girls as domestics, and a solution to their economic predicament was sought in arranging an early marriage for them.[52]

RESTRICTIONS ON INFANTICIDE, ABANDONMENT, AND THE KILLING OF CHILDREN

Although it was argued by Immanuel Jakobovits that infanticide was an unknown phenomenon among Jews, a careful examination of the medieval sources shows that this was not the case. Without understanding the Church's position on this issue, it is impossible to make sense of the Jewish response; and we shall now proceed to sketch the European Christian background. Synodal legislation from Mainz of 853 C.E. and penitential handbooks from Worms of the eleventh century were concerned with the overlaying of infants, that is, of the mothers intentionally or accidentally smothering them when feeding them in bed at night; both towns, it should be noted, were also leading rabbinic centers. But it was not until the eleventh and twelfth centuries that the campaign of the Church against the exposure and overlaying of infants gathered momentum. This can best be seen in the successive synods of the English Church in the thirteenth century, which sought not only to punish delinquent parents whose negligence had resulted in their children's death but to admonish ignorant parents. Mothers were warned not to take their babies into their beds to prevent them from overlaying them, and parents were also advised not to leave their infant children alone in the house because of the danger from fires or near to water without someone supervising them.[53]

---

52. Marc Saperstein, *Decoding the Rabbis: A Thirteenth Century Commentary on the Aggadah* (Cambridge, Mass.: Harvard University Press, 1980), p. 39. Goitein, *Community*, pp. 61 and 62. Jacob Katz, *Tradition and Crisis: Jewish Society at the End of the Middle Ages*, trans. Bernard Dov Cooperman (New York: Schocken Books, 1993, p. 116. Goitein, *Family*, pp. 306 and 307.

53. Zefira Entin Rokeah, "Unnatural Child Death Among Christians and Jews in Medieval England," *Journal of Psychohistory* 18, no. 2 (Fall 1990): 203, 224, and 225

In response to this heightened concern in the Church to the problem of overlaying, the rabbis began to take action in Germany in the thirteenth century. An early thirteenth-century rabbinic responsum bluntly stated that "women who find their infants dead near them in bed are considered to be malicious and should be treated severely." Nevertheless, Ephraim Urbach discovered that it was only in the late thirteenth century that rabbinic authorities began to deal extensively with the issue of overlaying. R. Meir of Rothenburg (1215–1295) declared that if a mother nursing a child was going to sleep, she should ensure that she did not fall asleep with her child, for this was akin to a criminal act. On the other hand, the later Polish authority R. Slonik (c. 1550–c. 1619) sought to differentiate between this situation and one where a maid placed a child in its mother's arms, at the same time putting the mother's breast in the baby's mouth; later the child was found dead. The maid claimed that the mother cursed her when she originally handed her the child, but the mother stated that she could not remember anything, and the decision here was that the mother should be dealt with leniently. In another earlier case of overlaying, the Maharil (1355–1427) decided that he could not be too strict with the wife, as she was only a child herself. Among the penances ordered by the rabbis were the observance of many fast days and abstaining from meat and wine during the week as well as prohibiting a mother from taking her child into bed, the last in line with the exhortations of the Church.[54]

Aside from the problems connected with overlaying, the group of infants who were most at risk were the illegitimate infants of unmarried mothers. An analysis of records from Nuremberg from 1513 to 1777 demonstrates that of the eighty-seven women executed for infanticide, all except four of these unfortunates were unmarried girls. Illegitimate children enjoyed a superior status among Jews; in any case their percentage was much smaller than in the surrounding population, so that the deliberate murder of illegitimate infants was seldom encountered among Jews. Jewish communal ordinances in Crete in 1238 specified that because men entered the "houses of their future father-in-law to eat and drink there," it "happens that as a result indiscretions are committed, and this has led

---

note 139 (hereafter cited as Rokeah, *Unnatural Child Death*). McLaughlin, *Survivors*, pp. 120, 121, 156 note 102, and 157 note 104.

54. Rokeah, *Unnatural Child Death*, pp. 205 and 226 note 149. Ephraim E. Urbach, "Unintentionally Caused Death and Cradle Death," (Hebrew) *Assufot: Annual for Jewish Studies* 1 (1986–1987): 319–332, but particularly pp. 321–323.

even to an attempt at abortion and to infant-murder." Again, Meir of Rothenburg, in a responsum dated 1271, mentioned a dissolute Jewish wife "who bore a bastard daughter by a Gentile and then killed her child" during her husband's absence on a lengthy business trip. However, such instances were isolated and rare.[55]

According to John Boswell, "There is little indication that Jews abandoned their offspring in the High Middle Ages . . .", whereas in medieval Europe this was a major social problem, with the foundation of homes for foundlings becoming increasingly common. Maimonides' examination of the issue of an abandoned child in the *Mishneh Torah* was little more than a réchauffé of talmudic material, so that it is doubtful whether his discussion had more than theoretical relevance. Instances of Jews abandoning their offspring during the medieval period were rare. Ninth-century chronicles from Languedoc in Southern France related that Christians and Jews sold their children into slavery on account of the disruptions caused by the Muslim invasion of Spain in 711 C.E. Salo Baron reported an account in a different French chronicle that claimed that because of the fiscal oppression due to the despotic rule of Hisham 1 (788–796 C.E.) in Spain, many Jews and Christians "sold their sons and daughters into slavery, and only a few remained living in great poverty." From the ample documentation surviving in the Cairo genizah, it appears that Jewish orphans in medieval Egypt were a communal responsibility eligible for distributions of bread and other benefits twice a week, and they were not left sleeping rough in the streets.[56]

We now turn to an examination of the medieval ritual murder allegations against the Jews, as it may reveal the underlying similarities and differences in Jewish and Christian family life during the Middle Ages. Because there was little emotional bonding between parents and children among

---

55. William Langer, "Infanticide: A Historical Survey," *History of Childhood Quarterly* 1, no. 3 (Winter 1974): 353–365. Magdalene Schultz, "The Blood Libel: A Motif in the History of Childhood," in *The Blood Libel Legend*, ed. Alan Dundes (Madison: University of Wisconsin Press, 1991), p. 285 (hereafter cited as Schultz, *Blood Libel*). Rokeah, *Unnatural Child Death*, pp. 225 and 226 note 146.

56. John Boswell, *The Kindness of Strangers: The Abandonment of Children in Western Europe from Late Antiquity to the Renaissance* (New York: Pantheon Books, 1988), pp. 217, 350, and 351. Salo Baron, *A Social and Religious History of the Jews* (New York: Columbia University Press, 1957), Vol. 3, pp. 169 and 312 note 56. Goitein, *Family*, p. 305.

the general population in the Middle Ages, there was a primitive process of splitting in early childhood; hence the later recurrent images of the good child, the murder victim, who was equated with the young Jesus, and the bad father, the Jew or Jesus' father. In the later Oedipal phase of childhood, there was hostility between sons and fathers because the fathers feared that their heirs would supplant them. At the same time, the Oedipal constellation triggered the underlying pathology of splitting, and the demonization of the bad father, the Jew. Sometimes the murderous rage of the fathers led to the death of a child, who was persistently ill-treated and beaten to death or so badly neglected that he died in an accidental death.

An examination of thirteenth-century eyre or circuit court rolls by Zefirah Entin Rokeah established that despite the inclusion of three hundred Jewish names, none were accused of being involved in "the death of children [under the age of twelve] from fire, from scalding, through overlaying, or from animals. Nor, with the possible exception of the drowned Sampson son of Josceus, do I know of any case where . . . a Jew was associated with the accidental death of a Jewish child." All the foregoing were common causes of the death of children in thirteenth-century England, particularly death by drowning in streams and ditches or death caused intentionally by an adult or older child. The only Jewish case of an accidental drowning was of Sampson son of Josceus of York, who fell into a well or pit outside Norwich castle while picking flowers and who died as a result.[57]

Although, as we have seen in the previous chapter, the majority of the population in traditional society accepted with some equanimity the death of children under the age of three years, the sudden death of older children was viewed as disturbing and with some morbid horror. In the twelfth and thirteenth centuries, the Church in Western Europe espoused the doctrine of transubstantiation, whereby the bread and wine utilized by the priest during the mass was said to become transformed into the flesh and blood of Jesus; and the eucharist became a magically charged ceremony with dire consequences for the marginal figures and outsiders in Christian society—old women, who were denounced as witches, and Jews, who were denigrated as demons. Thus the unexplained disappearances or deaths of children, mostly boys aged between three and twelve years, who were depicted in the art of the Romanesque period as youthful angels and Church

---

57. Rokeah, *Unnatural Child Death*, pp. 189, 190, 204 and 205.

attendants, were attributed to the malign action of the Jews and witches. Parents of children who died from neglect, in accidents, or from persistent battering often denied their hostility to their own children and projected it collectively onto members of the local Jewish community, many of whom were condemned to death on fabricated ritual murder charges. Examples of such accidental deaths were the boy who died in the Severn River at Pershore near Gloucester in 1168, "the poor scholar found dead in their latrines" and alleged by the Pope to have been killed by the Jews of France in 1205, and St. Hugh of Lincoln, a boy who probably "fell by misadventure into a well . . ."[58]

The ritual murder charges starting with the accusation in Norwich in 1144 focused for a century on an allegation that the Jews annually re-enacted the passion of Jesus at Passover-Easter by stealing a Christian boy aged between three and twelve and crucifying him. In 1235 in Fulda in Germany a startlingly novel accusation was leveled against the Jews, the blood libel, that is, that the Jews required the blood of a Christian boy, whom they allegedly murdered for their own ritualistic purposes. Incidentally, the Fulda incident fits into this category of accidental and negligent deaths, as five boys died in a fire in a mill when their parents left them to attend Church on Christmas Day. The Christians of Fulda, aware that Jews carefully watched over their offspring and that they were reluctant to abandon them, projected their envy and guilt onto the local Jewish population for their failure to save the innocent and pure children. In Christian eucharistic fantasies in Central and Eastern Europe, the Jews were said to need the blood of a young boy for the baking of matzah at Passover or "the blood of a Christian was [alleged to be] a good remedy for the alleviation of the wound of circumcision." Thus by a process of projection Jews were accused of consuming the flesh and blood of a sacrificial victim, the dead child, who was regarded as being akin to the Christian savior. Until these projective fantasies could be overcome, children continued to be ill-treated in many Christian families especially in Central Europe. At an official level in Germany, the emperors and the legal profession, with the added help

---

58. R. Po-chia Hsia, *The Myth of Ritual Murder: Jews and Magic in Reformation Germany* (New Haven: Yale University Press, 1988), pp. 9 and 11 (hereafter cited as Hsia, *Myth*). Zefira Entin Rokeah, "The State, the Church, and the Jews in Medieval England," in Shmuel Almog, *Antisemitism Through the Ages* (Oxford: Pergamon Press, 1989), p. 106. Gavin I. Langmuir, *Toward a Definition of Antisemitism* (Berkeley and Los Angeles: University of California Press, 1990), pp. 241, 262, 270, and 271 (hereafter cited as Langmuir, *Antisemitism*).

of the Protestants after the Reformation, undermined the credibility of the ritual murder charges in the fifteenth and sixteenth centuries; but at a popular level, ritual murder allegations survived well into the twentieth century in the Catholic Rhineland and Poland.[59]

In turn, the medieval Christian emphasis on the magical elements of the eucharist ceremony, the transformation of the wafer and the wine into the flesh and blood of Jesus, and the doctrine of the redemptive qualities of the blood of the Christian savior may have affected German Jewry. Despite a more active involvement in the rearing of their children than their Christian neighbors, there was a similar lack of empathy (Magdalene Schultz) and sometimes the same murderous Oedipal fantasies and drives against their own children. How else are we to explain the slaughter of Jewish children by their parents during the First Crusade in 1096 rather than permit a temporary conversion until the situation eased, as happened in the Muslim lands, and the graphic descriptions of these sacrifices in the Hebrew Chronicles? There was almost no precedent for these actions either in Jewish history, apart from the isolated instance of Massada, or in halachah. Nor were such ritual slayings of children repeated during the Holocaust.[60]

Yet the Hebrew Chronicles extolled the actions of the Jewish martyrs who killed their own children, a tactic designed to shock readers and to hasten the heavenly redemption of vengeance. Isaac ben David, a prominent Jew in Mainz, after a hasty conversion to save his children regretted his action and

> the pious one asked his children: "Do you wish that I sacrifice you to our God?" They said: "Do what you will with us" . . . Isaac the saintly one took his two children, his son and his daughter, and led them through the courtyard at midnight

---

59. Langmuir, *Antisemitism*, pp. 237–281. Joshua Trachtenberg, *The Devil and the Jews: The Medieval Conception of the Jew and Its Relation to Modern Anti-Semitism* (Philadelphia: Jewish Publication Society, 1983), pp. 147, 149, and 150. Jeremy Cohen, *The Friars and the Jews: The Evolution of Medieval Anti-Judaism* (Ithaca, N.Y.: Cornell University Press, 1983), p. 239. Hsia, *Myth*, pp. 226–228. Edward Timms, "Between Holocaust and Symbiotics: New Approaches to German-Jewish Studies," *Jewish Quarterly* 154 (Summer 1994): 57 and 58. James F. Harris, *The People Speak! Antisemitism and Emancipation in Nineteenth Century Bavaria* (Ann Arbor: University of Michigan Press, 1994), p. 29. *The Blood Libel Legend*, ed. Alan Dundes (Madison: University of Wisconsin Press, 1991), passim.

60. Schultz, *Blood Libel*, p. 285. David Biale, "Blood Libels and Blood Vengeance," *Tikkun* 9:4 (July/August 1994): 19. (hereafter cited as Biale, *Blood Libel*).

and brought them to the synagogue before the holy ark, and slaughtered them
there for the sanctification of the great name, the sublime and exalted God, who
commanded us never to deny his awe . . . and to cleave to his holy Torah. . . . He
spilled their blood on the pillars of the holy ark, so that they would come as a
memorial before the unique and everlasting King and before the throne of his glory.
[He said:] "May this blood serve me as an atonement for all my sins."

Again, Rachel from the same town killed all her four children, without
mercy, before dying herself:

The woman took the lad and slaughtered him—he was small and exceedingly
comely. The mother spread her sleeve to receive the blood; she received the blood
in her sleeves instead of in the [Temple] vessel for blood. The lad Aaron, when he
saw that his brother had been slaughtered, cried out: "Mother, do not slaughter
me!" He went and hid under a bureau. She still had two daughters, Bella and
Matrona, comely and beautiful young women. . . . They stretched forth their necks
and she sacrificed them to the Lord God of Hosts . . . she . . . called to her son:
"Aaron, Aaron, where are you? I shall not have mercy nor pity on you as well."
She pulled him by the leg from under the bureau where he was hidden and she
sacrificed him . . .[61]

Israel Yuval has recently suggested in a controversial article as summarized by David Biale that "the medieval Rhineland Jews believed [similar to
the medieval Christians] that the blood of the martyrs would reach
the divine throne, where it would stain God's coat and act as a magical agent
to cause Him to avenge his slaughtered children." So too, the *Sefer H.asidim*
proclaimed that if anyone had been martyred in a house, the blood stains
should not be hidden. "As long as the blood is not covered, God will take
vengeance and when it is covered He will not hurry to avenge." Hence the
killing by the Jews of their own children owed something to the Christian
ideas of blood and redemption that were circulating in medieval Europe.
Yuval's other assertion that the continental Jews' willingness to slaughter
their own children unleashed the charges of the ritual murder of Christian
children has also been accepted by many historians. New research demonstrates that the ritual murder accusations first originated in the German speaking lands in the early twelfth century, not in England as previously thought.[62]

---

61. Chazan, *First Crusade*, pp. 103–105, 111, and 112.

62. Israel Jacob Yuval, "Vengeance and Damnation, Blood and Defamation: From
Jewish Martyrdom to Blood Libel Accusations," *Zion* 58, no. 1 (1993): 33–90. Biale,
Blood Libel, pp. 39 and 40. For the controversy see *Zion* 59, no. 2–3 (1994). Willis
Johnson 111 lecture to the Jewish Historical Society London on "Recent work on the
English origins of the Blood Libel" 27th June 1996.

What arguments did the Jews in the Middle Ages use to justify the killing of their own children? The notion that Isaac was almost slaughtered by Abraham was advanced in the Hebrew Chronicles and liturgical poems to buttress the view that taking the life of members of one's own family was permissible in certain desperate situations. "Please inquire and find out as to whether there ever was such a mass *aqedah* [binding in preparation for a sacrifice] from the days of Adam; have there ever been eleven hundred *aqedot* in a single day, all of them like the *aqedah* [binding] of Isaac son of Abraham? A single one performed on Mount Moriah shook the world . . ." Moreover, R. Tam, a twelfth-century Tosafist, praised the four hundred youngsters mentioned in the Talmud, "who were taken captive for immoral purposes and threw themselves into the sea." When R. Meir of Rothenburg was asked whether atonement was required by a man who killed his wife and children with their consent, he replied as follows: "This is a matter whose permissibility has been widely accepted, for we have heard of a great many rabbis who slaughtered their sons and daughters. . . . And anyone who requires atonement for this is besmirching the name of the pious men of old." Another apologist held that "we fear lest such children [who cannot distinguish between good and evil] be assimilated bodily among the gentiles as they mature. It is better that they die in innocence than that they later die in guilt."[63]

Even in the late fifteenth century, preachers addressing a Spanish audience mulled over the relevance of the sacrifice of Isaac for their contemporaries, as witness the following passage that appears in two distinct sources:

> Rabbi Hasdai [Crescas] said that Abraham's act had this significance: in preparing to sacrifice Isaac upon the altar, he prepared to sacrifice all the generations of his descendants, for it was already promised that *through Isaac offspring will be referred to as yours* (Gen. 21:12). . . . Through his actions he also taught us, as it were, that all those who want to be among the descendants of Abraham must be prepared to offer their lives for the sanctification of God's Name when the proper time comes. . . . Every Jew should think that, being from the seed of Abraham, a father should be prepared to kill his child . . . as Abraham did, in order to fulfill the will of his heavenly Father.

We can now discern that the murderous rage directed against their offspring by medieval Jewish parents was not unique to Germany for a short

---

63. Salo Baron, *A Social and Religious History of the Jews* (New York: Columbia University Press, 1957), Vol. 4, p. 144 (hereafter cited as Salo, Baron, Vol. 4). Chazan, *First Crusade*, pp. 156–158. David Berger, *The Jewish Christian Debate in the High Middle Ages* (Northvale, NJ: Jason Aronson, 1996), p. 26.

period of time, but later affected the Sephardim as well and sprang from the basic personality structure of the medieval Jew.[64]

Other medieval Jewish authorities were not so certain about the merits of mass suicide. One of the German rabbis who had killed many infants was challenged by another rabbi, who "called him a murderer. . . . The [second] rabbi said: 'If I am correct, let that rabbi be killed in an unusual way.' Thus it was. . . . Subsequently the persecution subsided. If he had not slaughtered those infants, they would have been saved." Modern historians also share these doubts as to whether the Almighty "required the medieval German Jews to sacrifice themselves and their children."[65]

Having dealt with the martyrdom of Jewish children, we now turn to the question of the seizure of Jewish children and their forced conversion by Christians. Thomas Aquinas (c. 1225–1274) reformulated the prevailing moderate position of churchmen on the contentious issue of the forced conversion of Jewish children: "It was never the custom of the Church to baptize Jewish children against the will of their parents. . . . There are two reasons for this custom: One is on account of the danger to the faith [of these children when they come of age. The other because] it is against natural justice." Nonetheless, the Pope in 1201 proclaimed that once children were baptized, even without their parents' consent, they had to remain in the Christian faith. Such attitudes were of long standing, and Jews in Northern France as early as the ninth century sent their children to Arles to make them safe from the pressure to convert to Christianity. During the onslaughts against the Jews from 1096 onwards and the troubled aftermath of these pogroms, there was disruption of Jewish family life and a constant leakage of Jewish children from the faith of their fathers. For instance, when the Jews were massacred in Rouen during the First Crusade, a child was rescued and fostered by a local aristocratic family, ending his days as a devout monk at Saint-Germer. In the eleventh century a count of Macon seized a Jewish boy and made certain he was brought up as a Christian; in the following century Hermann, a Jewish apostate, kidnapped his seven-year-old brother and left him in a monastery at Flonheim. In Friedburg during the sixteenth century the Christian guardian of a Jewish boy refused to return him to his father, claiming that he desired to be baptized. Without doubt, we have only the most frag-

---

64. Marc Saperstein, *Jewish Preaching 1200–1800: An Anthology* (New Haven: Yale University Press, 1989), p. 83.

65. Chazan, *First Crusade*, p. 157. David Abulafia, *1492: The Expulsion from Spain and Jewish Identity* (London: Leo Baeck College, 1992), pp. 29 and 30.

mentary knowledge about the scale of such conversions, but they must have been appreciable after a riot had decimated a Jewish community and caused its dispersal, and the known instances of the conversion of children could be multiplied many times over.[66]

In the thirteenth century the Franciscans appear to have been aware of the martyrdom of Jewish children at the hands of their parents, so much so that they hardened the line of the Church on the issue of forced conversion. Duns Scotus (c. 1270–1308), a Franciscan schoolman, maintained that a ruler had the right to promote the compulsory conversion of Jewish minors because of his assumption that they would otherwise be condemned to perdition, especially if they suffered an early death inflicted by their own parents. Thus it was necessary to remove newly baptized children from the homes of their parents and have them brought up in a proper Christian environment elsewhere to prevent any relapses. According to a Continental Jewish source under the influence of this doctrine, when the Jews were expelled from England in 1290, many children were prevented from leaving with their parents and were forcibly converted to Christianity. Again, in 1493 when Portugal was inundated with Jewish refugees from Spain, the government forcibly baptized a large number of children, separated them from their parents, and shipped some seven hundred youngsters to the sugar island of São Tomé in the Gulf of Guinea, so that they should be far removed from any Jewish community. Influenced like so many other fifteenth- and early sixteenth-century intellectuals by the earlier Franciscan debate on the subject of conversion, Ulrich Zasius in 1508 supported the view that "the prince or anyone else in authority over Jews not only may, but he ought to cause, Jewish children to be baptized. . . . The second conclusion is . . . any good Christian may, and ought to, under any circumstances, baptize a child of a Jew or heathen without parental consent."[67]

In 1497 the Portuguese government not only issued a decree forcibly baptizing all Jewish children between the ages of four and fourteen and

---

66. Salo Baron, *A Social and Religious History of the Jews* (New York: Columbia University Press, 1965), Vol. 9, pp. 15 and 16 (hereafter cited as Salo Baron, Vol. 9). Salo Baron, Vol. 4, p. 55. McLaughlin, *Survivors*, pp. 122 and 160 note 123. Hsia, *Myth*, p. 112.

67. Mary Minty, "Kiddush Ha-Shem in German Christian Eyes in the Middle Ages," *Zion* 59, no. 2–3 (1994): 209–266. Salo Baron, Vol. 9, pp. 16 and 17. Hsia, *Myth*, pp. 112–119. Salo Baron, *A Social and Religious History of the Jews* (New York: Columbia University Press, 1957), Vol. 5, p. 113, and Vol. 11, 1967, p. 247. David Brion Davis, "The Slave Trade and the Jews," *New York Review of Books* 41, no. 21 (22 December 1994): 15.

removing them from their parents' control, but applied the decree to many youths and maidens up to the age of twenty. In contrast to the situation in medieval Germany, the conversion of families was far more widespread than the resort to the extreme option of mass suicide. One notable exception was Abraham ibn Zachin, who killed himself and his children to sanctify the divine name. Friendly Christian neighbors sometimes assisted Jewish families by taking in their children and so nullifying the implementation of the decree. However, most of the children who were dispatched to the island of São Tomé perished from privation and disease.[68]

On the other hand, the Venetian government, after a Jewish baby was baptized against the will of its mother in 1616, challenged the right of the papacy to enforce such conversions and resolved to return Jewish minors to their fathers. Further, in Bordeaux in the 1720s, a Christian maid baptized the three daughters of a communal leader, Abraham Mezes, who never secured their return, although the community extracted a royal decree forbidding the Church to accept converts under the age of twelve. Until the French Revolution, Jewish children in the town of Carpentras were frequently abducted and baptized throughout the eighteenth century. In 1858 there was the notorious Mortara case in Italy, when a Christian servant girl in Bologna claimed that she had some years previously secretly baptized a one-year-old baby, Edgardo Mortara, whom she thought was dying. As a result, the young boy was apprehended by the police and spirited away to Rome to be brought up as a Christian, despite worldwide protest. There were a number of forcible conversions of Jewish children in Rome in the 1860s, which were only partially redressed by the Italian government some years later, when the Papal State was vanquished in 1870. Nevertheless, these conversions were not quite a last splutter of waning papal political power, as witnessed in, among others, the Finaly case in France in 1953. Thus progress by the secular state authorities in checking the excessive proselytizing zeal of the Church, which was directed at Jewish children, was intermittent, so that it was only in the second half of the twentieth century that effective curbs were applied against the forcible conversion of minors.[69]

---

68. Heinrich Graetz, *History of the Jews* (Philadelphia: Jewish Publication Society, 1946), Vol. 4, pp. 371 and 373–378. Cecil Roth, *A History of the Marranos* (New York: Schocken Books, 1974), pp. 57–61.

69. Riccardo Caliman, *The Ghetto of Venice* (New York: M. Evans and Co., 1987), pp. 124 and 125. Arthur Hertzberg, *The French Enlightenment and the Jews* (New

In Russia under Tsar Nicholas I it has been estimated that some 70,000 Jewish recruits were drafted into the Russian army from 1827 to 1854, of whom 50,000 were below the age of eighteen. While the Russian authorities indicated that they preferred underage recruits, who were sent to special Cantonist battalions, there is no evidence that they put pressure on the heads of the Jewish community, who voluntarily complied with their wishes. What was a new phenomenon in the nineteenth century was the fact that the Jewish leaders were in a sense accomplices in the government's policy of enforced conversion. There was the widespread enlistment of children under the age of twelve, who were snatched from their poverty-stricken families by teams of kidnappers known as *khappers* in Yiddish. The writer Y. L. Katsenelson denounced these men, declaring that "all the *khappers* were in fact Jews, Jews with beards and sidelocks. . . . In the past, there were Gentiles who held a cross in one hand and a knife in the other, and said: 'Jew, kiss the cross or die,' and the Jews preferred death to apostasy. But now there come Jews, religious Jews, who capture children and send them off to apostasy." Once in the army the children were subjected to beatings and torture unless they converted, were not allowed to wear tefillin or pray, and were fed on food cooked in lard and given pork to eat. Not surprisingly about 25,000 of these youngsters apostasized, but they often remained alienated when they were discharged from the army. The grandfather of Lenin was one of these Jewish Cantonists.[70]

There is one final topic regarding the treatment of children that we must briefly deal with: homosexual relations between adult males and boys. In Spain, particularly in the Muslim period, love of boys was a common theme in Hebrew verse, as it was in ancient Greek, medieval Muslim, and Christian poetry. What interests us was the departure from the norms of Judaism, which condemned homosexuality, particularly the Greek type of relationship involving love between men and boys; and the concentration in much of the writing of four of the greatest medieval Spanish Jewish poets, Samuel Ibn Nagrillah, Solomon Ibn Gabirol, Moses Ibn Ezra, and Judah Ha-Levi on the love of young boys, who had not reached puberty

---

York: Columbia University Press, 1968), p. 226. Marianne Calmann, *The Carrière of Carpentras* (Oxford: Oxford University Press, 1984), pp. 188–192. Vogelstein, *Rome*, pp. 343, 344, 355, and 356. Cecil Roth, *The History of the Jews in Italy* (Philadelphia: Jewish Publication Society, 1946), pp. 471–472.

70. Michael Stanislawski, *Tsar Nicholas I and the Jews: The Transformation of Jewish Society in Russia 1825–1855* (Philadelphia: Jewish Publication Society, 1983), pp. 23–39.

and whose cheeks were not covered with hair. So too, the courtier and poet Todros ben Judah Halevi (1247–c. 1306) set out the advantages of love for youths over that for women. Homosexuality was widespread in Muslim Spain and was found on a lesser scale in the Christian North, so that Jews were often susceptible to the latest sexual fashion. We hear in one responsum from Spain about a cantor who was removed from office partly because he was consorting with prostitutes, partly because it was reported that he had sexual relations with a youth. In Aragon in 1328 three Jews charged with sodomy were released on the order of Alfonso IV, but another Jew was executed in 1374 for homosexual offenses. Many of these acts would now be classified as the sexual abuse of children, but we would stress that this phenomenon was little known in other medieval Jewish communities.[71]

CONCLUSION

On the positive side, there was the growth of the individual personality in Western Europe in the late eleventh and twelfth centuries, with emphasis placed on inner motivation and a degree of emotional development. The elaborate devices to protect the child during the watch-night and at the circumcision, the first cradling ceremony after the circumcision, the induction of the growing boy into the heder, the almost universal proliferation of these Jewish elementary schools, all attest to the love and concern of medieval Jewish parents for their children. On the other hand, Issachar Ben-Ami explained that in traditional society "the infant joins not only the family group, but also a wider framework. His birth, his existence, and his life are the fruit of communal effort and not just that of the parents." The birth and gradual maturity of the child ensured communal renewal and expansion. Through the civilizing process the group-based mentalities so prominent in Jewish communities in the earlier Middle Ages gradually disappeared in Western Europe. Did this, in fact, mean that certain ties of closeness, of empathy, were lacking in the medieval Jewish family, as Magdalene Schultz has suggested? We have noted how in the early mod-

71. Norman Roth, "'Deal Gently with the Young Man': Love of Boys in Medieval Hebrew Poetry of Spain," *Speculum* 57, no. 1 (1982): 20–51. Yom Tov Assis, "Sexual Behaviour in Medieval Hispano-Jewish Society," in *Jewish History*, ed. Ada Rapoport-Albert and Steven J. Zipperstein (London: Peter Halban, 1988), pp. 50 and 51.

ern period the bar mitzvah ceremony developed among Ashkenazi communities with increased attention paid to the child, how the circumcision rite became an intimate family affair, and how the initiation ceremony into the heder shrank in significance. All these examples seem to indicate the deeper intimacy of family life during the early modern period and support Schultz's contention. Moreover, the evolution of the romantic concept of the pure, unsullied child was impeded during the Middle Ages because of the projected fantasies of Christian and Jewish parents: the only pure children were the alleged victims of Jewish ritual murders or child martyrs from Jewish families who acquiesced in their own slaying.[72]

On the other hand, the much higher rates of infant survival among Jews when records commence, the tendency for wet nurses to stay with their infant charges in their employers' homes, the almost complete absence of the deliberate murder of infants by Jews, except during a medieval pogrom when parents were trying to protect children from conversion, the reluctance of Jews to abandon their children, and the much lower accident rates for children because of their constant supervision—all these factors point to a higher and perhaps more caring standard of medieval Jewish family life. In sixteenth century Italy R. Meir Katzenellenbogen, commenting on the aggadic passage that small children should be brought to listen to sermons even when they did not understand them, remarked that this was obvious. For "even if parents were not commanded to bring their pre-school children [to the synagogue], they would bring them of their own accord out of fear lest they be harmed if they are left at home with no adult around." Again, if the elementary school was almost universal among medieval Jews, this meant that young boys tended to be under adult surveillance for most of the day, thus reducing the chance of accidental mishaps. Scattered throughout the last two chapters are many examples of the active and caring involvement of both Jewish parents in the rearing of their young children, particularly toddlers, which undermines Ariès' conclusion about such interaction being scarcely existent in medieval society.[73]

---

72. Issachar Ben-Ami, "Customs of Pregnancy and Childbirth among Sephardic and Oriental Jews," in *New Horizons in Sephardic Studies*, ed. Yedida Stillman and George K. Zucker (Albany: State University of New York Press, 1992), p. 261 (hereafter cited as Ben-Ami, *Customs*).

73. Marc Saperstein, "Italian Jewish Preaching: An Overview," in *Preachers of the Italian Ghetto*, ed. David B. Ruderman (Berkeley and Los Angeles: University of California Press, 1992), pp. 32 and 33.

Does this evidence also contradict Schultz's conclusion about a certain lack of empathy for their children shared with their Christian neighbors? No, not completely. If relations between parents and children had been less stiff and formalized and less hierarchical, and if Jewish parents in medieval Germany had not possessed a primitive, murderous rage, they would not have massacred their own children before committing suicide themselves. Against this must be balanced the solicitude of Jewish mothers and the maternal warmth of Jewish fathers and the self-questioning in pietist circles, which after many generations of effort grew increasingly stronger in the late Middle Ages and may have produced a qualitative change in the range of emotional feeling in the Jewish family by the sixteenth century that could be classed as empathic. In short, what we are asserting was that with the strengthening of ego controls the murderous fantasies of fathers could not be enacted; hence the response of the Sephardi fathers after the expulsion from Spain was more muted than that of the Ashkenazim in Germany at the time of the Crusades; hence the late medieval period in Northern Europe saw major developments in childrearing practices, which in turn triggered vital changes in the early modern era.

During the Middle Ages, the important divisions in a person's life were those at the age of five or six years, marking a distinction between infancy and childhood, and those around twenty-eight and thirty, when respectable and economically established adults were differentiated from adolescents. As Robert Bonfil has admitted, there was a "lack of a rite of passage to the age of majority" in the Jewish community in Renaissance Italy. Marriage for girls and apprenticeship and talmudic studies for some boys were sometimes ineffective boundary markers of puberty or the escape into adult life. For instance, young adolescent girls who married men ten years their senior were treated as juveniles by their husbands and behaved in a deferential manner toward them.[74]

---

74. Ben-Ami, *Customs*, pp. 254 and 264 note 6, where he cites among others Elie Malka, *Essai de folklore des Israelites de Maroc*: "When the child reaches the age of five years, people celebrate with a family feast, in the course of which cakes and tea are served. The child ceases to be a baby. The child now enters into the new category of small boys or small girls." Robert Bonfil, *Jewish Life in Renaissance Italy* (Berkeley and Los Angeles: University of California Press, 1994), p. 256.

6

Children in the Early Modern Period

CHILDBIRTH AND INFANCY

In the seventeenth and eighteenth centuries there was the inauguration of a new genre in Jewish literature, the composition of lengthy personal memoirs, which afford us a much deeper insight into European Jewish family life. Thoughts and feelings previously concealed from us during the medieval period, which can at best only be guessed, can now be retrieved and removed from the shadows, particularly from the insights contained in the autobiography of Glückel of Hameln (1646–1724), the only female representative among a cohort of male authors. We shall then sift through these Jewish memoirs to test the hypotheses advanced in our previous two chapters dealing with the Middle Ages and try to evaluate whether or not there were any vital changes in childrearing practices in the early modern period.

Having been betrothed at twelve years, Glückel was married some two years later in 1660. In all, Glückel gave birth to fourteen children, twelve of whom survived into adult life and five of whom married into the most illustrious Jewish families in Europe, while one infant died shortly after birth and a much beloved daughter died as a young child. On the other hand, in the eighteenth century R. Jacob Emden (1698–1776) married three times, his wives bearing him a total of twenty children. Of the children produced by his first wife only three outlived Emden, and he was not survived by eleven children born between 1733 and 1751, most of whom died in infancy. Yet Emden's parents had a total of ten children, all of whom survived into adult life. So too, Ber of Bolechow (1723–1805) in his memoirs mentioned a certain R. Saul, a farming expert and leaseholder, who had "ten fine sons and one daughter. All his children married into families of Rabbis and other notable people." A new phenomenon in this period was the frequent survival of large families of children into adult life, even if other less fortunate families continued to be decimated by age-old epidemic and other diseases. Both evidence culled from these Jewish autobiographies and a careful demographic analysis of the Jewish population in the Polish town of Opatów by Gershon Hundert seem to indicate that the surge in the Jewish population of Central and Eastern Europe in the seventeenth century, followed by an even greater increase in the next century, was mainly concentrated in the households of the Jewish elite.[1]

Let us now turn to what Glückel has to say about the births of her own children. By the time she was fifteen, Glückel had given birth to her first child, a "beautiful healthy baby" daughter called Zipporah. Many of Glückel's births were uneventful, but it is not so much these instances that we are concerned with as those that resulted in complications. Distraught at the death of her young daughter Mattie, when she was pregnant with Hannah, Glückel became "dangerously ill and the physicians doubted my recovery and wished to resort to the last, most desperate measures." Ordering her husband to dismiss the doctors and relying on the help of the Almighty,

---

1. *The Memoirs of Glückel of Hameln*, trans. and ed. Marvin Lowenthal (New York: Harper and Brothers, 1932), p. XVII. Jacob Joseph Schacter, *Rabbi Jacob Emden: Life and Major Works*, Harvard Ph. D. Thesis, 1988, Vol. 1, pp. 181 and 182 (hereafter cited as Schacter, *Life of Emden*). *Memoires de Jacob Emden ou l'anti-Sabbatai Zewi (Megillat Sefer)*, trans. and ed. Maurice-Ruben Hayoun (Paris: Les Editions du Cerf, 1992) (hereafter cited as Hayoun, *Emden*). *Memoirs of Ber of Bolechow (1732–1805)*, trans. M. Vischnitzer. (London: Humphrey Milford Oxford University Press, 1922), p. 69 (hereafter cited as *Ber of Bolechow*). Gershon David Hundert, *The Jews in a Polish Private Town: The Case of Opatów in the Eighteenth Century* (Baltimore: Johns Hopkins University Press, 1992), p. 76 (hereafter cited as Hundert, *Opatów*).

Glückel gave birth to a bonny daughter without any of the expected complications.[2]

So too, what at first appeared to be grave difficulties surrounding the births of two sons quickly resolved themselves. "His birth [that of Glückel's son Leib] was unusual. When he came into the world he lay groaning for twenty-four hours, so that the midwife and all the women thought that he would not live. But it pleased the Lord that the child should improve day by day . . ." More problems were encountered after the birth of another son called Joseph. "At length they [the women] informed me that the baby had brown spots over his head and body. . . . I saw that not only was he covered with spots but that he lay like a lump of clay, not moving an arm or leg, just as though his soul had departed. He would not suckle or open his mouth . . ." Remembering that she had neglected to eat any medlars, although she had fancied sampling the fruit before his birth, Glückel now instructed a servant a few days after her son's birth to purchase some medlars, a fruit related to the pear family. "When she [the nurse] squeezed a little of the medlar between the baby's lips, he opened his mouth so eagerly, as though he wanted to swallow it whole, and sucked away all the soft part. Before this he had not opened his mouth wide enough to take a drop of milk or sugar-pap such as one gives to babies. The nurse handed the child to me in bed, to see if he would suck. As soon as he felt the breast, he began to suck with the strength of a three-month babe . . ."[3]

Usually parturient women in the more affluent Jewish households were more physically robust, as they were better fed, and had better medical attention and other help, so that on the whole they coped with the exigencies of childbirth, and their own and their infants' survival rates tended to be higher. Nevertheless, there were certain limits to a doctor's skill in the early modern period, and even sustained help could be of no avail. In the seventh month of her next pregnancy, Glückel developed a fever that she passed on to the infant she was carrying, and despite all efforts, he died fourteen days after birth from the same fever. On the other hand, skilled obstetrical care eased the birth of Ber of Bolechow as well as Leon Modena (1571–1648), who admitted in his autobiography that "my mother experienced great difficulty in childbirth" [as he probably was a premature

---

2. *The Life of Glückel of Hameln*, trans. and ed. Beth-Zion Abrahams (London: East and West Library, 1962), pp. 39 and 76 (hereafter cited as Abrahams, *Glückel*).

3. Abrahams, *Glückel*, pp. 91 and 101–103.

baby]. I was born in the breech position, my buttocks turned around facing outward, so that calamities turned upon me even at the beginning." Solomon Ufenhausen, in a Yiddish work published in 1615, noted that Christian midwives were frequently employed by Jewish mothers, while Christian households also availed themselves of the services of Jewish midwives.[4]

Contaminated water supplies and overcrowded living conditions in the ghettos or Jewish quarters in towns meant that disease was rife among the Jewish population of Early Modern Europe and among the most vulnerable sections of the population were young children. Describing incidents from his early childhood, Jacob Emden sketched a typical portrait of a sickly and ailing child from this era. We can begin to understand why so many children died under the age of five and before reaching adulthood. He wrote:

> The first [problem] was a rash that appeared on the flesh of my face which covered it from side to side in a manner that put me in jeopardy, almost beyond despair. God sent his word and healed me without it leaving any trace or damage on my face and no scars at all. Secondly, a leprous boil appeared on my penis which blocked the urinary tract for some time in a manner that caused my parents worry, sorrow and great sighing because of me. Thirdly, onerous boils covered all my legs, similar to the boils of Job, with ugly pain. God delivered me from all these, aside from other evil and serious maladies found in all childhood, like pimples, pox, measles and teething. I was especially prone to swollen tonsils, colds, coughing and burning urine; sometimes also small pimples and red speckles.[5]

By the sixteenth century, smallpox and measles had established themselves as the most virulent childhood diseases, from which many children succumbed. A medical book in 1775 considered that ninety-five in every hundred people were affected by smallpox and that one in seven persons died from it. Although the Venetian R. Leon Modena fell a victim to smallpox as a young child, he made a full recovery, unlike his son Abraham

---

4. Hundert, *Opatów*, p. 76. Abrahams, *Glückel*, pp. 103 and 104. *Ber of Bolechow*, p. 72. *The Autobiography of a Seventeenth Century Venetian Rabbi Leon Modena's Life of Judah*, trans. and ed. Mark R. Cohen (Princeton, N.J.: Princeton University Press, 1988), pp. 82 and 193 (hereafter cited as *Leon Modena*). Israel Zinberg, *A History of Jewish Literature: Old Yiddish Literature from Its Origins to the Haskalah Period* (New York: Ktav, 1975), Vol. 7, p. 168 (hereafter cited as Zinberg, *Old Yiddish Literature*).

5. Schacter, *Life of Emden*, p. 27.

and later still a grandson, both of whom died. There were many other young victims of the disease in the ghetto: "A year later, on . . . [7 March 1596], the boy [Abraham] became ill with smallpox," Modena recalled, "during an outbreak in which more than seventy boys and girls in our holy community died within six months and he returned to the Lord who had given him [to us]. My other two sons were also ill with that disease and were in great danger, but God graciously spared them for me, may he be blessed, forever."[6]

Progressive Jewish opinion in the latter part of the eighteenth century supported the new measures taken to combat smallpox, including inoculation, and Moses Mendelssohn secured an authoritative rabbinic responsum in its favor. In the Netherlands a Jewish physician in 1799 was the first doctor to inoculate children with cowpox as a preventive measure. Moreover, David ben Meir Frieshausen (c. 1750–1828) in his ethical will exclaimed,

> Hurry, without delay, to save your children from the deadly smallpox by giving them the illness called cowpox, which saves human beings from the more dangerous smallpox. . . . I know that some of our leaders regarded as wise and pious have forbidden cowpox infusion, but this is due to error. Their mistake stems from the fact that earlier treatments used to utilize matter from children who were only mildly ill of smallpox to treat unaffected children as a preventive. Some of the children so treated sometimes died from this treatment, so the rabbis banned it, rightly. But the more modern treatment, with cowpox, is different. All that happens is that a slight fever develops, and then the child is immune to smallpox.

Immunization against smallpox did not become widespread in Continental Europe until the nineteenth century, when the death rate from the disease fell.[7]

Because of the lack of a clean water supply, both children and adults in early modern Europe, like the inhabitants of the Third World of today,

---

6. William H. McNeill, *Plagues and Peoples* (Harmondsworth: Penguin Books, 1979), p. 114 (hereafter cited as McNeill, *Plagues*). Fernand Braudel, *Capitalism and Material Life 1400–1800* (London: Weidenfeld and Nicholson, 1973), p. 43 (hereafter cited as Braudel, *Material Life*). *Leon Modena*, pp. 83 and 97.

7. Israel Zinberg, *A History of Jewish Literature: The Berlin Haskalah* (New York: Ktav, 1976), Vol. 8, pp. 85 and 86. Mozes Heiman Gans, *Memorbook: Pictorial History of Dutch Jewry from the Renaissance to 1940* (Baarn: Bosch and Keuning, 1977), p. 301 (hereafter cited as Gans, *Memorbook*). Jack Reimer and Nathaniel Stampfer, *Ethical Wills: A Modern Jewish Treasury* (New York: Schocken Books, 1983), pp. 5 and 6. McNeill, *Plagues*, pp. 230–233.

were afflicted by worms in their digestive systems, resulting in debilitating disease and chronic ill health. "I was also troubled by worms [as a young child under the age of four]," Modena confessed, "and a certain woman gave one mineral oil to drink, from which I passed out and almost remained permanently unconscious." Incidentally, Jacob Emden, in his early twenties, was struck down by a fever caused by such a worm in Amsterdam in 1722. His description of his illness is so graphic that it must be recounted in full, as we can imagine that the consequences of the affliction were just as anxiety-making for young sufferers. "Then I fell into a second feverish illness . . . which plagued me for several months . . ." Emden commenced his account.

> As the days of my sickness extended, a worm several *amot* [cubits] long, which had constantly been piercing my intestines, emerged from me through my anus. This is how I felt for the past year. It appeared to me (as though) a living object was piercing my body on the right side, opposite the loins near the kidneys . . . the fever turned out to be beneficial because of the constant cleansing which the doctor did for me. His intention was to eliminate the cause of the fever by purging the turbid substance in the blood. The presence of the very long worm, which apparently was the cause of the fever, did not occur to him. I had to extract it with my hand because it could not emerge all at once. It remained suspended from my posterior and extended like a rope causing me trembling and anguish. I felt as though my intestines were being pulled out . . . It never occurred to me that it would be possible for such a long worm to grow in the stomach of a person.[8]

Great difficulty was experienced in discriminating between minor ailments, with such symptoms as a boil under the arm, and outbreaks of the plague. Glückel's eldest daughter was banished to a village and separated from her family when she was an infant, as a Polish Jewish female healer misdiagnosed her as suffering from the plague. Moreover, an anonymous writer described his experiences of the plague that broke out in Bohemia, particularly in Prague in 1680, when he was twelve years old. The count ordered all villagers with plague symptoms to flee to a lazaretto, a small wooden house with two rooms, in the midst of a big forest; but his father, fearing to remove his family to the forest because of bandits, kept his son hidden at home. "For three days and nights I had high fever, and was near to death," the writer declared. "Then a swelling broke out behind my ear

---

8. *Leon Modena*, p. 83. Schacter, *Life of Emden*, pp. 54 and 55. Braudel, *Material Life*, p. 51.

on the neck, which burned like fire, and all the members of the family became frightened." He was confined to a garret in his home, where food was brought to him at a distance and a plaster consisting of alum and the white of an egg was prepared for him, which he had to apply himself to an abcess. "I lay there alone day and night, and at that time I saw apparitions and dreamed dreams." Fortunately the fever subsided, although the place of the swelling still throbbed, but after a month he was well enough to mingle with the other members of his family. However, the bubonic plague disappeared in Western Europe in the early eighteenth century, followed by cholera a century later, thereby encouraging a population explosion. Despite centuries of urban living, the Jewish population was hardly more inured to these infectious diseases than the rest of the population.[9]

What do these memoirs and other sources tell us about the continuance of swaddling and the extent of breast-feeding? Glückel strongly hints that Jewish families were still swaddling babies and, narrating the problems encountered after her son Joseph's birth, Glückel remembered that "I called the nurse to unbind the baby and seat herself with him in front of the oven . . .", while the English traveler Paul Skippon, describing a circumcision at Rome in the seventeenth century, stated how before the ceremony could commence "the swaddling clothes . . . [were] unfolded . . ."[10]

Again, most mothers even in the better-off Jewish households in Germany and Italy, where they could afford servants, suckled their infants themselves and did not engage wet nurses for this purpose, except in emergencies. "As I was still so young [at the time of the birth of her first child]," Glückel later recalled, "my mother would not let me take my baby to my room at night. So, the baby was left in her room, where she and also her maid slept. My mother told me not to worry; if the baby cried she would send the maid with it for me to suckle it and later return the babe to its cradle." After a difficult confinement with her daughter Hannah, Glückel was weak and unable to attend to the needs of her child. "Daily I improved,"

---

9. Abrahams, *Glückel*, pp. 48–50. "Memories of an Unhappy Childhood," in Leo W. Schwarz, *Memoirs of My People: Jewish Self-Portraits from the 11th to the 20th Centuries* (New York: Schocken Books, 1963), pp. 107–110 (hereafter cited as *Unhappy Childhood*). Braudel, *Material Life*, p. 47. McNeill, *Plagues*, p. 163.

10. Abrahams, *Glückel*, p. 102. Abraham Cohen, *An Anglo-Jewish Scrapbook 1600–1840: The Jew Through English Eyes* (London: M. L. Cailingold, 1943), p. 292.

she explained, "and at length dismissed my nurse and wet-nurse and myself saw to all that was necessary for my household." Because Leon Modena's wife fell gravely ill after giving birth to a boy on 28 October 1593, her husband entrusted his infant son to a wet nurse: "But, because the milk had left . . . her [his wife's] breasts, I gave the boy Isaac to a Jewish wet nurse . . . for about eight months at considerable expense." Again, a generation later in 1629 Modena's daughter Diana gave birth to a girl and the family "turned her over to a wet nurse at great expense. . . . She died afterwards at the age of ten months," a sad fate, but the incidence of deaths was high for infants entrusted to the care of wet nurses. Moreover, Gershon Hundert pointed out that although wet nurses were sometimes found in Jewish homes in Eastern Europe in the early modern period, the plethora of Jewish and Christian ordinances forbidding such usage and the great expansion of the Jewish population in this period both point to the fact that this was a comparatively rare occurrence in Jewish households; as we have seen, this was unlike the situation in medieval Germany.[11]

A new feature in the early modern period was the rise in the number of illegitimate births in the overcrowded Jewish ghettos and even in more relaxed communities like Amsterdam. In Germany, Holland, Italy, and the Balkans, there were often Christian maids and sometimes wet nurses in the homes of well-off Jewish families. They on occasion fell pregnant after a casual liaison with the master of the house or his son. In Mantua, Italy, the Jewish community ensured that the seducer paid the cost of confinement and the care of the infant. In Poland and Berlin some of the maids with illegitimate offspring were Jewish. A decree was issued by the Prussian government in 1789 stipulating that whether or not the mother or father of the child was Jewish, children from mixed liaisons must be baptized. Quite a number of these children in Berlin were brought up in orphanages, thereby becoming lost to the Jewish community.[12]

---

11. Abrahams, *Glückel*, pp. 39 and 71. *Modena*, pp. 96, 97 and 133. Gershon David Hundert, "Jewish Children and Childhood in Early Modern East Central Europe," in *The Jewish Family: Metaphor and Memory*, ed. David Kraemer (New York: Oxford University Press, 1989), pp. 86 and 87 (hereafter cited as Hundert, *Jewish Children*).

12. Jonathan I. Israel, *European Jewry in the Age of Mercantilism 1550–1750* (Oxford: Clarendon Press, 1989), pp. 201–202. S. Simonsohn, *History of the Jews in the Duchy of Mantua* (Jerusalem: Kiryath Sepher, 1977), pp. 543–546. Steven M. Lowenstein, *The Berlin Jewish Community: Enlightenment, Family and Crisis,*

ATTITUDES TOWARD THE DEATH OF CHILDREN

We shall now examine the attitude of Jewish parents toward the death of young children in the early modern period with the help of relevant passages from the autobiographical material at our disposal. By far the best source for such a survey once again is Glückel's memoirs. She drew on two popular handbooks written in Yiddish for her intellectual inspiration, the *Brandtspeigel* of Moses Henoch Yerushalmi Altschuler (first edition in the 1590s) and the *Lev Tov* of Isaac ben Eliakum, published in Prague in 1620. Glückel advised her family that one should "have patience. If God sends you an affliction, accept it meekly and do not cease to pray. . . . My dear children be devout and good. . . . Should, God forbid, children and dear friends die, do not grieve too much, for you did not create them." And she uttered a comforting thought that was of medieval origin and was also shared by many pious Christians in the early modern era: ". . . nothing belongs it is only lent." Whereas Glückel said little about her son who died fourteen days after birth, she and her husband were inconsolable at the demise of a much-loved young daughter called Mattie, who died in her third year: "My husband and I mourned indescribably," Glückel declared, "and I feared greatly that I sinned against the Almighty by mourning too much, not heeding the story of Reb Jochanan. . . . I forgot that there were greater punishments. . . . We were both so grieved that we were ill for some time." After the subsequent birth of a daughter called Hannah, Glückel was slowly reconciled, and much the same attitude can be found among observant Christians in this period. Glückel continued, "And at last I had to submit and forget my beloved child, as is the decree of God, I am forgotten as a dead one to the heart."[13]

Leon Modena, as we would expect from our previous analysis in the medieval chapter, made little fuss in his autobiography when his infant daughter of seventeen days died: "After that my wife, may she be blessed above all women of the house, gave birth to a daughter in the Cividale house in the Ghetto Nuovo. . . . It was twilight on the Sunday of Hanukkah, which fell on . . . [December 22, 1596], but I did not have a chance

---

1770–1830 (New York: Oxford University Press, 1994), pp. 114–119 (hereafter cited as Lowenstein, *Berlin*).

13. Abrahams, *Glückel*, pp. 7 and 71. Linda A. Pollock, *Forgotten Children: Parent-Child Relations from 1500–1900* (Cambridge: Cambridge University Press, 1983), pp. 8 and 130 (hereafter cited as Pollock, *Forgotten Children*).

to name her, because after seventeen days she returned to her Father's house in her newborn state, expired, and died." Some years later in the summer of 1622, Leon Modena and his wife persuaded their daughter Diana and her husband together with their young son Isaac to come and live with them in Venice in their part of the house. "In Kislev [5]386 [November–December 1625], a son of my daughter Diana . . . died of smallpox," Modena sadly remembered. "His name was David. He was fourteen months old and had been my daily delight. My sorrow was so great that I left the lodgings I was in and went to live nearby . . ." Reeling from the death of two adult sons, Mordecai, who died from arsenic poisoning as a result of alchemical experiments, and Zebulun, who was murdered, Leon Modena became emotionally attached to his young grandson David, whom he no doubt viewed as a substitute son; and the depth of Modena's sorrow at the passing of the infant David illustrates the point already touched on in the medieval chapter, that there were a minority of parents who could not be comforted at the loss of an infant.[14]

The grief of parents at the death of adult children was very deep and unchanging whether the loss was sustained in the talmudic age, during the Middle Ages, or in the eighteenth century. Leon Modena agonized over the death of his son Mordecai, who had been a teacher of young children and a preacher in the synagogue, at the age of twenty-six. He exclaimed, "My bowels, my bowels I writhe in pain. The chambers of my heart moan within me as I come to tell you with twofold brokenheartedness about the death of my son Mordecai of blessed memory." Again, "Not a day passes that [his death] is not fresh to me, as if his corpse were lying before me. The saying, 'It is decreed that the dead should be forgotten by the heart,' does not apply to me, for it is today three years since his death, and wherever . . . I turn he is there before me." After the murder of his son Zebulun, who was almost twenty-one, Leon Modena explained how his blood-stained clothing was placed on his coffin. "This sight, and the sound of my cries and those of my woebegone wife, caused every heart and eye to shed tears. . . . His bloody state will never disappear from before my eyes for the rest of my life. My tears have been my bread, day and night. My soul refuses to be comforted, for there can be no consolation." So too, Glückel

---

14. *Leon Modena*, pp. 98, 128 and 129. Alexander Altmann, *Moses Mendelssohn: A Biographical Study* (Philadelphia: Jewish Publication Society, 1973), p. 99 (hereafter cited as Altmann, *Mendelssohn*). Mendelssohn's daughter Sara died at eleven months, an event that he recalled with tears some sixteen years later.

bade a poignant farewell to her adult son Zanvil, who died leaving a widow who presented him with a posthumous daughter. "The deep sorrow and heartache this was to me, only God knows. To lose so beloved a son, of such tender years. Can there be a greater grief?"[15]

During the medieval period certain Ashkenazi rabbis utilized the tale of Abraham's willingness to sacrifice Isaac when commanded by the Almighty as a precedent to impress parents to be ready to sacrifice their children rather than allow the forcible conversion of their families to Christianity. "There are people who say, 'Why should I always worry about my children?'" protested Glückel. "'Is it not enough that I saw to them when young? Brought them up well? Gave them fine dowries and made good matches for them? Now they can see to themselves' . . . This is quite right when children are in a good position and all goes well with them. But if, God forbid, things go badly which person with feelings would not bear the burden of his children and friends?" Such was the magnitude of Glückel's attachment and love for her children that she contested the position of the medieval rabbis and came to the opposite conclusion. "To my understanding it would have been much easier for Abraham had the Lord asked him to slay himself than he should slay his only son Isaac. For who can witness the doing-away of his own offspring?" Here was a sharp break with the ambiguities of medieval Jewish parenthood.[16]

Unlike the medieval accounts that glorified the martyrdom of children at the hands of their own devout parents, the chronicle of Nathan Hanover, which dealt with the 1648 massacres in Poland and the Ukraine, presented the death of children through the actions of the Cossacks as a horror story.

> Little children were killed at their mothers' breasts; they were chopped up and cut up like fish . . . or they were run through with spears, roasted over the fire, and then offered freshly roasted to their mothers. Pregnant women had their bellies torn open, their still unborn children were thrown into their faces, and into the ripped-open bellies live cats were sewn, and the hands of the women were cut off so that the miserable victims would not be able to remove the scratching cats. . . . In other places bridges were made of Jewish children, and then they rode over them with loaded wagons or threw them into wells and covered them with earth.

Perhaps Hanover's underlying message was that since the 1648 catastrophe was already preordained in the Psalms, there was the implication that

---

15. *Leon Modena*, pp. 111, 112, 120, and 121. Abrahams, *Glückel*, p. 169.
16. Abrahams, *Glückel*, pp. 9 and 10.

the martyrs did not die because of any sins on their part (David Roskies). This was a thoroughly old-fashioned view of history.[17]

Linda Pollock has contended that the high rates of sickness and mortality among children prior to the eighteenth century, so far from leading to a resigned and stoical attitude on the part of parents, in fact increased their levels of anxiety. She was unable to discern any fundamental shift in parents' concern for the welfare of their children after 1700, as evidence from sixteenth- and seventeenth-century sources showed that such deep-seated interest already existed. Parents also coped with their distress at the loss of their children in part by utilizing the psychological mechanisms of denial, by suppressing the belief that the children really had died, or by claiming that they were better off in heaven. Interestingly enough, R. Elhanan Kirchen published a popular work in 1707, in which he retold the well-known midrash of Beruriah concealing the death of their two young sons on the Sabbath, but added a new twist to the tale more in tune with eighteenth-century opinion, by denying that the children actually died. "Therefore God performed a miracle for them: when they were about to remove the bodies of the children at the end of the Sabbath, the children revived, because the parents had so cheerfully accepted what God had ordained." The low importance attached to the death of an infant, the savage emotional impact of the loss of an older child, even a stripling of three, and the searing emotional void at the sudden death of an adult child, all were attitudes of mind that we have encountered in Jewish sources for the Middle Ages and that persisted into the early modern period. Similar beliefs existed among non-Jews in England and America in the period 1600–1900, as has been amply demonstrated by Linda Pollock, who also suggested that some people could not find any solace at the death of young infants, a point with which the Jewish evidence concurs.[18]

CHILDCARE AND EDUCATION

Glückel invites us to share the innermost thoughts and feelings of a pious, socially upwardly mobile wife and Jewish mother living in Central Europe

---

17. Israel Zinberg, *A History of Jewish Literature* (New York: Ktav, 1965), Vol. 6, pp. 124 and 125. *The Literature of Destruction: Jewish Responses to Catastrophe*, ed. David G. Roskies (Philadelphia: Jewish Publication Society, 1988), p. 108.

18. Pollock, *Forgotten Children*, pp. 14–142. Zinberg, *Old Yiddish Literature*, p. 211.

in the latter half of the seventeenth and the early eighteenth centuries. Her first assumption was that "Almighty God . . . created us without sin [similar to Locke's concept of the mind as a blank page]—through the sins of Adam the Evil Spirit overpowers us . . . But gracious God threw us a rope for our guidance, to which to hold fast and so save ourselves. This is our Holy Torah." Everyone should accept punishment from the Almighty, "for suffering is a redemption for his body and merits the eternal world-to-be . . . ." Moreover, "A father loves his child; the same the nearest relatives one another. . . . Almighty God did all this in His infinite mercy that parents should love their children and help them to do right. And then the children seeing this from their parents, do the same to their children." Steeped in popular Yiddish ethical literature, Glückel had a belief that seemed close to the thinking of the medieval Spanish Jewish philosopher Ibn Paquda, whose ideas were plundered in these popular tracts: "how parents toil for their children while they, if they had trouble with their parents, as their parents with them, would soon tire." Glückel concluded, "That parents love their children is no surprise. We find the same among unreasoning creatures who have young and look after them until they are grown and can fend for themselves. And then they are left to themselves. We humans are in this sense better. We seek to support our children till they are grown; not only when they are small but as long as we live." Glückel consequently did not like being beholden to her children in old age; only reluctantly after her second husband had lost her fortune and died did she consent to reside with a loving and dutiful daughter.[19]

Family members were often close and supportive of one another. Leon Modena categorized his father, who died at the age of seventy-two, as someone who "loved his neighbours, was close to his relatives, and loved his wife, whom he honored more than himself." Having found a teaching position in Ferrara, Modena left his three-year-old son Zebulun behind in Venice, "for my in-laws and my brother-in-law Moses of blessed memory would not let him go." Equally we have seen a generation later how Leon Modena doted on his two young grandchildren, who came to live with him after he was desolated by the premature death of two adult sons. Families were enmeshed in ties of love and mutual obligation extending over the generations. Modena's daughters Esther and Diana came to stay with him in 1647 because of a chest illness and shortness of breath. "These past three months I have had my daughter Diana . . . here, but she and

---

19. Abrahams, *Glückel*, pp. 2, 3, 7, 8, 9, and 10.

Esther and my neighbour cannot adequately minister to my wife and me."
Under hostile pressure from outside, the ghetto communities often solidified
and there were many expressions of mutual self-help among neighbors.[20]

The idea of obligations between generations was already enunciated in
the medieval *Sefer Haredim* and reproduced almost in its entirety in
R. Abraham Danzig's (1748–1820) work *Hayye Adam*:

> . . . obviously a man ought to love his parents as himself, for they are included in
> "You shall love your neighbour as yourself." But the love of parents is compared
> to the love of God, as we read in the *Zohar*: "a man ought to do all for his mother
> and father and love them more than himself, and his soul and all he possesses
> ought to be held as nought in his zeal to do their will."
>
> Our sages have said that the obligations of a son toward his father are repay-
> ment of the debt owed the parents for their good nurture. . . . Part of this repay-
> ment must be that he love them strongly, as they loved him, and that he not con-
> sider them an unwelcome burden . . .
>
> "Honor" is a matter of thought, deed and speech.

Here we have a strong movement away from the conception of filial
obligation in the ancient world, where much more emphasis was placed
on honoring one's parents and less on loving them.[21]

Families in the early modern period were still fragile and sometimes
short-lived structures that rapidly disintegrated from the effects of the plague
or disease. Glückel's grandfather and several of his children died as a result of a plague. "My grandmother was left bare and destitute with two
unmarried daughters." They had "no bed to sleep on but plain boards and
stones . . ." Having gone to live with a married daughter called Gluck, "After
a time differences arose [between Gluck and her mother] because the
orphan grandchildren visited her often . . ." , and Glückel's mother Beila
and her grandmother went to live elsewhere, supporting themselves by
opening a workshop. When a generation later Glückel's son Zanvil died,
his widow gave birth to a posthumous daughter and later remarried. "She
[Glückel's granddaughter] is now about thirteen years of age and is said to
be an excellent child. She is with her grandfather, Reb Moses Bamberg."
Grandparents and other relatives regarded it as a religious duty to bring

---

20. *Leon Modena*, pp. 94, 103, and 165. Kenneth R. Stow, "The Consciousness of
Closure: Roman Jewry and its Ghet," in *Essential Papers on Jewish Culture in Renaissance and Baroque Italy*, ed. David B. Ruderman (New York: New York University Press,
1992), p. 394.

21. Gerald Blidstein, *Honor Thy Father and Mother: Filial Responsibility in Law
and Ethics* (New York: Ktav, 1975), p. 57.

up orphan children if one or more of their parents died. As the memoir of Isaac Thannhauser (born 1774 in Altenstadt, Bavaria) made clear, living with relatives could sometimes be most unpleasant: "One word from my uncle or from his wife and out of fright or fear I would have run through hell. It is most likely that if I had been forced to pass another half-year with this stingy woman, I would have been worn down by sorrow, hunger, chills, fever, and excess burdens . . ."[22]

Sometimes the second wife was so immature and inexperienced that she could not cope adequately with the rearing of the orphan children from her husband's first marriage, and when a mother died the family was often bereft of competent female carers, so that her death was quickly followed by that of an infant. The anonymous author from Bohemia claimed that "the [second] wife of my father was herself still a young child who did not know how to bring us up in cleanliness as is necessary with little boys, nor could she properly care for us when we were sick. We thank God and the help of our grandmother Lieble, and her good daughters, that we grew up at all. Even so, little Moses, who was only one year old, died." So too, once Jacob Emden's widowed mother had passed away, this was soon followed by the death of his three-year-old sister.[23]

Even in Poland in the eighteenth century, parents forsook the injunctions of the *Sayings of the Fathers* dating from the talmudic period against indulging young toddlers. Alexander Susskind ben Moshe of Grodno wrote that "I bear witness to myself that though I had many children I never kissed any of them, or took any of them in my arms; nor did I indulge with them in idle talk. The warning of the rabbis to beware of children's talk was constantly in my mind. But, alas! We see now with our own eyes that the father himself accustoms his children to idle talk." Here we once again come across the split in childrearing practices between the pietists and the masses, who loved their infants' chatter.[24]

---

22. Abrahams, *Glückel*, pp. 17, 19, and 169. *Jewish Life in Germany: Memoirs from Three Centuries*, ed. Monika Richarz and trans. Stella P. Rosenfeld and Sidney Rosenfeld (Bloomington: Indiana University Press, 1991), p. 68 (hereafter cited as Richarz, *Memoirs*).

23. *Unhappy Childhood*, p. 105. Schacter, *Life of Emden*, p. 52.

24. Nathan Morris, *The Jewish School: An Introduction to the History of Jewish Education* (London: Eyre and Spottiswoode, 1937), p. 174. Simha Assaf, *Sources for the History of Jewish Education* (Tel Aviv: Dvir, 1954), Vol. 1, pp. 270 and 271 (hereafter cited as Assaf).

An impartial non-Jewish Polish observer, Stanislaw Staszic, presented an idealized portrait of the Jewish family in 1789: "Family morals are incomparably stricter among the Jews; profligacy, dissipation, adultery and debauchery are not frequent among them; young people and unmarried men do not prevail over the fathers and husbands. They differ from all European nations among which they live by their reticence; drunkenness and gluttony do not exist, the young people are modest, there is faithfulness in marriage, the children warmly love their parents, and parents their children." While discounting the underplaying of the means used to discipline children within the Jewish family and its neglect of adolescent rebellion, we should listen to what it has to say about the love flowing within the Polish Jewish family, particularly that of the masses, who were freer to express their feelings. This account also neatly dovetails with Alexander Susskind's observations about the treatment of toddlers. Christian Wilhelm von Dohm, a German supporter of emancipation, also expressed admiration for the Jews in the 1770s for their "close bonding" in family life.[25]

Fathers were authoritarian and were treated with great reverence and respect by their children, although the authoritarianism was tempered with love. A good instance of this was the encomium of Leon Modena on his grandson Isaac, who was very much the substitute son, which we shall quote in full:

> The only comfort I have left in my misery is from my grandson Isaac . . . the son of my daughter Diana. . . . For about ten years, since the death of his father of beloved memory, I have reared him in my house, and he has been like a son to me. Now, at about eighteen years of age, he *obeys me* [author's emphasis], understands Scripture and Aggadah, and preaches in public, pleasing his listeners. He has a clean and easy craft in printing, which is . . . also the work of the Torah. I love him all the more because in his face and character traits he resembles in all respects my son Mordecai. . . . After my death, may he [God] grant me and my wife . . . our reward in the world to come for having raised an orphan in our home, with all the trouble and pain involved in child rearing.

---

25. Artur Eisenbach, *The Emancipation of the Jews in Poland, 1780–1870* (Oxford: Basil Blackwell, 1991), p. 99 (hereafter cited as Eisenbach, *Emancipation*). Ronald Schechter, "Translating the 'Marseillaise': Biblical Republicanism and the Emancipation of Jews in Revolutionary France," *Past and Present* 143 (May 1994): 131. According to Schechter, Isaiah Berr Bing stated that among Jews the authority of fathers was revered.

In contrast, Modena banished his errant fourteen-year-old son Isaac to the Levant for "behaving improperly [possibly with girls] with childish escapades." This action was high-handed and lacking in compassion on Modena's part, nor was it wise in that a young boy was removed from parental guidance at an impressionable age. So too, for some unknown reason Emden's father thwarted his son's desire at the age of fifteen to marry into a family of communal leaders. Dissembling his true feelings, Jacob Emden recorded that "I humbled myself to accept with love the decision of my revered father."[26]

Among seventeenth- and early eighteenth-century Jewish moralists there was a widespread consensus from Central and Eastern Europe through to England that parents should keep a certain distance from their children and that they should instill a modicum of fear into them in order to command their unswerving obedience, even when they were older. Gershon Hundert has pointed out that all these authorities drew on a work entitled *Sefer Ha-Musar*, which was composed in Algeria in the early sixteenth century and which in turn was based on a fourteenth-century Spanish text. Take for example the remarks of R. Joseph Yospa Hahn (d. Frankfurt 1637):

It happens that a little child will hit, curse and revile his parents and other important persons; and in most cases, fathers think that this is a clever act, it makes them laugh and they encourage them [the children] to go on doing it. It should not be so, as he will become accustomed to it and act in this way when he is older. They should frighten them [the children] from a very early age, so that they will listen to him when they grow up; but he should not implant excessive fear in them, especially not in young children, who are very tender-hearted . . . and every man should judge the disposition of his children and act accordingly; even if he knows the right measure of punishment, he should not inflict it continuously, as it will become a habit and not be effective. One should be sensitive; if they [the children] will always be angry, they will kick him and pay as much attention as a barking dog.[27]

Similar sentiments were voiced by R. Isaiah Horowitz (1555–1630), who stated that ". . . if the father rebukes his son early in his life with the

---

26. *Leon Modena*, pp. 105, 150, and 151. According to Schacter, *Life of Emden*, p. 44, "While young Jacob did not sit on his father's lap, he may very well indeed have been afraid of him."

27. Hundert, *Jewish Children*, pp. 82 and 83. Assaf, p. 82.

staff . . . and using fear while he is young . . . then he will be accustomed to fear his father always. . . . And since women are of a softer nature, they are obliged . . . to have brave hearts and not to spare the rod but to strike their sons even if they scream." Rivka Tiktiner confirmed this point by declaring that as the father was often engaged elsewhere, it was the mother who must attend to the education of their children, which included physical chastisement. Through the *Lev Tov* and the *Brandtspeigel,* Yiddish ethical tracts, this point of view in favor of corporal punishment was reaching a large lay audience, particularly of educated women in the seventeenth century. A century later the Vilna Gaon (1720–1797) urged his wife to train their daughters to conduct their conversation "in peace, love, affability and gentleness. I possess many moral books with German (versions); let them read them regularly. . . . For a curse, an oath, or a lie, strike them [their daughters; one text adds with cruel blows]; show no softness in the matter."[28]

The anonymous author of German origin of *Sefer Giddul Bonim,* which was published in England in 1771, opened with some remarks on the care of infants before he reverted to the themes of his Continental predecessors on the best method of discipline for children:

> Some doctors believe it to be good that children should be bathed in cold water on entering the world, and not to protect them, as is usually the case, from every draught, because this softens their nature and makes them weak and unhealthy. The habit in England of allowing children to go about in the severest cold without stockings and with chest bared is very healthy for them and strengthens their nature.
>
> Parents should avoid handing over their child to low-minded and immoral servants, who will often spoil the good intentions of father and mother by secretly permitting much that they on their part wished to withhold for the child's greatest benefit. This will not only teach the little ones a kind of theft but will arouse in them a hostility toward their parents, since they will believe that their father and mother are harder and less merciful to them than strangers. [From this it appears that the work was addressed to the more affluent sections of the Anglo-Jewish community.] It is also necessary that father and mother should not allow the child too much of its own will, and should not sympathise . . . too much if the child cries. . . . They should not have too close a relationship with their children and not overdemonstrate the love they have for them. By doing so the child would only lose its proper respect . . . for its parents. Nevertheless, they must not deal with it

---

28. Hundert, *Jewish Children,* pp. 87, 88, and 93 note 34. *Hebrew Ethical Wills,* ed. Israel Abrahams (Philadelphia Jewish Publication Society, 1926), Vol. 2, p. 316 (hereafter cited as Abrahams, *Ethical Wills*).

too harshly or in too terrifying a manner, lest the child lose its natural love for them.[29]

Accordingly there was a considerable congruence between the Jewish autobiographical accounts and the moralistic literature on the degree to which children should be disciplined by their parents. Reviewing chiefly Gentile English and American diaries and autobiographies, Linda Pollock came to the conclusion that methods of discipline varied little between 1500 and 1900, apart from the early nineteenth century, when there was a definite increase in the severity of punishment, particularly in Britain; otherwise, strict and indulgent parents were to be found in all these centuries. Her conclusions for the United States were challenged by Elizabeth Pleck, who asserted that whereas seventeenth-century manuals rarely advised moderation in corporal punishment, a new trend started in the following century with such books suggesting the limitation of punishment and the substitution of spanking for whipping. Spanking was a term introduced in the 1780s, although it gained wider circulation in the nineteenth century. We can utilize all these findings to illuminate Jewish opinion in this matter. In much the same vein, insofar as the use of a milder form of punishment was concerned, the son of the Chofetz Chaim (1838–1933) admitted that "when I was little and was naughty—especially when I insulted someone—[my father] would sometimes slap me in the face."[30]

To focus on the wider Jewish world, the business elite and rabbinic leadership in the seventeenth and early eighteenth centuries, like the non-Jewish world, advocated severe discipline, although the masses were inclined to be less tough. Even the sixteenth-century author of *Sefer Orech Yamim*, in rebuking his contemporaries, commented that "in this generation I have seen many children following their own inclinations faithlessly, with neither culture nor common sense. . . . The crime was committed by their parents, who acted without foresight and refrained from instilling discipline and awe in the children before they got too old to be disciplined."

---

29. *Remember the Days: Essays in Honour of Cecil Roth*, ed. John M. Shaftesley (London: Jewish Historical Society of England, 1966), pp. 147–149.

30. Pollock, *Forgotten Children*, pp. 143–202. Elizabeth Pleck, *Domestic Tyranny: The Making of American Social Policy against Family Violence from Colonial Times to the Present* (New York: Oxford University Press, 1987). Meir Munk, *Sparing the Rod, a Torah Perspective on Reward and Punishment in Education* (Bnei Brak: Mishor Publishing Co., 1989), p. 87 (hereafter cited as Munk, *Punishment*).

During the 1780s and perhaps a decade or two earlier in England, France, Holland, and the United States, less severe methods of punishing children were favored, which influenced members of the Jewish elite. In 1774 the Sephardim of Bordeaux abolished the use of the rod in the communal school, stating that it interfered with the educational process. However, in Eastern Europe and even more so in Germany, reliance on the well-tried methods of corporal punishment continued. A non-Jewish German called V. Kloeden, writing about his grandfather, claimed that his principle was that "children can never get enough beatings. That was not unusual in those days [around 1765]. The childrearing methods of that period are not at all equal to the modern ones [around 1830], because in schools, too, beating was considered to be the main thing in childrearing." A German Jewish source from the second half of the eighteenth century warned teachers not to strike children on the head or on the face or while suffering from a fit of temper.[31]

There is ample confirmation of the brutal punishment in the heder (private school) in the early memoir literature and the communal regulations. The anonymous seventeenth-century author from Bohemia mentioned that at the age of twelve he was boarded with a teacher at Herschmanik, where "he began to teach me Rashi, Midrash, haggadic texts, and the Sayings of the Fathers. He noticed that I could not read properly through the fault of my first teacher. . . . I was in great trouble, for the new teacher was of an irritable temper, and had neither composure nor common sense. He struck me and put me to shame, but did not make good my deficiency . . ." In early seventeenth-century Poland pupils in Jewish schools supported by communal funds were examined weekly, and if the unfortunate pupil supplied an incorrect answer, he was flogged by a beadle with a large cane. So too, in Worms the community regulations reiterated that children should be punished if they were lazy or failed to grasp what they were taught, by being made to wear a dunce's cap, smearing their face with black paint, being made to stand against a wall, and being subjected to physical chas-

---

31. Munk, *Punishment*, p. 130. Frances Malino, *The Sephardic Jews of Bordeaux: Assimilation and Emancipation in Revolutionary and Napoleonic France* (Tuscaloosa: University of Alabama Press, 1978), p. 25. Raffael Scheck, "Childhood in German Autobiographical Writings, 1740–1820," *Journal of Psychohistory* 15, no. 1 (Summer 1987): 411. Isidore Fishman, *The History of Jewish Education in Central Europe: From the End of the Sixteenth Century to the End of the Eighteenth Century* (London: Edward Goldston, 1944), p. 83 (hereafter cited as Fishman, *Jewish Education*).

tisement. All this evidence seems to indicate that Jewish pedagogical methods were affected by the example of harsh German educational techniques.[32]

In the next century, Jacob Emden, an excellent student, complained that "the majority of them [the teachers] were cruel and beat me without pity." Solomon Maimon (1754–1800) described how his brother was boarded with a schoolmaster "of some repute called Jossel" in Mir in Lithuania. "This man was a terror of all young people, 'the scourge of God'; he treated those in his charge with unheard-of cruelty, flogged them till the blood came, even for the slightest offence, and not infrequently tore their ears off, or their eyes out. When the parents of these unfortunates came to him, and took him to task, he struck them with stones or whatever else came to hand . . ." While not trying to discount the savagery of many heder teachers, it is interesting that the worst example of teacher-pupil violence was not based on the direct evidence of an eyewitness, and the account should be treated with caution. In fact, Ritchie Robertson, when comparing the memoirs of Maimon and Jakob Fromer warned that "the boundaries between autobiography and fiction are difficult to determine."[33]

Teachers had to curry favor and ingratiate themselves with both parents and pupils to ensure that the children stayed on at their heder and were not poached by a rival establishment, thereby lessening the propensity toward violence in their methods of instruction. On the other hand, the vast expansion of the Jewish population in Eastern Europe starting in the eighteenth century, when combined with short-term contracts for village teachers and the fierceness of competition for pupils, meant that schoolmasters often vented their frustrations on their charges. One late eighteenth-century source bemoaned that "there are more teachers than pupils, and therefore they do not succeed in earning even half a decent income. Their homes are bare of food and clothing. Some of them also do some business on the side, some of them give private lessons in the better homes. . . . And there are some who go abroad but find no students

---

32. *Unhappy Childhood*, p. 111. Fishman, *Jewish Education*, pp. 67–69. Herman Pollack, *Jewish Folkways in Germanic Lands 1648–1806* (Cambridge, Mass.: M.I.T. Press, 1971), p. 54 (hereafter cited as Pollack, *Folkways*).

33. Hayoun, *Emden*, p. 154. Schacter, *Life of Emden*, p. 27. *The Autobiography of Solomon Maimon*, trans. J. Clark Murray (London: East and West Library, 1954), p. 31. Ritchie Robertson, "From the Ghetto to Modern Culture: The Autobiographies of Salomon Maimon and Jakob Fromer," *Polin: A Journal of Polish-Jewish Studies* 7 (1992): 12–29.

there either, and their wives and children starve to death . . . another may beg alms from Jews wherever he goes, another will become a scribe . . ." As the Jewish population continued to soar in numbers, the situation in Eastern Europe as far as the impoverishment of teachers and the levels of punishment in schools were concerned deteriorated yet further in the nineteenth century.[34]

A mother was expected to influence her children's attitude toward study "by speaking kind words and arousing in their hearts the desire for learning . . ."; and Sabbatai Horowitz paid a tribute to his mother, stating that "I praise my mother, my teacher, my first instructor." It is well known that the medieval aristocracy sent their sons to other lords for a training in the knightly arts, and similarly in England apprentices were dispatched to strange households to acquire new skills, but these children were mostly adolescents; even so, this has unleashed a vigorous debate about unloving parents. Not so remarked on was the fact that Jewish pupils from the age of seven or nine were often sent far from home to board with a tutor in order to acquire the best or the cheapest religious education and were thus treated as miniature adults. Sometimes the conditions in these establishments were good, particularly in Italy, where they were run by grandmothers for their grandsons; sometimes they were deplorable, with young children being given unwholesome food and maltreated. In 1740 Jacob Emden lost a son called Zvi Hirsch at the age of seven, as he caught a severe chill on the journey to Hamburg, due to the neglect of his teacher, who was accompanying him. Despite occasional visits by fathers, the bad conditions in the teacher's home that were undermining their son's health and aptitude for study often went unrecognized. A relative's maidservants so "hated me and embittered my life," Modena recalled, that at one point he had to curtail his studies and return home.[35]

Perhaps Jewish historians need to debate the issue of the abandonment of young Jewish children by their parents in the early modern period in a

34. Fishman, *Jewish Education*, pp. 18, 19, 83, and 84. According to Munk, *Punishment*, p. 83, R. Eliyahu Hacohen of Izmir in Turkey (seventeenth century) complained, "There is a bad custom of ordering the teacher, in front of little boys who have been brought to the *Beis Midrash*, not to hit them. When the little children hear this, they misbehave deliberately." Benzion Dinur, "The Origins of Hasidism and Its Social and Messianic Foundations," in *Essential Papers on Hasidism*, ed. Gershon David Hundert (New York: New York University Press, 1991), pp. 122 and 123 (hereafter cited as Dinur, *Hasidism*).

35. Pollack, *Folkways*, pp. 51 and 62. Robert Bonfil, *Jewish Life in Renaissance Italy* (Berkeley and Los Angeles: University of California Press, 1994), p. 127 (here-

more thorough fashion than hitherto. It was one of the major discontinuities of Jewish childhood history, like the forced martyrdom of children by the medieval German Jews. On the other hand, as we have seen in the previous chapter, the development of the institution of the bar mitzvah in the early modern era marked the differentiation of adolescence from childhood and, with the population explosion, Jewish youth became much more vociferous.

Although children usually commenced their attendance at heder at the age of five, certain precocious children started their regular studies at three, when a father was supposed to teach his children the Hebrew alphabet. In Nikolsburg, children between the ages of three and five often attended the heder just to hear the lessons. One father charted his son's overeager progress as follows:

> At three Joseph encountered his Creator [in other words came into contact with the world of religion]. He began studying . . . [in 1560]. At four and a half he read the Haftarah in the synagogue. . . . At five and a half years he learned to write. At six he started wearing . . . [tefillin]. At eight and a half . . . he was studying the Alfassi [a digest of the Talmud studied by advanced students because the Talmud was banned in Italy]. At twelve and a half he began reading the Torah in the synagogue . . . and the same year he learned ritual slaughtering . . . During . . . [1571] he recited the morning . . . service in the synagogue.

Not to be outdone, Modena boasted with some degree of hyperbole that "people say about me 'when you were young you were like a grown man' . . . At the age of two and a half I recited the Haftara in the synagogue, and at the age of three I recognized my Creator and the value of learning and wisdom and was able to translate the weekly Torah portion [from Hebrew into Italian] and understand it."[36]

Most heder pupils in the early modern period studied the Bible, which was translated into the vernacular, the daily prayers, and at a later stage

after cited as Bonfil, *Italy*). *Unhappy Childhood*, p. 106. Hayoun, *Emden*, p. 316. George Duby, "The Aristocratic Households of Feudal France," in *A History of Private Life: Revelations of the Medieval World*, ed. George Duby (Cambridge, Mass.: Harvard University Press, 1988), Vol. 2, p. 76. Richard Barber, *The Reign of Chivalry* (Newton Abbot Devon: David and Charles, 1980), pp. 21 and 22. Mary Martin McLaughlin, "Survivors and Surrogates," in *The History of Childhood*, ed. Lloyd DeMause (London: Souvenir Press, 1976), pp. 128 and 129. Barbara A. Hanawalt, *Growing Up in Medieval London* (New York: Oxford University Press, 1994), p. 147. *Leon Modena*, p. 86.

36. Pollack, *Folkways*, pp. 52 and 65. Fishman, *Jewish Education*, p. 77. Bonfil, *Italy*, p. 130. *Leon Modena*, pp. 82 and 83.

the Pentateuch with the Rashi commentary. At the age of ten, pupils transferred their attention to the pages of the Talmud, sometimes with the gloss of the French medieval commentators, the Tosafists, and often without mastering the intermediate stage of the Mishnah. Critics headed by R. Loewe of Prague (c. 1530–1609) and his disciple R. Ephraim Lunshitz (1550–1615) attacked the deficiencies of the Jewish educational system then in vogue. Above all, they denounced "the barbaric order of study prevalent among us. . . . On studying the Bible and the Mishnah no emphasis at all is placed, and the study of the Gemara [Talmud] is also conducted in such a way that it can have no good result." Only sections of the weekly Torah portion, the *sidrah*, were covered, so that pupils had massive gaps in their knowledge of the Bible. Students not only failed to ascertain the plain meaning of the talmudic text because they began with the Tosafists' commentary, which was beyond their comprehension, but were also introduced to the intricacies of *pilpul*, talmudic dialectic, which again distorted the plain meaning of the text. In the eighteenth century, Isaac Wetzlar, partially influenced by the ideas of the German Christian pietists in his *Liebes Brief* (1749), repeated many of these criticisms, adding that like the Sephardim elementary pupils should study Hebrew grammar and the meaning of the daily prayers. When pupils were older, if they were unsuited to talmudic study, they should not be taught the *Ein Yakov*, a collection of stories from the Talmud with their fanciful interpretation of the Bible.[37]

Likewise drawing on the Sephardi example, Jacob Emden suggested that a child should be conversant with the Pentateuch, the prophets, and the rest of the sacred writings before he proceeded to learn about halachah, Jewish law; and he also regarded the study of Hebrew grammar as an important part of the curriculum. Yet this did not prevent him from subjecting his own seven-year-old son Zvi Hirsch to this pressure cooker system of learning. By then the child was absorbed in the study of the Talmud with the commentaries of Rashi and the Tosafists. All of these persons

---

37. Israel Zinberg, *A History of Yiddish Literature* (New York: Ktav, 1965), Vol. 6, pp. 89 and 90. Aharon F. Kleinberger, "The Didactics of Rabbi Loew of Prague," in *Scripta Hierosolymitana* (Jerusalem: Magnes Press, 1963), ed. A. M. Dushkin and C. Frankenstein, Vol. 13, pp. 32–55. Morris M. Faierstein, "The *Liebes Brief:* A Critique of Jewish Society in Germany (1749)" *Leo Baeck Institute Year Book* 27 (1982): 234 and 235 (hereafter cited as Faierstein, *Liebes Brief*).

were critics within the system, who found no fault with the basic design structure of elementary Jewish education.[38]

In the seventeenth century in Germany, Jewish tutors were found places in the households of wealthy merchants, where they instructed the children in religious subjects and the boys in the Talmud, and at the same time acquired business skills. Glückel mentioned "Michael, a young man from Poland who taught the children and later took a wife from Hildesheim and is now living there in great wealth and highly respected as the parnass. The same Reb Michael was a kind of household servant, as was then the practice in Germany when a young man was brought from Poland to teach young children." In the early 1770s, the number of the Polish Jewish private tutors employed in Prussia exceeded five hundred, and in 1772 a German-born teacher composed a treatise in which he requested Frederick the Great to ban the entry of these Polish Jewish tutors with their barbaric ideas.[39]

Not all Jewish boys received an adequate elementary education, although attempts were made to provide free communal schools for poor children and orphans or a payment was made to the teachers of such children. In early eighteenth-century Germany many impoverished Jews living in villages could not afford to pay for their children's education, but the communal leaders rejected their pleas for financial aid to rectify the situation. According to R. Joseph Stadthagen (d. 1715), the fault lay with the parents, who did not care whether or not their children received an education beyond the barest essentials, so long as a means of livelihood was found for them. At the same time in Poland preachers urged Jews to give larger amounts of bread to children who were going to heder on empty stomachs. In early seventeenth-century Prague, Landsofer reported that "the pupils abandon school to be at home, little disturbed that they have submitted to this foolish behaviour. . . . Such a state of affairs does not con-

---

38. Jacob Emden, *Migdal Oz* (Zhitomir: 1874) Section on the order of study, pp. 32 and 33. Hayoun, *Emden*, pp. 316 and 317.

39. Abrahams, *Glückel*, p. 51. Isaac Eisenstein-Barzilay, "The Background of the Berlin Haskalah," in *Essays on Jewish Life and Thought Presented in Honor of Salo Wittmayer Baron*, ed. Joseph L. Blau, Arthur Hertzberg, Philip Friedman, and Isaac Mendelsohn (New York: Columbia University Press, 1959), p. 194 (hereafter cited as Barzilay, *Berlin Haskalah*). Deborah Hertz, *Jewish High Society in Old Regime Berlin* (New Haven: Yale University Press, 1988), pp. 188 and 189 (hereafter cited as Hertz, *Old Regime Berlin*).

cern our contemporaries, for they are not ashamed that youngsters do not study sufficiently and lack adequate training in ethics, because they are preoccupied with the vanities of youth." In addition, because of the difficulties of the Polish economy in the mid-eighteenth century, many communities were unable to keep open a house of study (*bet ha-midrash*), a center of talmudic learning, and youths flocked in vain to Germany to continue their education. Due to the general economic malaise in Hungary, few students were able to prolong their schooling.[40]

Glückel's father ensured that "his daughters [were] taught religion and worldly things." Like other girls in Germany, she attended the heder with her brothers, and when writing about a Swedish-Danish war, she claimed to know little about its course because at the age of ten she was going to the heder "all day." In Nikolsburg in Moravia, girls were also taught reading and studied the prayer book but were excluded from anything more advanced, such as participating in those classes devoted to the study of the Pentateuch and Talmud. Women were expected to peruse ethical literature in Yiddish, such as the *muser-bikhel*, which covered a wide range of traditional source material. Emden complained bitterly about the bad custom of sending girls, sometimes on their own, to the heder for their religious studies, as boys could involve them in pranks. It was better that they had lessons at home or studied with a lady teacher, although not outside their home; otherwise they could end up as a prostitute. There was an exaggerated fear of exposing daughters to moral dangers by allowing them to walk in the streets. The Vilna Gaon instructed his wife that "the fundamental rule, however, is that they [their daughters] gad not about the streets, but incline their ear to your words and honor you and my mother and all their elders." Moreover, the communal authorities at Hamburg-Altona and Frankfurt enforced bans against Sabbath strolls by young women in the city streets outside the ghetto with a threat of withdrawing the permission to work for servant girls.[41]

---

40. Jacob Katz, *Tradition and Crisis: Jewish Society at the End of the Middle Ages* (New York: Schocken Books, 1993), pp. 328 note 8 and 329, note 10. Fishman, *Jewish Education*, pp. 24 and 25. Faierstein, *Liebes Brief*, pp. 234. Pollack, *Folkways*, pp. 58, 66, 74, and 75. Dinur, *Hasidism*, p. 123.

41. Abrahams, *Glückel*, pp. 14 and 19. Pollack, *Folkways*, pp. 63 and 64. Assaf, p. 206. Abrahams, *Ethical Wills*, p. 316. Raphael Mahler, *A History of Modern Jewry 1780–1815* (London: Vallentine, Mitchell, 1971), pp. 150 and 151 (hereafter cited as Mahler, *Modern Jewry*). Barzilay, *Berlin Haskalah*, p. 189.

A NEW WORLD FOR JEWISH CHILDREN?

It was asserted by both Lawrence Stone and J. H. Plumb that a new world for children was created in England in the second half of the eighteenth century. Although child mortality was still high at the close of the century, the elimination of the bubonic plague and the tentative measures being taken against the spread of smallpox both helped to reduce the childhood mortality rates, thereby encouraging parents to make a greater emotional investment in their children. Not only the aristocracy but the middle class, consisting of merchants and the professional classes, had more money to spend on their families. Before 1740, there were hardly any books specifically designed for children, but by the end of the eighteenth century hundreds of different titles on a vast range of topics poured from the printing presses each year. In the seventeenth century fathers still made toys for children, and we have the delightful story of Ber of Bolechow carving an ornate wooden sword for his stepson. In the following century shopkeepers sold a superior class of toy often manufactured with a didactic purpose, such as toy printing presses and farmyards, and the jigsaw puzzle was invented as a learning tool. The opposition of the liberal English philosopher John Locke to swaddling, wet-nursing, and flogging children and his theory of the child's mind being akin to "a piece of clean paper" (the environmentalist position) all gained wider currency in the eighteenth century, resulting in children being better treated and even indulged. One of the formative influences on Moses Mendelssohn, the father of the *haskalah*, was Locke. Whereas in the seventeenth century children wore adults' clothing after the age of seven, in the following century clothes purposely made for children became available. Despite all these improvements, children in England were still taught that they had a duty toward their parents and to detest cruelty.[42]

What was happening, however, in the palatial establishments of the Jewish bankers and entrepreneurs in the United States and Western Europe and in the more modest homes of those of middling rank during the second half of the eighteenth century? In this period a wealthy Jewish mer-

---

42. J. H. Plumb, "The New World of Children," *The Listener* (26 February 1976). J. H. Plumb, "The New World of Children in Eighteenth-Century England," *Past and Present* 67 (1975): 64–95. Lawrence Stone, *The Family, Sex and Marriage in England 1500–1800* (Harmondsworth: Penguin Books, 1979), pp. 254–299. (hereafter cited as Stone, *The Family*). *Ber of Bolechow*, p. 83.

chant class evolved in England, the United States, Holland, Germany, and France, with multifarious ties of family and trade. Lawrence Stone argued that forms of family structure were being created among the gentry and middle class in England that were less authoritarian, less sexually repressed, and more attentive to children and their needs. Yet, apart from instances here and there, it is difficult to discern a general pattern of actual Jewish families in Western Europe and the United States in which permissive modes of behavior predominated. Rather we witness the birth of a modified type of authoritarian family in which the father was still regarded as a figure of awe by his children but often acted by means of persuasion rather than force, and in which his love for his wife and children was more openly expressed.[43]

We can, perhaps, see this situation best in the Mendelssohn family in Berlin, where Moses Mendelssohn (1729–1786) held his wife Fromet in high esteem, referring to her as someone "whom I love more than father and child." This was a good example of a companionate marriage, in which there was increased affection between spouses with a consequent reduction in a husband's authority over his wife, but there was nonetheless a somewhat authoritarian way of rearing children. Dorothea Schlegel, one of Mendelssohn's daughters, writing some fifty years later to her brother Joseph on 25 November 1832, contrasted the rigid conditions prevailing in their own home with the freer family atmosphere in the country home of Nathan Meyer, a place where the Mendelssohn children spent part of their summer holiday. Dorothea remarked that

> Hinni is now the only one left from those gay childhood days when we were so often guests in . . . the parents' [the Meyers] house. That house with its garden, sheep, and cows, horse and carriage; the greater freedom as well as the greater respect and attention with which we, the children, were treated compared with what we were used to in our paternal home; all this appeared to me like the world of fairies. . . . All this is still vividly before my eyes whenever I recall it, especially the lovely mother [Joseph's future mother-in-law] who was of such inimitable, dignified patience and gentleness, and . . . [such] a striking contrast to our own somewhat impetuous, somewhat impatient mother.

Again Joseph, in an excited mood, dashed off a letter to his sisters in 1785, as "I am in an insufficiently sober mood to dare to write to them [his par-

---

43. Stone, *The Family*, pp. 411–414.

ents]. Reverence . . . restrains me from writing everything . . ." , which gives us an indication of the respect and awe that Joseph had for his father.[44]

Hence we should avoid a superficial reading of Mendelssohn family correspondence to construct a picture of a carefree, happy family with mild discipline, as the following examples can easily mislead. "God, be He Blessed, preserve you and our dear children," Mendelssohn wrote to his wife Fromet, "for a long and good life. . . . I greet my much beloved children. You cannot imagine how I feel when remembering them." So too, he penned another letter to Fromet suffused with tender sentiments about his offspring. "I greet . . . my dear children, God preserve them. Now I presumably love them all in equal measure, for they all come to my mind simultaneously when I think of home." Regarding Moses Mendelssohn as an authoritarian disciplinarian intent on imbuing his children with the work ethic would be to present an equally distorted view of him. He took a deep personal interest in the education of his children, particularly Joseph, giving him Bible lessons at the age of five and preparing the translation of the Pentateuch into German as a teaching tool for him. He also stressed that "I am not in favor of compulsion . . ." when it came to designing the educational curriculum for his children, even if it was generally weighted in favor of academic subjects. Moreover, Mendelssohn treated the education of his children with a playful sense of humor that must have colored his relations with them. "The rest of my children [apart from my son Joseph]," he advised Herz Homberg, "all turn out, for the time being, as we expected and, for the most desired: 'not long and not short, not wise and not foolish,' except my little son Nathan who calls himself the Wise, and whose wisdom consists at the moment in expecting sweetbread from Swa, gingerbread from Rabbi Samuel, and all else he needs from the cook." No doubt his youngest son Nathan, with whom his father romped around and was somewhat spoilt, had a different image of his father to that of his brothers and sisters.[45]

In the early eighteenth century R. Jonathan Eybeschutz (1690–1764) castigated those parents who allowed their children to be absorbed "in learning the French language, writing, arithmetic, and mixed dancing, and reduced the matter of Torah study to really not an hour in the day." His opponent R. Jacob Emden shared his opinions on this subject, reprimanding the "rich Jews of our [German] community [who] splash their money

---

44. Altmann, *Mendelssohn*, pp. 98, 723, and 724.
45. Altmann, *Mendelssohn*, pp. 99, 723, and 725–727.

to teach their sons and daughters the French language which makes them used to laughter, lightheadedness and bad language. . . . How much more is this the case when they teach them [their children] music." As early as the 1740s, the younger generation began to speak French and German at home, especially after commercial documents and notes could no longer be written in Hebrew or Yiddish in Germany. Eybeschutz, preaching in Metz in 1744, warned his congregants of the dangers to their morale that flowed from increasing wealth: "Because of our sins, there are some whose children are falling into bad ways. This is because these children are pampered and raised in the lap of luxury, and when they grow up they are unable to find the accustomed pleasures that they seek. It also leads them to mix with the Gentiles and learn their patterns of behaviour." Here was a clear denunciation of the permissive upbringing of Jewish children in Alsace-Lorraine in the 1740s, couched in general terms without citing specific examples of individual families, so that the diatribe may be somewhat exaggerated.[46]

By the second half of the eighteenth century, many opulent Jewish households in Germany not only retained the services of a tutor for Jewish subjects but also provided their children with a broad secular education. Benjamin Veitel Ephraim, born in 1742 to a coin millionaire, had private tutoring in Hebrew and the Talmud together with three months instruction in reading and writing German. Later he was tutored in French, English, and Latin, after which he read some key works of the Enlightenment and was instructed in geometry and algebra by a Jewish teacher. Bendavid, who was born in 1762, stated that his father's library in Berlin contained Judaica side by side with the New Testament, the Koran, and the works of Rousseau and Voltaire. He studied in a yeshiva until the age of thirteen with various Polish teachers, one of whom taught him Hebrew grammar and Maimonides' Aristotelian logic. He was given private instruction in writing, arithmetic, and bookkeeping. He was also taught by a French tutor, who gave him a grounding in Latin, while his mother had already coached him as an infant to read German. Steven Lowenstein discerned

---

46. Assaf, p. 205. Jacob Emden, *Bes Yakov* (Lemberg, 5674), reprinted in Israel, undated, p. 314. A. Schochat, "The German Jews' Integration within Their Non-Jewish Environment in the First Half of the 18th century," *Zion* 21 (1956): 207–235. Marc Saperstein, *Jewish Preaching 1200–1800: An Anthology* (New Haven: Yale University Press, 1989), p. 343 (hereafter cited as Saperstein, *Jewish Preaching*).

new ways of living among affluent Jews in Berlin in the 1770s, which went "beyond conspicuous consumption and luxury" by involving changes in dress, language, education, and socializing with Gentiles. Two playwrights blamed traditionalists opposed to educational reform "for the fact that the younger generation is turning to love affairs with Christians, gambling and high living."[47]

In the Jewish upper class in Germany in the seventeenth century, Reize Glückel's stepsister "knew French perfectly" and entertained her father's customers on the harpsichord, although such a secular education was not common then. By the 1750s, girls from affluent Jewish families were being coached by tutors in German, French, and English as well as being taught to dance and to play the harpsichord, the forerunner of the piano; they also subscribed to lending libraries to borrow and be amused by the latest fashionable novels. Henriette Herz, who was born in 1764, had such a thorough grounding in Hebrew that she mastered several rabbinic commentaries on the Bible. She also learned arithmetic, writing, geography, and French as well as attending a sewing class. In general Jewish girls from elite families had a poor Jewish education and were more influenced by novels than by the Yiddish ethical literature, which they could read had they so wished. Despite being very assimilated, Rachel Varnhagen's early letters were written in Yiddish. Breaking with past bans, many Jews started attending the theatre in Berlin in the 1770s, and Saturday promenades were now taken by men and women in Western Berlin, where Jews had not previously ventured. This was a significant break with the early eighteenth-century Jewish consensus that sought to restrict the movement of women. Yet even if a new, broader educational curriculum had been introduced among the Jewish elite and there was religious laxity in their homes, did these changes together constitute a revolution in Jewish childrearing practices by culminating in a more general permissive regime in Jewish households? To this question, there can be only the most tentative answer, which is yes.[48]

Todd Endelman depicted the children of the Prager family in England,

47. Steven M. Lowenstein, *The Berlin Jewish Community: Enlightenment, Family and Crisis, 1770–1830* (New York: Oxford University Press, 1994), pp. 43, 50, 51, and 101 (hereafter cited as Lowenstein, *Berlin*).

48. Abrahams, *Glückel*, p. 19. Hertz, *Old Regime Berlin*, pp. 172, 188, and 189. Lowenstein, pp. 48, 49, 51, and 52. Hannah Arendt, *Rahel Varnhagen* (New York: Harcourt Brace Jovanovich, 1974), p. 229.

who were Anglo-Dutch merchants with extensive ramifications in international trade, as being "raised to comfort and wealth and in a nontraditional, undemanding religious atmosphere . . ." When Yehiel Prager wrote in 1780, complaining that his son was learning too much Talmud in Amsterdam, his brother David replied: ". . . he will not learn too much Gemara [Talmud]. Nevertheless, it is no disgrace to be conversant with it, besides other fields of knowledge and languages." In 1783 the young Pragers journeyed from England to Philadelphia, taking with them a supply of kosher food, although their adherence to the dietary laws was slack. Their uncle Yehiel admonished them for avoiding the company of Jews after their arrival in the United States: "You know my opinions. Keep on good terms with people. You need certainly not keep company with low persons, but for God's sake don't avoid everyone." Above all else, the Pragers were concerned that members of the family should not give offense to fellow Jews, thereby jeopardizing the marriage prospects of younger members of the family. To the historian it is no easy task to conjure up the atmosphere in the Prager households. Were the children being lavishly bestowed with some of the wonderful new toys being manufactured, and were they participating in the wide range of children's games? Was lack of strictness in educating the Prager children in the Jewish religion and ritual merely one facet of their upbringing, or was it a more general symptom of the laissez-faire approach in their rearing?[49]

Benjamin Goldsmid's children were brought up on an estate in the English countryside at the end of the eighteenth century: "The Breakfast Room was fitted up with red morocco tapestry and gilt cornices, hung round with genealogical pictures of both sides of his family; many of them executed by the most eminent Masters, viz. WEST, SIR JOSHUA REYNOLDS AND BEECHY . . . In this room it was that he chearfully took his leave of his family and friends on the mornings when he came to town upon business." Moreover, "The Library was formed and arranged under the direction of his eldest son, abounding with a choice and numerous collection of the most famous Roman and English Classics . . . together with some very rare M. S. S . . ." As far as can be gleaned, Goldsmid ran his household in

---

49. Todd M. Endelman, *Radical Assimilation in English Jewish History 1656–1945* (Bloomington: Indiana University Press, 1990), p. 41 (hereafter cited as Endleman, *Radical Assimilation*). Gedalia Yogev, *Diamonds and Coral: Anglo-Dutch Jews and Eighteenth Century Trade* (Leicester: Leicester University Press, 1978), pp. 268–270.

a relaxed way, treating his servants "with respect," and his children's tutors were "more like friends than dependents"; and a favorite Jewish cook was allowed unusually to mix with the other guests after dinner. Presumably his family also benefited from Benjamin Goldsmid's affable and informal style before the onset of his mental illness. His son Lionel noted that "we had private Tutors in the house. English and Classic Masters, also French, German and Hebrew." Despite this, Goldsmid had in his library "a Law of Moses, with its sacred vestments . . . he kept all his family in the proper subordination of Religious decorum, and at particular times used to have Prayers performed in this Study-Room." Once again an indication of a family being directed by a patriarchal father, but not with much success, as another commentator remarked that the children were "by no means strict in their observance of the customs of their people."[50]

If we now turn to the memoirs of a member of "the middling class" like the boxer Daniel Mendoza, we gain some insight into the prevailing family atmosphere, which was less permissive than the childrearing practices of the Jewish grandees. His parents "contrived to bestow a tolerable education on all their children", and "as our family was large, my father was accustomed to place his children in different situations and employments very early in life [before they reached their teens]." Parental control was loosened over somewhat immature children, who were partially abandoned. The phrase that his father "would reprove me severely when it appeared that I had involved myself wantonly in a quarrel" hints at a strict disciplinarian.[51]

Jacob Rader Marcus characterized "the early republican period [in the United States] . . . [as] an age when children respected their parents or at least expressed themselves dutifully in their letters. The patriarchal mode prevailed; children were expected to obey; brothers dominated sisters." Even so, the family atmosphere seems to have been considerably freer than that prevailing in Western Europe. Nonetheless, because the hazzan Gershom Seixas presented a dignified public persona to his unruly con-

---

50. Levi Alexander, *Memoirs of the Life and Commercial Connections Public and Private of the Late Benjamin Goldsmid Esq of Roehampton* (London, 1808), pp. 96–99 and 118. Rachel Daiches-Dubens, "Eighteenth Century Anglo-Jewry in and around Richmond, Surrey," *Transactions of the Jewish Historical Society of England* 18 (1953–1955): 162 and 163. Endman, *Radical Assimilation*, p. 41.

51. *The Memoirs of the Life of Daniel Mendoza*, ed. Paul Magriel (London: B. T. Batsford, 1951), pp. 14 and 15 (hereafter cited as Mendoza, *Memoirs*).

gregants, this did not mean that he did not unwind at home and relax among his adoring family of fourteen surviving sons and daughters produced by two wives. Although he was in certain respects a permissive parent, his children did not seek to question his authority. "My children all love and fear me," he declared. "One of the little girls was an enfant terrible. She had two Aunt Judahs; one she liked, one she disliked. The child insisted upon referring to her favourite Aunt Judah by her first name, for, as she loftily informed the chuckling family: 'I've got one stinking Aunt Judah already." It is doubtful whether many Jewish children in Europe would have made such a cheeky comment with such aplomb at the time.[52]

Despite offering them a surfeit of advice on how they should conduct themselves, Jacob Mordecai, a widower who spent some time apart from his daughters, momentarily allowed his true feelings for them to be displayed. We cite this as yet another example of the new pattern of the loving authoritarian father who inculcated the desired modes of behavior through force of character and by implanting a modicum of fear in his children's hearts, yet lacing this all with his love and concern for them.

"Be good girls, mind your reading and writing, that you may be able to send me letters often, for I love you so dearly that I shall always be pleased when you can write to me. God bless you my dear children . . .", Jacob Mordecai wrote to Ruth and Ellen Mordecai on 4 September 1797. "Tell Ellen [one of his daughters] my lips have not diminished in consequence of the kisses she gave me, and that I long to press her to my heart. You are all equally dear to me and shall never know an abatement of my affection . . ."[53]

A similar warm picture of American Jewish family life, tinged with respect for parents, is created in the Gratz correspondence. Miriam Gratz referred to her children as "Our little Comforts." His wife having died, Barnard Gratz left for business in London in 1769, entrusting his orphaned daughter to the care of his sister-in-law Miriam.

"Dear little Rachel has escaped the small pox and is hearty," writes Miriam to Barnard. "She often talks of her 'dear little Daddy,' and wishes

---

52. Jacob Rader Marcus, United States Jewry (Detroit: Wayne State University Press, 1989), Vol. 1, p. 672. Jacob Rader Marcus, "The Handsome Young Priest in the Black Gown: The Personal World of Gershom Seixas," H.U.C. Annual 40–41 (1969–1970): 435 and 436.

53. Doris Groshen Daniels, "Colonial Jewry: Religion, Domestic, and Family Relations," American Jewish Historical Quarterly 66, no. 3 (March 1977): 389.

to see him, as, indeed, we all do. But how could it be otherwise when a person whom we all love and esteem, is at so great a distance from us. . . . I have a dear, good and kind husband, and a dear little, prattling niece, which is a great comfort. . . . I hope you make yourself entirely easy about Rachel and be assured she'll be as well taken care of by us as she possibly can be. Rachel gives her love to you and hopes that you won't forget her London doll . . . [Postscript] You must hurry home. . . . This is Rachel writing. As she begged me to let her write, I was obliged to guide her hand to please her . . ." Note the request from Rachel for the superior-made London doll.[54]

We now turn to a letter written by Rachel to her father a few years later, in which she tries to accommodate and internalize her father's values as regards education. It is bubbly but deferential in tone:

Hond. Father:-
. . . You mention in your letter about my minding schooling, which shall do my endeavors to learn as I know it is my dear daddy's desire. I have just begun to cipher [to use the Arabic numerals in mathematical calculations] . . . I am in Averdepois Weight and now can cast up anything. I should be very much obliged to my good Daddy if you see a pretty fan to get it for me, as they are very dear in this place; today I was at a French Colonel's funeral who was buried with all the Honors of war [this was during the American War of Independence] . . . I must conclude, Hond. Father, with wishing you every earthly felicity this world can afford.
Your Ever-Loving and Obedient Daughter,
Rachel Gratz[55]

If Simon Schama has brilliantly delineated the world of seventeenth-century Dutch childhood, showing the freedom and hidden adult constraints in play, it should come as no surprise that the children of Dutch Jewish patricians were similarly subjected to countervailing pressures. The wealthy Suasso family objected to the remarriage of Jeronimo's widow to a man of lower social status, and when a member of the family took the nine children into his own home, they were under strict instructions not to recognize their mother's children by her second marriage as close kin. To his mother's protestations, the eldest boy answered: "Mama, I shall pay you

54. Anita Libman Lebeson, *Jewish Pioneers in America 1492–1848* (New York: Brentano Publishers, 1931), pp. 178 and 180 (hereafter cited as Lebeson, *Jewish Pioneers*).

55. Lebeson, *Jewish Pioneers*, p. 180.

all the respect and obedience that a child owes to its mother, but as for what you have ordered me to do I would beg you humbly to excuse me. . . . It is our misfortune that our noble father lies under the earth and without doing violence to his memory and to our own self-respect we cannot obey your maternal orders." Her response was to order her children out of the house, while on the journey home "their eyes were full of tears." What was interesting about this episode was that Dutch family life was supposedly even more liberal than the English, yet in the West the deferential ties of children to fathers were still paramount.[56]

YOUTH AND LEISURE ACTIVITIES

Between 1525 and 1630, the Jewish population of Poland grew rapidly; it then slowed down because of the disruption caused by war until 1670, when it started to climb even more steeply in the eighteenth and nineteenth centuries. By 1764, the Jewish population of Poland numbered 500,000 and comprised about 5 percent of the total population. Unlike the stable sixteenth century, the conditions in eighteenth-century Poland were politically unsettled and concomitant with this instability was the disintegration of the economy. As a result, many Christian town dwellers left the urban centers for the countryside to eke out a living from agriculture. At the same time, Jews also began quitting the towns and moving into the villages, where they became artisans. The proportion of Jews living in small towns and villages in Poland reached its peak at the end of the eighteenth century, when it soared to 80 percent. So too, the proportion of persons under the age of twenty in the Jewish population of Poland was constantly growing, jumping from about a quarter in the eighteenth century to over 52 percent in 1897. In the unsettled conditions in seventeenth- and eighteenth-century Poland the ubiquitous and restless youngsters worried the communal leaders.[57]

---

56. Simon Schama, *The Embarrassment of Riches: An Interpretation of Dutch Culture in the Golden Age* (London: Fontana Press, 1988), pp. 481–561 (hereafter cited as Schama, *Dutch Culture*). Gans, *Memorbook*, pp. 237 and 238.

57. Hundert, *Jewish Children*, pp. 18 and 19. Gershon David Hundert, "Approaches to the History of the Jewish Family in Early Modern Poland-Lithuania," in *The Jewish Family: Myths and Reality*, ed. Steven M. Cohen and Paula E. Hyman (New York: Holmes and Meier, 1966), pp. 83 and 84. David Biale, "Eros and Enlightenment: Love

During the second half of the eighteenth century the Lithuanian Council requested local communities to set up centers of talmudic learning on no less than seven occasions. Every community was ordered to establish these centers for two boys and one youth for every ten taxpayers, as "boys and youth turn to idleness." At first the yeshivot were like the houses of study attached to synagogues, but later they became independent institutions not linked organically to the communities where they had been set up, and drew recruits from a wide area. Whereas the system of talmudic education was revitalized in Lithuania by the foundation of the Volozhin Yeshiva in 1802, in Poland the system of Jewish higher learning collapsed under the weight of the failing economy.[58]

Hence in Poland the new Hasidic movement throve in the interstices of the surviving and shrunken system for talmudic education. Both David Biale and Gershon Hundert posited a connection between the Jewish population explosion in Eastern Europe, the mass unemployment of juveniles, and the rise of Hasidism in the mid-eighteenth century. David Biale further claimed that the pressures of early marriage attracted large numbers of youths to become adherents of the Hasidic movement. In Eastern Europe the elite of merchants and rabbis ensured that most of their sons had married by the age of thirteen or fourteen, while the poorer Jews found partners for their children at fifteen or sixteen. Only the wealthy Jewish families could afford to support their children for several years after marriage, often to enable the young husband to pursue his talmudic studies. If the Jews shared with their neighbors this system of boarding newlyweds, only the Jews developed this institution known as *kest* as a means of financially underpinning higher education.[59]

Obsessed with fears about their sexuality and masturbation, some of the newly married youngsters flocked to the houses of study (*batei midrash*) or the courts of the Hasidic rabbi, the zaddik, where they could study Torah

Against Marriage in the East European Jewish Enlightenment," *Polin: A Journal of Polish-Jewish Studies* 1 (1986): 50 and 51 (hereafter cited as Biale, *Eros and Enlightenment*).

58. Hundert, *Jewish Children*, p. 19. Fishman, *Jewish Education*, pp. 33–37. Abraham Menes, "Patterns of Jewish Scholarship in Eastern Europe," in *The Jews: Their Religion and Culture*, ed. Louis Finkelstein (New York: Schocken Books, 1975), p. 202.

59. Biale, *Eros and Enlightenment*, p. 51. Hundert, *Jewish Children*, p. 19. Hundert, *Opatów*, p. 76. Max Weinreich, *History of the Yiddish Language* (Chicago: University of Chicago Press, 1980), p. 212.

and practice abstinence on the model of their mentor; and seek relief from the proper performance of their marital duties. It was stressed that most people attending the rabbi's court for a period of study during the festivals were young—one observer placed their average age at around twenty; and these youngsters were accused by their detractors of stealing from their wives and families to finance the trip, leaving them and their children "without food and without clothing." One model for the zaddik was Nachman of Bratislav, who as a newly married youth of thirteen gathered around him a group of married friends of a similar age and preached an ascetic attitude toward sex because of the anxiety produced by his early marriage. Moreover, kabbalists noted that nocturnal pollution involving the emission of semen resulted in the birth of demons, so that the custom arose in the seventeenth century of sons not accompanying their father's corpse to the cemetery in order to avoid being molested by illegitimate step-brothers. The Hasidic youths indulged in various manifestations of rebellion against their elders, such as turning somersaults in the street and dancing in synagogues, idling and smoking, overeating and drinking, and criticizing traditional scholars.[60]

Similarly in sixteenth century Verona and Asti in Northern Italy in 1619 confraternities were formed for Jewish youth under adult guidance. These transitional associations attempted to keep Jewish adolescents off the streets, particularly on a Sabbath afternoon, and to encourage their interest in traditional Jewish learning. They differed from the early twentieth century Jewish youth movement in alloting a low priority to outdoor and leisure activities. Jacob Marcus also noted a proliferation of mutual aid societies for youths in Central Europe in the late eighteenth century. These young men who had migrated far from home in search of employment wanted to ensure some financial support and medical care at times of illhealth, and were in revolt against the social controls imposed by their elders. One youngster having torn down a proclamation on a synagogue notice board, blew his nose in it!

The further east one traveled in Poland toward the more underdevel-

---

60. David Biale, *Eros and the Jews: From Biblical Israel to Contemporary America* (New York: Basic Books, 1992), pp. 129 and 130. Bernard D. Weinryb, *The Jews of Poland: A Social and Economic History of the Jewish Community from 1100–1800* (Philadelphia: Jewish Publication Society, 1973), pp. 283, 284, and 296. Gershom Scholem, *Kabbalah* (New York: New American Library, 1974), p. 322.

oped parts of the country, the higher was the percentage of Jewish craftsmen in the small towns. In the east the Christian guilds with their restrictive practices were less powerful, and this enabled Jewish youth to establish themselves in a wider range of crafts than was permissible in the big
cities. The bylaws of the guilds indicate that the majority of the Jewish
artisans were journeymen and apprentices rather than master craftsmen,
predominantly young persons. One would thus surmise that the majority
of those who journeyed eastward in search of work were juveniles. In the
large towns Jews dominated the occupations of tailor, furrier, cap-maker,
glazier, and butcher. The declining economy and mass unemployment bred
unrest among artisans, particularly apprentices. This economic hardship
fueled a series of revolts by artisans against the communal authorities, the
Kahal, in Minsk (1777 and 1782), Vitebsk (1783), Inowroclaw, Lublin
(1788), Vilna (1785–1790), and Leszno (1763 and 1792), with successes
for the artisans in a number of cities in western Poland. It is likely that
juvenile muscle spearheaded these revolts. Many of the underemployed
artisans and young persons worked as interlopers outside the guilds, which
were becoming increasingly obsolescent in the course of the eighteenth
century.[61]

Research into the Jewish guilds of Eastern Europe is only at a beginning, despite the pioneering investigations of Mark Wischnitzer. After the
age of thirteen the communal authorities ceased to have responsibility for
the education of orphans, and they were often apprenticed to a master to
learn a trade. We may thus take this as the age when apprenticeship contracts were first concluded. The term of apprenticeship varied from two
to seven years with the shorter, minimum term not being unusual. A tailor's
apprenticeship agreement from Cracow in 1750 specified that the master
tailor "undertakes to train [the youth] in sewing and cutting of every kind
of garment. He shall not conceal anything from him . . ." Boys from other
districts usually boarded with the master, his father paying for his room
and the food, although sometimes the master provided the meals free of
charge. The hours of work were long, stretching from sunrise to sunset in
summer and as many as five hours after it became dark in winter. Contracts tried to guard against the exploitation of the apprentice by stipulat-

---

61. Eisenbach, *Emancipation*, p. 33. Mahler, *Modern Jewry*, p. 284. Mark Wischnitzer, *A History of Jewish Crafts and Guilds* (New York: Jonathan David, 1965),
pp. 249, 258, 259, 272, and 273 (hereafter cited as Wischnitzer, *Crafts and Guilds*).

ing, for instance, that the apprentice was not to be forced to help with the housework. Nevertheless, there was a considerable amount of tension in the master's household between the master and his assistants, the apprentices and journeymen. In 1760 in Opatów an apprentice butcher broke his contract because he used to be beaten by his master. More important, the sources contain abundant complaints by masters against journeymen who had assaulted them and their wives, perhaps indicating underlying sexual tension in some of these disputes. Accordingly, the apprenticeship system, sometimes followed by a period as an unmarried journeyman living in the master's household, tended to inflate the years of adolescence from the early teens until the late twenties. On the other hand, it could be maintained that many youths were living away from home and separating from their parents in their early teens, forming new relationships, often later entering into partnership with their former masters, saving capital, and developing a degree of autonomy in preparation for marriage.[62]

Apart from a career as a rabbi, being trained as a merchant by one's father, and apprenticeship, other opportunities on the lower rungs of the occupational ladder were open to Jewish youth. During the eighteenth century the prestige of traditional learning was declining so much among the merchant elite in Western Europe that R. Eybeschuetz bemoaned the fact that wealthy men no longer sought Torah scholars as spouses for their disfigured daughters. Ascher Lehmann (1769–1858) as a lad of seventeen worked as a storeman for a well-to-do leather merchant in Prague. Here he was treated like a member of the family. "I had to go for walks with the beautiful daughter of the house on my arm, also to the theater, and always I had to go along when she went shopping. I could eat and drink as well as my master . . . " When Isaac Thannhauser's father died in reduced circumstances, he had to abandon thought of a career as a talmudic scholar and was harnessed by his father's family as a boy of thirteen to the pedlar's trade, for which purpose a stock of "buttons, eye glasses, big and small mirrors" and other similar objects were purchased on his behalf. However, in the late eighteenth century in Central Europe a career as an elementary teacher was regarded disdainfully as the lowest rung of the

---

62. Fishman, p. 77. Wischnitzer, *Crafts and Guilds*, pp. 262, 286, 266, 269, 271, and 286. Hundert, *Opatów*, p. 49. Mendoza, *Memoirs*, p. 15. Mendoza at the age of twelve was found a job with a glass-cutter, as a potential apprentice. The master's son was abusive and Mendoza "gave hime a severe thrashing."

occupational ladder, whereas the post of tutor of the Talmud in a wealthy household was still coveted. Thannhauser hated his wretched life as a pedlar and "sometimes thought of taking children for instruction, since I was capable enough at that time of being an excellent teacher, but in those days one was ashamed to be called *bocher* [Talmud student] or *rebbe* (a married teacher) and, to my great disadvantage, the prevailing arrogance held me back."[63]

Many of these other employment and educational opportunities in Central and Eastern Europe meant that a naive and somewhat inexperienced teenager might be living a long distance from his home. Adding this group together with those Jewish apprentices who boarded with their masters, we can now see that the adolescent experience in early modern Britain, where numbers of youths lived away from home, was not unique, but that similar conditions prevailed over large stretches of the European continent. Recent research has indicated that between a quarter and a half of the youths living in any given region entered into such service in stranger's households. It is doubtful whether a higher percentage of Jewish adolescents were so employed, so that the extent of the problem should not be exaggerated. If a Jewish youth in Central Europe was unfortunate enough to be trapped in a dead-end job, with bleak living conditions, he could sometimes break a short-term contract and move on, so long as he was not bound by an apprenticeship contract that tied him down for a longer period of time or caught in a web spun by malevolent relatives. Among the worst positions was that of an elementary teacher (*bocher*) tutoring a poor rural family in an isolated village. One such teacher reminisced:

> At four in the evening I arrived at a wretched house [in a Bohemian village] that had to be supported so that it wouldn't collapse. . . . Then a big pretty Jewish woman came out with five children. . . . In the evening the woman prepared a meal, a browned gruel, which tasted very good to me. At nine in the evening I had to climb a ladder with the two oldest sons. We got to the attic and lay down on a bed prepared for us. Since the blanket was too narrow for three persons, the sons took some sheepskins that were lying around there. . . . They even had a milk cow tied in back by the entrance hall, and also a calf for rearing. . . . I now began my instruction. There was the eleven-year-old son, who already began to read the *Aleph Bet* [the Hebrew alphabet] quite fluently. The second son, nine years old, didn't know much yet. . . . The seven-year-old daughter hardly recognized an Aleph. I said to the woman that the oldest son should start learning the *tefillah* [the prayers].

---

63. Saperstein, *Jewish Preaching*, p. 335. Richarz, *Memoirs*, pp. 56, 57, 66, 67, and 71.

But even here the unfortunate youth, who was bound by a short-term contract as a teacher, escaped by a subterfuge.[64]

What was the self-image of the Jewish adolescents in Central and Eastern Europe? If we rely on the evidence of moralistic writers and the communal ordinances, it appears that the frolics and boisterousness of youth was looked on askance by their critics. One writer urged rabbis to "admonish young men; otherwise, they will make carnival (celebrate Purim) the whole term"; and he warned the young men "that they should not always be after the girls." The *Brandtspeigel* (1590s) denounced "young girls flaunting themselves in front of men in the streets and at banquets, how loudly they speak and how shamelessly . . . one sees young women looking men straight in the eye, dancing." Much the same was said in 1727 by Elhanan Kirchan, who reproved the village Jews of Germany:

> In many villages women and virgins go about everywhere without a chaperon . . .
> There are also women who drink a great deal of liquor at a wedding or circumcision, As much as is required for a ritual bath, And carry on, at the same time, wanton talk and laughter with men and youths. As they do, so also do their daughters.

In Poland R. Joel Sirkes (1561–1640) referred to young men and women larking about by snatching handkerchiefs from each other, while dancing between men and women sometimes took place. Against these criticisms, it could be argued that all this was nothing more than youthful exuberance, expressing the vitality, beauty, and self-confidence of the swelling numbers of Jewish adolescents and that the Purim parades of youngsters in Poland as well as the other examples we have given were a completely new manifestation "of the will to take pleasure in life and enjoy it." This is in contrast with the situation in Paris, where a group of assimilationist Sephardi young bucks in the second half of the eighteenth century aped the nobility by carrying swords and dallied with Christian women.[65]

---

64. Richard Wall, "The Age at Leaving Home," *Journal of Family History* 3 (1978): 181–202. Michael Mitterauer, *A History of Youth* (Oxford: Blackwell, 1992), pp. 72–74. Richarz, *Memoirs*, pp. 54, 56, and 66–69.

65. Zinberg, *Old Yiddish Literature*, pp. 156, 288, and 290. Daniel Tollet, "The Private Life of the Jews in Old Poland," in *The Jews of Old Poland*, ed. Antony Polonsky, Jakub Basista, and Andrzej Link-Lenczowski (London: I. B. Tauris, 1993), p. 52. E. J. Schochet, *Bach, Rabbi Joel Sirkes: His Life, Work and Times* (Jerusalem: Feldheim Publishers, 1971), p. 197. Hundert, *Jewish Children*, p. 85. Arthur Hertzberg, *The French Enlightenment and the Jews* (New York: Columbia University Press, 1968), p. 161 (hereafter cited as Hertzberg, *French Enlightenment*).

We encounter a new problem in the seventeenth century—destitute children wandering into Lithuania from other parts of Poland. Seventy-five such boys were placed by the Lithuanian communal authorities in 1639 in educational institutions or apprenticed to a master to be taught a trade. After the Chmielnicki massacres of 1648, the large numbers of poor orphan boys who were drifting into vagrancy "were apprenticed to an artisan if they were willing to learn a craft."[66]

Having surveyed the working activities of Jewish youth, we now turn to their leisure pursuits, which developed prodigiously in the early modern period. Simon Schama's discussion of the seventeenth-century Dutch artist Cats contains a wonderful evocation of children's games: "hoop bowling, stilt walking, bubble blowing, somersaulting, blindman's bluff, hobby-horse riding, windmill and whirligig playing, knucklebones and marbles, and tops, for both whipping and unraveling. There was also mimic play, especially for girls—keeping house and playing with dolls—and in a version of the print . . . a mock militia company parade. Cats also added one important pastime somehow missing from Breugel's compendium—kite flying . . ." Unfortunately the Jewish evidence for this period is rather scrappy, apart from portraits of Dutch family groups that seem to show children with spinning-tops and the incidental reference to a doll. It is likely that children in wealthy Jewish families in Western Europe and the United States in the eighteenth century enjoyed many of these games. We also know that the Sephardi children in the Netherlands would skate on the frozen canals and lakes during the winter. In addition, Separdi and East European Jewish children played certain traditional pastimes on the various festivals. We should not assume that Jewish children in Central Europe were forced to concentrate on their studies all the time, as the twelve-year-old from Bohemia related how his father instructed him to throw fruit from a tree at village urchins "and jest with them" to show them that he was well. He would hardly be doing this if it was completely out of character for Jewish children.[67]

With the leisure pursuits of Jewish adolescents and young adults, we are on surer ground, particularly for southern Europe. A responsum from Mantua from 1560 sheds light on the history of tennis, as Jews already participated in the game. Moreover, in an Italian Hebrew comedy a boy

---

66. Wischnitzer, *Crafts and Guilds*, pp. 262 and 263.

67. Schama, *Dutch Culture*, p. 502 and 549. Gans, *Memorbook*, p. 237. Arthur Hanak, *Physical Education of Jews in the Middle Ages & Early Modern Times* (Tel Aviv: Maccabi World Union, 1987), p. 18. *Unhappy Childhood*, p. 109.

asked his carer for a loose-fitting garment, "so that I can move more easily when I play ball today." Two types of ball game were played: one was
much like handball but the ball was caught in a scoop attached to the wrist
and thrown against a wall, a form of the game of pelota; the other was
played in a court with a stone floor and the ball was struck by a racquet,
"small bows laced with guts, and netted with string." R. Moses of Provencal
decided that tennis could be played on the Sabbath, so long as hands were
used to return the ball rather than a racquet in case a player decided to
mend a broken string. This restriction was unimportant, as games were
frequently played with hands and tennis racquets came into more general
use only in seventeenth-century Italy. In Venice, despite Modena's protest, the rabbis persisted in their ban against playing with racquets on the
Sabbath. Restrictions were also placed on gambling on the outcome of
the game for money on the Sabbath, as nominal stakes were "converted
into cash." The responsum ended with the complaint that "it is not uncommon for the game to be conducted while the sermon is being preached in
the Synagogue . . ."[68]

Among the games played by Jewish children and adults in Carpentras
in southern France in the seventeenth century were *boules* (akin to bowling), skittles, cards, and *tarots*, a card game for telling fortunes. Communal regulations from 1645 forbade children to play *boules* and skittles,
except during the week following a wedding, before a circumcision, on
minor Jewish holidays, and during the two days of Purim. So too, there
were similar sumptuary laws in Hamburg-Altona, where playing with cards
and skittles was forbidden in 1726, except on Purim and the week of
Hannukah. In Metz, because repeated regulations against card playing had
been of little avail, a new rule was passed in 1777 stating that all those
who gambled or played cards and billiards within five miles of the city would
not be called up for three years to the reading of the Law. As we have
seen, the Jewish communities throughout Europe generally proscribed
certain leisure activities in the seventeenth century, but in Provence the
youthful Jewish courtship fraternities headed by the *prince d'amour* or
the *abbé de la jeunesse* flourished, despite attempts to limit them. It was
ordained by an arbitrator that "the Prince of Love, elected by young Jews,

---

68. Robert W. Henderson, "Moses Provencal on Tennis," *Jewish Quarterly Review*,
New Series 26 (1935–1936): 1–6. Cecil Roth, *The Jews in the Renaissance* (New York:
Harper and Row, 1959), pp. 28 and 29. Moses A. Shulvass, *The Jews in the World of
the Renaissance* (Leiden: E. J. Brill, 1973), p. 177.

may organise one dance during his year of office, on a day chosen by him," presumably with young boys and maidens dancing together.[69]

Everywhere Jews in early modern Europe were ignoring the age old restrictions against games and other forms of entertainment. In Amsterdam during the late eighteenth century, young Jews and other more supposedly staid citizens went much further by mingling with Gentiles in dance halls, clubs, music halls, and gaming houses, while the predilection of Dutch Jews for card playing and musing in coffeehouses was well known. In vain the Hamburg-Altona community issued regulations in 1726 that "boys and girls, and most emphatically servant boys and servant girls (were) forbidden to learn dancing with dancing masters." Both the Portuguese and the German Jews of Amsterdam were condemned in 1772 for attending the theatre and opera with their children. The fact that the Hamburg community banned attendance at operas in 1715 and the Furth community prohibited visits to a play or comedy in 1747 showed that long-standing restrictions no longer commanded the assent of wide sections of the German Jewish community. Henrietta Herz as a child in Germany participated in a musical play around 1772–1773 with an amateur Jewish troupe, after overcoming the objections of the communal elders. In Berlin and Prague even Orthodox Jews, particularly young persons, started frequenting the theatres. On the Sabbath Jews now strolled in the fashionable Tiergarten and Unter den Linden in Berlin; sometimes, however, these walks served as a cover for trysts between young Jewish women and Christian nobles.[70]

During the early modern period, when a city was afflicted by a plague or an outbreak of fire it was customary for rabbis to issue a decree banning card playing or dice throwing or other games of chance for a period of time as a mark of repentance, although by the eighteenth century these appeals ceased to be persuasive to the Jewish masses. In Frankfurt, after the conflagration of 1711, the rabbis forbade gambling games for fourteen years "except that they should be permitted to invalids and newly delivered mothers for their pleasure and to pass the time." The only other

---

69. Marianne Calmann, *The Carrière of Carpentras* (Oxford: Oxford University Press, 1984), p. 62, 86, and 162. Max Grunwald, *"Die Statuten der 'Hamburg-Altonaer Gemeinde' Von 1726,"* *Mitteilungen der Gesellschaft fur judische Volkskunde* 11: 1 (1903), p. 50. Hertzberg, *French Enlightenment*, p. 165. Michael Mitterauer, *A History of Youth* (Oxford: Blackwell, 1992), pp. 162–165.

70. Gans, *Memorbook*, pp. 209, 212, and 213. Mahler, *Modern Jewry*, p. 150. Lowenstein, *Berlin*, pp. 48 and 49.

exception was chess, which "some well-to-do Jews teach their children
. . . and have them instructed in it, for the reason that it does not so much
encourage greed but, on the contrary, sharpens the mind and requires
thought." R. Isserles (c. 1525–1572), in his gloss on the *Shulchan Aruch*,
permitted the playing of "a game with bone pieces, which is called *tschech*
[chess]" on the Sabbath, provided there were no monetary bets on the
outcome of the game. Chaim Azulai (1724–1800), summing up the views
of many rabbinic authorities, concluded that the playing of chess was permissible on the Sabbath only to lift melancholy.[71]

71. Victor Keats, *Chess, Jews and History* (Oxford: Academia Publishers, 1994),
Vol. 1, pp. 284–289. Shlomo Eidelberg, *R. Juspa Shammash of Warmaisa (Worms).
Jewish Life in the 17th Century Worms* (Jerusalem: Magnes Press, 1991), pp. 38
and 39.

7

Growing Up in Eastern Europe: Traditional Education

CHILDBIRTH AND INFANCY

Pregnant women were trammeled by a host of superstitions little different from those of the talmudic age and were careful to avoid glancing at ugly or misshapen persons in case their defects were imprinted on the fetus; nor would they eat cherries, as gorging on them was reputed to be responsible for the appearance of red birthmarks on babies. In traditional society in Eastern Europe, a midwife drawn from the local community and known as a *bobe* (grandmother) attended a woman when she gave birth. She was comparable in every respect to the handywoman who acted as a midwife in premodern English society. The *bobe* visited the pregnant woman weekly until the final stages of the pregnancy, when she called on a daily basis. On the actual day of the confinement, the men were ushered out of the house and the *bobe* was assisted in the delivery of the child by the female relatives of the parturient woman, who encouraged her to scream and push during the labor process. If necessary, the *bobe* would also do the housework and bathe and swaddle the baby. It was customary for her to visit the new mother for two to three weeks after birth to advise her as to what foods to eat to produce a plentiful supply of milk. The new mother would stay in bed for two or three weeks, where she would be pampered and in certain areas fed only on liquids. As in colonial society in America, childbirth in Eastern Europe was a social event, and the practice of women lying-in for several weeks after giving birth allowed them to recuperate and saved them from performing onerous household chores.[1]

Moses Marcuse, a Prussian-educated doctor who practiced in small Ukrainian towns, in his "Book of Remedies" *Sefer Refuot* (1789) launched a bitter diatribe against the traditional Jewish midwives:

> Why do you not persuade your husbands to let the midwives study from learned doctors, so that they should not kill you, make cripples of you. They [the midwives] kill many mothers along with their infants in childbirth, and they destroy many thousands of women with whom I have spoken; they become weak, sick, and crippled at the hands of the midwives, because of our many sins. How many men had to divorce their wives, though before their confinement they loved them much? . . . How many in confinement or thereafter become insane, melancholiac? How many become ill with epilepsy? How many have gotten tuberculosis, blood-poisoning, growths in the womb? How many become ill with jaundice, swellings, hernia? From how many do the midwives not tear the bladder out of their bodies or make a hole from which afterwards the urine cannot be contained . . . Can you imagine, dear women, how many thousands of women and children had to die young at the hands of the midwives? . . . they [your husbands] should let the midwives study.

While there was a degree of truth in such criticisms in that the midwives were not learning some of the new techniques that were becoming available, these assertions were partially misconceived, being motivated by a desire to diminish the role of these women at childbirth. They also dis-

---

1. Mark Zborowski and Elizabeth Herzog, *Life Is With the People: The Culture of the Shtetl* (New York: Schocken Books, 1978), pp. 313 and 314 (hereafter cited as Zborowski and Herzog). Lara V. Marks, *Model Mothers: Jewish Mothers and Maternity Provision in East London 1870–1939* (Oxford: Clarendon Press, 1994), p. 55 (hereafter cited as Marks, *Model Mothers*). Ghitta Sternberg, *Stefanesti: Portrait of a Romanian Shtetl* (Oxford: Permagon Press, 1984), pp. 124–126 (hereafter cited as Sternberg, *Stefanesti*). Richard W. Wertz and Dorothy C. Wertz, *Lying-In: A History of Childbirth in America* (New York: Free Press, 1977), pp. 1–28 (hereafter cited as Wertz, *Lying-In*).

counted the boost to the morale of expectant mothers, who were being cared for by midwives whom they knew well and could rely on.[2]

So too, Maurice Fishberg, writing in 1911, made similar criticisms, claiming that recent data showed "that only in two out of ten instances are the Jews more favourably situated in respect of the proportion of still-births. Only in Amsterdam and in Frankfurt-on-Main is the percentage smaller among them than among the Christians, while in Bulgaria, Warsaw, and Bucharest they have even a larger proportion of still-births. . . . In other words, in Eastern Europe, where child-birth is attended by ignorant midwives, the proportion of still-births is larger than in Western Europe, where either physicians or trained midwives are, as a rule, in attendance." Nevertheless, as we shall see later, there is a strong suspicion that these figures mask a high rate of infanticide for children born to unmarried mothers, which had nothing to do with the poor skills of midwives. In Galicia before the First World War in the shtetl of Sniatyn, the midwife called on the services of a doctor only in the case of an emergency, but other small towns were without a single physician; for instance, Vetka in White Russia could only boast several folkhealers, *feldshers*, and two pharmacists. As soon as new opportunities for training as midwives were created in Eastern Europe, Jewish women quickly availed themselves of these facilities. No fewer than 25 percent of the midwives in training in Russia in 1910 were Jewish, an astonishing figure, and such training meant that they could live and seek employment outside the Pale of Settlement.[3]

Moreover, when an expert in medical history was asked when it was statistically safer for patients in general to rely on the attendance of doctors or not, his answer was about 1925. It has also been asserted by a

---

2. Israel Zinberg, *A History of Jewish Literature: The Berlin Haskalah* (New York: Ktav, 1976), Vol. 8, p. 163.

3. Maurice Fishberg, *The Jews: A Study of Race and Environment* (New York: Walter Scott, 1911), pp. 241 and 242 (hereafter cited as Fishberg, *The Jews*), pp. 241 and 242. Joachim Schoenfeld, *Shtetl Memoirs: Jewish Life in Galicia Under the Austro-Hungarian Empire and in the Reborn Poland 1898–1939* (New York: Ktav, 1985), p. 27 (hereafter cited as Schoenfeld, *Shtetl Memoirs*). Don Gussow, *Chaia Sonia* (New York: Bantam Books, 1981), pp. 18 and 78. Samuel C. Ramer, "Childbirth and Culture: Midwifery in the Nineteenth-Century Russian Countryside," in *The Family in Imperial Russia*, ed. David L. Ransel (Urbana and Chicago: University of Illinois Press, 1978), p. 228.

medical historian that illiterate black midwives in Virginia caused less danger of infection at childbirth than doctors until the close of the nineteenth century. My own mother had her first confinement at home in 1928 and was allowed by her doctor's neglect to run some four weeks over the term, losing a baby boy called David after a month through some infection she transmitted to him, and she herself became dangerously ill for a year. Again, the maternal death rate for England and Wales averaged between 3,000 and 4,000 maternal deaths a year, hardly falling between 1855 and 1934. Because general practitioners interfered more than midwives when a patient was in labor, they were far more likely to infect the mother. The main cause of these deaths was puerperal sepsis, which was effectively combated only in 1936 with the introduction of sulfonamides.[4]

We now turn briefly to the subject of circumcision. In traditional society in Eastern Europe, on the day before the circumcision the teacher from the local heder attended at the baby's home with his class for the *krishmaleinen* (the recital of the *Shema*) around the cradle in order to bring good luck to the baby and to protect him from malign influences. After the psalms had been chanted, the father distributed honey cake to the male students and little girls also joined in the scramble for these goodies.[5]

It was only in the nineteenth century with the modernization of Jewish communities and the rise of assimilation that the question of the circumcision and conversion of vast numbers of minor children of Jewish fathers and Gentile mothers was acutely posed. For instance, in January 1801 the *mohel* Joseph ben David circumcised the infant son of a Sephardi father and a non-Jewish mother in Paris. Pious *mohalim* in Central Europe in the first half of the nineteenth century regularly circumcised the sons of Gentile mothers. Although this was halachically permissible, Samson Raphael Hirsch (1808–1888) thought there were sound reasons why this practice should no longer be allowed and carried Orthodox opinion with him. However, R. Yehuda Leib Zirelson, former chief rabbi of Bessarabia and a founder of Agudat Yisrael, "permitted a mohel to circumcise, and

---

4. *Medicine and Society in France: Selections from the Annales*, ed. Robert Forster and Orest Ranum (Baltimore: Johns Hopkins University Press, 1980), p. ix. Wertz, *Lying-In*, p. 13. Marks, *Model Mothers*, pp. 88 and 89.

5. Yekhiel Shtern, "A Kheyder in Tyszowce (Tishevits)," in *East European Jews in Two Worlds: Studies from the Yivo Annual*, ed. Deborah Dash Moore (Evanston, Ill.: Northwestern University Press, 1990), p. 55 (hereafter cited as Shtern, *Heder*). Sternberg, *Stefanesti*, pp. 126 and 127.

not convert, the child of a Jewish father and a non-Jewish mother . . ." Under talmudic law, a child under the age of bar mitzvah might be converted by immersing him in a ritual bath at the direction of a rabbinic court (Ketubot 11a). One may perform an act on someone else's behalf, so long as it is to his advantage, and conversion to Judaism was regarded as a privilege (a *zechut*). Relying on the argument that there is no advantage for a potential convert to grow up in a nonreligious home, modern Orthodoxy has clawed back the liberal rules of Halacha. One critic has asserted that through this approach "Orthodox Jewry is becoming a fortress separated from the general Jewish community. . . . As long as Halakha provides a device to properly convert children of intermarriage, it should be utilized aggressively to make contact with vast numbers of Jews."[6]

Swaddling the bodies of newborn infants in tight bands for the early months of their life started to disappear in England from the mid-eighteenth century, followed by France a decade or two later. In German cities the custom continued, despite the condemnation of doctors, into the 1840s. In the *Me'asef*, the organ of the German Jewish enlightenment, reformers protested in 1811 that "his [the baby's] hands and feet are bound by bands of linen so that he cannot turn this way or the other way, and is unable to move any of his members, and his freedom is robbed from him." Jewish doctors in Eastern Europe, such as Studentski in 1876, railed against the practice of swaddling "the child from head to foot in bands. . . . Many times did I reprove the midwives about this . . ." Among the Jews in Kurdistan the child was completely immobilized by the swaddling process in a cradle, so that a reed urine-tube had to be attached by wax to the child's genitals to enable the fluid to drain into a clay pot. Nonetheless, in spite of the swaddling bands the infant was physically freer in Eastern Europe, where at an early stage its arms were untied and the general restraints relaxed and it was constantly picked up by members of the family who rocked and serenaded it with lullabies. This regime of swaddling, against which there were no serious inroads in Eastern Europe until the

---

6. Jonathan Helfand, "A German *Mohel* in Revolutionary France," *Revue des Etudes Juives* 143 (July–December 1984): 367–369. Mordechai Breuer, *Modernity Within Tradition: The Social History of Orthodox Jewry in Imperial Germany* (New York: Columbia University Press, 1992), pp. 253 and 254 (hereafter cited as Breuer, *German Orthodoxy*). Andrew M. Sacks, "The Conversion of Children from Inter-Married Familes in Israel," *Berit Mila Newsletter* 6, no. 1 (13 May 1994): 8–10. Michael Rose, "Conversion: Crisis or Opportunity," *Jewish Quarterly* 154 (Summer 1994): 68–69.

interwar period, encouraged passivity in infants, which was compatible with growing up in a society in which there was little social change. The degree of swaddling was much more severe among the Jews of Kurdistan, where authoritarianism in family life was much more prevalent.[7]

In middle-class Jewish families in Eastern Europe, such as that of Vera Weizmann and Arthur Rubinstein, it was sometimes the custom of mothers to hand their infants over to the care of wet nurses who sometimes had their own illegitimate children. In colonial America children were nursed for a year and sometimes for two years, and in Eastern and Central Europe in the early nineteenth century children were breast-fed for similar lengths of time. By the beginning of this century, Jewish children in Eastern Europe were usually suckled for about a year, but probably for a shorter period of time than in the recent past.[8]

TRADITIONAL LEARNING: THE HEDER

From the first, the baby boy in the *shtetl* in Eastern Europe was familiarized with the world of Jewish culture with its focus on learning through its chosen instruments, the home and the Jewish elementary school, the heder (literally meaning a room). As we have seen, the amulets that adorned the birth chamber with the psalms were purchased from the local schoolteacher, the *melamed*; and children from the nearby heder recited the credo of the Jewish faith, the *Shema*, "Hear O Israel, the Lord our God, the Lord is One," to the sleeping infant boy on the day before his circumcision. A special kind of honey cake (*reshete*), on which the teacher drew a little fish with the words *Mazel tov* and which he dotted with many little holes to represent an iron sieve, was baked for the circumcision. All these symbolic actions ensured that the infant was almost enrolled as an honorary pupil of the heder, thereby integrating him into the community and enhancing its unity.[9]

Once the baby passed into its mother's hands again after the circumci-

---

7. Abraham Stahl, "Swaddling: Its Disappearance as an Illustration of the Process of Cultural Change," *Koroth* 8, no. 1–2 (June 1981): 285–298.

8. Vera Weizmann, *The Impossible Takes Longer* (London: Hamish Hamilton, 1967), p. 7. Arthur Rubinstein, *My Young Years* (New York: Alfred A. Knopf, 1973), p. 4 (hereafter cited as Rubinstein, *Young Years*). Wertz, *Lying-In*, p. 3.

9. Shtern, *Heder*, p. 55.

sion, she principally cared for it during the next three to five years of its life and sang lullabies to her infant son, urging him to fulfill her cultural expectations and ambitions for him when he grew to manhood:

> Sleep soundly and sweetly till the day has begun.
> For under the bed of good children at night
> There lies, till the morning, a kid snowy white.
> We'll send it to market to buy *sechorah* [merchandise],
> While my little lad goes to study *torah*.
> Sleep soundly at night, and learn *torah* by day;
> Then thou'lt be a Rabbi when I have grown grey.[10]

From the early nineteenth century onwards, there were many variations on this paean to Torah learning, which would, it was hoped, enable the infant to have a secure economic base and join the ranks of the communal elite of scholars and merchants. Another lullaby commenced,

> My Yankele shall learn the Law,
> The Law shall baby learn,
> Great letters shall my Yankele write,
> Much money shall he earn.
> A pious Jew will Yankele be . . .

In scholarly households, the father sometimes held his infant on his lap before he could talk, accustoming him to listen to the sing-song intonation of talmudic study and to respect holy books, which could not be hurled playfully onto the floor.[11]

We must now pause to consider the structure of the Jewish family in the shtetl and the interrelationships between parents and children. Writing of a childhood in the 1870s and as someone stemming from a com-

---

10. William Moses Feldman, *The Jewish Child: Its History, Folklore, Biology & Sociology* (London: Balliere, Tindall, and Cox, 1917), p. 196 (hereafter cited as Feldman, *Jewish Child*).

11. Feldman, *Jewish Child*, p. 199. Ruth Rubin, *Voices of a People: The Story of Yiddish Folksong* (Philadelphia: Jewish Publication Society, 1979), pp. 32–34. Some late nineteenth-century lullabies show strife in the household, with Jewish mothers opting for traditional religious values while the fathers exposed to the influence of the enlightenment or socialism scorned them. Mark Zborowski, "The Place of Book-Learning in Traditional Jewish Culture," in *Childhood in Contemporary Cultures*, ed. Margaret Mead and Martha Wolfenstein (Chicago: University of Chicago Press, 1964), p. 124 (hereafter cited as Zborowski, *Book-Learning*).

fortable family in Swislocz, Shmarya Levin (1867–1935) confessed that a boy "saw his parents only for half an hour in the morning—before first prayers—and then for an hour in the evening [after attending heder all day], before he went to sleep. So it happened in the majority of cases there was little intimacy beween parents and children, and even brothers if they happened to be learning in different *cheders*. As between brother and sister there was even less opportunity for the ripening of friendships and affection." Further, "My father was a stern, silent man. . . . It was dull, staying alone with father in the house, for he was always absorbed in his affairs, and seldom had a word for me. And in general he spent little time with his children." Again, Selman Waksman recalled that he and his father "were good friends, but not comrades. We seldom played games or engaged in activities that would bring us close together." Here was the emergence of the pattern of the remote father unable to communicate effectively with his sons. There was also a large group of Jewish fathers and grandfathers who were old-fashioned and strict disciplinarians.[12]

The philosopher Morris Raphael Cohen, who was born in 1880 or 1881, described his grandfather with whom he boarded for a number of years during his childhood as someone who "belonged to the stern old school that did not encourage the outward expression of affection." On one occasion, the young Cohen was unjustly accused of inciting an assault on another heder pupil, for which he was placed on the bench by the teacher "and the regular punishment was administered before the whole class as an admonitory example to all." By chance Cohen's grandfather arrived at the heder some thirty minutes later, but before he could assert that the accusation was unjust and a spiteful fabrication, his grandfather ordered the *melamed* to whip him again. The unfairness of what his grandfather did still rankled with Cohen some sixty years later. Joseph Patai (1882–1953), who grew up in a small village community in Hungary, asserted that his father "believed, worked, and struggled, but spoke little. And if he spoke, his word was a patriarchal command, with respect to which there

---

12. Shmarya Levin, *Childhood in Exile* (London: George Routledge, 1935), pp. 63 and 64 (hereafter cited as Levin, *Childhood*). Selman A. Waksman, *My Life with Microbes* (London: Robert Hale, 1958), pp. 32 and 33. See Samuel Chotzinoff, *A Lost Paradise: Early Reminiscences* (London: Hamish Hamilton, 1956), pp. 20, 21, 72, and 73 (hereafter cited as Chotzinoff, *Early Reminiscences*) for an example of a strict father; and Morris Raphael Cohen, *A Dreamer's Journey* (Glencoe, Ill.: Free Press, 1949), pp. 29, 37, and 38 (hereafter cited as Cohen, *Dreamer's Journey*).

could be no criticism, no offering of opinion, but only obedience." What this meant was that Joseph Patai as a boy of five or six was sent to heder with a younger brother unaccompanied by any adult, despite a heavy snowfall, and twice was unable to locate a plank over a brook they had to cross, as a result of which they fell through the ice and arrived home with their clothes drenched. Only on the third occasion, after numerous changes of clothing, did their father conduct them safely across the brook with a shovel to clear the snow from the plank, parting with the words "Now go to heder!" Yet none of this was mentioned in Joseph Patai's autobiography; the revelations had to await his own son's memoirs, and this suppression of evidence regarding father's true character may well have been a common pattern.[13]

These themes of the "loss of father and separation from the mother" or "the absence of the father and a mother handicapped by illness" were elaborated by three East European masters of Hebrew literature: Mendele Mokher Seforim (S. J. Abramowitz, 1835–1917), Hayyim Nahman Bialik (1873–1934), and Samuel Joseph Agnon (1888–1970). Mendele at the age of thirteen or fourteen was devastated at the disintegration of his family when his father died and he had to live apart from his mother, who was unable to support him. He repeatedly returned to an *aggadah* concerning R. Jose, who exclaimed, "Woe to the sons exiled from their father's table!", linking this refrain to his own life. Having lost his father at an earlier age than Mendele and also cut off from his mother, Bialik sought to overcome his trauma by escaping into a dreamlike world of ancient rabbinic legend and then imagining his own East European home as an extension of this world. So too, Agnon poignantly remarked that "when I was a child of six or seven, my father of blessed memory went to the fair in Lashkowitz. As I missed him very much I was sad all the time. One evening I came home from *heder* overcome with longing. I pressed my head against the wall and cried: Father, father, where are you, I have loved you deeply . . ."[14]

---

13. Cohen, *Dreamer's Journey*, pp. 29 and 36–38. Joseph Patai, *The Middle Gate: A Hungarian Jewish Boyhood* (Philadelphia: Jewish Publication Society, 1994), p. 30 (hereafter cited as Joseph Patai, *Middle Gate*). Raphael Patai, *Apprentice in Budapest* (Salt Lake City: University of Utah Press, 1988), pp. 42–44.

14. David Aberbach, "Aggadah and Childhood Imagination in the Works of Mendele, Bialik, and Agnon," in *Jewish Education and Learning*, ed. Glenda Abramson and Tudor Parfitt (Reading: Harwood Academic, 1994), pp. 233–241.

As the Jewish mother in Eastern Europe had an intensive relationship with her infant son for only a few brief years until he was handed over to the dominance of the all-male world of his father and the whip of the heder teacher, she became fixated on the pre-oedipal stage of her son's development, being concerned with feeding and sustaining a fragile creature in a hostile world where infectious disease and anti-Semitism were endemic. She was thus in the main not the educator of her son but the source of supply of breast-milk and solid foods, hence her obsession with the delicate constitution of her son and of the need to overindulge him with good food. Peretz has a wonderful story in which a young mother prematurely ravaged by poverty joyfully listens to her other-worldly husband chanting the Talmud, but then remembers everything in their home has been pawned and that "the baby is ailing and there isn't a drop of milk in the house." A row ensues, in the course of which she is about to hang herself, when she sees the child about to tumble out of the cradle. Stunned, she offers her withered breast to the child. "There, you glutton . . . There, sip away—torture me." All this hostility between mother and infant competing for the meager resources of the family had to be suppressed, just as when children were older in Eastern Europe they were not permitted to answer their mothers back. Thus mothers turned this hostility inwards and projected it onto their own children, whom they accused of killing them by their bad behavior, while they were making so many sacrifices on their child's behalf. If mothers related to their children as providers of food, in the better economic conditions prevailing in Western Europe and the United States for immigrant families this obsession with food supply and their children's care translated into significant gains for their children's health.[15]

On the other hand, girls in Eastern Europe tended to be spoiled by their fathers, who would mostly only reprimand them in gentle terms, leaving the task of severely disciplining them to their mothers. If these mothers came from working-class families, they tended to be harassed, slaving from dawn to late in the evening in the market or on a never-ending list of household chores for a large family. The fathers were sometimes unworldly, pious

---

15. Martha Wolfenstein, "Two Types of Jewish Mothers," in *Childhood in Contemporary Cultures*, ed. Margaret Mead and Martha Wolfenstein (Chicago: University of Chicago Press, 1964), pp. 424–440. Sylvia Barack Fishman, *Follow My Footprints: Changing Images of Women in American Jewish Fiction* (Hanover, N.H.: Brandeis University Press, 1992), pp. 17 and 18.

and scholarly individuals who had opted out of the labor market, which left their wives with little choice but to be the family breadwinner. Fathers in the shtetl could be affectionate, soft, nurturant, and caring individuals, but there were many who were harsh and restrictive disciplinarians and somewhat rejecting of their daughters if they hankered after a modern lifestyle. Under pressure from the incessant demands of a number of babies born in quick succession, the working-class Jewish housewife quickly enrolled her eldest daughter as a substitute mother to look after the youngest children. One woman recollected that the "trouble is, the parents did not have time. There was a lot of work. Already they had three smaller children than I. My mother was always cursing and angry and she was frustrated. . . . You have to let it out on somebody, so she always let it out on me."[16]

Whereas boys were pampered and petted by their mothers, girls were obliged to treat their mother's kitchen as a schoolroom. "There she [a young girl] learned to bake and cook and manage, to knit, sew, and embroider; also to spin and weave in country places. And while her hands were busy, her mother instructed her in the laws regulating a pious Jewish household and in the proper conduct for a Jewish wife . . ." wrote Mary Antin (1881–1914). Even girls as young as six were soon initiated into the art of scrubbing floors.[17]

Within Eastern Europe, the pre-heder years were seen as a paradise from which children were torn away, and hence according to David Biale the remote parents were idealized and the garden of Eden at home was contrasted with the brutal conditions extant in the heder. Although these themes were originally explored by Guenzburg and Gottlober, the same motifs reoccur in the work of Shmarya Levin (1867–1935) and Abraham Cahan (1860–1951). Recalling his pre-heder days, the latter remarked that "Podberezy was a small town. It ended a few steps from our house and there the meadows and fields began. I remember the grass and the flowers and the soft breeze and how I enjoyed them. I remember all the mysteries. I knew the name of only one kind of bird—the chirping sparrows—but not the others with their different calls and plumages." In a novel by S. Ben Zion published in 1904, according to Naomi Sokoloff, "*Heder* discipline

---

16. Sydney Stahl Weinberg, *The World of Our Mothers* (New York: Schocken Books, 1988), pp. 27, 30, 31, 38, and 39 (hereafter cited as Weinberg, *World of Our Mothers*).

17. Weinberg, *World of Our Mothers*, pp. 35 and 36. Mary Antin, *The Promised Land* (Princeton, N.J.: Princeton University Press, 1985), p. 34.

becomes a form of bondage and cruel near-sacrifice of the young, while Gentile boys from the village, at liberty to roam barefoot in the country-side, appear as 'bnei horin,' free men."[18]

Boys were enrolled in the beginner's heder (dardeki heder), where they were taught the Hebrew alphabet and prayers between the ages of three and five years. Shmarya Levin went through the heder initiation ceremony in 1871 at the age of four, when he was enveloped in his father's tallit (prayer shawl) and carried to the heder to mark his spiritual rebirth and his separation from the world of women. In Swislocz in the 1870s these Jew-ish elementary schools contained ten to fifteen pupils; elsewhere they usually numbered twenty children, although in some places as many as seventy to eighty children were enrolled. The heder, which was often no more than a single room, was also the teacher's home, where he lived and slept. It was often denounced by critics as poorly lit and insanitary. School lasted from 8 A.M. to 6 P.M. for five days a week with an extra half day's school on Fridays. The children were divided into small groups who were instructed by the teacher for short intervals during the day, after which they were supposed to revise but often used this as an opportunity to relax. The teacher was assisted by a belfer (helper), who not only carried small chil-dren on his back to and from school but sometimes brought them packed lunches or helped with the teaching.[19]

To aid the children in grasping and retaining a knowledge of the indi-vidual letters of the Hebrew alphabet, the shapes of these letters were compared to familiar objects or the limbs of the body. The first printed textbook to outline this method of instruction was the Sefer Torat Haim of Abraham Haim Shur (d. 1639), who for example depicted the letter alef as a water carrier and the beys as having "a wide-open mouth." Nonsense sentences were composed out of the letters of the alphabet,

---

18. David Biale, "Eros and Enlightenment: Love Against Marriage in the European Enlightenment," Polin (1986): 53–54 (hereafter cited as Biale, Eros and Enlightenment). The Education of Abraham Cahan, trans. Leon Stein, Abraham P. Conan, and Lynn Davison (Philadelphia: Jewish Publication Society, 1969), p. 8 (hereafter cited as Cahan, Memoirs). Levin, Childhood, pp. 43, 52, and 53. Naomi B. Sokoloff, The Child in Modern Jewish Fiction (Baltimore: Johns Hopkins University Press, 1992), pp. 10–12 (hereafter cited as Sokoloff, The Child in Jewish Fiction).

19. Zborowski and Herzog, pp. 88 and 89. Levin, Childhood, pp. 44, 47, 49, and 50. Schoenfeld, Shtetl Memoirs, pp. 46–48. Zborowski, Book-Learning, pp. 124 and 125. A. J. Brawer, "Study and Play in the Heders of Galicia," Edoth 2, no. 1–2 (October 1946–January 1947): 12 and 13 (hereafter cited as Brawer, Heders of Galicia).

which the children recited according to traditional rhythmic chants under the guidance of the teacher's assistant, the *belfer*. This was one of the many educational techniques borrowed by the rabbis of the talmudic age from the Greeks, who were very fond of mnemonic devices to stimulate memory. Even the recital of such beginner's exercises in learning to read in the heder as Bo, Ba, Be may not be accidental and may owe something to Greek antecedents. During the eighteenth and nineteenth centuries, the teachers were aided by printed alphabet charts, based on Christian models, which contained the whole alphabet, various permutations of the letters of alphabet, the *Shema*, and prayers before and after eating. With the aid of a *taytl*, a pointer, the teacher traced the contours of a letter on one of these charts or from the special opening page of a prayer book for each individual child for ten- or fifteen-minute sessions during the day. In fact, textbooks for teaching reading did not become common until after the First World War, when the traditional pedagogic methods were abandoned.[20]

Having passed this stage of the learning process after two years or less, the pupil now became a member of a *chumash heder*, where he was taught the Pentateuch. On joining this heder, the little boy attended a fresh initiation service. On the selected day the teacher sat at a table laden with a honey cake, brandy, and nuts and on the right side of the teacher was the boy's father, while all around them the other male guests were seated. Again, the boy's mother and the other female guests stood at a distance, emphasizing the boundary between the men's and the women's worlds, which had been imposed at the time of the circumcision and the previous heder initiation ceremony. Three older boys would be trained to recite special blessings over the little boy who was commencing the study of the Torah, while he was coached to participate in a lengthy stereotyped dialogue with the teacher and taught to read and translate the first chapter of Leviticus from Hebrew into Yiddish word for word. Portions of this ceremony may have been borrowed from the medieval heder initiation service.[21]

---

20. Diane Roskies, "Alphabet Instruction in the East European Heder: Some Comparative and Historical Notes," *Yivo Annual of Jewish Social Science* 17 (1978): 21–53 (hereafter cited as Roskies, *Alphabet Instruction*). Judah Goldin, *Studies in Midrash and Related Literature*, ed. Barry L. Eichler and Jefferey H. Tigay (Phildelphia: Jewish Publication Society, 1988), pp. 205 and 206.

21. Shtern, *Heder*, pp. 57–60.

Henceforth the pupils in groups of four or five studied the opening sections of the Torah reading, which changed week by week. When he had acquired some proficiency at translating a text word for word, a pupil was taught to grasp the meaning of entire sentences. Having mastered this, the pupil passed on to the study of the Rashi commentary on the Torah. Finally, at about the age of ten and in some places when they were younger, boys entered a Talmud heder, where they were taught the Mishnah and then the Talmud with its commentaries. Although boys were taught the rudiments of arithmetic in the heder, they were not given lessons in writing unless their families belonged to the intellectual or mercantile elite. When Morris Cohen's mother begged her father to obtain instruction for him in writing Yiddish, he replied: "My dear daughter, I am giving your son Torah—the substance of life. The trimmings can come later." More-over, the novelist Mordecai Spektor recalled that "my sister was sent to Avrom the *Shrayber* (writing teacher) but I wasn't. I was supposed to study just Gemara [Talmud] with the Rabbi and not trouble my head with silly ideas like writing . . ." On the other hand, in Galicia in the late nineteenth century A. J. Brawer remembered that at the age of nine he went to a special teacher during the midday break from heder to learn German and Hebrew calligraphy and arithmetic, and this became common practice prior to the First World War.[22]

In many areas special elementary schools, hadarim, were opened for girls. In Tyszowce the girl's heder was in the same building as the boy's but in an adjoining room; elsewhere girls could attend a boy's heder or in wealthier families had private tutors. In Tyszowce the curriculum for girls consisted of the prayer book, women's prayers in Yiddish (*tekhines*), the *Tse'ena Ureena* (material from the *aggadah*), and *Nachlas Tsvi* (a Yid-dish ethical and mystical tract), although they were not given *chumash* lessons. Girls, however, were often taught arithmetic and how to write

---

22. Shtern, *Heder*, pp. 60–62. Schoenfeld, *Shtetl Memoirs*, pp. 47 and 48. Zborow-ski, *Book-Learning*, p. 127. Louis Ginzberg, *Students, Scholars and Saints* (Philadel-phia: Jewish Publication Society, 1960), p. 24 (hereafter cited as Ginzberg, *Students*). Stephan A. Brumberg, *Going to America: Going to School, The Jewish Immigrant Public School Encounter in Turn-of-Century New York City* (New York: Praeger, 1986), p. 29 (hereafter cited as Blumberg, *School Encounter*). Shaul Stampfer, "Gender Differ-entiation and Education of the Jewish Woman in Nineteenth-Century Eastern Europe," *Polin* 7 (1992): 65 (hereafter cited as Stampfer, *Education of the Jewish Woman*). Brawer, *Heders of Galicia*, pp. 77 and 78.

business letters, one popular textbook opening with the words "I went to Odessa to purchase merchandise." On the basis that girls studied for about four years, a much shorter period of schooling than that for boys, Shaul Stampfer calculated that in 1894 the ratio of heder attendance was one girl for every eight boys; but even this is misleading, as attendance by girls was three times as high in southwest Russia as in central Poland. Women also learned to read with help from relatives and friends. Hence female literacy was more widespread than commonly supposed.[23]

What of the harsh discipline prevailing in the heder? Whereas the whip as a means of punishment was disappearing in Europe and America during the nineteenth century, it still remained an essential pedagogic tool in both the homes and classrooms of German Gentiles and in Jewish elementary schools in Eastern Europe. The lash was used so frequently that pupils often did not react when beaten. Shmarya Levin (1867–1935) added that whereas teachers in larger heders had a leather lash, teachers in smaller establishments had to make do "with the straws of a broom." If the class became rowdy, the helper lashed out in all directions, not caring whom he hit. A worse punishment was a whipping on the buttocks. Abraham Cahan (1860–1951) was a pupil at the heder of his Uncle Mende, who used to joke when giving a pupil a drubbing by exclaiming with each blow, "Here are the noodles" and then, "Here is some pepper and salt." One cocky pupil in the midst of the whipping, fearing a short measure, pleaded, "It needs more salt." One of Morris Cohen's teachers preferred using his walking stick to chastise pupils, instead of relying on his fists or a strap. Many sources mention heder teachers who pinched their pupils or pulled their hair. Sometimes the teacher's wife would apply butter to any facial injuries resulting from a bout of pinching or slapping to avoid complaints from parents. If a pupil made a mistake or committed a misdemeanor, the teacher cuffed him or hit him with a lash. So too, Hugo Mandelbaum (b. 1901 in southern Germany) confessed that in the secular village school that he attended, "Hazelwitch rods were always on hand, to be used to correct mistakes in spelling or arithmetic, as I well know from personal experience." Above all, as Joachim Schoenfeld so vividly recalled, "the rebbe often used a belt, stick, or *kantshik* (whip) to inject, through the

---

23. Stampfer, *Education of the Jewish Woman*, pp. 63–87. Abraham P. Gannes, *Childhood in a Shtetl* (Cupertino Calif.: Ganton Books, 1993), pp. 102–104 (hereafter cited as Gannes, *Childhood*).

bottom part of the child, the knowledge which might not go straight into the child's head."[24]

On Thursdays there was frequently tension in the teacher's home and classroom because of financial pressures. A. S. Sachs reminiscing about his childhood declared that "it was a rare thing for a Thursday to pass peacefully, without scoldings, kicks and blows, without whippings and weepings. '*Goy*! Stupid! Imbecile!' were some of the pet names the rebbi showered upon his pupils on Thursdays."[25]

David Biale has pointed out that "in most of the memoirs, the writers never admit to having been beaten by their parents, while the *melamed* invariably metes out corporal punishment." How are we to resolve the contradiction of supposedly gentle parents allowing, no, almost encouraging, teachers to be strict disciplinarians and to thrash their children? Rudolph Loewenstein asserted that Jews, because of the anti-Semitic environment around them, built many psychological defenses against their own aggressive tendencies. Accordingly parents had to allow impoverished outsiders, the elementary teachers who were full of frustration and resentment, to unleash their own aggression against the children. In fact, Samuel Chotzinoff noted that his father, who ran a heder, built up a reputation as a specialist disciplinarian to whom parents brought recalcitrant boys. In one such case, he beat a boy with a leather belt, while exclaiming: "So!—you are good in che—der—and bad at—home!—You thought—you would never—be found—out!—This will—teach—you . . ."[26]

Brawer, who went to a heder in Galicia 1888–1899, singled out a punishment known as the *kune*, in which the offender was partially un-

---

24. Lloyd deMause, "The Evolution of Childhood," in *The History of Childhood*, ed. Lloyd deMause (London: Souvenir Press, 1976), p. 42. George M. Kren, Review of *Schlage als Strafe: Ein Bestandteil der heutigen Familiehsitte in Volkskundlicher Sicht, Journal of Psychohistory* 6, no. 1 (Summer 1978): 140–142. Levin, *Childhood*, pp. 48, 49, 61, and 183. Cahan, *Memoirs*, pp. 14 and 15. Cohen, *Dreamer's Journey*, p. 43. Zborowski and Herzog, p. 90. Hugo Mandelbaum, *Jewish Life in the Village Communities of Southern Germany* (Jerusalem: Feldheim, 1985), p. 43 (hereafter cited as Mandelbaum, *Southern Germany*).

25. A. S. Sachs, *Worlds that Passed* (Philadelphia: Jewish Publication Society, 1943), pp. 6–8 (hereafter cited as Sachs, *Worlds*).

26. Biale, *Eros and Enlightenment*, p. 54. Rudolph Loewenstein, *Christians and Jews: A Psychoanalytic Study* (New York: International Universities Press, 1951), pp. 169–172 (hereafter cited as Loewenstein, *Christians and Jews*). Chotzinoff, *Early Reminiscences*, p. 21.

dressed and encircled by other pupils who beat him with sticks. Yekhiel Shtern described the three worst punishments, which no longer existed in his day, as the "whipping of the naked buttocks with wet, salted reeds"; "stuffing the mouth with a wooden peg"; and most dreaded of all, the punishment known as being made into "a bundle." The victim's face was blackened with soot, while his hands were tied and a broom and paddle were placed under his arms. Rags were tied in a bundle and attached to his back. To the jeers of his classmates, who shouted, "Bundle maker! bundle maker!" the culprit was paraded around on a table or on top of a cupboard. It seems reasonable to conclude that the most draconian punishments had been abolished by the early twentieth century.[27]

Pupils, so far from being intimidated by a whipping, often refused to utter any cries when struck so as not to acknowledge the rebbe's victory. On the other hand, parents were likely to support the teacher if he inflicted what was then considered to be a reasonable degree of punishment; and Shmarya Levin tried to avoid being slapped across the face by one brawny teacher, who left tell-tale marks on the face, so as to escape having to answer embarrassing questions at home. Moreover, Abraham Cahan added that "the cheder . . . is a holy place. The children dare not tell of the punishments and the parents dare not interfere with the melamed's authority. How can that authority be effective without slaps, pinches, and blows? To end punishment would be to end the discipline that insures that a youngster will grow up with learning and self-control. It is not easy to differentiate between necessary discipline and sadism." Marion Kaplan has argued that in Imperial Germany, "Jewish parents were less strict—and possibly more affectionate . . ." to their children than their neighbors to their own offspring. We would suggest that the new ideas about reducing corporal punishment being formulated in Western Europe infiltrated into Jewish circles in Germany and thence into the hadarim of Eastern Europe in the late nineteenth and early twentieth centuries. Selman Waksman mentioned that his mother did not spoil him, "but would discuss with me what was good and what was bad. Woe to the [heder] teacher who would dare to lay a hand on me for some childish prank! This happened once, and I was immediately removed from that school and placed in another." Again, Abraham Gannes (b. 1911), writing about the shtetl of Winograd in the Ukraine declared that "I do not remember ever seeing Reb Hersheleh use

---

27. Brawer, *Heders of Galicia*, p. 76. Shtern, *Heder*, pp. 68 and 69.

it [the cat-o'-nine-tails] or at least he never used it on me. The very fact that it was hanging on the wall within our sight put the fear of the Lord in all of us."[28]

Despite the fact that children were supposed to learn the whole time and that children were sometimes rebuked if caught playing in the street the schoolchildren subverted the heder system and utilized it for their own purposes to achieve the maximum time for leisure activities. All the child's energy and creative imagination went into play. Spontaneous play, mostly unsupervised by adults apart from a few religious recreational festivities, was the domain of the East European child. Writing of his heder years, Yekhiel Shtern described a whole series of games improvised around the ramshackle premises in which the schoolroom was housed, including catching pebbles that were bounced off the roof of an adjoining building, riding a horse consisting of wooden beams laid across a fence in the grounds of the heder and turning somersaults across these same beams; and wearing the sheet that concealed the teacher's living quarters from the classroom to play hide-and-seek or to imitate the cantor praying in a *tallit*. According to Shtern, when the child was not at his teacher's table for a few, short sessions a day, he was busy playing, while he was equally active when the teacher lingered at afternoon and evening prayers. Other accounts of heder days tell similar stories, even if play time was more limited than Shtern recalled. Sachs remembered that when children saw their teacher with knitted brow, totally absorbed by some intricate point, they would start revising their lesson at the top of their voices until he told them to desist and go into the courtyard for a rest; and if there were beautiful white pigeons outside or the hurdy-gurdy man with his box of magic views or acrobats performing, the heder children would invent a thousand excuses to join them. Of only one of the hadarim that he attended, Morris Cohen reported that "though we were in school practically all day, instruction was only occasional. The rest of the time we were either in the yard or sitting or walking about and talking in the classroom without any particular plan." At the Talmud heder that Chaim Aronson (1825–1888) joined, "the

---

28. Levin, *Childhood*, pp. 39, 183, and 184. Cahan, *Memoirs*, p. 26. Marion A. Kaplan, *The Making of the Jewish Middle Class: Women, Family, and Identity in Imperial Germany* (New York: Oxford University Press, 1991), pp. 61–63 (herafter cited as Kaplan, *German Jewish Middle Class*). Selman A. Waksman, *My Life with the Microbes* (London: Robert Hale, 1958), p. 32. Gannes, *Childhood*, p. 86.

melammed was an old man, worn out from teaching, who allowed us to play outside in the yard."[29]

Not only Shtern, but A. J. Brawer and Regina Liliental of Warsaw also provided detailed descriptions of children's games in the shtetl. Well-known games were *beknbroyt* ('pussy wants a corner'), in which four children stood in the corners of an imaginary square with a fifth child standing in their middle whose objective was to seize one of these corner places as the other children moved. *Kichke-pale* (similar to a game called 'peggy') was played with a *kichke*, a small peg pointed at both ends and the *pale*, a large stick, which was used as a bat to strike the peg as many times as possible as it became airborne. The other player's object was to seize the peg and return it to a plate that served as base. Another popular game was *iks, miks, driks* ('tick-tack-toe'), which was similar to the English game of noughts and crosses. On Sabbath and festival evenings in small towns, boys would split into two armies and fight for control of a hill. One side at the top of the hill would cast off their clothes and hurl them at the opposing army that was storming the position. Boys also see-sawed, slid down planks, played blind man's buff, and used their shoes as skates on frozen rivers and ponds to accomplish dangerous acrobatic maneuvers on the ice. On fine summer days, Aronson played with other children imitating pupils and the teacher at a heder, complete with a lash and stocks over which the victim had to lie to be whipped. During hot summer days the *belfer* would lead the pupils to the river to teach them how to swim, so that Jewish children sometimes acquired a skill that was often unknown to the peasants among whom they lived. Boys were fascinated by soldiers marching on the parade ground and spent much time watching them, as well as police arresting thieves; both the activities of the soldiers and police were mimicked in childish games. Boys' pranks could sometimes be cruel, reflecting the sadistic world around them. Aronson admitted with regret that he and a group of friends had once chopped the tail of a cat in half with an axe.[30]

---

29. Shtern, *Heder*, pp. 51–54. Sachs, *Worlds*, p. 9. *A Jewish Life under the Tsars: The Autobiography of Chaim Aronson, 1825–1888*, trans. and ed. Norman Marsden (Totowa, N.J.: Allanheld, Osmun, 1983), p. 27 (hereafter cited as Aronson, *Autobiography*).

30. Shtern, *Heder*, pp. 63–68. Brawer, *Heders in Galicia*, pp. 21 and 22. Regina Liliental, "*Das Kind bei den Juden*," *Mitteilungen zur judischen Volkskunde 26*, no. 2 (1908): 41–55. Levin, *Childhood*, pp. 70, 236, and 237. Sternberg, *Stefanesti*, pp. 162–171. Ginzberg, *Saints*, pp. 31 and 32. Brawer, *Heders of Galicia*, p. 84. Aronson, *Autobiography*, pp. 27, 31, and 32. Cahan, *Memoirs*, pp. 57 and 58. Gannes, *Child-

Girls imitated the social ritual of adults by acting the role of brides at weddings and housewives running a home; they dressed up in adult clothes and held tea parties. Whereas girls had dolls with which they played, saving shiny pieces of paper and colored bits of cloth for this purpose, boys in Eastern Europe lacked toys. Girls also skipped and played hopscotch outside their homes during spring and summer. They enjoyed a game of cat's cradle, making intricate patterns with a lengthy piece of string. Girls tossed a ball against a wall in a game called *bikel*, counting how many times they caught it as it bounced back. Jewish children in Germany in the late nineteenth century enjoyed a far richer assortment of toys, with dolls, doll houses, and miniature kitchens for girls, and train sets, guns, toy horses, and drums for boys. In the shtetl the best and perhaps only toy of a boy was a penknife, which he threw with extended blade into the floor. In fact, so deprived was the heder boy of toys that he sometimes ripped the buttons off his jacket to use them in a popular game, but girls and boys rarely participated in each others' pastimes.[31]

Around the Jewish festival cycle in Eastern Europe there were a large number of opportunities for Jewish children to amuse themselves. At Passover Jewish children played with colored eggs in a game borrowed from their neighbors, and there was a competition with opponents to see whose egg would crack first. Games with nuts were also popular on this festival. Five or six Brazil nuts or walnuts were placed in a row that an opponent placed at a distance tried to hit with a steel pellet, or you had to guess whether or not your challenger was holding an odd or even number of nuts in his hand. For Lag b'Omer fathers or the *belfer* helped boys to make bows and arrows, which they shot off into the air. There were outings to the woods to tap the sap of birch trees, which were slashed with a knife, after which the sap was drawn with a straw and sipped as a treat. For Shavuot the boys cut rushes for the synagogue floor, made flutes from reeds, and designed paper cutouts to look like roses, *reyzelekh*. On the

---

hood, p. 97. "Generally pets were forbidden. Playing with a dog took time away from Torah study and hence was taboo."

31. Shtern, *Heder*, pp. 66 and 67. Sternberg, *Stefanesti*, pp. 162, 164, and 165. Cahan, *Memoirs*, p. 35. Levin, *Childhood*, p. 117. Kaplan, *German Jewish Middle Class*, p. 58. Arthur Schnitzler, *My Youth in Vienna* (London: Weidenfeld and Nicholson, 1971), pp. 15 and 16 (hereafter cited as Schnitzler, *My Youth*). Mosheh Oved, *Visions and Jewels* (London: Faber and Faber, 1952), p. 34 (hereafter cited as Oved, *Visions and Jewels*). Brawer, *Heders of Galicia*, p. 85.

fast of Av children threw burrs at each other, brandished toy swords, and fired caps in wooden pistols. For Simchat Torah, the children made flags, and in some communities adults led a procession of children from house to house to collect cakes and fruit to eat. On Hanukkah and throughout the winter the children not only played with homemade spinning tops, dreydels, carved from wood or poured from molten lead, but tried their hand at various card games. For Purim the children put the finishing touches to rattles made by their fathers, and in Swislocz children purchased beautiful confectionery in the shape of toy soldiers and animals, which they played with for a few days before swapping. In Hungary for several weeks before Purim, children drew pictures to adorn the walls with scenes from the Scroll of Esther.[32]

A false antithesis was thus suggested in Jewish memoir literature between the prisonlike atmosphere of the heder and the liberating influence of nature, from which Jewish children were said to be excluded. If the evidence is re-examined it appears that the Jewish child was only partially banned from the garden of Eden. Despite the long hours of Judah Artzer's heder, Shmarya Levin still found time to go into the woods and listen to the secret communing of the trees. At the age of ten, Israel Kasovich day-dreamed in his Talmud heder: ". . . I would gaze at the blue sky through the window and think of Moliska with its beautiful river and high green-clad hill, where I bathed, picked berries and nuts, and fished, while here I sat cooped up like a bird in a cage. I missed my former outdoor life, I would have preferred to lie in the green grass and read story books as during the summer before." The imagination of the Jewish schoolchild was not only stimulated by the multifarious opportunities for play both inside and outside the heder, some of which were linked to the festival cycle, but it was also stirred by the dramatic retelling of biblical stories and tales from the *aggadah*. Joseph Patai devoted his memoir to stating how enchanted he was by the laws and legends he first imbibed when he began studying the tractate from the Talmud known as *Bava Metziah*, the Middle Gate. The fondest memories of Abraham Gannes were of the stories in and the midrashim woven around the heroes in the Pentateuch. Even Isaac

---

32. Levin, *Childhood*, pp. 64, 65, 66, 98, 177, and 178. Aronson, *Autobiography*, p. 39. Diane K. Roskies and David G. Roskies, *The Shtetl Book* (New York: Ktav, 1975), pp. 220, 222, and 223. Sachs, *Worlds*, p. 10. Article on Games, *Encyclopaedia Judaica* (Jerusalem: Keter, 1971), Columns 305 and 306. Joseph Patai, *Middle Gate*, p. 94.

Deutscher praised one teacher's account of the Exodus from Egypt, which brought into "our stuffy classroom the air and the smell and the breath of the Red Sea." By generating a special class of imaginative literature for children in the Victorian era, when its economy was sufficiently developed, Britain managed to treat its middle-class children as a special category in society rather than as young adults. In the hadarim of Eastern Europe the imagination of Jewish children was given some space in which to develop, but there were harsher pressures on youngsters to join the adult world quickly.[33]

Moreover, Chone Shmeruk has shown that outside the Jewish elementary schools a children's reading public for Yiddish literature came into existence between the sixteenth and eighteenth centuries. Certain books carried a note on their title page stating that they were "for young and old." These Yiddish chapbooks packed with "romances, fables, biblical stories," and travelers' tales were much more attractive for children to read than the new moralistic Hebrew literature created by the supporters of enlightenment in Germany for their schools. Even after the emergence of the enlightenment movement, children in large numbers continued to savor this popular Yiddish literature. Among the masses in Eastern Europe, a new concept of a separate world of childhood was slowly forming in the nineteenth century.[34]

On the other hand, Jewish children in somewhat assimilated upper-class households in Poland in the 1890s already fully participated in the new world that was specially designed to meet children's needs. Arthur Rubinstein (b. 1887), the son of a textile factory owner from Lodz, spent his early years with his adopted cousin Noemi, who lived next door. "A beau-

---

33. Sokoloff, *The Child in Jewish Fiction*, pp. 10 and 11. Levin, *Childhood*, p. 207. Israel Kosavich, *The Days of Our Years: Personal and General Reminiscence 1859–1929* (New York: Jordan, 1929), pp. 10 and 27 (hereafter cited as Kosavich, *Memoirs*). Isaac Deutscher, *The Non-Jewish Jew and Other Essays* (London: Merlin Press, 1981), p. 8. Joseph Patai, *Middle Gate*, pp. 21, 22, 31, 34–37, 42, 43, 67, 75, and 78. Gannes, *Childhood*, p. 87.

34. Arnold Paucker, "Yiddish Versions of Early German Prose Novels," *Journal of Jewish Studies* 10, no. 3–4 (1959): 151–167. Zohar Shavit, "The Function of Yiddish Literature in the Development of Hebrew Children's Literature," *Ha-Sifrut* 3–4: 35–36 (Summer 1986): 148–153. Zohar Shavit, "From Friedlander's Lesebuch to the Jewish Campe: The Beginnings of Hebrew Children's Literature in Germany," *Leo Baeck Institute Year Book* 33 (1988): 412–415. Dina Abramowicz, "On the Beginnings of Yiddish Children's Literature," *Judaica Librarianship* 3, no. 1–2 (1986–1987): 68–70.

tiful nursery, consisting of two big sunny rooms [in his aunt's house] filled with all sorts of toys, was our daily playground. A governess watched over our games and took us for walks; we had our meals together alternately at my aunt's or at my own house. Noemi . . . particularly liked playing husband and wife with me. . . . My piano playing made her gasp with admiration. I think we were probably the happiest children in the world." In addition, there was also a small minority of Jewish children growing up on landed estates who were excellent horsemen and swimmers, skilled at skating, and good shots.[35]

The East European heder was a prime example of the classical type of Jewish elementary school, which was constructed on the same pattern in all traditional societies. For instance, in the town of Shiraz in Iran the Jewish elementary school, which still existed in the 1930s, was called the *koto* or *maktab*. After the children grasped the alphabet and the essentials of the prayer book, they learned to chant the Torah and their teacher taught them a translation of the text in Judeo-Persian, which they intoned aloud. Whatever stage in their studies they had reached, the children were instructed in groups by a single teacher. Children might be taught the Mishnah and Midrash, but higher Jewish studies were excluded and they did not go on to learn the Talmud. Punishment was severe, culprits being chastised with a bastinado, a stick that was usually applied to the soles of a victim's feet. Similarly in Salonika, students were punished with a strap or a cane called a *palmatoria*, which was applied to the child's hands, feet, or buttocks, depending on the scale of his offense. Lesser offenses were dealt with by isolating the culprit or humiliating him in some way. In Kurdistan during the 1930s, Jewish elementary education was organized in the same way as Shiraz, although the types of punishment inflicted may have been even more brutal and children were thrashed rhythmically while the teacher chanted verses from the Psalms.[36]

---

35. Rubinstein, *Young Years*, pp. 6 and 8. Julia Namier, *Lewis Namier: A Biography* (London: Oxford University Press, 1971), pp. 15–17 and 32. Maurice Friedman, *Martin Buber's Life and Work: The Early Years 1878–1923* (London: Search Press, 1982), pp. 14 and 15. Theo Richmond, *Konin: A Quest* (London: Jonathan Cape, 1995), pp. 50–66.

36. Laurence D. Loeb, *Outcaste: Jewish Life in Southern Iran* (New York: Gordon and Breach, 1977), pp. 134 and 135. Michael Molho, *Usos y Costumbres de los Sefardies de Salonica* (Madrid-Barcelona: Instituto Arias Montano, 1950) pp. 116 and 117 (hereafter cited as Molho, *Customs of the Sephardim*). Erich Brauer, *The Jews of Kurdistan* (Detroit: Wayne State University Press, 1993), pp. 236–248.

"Our *chedorim* with their *melamdim* represent a copy in minature of the medieval inquisition applied to children . . ." fulminated the Russian Jewish newspaper *Voschod* in 1893. "Our Talmud Torah [an institution designed for orphans] makes an even sadder picture. . . . Its program consists of cold, hunger, corporal punishment and Hebrew reading." This onslaught was directed against the weakest link in the whole system of heder education. So too, Mendele Seforim (1835–1917) denounced the Talmud Torah, where "poor Jewish children, orphans, are driven into a hovel, a stable in truth, where they wallow in dirt and filth, where they are whipped and beaten as much as their poor bodies can stand, and where they learn not—not a single word. They are turned into miserable, unhappy people who are useless to God and man." Softening his earlier harsh critique of the heder system, Mendele praised his teacher Lipe Ruvens "as one of those inspired people of singular grace, blessed from the moment of their creation with good gifts: wisdom and talent and a compassionate heart, lacking in nothing but luck." Further, "Study was not the drudgery it is in most cases, when the master tries to force-feed the pupil by shouting, scolding, and beating, and the pupil must resort to lies and pretend he is absorbing his lesson when he is not. It was never that way with Lipe Ruvens. He taught so calmly and quietly that the lesson was rather like a conversation between two dear friends, where each one hangs on the other's words, and understands what is in his heart: a conversation that gives pleasure to both participants, and which both would like to extend, hour after hour."[37]

Louis Ginzberg, born in 1873 in Kovno, Lithuania, a product in part of this system of traditional elementary schooling, carried the defense of the heder a stage further. Writing in 1928, Ginzberg stated that "not only was the Heder as we have seen, a private institution in which parents were

---

37. Zvi Halevy, *Jewish Schools Under Czarism and Communism: A Struggle for Cultural Identity* (New York: Springer, 1976), pp. 48 and 49 (hereafter cited as Halevy, *Jewish Schools*). Shmuel Werses, "Jewish Education in 19th Century Russia," in *Jewish Education and Learning*, ed. Glenda Abramson and Tudor Parfitt (Reading: Harwood Academic Publishers, 1994), pp. 251 and 256. Mendele described a teacher in *Fathers and Sons* (1868) as "pug-nosed, of blotched complexion and spindly neck, wearing greasy pants and a *talit* dangling to his knees; a sweaty and soiled sash is wrapped around his middle. In his hand a cane, and on the table a sobbing boy with his breaches pulled down." *A Shtetl and Other Yiddish Novellas*, ed. Ruth R. Wisse (Detroit: Wayne State University Press, 1986), p. 295. Mendele Mocher Seforim, *The Parasite*, trans. Gerald Stillman (New York: Thomas Yoseloff, 1956), p. 164.

given an opportunity of choosing a teacher with a view to their children's needs and gifts, but the teaching was also personal in character. . . . The teacher usually occupied himself with no more than four children at a time." Moreover, "The Melamed was certainly more humane and gentle than most of the masters of the English schools, who till very recently ruled as tyrants. We may be quite sure he was not the brute pictured by the morbid imagination of certain Maskilim, whose animus against the Heder is probably to be sought in a hatred of the deeply Jewish atmosphere that prevailed there . . ." Franz Rosenzweig criticized the modern Western school for producing "fragmentary people, totally lacking orientation. . . ." In contrast, according to Nathan Morris the heder furnished the equivalent of a classical education: "The child is not only to be prepared for life, but from the beginning helped to live the life which is regarded as desirable." If the hadarim were condemned for employing methods of rote learning, the educational techniques utilized in the Russian gymnasia were just as antiquated. Moreover, Diane Roskies noted that if the test of educational effectiveness is used, the Yiddish literacy level of Jews in the Russian Empire was almost double that of the rest of the population, who were Russian speakers; and that insofar as reading instruction was concerned, the Jewish supporters of the enlightenment movement proposed reforms that had seldom been implemented in secular schools. Bialik ruefully admitted in 1912 that "The Heder is our mother. The Heder has nourished tens of generations. . . . We deserted the Heder and left it to its fate."[38]

Nor was this all. In 1863 the Society for the Promotion of Enlightenment Among the Jews of Russia was established in St. Petersburg under the leadership of the financier Yozel Gunzburg and other notables, aimed at directing the Jewish masses from above. It provided the funds for a few model hadarim in agricultural settlements in Russia plus a handful of modernized Talmud Torahs. In Odessa by the mid-1870s, where the influence of the proponents of enlightenment, the maskilim, was at its strongest, there was a successful attempt to introduce Russian and mathematics into the curriculum of the heder. This movement paralleled the much bigger Christian Sunday School organization, which introduced the study of Russian, mathematics, and the Bible into their classes, but which came to an abrupt end in the summer of 1862 because of difficulties with the authorities. For this reason the national elitist Jewish leadership refused to press

---

38. Ginzberg, Saints, pp. 25 and 26. Halevy, Jewish Schools, pp. 52 and 53. Roskies, Alphabet Instruction, pp. 46–48. Gannes, Childhood, p. 101.

the issue of heder reform, concentrating instead on opening vocational schools.[39]

Among the Zionists in Russia, efforts were made toward modernizing the curriculum of the traditional heder by establishing the *heder metukan* (reformed heder). According to Shmarya Levin (1867–1935), who must have attended the precursor of such a school in Swislocz in the mid-1870s, his teacher focused on the correct reading of Hebrew. During the first two terms at this, which was his third heder, they covered the whole of the Pentateuch, plus the Rashi commentary (which was studied independently), grammar, and writing. The hours were very long, up to ten hours a day in the heder in the winter and twelve in the summer, with longer hours after the first term; yet at the end of his stay at this heder, Levin was no more than seven or eight years old.[40]

As the Zionist movement in Russia mobilized the masses from below before World War I, more and more of these modernized hadarim were opened throughout the country, particularly in the south, where the Jewish population was economically better off. The driving force behind the spread of these hadarim was an organization based in Odessa. Chaim Weizmann and friends from his Zionist circle set up one of the first of these new schools in Russia in Pinsk in 1895. The curriculum varied from place to place; sometimes the instruction was in Yiddish, sometimes in Russian. A pupil from the *heder metukan* in the town of Keidan remembered that he studied Russian and that instruction in general subjects was in Russian, but that attention was also paid to the study of Hebrew grammar. Two of the five *hadarim* that David Ben-Gurion attended in Plonsk in the 1890s were modern ones, in which the Bible and Hebrew grammar were taught in Hebrew. To cater to the needs of these schools, two publishing houses began to issue a veritable flood of Jewish school textbooks on Hebrew grammar, Jewish literature and history, and the *aggadah*. Children's Zionist societies either instructed poor children to speak and write in Hebrew as in Plonsk or recruited pupils for teachers who taught Hebrew as a living language as in Steibtz. In the main, the comfortable Russian Jewish middle

---

39. Steven J. Zipperstein, "Transforming the Heder: Maskilic Politics in Imperial Russia," in *Jewish History: Essays in Honour of Chimen Abramsky*, ed. Ada Rapoport-Albert and Steven J. Zipperstein (London: Peter Halban, 1988), pp. 87–109. Steven J. Zipperstein, *The Jews of Odessa: A Cultural History, 1794–1881* (Stanford: University of California Press, 1985), pp. 130 and 135.

40. Levin, *Childhood*, pp. 200–205.

class sent its children to these schools with their secular, modern and Zionist, nationalist orientation. At times, as in Pinsk, these schools encountered violent opposition from the Orthodox Jewish elements in the town, and in small towns the traditional type of heder was too entrenched to be reformed. We shall shortly see how the creation of the *heder metukan* in Russia reproduced the developments in the transformation of the old-style heder in Western Europe in the late eighteenth and early nineteenth centuries into the modern Jewish school.[41]

In the small towns in Eastern Europe, the melamed, the Jewish elementary teacher, continued to be respected until the First World War. "What I remember from my mama, when we shared a teacher with other children in the village—this teacher was supposed to eat and sleep with us [for] two months," David Toback recalled in his memoirs. "One time in the morning a neighbour came to us, and my mother was sleeping on the straw and the teacher was lying covered over and covered under with two pillows on the bed. The neighbour said, 'You don't have pity on yourself. You're a mother of small children. Why are you tossing around on the straw and giving to the teacher the whole bed cover?' . . .

"For this whole big-shot, they used to sweep daily with a broom. For the rebbe's sake, they used to roast a chicken with coal. The women used to laugh, 'By the life of Sarah. This teacher's cuddled up in his diapers.' When would they roast a chicken if not when a child was being nursed."[42]

THE YESHIVA AND BET HA-MIDRASH

Whereas the Jewish masses went to the heder, only a small elite of children drawn from affluent and rabbinical families plus brilliant students from poor families went on to study the Talmud after the age of thirteen. Shaul Stampfer delineated the social mechanism that enabled this system of

41. Halevy, *Jewish Schools*, pp. 112–115. Jehuda Reinharz, *Chaim Weizmann* (New York: Oxford University Press, 1985), pp. 25 and 37 (hereafter cited as Reinharz, *Weizmann*). Shabtai Teveth, *Ben-Gurion: The Burning Ground 1886–1948* (London: Robert Hale, 1976), p. 14. Zalman Shazar, *Morning Stars* (Philadelphia: Jewish Publication Society, 1967), pp. 78 and 79 (hereafter cited as Shazar, *Morning Stars*). Jacob Tsur, *Sunrise in Zion* (London: George Allen and Unwin, 1968), p. 24.

42. David Toback's *Memoirs*. I am grateful to Carole Malkin for this reference and for permission to quote from her grandfather's unpublished diary.

selection to operate. Crucial factors were the quality of the heder teachers and the size of the class. The more opulent the family, the easier it was for them to attract the finest teachers and to stipulate a limit on the size of the class. M. L. Lilienblum (1843–1910) declared that "in 1857 [when he was fourteen years old] my father sent me to a *melamed* who was good etc. and he paid tuition of seven and a half rubles for six months, on condition that the *melamed* would not take more than six pupils . . ." Again, Shmarya Levin praised his uncle for founding a heder in Swislocz, where the teacher "promised that, he would not increase the number of his pupils beyond the four he set out with. . . . In other *cheders* the pupils numbered between ten and fifteen; they were divided into groups, so that the *cheder* became a school with several classes but with only one teacher. So that while the teacher would be occupied with one class, the other classes, even though they revised their lessons could relax. . . . But our *cheder* consisted only of one class, so that we were forever under the eye of the Rebbi, and we worked intensively through the ten and twelve hours." Thus the *gemara heder* rigorously tested pupils, and only those who had reached the standard of being able to peruse the Talmud on their own were selected for further study. Here the advantage lay with the small hadarim, where wealthy fathers could pay the teachers higher fees to compensate for the smaller number of pupils they enrolled. Of course, classes with few pupils gave these children considerable advantages when it came to mastering difficult talmudic texts.[43]

As the yeshivot were designed to combat modernity in Lithuania, they were a relatively late innovation, the first such institution being the Volozhin Yeshiva founded in 1802, but the new system of yeshivot began to flourish only in the second half of the nineteenth century. At the same time, Rabbi Israel Salanter (1810–1883) introduced the study of ethical literature, *Musar*, into some of the yeshivot in an attempt to make pupils delve into and come to terms with their unconscious by self-scrutiny, thereby bestowing on them an inner strength and making them more resistant to the allure of a secular education. He also established the first *kolel* in Kovno in 1876 to permit married men to devote themselves exclusively to advanced talmudic study, freed from financial worries. In the area around

---

43. Shaul Stampfer, "*Heder* Study, Knowledge of Torah, and the Maintenance of Social Stratification in Traditional East European Society," in *Studies in Jewish Education*, ed. Janet Aviad (Jerusalem: Magnes Press, 1988), Vol. 3, pp. 271–289 (hereafter cited as Stampfer, *Social Stratification*). Levin, *Childhood*, pp. 196 and 203.

the great yeshiva of Mir, teachers from the small towns nominated promising students to study with Reb Zaame, who ran a preparatory course in Talmud for the yeshiva of Mir. In Steibtz the brilliant Binyamin Leib, the son of the water-carrier, was awarded such a study scholarship. Thus did the Jewish elite try to absorb able recruits from the lower strata.[44]

Once young men started learning in the bet ha-midrash (study house) attached to the synagogue or, much less commonly, were admitted into a yeshiva, the students became entitled not only to eat their main daily meals on a rota basis with local families, but if they attended a yeshiva they received free instruction in the Talmud and its commentaries. This voluntary communal system of providing free subsistence for young men was known as "eating days." Although arrangements were made by the students and by the warden or beadle of the bet ha-midrash or yeshiva to provide the young men studying the Talmud with places to go for a daily meal, there were occasions when no such families were available and these young seekers after knowledge starved. Weighing up the evidence, David Patterson claimed that "in spite of its defects, therefore, the institution of the *Yesibhah* represents an extraordinary example of the voluntary maintenance of a widespread system of higher education, available to every boy, no matter how poor, with a modicum of intelligence and stamina." However, this generalization needs to be qualified by stressing that the hadarim turned out only a limited number of candidates suitable for higher learning and that even this number was reduced by the inability of certain aspirants to maintain themselves during this further period of prolonged study. Jacob Marateck (1883–1950) was so ashamed at "appearing like a beggar" and so horrified at the physical appearance of his fellow students, who were "stunted from malnutrition," that he quickly abandoned any intention of becoming a scholar.[45]

The view of the reformers, that there was too much emphasis placed on a talmudic education for poor boys who were bright, and too little

---

44. Hillel Goldberg, *Between Berlin and Slobodka* (Hoboken, N.J.: Ktav, 1989), pp. 15–35 (hereafter cited as Goldberg, *Berlin and Slobodka*). Shazar, *Morning Stars*, pp. 124 and 125.

45. David Patterson, *The Hebrew Novel* (Edinburgh: Edinburgh University Press, 1964), pp. 172 and 173 (hereafter cited as Patterson, *Hebrew Novel*). Shimon and Anita Wincelberg, *The Samurai of Vishogrod: The Notebooks of Jacob Marateck* (Philadelphia: Jewish Publication Society, 1976), pp. 21–25 (hereafter cited as Wincelberg, *Jacob Marateck*).

encouragement given to them to acquire the skills of a trade, gained wider currency during the second half of the nineteenth century. Nevertheless many of these trades were so glutted with labor that it was impossible to make a living from them.[46]

The novelist Samuel Braudes described how the system of "eating days" operated in Lithuania:

> These *Yesibhah* boys do not acquire their food and clothing in a normally digni-
> fied manner, but are forced to roam the town in search of sustenance. . . . When
> a lad arrives in search of learning he must first ensure a supply of food. . . . He
> trudges round from house to house with the plea: Would you be so kind as to
> provide a poor boy with a meal one day each week.
>
> We already feed one *Yesibhah* boy here—they will tell him, and off he will go
> to another house. There they may let him eat his fill on that occasion, but can't
> provide him with a regular meal each week—and so on from one house to the
> next. Usually he will only knock on the doors of the poor, for the rich will only
> provide meals for such boys as bring a letter of recommendation from the princi-
> pal or one of the managers of the *Yesibhah*. Eventually he will either fulfil his aim
> or he will become weary of the search and wait until some other pupil leaves the
> *Yesibhah* or finds a more attractive billet . . . it is not difficult to imagine that they
> entertain few scruples in resorting to flattery, slander or deceit if one of their com-
> panions is more favourably placed. . . . But still those who are sufficiently fortu-
> nate, even at the cost of such toil and humiliation, to find permanent meals for all
> seven days of the week are in a small minority. Some obtain meals for only six or
> five days each week, while many exist on four or even three.

Smolenskin added that at night the youths slept on the yeshiva tables and benches without any cover, each person sleeping in his own alloted place; elsewhere, as in the Rameiles yeshiva in Vilna, students made improvised beds "on platforms of board and [slept] with small hay or straw-filled sacks as their pillows."[47]

In Kovno in 1898 youths as young as ten and twelve traveled around together in pairs, seeking sustenance or cash to buy food. When Chaim Aronson (1825–1888) first came to Vilna at sixteen to study at the Rameiles yeshiva he was too shy to beg for his meals and at one point ate nothing for "two days except the porridge served at breakfast." As a yeshiva stu-dent Aronson was befriended by an affluent gentleman who taught him

---

46. Sol Liptzin, *Eliakum Zunser* (New York: Behrman House, 1950), pp. 30–32 (hereafter cited as Liptzin, *Zunser*). Wincelberg, *Jacob Marateck*, p. 24.

47. Patterson, *Hebrew Novel*, pp. 175–177. Cahan, *Memoirs*, p. 69.

German. "He himself lived in regal manner eating and drinking as he pleased, whilst fully aware that I was starving. In fact, on one occasion, during his lunchtime meal, he cut the top of a radish and threw it to the floor under the table; I waited until he had left, picked up the pieces and devoured them." In 1869, having reached the age of ten, Israel Kasovich (1859–1929) journeyed to Kurenitz to board with a teacher but for a time had to eat at the home of wealthy relatives who placed him on the corner of a table, a mark of contempt. ". . . every minute or so the children peeped in from another room, giggled, and disappeared. I choked on every morsel, felt homesick, and shed tears in profusion. The other four days I boarded in poorer homes, where the people were more friendly . . ." Later, when attending yeshiva, Kasovich complained that the people he ate with lived a long way from his study center and that "worse yet, they were wealthy people, the kind that served you your meals in the kitchen instead of the dining-room." At the yeshiva of Pressburg in Hungary, where there were many pupils, the majority of whom were poor and were "billeted on charitable people, who in proportion to their wealth, used to feed at their tables as many as fifteen or twenty [students] a day. . . . Those who could only obtain meals for two or three days, were assisted from the charitable contributions of the wealthier students and from endowments of ancient institutions bequeathed for the purpose."[48]

In Lithuania poor students on the whole were supported by the less affluent families, as wealthy Jews because of social snobbery were reluctant to have impoverished students dining with them. Hence in Vilna a saintly ascetic known as Simeon Kaftan collected coins in the main Jewish street, with which to purchase loaves of bread for famished students who were short of "eating days." On the Sabbath, he had a large pot in which he collected the tasty leftovers from Sabbath meals, which he distributed to hungry students. Such was the reputation for altruism of this beggar that his portrait hung in the Russian governor-general's office and 20,000 people came to his funeral.[49]

In Poland, where there were few yeshivot, most young men studied in the bet ha-midrash adjoining the synagogue or in the synagogue itself. "At

48. Aronson, *Autobiography*, pp. 80, 96, 97, and 297 note 180. Kasovich, *Memoirs*, pp. 24, 25, and 33. Cahan, *Memoirs*, p. 69. Heinrich Felbermann, *The Memoirs of a Cosmopolitan* (London: Chapman and Hall, 1936), p. 15 (hereafter cited as Felberman, *Memoirs*).

49. Liptzin, *Zunser*, pp. 27 and 28.

5 A.M. on a frosty winter day, when the city of Warsaw was still engrossed in slumber, hundreds of young men were already seated around tables in the study houses of Ger, Ostrowce, Sochaczow, and Radzyn, engaged in the study of the Law. This was the early morning lesson before prayers. The best preparation for prayers, it was said in these study houses, is a page of the Talmud." Unlike Poland, in Lithuania it was the custom for students to study in a locality other than their home town, although the following remarks when compared with other sources appear to be somewhat exaggerated.

> The Kapule synagogue served at the same time as a college, where young boys . . . supplemented their knowledge of the Talmud and the later authorities. In addition to the local boys, there also studied in the Kapule synagogue young married and unmarried out-of-towners. The inhabitants treated these newcomers with their tremendous thirst for study, very hospitably. No sooner did such a boy appear in the synagogue, carrying a walking stick in his hand and a bundle on his shoulders, than everyone surrounded him, greeted him, and immediately began supplying him with eating days. . . . Food—he had; books and candles—all that his heart desired; a royal shelter—the synagogue; a bed and a pillow—he had no need of, since he slept on the bench with his coat as a pillow.[50]

Many youths decided their own course of study in the bet ha-midrash, such as the particular tractate of the Talmud they wished to peruse, or they might want to consult works on the Kabbalah or philosophy. Whatever the case, they had to have the requisite knowledge to study the Talmud and its commentaries on their own; otherwise if they reached a difficult point in a volume, they always had the option of discussing it with an older and more experienced scholar, who was poring over books in the synagogue. "When I was thirteen," Bialik recalled,

> I passed from the jurisdiction of the teachers to my own, and began to study in the synagogue alone. Alone—because I was the only boy in the whole suburb who sat and studied in the synagogue except for the *dayyan* [rabbi's assistant], who bent over the Torah and prayers until midday. Otherwise there was no teacher there. . . . Alone with my old and new thoughts, my doubts and suppressed meditations, I sat there for many days . . . interrupting my study to sink into a mass of dreams and visions, contemplating relations and calculating the structure of the world, seeking meaning for myself and humanity.[51]

---

50. Abraham Menes, "Patterns of Jewish Scholarship in Eastern Europe," in *The Jews: Their Religion and Culture*, ed. Louis Finkelstein (New York: Schocken Books, 1975), p. 210 (hereafter cited as Menes, *Patterns of Scholarship*).

51. Menes, *Patterns of Scholarship*, pp. 210 and 211.

Israel Kasovich (1859–1929), having been placed in a small yeshiva by his brother, described what a typical day in his life was like:

> I used to sleep at the same synagogue as Mordecai, and after breakfast repair to my yeshivah, where I passed the whole day. The yeshivah I attended had an enrollment of over one hundred and fifty students of varying ages. I was the youngest among them. The tumult there—for . . . everybody studied at the top of his voice—was simply unbearable. To sit all day studying the Talmud amid such deafening noise simply dazed me, and more than once I fell asleep in the middle of my studies. The hours were too long and the studies too hard. Each day the Rosh Yeshivah [the principal of the yeshiva] would assign us a lesson in the Talmud, generally consisting of a single page, to be prepared for the next day; and the following day, when recitations were about to begin, there was complete silence in the yeshivah. The Rosh Yeshivah would then take up a position in the midst of us and call upon one of the students to recite the lesson. All would sit still and listen to the one reciting, while the Rosh Yeshivah made comments and corrected the student's mistakes; and if one did not know his lesson well, he was publicly reprimanded.

To assist him, Kosavich's brother tutored him, sometimes jolting him out of sleep in the early hours of the morning for this purpose: ". . . he would wake me up and coach me in my studies. I could scarcely keep my eyes open, I would yawn and hardly know what I was saying, until he would smack my face so hard I saw stars."[52]

From the 1870s there were drastic changes in the attitudes of some of the students enrolled in the yeshivot. At the Pressburg yeshiva in Hungary, "No student was allowed to study anything but the Bible and Rabbinic literature. Those who were detected showing proclivities for any secular knowledge were expelled from the College. The oldest and most trusted students were set to watch over the younger, upon whom a very strict surveillance was kept." Nevertheless, the reformist Hebrew press started to discuss including Russian and secular subjects in the curriculum of the yeshiva, and at Kelm under the influence of the *Musar* movement this idea first became a reality. After pogroms in the 1880s, in the great yeshiva of Volozhin there was a secret Zionist group, and students were not adverse to reading *haskalah* literature and Hebrew newspapers, although in many yeshivot anyone caught reading *Hashachar*, a secular newspaper, was immediately expelled. Again, there had been a revolt among students attending "the *mussar* yeshiva of Novahruduk: the long, fearful *Shaa* the angry students had hissed in unison one night, never stopping till Reb

---

52. Kasovich, *Memoirs*, pp. 32 and 33.

Yayzel, the ascetic head of the yeshiva, and his assistants fled in panic. Reb Yayzel had persecuted every student with Zionist leanings and his supervisors searched the boys' rooms for modern Hebrew books hidden in their boxes." Eliezer Ben-Yehuda was introduced to Hebrew grammar and *Robinson Crusoe* by the head of his yeshiva at Polotsk, after which "I was drawn more and more by the seductive heresy of the enlightenment, even though I still attended the rabbinical seminary diligently and plunged ever deeper into the study of Gemara, commentaries, Tosafot, and Posekim by day and by night—there happened to me what was bound to happen eventually, and what happened to most youths in those times after they had tasted enlightenment: I abandoned the rabbinical seminary . . ." Instead of joining some Hasidic order or continuing with their study of the Talmud, as they would have done in the past, alienated Jewish youth, often living away from home and susceptible to peer group pressure, now turned in the 1880s and 1890s to socialism and Zionism.[53]

The Jewish masses, on the other hand, despite their loyalty to Jewish tradition, were neither by training nor inclination suited to the study of the Talmud. Most Jewish men belonged to sacred societies for the study of the Psalms or the Midrash, not the intricacies of the Talmud. Even the inducement that young Jewish males would not be seized for forcible induction into the Russian army by professional kidnappers to make up the compulsory quotas on the Jewish community, if they were studying in a bet ha-midrash, was not enough to tempt large numbers into the voluntary study of the Talmud. As far as the impressment of Jewish youths into the Russian army was concerned, "Many private individuals took part in this traffic. They would seize young children and sell them to the community 'bosses,'" Eliakum Zunser noted. Further, "Hundreds of 'sales of Josephs' occurred daily. The lesser rabbis of the small towns gave supine assent to such outrages, with the argument that it was 'more pious' to protect the children of their own towns."[54]

Aryeh Litvinovsky was told by his father that as he (the father) was an orphan without protectors, the Jewish community wanted him to serve in

---

53. Felbermann, *Memoirs*, p. 15. Patterson, *Hebrew Novel*, p. 179. Goldberg, *Berlin and Slobodka*, p. 26. Menes, *Patterns of Scholarship*, p. 205. Shazar, *Morning Stars*, p. 86. Eliezer Ben-Yehuda, *A Dream Come True*, trans. T. Muraoka and ed. George Mandel (Boulder, Colo.: Westview Press, 1993), p. 21.

54. Stampfer, *Social Stratification*, p. 283. Eliakum Zunser, "How I Wrote My Songs," in *Memoirs of My People: Jewish Self-Portraits from the 11th to the 20th Centuries*, ed. Leo W. Schwarz (New York: Schocken, 1963), pp. 223 and 224.

the Russian army to help make up their local quota of recruits. "He slept in the fields, in the woods among wild animals, because he didn't dare show his face in the town for fear of betrayal." Having been held in shackles for three months in a synagogue awaiting induction, he escaped but he was soon recaptured and secured to a large log with a fellow recruit. "And here they sat, ate, drank, slept and performed their bodily functions." The guards, thinking that they would not dare escape because they were weighed down by the large log, did not bother to lock the door of their room, from which they fled into the woods one night. Here a pack of wolves attacked them, devouring the companion of Litvinovsky's father and merely leaving his boot attached to the log, while miraculously leaving his father unscathed. Akiba Zunser was another Jewish Cantonist who was fraudulently baptized while he slept. Whippings, starvation, and other tortures were not sufficient to make him abjure his faith and he defiantly put on tefillin. On being discharged from the army, he secretly married a Jewish girl and raised his children as Jews, for which he was imprisoned in 1884 and vanished without trace. Such was the fate of some poor Jewish youths in nineteenth-century Russia.[55]

---

55. Aryeh Litvinovsky, *From Times Gone By: Reminiscences and Ideas* (New York: Bernice and Jerry G. Rubenstein Foundation, 1985), pp. 19–22. Liptzin, *Zunser*, pp. 52 and 53.

8

Growing Up in Central and Eastern Europe: A Modern Education

APPRENTICESHIP

The Jewish elite in France, Germany, Russia, and England were concerned with encouraging the masses to move from peddling and employment in the petty trades into agriculture and handicrafts. The French Revolution abolished the corporate structure of society, including the guilds, thereby undermining the basis on which the apprenticeship system rested. In 1810 the leaders of the Paris Jewish community set aside funds for the apprenticeship of poor Jewish children, and further schemes were undertaken in Bordeaux and Metz, where apprenticeship as well as industrial training were connected with the elementary school system. Moreover, in many parts of France associations, *sociétés de patronage*, modeled on similar Christian bodies were set up by Jews to assist the poor from their community in drawing up apprenticeship contracts in a satisfactory form, to monitor the progress of the apprentices, and to provide additional training for them outside the workshop. They subsidized the apprentices and sometimes provided accommodation for them as well as aftercare. A matter that engaged the attention of these associations was to ensure that the Jewish apprentices did not have to work on the Sabbath; in Lyons, community leaders sent their apprentices to the trade schools of Mulhouse and Strasbourg rather than place them with local Christian masters because of the risk to strict Sabbath observance. In Paris the *école de travail* or trade school was established in 1865 to house orphans and children from broken homes. In 1854 Gerson Lévy praised the German-Jewish schools for teaching general subjects in the morning and giving vocational training in the afternoon; and during the 1850s the French school system started to promote more vocational training.[1]

The French Jewish leadership, like their Gentile counterparts, stressed the necessity of the social regeneration of the poor by apprenticing their children and by instilling both a work ethic and a spirit of patriotism in the young. They were to be taught to be deferential to their social superiors and grateful to them for preserving them from indolence. They were to be protected not only from the obscene conversations of the workshop but from a life of vagabondage that was associated with the itinerant trades. Jewish apprentices in Paris in 1886 were warned to keep away from the twin snares of cafes and cabarets as something that could corrupt them and disrupt their potential for hard work. Besides giving them necessary instruction for their future employment, the Foundation Bischoffsheim aimed at entertaining their students and keeping them off the streets by providing classes in gymnastics, dancing, singing, music, and sewing. To wean the young apprentices away from the trashy literature they were reading, a lending library was opened in which the novels of Jules Verne and Erckmann-Chatrian were the most popular items, but few Jewish books formed part of the collection.[2]

More as a result of growing industrialization in France than the campaigns of these voluntary associations, the percentage of Jews in Paris engaged in petty trading, chiefly peddling and street trading, declined from 52 percent in 1809 to 19 percent in 1872. It has also been estimated by Paula Hyman that the trade schools in Strasbourg and Mulhouse had trained

---

1. Lee Shai Weissbach, "The Jewish Elite and the Children of the Poor: Jewish Apprenticeship Programs in Nineteenth Century France," *AJS Review* 12, no. 1 (Spring 1987): 123–142 (hereafter cited as Weissbach, *Apprenticeship*). Zosa Szajkowski, *Jewish Education in France, 1789–1939* (New York: Conference on Jewish Studies, 1980), p. 15.

2. Weissbach, *Apprenticeship*, pp. 135–142.

750 graduates between them by 1870, not sufficient to make a significant inroad into poverty among the Jewish rural population in Alsace.[3]

In Prussia in the early 1780s, Dohm advocated the right of Jewish craftsmen to work outside the guilds as a means of combating their restrictions, and he was also of the opinion that they should be allowed to engage in agricultural pursuits. In Baden an edict stated in 1809 that Jews "on completing their schooling be trained and brought up, like Christian children, for a decent livelihood and trade in the state, in agriculture or manual crafts of all kinds, in accordance with the general rules. Should guilds or master workmen dare to offer obstruction, the police authorities are responsible for seeing to it that this law is carried out . . ." Since the 1820s the Jews had set up associations in Germany to promote the movement of their coreligionists into the crafts and agriculture, and by 1850 there were thirty-nine such societies for restructuring Jewish occupations.[4]

Everywhere difficulties were encountered in Germany in placing apprentices with Christian masters who demanded payment of exorbitant fees if they were to find vacancies for Jewish apprentices. Even when young Jews had been successfully trained, they could not find a suitable opening in the trade and searched for economic opportunities elsewhere. For example, although the father of Eduard Silbermann was a clothworker, he became a traveling salesman, part-time farmer, and hop-grower. Philipp Tuchman (1810–1883) was apprenticed as a tanner, but "so many difficulties were caused him by the guild, however, that he lost his desire to practice the craft, and upon grandmother's encouragement he turned to the hop business." The restrictions on the freedom of movement of Jews in Southern Germany hindered their ability to practice the trades for which they had been trained. According to Eduard Silbermann, who was born in 1851, "The efforts of the Bavarian government to bring the Jews into the crafts

---

3. Weissbach, *Apprenticeship*, p. 141. Paula E. Hyman, *The Emancipation of the Jews of Alsace* (New Haven: Yale University Press, 1991), pp. 113–115.

4. Jacob Katz, *Out of the Ghetto: The Social Background of Jewish Emancipation 1770–1870* (New York: Schocken Books, 1978), p. 60 (hereafter cited as Katz, *Out of the Ghetto*). Adolf Kober, "Emancipation's Impact on the Education and Vocational Training of German Jewry," *Jewish Social Studies* 16, no. 1 (1954): 4 and 5 (hereafter cited as Kober, *Education Part 1*). Adolf Kober, "Emancipation's Impact on the Education and Vocational Training of German Jewry," *Jewish Social Studies* 16, no. 2 (April 1954): 156 and 157 (hereafter cited as Kober, *Education Part 2*). David Sorkin, *The Transformation of German Jewry 1780–1840* (New York: Oxford University Press, 1987), pp. 117–119 (hereafter cited as Sorkin, *German Jewry*).

were in the main unsuccessful. Centuries-old customs and character traits were not easily eliminated by a legislative act . . . they took up trades that were more related to business and from which the transition to business or industrial enterprise was easier. Thus the clothmakers later became dry-goods dealers and fabricants, the tailors became clothing manufacturers, the shoemakers became dealers in footwear, etc." Nonetheless, a limited measure of restructuring was achieved in Bavaria, where in 1842 of the 61,000 Jews living there, 4,700 were employed in handicrafts and 1,200 in agriculture, that is, almost one-fifth of the male Jewish population. Again, in Wurttemberg 85.5 percent of the Jews were described as hucksters in 1812, but by 1852 this proportion had dramatically shrunk to 17.7 percent. In Northern Germany where the Central Association for Colonization of Jews was established in 1846, 1,064 Jews who were mainly destitute craftsmen had their hopes of becoming farmers dashed because the Prussian government reneged on its promise to allocate land at low rentals.[5]

With the industrial revolution in Germany in the nineteenth century and the growth of commerce, there were more opportunities for Jews in manufacturing and commerce, which they quickly seized; but the attempted restructuring of Jewish occupations, by moving them into handicrafts and agriculture, remained an anachronistic and unrealistic notion, unsuited to a modern industrial state. After the middle of the nineteenth century Jews migrated into medium-sized and large cities, where there were better economic prospects, and by 1910, 58 percent of the Jews in Germany were urbanized. At the same time, many of the wandering paupers and unemployed craftsmen left for America, London, and Paris. Although the percentage of Jews employed in trade and business in Germany hardly altered, falling from 65.2 in 1895 to 61.3 in 1933, more Jews joined the ranks of the prosperous middle class as they brilliantly adapted to the complex

---

5. Katz, *Out of the Ghetto*, p. 182. *Jewish Life in Germany: Memoirs from Three Centuries*, ed. Monika Richarz and trans, Stella P. Rosenfeld and Sidney Rosenfeld (Bloomington: Indiana University Press, 1991), pp. 80, 81, 88, 106, and 107 (hereafter cited as Richarz, *German Jewish Memoirs*). Kober, *Education Part 2*, p. 163. Reinhard Rurup, "Jewish Emancipation and Bourgeois Society," *Leo Baeck Year Book* 14 (1969): 81 and 82. Julian Bartys, "Grand Duchy of Poznan under Prussian Rule: Changes in the Economic Position of the Jewish Population 1815–1848," *Leo Baeck Institute Year Book* 17 (1972): 203.

needs of industrial society. The same developments occurred simultaneously among other Jewish communities in Central Europe. It was the children of these entrepreneurs who attended the high schools in increasing numbers in the decades before and after the First World War and who swelled the ranks of the professions.[6]

In Eastern Europe, orphan children were educated in the Talmud Torah, which had a curriculum designed to ease their rapid integration into the workforce. Hebrew and religious studies were kept to a minimum, while there was more emphasis placed on the study of the language of the country and arithmetic. In 1880 an organization known as ORT, Society for Manual and Agricultural Work among Jews, was instituted in St. Petersburg by Baron Horace Gunzburg. Despite the restrictions of the tsarist regime, it initiated the establishment of small workshops for tailoring, shoemaking, and carpentry within the Talmud Torah and also responded to requests for help from individuals. At the same time, the society assisted Jewish craftsmen to move from the Pale of Settlement into the interior of Russia. Because its operations were only on a small scale in Russia before the 1914–18 war, it is doubtful whether it contributed much to the restructuring of Jewish occupations.[7]

It was very difficult for Jews in Russia and Poland to acquire skills outside the three trades mentioned above and to create a profitable enterprise. Take the case of clockmaking and the watch repairing business. Jacob Marateck was apprenticed at the age of twelve to a watchmaker for six years, but his master bluntly informed him that he would have to attend to household chores and minding the baby for the first two years, without being taught anything, and nothing came of the contract. Moshe Oved was apprenticed at seventeen "in a lucky hour" to a repairer of watches and jewelry in Alexandrova, a bustling frontier town, yet he soon fled to England to seek his fortune. Finally Chaim Aronson, as a young married man, picked up the rudiments of clockmaking in a three-month self-imposed crash course. His master concealed certain things from him and he discovered, despite appearances to the contrary, such as the daughter having daily piano lessons, that his employer Sholem Vildoyer "was poor and his income small, so that at times there was no food in the house, not even

---

6. Richarz, *German Jewish Memoirs*, pp. 8–10.

7. Zborowski and Herzog, pp. 102–104. Article on Ort, *Enyclopaedia Judaica* (Jerusalem: Keter Books, 1971) Columns 1481 and 1482.

dry bread." On the other hand, Abraham Cahan was apprenticed to a highly skilled carver in a thriving furniture business, but his bad language so shocked the young apprentice that he resolved never to return.[8]

When we examine the attitudes of Anglo-Jewry to apprenticeship, we find the same concerns that troubled Continental Jewry. Only children from the respectable poor were accepted for education and apprenticeship, and the records for the Ashkenazi Orphan Charity School show that from the 1790s efforts were made to apprentice children from such families. Later, in 1867, the Jewish Board of Guardians established a workroom in London for training girls in dressmaking, shirt- and collar-making, and embroidery, the last attracting a superior class of girl but not the working-class girl for which the course was intended. In 1873 the board began to make provision for the apprenticeship of boys, recruiting 200 annually by 1900 and placing over 400 in 1907 before this figure gradually declined to 300 in 1913. While in theory the board was supposed to be keeping boys out of the overcrowded tailoring and shoemaking trades, in fact it was sometimes wastefully finding vacancies for them in these trades. Up to 50 percent of the apprentices, who were indentured, failed to complete the seven-year term of their contract. Part of the problem was the lack of adequate supervision by the board and the necessity for apprentices to repay the premium money lent to their parents by the Board out of their meager earnings. Of the 4,000 or 5,000 Jewish children annually leaving elementary schools in London, Vivian Lipman estimated that the board could not have apprenticed more than 10 percent, but of this last total almost half dropped out of such employment.[9]

Once again the communal elite's impact on the restructuring of Jewish occupations was negligible. Of more significance was the example of Jewish endeavour on the national scene with the setting up of the Apprenticeship and Skilled Employment Association in 1907, in which Ernest Lesser

---

8. Wincelberg, *Jacob Marateck*, pp. 45–50. Oved, *Visions and Jewels*, pp. 36 and 37. Aronson, *Autobiography*, pp. 162–167 and 170. Cahan, *Memoirs*, pp. 67 and 68.

9. Siegfried Stein, "Some Ashkenazi Charities in London at the End of the Eighteenth and the Beginning of the Nineteenth Centuries," *Transactions of the Jewish Historical Society of England* 20 (1964): 63–81 (hereafter cited as Stein, *Ashkenazi Charities*). Vivian Lipman, *A Century of Social Service 1859–1959: The History of the Jewish Board of Guardians* (London: Routledge and Kegan Paul, 1959), pp. 119–123. Eugene C. Black, *The Social politics of Anglo-Jewry 1880–1920* (Oxford: Basil Blackwell, 1988), pp. 80–84.

of the United Synagogue and Lily Montagu played leading roles to revive apprenticeship; and the creation of the East London Apprenticeship Fund in 1887, which was modeled on the board's industrial committee, to work among Christian children in the East End. Summing up, we would conclude that the industrialization of Central Europe and the migration of the impoverished German and East European Jews to the West, rather than the clumsy attempts at social engineering by communal elites, contributed to the rise of West European and American Jewry to middle-class status.[10]

SECONDARY EDUCATION: *REALSCHULE* AND GYMNASIUM

During the French Revolution and the Napoleonic era the *maskilim* and their supporters among the bankers and merchants established schools and temples throughout Germany to propagate the ideas of the Jewish enlightenment. The earliest advocates of secular education among Jews, however, were the doctors, who had been permitted to study at German universities since the last quarter of the seventeenth century. The first such school was the Berlin Free School (1778), followed by other schools in Breslau, Dessau, Seesen, and Frankfurt, and in Wolfenbuttel, where the local heder was transformed into a school in 1807. The Berlin school was the model for other such schools not only throughout Germany but for schools in Austria, Bohemia, Hungary, and Italy. The German-Jewish schools aimed to turn their pupils into productive citizens and awaken their moral feelings. They placed their emphasis on vocational training to qualify their students for careers in commerce and resembled the *Realschulen* rather than the gymnasium, the grammar school. Thus instead of teaching Greek and Latin like the grammar schools, they concentrated on instruction in German, English, and French, the languages of business. Apart from Dessau, the schools never attracted more than 20 percent of the potential school population, and between 20 and 40 percent of the pupils were recruited from poor families, so that fees for tuition could not be

---

10. H. W. Jevons, "Apprenticeship and Skilled Employment Committees, with an account of the Work of the Cambridge Boys' Employment Registry," in *Continuation Schools in England and Elsewhere*, ed. M. E. Sadler (Manchester: Manchester University Press, 1907), pp. 455 and 456. Apprenticeship and Skilled Employment Association, *Annual Reports*, 1908–1913.

charged. Nevertheless, by 1850 it has been estimated that 50 percent of Jewish schoolchildren studied in Jewish elementary schools.[11]

Unlike the hadarim, the schools abandoned Torah study and the scrutiny of sacred texts, substituting in their place the teaching of the moral and ethical content of Judaism and the obligation to learn a special Jewish catechism. They replaced the bar mitzvah ceremony by a confirmation service borrowed from the Christian church to make certain that their pupils had thoroughly imbibed the moral precepts that were being taught. Everywhere in Germany, the law prohibited hadarim located in teachers' homes that were not regulated by the state, so that by the middle of the nineteenth century the old-style Jewish elementary schools had disappeared in Germany. Exceptionally, in Berlin and Cologne, there were special schools where the Talmud was taught. In Western Europe, too, at the beginning of the nineteenth century the study of the Mishnah and Talmud was generally being eradicated from the curriculum of the Jewish school, as can be seen from the complaint of the English chief rabbi Solomon Hirschell in 1803 about the London Orphan Charity School.[12]

In Germany Jews went to grammar schools in increasing numbers in the second half of the nineteenth century. In Frankfurt six Jewish boys attended the gymnasium in 1789–1790. Although only a handful of privileged Jewish boys were enrolled in a gymnasium in Breslau in 1789, by 1837 their numbers had risen to 150. No less than 15 percent of Berlin's gymnasia students were Jewish in 1867. Moreover, whereas in 1886, 46.51 percent of Jewish schoolchildren in Prussia supplemented their elementary education by attending middle or secondary schools, by 1906 this percentage had risen to 58.91; and the number of Jewish children in such Prussian schools totaled 34,815. When Max Bodenheimer's (1865–1940) interest in literature was rekindled, he switched from the *Realgymnasium*, where he was being trained for a career in business, back to the gymnasium with its emphasis on the study of the classical languages.

---

11. Kober, *Education Part 1*, pp. 5–10. Sorkin, *German Jewry*, pp. 125–130. Arthur Galliner, "The Philanthropin in Frankfurt: Its Educational and Cultural Significance for German Jewry," *Leo Baeck Institute Year Book* 3 (1958): 169–186.

12. Sorkin, *German Jewry*, pp. 128 and 129. Michael A. Meyer, *Response to Modernity: A History of Reform Judaism* (New York: Oxford University Press, 1988), p. 40. Max Breuer, *Modernity Within Tradition: The Social History of Orthodox Jewry in Imperial Germany* (New York: Columbia University Press, 1992), pp. 93 and 102 (hereafter cited as Breuer, *Orthodox Jewry*). Arthur Ruppin, *The Jews of Today* (London: G. Bell, 1913), pp. 121 and 122 (hereafter cited as Ruppin, *Jews of Today*). Stein, *Ashkenazi Charities*, p. 69.

As his two sisters attended the municipal secondary school for girls in Magdeburg, Arthur Ruppin (1876–1943) was entitled to a free place at the Kaiser Wilhelm Gymnasium, to which he transferred in 1888. Ruppin was unable to do much homework, partly because his parents could not afford the textbooks, partly because he had to go peddling with them. In earlier decades Hermann Makover (1830–1897) encountered similar problems as regards the purchase of textbooks and through poverty often went to school without breakfast.[13]

Ruppin admitted that "in Magdeburg, I was exposed to anti-Semitism from my schoolmates for the first time; in Rawitsch it had been unknown. In the secondary school and—though to a lesser extent—in the Wilhelm Gymnasium, friendships between Christian and Jewish children did exist, but every class also had a few anti-Semites who avoided having anything to do with the Jews or tried to make things unpleasant for them." Apart from a few exceptions, most of the teachers had been brought up in the liberal era and held the anti-Semitism in the school in check. Even so, there was sufficient anti-Semitism in the school to encourage the Jewish boys to make friendships within their own circle. Again, Max Bodenheimer "soon realized that the deadly fungus of Jew-hatred was developing among my schoolmates. Some of them had a secret society from which Jews were excluded. I had no interest in the drinking bouts of this club . . ." During his time in the upper form in the gymnasium, Bodenheimer joined a middle-class dancing club, but after an anti-Semitic incident involving one of his friends, he resigned from it. By way of contrast Gershom Scholem (1897–1982), who attended a gymnasium in a big city like Berlin, reported that he suffered more teasing on account of his jug-handle ears than much anti-Semitic hostility from his schoolfellows, and he counted three non-Jewish chess enthusiasts among his friends.[14]

In Frankfurt Samson Raphael Hirsch founded an Orthodox school in

---

13. Kober, *Education Part 1*, p. 26. Calvin Goldscheider and Alan S. Zuckerman, *The Transformation of the Jews* (Chicago: University of Chicago Press, 1984), p. 86 (hereafter cited as Goldscheider and Zuckerman). Ruppin, *Jews of Today*, pp. 126 and 127. Max Bodenheimer, *Prelude to Israel: The Memoirs of M. I. Bodenheimer* (New York: Thomas Yoseloff, 1963), pp. 40 and 41 (hereafter cited as Bodenheimer, *Memoirs*). Arthur Ruppin, *Memoirs, Diaries, Letters* (London: Wiedenfeld and Nicholson, 1971), pp. 26 and 27 (hereafter cited as Ruppin, *Diaries*). Richarz, *German Jewish Memoirs*, p. 153.

14. Ruppin, *Diaries*, p. 28. Bodenheimer, *Memoirs*, pp. 42 and 43. Gershom Scholem, *From Berlin to Jerusalem: Memories of My Youth* (New York: Schocken, 1988), pp. 63 and 64 (hereafter cited as Scholem, *Memories of My Youth*).

1853 that combined Torah with modern culture (*Torah im derekh eretz*). By 1878, it secured state recognition as a nonclassical secondary school (*Realschule*), and its numbers grew steadily from 487 in 1886 to 766 in 1923–1924. It was a model for similar schools established in Mainz in 1859 and for Furth in 1862, which achieved secondary school status later, as did other schools at Hamburg and Halberstadt. Other Orthodox secondary schools were opened in Leipzig in 1913, catering to a large East European Jewish population, and in Berlin in 1919. Around 1872 there were in addition 674 Jewish elementary schools in Germany, but after this date their number started to decline. Moreover, it was estimated that in 1901 out of 17,085 Jewish children attending non-Jewish elementary schools in Prussia, a mere 3,530 received some religious instruction in school, although there was an Orthodox supplementary religion school in Berlin and some other towns for such pupils. In Southern Germany the children sometimes attended an Orthodox communal religion school from 4 to 6 P.M. after their state school had finished for the day. They were taught to translate the *chumash* and prayer book, to read and write Juedische-Deutsch, and to understand the elements of Hebrew grammar and some Jewish history; additionally they had to memorize the Ten Commandments and the Thirteen Principles of Faith.[15]

In Vienna, the Austrian capital, Jewish merchants and industrialists were determined to send their sons to the gymnasia. In the decades before World War I, whereas only 10 percent of the capital's population was Jewish, 30 percent of the pupils attending the most prestigious high schools, the gymnasia, were of Jewish origin. Despite the massive increase in the Jewish population of Vienna between 1875 and 1910, the proportion of Jewish students attending these schools remained constant at 30 percent. Of this Jewish student total, two-thirds attended grammar schools in three districts of Vienna with large Jewish populations, where between 40 and 80 percent of one's classmates could be Jewish. While in the gymnasium eight hours a week were devoted to the study of Latin and between four and five hours to Greek, only three hours a week were spent on science and mathematics. Jewish studies were given short shrift, with a teacher coming to the school for a couple of hours a week. "Rabbi Schmiedl was the first teacher of the Jewish religion to appear at our school," Arthur Schnitzler (1862–1931) declared, "a good-natured little man who made life easy for

---

15. Breuer, *Orthodox Jewry*, pp. 91–125. Kober, *Education*, pp. 23–30. Hugo Mandelbaum, *Southern Germany*, pp. 38–41.

us. . . . If there was too much chatter and restlessness, he would jump up and down on the rostrum in despair, whimpering over and over again, 'But this isn't a school!' while we went on talking unconcernedly. After him, Dr. David Weiss took the reins into his hands. He was a scholarly, irascible and spiteful man, who with shrieking severity tried to enforce the respect that was perhaps unjustly denied him." Possibly because careers in engineering and certain sections of industry were less open to Jews, fewer Jewish students attended the *Realschule*, preferring a classical education that enabled them to pursue careers in the law and medicine. As early as the 1870s, Schnitzler noted the separation between the Jewish and Christian boys in the gymnasium he attended in Vienna, a division that deepened in future decades with the growing anti-Semitism in the city. The Viennese authorities were much more generous with the provision of free tuition for poor pupils than the German education authorities, so that it was not long before the children of poor Jewish immigrants from Galicia, such as Manes Sperber, started attending these schools.[16]

Although in the Rhine province a law was passed in 1824 that Jewish pupils, who attended school on Sabbaths and festivals, were to be exempted from doing things contrary to their religious conscience, these children nevertheless encountered difficult situations in schools. In Saxony and in Prussia, Jewish pupils were not exempted from writing on the Sabbath. In the 1870s the situation for Jewish pupils worsened partly because of civil service regulations to ensure uniformity throughout the country and partly because of the vociferous anti-Semitic agitation. By 1884 the *Israelit*, a German Jewish newspaper, could admit that "only a small minority of Jewish pupils" refrained from using a pen on the Sabbath. Despite all this pupils could obtain certain permissions not to attend school and not to write on the Sabbath, if the parents wrote to the school administration at the beginning of the school year giving the dates of all the festivals when their children would be absent from school. In places where there was no Jewish school, even Orthodox parents were reconciled to their children going to school on the Sabbath. Samuel Spiro (1885–1960), who attended a gymnasium in Hersfeld, where there was no *eruv*, "had to take the books that I needed for classes to the caretaker of the Gymnasium on Friday and

---

16. Marsha L. Rozenblit, *The Jews of Vienna 1867–1914* (Albany: State University of New York Press, 1983), pp. 99–125 (hereafter cited as Rozenblit, *Vienna*). Arthur Schnitzler, *My Youth in Vienna* (London: Weidenfeld and Nicholson, 1971), pp. 63 and 68 (hereafter cited as Schnitzler, *My Youth*).

fetch them from him again on Sunday. I did it unwillingly, since I was ridiculed for it by my schoolmates, including the Jewish ones. Naturally, the Jewish pupils did not write on the Shabbat. Only a single teacher took offense at that; all of the others respected our religious sentiments." So too, when Chaim Weizmann joined a *Real-Gymnasium* in Pinsk, he promised his grandfather that he would not write in class on the Sabbath.[17]

Under Nicholas I in 1844 a law was promulgated in Russia that in addition to attending general state schools, Jews could establish their own primary schools and two theological seminaries corresponding in standard to the gymnasium. On the whole, the bulk of the Jewish population tended to boycott these schools, since they feared the underlying intentions of the Russian government. In 1852 in the city of Shklov, with a Jewish population in excess of ten thousand, only twenty-seven pupils were enrolled in these schools. By the 1860s Jewish children fostered the ambition of entering the general government schools rather than the special Jewish ones. In 1864 the poet Judah Leib Gordon wrote to a friend that "I remember that in your city there was one Jewish student in the gymnasium. The youth would walk to school stealthily. He never appeared in the street in his student uniform, but would always leave it with the janitor of the gymnasium. He would come to school attired in his orthodox garb. Once there, however, he would change his uniform, hide his earlocks behind his ears, and become a completely different person. . . . Today, however, there is not a town where Jewish children do not drink the refreshing waters from strange fountains. And they do it openly, without embarrassment." In 1853 there were still only 159 Jewish pupils enrolled in all the gymnasia throughout Russia, while by 1870 this number had risen to 2,045, or 5.6 percent of the whole student body, and by 1880 7,004 Jewish pupils were going to gymnasia, or 12 percent of the total enrollment. Reasons suggested by Steven Zipperstein for this new enthusiasm for high schools by Jewish parents were: a law of 1874 which shortened the period of military service for persons with a secondary education and higher degrees who served as officers, growing urbanization, and an actual increase in the number of such state schools, but this omits the motivation of the pupils themselves.[18]

---

17. Breuer, *Orthodox Jewry*, pp. 96, 106, 314–317. Richarz, *German Jewish Memoirs*, p. 205. Reinharz, *Weizmann*, p. 21.

18. Louis Greenberg, *The Jews in Russia* (New York: Schocken, 1976), Vol. 1, pp. 31–37 and 81–83. Steven J. Zipperstein, *The Jews of Odessa: A Cultural History,*

In the 1860s Jewish parents in Pinsk, as in other parts of Russia, started sending their children to high school, and by the end of the 1870s almost 40 percent of the seventy pupils in the *Real-Gymnasium*, which emphasized the sciences in its curriculum, were Jewish. Chaim Weizmann (1874–1952) joined this school in 1885, where he was inspired by the chemistry teacher Kornieko. "He had managed to assemble a little laboratory, a luxury which was then almost unknown in Russian high schools. His attitude towards his pupils was in wholesome contrast with that of the other members of the staff. He was a decent, liberal-minded fellow, and treated us like human beings. He entered into conversation with us, and did his best to interest us in the wider aspects of natural science . . . there grew up a kind of friendship between pupils and teacher—a state of affairs unimaginably rare in the Russian schools of that day." Weizmann was at school from 9 A.M. to 2.30 P.M., after which he did his homework, had some instruction with a Hebrew teacher, and tutored the young son from a wealthy family. Like Shmarya Levin and other Jewish boys, Chaim Weizmann discovered that the school course in ancient Slavonic was difficult and unappealing. Despite the excellence of Kornieko as a teacher, when Weizmann studied science in college in Germany, he had to work late into the night "to fill the gaps in my scientific and general education, which was far behind the standards of the German high schools."[19]

Although he was a brilliant student, Shmarya Levin (1867–1935) found the entry into a Russian high school harder than Weizmann. He was smitten with envy when he saw his old childhood friend Bendet Getzov parade around Swislocz in his new outfit: "He came in his royal robes, that is, in the smart uniform of the Russian student: a blue jacket with silver buttons, the high coat-collar set with silver stripes, and a silver badge on his cap." Here and in similar comments from Abraham Cahan we can see a complete break with the negative attitudes of the Jewish population in the first half of the nineteenth century. Moreover, Smolenskin asserted that through adolescent peer group pressure "many parents have allowed their sons and daughters to study secular subjects and languages, not from the conviction that such knowledge graces its possessor, and may even on occasion prove valuable, but solely because their sons and daughters

1794–1881 (Stanford, Calif.: Stanford University Press, 1985), p. 129 (hereafter cited as Zipperstein, *Odessa*).

19. Reinharz, *Weizmann*, p. 20. Chaim Weizmann, *Trial and Error* (London: Hamish Hamilton, 1949), pp. 32–35 and 49 (hereafter cited as Weizmann, *Autobiography*).

have complained that the children of some relative or neighbour are learning them, and taunting them for not taking part."[20]

Twice Levin had to abandon efforts to gain admission to high schools, once at Dinaburg because his knowledge of Russian was deficient, the other time at Vilna for the same reason. Finally, he squeezed into the *Realschule* at Minsk by a fluke because he successfully answered a question on quadratic equations that was outside the curriculum by perseverance and brute logic. He prepared for this school rather than a gymnasium, as he had doubts as to whether or not he could master the classical languages. Again, he had the good fortune to alight on an inspiring teacher, Kurilko, who taught mathematics and who demanded "industry and exactitude" of his pupils. Shmarya Levin admitted that "in the actual conduct of the school we came across very little anti-Semitism." Both Levin and Weizmann were of the opinion that most of the teachers were bureaucrats more interested in advancing up the professional ladder than enthusing or relating to their pupils. In addition, the schools were harassed by police called "Assistant Class Educators" who kept the pupils under surveillance by day, patrolled the streets in the evening, and visited their homes at night to monitor what literature they were reading and to ferret out by seemingly innocent questions whether or not they were engaging in any antigovernment activities.[21]

In Minsk in 1880 or 1881, Levin had also met youths from distant parts of the province, who were mainly older than he was and who were preparing for the school entrance exam. "They had studied Hebrew and the Talmud up to their fifteenth and sixteenth years, and had come—at a more advanced age than I—to the conclusion that these studies would bring them nowhere. . . . But they had now become fanatical enthusiasts of the Russian language and literature."[22]

In the early 1870s only a handful of Jewish boys from Russified families attended Vilna's gymnasium, but attitudes among traditional Jewish families toward providing a secular education for their children were changing rapidly. In August 1874 fifty or sixty extra Jewish pupils were enrolled in the gymnasium, which underwent a period of expansion by the addition of a pre-gymnasium with six classes. In Vilna children from wealthy,

---

20. Shmarya Levin, *Youth in Revolt* (London: George Routledge, 1935), pp. 45–47 (hereafter cited as Levin, *Youth*). Cahan, *Memoirs*, pp. 74 and 75. Paterson, *Hebrew Novel*, p. 162.

21. Levin, *Youth*, pp. 113–123 and 127. Weizmann, *Memoirs*, pp. 33–35.

22. Levin, *Youth*, pp. 100–102.

modern Jewish families or from poor nonreligious ones attended the Rabiner school, one of the theological seminaries, which was abolished in 1873 and replaced by a teacher training college. The other students were former yeshiva students from the provinces who had broken free of parental control. A diploma marking completion of eight grades qualified a pupil for admission to a medical college, which was why the children from better-off Jewish families studied there. Otherwise the pupils qualified as teachers, or if they stayed at the school for ten grades, as crown rabbis able to preside at official functions.[23]

What was it like to be a student at the Vilna Teacher Training Institute for Jewish instructors in the 1870s? All the pupils were issued gray jackets and trousers together with coarse linen undershirts and pants. They did daily gymnastic exercises before lunch, after which they paraded in the gymnasium and then marched into the dining hall. The bed linen was changed weekly. "Everything was clean and beautiful, more so than in our homes." Even so, pupils were taken to the public baths only once every two weeks. Meat, mostly roast beef, was served daily in contrast to the pupils' homes, where this would be a Sabbath luxury. The blessings on the food were recited in Russian, although there was a synagogue that was utilized on the Sabbath. Yiddish speaking was forbidden in the interests of an intensive effort to Russify the students. Because pupils were not allowed outside the premises during the week, there was an oppressive, gloomy air pervading the Institute, which was not improved by the pedagogical methods adopted by the teachers. Even if the Russian educational system was closely modeled on the German one, it was an inferior irritation. Instruction was by the rote learning method little different from the techniques employed in the traditional heder. Pupils were expected to memorize their textbooks and deviations from these in their answers were penalized when marks were awarded. Apart from three teachers, there was little originality or fire in their presentation of their lessons. One of the outstanding teachers was Joshua Steinberg, who taught Hebrew grammar and Bible; he sometimes delighted students with "his philological revelations and historic parallels" when teaching the Prophets.[24]

23. Cahan, *Memoirs*, pp. 74–76 and 80.

24. Cahan, *Memoirs*, pp. 106–139. Hirz Abramowicz, "A Jewish Teacher in Czarist Russia," *Yivo Annual* 19 (1990): 336–344 (hereafter cited as Abramowicz, *The Jewish Teacher*).

In Odessa there were more Jewish high school students than in any other Russian city, their number reaching 1,377 in 1880. In certain schools they were the dominant majority. In the second gymnasium 215 of the 300 pupils or 71.6 percent were Jewish, while in the third gymnasium their numbers were even greater, 265 or 72 percent of the total student body of 368. A commercial school attracted even more Jewish pupils, 77.9 percent of the student body. Trotsky attended St. Paul's *Realschule* in Odessa, a school with a multinational staff and a liberal and tolerant atmosphere.[25]

In spite of the hardships they encountered in seeking a high school education, Abraham Cahan, Shmarya Levin, and Chaim Weizmann belonged to a lucky transitional Jewish generation born between two periods of reactionary rule. Under a tsarist decree issued in 1887, the number of Jewish pupils in primary and secondary schools was limited to 10 percent, even though the Jewish population was concentrated in the Pale of Settlement, where they comprised between 30 and 80 percent of the population in the towns. To gain entry to the schools for their children, wealthy parents either bribed officials or hired ten non-Jewish candidates to sit the entrance exam for the school, thereby creating a place for a favored Jewish candidate. Having been thwarted when they tried to secure admission into secondary schools, Jewish pupils relied on private tutors and obtained a diploma by external examination, which entitled them to seek a university education. As the Russian universities had a Jewish quota of 10 percent in the Pale, 5 percent outside it, and only 3 percent in St. Petersburg and Moscow, Jewish students flocked abroad to study, to Switzerland, Germany, and France. To secure the opportunity of studying abroad, young Jewish men without means starved as they tried to cover the syllabus, and there were men as old as thirty called "the eternal externes" still struggling to obtain their school graduation certificate. According to Chaim Weizmann, "The women students [studying abroad] were almost as numerous as the men. . . . Medicine was the favourite study, for it offered the most obvious road to a livelihood; besides, it was associated with the idea of social service. . . . Engineering and chemistry came next, with law in the third or fourth place." Before his academic plans were disrupted by

---

25. Zipperstein, *Odessa*, p. 130. Isaac Deutscher, *The Prophet Armed Trotsky 1879–1921* (New York: Vintage Books, 1954), p. 13.

the imposition of the *numerus clausus* in the Russian universities, Levin had intended to study engineering.[26]

Moreover, after the Russian Revolution of 1905, there were gains for the Jewish community that the government could not completely undo. The quota system imposed in 1887 restricting the number of secondary schools for Jewish children was also undermined by granting Jews the right to open high schools for Jewish children, staffed by Jewish administrators and teachers. Among the centers opened were schools in the cities of Vilna, Minsk, Homel, Warsaw, Odessa, Bialystok, and St. Petersburg, which had substantial Jewish populations. Hampered as they were by the official curriculum, there were a few inspired teachers, such as Chaim Fialkov, who yet managed to go outside the syllabus and instill a love for Hebrew and Jewish studies in their pupils. So long as the chief of the educational district was present during the exams, Jewish students could receive their diplomas. Hirsz Abramowicz was informed by Anatoli Gurovich that he wanted to open a new Jewish school in Bialystok, as the existing one was of poor quality, and he arranged for the Jewish card-playing crony of the anti-Semitic administrator of the Vilna educational district to persuade his friend to issue a license for the new school in 1913.[27]

Before leaving the topic of secular education, we must turn to the vexed question of whether or not there was any connection between the Jews' traditional veneration for talmudic learning and the alacrity with which they turned to secular learning and flooded into the new secondary schools and universities. This was a key factor in Jewish social mobility, first in Central Europe and Russia and later in the United States and Britain. That there was any significant link between the two traditions has been denied by Calvin Goldscheider and Alan Zuckerman, who noted that Jews were disproportionately concentrated in European cities in the late nineteenth century, thus enabling large numbers of Jewish children to attend high schools, from where they proceeded to university. By 1901, Jewish pupils comprised 8 percent of the Prussian gymnasia enrollment and 15 percent of the student body in the equivalent Austrian schools. Further, in 1896 there were 2,700 Jewish students in Austrian universities or 17 percent of those

---

26. Levin, *Youth*, pp. 146–152. Weizmann, *Autobiography*, p. 50. Abramowicz, *The Jewish Teacher*, pp. 349 and 350.

27. Abramowicz, *The Jewish Teacher*, pp. 350–354.

enrolled, whereas the Jews accounted for only 3–4 percent of the population of Austria. Nevertheless, a recent examination of Prussian university statistics by Norbert Kampe has shown that there was no evidence to connect the degree of urbanization among Jews to the level of university enrollment, as East Prussia, where the urban population reached only 25 percent, had the highest index for university study among Jews. Carl Schorske held that in the case of Vienna the Jews were driven by the social need to participate in high culture; hence businessmen encouraged their sons to enter the liberal professions. By acquiring an aesthetic cultural polish, Jews such as Herzl hoped to show that they had an affinity with aristocratic values. But if as Steven Beller has argued, the Jews introduced high culture to the aristocracy through the salons, then this proposition appears to be untenable; moreover, it should be stressed that Martin Buber (b. 1878) was also a dandy and aesthete as a student in Vienna but was brought up by his grandparents, who lived on a large estate near Lvov (Lemberg) in the style of a gentry family.[28]

Beller has further asserted that the Jews transferred their traditional love of learning of the sacred to the subject matter of secular culture, while within the Austrian Jewish cultural elite there was usually in childhood some ambitious and inspirational family member directly linked to the ancient tradition of talmudic study. From the 1870s onwards in Eastern Europe and in Austria, where there were many migrants from the outlying provinces of the empire to Vienna, Jewish youths were steeped in the traditions of both sacred and secular learning. In the Leopoldstadt district of Vienna, with a poor and mainly Orthodox Jewish population, 50.4 percent of the pupils in one gymnasium in 1910 received free tuition, thus giving us a measure of how these secondary schools were being used as vehicles for social mobility, just as similar schools were utilized a decade later by Jewish immigrants in the United States. Much the same situation can be found in East Prussia and Russia. Abraham Cahan, who studied

---

28. Goldscheider and Zuckerman, pp. 85–87. Ruppin, *Jews of Today,* pp. 124–133. Norbert Kampe, "Jews and Antisemites in Universities in Imperial Germany: (1) Jewish Students: Social History and Social Conflict," *Leo Baeck Institute Year Book* 19 (1985): 357–394 (hereafter cited as Kampe, *Students*). Carl E. Schorske, *Fin-De-Siecle Vienna: Politics and Culture* (Cambridge: Cambridge University Press, 1985), pp. 148–150. Steven Beller, *Vienna and the Jews 1867–1938: A Cultural History* (Cambridge: Cambridge University Press, 1990), pp. 96 and 97 (hereafter cited as Beller, *Vienna*).

the Talmud from the age of eight until he was fourteen stated that "as mental exercises the tractates were useful. I had learned to reason so that I later found the most rigorous reasoning required in arithmetic easy." So too, Shmarya Levin thought that his prowess at mathematics owed little to his tutoring in secular knowledge but much to the heder boy "whose mind had been trained and sharpened in childhood on Jewish studies." At the end of the nineteenth century there appear to be indications that children from traditionally minded and poor families in the small towns of East Prussia, who were highly motivated, used higher education as a means for rapid upward social mobility. In an important article by Miriam Slater entitled "My Son the Doctor: Aspects of Mobility Among American Jews" (1969), she attempted to demolish the thesis that there was any continuity between the great value placed on learning in the shtetl and Jewish upward social mobility in the United States. We have already seen that the rabbinic and the business elite were intertwined in Eastern Europe, and her reading of Zborowski and Herzog fails, as she attempted to portray a false antithesis between rabbinic learning and wealth. She gave insufficient attention to the social changes occurring in the Austrian Empire and Eastern Europe in the second half of the nineteenth century, which interacted with a living tradition of Jewish scholarship.[29]

THE GERMAN JEWISH FAMILY

We now turn to a discussion of how children were brought up in middle-class German Jewish families. Hermann Makower (1830–1897) in his memoirs described the old patriarchal type of family, organized on hierarchical lines, which was disappearing in the late nineteenth century. At his gymnasium Makower became friendly with Conrad Meyer, the son of the head of the Berlin Jewish community, who was then a very wealthy individual.

> His father was a somewhat odd man, an aristocrat, tight-laced, at home an absolute, patriarchal ruler, strict and firm, and intolerant of other views. His 'written'

---

29. Beller, *Vienna*, pp. 90–105. Cahan, p. 72. Levin, *Youth*, p. 114. Kampe, *Students*, pp. 364–368. Rozenblit, *Vienna*, pp. 110–125. Miriam Slater, "My Son the Doctor: Aspects of Mobility Among American Jews," *American Sociological Review* 34 (1969): 359–373.

permission was required for me to be allowed to visit his children, so anxiously did
he seek to ward off all harmful influence from alien elements. The family was respected and widely known; everything possible was done for the children's education, but a quickening breath of freedom and gaiety were lacking. This pedantry
extended to the private tutor, a medical student, and although the social niceties
were strictly adhered to, there was a certain coldness in the home, and the spirit
remained unfulfilled. . . . I owe much to that home . . . I was introduced into a family
that practiced an ordered, strict upbringing.

The head of the family, who "regarded himself as a pious man in the orthodox sense, strictly observed the dietary laws, the holidays, and the like,"
but even so he had departed somewhat from the minutiae of the Jewish
faith observed in the small towns. The dourness of the family, the stress
on education, and the authoritarian rule of the father all remind one of the
pre-eighteenth-century Jewish household.[30]

Gerson Bleichroder (1822–1893), the leading German-Jewish banker
who mobilized funds for Bismarck's wars and the creation of the German
Empire, reflected in old age that he had brought up his children in too
permissive a manner. Looking back on his life, Bleichroder painted a picture of a happy childhood, of a close relationship with his mother, the
ideal woman, who would read the novels of James Fenimore Cooper or
Bulwer Lytton to him, and of idyllic summer holidays spent in a rented
house in the country. He also gave examples of his filial devotion to his
father, for whom he purchased an estate in the village of Pankow for the
summer vacations. After a conversation, Bleichroder's secretary noted "that
in the education of his own children he [Bleichroder] had come to recognize, with the best intention and reflection, that a different method would
be more appropriate for the present age, and hence he did not tie them to
the house, gave them even in their younger years greater freedom, and
did not so anxiously shield them from all contact with the modern world.
I meant well, but now I have to recognize that I was wrong." The children
had an indulgent and permissive childhood, but Bleichroder was a busy
man who probably saw little of his offspring. Hans was so spoiled and
difficult that he had to be moved from gymnasium to gymnasium. Later,
thanks to his father's influence and his own determination, he became a
reserve officer in a prestigious Guards regiment from which he was igno-
miniously cashiered. Bleichroder's other sons also became officers in im-

---

30. Richarz, *German Jewish Memoirs*, pp. 154 and 155.

portant regiments, while his children mixed in aristocratic circles, and some of them married into the nobility, bringing up their own children as Christians. Old and blind, Bleichroder was neglected by his sons, who lunched at clubs with their friends and mistresses. His loyal secretary remarked that "must he not from time to time have a feeling of loneliness? Are there not days when he barely sees or talks to one of his four children . . . ?" We would cite the Bleichroder household as an example of the new upper-class, permissive Jewish family, examples of which abound from the late eighteenth century onwards and which became even more widespread in Germany among middle-class families in the decades before the First World War.[31]

During the period 1890–1914, German Jewish women in bourgeois families rarely went to work like their grandmothers and mothers, leaving them with ample time to run their households and to spend with their children. Fathers toiled for long hours in their businesses or were frequently away from home on commercial ventures. In their absence, control over the children was left to their wives, who were often stricter disciplinarians and did not shy away from slapping their children when they thought it necessary; even so, the punishment meted out by them was not severe when compared with the harsh discipline of the patriarchal father and the tyrannical schoolmaster of the recent past. In contrast, German Jewish bourgeois fathers, like their East European counterparts, were sometimes mild and indulgent insofar as disciplining their children was concerned. Thus in bourgeois families it was not only the absorption of the ideas of Locke and Rousseau that were producing more relaxed styles of rearing their children, but a newfound affluence as well as the decay of the family workshop and the absence of the home over the family store that made the father a distant and nonthreatening figure. Instead, with Jews among the first to avail themselves of the new means of contraception that were becoming available, there was a consequent shrinkage of the number of children in middle class Jewish families, a rise of the cult of motherhood, and a new dominance of the Jewish mother. Moreover, the well-educated

---

31. Fritz Stern, *Gold and Iron: Bismarck, Bleichroder and the Building of the German Empire* (London: George Allen and Unwin, 1981), pp. 485–493. David Landes, "Bleichroders and Rothschilds: The Problem of Continuity in the Family Firm," in *The Family in History,* ed. Charles E. Rosenberg (Philadelphia: University of Pennsylvania Press, 1975), pp. 95–114.

bourgeois Jewish mothers hastened the process of assimilation by laying so much stress on the inculcation of German culture and manners.[32]

Let us focus on one middle class German Jewish family in Berlin in the 1890s, the household of Joseph and Helene Eyck. Joseph was a grain broker with a large household to maintain, consisting of his wife, six children, a cook and maid, and a nanny for his offspring. Until he secured a job as manager of a Berlin brewery the finances of the family were often precarious. Helene was well educated, an admirer of Goethe, and utterly devoted to her domestic duties, with primary responsibility for the upbringing of their children. She sent the children to a nursery school where the teacher was trained in the Froebel methods of not interfering with the natural development of the child. Helene curbed negative character traits in her children, such as laziness and quick temper, without pushing them hard academically. Under strain from business and financial worries and the need to live with all the status symbols of a middle-class household, the couple were nervous and perhaps overreacted to misbehavior on the part of their children, although a warning was given before corporal punishment was eventually resorted to. On the move from the small town in East Prussia where he was brought up, Joseph shed his Orthodoxy, and the family character of Friday nights and the boys' bar mitzvah ceremony was stressed rather than their religious elements.[33]

Helene espoused the romantic concept of childhood innocence. "If only one could for a long time preserve for them untroubled their childlike nature and their genuine cheerful spirit; if only their contact with their fellow students [through anti-Semitism] would not break this bloom and the hazy veil of poetry, which is only found in the soul of a child, and drive them all too soon from this children's paradise . . ." she wrote. Whereas the East European Jews contrasted the paradise of playing in the fields and forests with the shortcomings of the heder, the emancipated German Jews dreaded their children's leaving the wondrous world of the nursery and primary school for entry into the secondary school system because of the anti-Semitism prevailing there. In the spring of 1892 Helene recorded in her diary that

---

32. Marion A. Kaplan, *The Making of the Jewish Middle Class: Women, Family, and Identity, in Imperial Germany* (New York Oxford University Press, 1991), pp. 49–63.

33. Frank Eyck, "A Diarist in Fin-de-Siecle Berlin and Her Family: Helene, Joseph and Erich Eyck," *Leo Baeck Institute Year Book* 37 (1992): 287–307 (hereafter cited as Eyck, *Diarist*).

... probably he [Ernst] will be going from Easter onwards to school [apparently to the *Friedrichsgymnasium*], to which I am reluctant to send him as at the present an indescribable antisemitism prevails there from which the boys of the middle forms, to which Erich belongs, suffer very much; for not only do the fellow-students show an incredible impudence, but . . . the form master is so inconsiderate as to punish a boy who had used the word "Goy" to defend himself more severely than the Christian students who had uttered the most incredible insults . . .

By creating a close and affectionate atmosphere at home, Helene hoped to give her children sufficient self-esteem to insulate them from the anti-Semitism of the outside world.[34]

How unlike the half-Jewish household of Thomas Mann, who was the scion of a line of Lubeck burghers. Golo Mann was overawed by his father until he was eighteen: "When we were children there was no warm, cordial, relaxed feeling of trust." Attempts to join in adult conversations were rebuffed. When Michael Mann was six, his father purchased a new car, and Michael unwisely took off the brakes, thereby damaging the car, which crashed into a wall. His father thrashed him with a walking stick that the boy was carrying. Thomas Mann would brook no argument from his children. A daughter, Monika, remembered that "if I was naughty, he would shame me with an admonishing lift of his brow, a gentle tap of his ring and fingernails, and his clear-sighted, penetrating look."[35]

Assimilation in the middle-class German Jewish households prior to World War I went to bizarre lengths. Although belonging to such a family, Gershom Scholem (1897–1982) from his youth was interested in Jewish culture and Zionism. Since his grandparents' day, Christmas was celebrated with a tree, a roast goose or hare, and the distribution of presents to relatives and friends with the excuse that this was a German national holiday rather than a Christian festival. Hanging on the Christmas tree one year was a framed picture of Herzl, Scholem's present. In the summer of 1909, when Gershom Scholem was twelve, he roller-skated through the streets of Berlin, weaving through the traffic and already showing a marked independence of character. Thus, unlike his brothers, Scholem insisted on learning Hebrew and could recite the blessings on being called up to the reading of the Torah at the time of his bar mitzvah, instead of having to read the Hebrew words from a transliterated text. Incidentally, his father

---

34. Eyck, *Diarist*, pp. 294 and 295.
35. Ronald Hayman, "In Pursuit of Thomas Mann," *Times Literary Supplement*, 9 September 1994.

insisted that all his sons had to wait until their fourteenth birthday before he would allow them to celebrate this event, as he seemed to be viewing it in terms similar to that of a Protestant confirmation ritual. Even so, many of these assimilated German Jewish families betrayed vestiges of the authoritarian personality type in that they had a xenophobic hatred of foreigners, particularly East European Jews, who could not be accepted as narcissistic reflections of themselves.[36]

Steven Lowenstein distinguished two types of families among the German Jews who migrated to Washington Heights in the 1930s.

> In some families the traditional German strictness in bringing up children and the patriarchal style of family decision making were preserved, while in others these traditions were very much relaxed. Although the status of wives may have been improved by the fact that so many of them worked outside the home, a great deal of formal prestige remained with the father. In many families the father sat at the head of the table, and in some families no one else was permitted to sit in his chair. He was usually served his food first. . . . In traditional families the children rose from their seats in the synagogue when their fathers were called to the Torah. In most Orthodox German-Jewish families, both parents blessed the children on the Sabbath and holidays by laying their hands on their heads (a custom practically obsolete among American Jews). In some families meal times were set rigidly by the clock with no leeway allowed for a child's deviation from schedule; those who did not arrive on time risked missing a meal. Although these traits characterized some German-Jewish families well into the 1960s, many other families exhibited only a few or none of them. Articles in the German-Jewish press [in America] demonstrate that, from an early date, parents had a hard time enforcing European rules in the more permissive atmosphere of New York.[37]

In any case it has been suggested that a distinction must be drawn between the old-style patriarchal and authoritarian father, who inculcated "compulsive obedience" in his children and deference to elders because of the force they could wield, and the modern conservative, traditionalist father, who no longer believed in the efficacy of corporal punishment, as this could damage the inner sense of worth of the child. Nonetheless, the traditionalist conservative encouraged his children to be honest and to

---

36. Scholem, *Memories of My Youth*, pp. 28, 37, and 38. For a secular German-Jewish family in the 1930s, see Peter Gay, "The German-Jewish Legacy—and I: Some Personal Reflections," *American Jewish Archives* 40, no. 2 (1988): 203–210.

37. Steven M. Lowenstein, *Frankfurt on the Hudson: The German-Jewish Community of Washington Heights 1933–1983* (Detroit: Wayne State University Press, 1989), pp. 195 and 196.

respect family and religious values. It may also be questioned whether the trappings of power enjoyed by the father in Orthodox German Jewish families were real or in many cases nothing more than symbolic manifestations of an authority that no longer existed.[38]

YOUTH IN REVOLT

Maybe, as David Biale has observed, there was a psychological process of "splitting" in the Kleinian sense by children in the shtetl, contrasting the soft world of their parents' home with the harsh realities of the heder, or as Rudolph Loewenstein suggested the ego defenses against aggression among Jewish parents were too constraining for them to be strict with their own children. Whatever the reason, Jewish fathers emerged with the dual qualities of being both nurturing and, in many cases, only mildly authoritarian; and mothers were often idealized as being more intelligent, more forceful and more practical than their husbands. Moreover, middle-class Jewish fathers who were merchants or connected with the lumber trade were away from home for long periods of time, as were religious fathers. The children thus developed as self-willed and independent. Yaakov Katzenelenbogen as a young child came home from heder one day and informed his parents that henceforth he wished to be known as Dadel and that he would not desist from making a clatter with pots on the kitchen table until they agreed. When he suddenly left his job as an apprentice, Abraham Cahan's father denounced him as "a samovlietz or hefker yung, a headstrong or dissolute youth," but failed to budge him. Parents in East European Jewish families, such as the Weizmanns and to a lesser extent the Levins, could be surprisingly nondirectional as far as the choice of school or career was concerned. Open any East European festival prayer book and turn to the memorial prayer and you will see how important grandparents, uncles, and aunts were. Extended families tended to cluster around the grandparents' home, and it was often the intervention of a perceptive grandfather, modernizing uncle, rabbi, or teacher that persuaded parents to allow their child to embark on some new course.[39]

---

38. Daniel Burston, *The Legacy of Erich Fromm* (Cambridge, Mass.: Harvard University Press, 1991), pp. 112–115.

39. Biale, *Eros and Enlightenment*, pp. 53 and 54. Loewenstein, *Christians and Jews*, pp. 169–172. Cahan, *Memoirs*, pp. 54, 55, and 69. Sperber, *Water Carriers*,

We should remind ourselves that in 1897 over 52 percent of the Jews in Russia were under the age of twenty. Children and adolescents were everywhere; they had a colossal impact on Jewish society, which they helped to shape. "The small group of Jewish pioneers of Enlightenment in Russia," Eliakum Zunser (1840–1913) asserted, "was surrounded on all sides by a powerful foe. . . . Communities ostracized them and turned them over to the military. The schism between parents and children grew wider and deeper from day to day. Jewish youths suffered terrible persecution. . . . They were the modern Maccabees. They unfurled the banner of Jewish nationalism and they carried it from town to town, village to village. Every city and hamlet contained a few of these heroes, who exercised great influence over their fellows and who recruited ever new adherents until a tremendous army was formed." Freed from parental control by studying in a yeshiva or some other religious establishment far from home or in an alien Russian school, Jewish youths were rapidly educated into new ways of thinking by peer group pressure. The May Laws of 1882 not only forced Jews out of the villages of Russia into the towns, where employment was scarce, but by heavily restricting the number of Jews who could enter the gymnasia and universities compelled Jewish youth to study abroad, where they became radicalized. Confident in their own numbers and in revolt against their parents and the violent anti-Jewish mobs, Jewish youths refused to rely any longer on the communal magnates from St. Petersburg to act as intercessors with the government and wrested power from them by the creation of the two mass Jewish parties, the Zionists and the Bund, the Jewish socialist party.[40]

Rebuffed in an attempt to ingratiate themselves with the Russian peasants by joining the Narodnik movement, the youthful Jewish intelligentsia recoiled and became more nationalist in outlook. Utopian farming communities were established by Am Olam groups in the 1880s in Louisiana, South Dakota, and Oregon in the United States, and funds were collected to start a small farming community in Gedera in Palestine in 1884. Without practical training in agriculture and technical expertise, all the American experiments failed, and although the colony in Gedera survived, it never became the prototype for a new social order. Nor was the first attempt to form a self-defense unit a success. In 1881 Jewish students addressed meetings in

---

p. 41. Shazar, *Morning Stars*, p. 90. Reinharz, *Weizmann*, pp. 12, 13, and 21. Levin, *Youth*, pp. 69 and 70. Rubinstein, *Young Years*, p. 7.

40. Biale, *Eros and Enlightenment*, pp. 50 and 51. Lipzin, *Zunser*, pp. 34 and 35.

the synagogues at Odessa to organize self-defense units to counter a possible pogrom, but unexpectedly the pogrom was unleashed on the following day, 3 May 1881, before any arrangements could be made.[41]

After the mid-1880s there was a huge influx of Jews into the socialist parties, youths who came from every strata of society, including three grandchildren of the Zionist tea magnate Wissotzky. Levin argued that "the higher degree of danger gave them [the socialists] a superior prestige in the eyes of the youth and particularly in the eyes of girls"; and that most young women sided with the socialists because they, unlike the Zionists, welcomed female members. Modern girls from well-to-do families as depicted by the novelist Smolenskin were not only taught to read and write and studied languages, but adopted the latest fashions in their dress and groomed their hair. According to Zalman Shazar, "the daughters of our good families were generally not interested in Zionists and Hebraists . . . cultivated girls who spoke Russian and prepared for examinations were almost all on the other side of the line, along with the visiting students, the externe-teacher, and, in time, the Bundist workers." If some secondary pupils were neutral as far as the two movements were concerned, the sons of rich parents were often content with the status quo. While undertaking a necessary minimum of schoolwork, "they spent their free time in amusements, card-playing, and often enough in drinking." Everywhere in the towns in the 1880s, there were still large groups of Jewish teenagers from comfortable families who had completed their Hebrew education without embarking on any secular studies. Known as "children of good family," they were waiting for a suitable marriage partner and to be launched in some business career.[42]

Weizmann addressed an important memorandum to Herzl in 1903, in which he analyzed the political allegiance of East European Jewish youth. The nub of his argument was that the Bund, the Jewish socialist party that combined a revolutionary fervor with the promotion of Yiddish culture, had many more adherents among the younger generation from intellectuals and the working class than the Zionists.

---

41. Louis Greenberg, *The Jews in Russia* (New York: Schocken, 1976), Vol. 2, pp. 166–172. Jonathan Frankel, *Prophecy and Politics: Socialism, Nationalism and the Russian Jews, 1862–1917* (Cambridge: Cambridge University Press, 1981), pp. 54, 55, 96, 97, 115, and 116 (hereafter cited as Frankel, *Prophecy and Politics*).

42. Frankel, *Prophecy and Politics*, p. 140. Levin, *Youth*, pp. 123–129. Patterson, *Hebrew Novel*, p. 154. Shazar, *Morning Stars*, p. 85.

The larger part of the contemporary younger generation is anti-Zionist, not from a desire to assimilate, as in Western Europe, but through revolutionary conviction. It is impossible to calculate the number of victims, or describe their character, that are annually, indeed daily, sacrificed because of their identification with Jewish Social Democracy in Russia. Hundreds of thousands of very young boys and girls are held in Russian prisons, or are being spiritually and physically destroyed in Siberia. . . . Almost all those now being victimized in the entire Social Democratic movement are Jews, and their number grows daily. They are not necessarily young people of proletarian origin; they also come from well-to-do families, and incidentally not infrequently from Zionist families. Almost all students belong to the revolutionary camp. . . . Saddest and most lamentable is the fact that although this movement [the Bund] consumes much Jewish energy and heroism, and it is located within the Jewish fold, the attitude it evinces toward Jewish nationalism is one of antipathy, swelling at times to fanatical hatred. Jewish children are in open revolt against their parents. The elders are confined within tradition and Orthodox inflexibility; the young make their first step a search for freedom from everything Jewish. In one small town near Pinsk, for example, youngsters tore the Torah Scrolls to shreds.

Nonetheless, Weizmann exaggerated the alienation of some of these youths from Jewish tradition and glossed over the fact that because the Bund had been swamped by an influx of youngsters of middle-class origin with heder and yeshiva backgrounds, it had adopted a new Jewish national stance in 1900; this culminated in 1906 in support for the principle of national cultural autonomy for the Jews.[43]

Part of the youthful rebellion was expressed in a positive way, by taking up arms against the participants in pogroms instead of trying to ignore anti-Semitic outrage, as their fathers had done in so many instances. Whereas the earlier pogroms in the 1880s had been mainly directed against property, those from 1903 to 1906 at Kishinev, Zhitomir, Kiev, and Bialystok were targeted against persons, claiming a total of 1, 230 Jewish victims. In response to these attacks, the Zionists and the Bund together with the more revolutionary socialist parties started organizing Jewish self-defense units, while Jewish emigration from Russia to the United States leaped from 37,011 in 1900 to 125,234 in 1906. In reaction to the new wave of pogroms in Kishinev in April and in Homel in September 1903, the Bundists and the Poale Zion formed a self-defense unit in Homel of 500 persons equipped with guns. Proud of their identity as Jews, members of the Poale Zion in the shtetl of Steibtz and the surrounding small

    43. The Letters and Papers of Chaim Weizmann, ed. Meyer W. Weisgal et al. (London: Oxford University Press, 1968), Vol. 1, ser. A, pp. 306 and 307.

towns of Svirzna, Baranovitz, Mush, Lechavitz, and Gorodzia spearheaded the organization of Jewish self-defense units, busily co-opting members of other Jewish parties to ensure that there was communal unity. In 1905 Jewish self-defense units were active in Zhitomir and Melitopol as well as in large towns such as Odessa, Kiev, and Riga. In Bialystok in June 1906, units of 400 men with rifles successfully beat off assaults in the side streets of the town. From their experiences gained while serving in Jewish self-defense units in Homel and Zhitomir as well as in foreign armies, the young pioneers who migrated to Palestine before World War I formed an armed organization, *Hashomer* (the watchman), to safeguard the Jewish settlements.[44]

If children had sufficiently internalized their idealized image of their parents or that of a deeply admired elementary teacher, despite the conflict engendered by the regimen of the heder, they adhered to either traditional Judaism or one of its secularised versions, particularly the ideology of the Zionist movement. His *melamed* Judah Artzer kept Shmarya Levin enthralled with Jewish culture, despite his negative experiences with other teachers. Chaim Weizmann admired Rabbi Motolianski, who taught him Hebrew composition and grammar as well as introducing him to the works of Mapu, Smolenskin, and Judah Leib Gordon, all part of the Jewish enlightenment. Brushing aside the admonitions of his rabbi, who feared that his faith would be undermined, Zalman Shazar, a precocious young hasid and a future president of Israel, had lessons with a Hebrew poet. A survey of immigrant men in Palestine in the 1930s indicated that a third of them had studied in heder or yeshiva, while over half of them spoke excellent Hebrew before their arrival. The experience of revolutionary and messianic ferment in Russia, the formative years spent in a progressive elementary school steeped in Jewish culture and Hebrew, and the concept of Jewish self-defense against the perpetrators of pogroms—all molded the basic personality structures of Russian Jewish youth in Palestine in the period 1904–1914 and helped in the course of generations to create a new type of Jew, the Hebrew-speaking macho male.[45]

---

44. Frankel, *Prophecy and Politics*, pp. 135, 147, 154, 155, 335, 336, and 368–370. Shazar, *Morning Stars*, pp. 150–152. Yigal Allon, *Shield of David: The Story of Israel's Armed Forces* (London: Weidenfeld and Nicholson, 1970), pp. 13, 29, and 30.

45. Levin, *Childhood*, pp. 207 and 208. Kasovich, *Memoirs*, pp. 10 and 27. Isaac Deutscher, *The Non-Jewish Jew* (London: Merlin Press, 1981), p. 8. Reinharz, *Weiz-*

Parallel with the Jewish youth revolt in Eastern Europe was a similar rebellion in Germany and Austria. The historian Michael Berkowitz summed up the Zionist revolt in the 1890s and the years before the First World War:

> Indeed, the contemporary European nationalisms comprised elements that may be characterized as rebellions of youth, and, simultaneously, "bourgeois anti-bourgeois revolts"; that is, young people who sought to distance themselves from the older generation, but nevertheless clung to many of its core values. Similarly, these young Zionists—who championed the reconstitution of a Jewish sovereignty, the revival of Hebrew, and a Jewish totality—advocated what may be seen as a "'traditional anti-traditional revolution."

Siegfried Bernfeld in 1914 called on young people to throw off the constraints of parents and school. These middle-class youngsters wanted to appropriate large parts of their Jewish inheritance, but at the same time desired to embrace Western culture, particularly its literature, art, and science.[46]

Jewish adolescents in Central Europe were in revolt against the vestiges of authoritarianism in their homes and the anti-Semitic hostility they encountered in their schools, particularly the gymnasia, and the universities. If Erich Eyck left school with life-long scars because of the anti-Semitic atmosphere prevailing there, Gershom Scholem was expelled from his gymnasium after the exposure that he had composed an antiwar protest in 1915. Again, there was a quantitative leap in the representation of Jewish students in German universities from the mid-1870s through to the 1880s, which in Prussia reached a peak of overrepresentation by a factor of 7.48 in the late 1880s, and then gradually subsided to 5.44 in the years 1911–1912. Between 1880 and 1895, anti-Semitic elements in Germany took over the leadership of the chief student fraternities. Coinciding with this, there was a crisis in the professional labor market in the 1890s, and a sharp political shift to the right in the attitudes of the academic and pro-

---

mann, pp. 10 and 11. Shazar, *Morning Stars*, pp. 82–86. Frankel, *Prophecy and Politics*, pp. 366–369.

46. Michael Berkowitz, *Zionist Culture and West European Jewry before the First World War* (Cambridge: Cambridge University Press, 1993), pp. 42, 43, 46–49, and 86–89 (hereafter cited as Berkowitz, *Zionist Culture*). George L. Mosse, *Germans and Jews* (London: Orbach and Chambers, 1971), p. 79 (hereafter cited as Mosse, *Germans and Jews*).

fessional classes. Confronted by this volatile situation, the dilemma of German Jewish youth was well expressed by Walter Rathenau, later the foreign minister: "In the youth of every German Jew there is a painful moment which he remembers all his life: when he becomes fully conscious for the first time that he has entered the world as a second-class citizen and that no ability and no merit can free him from this situation." Many adolescents thus grew up with personalities displaying schizoid features. Cora Berliner, writing in 1916, admitted this:

> Among the younger Jews we find many ill-adjusted and split personalities; they clearly sense that there are two different worlds that will not be united. Often a decision to convert to Christianity, the religion of the majority, or else to join the Zionist party is inspired by a longing to escape from that inner conflict so as to be able to fully develop one's potential on one of the two sides . . .[47]

Although the Jewish youth movement gained momentum after the First World War, it had its beginnings earlier. In Germany the Jewish youth organizations were influenced by the *Wandervogel* (migratory bird) movement, a national German association that venerated the Middle Ages and the mythic German past as opposed to industrial civilization and believed that members could find a genuine and true response in nature, "the landscape of the Volk." Many of these ideas were espoused by Zionist theorists and appealed to the agricultural pioneers and the founders of the kibbutz movement in Israel. Arthur Ruppin, a future Zionist technocrat, asked in his diary in 1894, "Why does the farmer lead a happier life than the city-dweller, why is he healthier, why is he more content, why is the love of God . . . still alive in him? Because he lives in inner feeling with nature, to which he strives to adapt as closely as possible, because he has occasion daily to see in the working of nature the hand of God." Ravnitski claimed that "working the soil . . . will heal the fractured bodies of the sons." Moreover, Martin Buber suggested that Jews had "to feel as though they are an organism and to aspire to harmonize their powers, to invest as much soul in walking, singing, and working as in solving intellectual problems,

---

47. Bruno Bettelheim, *The Children of the Dream* (New York: Avon, 1970), p. 35. Lewis S. Feuer, *The Conflict of Generations: The Character and Significance of Student Movements* (London: Heinemann, 1969), p. 12. Eyck, *Diary*, p. 295. Scholem, *Memories of My Youth*, pp. 60 and 61. Kampe, *Students*, pp. 357–394. Chaim Schatzker, "Martin Buber's Influence on the Jewish Youth Movement in Germany," *Leo Baeck Institute Year Book* 23 (1978): 158 and 159.

and to derive pleasure out of pride and love for a healthy and perfect body."[48]

"All Jewish youth movements stressed physical fitness, courage and self-respect, in direct contrast to the image of the degraded Jew." Until the 1880s, when they were infiltrated by anti-Semitic nationalists, the German gymnastic associations were liberal and attracted many Jewish adherents; so much so that it was estimated at the beginning of the decade that 5 percent of their members were Jews. Thus Austrian and German Jews, who were excluded from the German sports club in Turkey, set up the Israelitischer Turnverein (Israelite Gymnastic Association) in Constantinople in 1896. The first European Jewish sports club was the Bar Kochba in Berlin (1898), followed by the Hagibor in Prague and Hakoah in Vienna (1909), which started as a football club. David Wolffsohn, the Zionist leader, decided to form Hakoah as a sports club that would admit only Jews. Again, Fabius Schach, an early German Zionist, in 1893 urged Jews to cultivate "the manly virtues" and to shape themselves by physical exercise to "look the world in the eye, in a forthright and courageous manner, and demand rights rather than sufferance." In the Second Zionist Congress in Basle in 1898, Max Nordau made his "muscular Jewry" speech, in which he asserted that "we Jews possess an exceptional gift for physical activity." Further, "This may appear paradoxical, since we have been accustomed to view ourselves in the mirror that our enemies have held up to us, and to discover any number of physical defects and blemishes. When, however, Jews engage in physical culture, our defects vanish, our posture improves and our muscles become strong. The more Jews achieve in the various branches of sport, the greater will be our self-confidence and self-respect. We must cultivate a Judaism of muscles!" What happened was that the Zionist movement in part took over thriving Jewish sports organizations and the support of the Zionists boosted the expansion of these clubs, culminating in a gigantic gymnastics display by two thousand per-

---

48. Walter Laqueur, "The German Youth Movement and the 'Jewish Question,'" *Leo Baeck Institute Year Book* 6 (1961): 193–205. Mosse, *Germans and Jews*, pp. 77–115. Derek J. Penslar, *Zionism and Technocracy: The Engineering of Jewish Settlement in Palestine 1870–1918* (Bloomington: Indiana University Press, 1991), pp. 89 and 90 (hereafter cited as Penslar, *Zionism and Technocracy*. Shmuel Almog, *Zionism and History: The Rise of the New Jewish Consciousness* (New York: St. Martin's Press, 1987), pp. 109–114 (hereafter cited as Almog, *Zionism and History*). Mosse, *Germans and Jews*, pp. 85–89.

formers in front of a crowd of 25, 000 at the Eleventh Zionist Congress in 1913. The events ended with the recitation of the motto of the gymnasts: "We fight for Judah's honor/Full strength in youth/So when we reach manhood/Still fighting ten times better." By training for perfection at gymnastics and fencing, the Zionists in Central Europe aimed at creating a new type of Jewish man, which overlapped with similar concepts evolving among the East European Jews.[49]

In Austria the German national student fraternities began expelling Jews because of rising anti-Semitism, and conflicts occurred between the German student groups and members of radical-liberal *Landsmannschaften*, associations of those coming from the same area, some of which were mainly Jewish. Clashes erupted on a daily basis between individuals in the lecture halls, corridors, and laboratories of the universities. Theodor Herzl joined one such student fraternity, the Albia, in 1881, although he later resigned from it when members associated themselves with an anti-Semitic demonstration. The first Jewish student nationalist organization, Kadimah, was formed in 1882, and by the early 1920s there were twelve such Zionist fraternities in the University of Vienna. Starting as an academic organization with the usual beer drinking sessions, when student songs were lustily bawled, the Vienna Kadimah, stung by taunts, reversed its policy in 1893 and demanded satisfaction by a duel when its members were insulted, and selected six expert swordsmen to uphold the honor of the fraternity. "Their aim was to show the world that Jews could hold their own in duelling, bawling, drinking and singing just like other people . . ." wrote Arthur Koestler, himself a member of one such body. The founders of Kadimah "spent eight hours a day for six months learning the art of duelling with cavalry sabres before their first appearance, complete with 'colours' and trappings in the Great Hall of Vienna University." The German students provoked a riot that "led to a series of duels, in which the Kadimites made mincemeat of their opponents." It should be added that the anti-Semitism among student bodies was so virulent that it encouraged Jews to become duelling champions. Among these the most outstanding was Dr Jeno Fuchs

49. Sarah Honig, "Unquenched Vitality," *The Jerusalem Post Magazine*, 27 March 1987. Scholem, *Memories of My Youth*, p. 9. Joseph Hoffman, "Muscular Vitality," *The Jerusalem Post Entertainment Magazine*, 19 August 1988. Erich Juhn, "The Jewish Sports Movement in Austria," in *The Jews of Austria*, ed. Josef Fraenkel (London: Vallentine Mitchell, 1967), pp. 161–164. Almog, *Zionism and History*, pp. 108–117. Berkowitz, *Zionist Culture*, pp. 107–109.

(1882–1955) from Hungary, who won several gold medals in the Olympic games for fencing.[50]

By passing the Waidhofen declaration in 1896, insisting that Jewish students were "without honour or character," the tactic of the German nationalist students was to deprive Jews of the opportunity of becoming officers in the reserve and to exclude them from teaching and the legal profession and from becoming bureaucrats. That was why Jewish students so stoutly resisted the attempt to relegate them to the category of a non-person unworthy of being a fit opponent in a duel.[51]

The upheavals of the First World War continued the radicalization of Jewish youth. "The members of Hashomer [a socialist Zionist party], almost all of them high-school and university students, came from bourgeois or petty-bourgeois families who had fled to Vienna from Galicia or Bukovina," wrote Manes Sperber in his memoirs, which echoed the analysis of Berkowitz.

> Their social status could have led them to a certain kind of assimilation, a gradual estrangement from Judaism, from its faith and customs. But here, the organization reached into the lives of these young people and their families in an astonishingly contradictory way. The conscious or unconscious tendency toward assimilation left room for a firm desire to be actively Jewish. At the same time, the younger generation alienated itself from their elders, openly attacking their traditional way of life and thereby them. The generation gap that threatens immigrant families everywhere was made almost inevitable by Hashomer and remained generally incomprehensible to our parents. They had feared that their children might move away from Judaism and thus from them. This alienation came about, not because the children assimilated, but because they wished to be different from their mothers and fathers . . . we boys, in order to find ourselves in the midst of an urban, cosmopolitan civilization, wanted to retain certain things from the shtetl, but not belong to it anymore.

These youngsters concentrated on speaking Hebrew, studied Zionist history and the geography of Palestine, drilled in the Vienna Woods in Hebrew, and went for hikes on Sundays holding aloft their blue and white Zionist

---

50. Kampe, *Students*, pp. 377–383. Julius H. Schoeps, "Modern Heirs of the Maccabees: The Beginning of the Vienna Kadimah, 1882–1897," *Leo Baeck Institute Year Book* 27 (1982): 159–170 (hereafter cited as Schoeps, *Vienna Kadimah*). Alex Bein, *Theodore Herzl* (Philadelphia: Jewish Publication Society, 1945), pp. 30–42. Arthur Koestler, *Arrow in the Blue* (London: Collins, 1952), pp. 82 and 83. Andrew Handler, *From the Ghetto to the Games: Jewish Athletes in Hungary* (New York: Columbia University Press, 1985), pp. 30 and 31.

51. Schoeps, *Vienna Kadimah*, pp. 166 and 167.

flag, daring opponents to challenge them to a fight. With the coming of the Russian Revolution in 1917, many of these youths from Hasidic families switched their allegiance to Marxism, shifting from religious to secular messianism.[52]

Both the Eastern and Central European youths wanted to return to the certainties of childhood, to paradise or the realm of nature in order to complete an inner healing process of the split in their personalities, thereby creating, with the aid of new Western technology imported from Germany, the kibbutz movement. Its other source was the socialist messianism of the East European youths of the Second Aliya (1904–1914).[53]

---

52. Sperber, *Water Carriers*, pp. 131–133.
53. Penslar, *Zionism and Technocracy*.

9

Growing Up in Britain and America: Childhood and Education

INFANCY

From the early part of this century, social scientists have vigorously debated why Jews had lower infant mortality rates than their Gentile neighbors, but it has been extremely difficult to isolate the reasons for these differences. In Frankfurt-on-Main in 1905, the mortality of infants under the age of one among Protestants was 29.27 per 1,000 and under five years 39.09 per 1,000, whereas the rates for Jews were considerably smaller, 12.33 and 14.33. In Hungary the death rate of infants under one year per 1,000 births among Catholics was 166.5 as against 98.2 among Jews. In Amsterdam in 1900 the survivors for the first year among Jews numbered 907 out of 1,000 newborn babies, while for Christians the figure was only 861. More than this, the low death rates for Prussia between 1893 and 1897 of Jewish children were outstanding in Europe, with 3.96 Jewish children under fifteen dying per 1,000 of the population as compared with 11.47 Christian children. In Galicia, however, where the Jews lived under conditions of the direst poverty at the start of the century and in Vilna, Jewish infant mortality was higher than that of their neighbors. For instance, in Lvov (Lemberg) during 1901–1902, 870 out of 1,000 Christian babies survived into their second year as against 866 Jewish infants. What all this and subsequent research revealed was that the sharp decline in Jewish infant mortality, an event that inaugurated a new era in childhood history, went back in Europe to developments in the nineteenth century.[1]

Although the Jewish illegitimacy rates remained low in the small towns and rural areas in Central and Eastern Europe, they were high in some of the big cities. In Vienna in the early 1870s, 83 percent of the Jewish found-lings died because only the most wretched wet nurses would agree to breast-feed them. Only by the action of the Viennese community in offering rich financial rewards to a superior class of women to suckle these children was the death rate of these unfortunate infants reduced to 29 percent. Otherwise, only well-to-do Jewish families in Germany and elsewhere tended to hire wet nurses for their infants.[2]

Again, during the interwar period there was a rise in the number of Jewish mothers giving birth to illegitimate children in Eastern Europe, even if the level was lower than that of the surrounding Gentile population. In the 1920s and 1930s the number of illegitimate births among Jews in Warsaw and Lodz was so high that U. O. Schmelz asserted that it prob-ably represented "a crude form of birth control . . ." for "the very high ratios of reported stillbirths to livebirths for illegitimate children in War-saw, Lodz, Vienna, Bohemia and Moravia in some part of the 1920s, and in Vienna even earlier, must in all likelihood, again be understood as due to induced cases . . . [that is, infants who were deliberately killed]," as their existence conflicted with their mothers' warped but strong moral code. We will recall from an earlier chapter Maurice Fishberg's concern about

---

1. Maurice Fishberg, *The Jews: A Study of Race and Environment* (New York: Walter Scott Publishing Co., 1911), pp. 259–261 (hereafter cited as Fishberg, *The Jews*). Arthur Ruppin, *The Jews of Today* (London: G. Bell, 1913), pp. 75–81 (hereafter cited as Ruppin, *Jews of Today*). U. O. Schmelz, *Infant and Early Childhood Mortality Among the Jews of the Diaspora* (Jerusalem: Institute of Contemporary Jewry, 1971), pp. 1–83 (hereafter cited as Schmelz, *Infant Mortality*). Gretchen A. Condran and Ellen A. Kamarow, "Child Mortality among Jewish Immigrants to the United States," *Journal of Interdisciplinary History* 22, no. 2 (Autumn 1991): 223–254.

2. Valerie Fildes, *Wet Nursing: A History from Antiquity to the Present* (Oxford: Basil Blackwell, 1988), p. 221.

such deaths, which he mistakenly attributed to the lack of skill of the midwives.[3]

We would suggest that the socially mobile Jewish population of Western Europe and the United States, with their rising standard of living, had superior methods of rearing their children and low mortality rates, while the most impoverished strata of the Jewish population in Central and Eastern Europe at the beginning of the century had high infant mortality rates. Sometimes these poor Jewish fathers and mothers had a low standard of infant care; sometimes they were excellent parents, but their efforts were undermined by long bouts of poverty. Golda Meir (1898–1979) in her autobiography mentioned that "my mother had other troubles. Four little boys and a girl all fell ill. Two of them died before they were a year old, two of them went within one month." Conditions only improved when the wealthy family for whom Golda's mother had been hired as a wet nurse insisted that a nurse was to teach her "the rudiments of child care," that she changed her accommodation and ensured that she had enough to eat. Arthur Ruppin (b. 1876) described his childhood in Magdeburg between 1887 and 1890 and recounted that "my mother devoted the utmost care to every child, but poverty was more effective than her care, and four of the babies succumbed to the bad conditions. They usually died at the age of four months, and the new babies also died at that age. If they stayed alive beyond the fourth month, in spite of being inadequately nourished on fresh and condensed milk, they survived." It was the well-to-do Jewish bourgeois families in Central Europe and elsewhere in the nineteenth century who had large numbers of children surviving into adult life. For example, Hanle Kohn (1803–1880) from Bavaria had eight sons and seven daughters, all of whom outlived their father, except a son who died from an infectious disease at twenty-six.[4]

Among other reasons proffered for the lower infant mortality rates among Jews were the higher standards of cleanliness in their homes. Jew-

---

3. Schmelz, *Infant Mortality*, pp. 50–55. Fishberg, *The Jews*, pp. 241–242.

4. Golda Meir, *My Life* (New York: G. P. Putnams' Sons, 1975), p. 16. Arthur Ruppin, *Memoirs, Diaries, Letters* (London: Weidenfeld and Nicholson, 1971), pp. 24 and 25. Goitein, *Family*, pp. 240 and 478 note 115. Ruth Dudley Edwards, *Victor Gollancz: A Biography* (London: Victor Gollancz, 1987), pp. 134 and 135 (hereafter cited as Edwards, *Gollancz*). Edwards pointed out that Henrietta Solomon was one of twelve children of a prosperous leather merchant and that her daughter Susan, who married Herbert Bentwich, herself gave birth to twelve more children.

ish religious law sanctioned the washing of hands before and after meals, bathing before the Sabbath, and the ritual bath; and the dietary laws made Jewish mothers more careful in food preparation. In this context we should note that the *Brandtspeigel* (1590s) urged that if a woman was pregnant or nursing a child, she should make certain that the infant was receiving clean and pure food, so that the child would not become constipated or suffer from diarrhea. Such mothers were also warned against walking in filthy places and in areas that had deposits of sewage or had noxious smells. This Yiddish ethical literature was extensively read in the eighteenth century by women from business and rabbinic families, but it is doubtful whether all the ideas about the importance of cleanliness had percolated down to the lower classes in Eastern Europe. Dr. Marcuse, also writing in Yiddish in 1789, protested against the practice of the Jewish population leaving dung-heaps outside their doors, as abscesses and scabies resulted from uncleanliness, and when the sun came out, flies teemed in the air. "Our children walk about in the filth or play not far from it, and they become sick." Further, "You should keep them [babies] very clean and not let them lie wet. You should let the rooms where new mothers lie with their weak little children be clean, dry, and disinfected with sulphur." Again, Dr. Elkan Isaac Wolf not only urged in 1777 that a child should be kept clean by frequent washing, but that its room should be ventilated three times a day and that babies should be taken out into the open air in winter even in cold weather. Further, Chaim Aronson (1825–1888), when he was a young man, lodged with a Jewish watchmaker in Courland in a house that he specifically described as being "kept tidy and clean, in the usual German [modern] manner"; the inference is that not all Jewish homes then matched this standard. Abraham Cahan also spoke about the home of one of his childhood friends in Vilna, where "the floors . . . were as spotlessly clean as the table on which they ate. This was not usually the case in more old-fashioned households." Moreover, "By the 1840's the Jews [in France] had adopted many of the French behavioral norms. Observers often cited changes in Jewish behaviour, e. g., greater regard for personal cleanliness and appreciation of modern secular education."[5]

---

5. Deborah Dwork, "Health Conditions of Immigrant Jews on the Lower East Side of New York City: 1880–1914," *Medical History* 25, no. 1 (1981): 29 (hereafter cited as Dwork, *Health Conditions*). Assaf, pp. 54 and 55. Israel Zinberg, *A History of Jewish Literature: The Berlin Haskalah* (New York: Ktav, 1976), Vol. 8, pp. 158–165. Feldman, *Jewish Child*, pp. 200 and 201. Aronson, *Autobiography*, p. 163. Cahan,

We would conclude then that the Jewish immigrants to Britain and the United States came with mixed views on the standards of hygiene they should adopt. This is partially reflected in the differing assessments as to whether Jews in the immigrant catchment areas were cleaner than their neighbors or not, although the bulk of the observers came to a positive conclusion. In 1902 Fishberg declared that "in fact, of the homes of the poor population of the city [New York], the Jewish home is the cleanest"; and Lilian Brandt concurred a year later by asserting that Jewish homes were cleaner than Italian ones. At the turn of the century American sociologists found 82.5 percent of the Polish immigrant families were living in one room as compared with 58.6 percent of Jewish families. The larger the premises were, the easier it would be for families to maintain reasonable standards of hygiene, but these statistics may also be indicating that the Jews were more skilled and socially mobile than the rest of the population, more likely to be earning a higher income, more willing to pay a higher rent for spacious premises and more able to purchase greater quantities of nutritious food. Again, it was the practice of Jewish families in London in the early years of this century to make certain that if milk or water was given to young babies, it was always boiled. So too, in the United States the distinguished Jewish paediatrician Dr. Abraham Jacobi averred that mother's milk was best, but if that was unavailable raw, unpasteurized milk should not be supplied to infants; and the philanthropist Nathan Straus opened seventeen milk depots in New York by 1910 that annually dispensed four million bottles of pasteurized milk for infants.[6]

Moreover, Fishberg pointed out that "the Russian baths [in New York] are very numerous in the Jewish quarter, and very much frequented. 'I

Memoirs, p. 85. Calvin Goldscheider and Alan S. Zuckerman, The Transformation of the Jews (Chicago: University of Chicago Press, 1984), p. 50 (hereafter cited as Goldscheider and Zuckerman, Transformation).

6. Dwork, Health Conditions, pp. 8 and 30. Robert Morse Woodbury, Causal Factors in Infant Mortality: A Statistical Study Based on Investigations in Eight Cities (Washington: Government Printing Office, 1925), p. 116 (hereafter cited as Woodbury, Infant Mortality). Lara V. Marks, Model Mothers: Jewish Mothers and Maternity Provision in East London 1870–1939 (Oxford: Clarendon Press, 1994), p. 68 (hereafter cited as Marks, Model Mothers). Naomi W. Cohen, Encounter with Emancipation: The German Jews in the United States 1830–1914 (Philadelphia: Jewish Publication Society, 1984), pp. 307 and 380 note 20. Ionel Rosenthal and Baruch Rosen, "Nathan Straus' Contribution to the Dairy Industry in Palestine," Journal of Israeli History 15, no. 1 (Spring 1994): 91–99.

cannot get along without a "sweat" (Russian bath) at least once a week,'
many a Jew will tell you"; much the same was the case among the immigrant community in the East End of London. There were also public baths
within easy reach of the Jewish population in the East End, which one
boy remembered being taken to by his mother after school every Thursday. The majority of the Jewish immigrant population were receptive to
the new ideas about social and personal hygiene that were evolving in the
West, as similar notions were part of their own culture. In the East End of
London sanitary inspectors appointed by the Jewish Board of Guardians
and home helps from the Sick Room Helps Society raised the standard of
cleanliness in the poorest Jewish homes, as it was alleged that friends and
neighbors "having no sense of cleanliness or order in their own dwellings"
could not be entrusted with the task. Even so, Dr. Stallard, writing in the
1860s in Britain, declared that "the houses of the poor [Jews] are, on the
whole, cleaner and more tidy and more comfortable than amongst the poor
English. The children are always better clothed and more cleanly, their
ruddy faces presenting a strong contrast to the pale and scrofulous coun-
tenances of English children living in the same overcrowded courts." In
contrast, when Abraham Cahan was a pupil in the state-run Vilna Teacher
Training Institute in the 1870s, he remembered that "we were taken to
the public bathhouse every two weeks," a standard of personal hygiene
inferior to that common among Jews.[7]

Another factor frequently cited for the low infant mortality rates found
among Jews was their prolonged breast-feeding of their infants. In traditional society Sephardim in Turkey and Morocco breast-fed their infants
for two to three years and in Jerusalem around 1900 often for eighteen
months, while in Morocco at the end of the nineteenth century there were
instances of mothers visiting the heder to suckle their sons who were aged
between six and seven. David ben Meir Friesenhausen writing in Bavaria
in 1820 noted that "our sages have stated that the period for nursing
children is two years, but physicians in our day say there is no need for

---

7. Dwork, *Health Conditions*, p. 30. See Jerry White, *Rothschild Buildings:. Life
in an East End Tenement Block 1887–1920* (London: Routledge and Kegan Paul, 1980),
pp. 48 and 49 (hereafter cited as White, *Rothschild Buildings*), who says that children
and adults sometimes bathed in tin baths at home. Marks, *Model Mothers*, pp. 113–
119. V. D. Lipman, *A Century of Social Service 1859–1959: The History of the Jewish Board of Guardians* (London: Routledge and Kegan Paul, 1959), pp. 7 and 8. Cahan,
Memoirs, p. 110.

this—it is too troublesome for the mother—and many people listen to them
. . . do not listen to these physicians . . . Because during the first two years
the child is subject to various diseases. Experience teaches that during illness and fever the child will not reject the mother's milk which will then sustain
his life." Again, Dr. Moshe Studentski wrote a health guide in Hebrew called
"The Paediatrician" that was published in Warsaw in 1846, in which he
berated foolish mothers who refused to suckle their babies, suggesting that
these infants should be breast-fed for eighteen months and not be given meat
until they were two years old. He was also critical of the practice of adults
chewing scraps of food for their infants prior to feeding them.[8]

In London Dr. William Feldman, a general practitioner and physician
to St. Mary's Hospital for Women and Children, published in 1907 a book
in Yiddish entitled *The Child, Its Rearing, Development and Ailments*,
which was addressed to Jewish parents and nurses. A volume on similar
lines in English called *A Manual of Nursery Hygiene* and aimed at a wider,
more general audience followed in 1910. At the turn of the century it was
believed that Jewish mothers in the East End suckled their infants for considerably more than nine months; they also supplemented the breast milk
with other foods. So too, Charlotte Wolff, who was born in Germany in
1901, recalled that she had a Polish wet nurse whose milk "fed me for a
year, if not longer." Thus we can see that in the early part of this century
Jewish mothers were still accustomed to breast-feeding their babies for
over a year, even if they did not adhere to the nineteenth-century target of
eighteen months. Dr. Feldman advised on the contrary that babies should
be weaned at ten months, although he admitted that "many poor mothers, however, keep their children at the breast for a much longer period."
It was bad for children to be breast-fed for more than a year, he claimed,
on the spurious grounds that the milk did not contain enough iron or that
it began "to lose its proper proportion of fat (cream) and therefore the
child is liable to develop rickets, which . . . is partly due to a deficiency of
fat in the diet."[9]

8. Marks, *Model Mothers*, pp. 68–71. Abraham Stahl, *Family and Childrearing in Oriental Jewry* (Hebrew) (Jerusalem: Akadamon, 1993), p. 391. Yakov Yehoshua, *Home and Street in Jerusalem of the Old Days* (Jerusalem: Rubin Mass, 1965), p. 81. *Ethical Wills: A Modern Jewish Treasury*, ed. Jack Riemer and Nathaniel Stampfer (New York: Schocken Books, 1983), p. 6. D. Margalit, "Dr. Moshe Studentsky and His Book, 'Rofe Hayeladim' (1804–1883)," *Koroth* 4, no. 5–7 (December 1967): 363–388.

9. William Moses Feldman, *The Child, Its Rearing, Development and Ailments* (London: E. W. Rabbinowicz, 1907). William Moses Feldman, *A Manual of Nursery*

Anticipating many features of Truby King's later program of baby care, Dr. Feldman declared that "one of the worst mistakes mothers often make is to feed the baby each time it cries . . ." "Many children are little gluttons, and so long as the breast contains any milk they will not let it go . . ." until they vomit up the milk. Instead of demand feeding, as practiced by the immigrant mothers, Dr. Feldman recommended that the child's feeding times should be fixed at regular intervals of every three hours between the age of three and six months and then reduced to once every three and a half hours until it was weaned. It is doubtful whether many of Dr. Feldman's ideas made much headway in the immigrant Jewish community in the East End and perhaps fortunate, since a reduction in the length of breast-feeding for the infant would have reduced its protection against disease. Susan Tananbaum has noted that immigrant mothers attended the infant welfare centers in the East End less regularly than their daughters in the 1930s, as they were still deeply attached to the childrearing practices of Eastern Europe.[10]

Breast-feeding not only provided a baby with some immunity against infectious disease in the antibodies he absorbed with his mother's milk, but avoiding bottle feeding and contaminated milk protected the child from gastric and intestinal diseases, particularly epidemic diarrhea that was common in the summer months and led to the death of young infants. Effective legislation to safeguard the quality of milk was not introduced in England until 1914 and 1915. Nevertheless, it was pointed out that the Irish immigrants in Britain and the Polish community in the United States also practiced the prolonged suckling of their children, without enjoying the commensurate fall in their infant mortality rates. Hence other factors were responsible for this, particularly the diet of the different groups. Lara Marks has put forward the commendable hypothesis that Eastern European Jews had a diet of fish such as herring, fish oils, animal fat (schmaltz), eggs, cheese, butter, milk, and vegetables, which was rich in vitamins A and D. Because of the vitamin D in their diet, Jewish children in the schools in

---

Hygiene (London: Bailliere, Tindall, and Cox, 1910), p. 28 (hereafter cited as Feldman, Nursery Hygiene). Marks, Model Mothers, pp. 69 and 71. Kaplan, German Jewish Middle Class, p. 49.

10. Feldman, Nursery Hygiene, pp. 24, 27, and 36. Susan L. Tananbaum, "Making Good Little English Children: Infant Welfare and Anglicanization among Jewish Immigrants in London, 1880–1939," Immigrants and Minorities 12, no. 2 (July 1993): 190 (hereafter cited as Tananbaum, Anglicanization Among Jews).

Leeds in 1902 had a low incidence of rickets (5 and 7 percent), while Gentile children in the poorest districts of the city had a rate of 50 percent. When children had rickets, it meant that they were less physically robust and more susceptible to other virulent childhood diseases such as whooping cough and measles. Conducted on a surprise visit to two of the poorer schools in Leeds in 1904 by Dr. Hall, Sir John Gorst M.P., then a junior minister of education, saw for himself how "the two schools [one Jewish, the other Gentile] presented the most marked contrast in healthy appearance, cleanliness, neatness of clothes, and general brightness, though Dr. Hall declared that the parents of the two sets of children were equally poor and their homes equally dirty and over-crowded."[11]

A final explanation for the low infant and childhood mortality rates among Jews was the closeness of the family, mostly unaffected by the blight of alcoholism and venereal disease, and the caring values as regards the raising of children that this engendered. Gorst also noted that "on the steps of a Gentile school was a little girl of ten partaking of a cup of cocoa, administered by a poor ragged woman. It turned out on inquiry to be a Jewish child, who had been out of sorts at breakfast, and eaten nothing; its mother had brought up the cup of cocoa to the school, fearing her child might be faint and hungry, and unfit to do her lessons." We would mention a further example of good Jewish mothering from Manchester, where a woman burst into a packed classroom to give a breakfast consisting of a bagel and an egg to her daughter, who had just been released by a fever hospital, much to the girl's embarrassment. Jewish schoolchildren often received "a better quality lunch [from their parents] 'which often consists of a meat sandwich and a banana . . .'" Gorst stated that "Dr. Eichholz says that both Jews and Irish 'make a great point of caring for their young children'—it is in fact a matter of religious obligation with both . . ." What was important here was that the advantages gained by the Jewish mothers' prolonged breast-feeding of their infants were maximized by scrupulous attention paid to the schoolchild's nutritional and health needs. It appears that Jews adopted contraceptive methods earlier and on a wider

---

11. Schmelz, *Infant Mortality*, p. 50. Marks, *Model Mothers*, pp. 57, and 69–74. John Cooper, "The Bloomstein and Isenberg Families," in *The Jewish East End 1840–1939*, ed. Aubrey Newman (London: Jewish Historical Society of England, 1981), pp. 63 and 64 (hereafter cited as Cooper, *Bloomstein and Isenberg Families*). Woodbury, *Infant Mortality*, p. 114. John Eldon Gorst, *The Children of the Nation* (London: Methuen, 1906), p. 69 (hereafter cited as Gorst, *Children*).

scale than other ethnic groups, resulting in an "unusually low proportion of infants born at short intervals after preceding births." This meant that more attention could be devoted to each child and that, as Fishberg pointed out, more of them survived to maturity. In addition, fewer Jewish women participated in the workforce outside the home, releasing them to give their young children sustained and loving concern whether it was breast-feeding them longer or nursing them through illness when they were older. Studies from Leeds at the beginning of the century showed that Jewish schoolchildren were heavier in poorer areas than their neighbors' offspring, at least as tall in good neighborhoods, and often physically sturdier. This is supported by the fact that the tenth ward in Manhattan, with a high Jewish population, was the healthiest in New York with low mortality rates for measles and scarlet fever, both potentially lethal childhood diseases, and for tuberculosis, which could strike at any age.[12]

The rich diet of the Jewish population, their superior voluntary infant care services, their closer family cohesion and nurturing values—all were responsible for the low rates of infant mortality among Jews. Yet we would conclude overall that the lower infant mortality rates of Jewish immigrants may be reflecting their higher social mobility than other ethnic groups and their greater escape from the multifarious negative consequences of poverty.

FAMILY STRUCTURE AND CHILDREARING PRACTICES

The immigrant generation of American and British Jews between 1880 and 1920 tended to marry earlier and have bigger families than succeeding generations. Records from the Minneapolis Talmud Torah for 1910

---

12. Gorst, *Children*, pp. 69 and 70. Marks, *Model Mothers*, pp. 74, 75, 86, and 87. Tananbaum, *Anglicanization Among Jews*, pp. 186, 188, and 192. Rosalyn Livshin, "The Acculturation of the Children of Immigrant Jews in Manchester 1890-1930," in *The Making of Modern Anglo-Jewry*, ed. David Cesarani (Oxford: Basil Blackwell, 1990), pp. 88 and 89 (hereafter cited as Livshin, *Acculturation of Children*). "It was not an uncommon sight in those old East End days [in the 1920s and early 1930s] to see groups of kids waiting for hours outside pubs for their parents or their fathers to emerge. Many gentile families went hungry—then—because the money for food had gone on beer." Letter from Ralph J. Finn, *Jewish Chronicle*, 28 June 1985. Woodbury, *Infant Mortality*, pp. 113 and 117. Fishberg, *The Jews*, p. 262. See Arthur Greenwood, *The Health and Physique of School Children* (London: P. S. King, 1913), p. 86 table summarizing Dr. Hall's findings. Dwork, *Health Conditions*, pp. 25 and 27.

indicate that many Jewish families had five or ten children; and in 1919 the families of immigrant Jews in Boston, comprising an average of 5.28 persons, were still larger in size than the Irish and were almost as big as the Italian. For the second and third generation of American Jews, social and economic status became closely related to family size, although this was not the case with the immigrant generation. Jews employed contraceptives more effectively and on a wider scale than Protestants and Catholics in the United States during the 1930s, thus limiting the size of their families; and there were similar findings for the widespread use of artificial methods of birth control among British Jews in the 1920s. The second generation of American and British Jews, having benefited from a spell of secular education, were determined to advance economically into the ranks of the middle class by delaying the age of marriage and by having much smaller families than their parents, usually with not more than two children. By the third generation, the American Jews were college educated and in more secure professional and business positions, so that they were able to participate in the post–Second World War baby boom and sometimes have slightly larger families than their parents. Even so, the average size of Catholic and Protestant families in America in 1955 was 2.1 compared with 1.7 for Jews. Accordingly it could be argued that the speed of Jewish social mobility of the second generation in the United States may be linked in the first place to the control of fertility and the deliberate limitation of family size.[13]

Birth in the home was still extremely hazardous for immigrant mothers in the early years of the century. Before the First World War in London it was still the custom to plaster the walls of the bedchamber with amulets to ward off the depredations of Lilith and other demons, in line with East European practice. "What I remember though," a Mr. Shaw told his interlocutor, "was in the bedroom that my brother was born [in Gloucester

---

13. Sidney Goldstein and Calvin Goldscheider, *Jewish Americans: Three Generations in a Jewish Community* (Englewood Cliffs, N.J.: Prentice-Hall, 1968), pp. 116–118 and 124. Albert I. Gordon, *Jews in Transition* (Minneapolis: University of Minnesota Press, 1949), p. 194 (hereafter cited as Gordon, *Jews in Transition*). Stephan Thernstrom, *The Other Bostonians: Poverty and Progress in the American Metropolis, 1880–1970* (Cambridge, Mass.: Harvard University Press, 1973), p. 167 (hereafter cited as Thernstrom, *Other Bostonians*). Marks, *Model Mothers*, p. 86. Victor D. Sanua, "The Contemporary Jewish Family: A Review of the Social Science Literature," in *Serving the Jewish Family*, ed. Gerald B. Bubis (New York: Ktav, 1977), p. 14 (herafter cited as Sanua, *Contemporary Jewish Family*).

Buildings London in 1909]—and that went on everywhere, where they got them from I don't know—there were printed leaflets in Hebrew attached to the walls."[14]

Beginning in the 1870s, the American medical profession started recommending circumcision as a cure for an ever increasing number of male psychosexual conditions and maladies; so much so that in the 1870s 80 percent of American males were circumcised. Whereas before 1939 85 percent of upper-middle-class males in England were circumcised, this figure has currently fallen to less than one-half of one percent, as the operation was not provided free under the National Health Service. Perhaps the much larger number of Gentiles who are circumcised in the United States as compared with Britain, together with the rejection of circumcision because it is a marker of Jewishness, accounts for the virulence of the anticircumcision campaign in the latter country, headed by an organization known as NOCIRC. A new twentieth-century development was that while a few assimilated Jewish families eschewed the circumcision rite for their male infants, they nevertheless ensured that the children later celebrated their bar mitzvah.[15]

Ruth Benedict in 1949 found that Russian and Polish mothers viewed swaddling as a process to harden a child, whereas Jewish women provided the baby with a soft pillow and loose bindings, stressing instead the warmth and comfort of the child. Franz Boas noted that "the fact remains that among Hebrews there is a radical difference in the bedding and swathing of infants born abroad and of those born here [in the United States]." Moreover, we have suggested that the Jewish mother from Eastern Europe was orally fixated on her children, breast-feeding them for lengthy periods of time and boosting their self-confidence and feeling of optimism, a pattern that was repeated in even stronger terms by the immigrant mothers in Britain and America. As the prestige of the immigrant father waned, the strength of the mother as the dominant figure in the family grew, because she was the person who held the family together in the tough new environment. Despite all the hardships of immigrant life, the joint

---

14. Mr. and Mrs. Shaw, interview transcript deposited at the London Museum of Jewish Life, p. 4.

15. David L. Gohaller, "From Ritual to Science: The Medical Transformation of Circumcision in America," *Journal of Social History* 28, no. 1 (Fall 1994): 5–36. For the anticircumcision movement in the United States, see the *Berit Milah Newsletter*, 6:1 (13 May 1994), pp. 5 and 6.

income of the family when the father was working and from the contributions provided by the mother and the older children provided a more regular and plentiful supply of food than in the Old Country, which the mother distributed, particularly to the schoolchildren in the family. We have already cited a number of instances of the superior diet of such Jewish children in Britain. Sick children were watched over carefully by their mothers and pampered with choice tidbits; thus a new, healthier generation of Jewish children was raised in the opening decades of this century. So too, in America Jewish mothers "went to inordinate trouble and expense to provide their children with the 'best and freshest' food, the best medical care, the warmest clothing—at considerable sacrifice of other needs and wants."[16]

For conditions were still harsh at the end of the nineteenth century, as Jewish burial records from the West End of London for 1900 showed that 50 percent of the burials in the poorer districts were of children under the age of five, whereas the West London Reform Synagogue, which drew its members from a more affluent class had no child deaths. But it is likely that in Britain the increased provision of facilities for safeguarding both infant and child health significantly narrowed the effects of these class divisions between 1900 and 1920. In all this Dr. David Eder (1866–1936), the Zionist and psychoanalyst, played an outstanding role as an initiator of a network of school clinics in England.[17]

Certain authoritarian fathers who became successful businessmen imposed their decisions on the family and the mother tried to act as an intermediary, shielding her children from the whims and more arbitrary rulings of her spouse. In one such case, a father slapped his grown-up son, who was a university student, for not saying his prayers. In other cases, the wife would make many of the important family decisions while giving her

16. Sanua, *Contemporary Jewish Family*, p. 17. Franz Boas, *Race, Language and Culture* (New York: Macmillan, 1940), p. 69. Arthur Hertzberg, *The Jews in America: Four Centuries of an Uneasy Encounter: A History* (New York: Simon and Schuster, 1989), pp. 197 and 198 (herafter cited as Hertzberg, *Jews in America*). Zena Smith Blau, "The Strategy of the Jewish Mother," in *The Jew in American Society*, ed. Marshall Sklare (New York: Behrman House, 1974), p. 169 (hereafter cited as Blau, *Jewish Mother*).

17. Sidney Budd, "West End Jewry in Life and Death," in Gerry Black, *Living West: Jewish Life in London's West End* (London: London Museum of Jewish Life, 1994), pp. 242–252. *David Eder: Memoirs of a Modern Pioneer*, ed. J. B. Hobman (London: Victor Gollancz, 1945), and for the school clinics' campaign see the journal *School Hygiene* 1910–1915, of which Eder was editor.

husband the nominal credit for acting so perspicaciously. To outsiders it might appear that the husband's authority was still intact. More often the father was a member of a family that he could not support out of his own earnings, as a result of which his power shrank and he became an "angry but impotent patriarch," unable to enforce his religious values on other members of the family. It was estimated that in the United States after 1900 less than one in five immigrant families subsisted on the father's earnings alone. Kate Simon declared that "being long unemployed as I had noticed among the fathers of several friends, seemed to silence and emasculate them and they became quiet, slow-moving old women."[18]

One last means of bolstering the father's tottering authority was the use of corporal punishment, but if he was unemployed the father was often too passive to enforce his will; and in many cases his own religious practices had lapsed, so that there was little point in punishing sons for infractions of the Jewish religious code. Of my two grandfathers, one only resorted to physical punishment on a rare occasion, by striking one of my uncles with a strap when he played truant from grammar school; the other, much influenced by the liberal ideas current in Edwardian England, did not believe in using physical violence against his children. Discipline in both households was maintained by the father's verbal authority. After being unjustly caned by a master at the Jews' Free School, Ralph Finn commented that "I was eleven. I had never really been hit as hard as that in all my short term of living. My mother did not hit me at all. Zaida and Booba certainly didn't. Occasionally one of my brothers or sisters would cuff me." A respondent, Alfred Oliver, explained that his father would smack him from time to time, but that discipline in his home was much milder than in his infants' school, where the lady teachers regularly wielded a cane, or in heder, where the rebbe lashed out with a cat-o'-nine-tails. On the other hand, one informant from the East End told Jerry White: "Well, I remember as a kid they used to buy the straps, a little stick like this [about nine inches long] with four or six bits of leather hanging on it. They used to buy it down the Lane . . ." Undoubtedly there were immigrant families where discipline was harshly enforced, although both in Britain and the United

---

18. Sydney Stahl Weinberg, *The World of Our Mothers* (New York: Schocken, 1988), pp. 109, 110, and 130–133 (hereafter cited as Weinberg, *Our Mothers*). Gordon, *Jews in Transition*, pp. 222, 225, and 228. Gwen Gibson Schwartz and Barbara Wyden, *The Jewish Wife* (New York: Peter H. Wyden, 1969), p. 5 (hereafter cited as Schwartz and Wyden, *The Jewish Wife*).

States the immigrant communities relied on corporal punishment less and less as they adopted the new ideas on punishment prevalent in the wider society. Samuel Chotzinoff's father had problems in earning a good living in the United States, where "he came up against a newfangled idea among parents that [heder] teachers were not to administer corporal punishment."[19]

Hutchins Hapgood noted in 1902 that "in the new World the boy contributes very early to the family's support. The father is in this country less able to make an economic place for himself than is the son. The little fellow sells papers, blacks boots, and becomes a street merchant on a small scale. As he speaks English, and his parents do not, he is commonly the interpreter in business transactions, and tends generally to take things into his own hands. There is a tendency, therefore, for the father to respect the son." Indeed, it was a common saying that "in America, the children bring up the parents." According to one settlement worker, "soon we find [the child] rapidly assimilating himself with our institutions and customs. . . . The home then becomes to the child a place to sleep and eat. . . . It is no longer a home. . . . The Jewish mother . . . loves the child very much, so that after a time the child begins to control the parent instead of being controlled by her." Nevertheless, these writers somewhat exaggerated the autonomy of such a child from an immigrant family, as he was also subject to a series of countervailing pressures from his peer group in the streets and his teachers at school.[20]

Lincoln Steffens glimpsed the divide between immigrant fathers and American sons: "We would pass a synagogue where a score or more boys were sitting hatless in their old clothes, smoking cigarettes on the steps outside, and their fathers, all dressed in black, with their high hats, uncut beards and temple curls, were going to synagogue tearing their hair and rending their garments. . . . Their sons were rebels against the law of Moses . . ." Already in the 1880s Moses Weinberger denounced "our faithful Orthodox brethren, who pride themselves on not seeking reforms, and

---

19. Cooper, *Bloomstein and Isenberg Families*, p. 65. Ralph L. Finn, *Time Remembered* (London: Futura, 1985), pp. 26 and 27. Interview with Alfred Oliver, 23 July 1995. White, *Rothschild Buildings*, p. 152. Karen Taylor, "Blessing the House: Moral Motherhood and the Suppression of Physical Punishment," *Journal of Psychohistory* 15, no. 1 (Summer 1987): 431–452. Samuel Chotzinoff, *A Lost Paradise: Early Reminiscences* (London: Hamish Hamilton, 1956), p. 73.

20. Irving Howe, *The Immigrant Jews of New York 1881 to the Present* (London: Routledge and Kegan Paul, 1976), pp. 253 and 254. Dwork, *Health Conditions*, pp. 32 and 33.

revel in their own piety and righteousness, unhesitatingly allow their sons to grow up without Torah or faith. They don't mind that their children, while still babes, run after lucre, a life of pleasure, and all human gratifications—forgetting altogether their faith, Torah, and holy roots." Further, "during the time when the Hungarian or Polish Jewish youngster was brought to a level where he could understand the Prophets, and listen to rigorous biblical and legal studies, the American youngster is merely brought to the magnificent level of being able to stammer a few words of English-style Hebrew, to pronounce the blessing over the Torah, and to chant half the *maftir* [the weekly prophetic portion] from a text with vowels and notes on the day he turns thirteen—a day that is celebrated here as the greatest of holidays among our Jewish brethren. From that day onward a youngster considers his teacher to be an unwanted article . . . he forgets all the Torah that he has learned, including the blessings, the *maftir*, and, of course, the phylacteries." To put these observations into perspective, it is necessary to note that Alexander Dushkin estimated that there were 275,000 Jewish children between the ages of five and fourteen in New York in 1916, of whom only 65,000 or 23.5 percent were receiving some religious instruction. A number of Jews on arriving in America gradually forsook their identity, such as Armand Hammer's parents, who became Unitarians.[21]

In the 1920s and 1930s, the second generation of immigrant Jews in Britain and the United States moved out of the inner-city ghettos to areas of secondary settlement, to the Bronx and Brooklyn from the East Side of New York and to Hackney, Stamford Hill, and the North-West suburbs from the East End of London. Whereas in 1920 some 54 percent of New York's Jews lived in areas where at least 40 percent of the population was Jewish, by 1930 this number had risen to 72 percent. According to Gerald Sorin, Brownsville in the Bronx was a typical ethnically cohesive area of secondary Jewish settlement with many synagogues, *landsmans-*

21. Hertzberg, *Jews in America*, p. 197. *People Walk on Their Heads: Moses Weinberger's Jews and Judaism in New York*, trans. Jonathan D. Sarna (New York: Holmes and Meier, 1982), pp. 51 and 52. Arthur A. Goren, *New York Jews and the Quest for Community: The Kehillah Experiment, 1908–1922* (New York: Columbia University Press, 1970), pp. 88, 89, and 272 note 10. Mordecai M. Kaplan and Bernard Cronson, "First Community Survey of Jewish Education in New York City—1909," *Jewish Education* 20, no. 3 (Summer 1949): 113–116. Armand Hammer with Neil Lyndon, *Hammer: Witness to History* (London: Hodder and Stoughton, 1988), p. 58.

haftn of settlers from the same area of Eastern Europe organized in mutual-aid societies, an educational institution with a socialist orientation, and close-knit Jewish families. Although by 1940 only 9 percent of Brownsville's population attended synagogue regularly, on festivals synagogues were crowded and Jewish shops were closed. Irving Howe, who grew up in East Bronx, described how

> two or three blocks from where we lived stood the peeling McKinley Square The-
> atre, in which a company of Yiddish actors, as mediocre as they were poor, tried
> to keep alive . . . and as if to acknowledge reduced circumstances my own bar
> mitzvah took place not there [in the big synagogue], since that would have cost too
> much and probably made us feel uncomfortable, but in a whitewashed storefront
> *shul*, ramshackle and bleak with its scattering of aged Jews . . . its equivalents can
> still be found among the more exotic black denominations. A few blocks past the
> synagogue, on Wilkins Avenue, stood the loft in which a secular Yiddish school
> was run by the Workmen's Circle, a fraternal order more or less socialist in outlook.

Many second-generation Jews became secularized either as radicals with a new, internationalist outlook or as Zionists. Second-generation Jews, because of discriminatory employment practices, were concentrated in the garment industry and certain sectors of the building trade or were shop-keepers unless they had edged their way into white-collar jobs such as teaching, law, pharmacy, and social work. Equally as important, these Jews according to Sorin brought with them "a deeply embedded religious cul-ture, a long-standing commitment to community, and a centuries-old tra-dition of mutual aid"; and their ethnic values of *tikkun olam*, the improve-ment of the world, and *takhles*, "an orientation to ultimate outcomes," could be applied to socialist politics and trade unionism as much as business.[22]

---

22. Gerald Sorin, "Street Corner Jews: The Boys of Brownsville," *Yivo Annual* 19 (1990): 37–56 (hereafter cited as Sorin, *Street Corner Jews*). Gerald Sorin, *The Nur-turing Neighbourhood: The Brownsville Boys Club and the Jewish Community in Urban America 1940–1990* (New York: New York University Press, 1990), pp. 5, 12–16, and 19 (hereafter cited as Sorin, *Brownsville*). Will Herberg, *Protestant—Catholic—Jew* (Garden City, N.Y.: Anchor Books, 1960), pp. 185 and 186. Deborah Dash Moore, *At Home in America: Second Generation New York Jews* (New York: Columbia Uni-versity Press, 1981), pp. 13, 19–24, and 30. Irving Howe, *A Margin of Hope, An Intel-lectual Autobiography* (London: Secker and Warburg, 1983), p. 3. David Cesarani, "The Transformation of Communal Authority in Anglo-Jewry, 1914–1940," in *The Making of Modern Anglo-Jewry*, ed. David Cesarani (Oxford: Basil Blackwell, 1990), p. 137.

Having been born and educated in the West, the second immigrant generation were sufficiently anglicized or Americanized to reject the child-rearing methods of their parents, who had grown up in the shtetl, and were determined to bring up their children in a novel way. Contraception was even more widely used by this younger generation of parents, who decided to have fewer children, usually two, instead of the large familes of their parents with four, five, or more children; and the Jewish babies who were born in Britain or America in the 1920s or 1930s onwards were born in a hospital rather than in the home. Many mothers of the second immigrant generation still preferred to breast-feed, especially in Britain, although bottle-feeding became more popular. In Britain, Jewish mothers either read Truby King's handbook on baby care or learned his somewhat rigid methods from maternity nurses, whom they engaged for one month after their confinement. Truby King babies were fed regularly every four hours and were soon expected to sleep through the night; and if the infant cried, it was to to be pacified and not fed. This was in complete contrast to the shtetl, where infants were fed on demand and mothers rejoiced if their baby had a voracious appetite, exclaiming "I'm all dried up, he sucks me dry." Many mothers of the second immigrant generation now breast-fed for only six months; others suckled their children for eight or nine months.[23]

Polly Solomons reported that the mother of a large neighboring family in the East End "always had the baby in . . . [an old wooden] cradle . . . so she'd sit and cut out blouses on the table and with her foot she would cradle [rock] this baby to sleep." Here once again, as in the case of the need for amulets in the birthchamber, the immigrant mother adhered to the ideas on infant care that were most cherished in Eastern Europe. Whereas the shtetl baby spent much of his time indoors, where he was frequently picked up and fondled by both his parents, female relatives, and older siblings, the English or American Jewish baby in the 1920s and 1930s was kept for long hours in his pram outside in the garden or on a balcony, as fresh air and sunshine were held to be of supreme importance for his

---

23. Neil M. Cowan and Ruth Schwartz Cowan, *Our Parents' Lives: The Americanization of Eastern European Jews* (New York: Basic Books, 1989), pp. 177–209 (hereafter cited as Cowan and Cowan, *Parents' Lives*). Interview with Mrs. Ethel Levine and Mrs. R., 12 April 1995. Christina Hardyment, *Dream Babies: Child Care from Locke to Spock* (Oxford: Oxford University Press, 1984), pp. 176–179. Zborowski and Herzog, p. 325.

well-being. Catharine Brody, who grew up in a lower middle class household in Manhattan around the time of the First World War, stated that all the girls in her block took care of infants after school. "The babies came in baby carriages. We parked the carriages, generally at the edge of the sidewalk and placed kitchen chairs or footstools together." Parents of the second generation were terrified of the harm that could be wreaked by germs and sterilized the baby's bottle or food, thus withdrawing more from intimate contact with their baby. Fathers spent long hours away from the home in their businesses, leaving infant care to a larger extent in the hands of their wives than previous generations and sometimes became distant from their children, whom they loved deeply but were not always able to respond to emotionally. Childrearing became more impersonal, more consonant with the needs of industrial civilization and the rhythms of modern life. Hence the changes within the Jewish family produced the birth of those well-known stereotypes, the absent Jewish father and the overpowering Jewish mother.[24]

Despite criminal elements frequenting Brownsville, Jewish family values and communal institutions plus the idea of the athlete as a hero all kept the rate of juvenile delinquency to a low level. In these compact ethnic subcultures, parents were hardworking and anxious for their children to obtain good grades at school, and ensured by stern discipline that their progeny avoided vexatious situations. "As we left the house . . . parents constantly reminded us of two things," said one person who grew up in Brownsville in the 1940s, "'Don't get into trouble, and don't tear your trousers.' Every boy who misbehaved and got caught vividly recalled how his parents handled him when he got into trouble: lots of yelling, and often two beatings—one from mama and a more serious one later from pop."[25]

When analyzing the construction of the stereotype of the Jewish mother, Gladys Rothbell discovered that jokes about Jewish mothers were almost nonexistent in books during the 1920s and 1930s and that the creation of this image occurred only in America after the Second World War. Yet its roots went back to the period of the mass migration, when the prestige of the Jewish mother within the family was considerably enhanced; and

---

24. Polly Solomons, interview transcript deposited at the London Museum of Jewish Life, p. 13. Interview with Mrs. R. and Mrs. Ethel Levine. David Nasaw, *Children of the City: At Work and at Play* (Garden City, N.Y.: Anchor Press, 1985), p. 106. Cowan and Cowan, *Parents' Lives*, pp. 193 and 194.

25. Sorin, *Street Corner Jews*, pp. 46 and 47. Sorin, *Brownsville*, pp. 70 and 71.

these trends were intensified still further during the 1930s and after 1945 as a result of a Jewish population movement into the suburbs. Writing in 1932 Jacob Kohn remarked that "in Jewish circles in America particularly, there are signs of a new matriarchy—that is, signs that the mother of the family is looked upon as more highly privileged and more directly responsible as regards the training of children." In 1959 Rabbi Albert Gordon came to the same conclusion: "My observation of three decades . . . [is] that the wife, by virtue of her increased duties and responsibilities within the family, has become the modern matriarch of suburbia."[26]

"My husband seldom sees the children during the week," one such suburban housewife confessed. "He has to rush off to the office early in the morning. When he gets home, the children have usually had their dinner and are already doing their homework. Of course, he speaks with them and jokes with them. He even gets a quick report on how they are doing in school and with their music lessons. But he really doesn't know them very well." Seen from the vantage point of a youth, the same general picture emerges.

> Mother makes all the family decisions in our home. I really don't talk to Dad about my problems in school or about my friends, because I know that it is really Mother who knows what is going on with us kids. Oh, I don't mean to ignore my father. He's a fine man, all right. But I turn to him when I need more spending money, new clothes and for things like that. He looks at my report card and says whether he is pleased or disappointed. I try to please him. I know that he would do anything he can for me and all of us, but if things have to be done in our family, it's Mother who will do them. She really runs the family.

Fathers, apart from attending an occasional PTA meeting, were uninvolved in the flourishing voluntary and cultural activity in the suburbs that depended on the energetic support of their wives.[27]

---

26. Gladys Rothbell, "The Jewish Mother: Social Construction of a Popular Image," in *The Jewish Family: Myths and Reality*, ed. Steven M. Cohen and Paula Hyman (New York: Holmes and Meier, 1986), pp. 118–128 (hereafter cited as Rothbell, *Jewish Mother*). Jacob Kohn, *Modern Problems of Jewish Parents* (New York: Women's League of the United Synagogue of America, 1932), p. 119. Albert I. Gordon, *Jews in Suburbia* (Boston: Beacon Press, 1959), p. 59 (hereafter cited as Gordon, *Suburbia*).

27. Gordon, *Suburbia*, pp. 60 and 61. For the vital role of Jewish women in the PTA, see John R. Seeley, R. Alexander Sim, and E. W. Loosley, *Crestwood Heights* (Toronto: University of Toronto Press, 1956), pp. 286 and 287 (hereafter cited as Seeley, *Crestwood Heights*).

Thus there was a measure of truth in the stereotype of the "overpro-tective, self-martyring," guilt-inducing Jewish mother and the passive Jewish father. What Arnold Green wrote about the American middle-class child was especially apposite for the Jewish family. "The mother . . . is her . . . child's sole companion. Modern 'scientific child care' enforces a constant supervision and diffused worrying over her child's health, eating spinach, and ego-development; this is complicated by the fact that much energy is spent forcing early walking, toilet-training, talking, because in an inten-sively competitive milieu middle-class parents from the day of birth on are constantly comparing their own child's development with that of the neighbours' children." Teachers in the New York elementary schools had already complained about the competitiveness of the immigrant Jewish children, while admiring their ambition. Because of the anxiety and inten-sity of the second-generation Jewish mother, she produced guilt in her child that was a spur to achievement, as the child's aggression was directed toward scholastic success. Economically secure, the suburban wife devoted much of her energy to the rearing of her children, bombarding them with verbal stimulation from an early age and thus laying the groundwork for their later educational development. The American Jewish mother built up her child's ego, and the fact that his self-esteem was so high encour-aged him to keep on trying and achieving. As one mother put it, "Kids like to be nurtured. Anything they do, I want to be proud of. If they play Taps on the trumpet, I'll say 'Great, great, great!' If they make a sandwich and it's the driest thing in the world, I'll eat it." Moreover, in a survey of 5,000 high school students, Morris Rosenberg established that Jewish youngsters had higher self-esteem than children from the other religious denominations; and other research indicated that the ambitious aspirations of Jewish mothers for their children stimulated and stretched their off-spring's intelligence.[28]

If the father's role in the child's upbringing was somewhat more pas-sive, he served as a role model of consistent hard work and demanded the

---

28. Arnold Green, "The Middle-Class Male Child and Neurosis," in *Class, Status and Power: A Reader in Social Stratification*, ed. Reinhard Bendix and Seymour Mar-tin Lipset (Glencoe: Free Press, 1953), p. 296. Rothbell, *Jewish Mother*, pp. 122 and 123. Louis Birner, "Some Speculations on the Emotional Resources of the Jewish Fam-ily," in *The Jewish Family in a Changing World*, ed. Gilbert S. Rosenthal (New York: Thomas Yoseloff, 1971), pp. 307–320. Blau, *Jewish Mother*, pp. 168, 169, and 184. Schwartz and Wyden, *The Jewish Wife*, pp. 167–223.

same high standards from his children as his wife. On the other hand, for a number of the third generation their image of their fathers "is an unkind one of men so busy earning all that money could buy for their children, they had little time to be 'companionable' . . . Some of the sons have still not forgiven their fathers for devoting long hours to business rather than the 'finer things in life,' like their children." The enhancement of the Jewish woman's role within the family meant the disciplining of the children was left to her and that she relied on softer techniques, moral suasion and love rather than corporal punishment. While Jewish mothers were unconcerned with "independence training," they were permissive about discipline, enforcing it through a mixture of nagging and screaming, with some occasional slaps, but these were never aimed at the head. Some observers complained that certain suburban children were overindulged by their parents, as a result of which they emerged as "spoiled brats," but Gordon concluded that the "Jewish children in suburbia . . . are . . . generally, obedient and reliable students who perform their school and home duties in creditable fashion." Despite the lip service paid to the new permissive ideals as regards punishment, a Canadian survey of a wealthy suburb with a mixed Jewish-Gentile population published in 1956 showed that there were still some fathers who spanked and strapped their children, although it is unlikely that many of these harsh disciplinarians were Jewish.[29]

Whereas the synagogue in traditional communities was oriented toward adult activities, in the new suburban communities created in the United States in the 1950s and 1960s its aim was primarily to cater to the needs of the children. Within the suburban Jewish communities, parents wished to reinforce their children's Jewish identities by teaching them Jewish history and traditions. In 1949 in Park Forest, Illinois, a Jewish community with six hundred families, the new Reform synagogue held "Friday night services [which] generally attracted fifty to seventy-five people. A part of this attendance came from a core of forty more-or-less regular worshippers. The rest were celebrants of Yahrzeit services, or came for special reasons. Bar Mitzvahs . . . and social festivities often doubled or trebled

---

29. Blau, *Jewish Mother*, pp. 170–172. Judith R. Kramer and Seymour Leventman, *Children of the Gilded Ghetto: Conflict Resolution of Three Generations of American Jews* (New Haven: Yale University Press, 1961), p. 197 (hereafter cited as Kramer and Leventman, *Gilded Ghetto*). Gordon, *Suburbia*, 65, 66, and 73. Seeley, *Crestwood Heights*, pp. 170, 199, and 200.

attendance, with many of the extra worshippers coming from outside the village. High Holiday services attracted as many as 600 people." Four decades later regular synagogue attendance for the bulk of American Jewry was still minimal. In the suburb of Cleveland Heights was a synagogue housing the largest Conservative community in the country with a membership of two thousand families in 1985, but only 150 persons attended the shul on the Sabbath when no bar mitzvah was being held. Parents arranged for their children to be taught in religion classes in such a way that the children would not exert pressure on their parents to be more observant and pay more attention to Jewish ritual, as the parents wished to remain uninvolved. Judaism became child oriented. Candles were lit on Friday night to satisfy the needs of the child, while the happy festival celebrations were emphasized, not those that encouraged self-reflection and spirituality. In this way the bar mitzvah and the equivalent ceremony for girls, the bat mitzvah, which became fashionable in these suburban communities only after the Second World War, came for these boys and girls to foreclose the experience of a Jewish childhood and to sanction their future uninvolvement as adults. Marshall Sklare's optimistic reading of this development in 1967 was unconvincing, as the parents gave their children an ambivalent message about Jewish survival, which did not to a large degree take firm hold during the unstable years of late adolescence and college.[30]

The grandchildren of the immigrants to Britain and the United States rebelled against the rigid instructions in Truby King's manual, adopting Dr. Benjamin Spock's book on *Baby and Child Care* (1946) as their bible. In so doing they inadvertently returned to some of the child care practices of the shtetl, such as feeding the infant on demand and having a more tactile contact with their babies. "Three years before the publication of

30. Herbert J. Gans, "The Origin and Growth of a Jewish Community in the Suburbs: A Study of the Jews of Park Forest," in *The Jews Social Patterns of an American Group*, ed. Marshall Sklare (New York: Free Press, 1967), pp. 214–221 and 236–239. Herbert J. Gans, *The Levittowners: Ways of Life and Politics in a New Suburban Community* (London: Allen Lane, Penguin Press, 1967), p. 77 (hereafter cited as Gans, *Levittowners*). David Landau, "Faces of American Jewry: 5," *Jerusalem Post International Edition*, 13 April 1985. Marshall Sklare, *Jewish Identity on the Suburban Frontier* (Chicago: University of Chicago Press, 1979), p. 74. Paula E. Hyman, "The Introduction of the Bat Mitzvah in Conservative Judaism in Postwar America," *Yivo Annual* 19 (1990): 133–146.

Spock's" guide, "Eve [Gordon] had defied conventional wisdom by picking up Susan whenever she cried. 'It makes me nervous,' she'd explain to
relatives when they urged the rigid behaviourist dispensation of cuddles
and bottles prescribed by psychologist John Watson, who had counseled
two generations of [American] parents never to 'hug and kiss' their children . . . and who believed picking up a bawling infant would create a
grown-up with no self-control." Nonetheless, a new pattern of child care
evolved in that fathers participated to a greater degree than ever before in
the rearing of their children. They were present at the birth of their children, for me one of the most momentous events of my life; truly the grave
opens and the blue-grey mummified shape becomes pulsating life. A good
measure of the fathers' involvement was their physical care of their children, bottle-feeding the babies, burping them, helping to bathe them, and
changing their diapers. Both my children as infants attended the Well-Baby
Clinic in London, one of the services provided by the Hampstead Child
Therapy Clinic founded by Anna Freud, which was designed to attend to
the physical and emotional needs of normal children. Active workers at
the clinic whom my wife saw were the pediatrician Dr. Josefine Stross,
Freud's personal physician, and Mrs. Freud, who was Freud's granddaughter by marriage.[31]

Families had fewer children and they wanted the children who were born
to survive. To ensure this, medical technology and care reached a new
level of efficiency and helped sustain our son Zaki, who was born at twenty-
nine weeks. A disadvantage of the plethora of services for child care was
their intrusiveness and control of family life. Because our son was born
prematurely, he had to attend a clinic at the Royal Free Hospital when he
was two. Zaki was stubbornly silent throughout his session with the con-
sultant pediatrician, who thought that he was unable to speak and was
not developing properly. This was despite our assurances to the contrary.
To follow up the pediatrician's negative assessment, a health visitor was
dispatched to our home on several occasions, when Zaki again refused to
utter a word to her. A year or two later, still not believing our assurances,
the health visitor telephoned our son's school to check his development.
The school was amazed at her query.

---

31. Donald Katz, *Home Fires: An Intimate Portrait of One Middle-Class Family
in Postwar America* (New York: HarperCollins, 1992), p. 27 (hereafter cited as Katz,
Home Fires).

EDUCATION AND SOCIAL MOBILITY

American Jews advanced more rapidly to wealth and middle-class status than any other ethnic group in the United States. Stephan Thernstrom asserted that

> the achievements of the sons of the Russian Jewish immigrants [in Boston] were most extraordinary. Three out of 4 of them entered middle-class callings, a far higher figure than that for any other second-generation group [that is, the children of immigrants] or even for native-born Americans of native-born parentage. Second generation Jews, like their fathers, obtained far more than their share of proprietorships, but they were also highly successful at penetrating other white-collar callings as well; they out-ranked all other second-generation groups in both the professional and the clerical and sales categories.

What was the role of education in this social mobility for the migrants themselves and their children? By the 1930s many Jewish families were sufficiently well established to permit their college-educated sons of the third generation to become professionals or successful businessmen able to join the ranks of the upper middle class after 1945, when discriminatory barriers were lowered. Social trends among British Jews were similar, even if the whole process was somewhat slower, but such developments themselves mirrored the earlier transformation that occurred among Jews in the Austrian Empire and Germany prior to the Second World War. For certain American ethnic groups, such as the Greeks, Japanese, and above all, the Jews—cultures that placed an emphasis on individual achievement—education was a means to social mobility; but for other groups, such as the Slavs, Irish, and Italians, the families attained middle-class status by putting the children to work, sometimes as young as ten or twelve.[32]

Two seemingly incompatible explanations have been advanced for the social mobility of American Jewish immigrant families over three generations, roughly between 1880 and 1980. One hypothesis, put forward by Nathan Glazer, was that "the Jews, far more than any other immigrant

---

32. Thernstrom, *Other Bostonians*, p. 142. Joel Perlmann, *Ethnic Differences, Schooling and Social Structure Among the Irish, Italians, Jews & Blacks in an American City, 1880–1935* (Cambridge: Cambridge University Press, 1988), p. 122 (hereafter cited as Perlmann, *Ethnic Differences*). Charles E. Silberman, *Crisis in the Classroom: The Remaking of American Education* (London: Wildwood House, 1973), pp. 54–56.

group, were engaged for generations in the middle-class occupations, the professions and buying and selling . . . [which] are associated with a whole complex of habits. Primarily, these are the habits of care and foresight." Further, Judaism "emphasizes the traits that business men and intellectuals require, and has done so since at least 1, 500 years before Calvinism. . . . The strong emphasis on learning and study can be traced that far back, too. The Jewish habits of foresight, care, moderation probably arose early during the two thousand years that Jews have lived primarily as strangers among other peoples."[33]

The other view, formulated by Calvin Goldscheider and Alan Zuckerman, was a modification of a theory originally outlined by Arthur Ruppin to explain the rapid rise to middle-class status of Central European Jewry. Ruppin noted that "Jewish children . . . are four, eight and ten times out of proportion to their numbers in their percentage of scholars in the middle, secondary boys' and secondary girls' schools respectively. . . . This increase [in secondary education] is due to the growing prosperity of the Jews, to their interest in trades which demand education, and to their domicile in large towns where schooling is easier to obtain. These factors must be added to the already mentioned natural love of knowledge inherent in a Jew . . ."[34]

Goldscheider and Zuckerman were skeptical as to whether or not the immigrant Jewish population shared any middle-class values that influenced their attitude toward the worth of education, stressing instead the overriding importance of structural factors.

> Working in skilled occupations, Jews earned more money than did other immigrant groups. Their relative income and occupational security made it easier for Jews to invest in the schooling of their children. This combined with the permanency of their immigration, urban residence, and the availability and access to public education. Together, these structural factors explain why Jewish children were in school longer than other immigrant groups and why Jews accounted for relatively high percentages of those who attended schools and universities in the large cities of the Northeast [United States]. As in Western Europe, occupation, residence, and access account for educational attainment levels.[35]

---

33. Nathan Glazer, "The American Jew and the Attainment of Middle Class Rank: Some Trends and Explanations," in *The Jews: Social Patterns of an American Group*, ed. Marshall Sklare (New York: Free Press, 1958), pp. 138–146.

34. Ruppin, *Jews of Today*, pp. 126 and 127.

35. Calvin Goldscheider and Alan S. Zuckerman, *The Transformation of the Jews* (Chicago: University of Chicago Press, 1984), p. 168.

When Selma Berrol examined the data on the New York schools between 1880 and 1920, she discovered that the immigrant generation had
a perfunctory education in the United States and that the opportunities
were few for most of the second-generation until 1910. Only four years
of primary schooling were required from the age of eight to twelve until
1903, and papers entitling the recipient to work were not difficult to obtain. Throughout the 1890s, the schools on the Lower East Side, where
the bulk of the Jewish migrants settled, were swamped and classes with
up to a hundred pupils could be found, while in this period fifty to sixty
thousand pupils a year were refused admission to primary schools because
no places were available. The situation did not ease until 1910, after a
number of new schools had been built. There was also the suspicion that
truancy rates were high among poor immigrant Jewish families and that
children toiled in the home in some trade to supplement the family income.
Berrol claimed that "the absence of adequate secondary school facilities
made it impossible for most of the Jewish immigrants to use education as
the main road to upward mobility." Out of the quarter of a million Jewish
children in the New York schools in 1908, there were 2,549 in the first
year of high school and only 488 in the final year. In De Witt Clinton, the
first such high school in the city, East European Jewish names became
common only after 1916, so that there was no large influx of students
with a Russian or Polish Jewish background into City College until the
1930s, when they comprised 50 percent of those enrolled in the classes.[36]

The conclusion must be that the first generation of Russian New York
Jews started on the path to middle-class status partly because they already
had the trade skills to start small workshops and businesses, partly because,
and this is our contention, the heder education in the Old Country was
much more adequate than its critics alleged, endowing its pupils with sufficient numeracy and literacy to operate as entrepreneurs. In other words,
the heder system was equal or perhaps more than equal to a first-generation
American secular education.

Recently Joel Perlmann examined a sample of 12,000 persons drawn
from records in the town of Providence, Rhode Island, to evaluate their
scholastic achievements between 1880 and 1935. He found that 54 per-

---

36. Selma C. Berrol, "Education and Economic Mobility: The Jewish Experience in
New York City, 1880–1920," *American Jewish Historical Quarterly* 65, no. 3 (March
1976): 257–271. Selma Berrol, *East Side/East End: Eastern European Jews in London and New York 1870–1920* (Westport, Conn.: Praeger, 1994), pp. 83–96.

cent of American-born Jews attended high school in 1915, of whom 22 percent graduated, whereas only 36 percent of persons from other ethnic groups in Providence enrolled in high school and an even smaller percentage, 12 percent, graduated. Again, evidence from 1925 showed that 67 percent of the Russian Jewish boys who graduated from high school went on to study in a university. Thus one in four Jewish boys obtained a college education, while the attendance of boys from other ethnic groups was only half this amount. Moreover, Thernstrom discovered that in Boston in 1950, 44 percent of second-generation American Jews aged between 25 and 44 had attended college as against 27 percent of those with an advantageous English background, producing figures for college enrollment among Jews comparable with the data supplied for New York in the 1930s by Berrol. Records from Providence for 1915 showed that Russian Jewish boys achieved the highest secondary school grades, underscoring their competitiveness and ambition, fuelled by their impressive level of self-esteem and their insecure minority group status.[37]

When Perlmann critically reviewed the occupational advantages of the Russian Jews, he still found significant differences in their level of achievement as compared with other ethnic groups that could not be reduced to favorable circumstances conferred by family background or length of schooling. He accordingly inferred that these residuals could be explained only by cultural factors. If the tradition of learning enjoyed high prestige among all sections of immigrant Jewry, then it was clear that such values could be transferred to secular education in general, and the prestigious occupations associated with it, such as medicine and law. This was even the case when the immigrant generation was impoverished and on the whole not well versed in the methods of talmudic dialectic. Not only does Perlmann's conclusion tie up with the earlier findings of Thernstrom, who also located residuals that suggested "that Jews placed an especially high value on education and the careers it was the key to . . .", but it also dovetails with the historical research on education and Jewish social mobility in Prussia and Austria before the First World War. "The [Jewish] tradition of learning," Perlmann declared in an attempt to reconcile the respective positions of Glazer and Goldscheider and Zuckerman, "may well have influenced the length of schooling and the enrollment of boys in the classical

---

37. Perlmann, *Ethnic Differences*, pp. 142, 146, and 148. Thernstrom, *Other Bostonians*, pp. 172 and 173.

and other college preparatory programs [in which Jewish boys enrolled in large numbers, 45 percent as against 25 percent for other ethnic groups in 1915]. The traditional [Jewish] difference between male and female education, though it suffered considerable erosion, would explain the predominance of boys over girls in classical programs in high schools and in college enrollments." Further, Perlmann drew attention to the fact that the effect of the length of schooling was as important as social class in promoting the social mobility of second-generation American Jews, some of whom advanced into the lower reaches of the professions prior to the Second World War. In New York, acting as an accountant for the small Jewish businesses was a popular career choice between the wars, but the Depression of the 1930s disrupted the lives of the Jewish lawyers, the bulk of whom became a legal underclass.[38]

According to Marshall Sklare, "the choice of the public schools [by the Jewish immigrant generation] was a fateful decision, because granting primacy to secular learning undermined the assumptions on which the traditional [heder and yeshiva] system rested." In the 1920s and the 1930s afternoon schools that grew out of the congregational Talmud Torahs became an established feature of American Jewish education. In 1935 it was estimated that a quarter of the Jewish children were receiving some form of Jewish instruction, more than half of them in these schools, and that three-quarters of the Jewish children were given the rudiments of Jewish knowledge at some point in their school careers. With the growing embourgeoisement of the second-generation American Jewish community, there was a shift away from the Orthodoxy of their immigrant fathers and swelling numbers joined the Conservative camp. In 1966–1967, 44 percent of the affiliated Jewish children attended afternoon schools to further their Jewish education, 42 percent went to a Reform-style Sunday School, and 13 percent went to Jewish day schools, the majority of which were Orthodox. Jewish life, however, became increasingly secularized after the Second World War. "The afternoons of the [upper middle class] . . . [third generation Jewish] children are occupied with junior versions of country club activities as well as music and dancing lessons. There is

---

38. Perlmann, *Ethnic Differences*, pp. 148, 156, 157, 161, and 162. Thernstrom, p. 174. Kampe, *Students*, pp. 357–394. Rozenblit, *Vienna*, pp. 99–125. Jerold S. Auerbach, "From Rags to Robes: The Legal Profession, Social Mobility and the American Jewish Experience," *American Jewish Historical Quarterly* 66, no. 2 (December 1976): 249–284. Berrol, *East Side/East End*, pp. 104 and 105.

no time left for daily religious instruction," Judith Kramer and Seymour Leventman wrote in their study of one suburban community. So too, a sympathetic critic denounced the afternoon schools because "even when pupils complete the requirements established by the curriculum, they have no recognizable fluency in Hebrew and cannot understand more than carefully edited texts based on a limited vocabulary."[39]

The pattern of schooling in England for the Jewish immigrants and their descendants shared many of the features of the American experience. There was strong pressure on the children of immigrants to acquire fluent English at school; at the same time, Yiddish speaking was either proscribed or denigrated. Put in more positive terms, children were the mediators between the older generation and the wider society. Tina Lent, when she was six or seven, had to teach a group of older ladies English. ". . . I would have to address them in very correct Yiddish, which I wasn't very good at. . . . And then they would sit round in a circle and I had a little blackboard, you know the child board, and I would teach English. . . . Well, they couldn't write their name. They couldn't read to get on to a bus, they couldn't read the directions on a bus." Another woman called Frieda declared that "I can remember the thrill going to school, the thrill of integrating with children who spoke English, as opposed to the home in which Yiddish was the language that was spoken. Before very long—I was a very avid learning pupil—I was able to read and write and become not only the family secretary but secretary to all the friends and neighbours. Old kinsmen and kinswomen of my sister and my parents." While lessons in patriotism were instilled, there was also often little sensitivity shown to the religious scruples of Jewish children in state schools. One respondent declared that "I went to an English school at 4. And they said, infants go down on your knees and then when it came to prayers you had to sit down . . . this was the thing you had to do."[40]

---

39. Marshall Sklare, *America's Jews* (New York: Random House, 1971), pp. 157–167. Kramer and Leventman, *Gilded Ghetto*, p. 83.

40. Stephan F. Brumberg, *Going to America Going to School: The Jewish Immigrant Public School Encounter in Turn-of-the Century New York City* (New York: Praeger, 1986), pp. 82, 85, 111–115, 126, 127, and 130 (hereafter cited as Brumberg, *Going to School*). Tina Lent, interview transcript, p. 6; Frieda, interview transcript, p. 2; and an anonymous respondent, interview transcript, p. 3; all these Age Exchange Transcripts on childhood and schooling are deposited at the London Museum of Jewish Life.

"I remember the first day I went to school," another reminisced. "In those days teachers were very strict and possibly callous . . . a little boy began to cry very much indeed and the teacher pulled him out of his seat and there was a puddle on the floor. So she set him on her table and whipped his legs with a ruler and then shook him thoroughly by the arms. The little boy had wet the floor as no one had told him how to get to the lavatories." So too, the Cowans supplied a number of examples of brutal punishment by teachers in American schools, including hitting a pupil "with a pointer if we talked at the wrong time," cutting another pupil's hand with a ruler, and a school principal who would "beat the hell out of you."[41]

When the distinguished British social investigator Beatrice Webb interviewed a headmistress of a school in a Jewish area of London in 1888, she noted in her diary that "Jewish children much more alive than . . . Xtian [Christian] children: quick witted—vitality." So too, a Mr. J. Smith, the headmaster of Swan Street School, which had a mixed intake of Jewish and English pupils, had great expectations of the potential of these children of immigrants. "Thus if Smith was from time to time inclined to be 'short' with Jewish kids, it was because, as he once told my father," wrote Samuel Feld, "his dwindling hopes of producing academic success at Swan Street was through his Jewish pupils. Poverty in many Jewish homes was of course equal to that of the Gentile ones but he acknowledged that there was a certain something in the family life that tended to ensure progress. His expectations from his Jewish pupils were high and when success was apparent, his satisfaction [was] great." On the whole, however, the schools in Britain and America were seen as instruments for consolidating class divisions, apart from a few pupils of exceptional ability, and not as a general vehicle for promoting the social mobility of the masses. Thus the Anglo-Jewish establishment had very limited aspirations for the children of the Jewish immigrants. Lord Rothschild in 1905 quoted the headmaster of the Jews' Free School, who claimed that "a great deal too much time is devoted to subjects like advanced arithmetic, grammar, analysis, composition, poetry and music, while chemistry and physics should be struck out altogether." Further, Lord Rothschild doubted the need to teach arithmetic and algebra to "future bricklayers, cabinet-makers, cigar-

---

41. Anonymous respondent, Age Exchange interview transcript on childhood and schooling deposited at the London Museum of Jewish Life, pp. 8 and 9. Cowan and Cowan, *Our Parents*, pp. 87, 88, and 93.

makers, tailors and boot-makers, which is probably the highest ambition those boys wish to achieve."[42]

Of 2,399 children who gained Junior County scholarship awards in East London schools between 1893 and 1914, which entitled them to secondary education, 1,063 or 46 percent were Jewish. Many of these and later scholarship winners either did not take up the awards or abandoned secondary education before completing their studies because of economic hardship. Mrs. Kleinberg was unable to take up her scholarship at the Central Foundation School, as "Father signed papers, but mother refused—said she should be getting married soon." Ena Abrahams stated that her mother "got a Junior County Scholarship—bearing in mind that she came from Poland, you know,—came from a very poor immigrant family—she was on and off school a great deal, because her mother was always having children, or she was taking the younger children to hospital, or looking after them—and yet she got a Scholarship, in those days, but could never go, could never take it up—for two reasons: one—I think her parents did not understand the significance of a Scholarship: and the second thing was that they certainly could not afford it. She Left school at fourteen." Mark Finemen "decided to leave [Cowper Street] school at fourteen and a half years of age—the family being short of money." Recalling his life, a Mr. W. Massil stated that "until I joined him [his father, who was a skilled woodturner] later when I was 16, I went to Grammar School—Grocers . . . I was due to have an academic career as a chemist but my father was rather sick and I was persuaded by my mother to join him at the age of 16, after I'd done my matriculation. Chemistry was my subject. And that would have been in 1928."[43]

After the First World War, the sons of the immigrants who left school at fourteen or fifteen grasped some of the new market opportunities and started up successful businesses that enabled their families to move out of

42. Rosemary O'Day, "Before the Webbs: Beatrice Potter's Early Investigations for Charles Booth's Inquiry," *History* 78, no. 253 (June 1993): 239. Letter from Samuel Feld in the London Supplement of the *Jewish Chronicle*, 9 September 1983, and *Jewish Chronicle*, 26 May 1905.

43. Irving Osborne, "Jewish Junior County Awards in East London Schools, 1893–1914," (London: Centre for East London Studies, Queen Mary College, 1988), pp. 1–38. Mr. R. Kleinberg and Mrs. Kleinberg, interview transcript; Ena Abrahams, interview transcript, p. 1; Mark Fineman, interview transcript; W. Masil, interview transcript, p. 1; all these transcripts are deposited at the London Museum of Jewish Life. Berrol, *East Side/East End*, pp. 98, 99, 102–106.

the East End to Stamford Hill and to North-West London in the 1920s and 1930s. It was the business acumen of this generation that achieved solid enough financial stability to permit their sons of the third generation to study for the professions. By the 1920s, it was noted that in a "school chosen as representing the best neighbourhood, several of the Jewish children belonged to an economic class not usually represented in non-Jewish [local authority] elementary schools. One Jewish boy, for example, had just returned from a holiday on the Riviera; another had just spent his holiday motoring. Well-to-do Jewish parents are perhaps more ready to take advantage of the educational facilities provided by the State, and they are less enamoured of private schools than non-Jewish parents." It was also suggested that "commerce attracts Jews of good intelligence, men of calibre who, if they were non-Jews, would probably enter the professions." But this latter option was usually closed, for if families did not have a modernizing or Zionist ethic, immigrant parents dissuaded children from pursuing professional careers, fearing that this would estrange them from Orthodoxy.[44]

During the 1930s, racism triumphed in the German school system and in November 1938, Jewish children were excluded from German schools. Before this happened, a Jewish pupil would be hauled out in front of the class during a lesson on racial theory and the teacher "explained that my skull was several inches shorter than that of the others, which meant that I was inferior," one former pupil remembered. A different experience was encountered by others, who were sent out of the class for a time during a lesson and then dumbfounded with questions on new material, which the teacher had taught during their absence, to prove that Jewish children were not so intelligent after all.[45]

In Britain, Karl Pearson and Margaret Moul, in a lengthy paper submitted to the *Annals of Eugenics* in 1925, concluded that Jewish boys "are not as good as the boys of the medium or average schools, but are better than the boys of the poor type of school. What is definitely clear, however, is that our alien Jewish boys do not form from the standpoint of intelligence a group markedly superior to the natives. . . . Taken *on the*

---

44. A. G. Hughes, "Jews and Gentiles, Their Intellectual and Temperamental Differences," *Eugenics Review* (July 1928): 92 and 93 (hereafter cited as Hughes, *Jews and Gentiles*). Cooper, *Bloomstein and Isenberg Families*, p. 68.

45. "The Last Goodbye, the Rescue of Jewish Children from Nazi Europe: The Jewish Experience in the Second World War," an Exhibition at the London Museum of Jewish Life in the summer of 1995.

average, and regarding both sexes, this alien Jewish population is somewhat inferior physically and mentally to the native population." This research was flawed, partly because it was undertaken in 1913 when immigrant Jewish children were handicapped by their inadequate knowledge of the English language; and partly because different teachers estimated the intelligence of Jewish and Gentile pupils. To rebut these conclusions, the Jewish Health Organisation of Great Britain sponsored research in 1926 by A. G. Hughes and Mary Davies, who tested children in three schools. "The Jewish children, both boys and girls . . . at almost *every* age from 8 to 13, proved to be superior to the non-Jewish children, alike in intelligence and in attainments in English and arithmetic."[46]

Likewise in the United States in the mid-1930s, according to Oscar Handlin, "Americans ceased to believe in race, the hate movements began to disintegrate, and discrimination increasingly took on the aspect of an anachronistic survival from the past. . . . And newer developments in genetics and anthropology, in sociology and the other social sciences discredited racism. By 1940 it was difficult to find a serious, reputable American exponent of the racist views once so widely held." This was an overoptimistic reading of the situation in Western countries, where quotas on Jewish students only slowly disappeared and where H. G. Wells in 1939 "foresaw the 'systematic attempt to exterminate' European Jewry, but blamed this on the failure of German Jewry to assimilate." In the same year, Marie Stopes, the famous campaigner for birth control, wrote a letter to Hitler, sending him a copy of a volume of poems she had composed. Had Hitler invaded Britain a host of intellectuals would have abetted the Nazi programs, so long as myths abounded that any outstanding Jewish attainments in intelligence testing were due more to their early maturation than to any innate or acquired ability. In 1958 Max Lerner was still complaining, "As for the Jews and Catholics, they go to college in large numbers but their range of choice is restricted (especially for Jews) by an operative though silent quota system in many universities and professional schools."[47]

---

46. Karl Pearson and Margaret Moul, "The Problem of Alien Immigration into Great Britain, Illustrated by an Examination of Russian and Polish Jewish Children," *Annals of Eugenics* 1 (October 1925): 1–128. Hughes, *Jews and Gentiles,* pp. 89–94. J. Rumyaneck, "The Comparative Psychology of Jews and Non-Jews: A Survey of the Literature," *British Journal of Psychology* 21, no. 4 (April 1931): 404–426.

47. Oscar Handlin, *Race and Nationality in American Life* (Garden City, N.Y.: Doubleday Anchor Books, 1957), pp. 141 and 142. See Max Lerner, *America As a Civilization* (London: Jonathan Cape, 1958), p. 736.

By the 1930s, while some Jewish families were economically secure enough to avail themselves fully of the opportunities for higher education existing in the grammar schools, other families struggled to give their children a chance of an advanced education that they had been denied. By the 1930s, half the pupils in the Grocers' Company School for Boys in Hackney were Jewish, and this situation continued for over three and a half decades. Among its luminaries were Lord Arnold Goodman (1913–1995), the eminent solicitor, Sir Arthur Gold (a pupil 1928–1935), the honorary secretary of the British Amateur Athletic Board from 1962 to 1977, and Sir Alfred Sherman (a pupil 1931–1938) and a principal adviser to Margaret Thatcher when she was prime minister. Later pupils included the playwrights Harold Pinter and Steven Berkoff, Stanley Orman, who became the top scientist at the atomic research center at Aldermaston, and the historians Barry Supple and Geoffrey Alderman. Describing his childhood in London in the 1920s and 1930s spent within a compact ethnic enclave, W. Victor Sefton attributed much formative Jewish influence to Redman's Row Talmud Torah, where the instruction was in Hebrew, and to the new Zionist youth movement, the Habonim, as well as to his grammar school, where 60 percent of the pupils and most of his friends were Jewish. "We discussed and played and learned against an overall background knowledge of Yiddish as well as of English, of Hebrew classes in the evening, of *kashruth*, observed or ignored—at least we all knew what it was."[48]

By the 1940s and 1950s, the third generation of Jews were attending such nationally known public schools as St. Paul's, the City of London, and Haberdashers' Aske's School in large numbers, although some of these schools had a secret numerus clausus putting a ceiling on the number of Jewish applicants. One Jewish father was told by the acting high master of St. Paul's School that although his son had passed the Common Entrance examination, he could not offer him a place because the Jewish quota had been filled, but that he should apply again for the following term, when he would see what he could do; hence his son commenced at the school in January 1954. Similarly I remember a master saying to me when I was in

---

48. Ruth Rothenberg, "Old School Ties," *Jewish Chronicle*, 4 August 1995. W. Victor Sefton, "Growing Up Jewish in London 1920–1950: A Perspective from 1973," in *Studies in the Cultural Life of the Jews in England*, ed. Dov Noy and Issachar Ben-Ami (Jerusalem: Magnes Press, 1975), pp. 311–330 (hereafter cited as Sefton, *Growing Up Jewish*).

a junior form in the City of London in 1947 that "we cannot have too many of you [meaning Jews] at the school." Norman Bentwich (b. 1883), an Old Pauline, justified the later imposition of a numerus clausus on the somewhat specious grounds that "Jewish parents want the best education for their children and are inclined to choose a school which other Jewish parents have chosen, and so put on the headmaster the invidious task of deciding when there are enough." By the 1990s the City of London School was a multiracial community of whom 35 percent of the boys were Jewish, 12 percent Hindu or Muslim, and the rest English.[49]

On the whole, in the 1950s there was a liberal ethos among the staff in the City of London School, who at the sixth form level encouraged boys to enter Oxford and Cambridge, and I owe much to the inspired history teaching of Joseph Hunt and Bernard Ross. They treated pupils as adults, tried to stimulate them intellectually, and fostered original argument. Much the same point was made by Ronald Hayman about his upper form teachers at St. Paul's in the late 1940s; Mr. Harding, who instructed boys to jot down interesting quotations into a book and peppered essays with the comment "classy quote", and the language teacher, Mr. Fletcher, who devised small cards with French or German vocabulary to be learned at bus queues or while sitting in the toilet. Through the pedagogic skills of these teachers, primarily in the public schools but also in the state grammar schools, a large influx of Jewish boys entered the elite universities of Oxford and Cambridge after the Second World War. Among my Jewish contemporaries at the City of London School were Lord Lester, a leading constitutional lawyer, Brian Lapping, the producer of the important television program on British politics, *Question Time* and John Gross, the former editor of *The Times Literary Supplement*, as well as many future doctors, accountants, lawyers, and academics. Contrast the glittering career of David Lewis (1928–1994), who became professor of ancient history at Oxford, with that of Cecil Roth (1899–1970), who never received a fellowship from his Oxford College, both educated at the City of London School. Earlier the distinguished historian Sir Lewis Namier failed to win election to a fellowship at All Souls in 1911, despite being "the best man by far in sheer intellect" because "the Warden and majority of Fellows shied at his

---

49. Interview with Aubrey Silverstone, 27 August 1995. Norman Bentwich, *My Seventy Seven Years: An Account of My Life and Times 1883–1960* (London: Routledge and Kegan Paul, 1962), pp. 9 and 10. Thomas Hinde, *Carpenter's Children: The Story of the City of London School* (London: James and James, 1995), p. 129.

race," and Ephraim Lipson was passed over in the 1930s when the first professor of economic history was appointed at Oxford. The obverse side of this postwar Jewish success was the tenuous affiliation of the Jewish boys at these schools, where at St. Paul's "there were about 110 Jews [in 1945] in the school, but one table was enough to accommodate all the vegetarians." At Oxford, although by 1971 Jewish students numbered three or four hundred, only about a hundred of them were connected with the university Jewish society.[50]

Rabbi Solomon Schonfeld (b. 1912), when he was inducted into office as head of the Adath Yisroel Synagogues and his father's Jewish Secondary Schools Movement in 1933, ignored skeptics and built up his schools into the major force in Jewish education after the Second World War. From a total of 8,250 pupils in 1900, the number of such students in Jewish voluntary schools had declined to 3,000 by 1939. "Today, the idea that the Jewish day schools are necessary to Jewish survival is accepted even in Reform congregations," wrote Chaim Bermant in a tribute in 1982, "but such ideas were considered eccentric in the 'thirties, and even in the 'fifties, and anyone without the stamina, determination and self-assurance of a Schonfeld would have given up the cause as lost . . . but amidst all his struggles he failed to notice that others were beginning to do the same job, and perhaps even doing it better." As in the United States only the Orthodox provided day schools between the wars, but since 1945 the Jewish day schools' movement in Britain has mushroomed among the centrist United Synagogue and Reform congregations. A leading Jewish educationist, Salmond S. Levin, summed up the situation in Britain in 1984: "We have created schools—a few are good, but on the whole they are schools for Jews and not Jewish schools. In any event, the dichotomy between the school and the home most often creates a situation where even if a child learnt Judaism, it is not practised in the home. Above all, the periods for Jewish studies are not adequate. . . . That means for most of them two and a half hours' tuition a week for about 37 weeks in the year, largely by unskilled teachers." Looking back, one can see that one

50. Ronald Hayman, *Secrets: Boyhood in a Jewish Hotel 1932–1954* (London: Peter Owen, 1985), pp. 134–139. Irene Roth, *Cecil Roth, Historian Without Tears* (New York: Sepher-Hermon Press, 1982), p. 145. Julia Namier, *Sir Lewis Namier: A Biography* (London: Oxford University Press, 1971), pp. 100–101. Raphael Loewe, "The Evolution of Jewish Student Feeding Arrangements in Oxford and Cambridge," in *Studies in the Cultural Life of Jews in England*, ed. Dov Noy and Issachar Ben-Ami (Jerusalem: Magnes Press, 1975), p. 182.

of the great strategic failures in Jewish communities in both Britain and the United States during the 1920s and 1930s was the inability to establish an adequate number of Jewish day schools, when the committed Jewish population was so much more numerous. As early as 1943 Rabbi Schonfeld had bluntly commented: "Anglo-Jewry needs fifty Jewish day schools, and the Empire probably requires a similar number. British Jewry! What are you going to do about it? You have resources for elaborate houses, private and communal, for tombstones, furs, diamonds and pleasures. What about the well-being of your children and the future of your people?" If the similar developments in Jewish education for both countries are considered together, it was obviously the growth of the secular approach to education in these decades rather than the added disruption caused by the evacuation of 14,000 Jewish children into Gentile homes in Britain during the Second World War which produced a generation of "non-attached parents."[51]

UPPER-CLASS CHILDHOOD

Whereas Sir Anthony de Rothschild (1810–1876) was described by his daughter as having "the kindest heart and the most generous nature of anyone I have ever known," his wife Lady Louisa (1821–1910) was a brilliant conversationalist but somewhat dour and dutiful. When Constance was four, her mother fretted, exclaiming, "How much fonder she is of dissipation and dress than I was as a child." Just as in the wealthy eighteenth-century households, so Constance (1843–1931) and Annie (1844–1926), the daughters of Sir Anthony and Lady Louisa, did not attend school but were coached by a group of able tutors. Their whole upbringing was more cosmopolitan and wider than that bestowed on the scions of other aristocratic families. Dr. Kalisch instructed the girls in Hebrew, German, and philosophy, and was so admired by the girls that they consulted him about everything, including in later life their love affairs. Dr. Kalisch was a genial person who participated fully in the frolics and the charades his young charges played. "I wrote until the little Cat [Dr. Kalisch] came who looked as usual very merry. I thought him extremely talkative during our Hebrew

51. Chaim Bermant, "One of God's Coassacks," *Jewish Chronicle*, 19 February 1982. Salmond S. Levin, "The Changing Pattern of Jewish Education," in *A Century of Anglo-Jewish Life 1870–1970*, ed. Salmond S. Levin (London: United Synagogue, 1970), pp. 57–73. Letter of Salmond S. Levin, *Jewish Chronicle*, 25 May 1984.

lesson," Constance remarked in her journal. "After dinner . . . go to Bucklands," her sister Annie noted. "The little Doctor remarkably chatty; have a race with him, 'Shame to me he wins. All my boots fault.' Mrs. Fowler gives us very good wine; return have another race. Alas he won. Then we had a jumping match over a ditch." Mr. Jeremy tutored the girls in mathematics, Mr. Shepperson in drawing, and Mrs. Chappell and later Mr. Pauer gave them music lessons on the piano, while a series of young females from across the Channel taught them to speak fluent French. It was common in these upper-class Anglo-Jewish families for the children "to speak German as well as French with ease," as is mentioned in the biography of Lady Louisa Cohen.[52]

Despite their mother trying to pry into the confidential exchanges between adolescent girls, the Rothschild daughters seemed to have had a happy childhood and were not unduly cowed by their tutors. Annie in reply to Mr. Jeremy, who had a cough and apologized for his "barking," answered that "we have so many dogs here that one more does not signify." As young teenagers, "the [Rothschild] children this morning declared that they were so happy they did not know how to contain their joy." The girls sometimes played bagatelle with cues and balls on a special table with a semi-circular end at which there were nine numbered holes. Their lives were filled with visits to Rothschild cousins, with musical soirées, charades, and plays, in which Annie loved to act, balls and hunting parties. Describing an evening's entertainment at the home of Mayer Amschel de Rothschild at Mentmore, Constance wrote up the event in her journal in her own idiosyncratic spelling. "The bell rang, the curtain drew up and little Hannah [the daughter of Amschel] appeared in the garb of a sheppardess curtseying and saying a prologue quite distinctly and without fear. . . . When the play was over we all rushed into supper and from there to the hall where the dancing began. . . . We danced away till the end of the ball without sitting down once and returned after a most delightful evening at two o'clock." The girls participated in their first hunt at Mentmore. "I wanted to give the ponies a good gal[l]op," Annie explained, "but Papa was now and then frightened, and so we rode at a gentle pace to which the horses

52. Lucy Cohen, *Lady De Rothschild and Her Daughters 1821–1931* (London: John Murray, 1935), pp. 66, 79–81 (hereafter cited as Cohen, *Lady De Rothschild*). Derek Wilson, *Rothschild: A Story of Wealth and Power* (London: Mandarin, 1989), p. 218 (hereafter cited as Wilson, *Rothschild*). Hannah F. Cohen, *Changing Faces: A Memoir of Louisa Lady Cohen* (London: Martin Hopkinson, 1937), p. 74.

are very little accustomed. . . . When we approached the terrace we found a very gay scene assembled, more than a hundred redcoats on handsome spirited horses. . . . We rode first to one cover and then to another but no fox could be found until at last it was getting so late that we left the sportsmen and went back to Mentmore." It is evident that the Rothschilds did not share the view of such medieval sages as the Or Zaruah (1180–1260) that hunting with dogs like the Gentiles would debar a Jew from supping on a portion of the Behemoth and the Leviathan, the feast of the righteous in the world-to-come.[53]

Upper-class Anglo-Jewish families rapidly assimilated the values of the Quakers and Tory paternalism, which included a tradition of social service on behalf of the poor; later members of this elite consciously modeled themselves on the settlement movement and the Christian missions in the East End. Lady Louisa was friendly with Quakers and Anglican clergymen and was conversant with the New Testament and the latest heavy-weight Christian theological literature, having only a limited knowledge of her Jewish heritage. This was one reason why she encouraged her daughters' Hebrew studies. Among her friends were the novelist Thackeray, the poet and school inspector Matthew Arnold, Joachim, the conductor and composer, and Sir Arthur Sullivan, so that her daughters grew up in a privileged musical and literary atmosphere. Constance became an omnivorous reader, digesting in the course of a morning Macaulay's Milton, Southey's life of Lord Nelson, and the Civil Disabilities of the Jews. Influenced in part by some of her Christian friends, Lady Louisa resolved to work among the village poor at Aston Clinton and Halston and, unlike their cousins, the girls were encouraged to participate in this work. Soon Constance at the age of eleven, aided by her younger sister, was giving girls from the village elementary instruction, while they were attending classes in plaiting run by a few old women. Later Sir Anthony built a school for girls in Aston Clinton, and at Constance's request as a birthday present, a new infant's school for village children. From time to time Constance instructed children at the school; on one occasion she gave them a lesson all about armor, on another occasion she "taught the little things bits of poetry, which amused them immensely . . ." Constance and her sister also taught in the Jews' Free School in London, and when they discovered that children were instructed in only the first five books of the Bible, urged on by their mother

53. Cohen, *Lady De Rothschild*, pp. 75, 77, 78, 80, 83, 86, 89, and 95–98. Max Grunwald, *Vienna* (Philadelphia: Jewish Publication Society, 1936), p. 56.

and Dr. Kalisch they decided to cover the whole history of ancient Israel in a work on the *History and Literature of the Israelites* (1870).[54]

In addition, the girls always felt like outsiders in the Jewish community, having been unconsciously reared in a manner akin to that of pious Protestants. When Anthony de Rothschild was staying in his country house, there was a short family service on the Sabbath and there was a significant degree of Sabbath observance, such as no letter writing or horse riding, but on the Day of Atonement the womenfolk of the family stayed at home, as the walk to the synagogue was too far; and Constance developed a distaste for praying in a synagogue, much preferring the service in Westminster Abbey. "The place, the service, the singing, the sermon—all were so full of the true and real dignity of religion. It was the most stirring, and yet, most soothing. I should like to go weekly to hear such a service." Both girls also had an aristocratic upbringing that tore them from their Jewish roots; both girls later married non-Jewish husbands.[55]

After the Rothschilds became friendly with Prince Edward, there were reciprocal visits for shooting and dancing. Best of all, Constance enjoyed playing with the royal princes. "I had a fearful romp with the little princes, we taught them blind man's bluff and ran races with them. The eldest is a beautiful child, the image of the Princess, the second, the future King George V has a jolly little face and looks the cleverest. The Princess said to me, 'they are dreadfully wild, but I was just as bad.'" The Rothschilds had reached the apogee of social acceptability in Britain, yet at the cost of the estrangement of the younger generation from their Jewish roots and the loss of their Jewish identity.[56]

Sheila Conrad was born on 23 December 1910; her father, Reginald Myer, was a manufacturer of beds and her mother, Elsie (1877–1970), was the youngest of the six daughters of the banker Samuel Montagu (1832–1911), the first Lord Swaythling. She lived in a house in Westbourne Terrace that was on five floors. Until Sheila was twelve she was brought up by a nanny, "an absolutely wonderful Nanny," "a treasure." As in so many affluent households, her mother had difficulties in being able to breast-feed her. The nanny was assisted by "an under-nurse, she would have cleaned the nursery, fetched trays and—help." Sheila Conrad's mother had been reared by governesses,

---

54. Cohen, *Lady De Rothschild*, pp. 66, 67, 70, 99–103, and 113. Wilson, *Rothschild*, pp. 219 and 220.

55. Endelman, *Radical Assimilation*, pp. 81, 84, and 85.

56. Wilson, *Rothschild*, pp. 221 and 222.

and relations between Sheila and her mother may have been formal, lacking
in emotional warmth in the style of many upper-class English households,
with much of the young girl's affection lavished on her substitute mother,
her nanny. "Then [when the nanny left] we had a nursery governess, who
taught nothing but was a sort of chaperon and took us to lessons and that
sort of thing." Sheila used to visit her former nanny at Lord Allandale's, where
she was now working, and help with the babies; the present queen as a four-
year-old used to be invited to some of the birthday parties there, as she was
related. In Sheila's home in London, there were "2 housemaids and 2 parlour-
maids and a cook and a kitchen-maid and we had a charwoman who came
for emergencies, if there was a party to do extra—and a chauffeur. They lived
on the top floor, attic bedrooms. They had their own bathroom up there but
Nanny, of course, lived on our floor, and the Nursery maid . . . we had an
enormous drawing room, which was never used except, it was a double drawing room, and was only used for parties."[57]

Sheila Conrad belonged to a family whose religious affiliation weakened
over time but nonetheless remained firm; and she was actively involved in
Jewish club work. "Yes, my parents belonged to St. Petersburgh Place
[United Synagogue and Orthodox], then they moved to Berkeley St[reet,
a Reform synagogue] and then from there to Aunt Lily . . . [Montagu's]
St. John's Wood [Liberal Synagogue]." Moreover, "We didn't have 2 sets
of crockery or cooking things—but no unkosher food was cooked or
served"; and her brother did celebrate his bar mitzvah in St. Petersburgh
Place and was a member of the Jewish house in Clifton.

Sheila went to four schools in London. "The first school, the PNEU, was
nearly all cousins and just one or two friends of my aunt. There were only
about a dozen children. It was a little class, held in my aunt's house in
Pembridge Gardens. There were only about a dozen children. . . . But I only
stayed there until I was 10 I think, . . . Yes we were only girls and a few of
them about half of them were non-Jewish, at least half, because they were
friends." She later went to St. Paul's Girls' School, where she was informed
that her math was so peculiar that she would not be able to take any public
examinations, but she was good at literature. This school in the past had the
reputation of concentrating on girls of exceptional academic ability, we have
been informed, while at the same time undermining the others, even if they
were extremely talented and able. At fifteen, Sheila moved "to Miss Spalding
at Queensgate and there she was very keen on [the] History of Art, which I

---

57. Sheila and Eric Conrad, interview transcript deposited at the London Museum of
Jewish Life, pp. 2 and 9.

liked very much and languages [French and Italian] . . . I enjoyed the lessons but the girls to be truthful, were extremely snobbish. Many of them had their own cars driven by a chauffeur to fetch them and then [the cars were] handed over to the girl to drive away." Although she was meant to go to a finishing school in Switzerland like her cousins, she had an accident and after recovering went straight to Art School. "And I detested all of them [my schools]. Because I wanted to be a painter or . . . a writer, or something and I had too much school-work and I didn't like being so occupied with things that didn't really interest me."

"Well my father didn't really approve but he was told by someone whose advice he thought was wise, that if I married into an Army family or an Ambassadorial family that it was an advantage or even going to live somewhere abroad, it was easier to enter Society if you had been presented at Court." What this advice meant was that Sheila Conrad should risk entering the marriage market of high society, where there was a chance of marrying a young man with a chosen career in the army or diplomatic service, who in all probability would not have been Jewish, as even upper-class Jews aspiring to enter the diplomatic corps were looked on askance. An aunt on her father's side presented Sheila at the palace, probably by applying to the Royal Chamberlain for an invitation.

> Then you had to have a nice dress, which was absolutely regulation with a train which was 3 foot long and you had to have 3 Prince of Wales ostrich feathers which most people borrowed from somebody who had been before. They were cleaned and curled—re-curled. You had to have long, I think they were called 23-button white gloves—up above the elbow. And you could have a bouquet of flowers to carry or a fan—one or the other. I had a bouquet. . . . After you left the Palace you came home and either had a party at home or you went to a restaurant or grand hotel, like Claridges. . . . Because it . . . [was] over quite early . . . I didn't. You had to go about 5.30 to 6 and sit in a queue in the Mall for ages and ages. . . . In the Throne Room, your name was called and then there were 2 Chamberlains, with very long black sticks with a silver knob on the top, [a] very long, staff. They would poke your train so that it was straight out behind you . . . The King and Queen were sitting on your left, next to one another on a raised dias with the Prince of Wales and various members of the royal family around them. And you went I should imagine about 6 paces and made a very low curtsy to the King, who lent forward and smiled at me. . . . Then you got up and went another 2 paces and curtsied again very low to the Queen and then you went out of the room and went into the long galleries, where everybody was standing.

During the Season for the girls who were coming out into society, Sheila Conrad's family held a dance with a band in their spacious drawing room and they

used to have a sit-down supper in 2 rooms downstairs, because it was nicer. . . .
And other people had these parties and usually had the same waiters and wait-
resses, so they became quite friends because you met them at another house. And
when I was young the Season—one Season I had more than 20 between 20 and
30 dances during the Season. And sometimes one had them on the same evening
and then you went from one to the other. And it became the snobbish thing to do,
even if you hadn't been to one ball, to arrive late and say you had come from
another party. And also if you were bored you said you had to go on to another
party. I should think I went to many more Jewish [ones] because I've got such an
enormous family . . .[58]

An anonymous letter writer to the *Jewish Chronicle* claimed in 1895
that

Many German Jews in Britain, as well as others of the lowest Jewish strata, have
suddenly become rich recently. They are now aping the best class of English Jews
and sending their boys to preparatory schools in shoals, before they enter public
schools. It is, of course, not the fault of these young gentry that they have the most
pronounced vulgarities of their former surroundings. . . . They will, of course, go
into Christian houses [at school] and, being neither Christians nor Jews, will lower
and degrade our race. I was told by one of the assistant masters that this class is
sure to be looked upon with contempt, even by their schoolfellows, and that there
will one day be such an outbreak of anti-Semitism among the better classes as to
destroy all the good that has been done in this country.[59]

Despite such sentiments, Jewish boys from upper-class families continued to be sent away to boarding schools, the Montagu family having the
tradition of sending its sons to Clifton, where there was a Jewish house.
Edwin Montagu, when at the school in the 1890s, complained to his parents that Jewish boys were teased by other pupils. Of his school days in
Harrow in the 1930s, George Hayim wrote, "There were few Jews at
school and we were not discriminated against. The odd crack came out
and Dick [his brother] who was such a good boxer that he became Harrow's
boxing captain, had to hit a few blokes. But for such a school, there wasn't
all that much prejudice." Frederick Raphael, the novelist, has recounted

---

58. Sheila and Eric Conrad, interview transcript deposited at the London Museum of
Jewish Life, pp. 1–11. Bryan Montagu (b. 1916), interview transcript deposited in the
London Museum of Jewish Life, p. 3. As regards choices of career, "One was engineering and they [my teachers] didn't think my Maths would be good enough and the second
was Diplomacy, where I was advised that the chances of getting in there, when one was
Jewish, was very remote."
59. Letter signed S. H., *Jewish Chronicle*, 25 October 1895.

how he took the scholarship examination to Winchester. The headmaster, who was a clergyman, asked him, "What do you feel about going to chapel?" To this, Raphael replied that "'I don't mind at all going to chapel' . . . 'Ah,' he said, 'you go to chapel without caring about it, do you?' I got the impression this interview had somehow gone wrong . . ." At first, Raphael was informed that he had been awarded a scholarship, but then the headmaster of his preparatory school advised him that "I'm afraid there's been a mistake. They find they haven't got a place for you." In the end Raphael won a scholarship to another public school, Charterhouse. "There was a prevailing air of anti-Semitism at Charterhouse," Raphael explained. "A very thin boy in the house was given the nickname of Belsen . . ." When two British sergeants were killed in Palestine in 1947, "Suddenly, and without any warning nobody in the house spoke to me . . . they then talked about me as if I wasn't there, and I felt extremely isolated. This went on for a number of days . . . [At other times] People arranged for my jam to fall out of my locker and smash on the floor, or my possessions would be thrown out of my room. Once or twice I found shit in my boots."[60]

Both in Britain and the United States, boarding schools were hothouses for the rapid assimilation of children from opulent families. By arranging for their sons to be educated at the select Middlesex School near Concord, Massachusetts, which took only a limited number of Jewish boys, Felix and Paul Warburg ensured that "they would socialize with non-Jews and marry outside the faith." When Felix Warburg and his wife upbraided their son for his being cut off from his Jewish roots, he angrily exclaimed: "If you wanted us to stay locked in the Jewish community and be active solely in all their communal activities, you should have sent us to Horace Mann and Columbia instead of Middlesex and Harvard. Why should it surprise you that Bunker Hill means more to us than the days of the Old Testament?"[61]

We now turn to a brief look at the childhood of Dorothy Schiff, who was born on 11 March 1903 and was the granddaughter of the wealthy American banker and philanthropist Jacob Schiff. In her house at 932

---

60. Naomi B. Levine, *Politics, Religion, and Love* (New York: New York University Press, 1991), p. 31. George Hayim, *Thou Shalt Not Uncover Thy Mother's Nakedness: An Autobiography* (London: Quartet Books, 1988), p. 45. "The Worst of Times: Frederick Raphael Talks to Danny Danziger," *Independent*, 1 March 1993.

61. Ron Chernow, *The Warburgs: A Family Saga* (London: Plimlico, 1995), p. 314.

Fifth Avenue, New York, there were two nurseries, a day one that served as a playroom and a sickroom, if she fell ill, and a night nursery, where she slept. She had a strict Canadian nurse who would check as to whether or not she was sleeping soundly, and if not, she was spanked. To prevent her sucking her thumb as an infant, she wore a device that was then utilized, aluminum mitts. In the 1920s in London, the wife of the publisher Victor Gollancz (1894–1967) had to curb the enthusiasm of their daughters' nanny, who was also a stern disciplinarian, for corporal punishment. Because of her mother's dread of Dorothy and her brother picking up an infection, there was first a routine of tutors at home in French, German, and carpentry. Later Dorothy was sent to the Brearley School. "Once I was dressed, it was down the front stairs quietly to the breakfast room," Dorothy recalled. "After that came good-mornings to our father and mother, who had separate rooms. . . . Then came the potty business which seemed to take hours, followed by that awful line 'Let me see what you've done—there's nothing in it.' Everything retreated, and that meant punishment—laxatives, purges—and so the day began." Sometimes Dorothy was invited out by girls for lunch in their Upper East Side homes. "Their brownstones were smaller with only an Irish maid to serve lunch, but the food was much better—hot chocolate with whipped cream instead of our ice water. Occasionally, mothers would appear at these lunches, less fashionably dressed than mine, but kind and nice. . . . No parents were visible at supper, which John [her brother], I and our governess had in the breakfast room. We had to finish everything on our plate. . . . The only time we had meals with our parents was Sunday lunch."[62]

A Miss Clemens would give the children instruction in the Old Testament, and their grandfather Jacob Schiff would come to the house every Friday night to bless them. The Jewish observances adhered to in her parents' household were minimal, and Dorothy had a sullen resentment of Judaism, as her mother seems to have possessed a considerable degree of Jewish self-hatred. Dorothy never dared tell her grandfather that she was reading the New Testament, nor that she sometimes accompanied a school friend to St. Bartholomew's Episcopal Church on Park Avenue. "Grandpa Schiff didn't permit it [the celebration of Christmas]. It was pathetic—no tree—and we had to wait for New Year presents, which is

---

62. Jeffrey Potter, *Men, Money and Magic: The Story of Dorothy Schiff* (New York: Coward, McCann and Geoghegan, 1976), pp. 25, 27, 29, and 30 (hereafter cited as Potter, *Dorothy Schiff*). Edwards, *Gollancz*, p. 202.

what our Christmas presents were called. Friends . . . didn't have a Grandpa Schiff lurking in the background, coming each night at Hannukkah to light a candle. My mother would have had Christmas, but my father was too frightened of his father." A later American study undertaken in the 1950s found that "among the country club set, the higher the income the more likely the family is to have [Christmas] trees and exchange gifts [within the family] . . ." Dorothy and her brother had a joint bar mitzvah–bat mitzvah ceremony celebrated by a rabbi in the library of her parents' mansion on Long Island, at a distance from the companionship of other Jews, and the event did not engender any feeling of kinship with her people in Dorothy.[63]

Although Dorothy and her brother were brought up by nurses and governesses, he felt that they were "close to their parents," but perhaps Dorothy was more skeptical about this. Dorothy as a young girl enjoyed physical contact with her father. "When I was still preschool, I used to roughhouse with him in the library; I'd be in his lap in a big armchair, and I would tickle him under the chin or something. We'd laugh together with my mother sitting there sternly, and then we'd get quite violent, she'd put a stop to it, saying, 'That's enough, Dolly—you're playing too rough' . . . I think I must have been a hyperactive child. I was always rushing up to everyone, flinging my arms around them, usually to be pushed away." The more she craved for affection, the more her parents seemed to withdraw and become remote. After her freshman year Dorothy Schiff left Bryn Mawr and joined the debutantes' circuit, being vetted by J. P. Morgan's sister for membership of the Junior League. "Once you were on the list, you were invited to endless parties, a lot of them at the old Ritz Carlton. . . . These parties, which my mother thought so important for me, drew the fortune hunters and no-goodniks." While her father liked Lewis Strauss as a potential suitor, her mother despised him as "a [Jewish] shoe salesman from Richmond, Virginia"; but when he was invited to one of Dorothy's parties, he was appalled to find no Jews there and went home. Like many members of the Rothschild family, Dorothy Schiff had little real sense of Jewish identity in her childhood, a phenomenon that was to affect many children from ordinary middle-class families in Britain and America after the Second World War.[64]

---

63. Potter, *Dorothy Schiff*, pp. 28 and 35. Kramer and Leventman, *Children of the Gilded Ghetto*, p. 93.

64. Potter, *Dorothy Schiff*, pp. 40, 50, and 53.

10

Growing Up in Britain and America: Leisure Activities

STREET LIFE

The children of the Jewish immigrants from Eastern Europe to the United States spent much of their leisure time and their early working life, when they filled a variety of part-time jobs to supplement the family income, on the streets of the city. Here the Jewish children were subjected to many of the same working-class concerns as their Irish, Polish, and Italian counterparts, but nevertheless differences in their life at home and religious background ensured that the progeny from all these disparate immigrant groups grew up in tightly knit ethnic communities with distinctive institutions, symbols, and values. At the same time they acquired some looser, overarching cultural ideals that welded them into one generation of Americans. To social reformers and their wealthy backers, street life was well supplied with temptations and dangers that could propel youths into a dissolute life of crime and idleness. Cary Goodman argued in his *Choosing Sides* (1979) that the reformers in the United States tried not only to create a network of playgrounds, vacation schools, and evening recreation centres to take

children off the streets of New York, but to socialize the younger generation and make them amenable to the capitalist values of industrial civilization. Further, he suggested that the industrial elite felt threatened by the
freedom of street life, a part of working-class culture that they could not
control.[1]

Whatever the intentions of the reformers, the children and their mothers, according to David Nasaw, preferred the city streets to the playgrounds
in the parks and the amenities provided by the settlement houses. In New
York it was estimated that 95 percent of the children utilized the streets
for play rather than the alternative supervised facilities supplied elsewhere.
It was the same in Cleveland and Milwaukee, where only 4 percent of the
children attended these leisure centers, which were not always within easy
reach of the majority of the children. Both Seward (1899) and Hamilton
Fish (1900) Parks in New York contained outdoor gym equipment, facilities for basketball, athletic tracks, and the usual provision for smaller children. While the children loved the equipment available in the playgrounds
and in the evening recreation centers in schools from seven until ten or
eleven at night, they resented the adult supervision, and the evening centers never became popular. Even Goodman had to confess that sometimes
where children availed themselves of the alternative facilities, they often
subverted the system by mocking the enforced ideals of social harmony at
a vacation camp run by the Educational Alliance, an organization sponsored by well-heeled German Jews; and by literally pricking pomposity,
by sticking pins into a platform speaker at the opening of Hamilton Fish
Park in 1900 and sabotaging the brass horns of the band by filling them
with paper balls.[2]

The street then was an ideal playground, where mothers could watch
their children playing, just as older brothers and sisters looked after younger
siblings joining in the street games and fun. Because the streets were always
full of family members, neighbors, and nearby shopkeepers, they were
always well policed, and if something untoward happened to a child or,

---

1. Cary Goodman, *Choosing Sides: Playground and Street Life on the Lower
East Side* (New York: Schocken Books, 1979), pp. 6, 7, 14, 15, and 29 (hereafter
cited as Goodman, *Choosing Sides*). David Nasaw, *Children of the City: At Work
and at Play* (Garden City, N.Y.: Anchor Press, 1985); see the Preface (hereafter
cited as Nasaw, *City Children*).

2. Goodman, *Choosing Sides*, pp. 26, 27, 29, 45, 98, and 99. Nasaw, *City Children*, pp. 36 and 37.

worse still, he was assaulted, help was near at hand. A perennial air of excitement enveloped the street. "'What's-a-matter?' was a perpetual query as we were attracted by a sudden frantic exodus from a tenement," Samuel Chotzinoff reminisced about Stanton Street, "the clang of an ambulance as it drew up in front of a house, a person deliberately running, pursued by a crowd, a runaway horse and wagon, a policeman forcibly propelling a drunk and twisting his arm until the wretch screamed with pain, an altercation through open windows between next-door neighbours." As Stanton Street on the Lower East Side was one block from the Bowery, Chotzinoff would venture there with a few friends to view the drunks and criminals and the elevated railway. Sometimes female tramps would stray into Stanton Street from the Bowery. "The poor, dirty, ragged creatures would come reeling into our block, cursing and swearing, and we would run after them," Chotzinoff declared, "calling out 'Mary Sugar Bum!' . . . and they would threaten us grotesquely with their fists . . ."[3]

George Burns, the comedian, who lived on the East Side as a child, claimed that "our playground was the middle of Rivington Street. We only played games that needed very little equipment, games like kick-the-can, hopscotch, hide-and-go-seek, follow the leader. When we played baseball we used a broom handle and a rubber ball. A manhole cover was home plate, a fire hydrant was first base, second base was a lamp post, and Mr. Gitletz, who used to bring a kitchen chair down to sit and watch us play, was third base." Isidore Kanowitz, another Lower East Side resident, added that "it didn't mean nothin' playin' baseball in those days. We used to get a five-cent bat and a two-cent ball and play barehanded in the middle of the street. Sometimes we'd get chased by a storekeeper who was afraid we'd break a window." Burns described how these sessions in the street were brought to a close. "At nine o'clock in the evening my mother would holler out of the window, 'Come on up children, it's time to go to bed!' We'd all rush up, and my mother would stand there with the door open. Sometimes I made it, sometimes I slept in the hall."[4]

The center of the street was the boys' territory, where boys of ten and upwards played baseball, lit bonfires, especially on election days when they could not be chased by the police, played marbles, and shot craps. Gangs

---

3. Goodman, *Choosing Sides*, p. 13. Nasaw, *City Children*, pp. 20, 21, and 29. Samuel Chotzinoff, *A Lost Paradise: Early Reminiscences* (London: Hamish Hamilton, 1956), pp. 69 and 70 (hereafter cited as Chotzinoff, *Reminiscences*).

4. Nasaw, *City Children*, p. 30.

of young boys played follow the leader, hurling themselves over milk cans and fire pumps, as is illustrated by this episode from the novel *Call It Sleep* by Henry Roth. "'Jump on Johnny Pump!' commanded Sidney leaping up on the two stumpy arms of the fire-plug. 'One two t'ree! Yee!' He jumped off. . . . Arrived at the barber-pole . . . [Sidney] wound around and round the pole until he stood tiptoe and the band he traced was beyond his reach. When the others had accomplished this feat, he crouched down [and] . . . poked his head into the doorway and chanted in a croaking voice. 'De monkey's in de ba'ba shop!'" Among boys, playing craps and lighting fires were the two most popular pastimes, while a 1913 survey discovered that only 13 percent of the games played by the children were team games. If Jewish evidence from the East End is anything to go by, toys were also scarce for the children on the East Side, a fact perhaps indicated by the continuing popularity of the German and East European game of buttons. Girls kept more to the sidewalks, where they skipped to various rhymes and bounced balls, sometimes played potsy, and only occasionally participated in their brothers' games.[5]

"We turned on the fire hydrant in summer," remarked Michael Gold of his New York childhood, "and splashed in the street, shoes, clothes and all. Or went swimming from the docks. Our East River is a sun-spangled open sewer running with oily scum and garbage. . . . Often while swimming I had to push dead swollen dogs and vegetables from my face. In our set it was considered humor to slyly paddle ordure at another boy when he was swimming." The popularity of swimming to escape the summer heat of New York was not an indulgence of a new craze but was a sporting skill acquired by many Jewish families in Eastern Europe and naturally adopted by their children.[6]

During the 1940s and 1950s, Jewish children growing up in Brooklyn still amused themselves on the streets until their mothers shouted for them to come home; and it is untrue that the organized play movement superseded street life after 1918, once families had started moving out of the Lower East Side. "We played stickball, punchball, hide-and-go-seek, and

5. Nasaw, *City Children*, pp. 24, 26, and 29. Henry Roth, *Call It Sleep* (New York: Mayflower-Dell, 1967), pp. 87 and 88. Sefton, *Growing Up Jewish*, p. 322. William Wells Newell, *Games and Songs of American Children* (New York: Dover Publications, 1963), p. 187.

6. Michael Gold, *Jews Without Money* (New York: Carroll and Graff, 1984), p. 39 (hereafter cited as Gold, *Jews Without Money*).

of course, basketball and softball till after dark," asserted Roger Green. "Our block was known for that kind of street activity." According to Jerry Stiller, "We played ringolevio and kickety-can-hide-go, which means you kick the can and hide before the guy who's It picks up the can. And Johnny-on-the-pony. . . ." Girls' games remained less boisterous. "We played potsy and hopscotch and jump rope and double-dutch jump rope . . ." declared Joyce Shapiro Feigenbaum. "I lived in this crowded little apartment [in Brooklyn]. . . . I spent every moment I could outside, even in the winter-time. The streets were my sanctuary." On days when it rained, boys shel-tered in the common parts of the building and played cards and shot dice. There was still much improvisation to obtain the necessary equipment for games. Broom and mop handles were broken under car wheels to obtain bats for stickball, just as aluminium foil or silver paper and cellophane were scrunched up to make balls. On the streets the boys formed tightly bonded communities of "peer interdependence."[7]

Cars did not cause too much of a problem for the ball players in Brook-lyn, as not too many people owned such vehicles at the time. Several former members of the Brownsville Boys Club "who grew up together on Chris-topher Avenue remember that one Sunday when they were organizing for a punchball game, they realized that a car—itself unusual on that street in the 1930s—was parked on what would have been first base. When they went to ask the driver to move, they discovered he was dead—shot in the head. These Brownsville boys, apparently not *too* terribly surprised, and certainly undeterrable, released the brake, pushed the car, and played ball!" Thus the boys took for granted the highly visible presence on the streets of Brownsville of Jewish criminals from such gangs as Murder Inc.[8]

In London in the opening decades of the century, Jewish children from immigrant families learned to play cricket and football in the side streets, where there was not too much traffic. My uncle, who lived in the Com-mercial Road in the East End, played cricket in Exmouth Street, using a lamppost as a wicket. Similarly in Soho, the Jewish immigrant quarter in the West End, "All we worried about was football and cricket," declared

7. Myrna Katz Frommer and Harvey Frommer, *It Happened in Brooklyn: An Oral History of Growing Up in the Borough in the 1940s, 1950s, and 1960s* (New York: Harcourt Brace, 1993), pp. 18–28. Gerald Sorin, "Street Corner Jews: The Boys of Brownsville," *Yivo Annual* 19 (1990): 42 (herafter cited as Sorin, *Boys of Brownsville*).

8. Sorin, *Boys of Brownsville*, p. 40.

one respondent. "When we played cricket in Poland Street there was a traffic island which we used as a wicket. If the ball was hit straight it would go down the ladies' lavatory and we had to go down and ask for it back. The woman in charge was a tartar, so I hated fielding there." Other games that occupied boys were marbles, rounders, and tibby, in which a contestant had to hit a four-inch pointed piece of wood with a bat. Louis Golding observed in his novel *Magnolia Street* how the national English games accelerated the process of anglicanization in the younger generation. "In these few years of their boyhood and girlhood, they had become more impregnated with English than other foreigners might in two generations. He saw small boys conforming to the type of the small boys opposite. They played football and cricket, and studied the team scores with, if anything more passion. They became, or yearned to be 'sports,' and 'decent chaps.'"[9]

As in New York, the streets of London in the early years of the century could be exciting places of fun. One person remembered that in the Jewish area of the West End,

> first the cats' meat man came round. You threw him a penny and he hurled a piece of meat into your doorway. Then the muffin man came, then at teatime a Jewish man from the East End with cakes and biscuits in a basket and little sweet bagels on a string. Rag-and-bone carts came round, offering ornaments in exchange for junk. Then there were barrel organs. There was one organ-grinder who dressed up as a gipsy and had a parrot; when you put a penny in his tin the parrot jumped in a box and gave you a folded-up paper [prediction of your] fortune. There were musicians, like the blind violinist and his daughter who sang.

Children in the East End after nightfall would suspend a piece of yarn across a narrow street and knock hats off people's heads. The rag-and-bone man would offer children balloons when collecting old clothes, and my mother as a young child followed one such man and became lost.[10]

According to Harpo Marx, "School didn't teach you how to collect tennis balls, build a scooter, ride the El trains and trolleys, hitch onto delivery wagons, own a dog, go for a swim, get a chunk of ice or a piece of fruit—

---

9. Interview with Michael Cooper, 25 April 1995. Jerry Black, *Jewish Life in London's West End* (London: London Museum of Jewish Life, 1994), pp. 44 and 45 (hereafter cited as Black, *Jewish West End*). Marks, *Model Mothers*, p. 34.

10. Black, *Jewish West End*, p. 45. Interview with Mrs. Kate Cooper, 15 November 1976.

all without paying a cent. . . . School simply didn't teach you how to be poor and live from day to day." Outside the home, the schools, and the hadarim, there was the world of the streets, where some American Jewish boys indulged in petty pilfering, hitched risky rides on the backs of wagons, and gambled. Samuel Ornitz, in an autobiographical novel, described this world of petty thievery. "During these days of unemployment our dining is almost an empty form. But the gang knows how to supplement the scanty home provender. Wares on pushcarts, stands, and in shops yield to nimble fingers and magically disappear in capacious pockets. . . . Chunks of black bread, potatoes, smoked fish, fruit in season, and a variety of other eatables diversify the day's forage. . . . I am the cover guy. . . . I distract the owner and screen the thief." A similar tale from his youth was recorded by Michael Gold. "Nigger [the leader of the juvenile gang] ran the fastest, so he would march up to a pushcart and boldly steal a piece of fruit. The outraged peddler chased him, of course, which was the signal for us to grab fruit and run the other way."[11]

Boys naturally gravitated into the juvenile gangs in their neighborhood. Each gang was recruited from the same street for a distance of two blocks; and although there were fierce clashes with gangs from other ethnic groups, territorial disputes between Jewish gangs were not uncommon. David Nasaw has pointed out that there were two ideologies in conflict, one enforced by the home and school that stealing was wrong, the other that minor infractions of this kind were common and harmless, and that your first loyalty was to your friends and members of your gang, not to the police and the law. The criminologist E. H. Sutherland suggested that "the age of maximum criminality lies . . . in the young adult period of life. This period is not clearly defined, for delinquency or criminality increases from the age of ten to about nineteen, where it remains fairly constant until the age of twenty-seven, after which it decreases sharply with advancing age." If many of these Jewish youth gangs only indulged in the occasional prank, there were "rough gangs" in New York that entered the world of crime by encouraging pickpocketing, stealing, and extorting money from shopkeepers on the pretext of offering them protection; they learned to shoot craps and hung around poolrooms, where there were not only billiard tables but facilities for betting on horses. So too, there were Jewish prostitutes on

11. Nasaw, *City Children*, p. 26. Samuel Ornitz, *Allrightniks Row, "Haunch, Paunch, and Jowel," The Making of a Professional Jew* (New York: Marcus Wiener Publishing, 1985), p. 30. Gold, *Jews Without Money*, p. 38.

the Lower East Side, and one woman, who was a neighbor of such a prostitute, informed Lincoln Steffens that her eldest daughter told her "that
she will go into that business when she grows up; she says it's a good
business, easy, and you can dress and eat and live." Few of the roughest
gang members from the Lower East Side, however, drifted into a life of
permanent criminality; as adults they usually married and led respectable,
hardworking lives.[12]

If a boy of eleven or somewhat older was misguided enough to wander
into the territory of another ethnic minority in the Lower East Side without the protection of his friends, he could be assaulted or "cockalized."
Harry Golden explained in his memoirs that "a year later, three of these
Irish buckoes caught me when I dared a similar venture [of straying into
their territory]. They 'cockalized' me. There are hundreds of men in their
sixties who know what it is to be cockalized. . . . The enemy kids threw
the Jew to the ground, opened his pants, and spat and urinated on his
circumcized penis while they shouted, 'Christ killer.'"[13]

A factor that kept the children of the immigrants on the path of re-
spectability was the fact that after the age of eleven or twelve these children, according to David Nasaw, "went to work in the downtown business, shopping, and entertainment districts where, every afternoon after
school, they scavenged for junk, blacked boots, peddled gum, candy, and
handkerchiefs and hawked the latest editions of the afternoon dailies."
Three-quarters of the newsboys in New York at the turn of the century
were East European Jewish or Italian, including people like Morris Raphael
Cohen, Irving Berlin, and David Sarnoff. The boys also worked during the
summer holidays. Irving Howe recalled that "once I carried rolls of lino-
leum for a storekeeper, who suffered from a hernia, but after a day or two
he fired me, saying in his kindly-sour way that there was no need for me
to get a hernia, too. Another time I found a few days' work distributing
circulars for a supermarket, but again was fired because the manager suspected . . . that some of the circulars were ending up in sewers." Al Jolson
and his brother purchased watermelons at the docks at the wholesale price
and sold them on the streets, while singing a catchy ditty. Boys were ad-

---

12. Nasaw, *City Children*, p. 26. Gold, *Jews Without Money*, pp. 47 and 48.
Albert Fried, *The Rise and Fall of the Jewish Gangster in America* (New York:
Columbia University Press, 1993), pp. 1–41 (herafter cited as Fried, *Jewish Gang-
ster*).

13. Nasaw, *City Children*, p. 34.

vised by more experienced adults how to sharpen their patter to suit an American audience, who would be more inclined to buy from such cute kids. Entertainers such as Fanny Brice, Eddie Cantor, and George Burns perfected their art on the streets, performing in front of friends and neighbors and then moving on downtown to more select audiences.[14]

In London, Jack "Kid" Berg, who was born in 1909, as a child of six or seven roamed the streets in search of additional ways of earning pocket money. "I used to go to Fenchurch Street station, Liverpool Street station . . . and help people to carry their bags to the buses, to trams or taxis, wherever they wanted to go. There were plenty of other kids doing that— the porters whose jobs and tips we were pinching used to chase us all over the station." At other times he would go to the Strand and hail taxis for passengers, who gave him a tip, which led to him becoming embroiled with hotel porters angry at a lucrative source of income being filched from them.[15]

If the streets taught children of the immigrant generation the inner workings of the free market and the shortest route out of the ghetto, they were also places where the children learned to become consumers. While handing their parents some of their earnings, they retained enough money to patronize the pushcart vendors, the candy stores, the nickelodeons, and the music halls. The streets also engendered a spirit of optimism in the children, teaching them that they could succeed by a combination of hard work allied to ingenuity. If Jewish children of the second generation chose a number of alternative routes to escape from the ghetto apart from the more usual one of a career in business or in some petty white-collar job, they drifted into crime and prostitution, and they sometimes rose to great prominence in professional sport, particularly boxing, and also in the entertainment industry. The worlds of sport, prostitution, and crime, however, were largely a one-generation phenomenon, possible career choices for the children of Jewish immigrants desirous of rapid social ascent, but ones that their successors tended to ignore.[16]

---

14. Nasaw, *City Children*, pp. 48–69 and the Preface. Irving Howe, *A Margin of Hope: An Intellectual Autobiography* (London: Secker and Warburg, 1982), p. 6.

15. John Harding with Jack "Kid" Berg, *Jack Kid Berg: The Whitechapel Windmill* (London: Robson Books, 1987), p. 22 (hereafter cited as Harding, *Jack Kid Berg*).

16. Nasaw, *City Children*, see the Preface. Fried, *Jewish Gangster*, pp. 11 and 287.

SPORT

In 1913 the American sociologist Edward Ross stated that "on the physical side the Hebrews are the polar opposites of our pioneer breed. Not only are they undersized and weak muscled but they shun bodily activity and are exceedingly sensitive to pain." To rebut such widespread calumnies, the German Jews long settled in America established the Young Men's Hebrew Association (1874), the Educational Alliance (1891), and the Chicago Hebrew Institute (1903), which among their other activities encouraged Jewish prowess at sport by providing proper facilities. For instance, the grounds of the Chicago Institute, which were opened in 1909, contained a baseball diamond, handball and tennis courts, a gymnasium, and a track for athletics. It may also be the case that the German Jews in America were influenced by the Jewish sports movement in Central Europe, which was growing rapidly prior to the First World War. In 1929 Joseph Proskauer noted that having successfully taken the requisite steps to Americanize the East European immigrants, they now had "to deal almost entirely with the needs of young American manhood . . . entitled . . . to facilities and leadership which will enable them to maintain their ties with the religious and social traditions of their forefathers and at the same time . . . enjoy those activities of mind and body which will give spice and zest to healthy youth." During the interwar period, there was a huge expansion of Jewish community centers, a proliferation of YMHAs, and the support of the settlement houses and the school system, all of which provided excellent facilities for Jewish athleticism. By 1942 one writer suggested that the Jews "have more gyms and playgrounds at their disposal and use them more than any other group."[17]

Fighting skills were acquired on the streets of the inner city ghettos by the toughest and roughest Jewish youngsters, who later became amateur and professional boxers and sufficiently socially mobile to advance far beyond the blighted inner-city areas where they grew up. Jewish boys had to learn to be pugnacious in the inner-city areas in the early decades of the century because they were constantly being challenged by boys from

---

17. Peter Levine, *Ellis Island to Ebbets Field: Sport and the American Jewish Experience* (New York: Oxford University Press, 1992), pp. 11–25 (hereafter cited as Levine, *American Jewish Sport*). Gerald A. Gems, "Sport and the Forging of a Jewish-American Culture: The Chicago Hebrew Institute," *American Jewish History* 83, no. 1 (March 1995): 18 and 19.

other ethnic groups when going to school, when using the public baths or swimming pools, and when trying to retain their pitch for selling newspapers or other articles. In Chicago, gangs of Polish youths crossed the boundaries into the Jewish areas of the city to assault businessmen and pedestrians, provoking rival gangs of Jewish boys to organize in social and basement clubs in order to retaliate against them. One such group of Jewish youths was the Miller gang, a quarter of whom were boxers, and whose successful exploits restored Jewish pride. Louis Wallach, later a famous lightweight fighter under the name of Leach Cross, organized a Jewish street gang with friends for self-protection, as they were frequently set on and pummelled by Irish youths when going to high school. Meyer Levin, who lived on the fringes of an Italian area of Chicago, remembered occasional knives being flashed and stones being thrown by Italian boys, and on one occasion knocked down an Italian youth in a rage when he was called a sheenie. Benny Leonard, later a world champion fighter, lived near the public baths on the Lower East Side, recalling that "you had to fight or stay in the house when the Italian and Irish kids came through on their way to the baths." Jackie Fields, a gold medalist in the 1924 Olympics, described how as a child he had "Stanford Park three blocks away where you had to fight your way to the swimming pool because the Italians, the Polish, the Irish, the Lithuanians were there. . . . 'What are you doin here, you Jew bastard?' 'Hey, Kike.' You know. We'd start fighting right away." Another Jewish pugilist, Kid Herman, remembered a challenge from another newsboy, who tried to eject him from his regular place. "I told him to move on, that this was my block. Then he wanted to fight me. I hit him and he ran away. . . . We had to learn to fight in those days if we wanted to hold our business."[18]

Learning the rudiments of boxing on the streets, some of these ambitious second-generation Jewish youths graduated to the Educational Alliance or settlement house gyms, where they received coaching from expert trainers, and then became professional boxers. Whereas there were no American Jewish boxing champions in the 1890s and four between 1900 and 1909, by 1928 the East European Jewish pugilists dominated the world

---

18. Steven A. Riess, "A Fighting Chance: The Jewish-American Boxing Experience, 1890–1940," *American Jewish History* 74, no. 3 (March 1985): 228, 232, 235–239, and 244 (hereafter cited as Riess, *Jewish-American Boxing*). Meyer Levin, *In Search* (New York: Paperback Library Inc., 1961), p. 12. Levine, *American Jewish Sport*, pp. 148 and 149.

of fisticuffs. Many of these Jewish prize fighters regarded themselves as representatives of their people, Barney Ross for example having a Star of David sewn on his shorts, and attracted a large Jewish following who took pride in their victories in a world in the 1920s and 1930s shattered by the rise of anti-Semitism and Hitler. In turn the wide hostility to Jews strengthened the determination of these boxers. "You take a Jewish boy and sooner or later his race is decried. . . . The knowledge that more than one Jew is on trial when he fights gives him an incentive for training more faithfully and taking greater pride in his work." Before one such fight, Barney Ross stated that "the news from Germany made me feel I was . . . fighting for all my people." The success of Jewish boxers confirmed their toughness, was a defiant answer to anti-Semites, and symbolized the Jews' ability to thrive in an unfriendly world. No wonder the outstanding world champions such as Benny Leonard and Barney Ross were folk heroes to the immigrant masses and their children, and there were ten such Jewish title holders between 1930 and 1939. In London the world champion Ted "Kid" Lewis was famous for scattering gold and silver coins to children in the East End. Some of the Jewish fighters lived lavishly. Barney Ross dissipated most of his earnings of $500,000 on gambling debts, and Ruby Goldstein was driven to training sessions by a chauffeur and dined at the best restaurants and speakeasies; both sometimes consorted with gangsters. Because of the social mobility of second- generation Jews, their children often attended high school and looked to careers other than prize fighting for reward.[19]

Another sport in which Jews excelled was basketball, which they dominated in the 1930s. In 1936 Stanley Frank claimed that no game was so well suited to Jews because it demanded "the characteristics inherent in the Jew . . . mental agility, perception . . . imagination and subtlety." Crammed into the inner-city areas, where there were few parks or facilities, the children from the Jewish immigrant communities found it more difficult to develop proficiency at baseball or football, which required bigger playing fields than basketball and boxing (which could be practiced in a settlement house or gymnasium. Jewish boys, however, played basket-

---

19. Riess, *Jewish-American Boxing*, pp. 234–247 and 253. S. Kirson Weinberg and Henry Arond, "The Occupational Culture of the Boxer," in *The Sociology of Sport: A Selection of Readings*, ed. Eric Dunning, p. 286 (London: Frank Cass, 1971). Morton Lewis, *Ted Kid Lewis* (London: Robson Books, 1990), p. 3 (hereafter cited as Lewis, *Ted Kid Lewis*).

ball in Brownsville in the street in the early 1900s, improvising by using dustbins, but their coreligionists were more fortunate in South Philadelphia, where "every phone pole had a peach basket on it." Having worked hard and concerned that their family had enough to eat, the immigrant parents distrusted their son's obsession with playing basketball, preferring him to become "a doctor or a lawyer or a musician . . ."; they were primarily concerned with their child's education and were less insistent on his degree of religious observance. Keen basketball players either did not come from observant families or if they did, lapsed in their degree of religious commitment by playing on Friday night or Saturday. Peter Levine declared that second-generation youths used their infatuation with basketball as a "middle ground," where they retained certain Jewish values while at the same time selecting which American traditions they wished to absorb. Yet by sometimes playing basketball games on Friday nights, frequently with other Jewish teams, and by attracting a large crowd of Jewish supporters, it could be argued that this sport to a certain extent weakened Sabbath observance and religious commitment among second-generation Jews.[20]

Until the late 1920s the Jewish basketball players were usually members of club and community teams. When the American Basketball League resumed its activities in 1933 in the northeastern United States, Jewish players dominated professional basketball for the rest of the decade; they sharpened their skills in outstanding college teams, such as New York University and City College; and the two foremost teams in the professional league were Jewish, the Jewels and the SPHA (South Philadelphia Hebrew Association), whose players wore an insignia on their shirts consisting of a Magen David together with the team's initials in Hebrew. During the years of the Depression, the professional players among the Jews found that their earnings from basketball were a useful supplement to the income from their regular jobs. Again, these Jewish teams had a large ethnic following from their neighborhoods, and a standard feature was the dance after the match, where Jewish adolescents mingled and sometimes dated. Sport, therefore, tapped into collective Jewish religious and communal feeling and gave it a more secular focus for some second-generation Jews.[21]

Immigrant Jewish parents, whether in Britain or America, often viewed their children's passion for ball games or the wider world of sport with some distaste. When my mother played tennis or hockey, her father would

---

20. Fried, *Jewish Gangster*, p. 228. Levine, *American Jewish Sport*, pp. 26–51.
21. Levine, *American Jewish Sport*, pp. 52–86.

chide her with the phrase "again with the sticks" (*varter mit der steckness*). The brother of Victor Sefton was called a *spielkatz*, a playful cat, by his mother because of his athletic skills, and it required a visit of his elementary teachers to their home for him to be allowed to play football for the school team. Exceptionally, there were studious youths like Selig Brodetsky, who "didn't play much, because I was a boy who liked reading and studying." In 1903 the Yiddish daily the *Forward* devoted an editorial to the merits of baseball. "A father writes a letter about baseball and asks our advice. He sees baseball as a foolish and wild game. . . . The majority of our immigrant parents have such an opinion about this matter. . . . 'Here in the gorgeous America, big people play baseball. They run around after a piece of suede and fight with themselves because of this like small boys' the father writes! . . . [Cahan, the editor, answers:] Let your boy play baseball and become excellent in playing the game. It should not interfere with their studies and they should not become dragged down in bad company . . ."[22]

Baseball was America's national game, which was meant to instill values such as competitiveness, team spirit, and the recognition of merit. Although baseball was not as popular as basketball with the children of immigrants prior to the First World War because it required much larger sporting facilities, it gained in popularity with youngsters in the 1920s and 1930s, as more baseball diamonds became available to practice on. Philip Roth, who was born in 1933, noted that participation in sports teams "separated us from the faint, residual foreignness still clinging to some of our parents' attitudes and . . . validated our own spotless credentials as American kids." Further, "I was an average playground [baseball] player, and the mitt's enchantment had less to do with foolish dreams of becoming a major leaguer, or even a high school star, than with the bestowal of membership in a great secular nationalistic church from which nobody had ever seemed to suggest that Jews should be excluded." American football in contrast was played in universities and colleges that originally restricted Jewish entry and thus was a sport never very attractive to Jews.[23]

Like the boxers, the star baseball players, such as Hank Greenberg, were representatives of their people, tough persons who undermined the stereotyped image of the trembling and fearful Jew in the 1930s and gradu-

22. Cooper, *Bloomstein and Isenberg Families*, p. 65. Sefton, *Growing Up*, p. 322. Goodman, *Choosing Sides*, p. 89.

23. Levine, *American Jewish Sport*, pp. 87–97. John M. Hoberman, "Why Jews Play Sports: Do Sports and Jewish Values Conflict?" *Moment* (April 1991): 38.

ally reconstructed the image of the American Jew into that of a robust fighter. Professional Jewish baseball players, like the Jewish footballers in Continental Europe, stood up to anti-Semitic taunts from the crowd in the 1930s and harassment from their teammates and opposing sides. It is true that Hank Greenberg did not play a game that clashed with the Day of Atonement, but he and Harry Eisenstat sought rabbinical dispensation for participating in a game on the Jewish New Year, and Greenberg eventually lost interest in religion, not bringing up his children as Jews. Even so, Greenberg continued to attend testimonial dinners given in honor of prominent Jewish sportsmen, but he married a Gentile actress as his second wife and there was no Jewish element in his funeral service. Perhaps the career of Greenberg was important in that it symbolized the ambivalence of many of these Jewish sporting heroes, the increasing distance of many second-generation Jews from their faith, their growing secular outlook, and their casual attitude to the transmission of any Jewish heritage to the next generation.[24]

In Britain the participation of Jews in sport followed the American pattern in certain respects, with enthusiasm being shown by youngsters in school, but apart from boxing, few members of the second generation became professional sportsmen. One respondent, who lived in the East End, stated that "in those days we first had the Jewish Athletic Association which was composed of all the Jewish Schools, which all joined together into an association as the name implies. And they used to compete with each other in sports, football, cricket, or what have you. Boxing was popular. In some of the schools there were Gymnasiums—particularly in the school that I went to—which was the Jewish Free School . . . [it] had its own Gymnasium with all the athletic apparatus—a boxing room, climbing ropes, ladders and everything, dumbells and Indian clubs and so on . . ." Alexander Flinder (b. 1921), who attended Pulteney School in Soho, in which 95 percent of the boys were Jewish, recounted a wonderful story of how the interschool swimming championships for Westminster fell on Yom Kippur. With great difficulty, the headmaster of his school had the start of the swimming gala delayed until after the termination of the fast and then collected his team of Jewish boys by taxi, fortified them with some "light refreshments," and rushed them to the swimming baths, where they

---

24. Levine, *American Jewish Sport*, pp. 131–143. Edward S. Shapiro, *A Time for Healing: American Jewry Since World War II* (Baltimore: Johns Hopkins University Press, 1992), pp. 10–15.

vindicated his confidence in them by winning the championships for the school for the first time. Rabbi Ferber, relying on the rabbinic dictum that it was "the duty of every man to teach his child to swim," praised the head for "performing the mitzvah for hundreds of boys and their fathers." Here talmudic tradition coincided with secular educational values.[25]

As in New York, Jewish boys encountered hostility from Gentile gangs on the street if they ventured out of their area, and gyms flourished in the Jewish quarter of the East End and "fight halls such as the Judean Club, Wonderland and Premierland proliferated . . ." Both Ted "Kid" Lewis and Jack "Kid" Berg developed their skill as prize fighters in juvenile street gangs, mirroring the experience of the Jewish boxers in the United States. Bud Flanagan (b. 1896), a member of the famous British comedy act "The Crazy Gang," reported that around 1910 he went to school playing fields in Victoria Park, which was situated in Bethnal Green, some two and a half miles from the Jewish part of the East End. "To get to the park," Flanagan noted, "we had to cross a street called Russia Lane, and on Friday afternoons when we played our matches, the Christian kids in this area used to lie in wait for us. We knew it and each of us carried a cricket stump or a bat. We fought our way through because other Jewish schools used to meet us near Russia Lane and we advanced in strength." A decade later the situation had little changed. According to one informant from the East End, his school had a weekly sports session in Victoria Park in the 1920s, where they would be assailed by gangs of Gentile youths throwing stones with such venom that in the end the outings for games were cancelled. Whereas hardly any Jewish lads became professional footballers and crick-eters, because the pay and prospects were so poor between the wars, there were richer pickings to be gleaned from a career in boxing; and a galaxy of talent was nurtured in the East End, including Ted "Kid" Lewis, welter-weight champion of the world from 1915 to 1919, and Jack "Kid" Berg, world junior welterweight title holder in 1930, who successfully defended his title nine times until his defeat by Tony Canzoreni. Behind them stood an array of lesser talents, men such as Harry Mason, British lightweight champion 1925, Harry Mizler, the 1934 British lightweight champion,

---

25. Age Exchange Transcripts, p. 14, London Museum of Jewish Life. Alexander Flinder, "The Yom Kippur Swimming Gala, " *Jewish Quarterly* 146 (Summer 1992): 49–51.

and Harry Lazaar, and able amateurs such as Sidney Silverstone, flyweight champion of the British army in India.[26]

In Germany, Jewish proponents of the need for physical fitness followed the nationalistic aims of the wider sports movement, stressing the aim of physical fitness through mass participation in gymnastics to benefit their own community. They detested the English sporting tradition, which they claimed led to unhealthy competition between individuals and the vain pursuit of records. In opposition to the Germans, Lajos Domeny, a young Hungarian Zionist leader, established the first Jewish sports club in Budapest in 1906 known as Vivo es Athletikai Club (VAC), which in addition to swimming, fencing, and gymnastics also encouraged members to participate in football, table tennis, wrestling, and boxing. When he moved to Vienna, a past president of VAC, Dr. Lipot Weiss, suggested the formation of a club with similar interests, leading to the foundation of Hakoah in 1909. Many of the new Central European sports clubs were Zionist in orientation and embraced the ideology of assertive middle-class youth in revolt against assimilationist parents or more traditional parents, who had little interest in physical recreation.[27]

---

26. Obituary of Jack Kid Berg, *Times*, 23 April 1991. Bud Flanagan, *My Crazy Life: The Autobiography* (London: Frederick Muller, 1961), p. 22. Interview with Alfred Oliver, 10 September 1995. Lewis, *Ted Kid Lewis*, p. 5. Harding, *Jack Kid Berg*, pp. 29–31. Brian Glanville, "Leagues Apart, Football Favourites," *Jewish Chronicle Colour Magazine*, 28 September 1984, pp. 25–26. "Money rather than talent was at the bottom of it. Jewish boys from Stepney went out and fought for a few shillings because their families were starving, and because if they stuck to it there was big money to be made. By contrast professional footballers were pegged till 1961 to the ludicrous maximum wage ..." Monty Modlin talking to William and Dolly Moss. London Extra, *Jewish Chronicle*, 28 September 1984. Arnold Wesker, *As Much As I Dare: The Autobiography (1932–1950)* (London: Century, 1994), p. 66 (herafter cited as Wesker, *Autobiography*). Interview with Bertram Silverstone, 11 October 1995.

27. George Eisen, *The Maccabiah Games: A History of the Jewish Olympics*, Ph. D. Thesis, University of Maryland, 1979, pp. 53–55 (hereafter cited as Eisen, *Maccabiah*). Andrew Handler, *From the Ghetto to the Games: Jewish Athletes in Hungary* (New York: Columbia University Press, 1985), pp. 42–43 (hereafter cited as Handler, *Hungarian Jewish Athletes*). Heidi Zogbaum, "Hakoah Wien: Jewish Sport Before 1938," 8, no. 2 (*Australian Journal of Jewish Studies* (1994): 44, 48, and 49 (herafter cited as Zogbaum, *Hakoah*).

On the Continent of Europe the most outstanding Jewish sports club was Hakoah of Vienna. Although assimilationist parents wanted their children to take up sports such as riding, polo, tennis, or fencing, the Zionist youngsters were most enthusiastic about the English game of football, but it was not until after the First World War that soccer drew huge working-class crowds in Vienna. With victories over West Ham, English cup finalists in 1923, and winning the Austrian league championships in 1925, Hakoah's football team reached its apogee. Maccabi Brno in Czechoslovakia also fielded one of the best soccer teams in Central Europe in this period, while between 1919 and 1926 seven of the eleven players in Hungary's national team were Jews. Because football was a new sport in Central Europe between the wars, Jews gained an early and short-lived prominence at the game. When Hakoah played against and thrashed football teams with many working-class supporters, their players risked serious assault, so that athletes from the other sections of the club used to accompany the football team to protect them. Later, wrestlers and boxers guarded the Hakoah swimming team when it took part in tournaments because of threats of violence from anti-Semitic groups. Although the enmity from spectators and the opposing teams was greater in Austria than in the United States, it evoked the same response, vigorous training by Jewish athletes, a stress on supreme physical fitness, and a determination to win while wearing a Magen David enclosing a large H emblazoned on their outfits. Both the Hakoah swimming and water polo teams were unbeatable in Central Europe in the 1920s, reaching world class standards, and their players regularly had places in the Austrian national teams. Hagibor of Prague, a club that was set up in 1912, also had excellent swimming and water polo teams.[28]

We see thus that in the interwar period, the interest of the younger generation of better-educated and more emancipated Jews in sport deepened and that it was one of the factors that modernized the basic personality structure of the Jews, giving them the self-confidence to confront anti-Semitism head on. Even the Jews in Warsaw in this period could boast a sports paper in Yiddish. It also imbued Jews with a martial spirit. At the

---

28. Zogbaum, *Hakoah*, pp. 44–65. Joseph C. Pick, "Sports," in *The Jews of Czechoslovakia* (Philadelphia: Jewish Publication Society, 1971), Vol. 2, pp. 185–188. Erich Juhn, "The Jewish Sports Movement in Austria," in *The Jews of Austria*, ed. Josef Frankel (London: Vallentine Mitchell, 1967), pp. 161–164.

close of the First World War, the Maccabi clubs organized Jewish self-defense units in Warsaw, Budapest, and Zagreb equipped with knives and axes. In Palestine, Maccabi members poured into the new Jewish legion. In Russia, Maccabi Simferopol, which like many of these clubs emphasized Jewish education, migrated en masse to Palestine; its members included Yitzhak Sadeh, later commander of the Palmach. All this, according to George Eisen, led to "the creation of the modern Jewish military tradition, which coalesced into the creation of a semi-legal Jewish defense organization in Erez Israel, the Haganah," although we should remember that the Jewish military movement in Palestine antedated the First World War and had additional roots. These sports clubs were an ideal venue for youngsters with a more secular Zionist identity to meet and some of them had wonderful facilities. For instance, the premises of Hakoah in Vienna had seats for 2,500 spectators and standing room for 35,000, it included a restaurant, and the club supported its own first-rate orchestra. If we take into account the outstanding achievements of Jewish sportsmen and women in Central Europe in the 1920s and 1930s, the Jewish dominance of boxing and basketball in the United States becomes less idiosyncratic and more understandable in this wider context.[29]

Barred from exclusive Protestant clubs in the United States in the early decades of the century, wealthy German Jews initiated the building of fifty-eight country clubs in twenty states by 1926. A year earlier the Progress Club of New York purchased a huge estate overlooking the Long Island Sound that contained two golf courses, a swimming pool, and facilities for playing polo and billiards and a pond in which members could fish. To distinguish themselves from their poorer East European brethren, the German Jews cultivated their skills at sports such as golf, tennis, polo, grouse shooting, horseback riding, and yachting, which demanded a considerable outlay on clothes and equipment. They ensured that membership dues were high and out of the reach of most immigrant families. At the Inwood Country Club, the German Jews in 1920 took "full advantage of the possibilities for sport to such an extent on Saturday afternoons . . . [that] the players must leave the tee on a three minute schedule or miss the opportunity to play"; and some clubs even staged balls and parties for Christmas. These German Jews did practice an anemic form of Reform Judaism and sometimes supported Jewish charities, but these upper-class

---

29. Eisen, *Maccabiah*, pp. 66–70. Zogbaum, pp. 48–51.

Jewish youth aped the leisure activities of the ruling elite and desacralized the Sabbath, making it relatively easy for them to assimilate.[30]

Jews in Britain encountered the same problems, particularly when they tried to enter golf clubs. Upper-class athletic Jews, however, were accepted by Gentiles, provided their Jewishness was not too obtrusive. Sheila Conrad claimed that "what was unusual, slightly unusual about them [her parents], they were both extremely athletic. My mother [Elsie Myer, nee Montagu, who was born in 1877] was reserve for England at hockey and she and Auntie Mamie belonged to one of the first hockey clubs, and my mother played cricket for Middlesex, Aunt Mamie was the one who did things with my mother. They both rode, my parents, very well, and played golf and my father [Reginald Myer, born in 1879] used to win tennis tournaments, which was all slightly unusual for Jews at that period." Further, her parents "used to go on riding holidays in the West country. No, there was no problem about them joining any clubs because they were Jewish. And my mother was a member, practically, and I and my sister were members practically all our lives of Royal Surrey Golf Club, which has a reputation of being anti-semitic but we never noticed anything at all there, they accepted us very politely. Perhaps because she was well-known as a—people had seen her play cricket for Middlesex [Ladies Team] and so on." Sheila Conrad's cousin Ivor Montagu (1904–1984) represented Britain at table tennis and established the first world championships in London in 1926. Wellesley Aron (1901–1988) went to Perse School Cambridge, where he distinguished himself at athletics and boxing, bringing many trophies home for sport instead of scholarship, much to his mother's disgust, as she placed more value on a classical German education. When he went up to Cambridge, he at first concentrated on athletics, employing the same coach as the sprinter and Olympic gold medalist Harold Abrahams. The latter, according to Aron, was a go-getter who passed himself off as a Protestant at university. As a young man, Wellesley Aron spent several vacations with his half-sister Vio in Devon, "sailing, cricketing, riding and playing tennis"; his sister carefully concealing the fact that Aron was Jewish.[31]

---

30. Peter Levine, "The American Hebrew Looks at 'Our Crowd': The Jewish Country Club in the 1920s," *American Jewish History* 83, no. 1 (March 1995): 27–49.

31. Sheila and Eric Conrad, interview transcript deposited at the London Museum of Jewish Life, pp. 1 and 2. Obituary of Ivor Montagu, *Times*, 7 November 1984. Helen Silman-Cheong, *Wellesley Aron: Rebel with a Cause: A Memoir* (London: Vallentine Mitchell, 1987), pp. 11–13 and 19–21 (hereafter cited as Silman, *Wellesley Aron*). Wellesley Aron tape of interview deposited at the London Museum of Jewish Life.

Once Jews moved out of the compact, ethnic neighborhoods, where they lived in areas of secondary settlement between the wars and dispersed to the suburbs in the 1940s and 1950s, they no longer opted for careers in sport and treated it on the whole as a recreational activity. Their second-generation parents insisted that they concentrate on their studies and obtain the requisite grades for college now that some of the occupational barriers to Jews were crumbling; and prominent Jewish athletes and boxers with national and international reputations became fewer. Since the late 1940s, there has been a great expansion in community centers in the United States, the bulk of whose members were attracted by the excellent sports facilities; at the same time there was an attempt to impart Jewish education and culture. Philip Roth remembered that at the nearby park in Newark, New Jersey, where he grew up, in the 1940s "his friends hung around on Sunday mornings, watching with amusement as the local fathers—the plumbers, electricians and produce merchants—kibitzed their way through the weekly softball game." When Herbert Gans started living in the suburb of Levittown in 1958, he observed the same pattern among second-generation Jewish men of relaxing by playing softball together on Sunday morning. In the United States in the 1950s and 1960s, golf and tennis also became popular with Jews as recreational activities, a pattern that was to some extent followed in England, where Sydney Obrart (1919–1995) established the JNF golf championships in the 1950s. In Cleveland, Jews forced their way into the exclusive Union Club, but most Jews with a hankering for a country-club lifestyle preferred to play golf with their coreligionists in the four golf clubs that had been formed by the 1980s.[32]

If any activity was dropped by third-generation Jews with the connivance of their sports-loving parents, it was heder and Jewish education for games. Leslie Epstein, who grew up in Los Angeles, admitted that "I also went to Sunday school for a while, but got thrown out. . . . But basically I preferred playing tennis. My parents didn't mind when I stopped going . . . [They] had been given the typical strict upbringing, and they broke free . . ." Again, a New York film producer remembered that he "went to Hebrew school for three years to have a Reform bar mitzvah. . . . But after

32. Levine, *American Jewish Sport*, pp. 234–279. Herbert J. Gans, *The Levittowners: Ways of Life and Politics in a New Suburban Community* (London: Allen Lane, Penguin Press, 1967), pp. 77 and 78. Sydney Obrart, obituary, *Jewish Chronicle*, 8 September 1995. David Landau, "Faces of American Jewry: 4," *Jerusalem Post International Edition*, 6 April 1985.

that, there was a choice, and I stopped right away. I hated Hebrew school; it wasn't special, like sports or wrestling practice, and it wasn't fun, and my family in no way reinforced it as a value. Both my grandmothers kept kosher homes, the Sabbath, candles, everything." Moreover, Mike Epstein, a professional baseball player, related that his young son, who desired to follow in his footsteps, decided not to enroll in Hebrew classes, as the time for religious instruction conflicted with baseball games that he wished to watch.[33]

YOUTH MOVEMENTS

Werner Mosse pointed out that many historians assumed that the burgeoning youth movement before the First World War was purely a German phenomenon, but that there was a parallel Boy Scout movement in Britain that in certain respects resembled the Central European movement. The Boy Scouts were attuned to nature and the countryside rather than the big city, while their organization was more authoritarian than that of the German ramblers, with members having to be loyal to the king, officers, and employers. In Germany the *Wandervogel* began as an association of a group of hikers in the Berlin suburb of Steglitz in 1896 and the movement spread rapidly throughout Germany prior to 1914. By roaming in groups throughout the countryside, the *Wandervogel* believed that they could escape from the control of patriarchal fathers and authoritarian teachers. They rejected the leadership of adults and thought that youths should come together spontaneously and form their own associations under the guidance of charismatic leaders of their own age; they wore distinctive rambling clothes, had their own repertoire of songs, and led a group life around the campfire. Within the *Wandervogel* there were anti-Semitic elements that tried to exclude Jewish members, but they became increasingly marginalized. After 1916, the *Wandervogel* and the Free German Youth movement became radicalized under socialist and internationalist pressure until their disintegration in 1921–1922. Although Jewish families tended on the whole to be less authoritarian than their neighbors, they were not completely free of these traits, and in addition Jewish pupils in secondary schools suffered from both the authoritarianism of many teachers

---

33. Sara Bershtel and Allen Graubard, *Saving Remnants: Feeling Jewish in America* (New York: Free Press, 1992), pp. 19 and 23. Levine, *American Jewish Sport*, p. 242.

and their increasing anti-Semitism, so that in turn they flocked into the *Wandervogel* or new Jewish youth movements that were modeled on the German ones.[34]

When the *Blau-Weiss* (Blue-White) youth association was formed in Germany in 1912, one historian has claimed that it was "simply another *Wandervogel* band and only vaguely Zionist." Another movement, *Hashomer Hazair*, which emerged in 1916 in Galicia, was deeply influenced by German and Polish romanticism, and there was a strong emotional bond between members, who were inclined "to poeticize life"; and it was not until after the First World War that there was an interest in practical Zionism and preparation for life in the Yishuv. Other youth associations set up in Germany during the First World War were *Jung-Judischer Wanderbund* (JJWB) and the *Kameraden*, whose names betray their ideological affiliation to the *Wandervogel*. One of the offshoots of the *Kameraden* was *Werkleute*, whose members read the writings of Martin Buber and Stefan Georg. This was, therefore, a generational revolt against the vestiges of authoritarianism remaining in the German Jewish family.[35]

Walter Laqueur has argued that the Zionist movement may have appeared to share many of the assumptions of "the *volkisch* camp, with their emphasis on race, blood and soil . . ." but that this was not the case; for when Martin Buber spoke of the "voice of the blood" he did not give the concept the same connotation as Nazi racial theorists, who stressed the purity of the blood. For instance, Buber asserted in 1917 that "people means unity of blood and fate . . . the unity which embraces us, and we must see ourselves as capable of facing its mystery and greatness, its complexity and contradictions." Yet there appeared to be some congruence between the romantic and volkish ideology of the *Wandervogel* and the Zionist youth, such as the belief in the Jewish people functioning healthily only on its own soil and the critique of a society based on mechanistic

---

34. Discussion on the Youth Movement, *Leo Baeck Institute Year Book* 19 (1974): 105. Walter Laqueur, "The German Youth Movement and the 'Jewish Question,'" *Leo Baeck Institute Year Book* 6 (1961): 193–205.

35. Joan Dash, *Summoned to Jerusalem: The Life of Henrietta Szold* (New York: Harper and Row, 1979), p. 238 (hereafter cited as Dash, *Henrietta Szold*). Jehuda Reinharz, "Hashomer Hazair in Germany (1)," *Leo Baeck Institute Year Book* 31 (1986): 173 and 174 (hereafter cited as Reinharz, *Hashomer Hazair* (1). Chaim Schatzker, "The Jewish Youth Movement in Germany in the Holocaust Period (1): Youth in Confrontation with a New Reality," *Leo Baeck Institute Year Book* 32 (1987): 157 (hereafter cited as Schatzker, *Youth and New Realty*).

relations between men that could be repaired only by building a true, organic community of members on the land who shared the same inner conviction—hence the goal of forming a kibbutz. In 1898 Arthur Ruppin, who was later a leading technocrat advocating the foundation of kibbutzim, mused that "only a people engaged in agriculture can be healthy, only a state with the majority of its people engaged in agriculture constitutes a firmly bound, organized whole. Agriculture is the wellspring of mankind. England and other states [whose agricultural populations are steadily declining] will always present only an aggregate of individual people who have been haphazardly thrown together." Whereas the first wave of kibbutz pioneers had been influenced by Russian populism and Tolstoy, those who came to Palestine in the 1920s were more indebted to Wyneken and Bluher, the theorists of the *Wandervogel* movement.[36]

Under the impact of the worsening economic position of Germany in the 1920s and the growing anti-Semitism, many of the German Jewish youth movements switched to Zionism and socialism, although a small corps clung tenaciously for a time to the illusion that they could reach some form of accomodation with the Third Reich. During the difficult years after 1933, the Jewish youth movement shielded thousands of new members from the "reproaches, irritation, and tensions" of the parental home and offered them "security, warmth, courage, the spirit of action, the joy of youth and existential values." The JJWB–*Brith Haolim* from the late 1920s until 1933 was the German youth movement most closely identified with *Hechalutz*, an umbrella organization set up in Russia during the First World War to encourage members to go on *hachscharah*, preparatory agricultural training for life on a kibbutz. Many of its members came from families of East European migrants who had settled in Germany. The *Habonim-Hanoar Hahaluzi*, which was established in 1933 after the merger of JJWB–*Brith Haolim* with *Kadimah*, then continued this work. The majority of the membership of *Kadimah* came from assimilated families and were attracted by the Communist party, to which they would have naturally gravitated had not the youth group restored some semblance of their Jewish identity.[37]

---

36. Walter Laqueur, *Out of the Ruins of Europe* (London: Alcove Press, 1971), pp. 123–135. Avraham Shapira, "Buber's Attachment to Herder and German 'Volkism.'" *Studies in Zionism* 14, no. 1 (Spring 1993): 1–30. Derek J. Penslar, *Zionism and Technocracy* (Bloomington: Indiana University Press, 1991), p. 89.

37. Chanoch Rinott, "Major Trends in Youth Movements in Germany," *Leo Baeck Institute Year Book* 19 (1974): 77–95. Chaim Schatzker, "The Jewish Youth Move-

Transformed by the worsening plight of the Jews in Germany and their internal development into a close community, other Zionist youth movements, such as *Werkleute, Zofim* (scouts), and *Makkabi Hazair* also encouraged their members to stay at *chalutz* hostels and to undertake a course on a training farm before going to the Yishuv. Among the youth movements in Germany that were aligned to Orthodoxy were *Bachad* (*Brit Chalutzim Datiim*), which was instrumental in founding a training farm at Rodges in 1927, and *Esra*, the youth wing of Agudat Yisrael. One of the largest and most active of the Jewish youth movements in Eastern Europe with over 50,000 members was the Marxist-Zionist *Hashomer Hazair*, but it was only transplanted to Germany in 1931, where it became a small, elitist movement with a membership heavily drawn from ex-gymnasia pupils and university students with an emphasis on specialized vocational training for kibbutz life in Palestine. This aim was opposed by *Hechalutz*, which wanted to train members of the middle class for work as laborers on the new settlements. There was also a clash between the ideologists in *Hechalutz* who despised the scouting activities of the Zionist youth organizations as being frivolous and the leaders of the latter, who regarded the games as reinvigorating the spirit of the youth. By the late 1920s the infrastructure for *hachscharah* was completed in Germany, so that much larger numbers could be absorbed for training after 1933 when Hitler became chancellor. *Hechalutz*, which was a struggling organization in Germany with 500 members, suddenly had a mass membership of 14,000 in 1934. From 300 persons undergoing agricultural *hachscharah* in 1930 the numbers had leaped to 5,000 by 1935. Some 3,000 German Jewish youngsters were also saved by Youth Aliya. In 1932 *Betar*, the youth wing of the Revisionist party that was active in Eastern Europe, started to organize the transport of illegal immigrants to Palestine. They

---

ments as an Historical Phenomenon," in *Sects, Religious Movements, and Political Parties,* ed. Menachem Mor (Ohama, Neb.: Creighton University Press, 1992), pp. 149–164. Sarah Honig, "Unquenched Vitality [the pre-War Jewish youth movements]," *Jerusalem Post Magazine,* 27 March 1987 (hereafter cited as Honig, *Unquenched Vitality*). Dash, *Henrietta Szold,* pp. 229–281. Schatzker, *Youth and New Reality,* pp. 157–208. Chaim Schatzker, "The Jewish Youth Movement in the Holocaust Period (11): The Relations Between the Youth Movement and Hechaluz," *Leo Baeck Institute Year Book* 33 (1988): 301–325 (hereafter cited as Schatzker, *The Youth Movement and Hechaluz*). Reinharz, *Hashomer Hazair (1),* pp. 173–207.

numbered 15,000 by 1941, while *Hechalutz* smuggled in another 7,000 persons.[38]

In Britain, upper-class Jewish ladies established a network of clubs to "civilize and spiritualize" adolescent Jewish girls from immigrant families who lived in Soho and the East End. Lady Magnus founded the prototype organization, the Jewish Girls' Club, in 1888, which was followed by Lily Montagu's West Central Jewish Girls' Club and the Butler Street Jewish Girls' Club under the patronage of Lady Sassoon and direction of Nettie Adler early in the new century. All these clubs emphasized Bible lessons, needlework, cookery, gymnastics, and a thrift club in an effort to train and mold the girls' character. If girls were bereft of parents or guardians or temporarily unemployed, they could lodge in the Harris Home in the West End, which was opened in 1902, for a small payment. Contemporary opinion viewed the clubs as a safety vehicle for keeping young Jewish working-class girls out of sexual entanglements, with which they could not emotionally cope. Great care was taken to ensure that the clubs were single-sex institutions where the young men and women were kept apart or on the rare occasions when they mingled were closely chaperoned. The aim was to wean factory girls away from crude utterances and to turn them into ladies of refinement and discernment like their mentors.[39]

Boys' clubs were instituted a decade later than girls' clubs, the Brady Boys' Club being inaugurated in 1896, followed by the West Central Lads' Club in 1898, then the Stepney Jewish Lads' Club, and the Victoria Boys' Club in 1901. Here there was a widespread fear of gangs of boys loafing in the streets and stealing from stall-holders, which culminated in a letter of complaint from the bishop of Stepney to the chief rabbi in 1901. To channel the energy of these young boys, the clubs concentrated on athletic activities and provided facilities for gymnastics and for playing football and cricket, although they also staged debates and members could

---

38. Honig, *Unquenched Vitality.* Joseph Walk, "The Torah va' Avodah Movement in Germany," *Leo Baeck Institute Year Book* 6 (1961): 236–256 (hereafter cited as Walk, *Torah va' Avodah*). Schatzker, *The Youth Movement and Hechaluz*, pp. 301–325. Reinharz, *Hashomer Hazair*, (1) p. 181. Jehuda Reinharz, "Hashomer Hazair in Germany (11): Under the Shadow of the Swastika, 1933–38," *Leo Baeck Institute Year Book* 32 (1987): 183–229.

39. Eugene C. Black, *The Social Politics of Anglo-Jewry 1880–1920* (Oxford: Basil Blackwell, 1988), pp. 133–141 (hereafter cited as Black, *Anglo-Jewry*). Lecture of Susan Tananbaum on "Education for Citizenship: Schools, Clubs and the Role of Gender in the Jewish East End," 2 June 1994.

sometimes borrow books. In 1899 the Jewish Athletic Association (later the Association of Jewish Youth) was set up. It arranged sports matches between schools with large numbers of Jewish boys and girls and later between its affiliated clubs so as to avoid matches on the Sabbath. Clubs frequently ran job placement schemes for their members. Before boys' clubs were started, the community invested its efforts in training immigrant youth by forming the Jewish Lads' Brigade in 1895 to instill habits of honor, cleanliness, and orderliness" and "to improve the physique . . . of our boys." In contrast to girls, who had to conform to a genteel feminine model, boys were to have their ghetto bends ironed out and to become manly and tough, a viewpoint shared by middle-class Zionists and upper-class anglicanized Jews. Many of the boys' and girls' clubs were run by upper class individuals with charismatic personalities on rigid, semi-authoritarian lines, allowing club members little say in the running of the organization and bent on imbuing members with suprapatriotic values and a love for the British Empire that was so exclusive that Zionist aspirations were shunned. Despite Basil Henriques' commanding personality and stern anti-Zionist stance, it was said that much of his philosophy had little impact on youth and that more members of his Oxford and St. George's Club went to fight in the Spanish Civil War and in 1948 for the fledgling state of Israel than volunteers from other clubs.[40]

In 1928 a Cambridge friend invited Wellesley Aron to inspect a Jewish youth club in Bethnal Green in order to evaluate its activities because of his past work with adolescents. "He went along one evening and watched the youngsters playing chess and table tennis, doing gymnastics, folk dancing and other activities. On the top floor of the converted house he found two boys reading. One said he was studying the Talmud, the other Jewish history." Asked for his reaction, Aron retorted that the club lacked any commitment to Jewish culture and hardly warranted the description of Jewish in its title. He, therefore, founded an organization called *Habonim* in 1929 that was consciously modeled on the Boy Scouts movement of Baden-Powell, of whom he was an admirer and whose methods he had absorbed while serving as leader of the 36th Stepney Jewish Scout Troop. Aron had refashioned his troop into an exemplary organization, the winner of interscout competitions. But instead of teaching youngsters in the *Habonim* woodcraft, camping, path finding, and other matters that in

---

40. Black, *Anglo-Jewry*, pp. 141–147. Interview with Montague Richardson, 30 November 1995.

themselves had no Jewish relevance, Aron looked for ways in which to substitute a Jewish cultural content or give these scouting techniques a fresh, Jewish orientation. Aron insisted on recruits to the movement learning a basic vocabulary in modern Hebrew, the geography of Palestine, and a potted version of Jewish history that he devised with the assistance of Cecil Roth and Sir Leon Simon. Besides this they had to construct a brick out of cardboard decorated with the symbols of the ancient Jewish tribes, their local group, and anything else culled from the *Jewish Encylopaedia*. At every meeting, according to Victor Sefton, the groups had "a dedication, a games and a drama period [on some theme from Jewish life], a sing song and various discussions . . ."[41]

Alexander Flinder joined a *Habonim* group in 1932 in Poland Street in the West End when he was eleven. "No, we were not mixed," he declared, "there was a girls *Gedud* (troop) and the boys *Gedud* but we used to mix at camps, we used to have mixed functions, but actually the *Gedudim* were separate." He later stated that "Yes, the strange thing was in many ways I probably learned more about the essence of being Jewish from Habonim than I did actually from cheder . . . other than from Bet Hasefer. . . . The Habonim and the Bet HaSefer was learning Hebrew songs and something of the history of the Jewish people other than that of the Bible, so that to this day I can remember any Yiddish songs which was a nice thing . . . and Hebrew songs. . . . So in many ways one had a feeling of Jewish identity rather more from Habonim peculiarly enough than one did from cheder, in many ways." Similarly Louis Rabbinowitz, an Orthodox rabbi, observed in 1937 that "it was always possible to detect among children attending religion classes those who were also members of the Habonim movement. They were pulsating with an interest for all things Jewish which somehow their classes failed to infuse in the young people who attended them." So too, Arnold Wesker (b. 1932), the playwright who was also a member of *Habonim*, claimed that while the left-wing *Hashomer Hatzair* regarded it "as nothing more than a Jewish boy-scout movement," the *Habonim* provided him "with some of the happiest days of my life—companionship, soul mates, gaiety, a sense of purpose, and a deeper awareness of what it meant to be Jewish."[42]

---

41. Silman, *Wellesley Aron*, pp. 17–19 and 48–55. Sefton, *Growing Up*, pp. 325 and 326.

42. Alexander Flinder, transcript of interview deposited at the London Museum of Jewish Life, pp. 8 and 9. *Jewish Chronicle*, 3 December 1937. Wesker, *Autobiography*, p. 155.

The highlight of the year was the *Habonim* camp, *Machaneh*, in the countryside, for which youngsters mainly from working-class homes contributed for weeks to scrape together the total required payment of thirty shillings. While the first camp was started in 1932, "The Big Jamboree" in Oakley in 1939 attracted fifteen hundred members. During the Second World War, "there were numerous weekend and summer camps, attended by hundreds of Habonimniks. My first, at Burgage in 1943, had around 600 participants," wrote Gerald Jackman. Asher Benson described one such camp from the 1930s, stating that "we had cultural and social programmes. We discussed Palestine, Zionism, Socialism, Communism, and a dozen other -isms. We sang Hebrew songs, danced Hebrew dances, and drilled in Hebrew. We scouted, we rambled, and 'zigged' [staged short sketches, parodying current events]. . . . It was the period of the Tower and Stockade expansion of the yishuv in Palestine, when, overnight, new settlements were established by chalutzim. At camp we built our own tower and stockade . . ." Along with the idea of camping there was an emphasis on scouting skills, "tracking, observation, and bridging," the ability to assemble the bell tents held up by a central pole, and proficiency at tying five knots—all a clear borrowing from Baden-Powell. In addition, Chaim Lipschitz, one of the first leaders of *Gedud Trumpeldor*, the original branch of the movement, had been a language student in France, where he had encountered a Jewish scouts' association, the *Eclaireurs Israelites*, which among its other activities taught its adherents Hasidic and Zionist folk dances.[43]

Through pressure from such stalwart Britons as Neville Laski, Wellesley Aron, despite misgivings, was forced to include a declaration of loyalty to the Crown and the British Empire in the promise pledged by members to the movement. That was why Shimon Barzilai, one of the founders of Kibbutz Kfar Blum, recalled that early *Habonim* was "not a Zionist movement at all. We made it into a Zionist movement—but the founders, they wanted us to be good British citizens, I think they wanted a sort of Jewish

---

43. Asher Benson, "Menachaneh Memories," *Koleinu* 14, no. 3 (July 1994): 18 and 19, and Linzi Frankel, "Menachaneh Magic" in the same issue of *Koleinu*, pp. 20 and 21. Jenni Frazer, "Zionist Youth Group is 65 Years Young," *Jewish Chronicle*, 7 October 1994 (hereafter cited as Frazer, *Zionist Youth*), and letter from Gerald Jackman, *Jewish Chronicle*, 21 October 1994. Interview with Montague Richardson, 30 November 1995. Paula Hyman, *From Dreyfus to Vichy: The Remaking of French Jewry 1906–1939* (New York: Columbia University Press, 1979), pp. 191–198.

Boy Scouts." In 1933, after pressure from leaders of local groups, a number of militant Zionists joined the executive of the *Habonim* and rewrote the official handbook to allow these local branches to develop on Zionist lines. Again, the first leaders of the movement were young second-generation Jews of East European descent, not upper-class British Jews, and the whole atmosphere in the *Habonim* was freer, less sexually repressed, and somewhat irreverent with a mocking air at authority. Not surprisingly, one member of a *Habonim* group in West Ham admitted that in the 1930s they despised the somewhat hidebound Jewish club members. At the same time, the *Habonim* were used as "shock troops," with only partial success in the East End, to try to combat the conversion of so many working-class Jewish youths to Communism.[44]

What revitalized the Anglo-Jewish youth movements was the influx of refugees in the late 1930s from the Continent, so that the number of *Habonim* members opting for agricultural training was swollen, the *B'nei Akiva* became a national organization for religious youth, and the Maccabi movement was put on a firm foundation. With the arrival of Continental refugees in England and a keen interest from some *Habonim* members in *hachscharah*, the Zionist Federation in Britain established a branch of the *Hechalutz* movement in 1934. The David Eder training farm in Kent was chiefly filled by members of the *Habonim*, who were joined by sixty German refugees in 1938, while before the onset of the Second World War some forty members of the *Habonim* had gone on aliya to Palestine. All the remnants of the Continental youth movements with the exception of the *Hashomer Hazair* and the religious *chalutzim* merged to form the *Mishmar Habonim* with a program of aliya and life on a kibbutz, eventually uniting with the British movement in 1943. During the war the membership of the David Eder Farm was exclusively British in composition, as it was in the middle of a restricted area, but Continental *haverim* were to be found at the movement's three other *hachscharah* centers, Gorsey Leaze and Latton in Wiltshire, and Newport-Pagnell in Buckinghamshire. Some of the youngsters undergoing agricultural training were a part of a much larger contingent of 10,000 children from Germany who had been offered shelter in Britain before the war, the *Kindertransporte*. Out of

---

44. Silman, *Wellesley Aron*, p. 53. Respondent at the Susan Tananbaum lecture on 2 June 1994. Frazer, *Zionist Youth*. David Cesarani, *Zionism in England 1917–1939*, D. Phil Thesis, Oxford, 1986, pp. 380 and 388–395 (hereafter cited as Cesarani, *Zionism in England*).

these centers associated with the *Habonim* came ideologically motivated persons who contributed to the building of four kibbutzim, Kfar Blum, Kfar Hanassi, Beit Ha'emek, and Amiad. At the same time, three kibbutz-style youth hostels were opened by the *Habonim* during the war in towns on the Devon coast to accommodate 140 children evacuated from London, who grew up in a Jewish atmosphere.[45]

In Germany in the winter of 1928 Young Mizrachi created an educational youth movement called *Brit HaNoar* (Youth League) and a branch of the *Hechalutz Hamizrachi Federation*, resulting in the foundation of a religious Zionist and socialist organization, the *Bachad*. In 1937 two branches of a religious youth organization called *B'nei Akiva* had been set up in England, drawing their inspiration from Germany and the Yishuv, where this name was used. In November 1938, Arieh Handler (b. 1925), the director of the Berlin Youth Aliya, was on a mission to Palestine to urge religious bodies to increase their absorptive capacity of refugees when he received a coded cable from Dr. Burg that following the outbreak of violence against Jews on Kristallnacht he should not return home, because he would be arrested by the Gestapo. He, therefore, went to Britain to open a Youth Aliya office in London at the end of the year and became involved in youth work for the Young Mizrachi, which had become radicalized by the influx of refugees from Germany and affiliated to the religious labor movement, *HaPoel HaMizrachi*. Within a year or two there were active *B'nei Akiva* groups in London, Stamford Hill, Willesden, and Golders Green, followed by more branches in the provinces, Manchester, Liverpool, Leeds, Glasgow, and Edinburgh, so that by 1941 the movement had swiftly grown into a national organization. Teddy Kollek, who worked for a short time in England as a *shliach* for the *Habonim*, accused Arieh Handler of depleting his organization of Orthodox members. The *B'nei Akiva* sprang from three different sources, the British scouting tradition, the idealism of the German religious and socialist Zionists, *HaPoel HaMizrachi*, and the Hasidic fervor of the Polish Jewish youth movement, *Shomer HaDati*, which was favored with the charismatic leadership of Shmuel Chaim Landau. Soon 2,000 members were attending the sum-

45. Cesarani, *Zionism in England*, pp. 383–386. Series of articles in the "Habonim Jubilee Supplement," *Jerusalem Post*, 14 May 1979. Jeremy Leigh, *A History of Habonim in England 1948–1950*, University College London, M.A. Thesis, 1990, p. 59 (hereafter cited as Leigh, *History of Habonim*). *Jewish Chronicle*, 29 December 1995.

mer and harvesting camps of the *B'nei Akiva*. A moderate Orthodox stance was adopted by the leadership of the organization and each branch had, unusually, a mixed membership of boys and girls on the same lines as the parent German organization. Handler not only created the *Bachad* movement for older youths but raised the necessary funds to open *hachscharah* centers, among them one at Thaxted, which led to the foundation of kibbutzim at Lavi and Tirat Zvi.[46]

During the 1930s branches of the Maccabi, the Zionist-oriented Central European Jewish sports movement, were started in Britain, the Northern Maccabi Council being formed in 1936 and the South London Maccabi being established a year earlier. Lionel Schalit, a Cambridge friend of Wellesley Aron, formed the Bar-Cochba Association, which hired playing fields in Streatham for rugby and football as well as other sports, and led the British contingent to the first Maccabiah games in Eretz Israel in 1932. Although in the early 1930s the membership of the Maccabi Association London climbed to 2,000, it rapidly began to dwindle as members were dissatisfied with the provision of facilities for outdoor sports, while indoor sports were neglected. Each sports section was compelled to make its own arrangements, and the swimming section founded in 1933, for instance, operated out of the Holborn baths. To obviate these difficulties, Maccabi House in West Hampstead was opened in 1937 to cater to new suburban Jewry with a fully equipped gymnasium, a boxing ring and punch balls, facilities for judo, and a section for rhythmic exercises for ladies under the guidance of a Continental instructress. Among the cultural activities were the learning of Modern Hebrew, amateur dramatics, a choir, and orchestra. Alexander Flinder recalled "the famous Hungarian and Viennese Maccabi and Bar Kochba came over to play us water polo, so I remember playing against Hakoah and Bar Kochba Bratislava in the thirties. They were the . . . top champions." Many refugee sportsmen from the Continent joined the Bar Kochba Club in Hampstead; others were made welcome at the nearby Maccabi House. Much of the emphasis in the Maccabi movement was on self-defense, its members joining Zionist youth groups and Communists in confronting Fascist marches through the East End of London in the 1930s, and a flying battalion under Fred Oberlander, an

46. Cesarani, *Zionism in England*, pp. 395 and 396. Walk, *Torah va' Avodah*, pp. 251–253. Interview with Arieh Handler, 1 December 1995. *Jewish Chronicle* article on the outbreak of the Second World War, 8 September 1989. Harry Schwab, "Down Memory Lane," *Jewish Review* 15, no. 4 (September 1995): 13.

international wrestler, protected Jews when there was a fresh resurgence of anti-Semitism after 1945. Through participation in the Maccabiah games in Israel every four years, the movement helped members revive their own Jewish identities, even when they came from assimilated families, and some sportsmen settled in Israel, where they became active in its athletic and cultural life.[47]

During 1950 the clubs in the Association of Jewish Youth, which boasted a membership of 13,000, still dominated the Jewish teenage scene in England, but the association went into decline and merged with Norwood in 1995. The most dynamic elements in the Anglo-Jewish youth movement just over four decades ago were the Zionist organizations, the *Habonim* with 3,000 members, and their more religious rivals, the *B'nei Akiva* with 2,000 members in their junior organization plus another 750 members in their senior organization, the *Bachad*. Since then the current membership of the *Habonim* in a shrinking Anglo-Jewish population in 1995 stands at 850 and the *B'nei Akiva* at 1,500. Both the *Habonim* and the *B'nei Akiva* emerged as youth subcultures, rejecting the values of Anglo-Jewish society. *Habonim* strengthened both Jewish values and social consciousness among the young by dwelling on the importance of making *aliya*, that is, immigrating to Israel for life in an ideal kibbutz society, which, while only achieved by the few, was the goal of many others. Those who did not depart for Israel were left with a lasting concern for social justice and an attachment to Jewish culture. One criticism of the American *Habonim*, which may be valid for Anglo-Jewry, was that by losing its autonomous indigenous leadership and by falling under the control of *shlichim*, emissaries sent from Israel, the movement lost its inner dynamic and lapsed into passivity and its members tended to become more immature.[48]

B'nei Akiva in the 1980s imbued its members with new religious zeal, so that they rejected the socialism of its founders and centrist Orthodoxy of their parents for a return to the talmudic sources and a scrupulous

47. Silman, *Wellesley Aron*, p. 57. *The Jewish Year Book 1933*, ed. S. Levy (London: Jewish Chronicle, 1933), p. 135. Interview with Fred Worms, 6 December 1995, and Brochure of the Maccabi Association London to mark the opening of Maccabi House in 1937. Profile on Fred Worms, *Jerusalem Post*, 2 May 1982. Sidney Bunt, *Jewish Youth Work in Britain: Past, Present and Future* (London: Bedford Square Press, 1975), pp. 20, 21, 26, 88, 89, and 175–176.

48. V. D. Lipman, *Social History of the Jews in England 1850–1950* (London: Watts, 1954), pp. 180 and 181. Leigh, *History of the Habonim*, pp. 17–60. Yehuda Riemer, "The Habonim Youth Movement As a Research Topic," pp. 53–58.

observance of the minutiae of halachah. For the boys, this meant spending a year in a kibbutz and yeshiva in Israel before proceeding to university; for the girls, a similar stay in Israel at a religious seminary, from which they emerged with a more traditional way of thinking and a more conservative style of dress. Again, a minority of *B'nei Akiva* members chose to settle in Israel, but the larger majority remained in Britain with stronger Jewish convictions than their parents. Without the attraction of building up the land and becoming a pioneer, the number of *Habonim* members with a secular approach going on aliya to Israel, which was once greater than that of their rivals, has dropped, whereas the religious lure remains and the *B'nei Akiva* now sends a higher number of its members to Israel. According to one estimate, over 3,000 *Bachad* members, who have graduated from the *B'nei Akiva* to the senior organization, have gone on aliya, with possibly an additional 1,000 *chaverim* from the related *Torah Va'Avodah* movement settling in Israel. Within Israel itself, the *B'nei Akiva*, with 50,000 members, is one of the largest and most powerful youth movements. Many of its members follow a well-trodden path through religious high school, the youth movement, and "service in the army via the *hesder* [yeshiva] route," where army service can be combined with study. Here they are influenced by rabbis and other leaders who believe in a divinely ordained Greater Israel and sometimes encourage defiance of the government at various levels of belligerence to achieve this.[49]

Within Anglo-Jewry in the early 1990s, the majority of Jewish youth had deserted the youth clubs and preferred going to night clubs, licensed premises that sold liquor, or other commercial establishments, spilling out onto the streets at 10:30 or 11 P.M. when the public houses closed. This phenonemon was not limited to the streets of Golders Green and Hampstead in London, particularly on a Thursday night, but similar open-air gatherings occurred in other parts of the capital and in Manchester, Leeds, and Birmingham. The youngsters, who congregated on the streets in North-West London, were chiefly aged between sixteen and eighteen and tended to meet for up to a maximum of an hour and a half, after socializing elsewhere with a smaller group of friends. According to Micah Gold,

> Meeting in Golders Green is seen by many of the young people as a way of keeping in touch with Jewish friends while they study, work and mix with a

---

49. Interview with Arieh Handler, 1 December 1995. Jenni Frazer, "Free Speech and Silence [interview with Stuart Cohen]," *Jewish Chronicle*, 8 December 1995.

wider community during the rest of the week. It is also seen as a way of meeting new Jewish friends and possibly Jewish partners. . . . Some referred to the "religion aspect" or observance of religion and their dislike of practising it. It seems almost as if they want to keep their Jewish identity and have strong feelings about the community they belong to but at the same time are not too interested in observing a religion.

Hence there is a large group of Jewish youngsters proud of their Jewish identity who mix socially only with other Jews; this creates emotional ties that in turn reinforce their feelings of ethnic solidarity, enabling them to experience a new, more secular form of Jewish childhood; other young Jews with a weak or nonexistent religious affiliation hardly mix with their fellow Jews and miss the magic of a Jewish childhood.[50]

---

50. Micah Gold, *"Off Centre" A Study of Jewish Youth in North West London* (1991), pp. 8–10, 19, 25, and 34–44. Micah Gold, *Maccabi Street Project: A Two Year Evaluation June 1992 to July 1994* (February 1995), p. 17. Studies commissioned by the Maccabi Association London and the Maccabi Union of Great Britain. For a study of Manchester Jewish youth, see the *Jewish Chronicle*, 30 June 1995 and 14 July 1995.

Conclusion

The distinctive characteristics of Jewish childhood evolved in the biblical period with the institution of the rite of circumcision for infant males and the ban on child sacrifice supported by the powerful message of the *Akeda*, in which Abraham's zeal to sacrifice Isaac was thwarted at the last moment. The unconscious dimensions of this narrative seem at one level to offer us a precious insight into the changing psyche of the Jewish family at a critical stage of its development. By creating the symbolic castration of circumcision, Jews ritualized the interfamily strife of the Oedipus conflict, thus giving women more space to enhance their own roles. Men emerged as more nurturant in their role as fathers, and women with a higher status than females in surrounding nations, perhaps less angry and frustrated and more solicitous as mothers.

To meet the challenge of Graeco-Roman civilization in the talmudic age, the Jews borrowed one of its key institutions, the primary school, and adapted the heder for its own purposes as the chief vehicle for transmitting the heritage of the Torah from generation to generation. This school, which was mainly for boys from the age of six until twelve or thirteen years, rapidly developed into an almost universal institution within Jewish communities. Its aim was to teach boys to read and to translate from the Torah, the Prophets, and other later writings. At first boys were expected to recite portions of the Torah during the synagogue service on the Sabbath or to accompany the reading from the Torah with an Aramaic translation; later this was modified in the early modern period to reading a portion from the Pentateuch and Prophets on the Sabbath closest in time to his thirteenth birthday. Other features of Judaism during the talmudic age grew out of its earlier concerns, particularly its campaigns against infanticide and abortion and its hostility to the seduction of minors by predatory males—all these issues helped to define the cultural contours of Jewish family life and to differentiate Judaism from Hellenism and the value system of the pagan world.

When we surveyed the Middle Ages and the early modern period, we discussed certain discontinuities in Jewish childhood history. On the one hand, because of an almost universal primary school system for boys during the medieval period, they tended to be better educated, more carefully supervised and watched over than their neighbors' children; on the other hand, because of a narcissistic identification with their children and a failure to separate, Jewish parents sometimes slaughtered their own children during the disturbances provoked by the Crusades rather than allow them to feign conversion to Christianity until the hostility subsided. Such temporary conversions were not unknown in the Islamic lands. With the bolstering of ego controls in the early modern period, the murderous Oedipal fantasies of fathers were suppressed.

During the seventeenth and eighteenth centuries but extending into the modern age, we noted another discontinuity, the fact that children as young as seven or nine were boarded a long way from home to study at heder, and the growth of the system of "eating days," especially for those enrolled in a yeshiva. Here, although children and adolescents were meant to be provided with daily meals in different homes while they studied, the system was flawed and they sometimes starved. Despite this and the difficulties of some apprentices living in their master's household, we should be careful not to exaggerate the scale of the problem, for it was more commonly encountered in Lithuania than Poland and in any case affected only a minority of youngsters.

During the modern age, the system of universal heder education and talmudic study for the elite, which had sustained Jewish culture for 1,700 years, started to unravel, first in Germany from the 1780s and then in

Eastern Europe in the second half of the nineteenth century. We assessed the impact of a Western education on Jewish children in Germany, Austria, and Russia, contrasting it with the traditional heder education in Eastern Europe, which continued until the First World War. The latter system of instruction still had considerable pedagogic merits, even if it was compared with the Western primary school, and underwent a radical transformation at the end of the nineteenth century through the impact of Zionism. With inspirational teachers, such education could still nourish a child's imagination. If a boy or girl was brought up in a religious household in Eastern Europe that kept a kosher home and celebrated all the weeky and seasonal rituals of the Jewish year, as was usually the case, and then received a heder education, there could be little doubt that they had experienced a Jewish childhood.

When, however, large numbers of Jews migrated from Eastern Europe to Britain and the United States from the 1880s until the 1920s, the new communities came under intense pressure to modernize and to jettison a well-tried system of education before they had time to evolve the framework of a system to replace it. Ahad Ha'Am argued that there was little difference between the Orthodox and Reform movements in the West, since even Orthodox communities no longer had a *bet ha-midrash* adjoining the synagogue. If then in the immigrant communities in the West a heder education was no longer always the chief marker of a Jewish childhood, were there other differences in the upbringing of Jews and Gentiles in the modern age? And if there were such distinctions, what were they? We focused in the first instance on the wonderful standards of infant care that had as a consequence the greater survival of Jewish babies, but such superior methods of care did not end there, as they continued throughout childhood. Clearly, rather than a recent development, this cultural trait may be traced back to the nineteenth century, possibly to the Middle Ages. Moreover, within the suburban Jewish family in the West, mothers played a key role in enhancing the achievement motivation of their children. Again, almost alone the Jews had a universal system of primary education for boys during the Middle Ages, while talmudic education for the elite carried immense prestige. This cultural hankering for education, when combined with the migration of the Eastern European Jewish population to large cities in the West with the most advanced educational facilities, resulted in the rapid social mobility of the Jewish population.

The families of the Jewish immigrants to Britain and the United States underwent a number of generational transformations. Undermined often by lack of steady work, the immigrant fathers relaxed their control over their children, many of whom were not offered a religious education and whose formative influences were the secular school and the peer group that roamed the streets. But the lives of the younger generation were shaped overall by the vibrant immigrant culture. Young men were clean-shaven, while newly married wives displayed their hair without any form of covering, both becoming invisible Jews. Following the First World War, many of the immigrant families moved out of the East End and East Side in the 1920s and 1930s to the areas of secondary settlement, where they lived in ethnic enclaves. Synagogue attendance on the Sabbath declined precipitously, although the population was still bound together by the secular ties of politics, including Zionism, and sport together with the Yiddish language and East European Jewish food. Close friendships before the Second World War were still confined to Jews.

A teacher by the name of M. Bloch claimed in 1937 that "the late Rev. A. A. Green said that Hebrew education was neglected because the parents took the children away into the country on Sunday morning, and it was a case of 'Pentateuch versus Petrol.' Nowadays . . . It is 'Pentateuch versus Parents.' Any excuse, it seems, has the sanction of the father and/ or mother, and the child abstains from attending Hebrew Classes." So too, Henry Goldring, whose family ran a bakery business in London, related how his "grandmother wore a *sheitel*, a wig, for the whole of her married life, and . . . the family was conducted on ultra Orthodox lines until the children got rather affluent in the motor-car era, in the 30s, and, then the family outings began, which included football matches with the strict disapproval of the elderly . . ."[1]

During the 1930s and the following two decades, a process briefly interrupted by the war, the children of the immigrants, who had prospered in business or in white-collar jobs, went further afield to the suburbs, where a child-centered religion evolved with great emphasis on the bar mitzvah and the equivalent ceremony for females, the bat mitzvah. Having received a secular education and having had their physiques improved by participation in sport and gymnastics, enthusiasts for muscular Judaism, young Jews, were now more self-confident and determined to prise open entry to the higher reaches of the professions. Not only the Jewish mind but the Jewish body was reinvented as a result of the modernization process.

---

1. Letter from M. Bloch *Jewish Chronicle*, 3 December 1937. Henry Goldring interview transcript deposited with the London Museum of Jewish Life, p. 3.

Qualities such as "pushfulness" and "aggressiveness," which were frequently denounced as vices of Jews by anglicanizers like Dayan Gollop, were what enabled the younger generation to breach the walls of privilege. Careers in the higher ranks of the professions as corporation lawyers, academics, and surgeons came within the reach of Jews after the Second World War, while a minority secured prestigious positions in Columbia, Harvard, and Yale a little earlier. On the one hand, the forms of secular Judaism sometimes dissolved ancient ethnic ties, and friendships developed with members of other groups, leading to a galloping rate of intermarriage from the 1960s. This is important insofar as the children who were the products of these marriages often led fragmented Jewish lives, as is illustrated in Emma Klein's recent book, *Lost Jews*. On the other hand, for families who were interested there were now more Jewish day schools and Zionist youth movements, organized trips of young people to Israel, and in the United States summer camps with an intensive Jewish orientation. After the Six Day War in 1967, a new pride in being Jewish emerged among the youth, who started wearing a knitted *kipah* (skullcap) in the street. New positive forms of Jewish childhood were being created.[2]

From the eighteenth century onwards, the proportion of youth within the Jewish population structure increased dramatically within Central and Eastern Europe. These adolescents flocked into a series of innovative movements, Hasidism, Zionism, socialism, and the youth associations, between the Wars, infusing them with the dynamism to reshape the course of modern Jewish history. Whereas prior to the eighteenth century Jewish history was child-centered, starting with the ceremony for the initiation of boys into the heder that ushered in a Jewish learning process for life, the modern emphasis shifted in favor of youth, who had their own agenda and wrested the initiative from their elders.

---

2. Dayan Gollop at the Preachers' Conference, *Jewish Chronicle*, 8 July 1938. Jerold S. Auerbach, "From Rags to Robes: The Legal Profession, Social Mobility and the American Jewish Experience," *American Jewish Historical Quarterly* 66, no. 2 (December 1976): 249–284. Lewis S. Feuer, "The Stages in the Social History of Jewish Professors in American Colleges and Universities," *American Jewish History* 71 (June 1982): 432–465. Seymour Martin Lipset and Everett Carll Ladd Jr., "Jewish Academics in the United States," in *The Jew in American Society*, ed. Marshall Sklare (New York: Behrman House, 1974), pp. 255–288. Suzanne Klingenstein, *Jews in the American Academy 1900–1940: The Dynamics of Intellectual Assimilation* (New Haven: Yale University Press, 1991). Emma Klein, *Lost Jews: The Struggle for Identity Today* (London: Macmillan, 1995).

From time to time we have touched on gender issues, without spelling out in detail how the childhood of Jewish girls differed from that of their brothers. In a sense the clearly demarcated boundaries of the life of a Jewish boy defined both his own childhood and that of his sister because of the symbiotic relationship between them. In another sense, there was a gulf between their childhoods that has been bridged only in the modern age. During the talmudic era, girls were excluded from being called up to reading from the Torah, thus making their attendance at the Jewish primary school less necessary; yet nonetheless, they studied in the heder in medieval Egypt, and girls from rabbinic families in Western Europe were taught their prayers. During the Middle Ages and in immigrant families in the modern period, girls were allocated domestic tasks at an early age, which included minding younger siblings and babies, but in Central Europe in the seventeenth and eighteenth centuries and in Eastern Europe later, they also studied in hadarim in appreciable numbers, even if it was for a short period of time. Whereas boys were educated in yeshivot in Poland, their sisters often received an extensive secular education, leaving them sometimes with a shallow knowledge of Jewish traditions. To circumvent this problem, Sarah Schenirer (1883–1935) founded a network of Orthodox schools for girls, the Beth Jacob movement, in 1918. Moreover, once the East European immigrant families in Britain and the United States had moved to areas of secondary settlement and beyond into the suburbs, girls shared a usually attenuated form of Jewish education with their brothers, a Jewish rite of passage at adolescence, and a school and college life. Sometimes they embarked on their own careers—for example as schoolteachers—which gave them financial independence and even on occasion sexual freedom.[3]

There are a number of other topics that we could not explore in depth because of limitations of space, namely the plight of orphans, Jewish youth in Nazi Europe, and children in kibbutzim, but it is necessary to say a few words about them. In recent years detailed research has started on recon-

---

3. Shoshana Pantel Zolty, *"And All Your Children Shall Be Learned," Women and the Study of the Torah in Jewish Law and History* (Northvale, N.J.: Jason Aronson, 1993), pp. 263–300. For examples of the sexual freedom of Jewish women in the 1930s, see Harvey J. Graff, *Conflicting Paths: Growing Up in America* (Cambridge, Mass.: Harvard University Press, 1995), pp. 320–326 and the Mass Observation Archive in the University of Sussex TC Anti-Semitism Box 2, File A, "Saturday Night with Three Jews," 1939, indicating the relaxed sexual mores of some Jewish girls in suburban London.

structing the lives of Jewish children in orphanages in Britain and the United States and describing the shift in policy of closing these homes by providing financial assistance to single parents to enable them to keep their children or, where this option was not available, encouraging their fostering. Some children praised the care they had received in the orphanages, others complained about the poor food and harsh discipline with youngsters being caned on their birthday, yet others had a mixture of criticism and praise. After the First World War and the disturbances in the Ukraine during the Russian Revolution, tens of thousands of Jewish children were orphaned and abandoned. Both the Federation of Ukrainian Jews in London, a high-powered body of Anglo-Jewish notables, and the American Joint Distribution Committee were of the opinion that it was impracticable and too costly to remove huge numbers of orphans from the Ukraine and its contiguous areas for adoption overseas. "He [Boris Bogen], says that for over a year the Joint Distribution Committee has been considering the problem of the orphans," wrote A. M. Kaizer in London to Isaac Ochberg in Cape Town on 24 February 1921, "and it has come to the conclusion that it will cost considerably less to maintain the orphans on the spot than to take them out of the Ukraine and settle them elsewhere." Nevertheless, other East European immigrants who had grown up in these lands and were closer to the grass roots were not so sanguine about the future prospects of these children, and worked incessantly in Canada, South Africa, and Britain to save some hundreds of these orphans, by allowing them to start a new life elsewhere.[4]

As far as the Holocaust is concerned, one and a half million children perished, which is by far the greatest discontinuity in Jewish childhood history and unique in scale for any people. Deborah Dwork has painstak-

---

4. Hyman Bogen, *The Luckiest Orphans: A History of the Hebrew Orphan Asylum of New York* (Urbana: University of Illinois Press, 1992). Reena Sigman Friedman, *These Are Our Children: Jewish Orphanages in the United States, 1880–1925* (Hanover, N.H.: Brandeis University, 1994). *What About the Children? 200 Years of Norwood Child Care 1795–1995* (London: London Museum of Jewish Life, 1995). For examples of sadism in Jewish orphanages, see the transcript of the interview of Rose Mitchel deposited at the London Museum of Jewish Life, pp. 13 and 14 and Robert and Michael Meeropol, *We Are Your Sons: The Legacy of Ethel and Julius Rosenberg* (Urbana and Chicago: University of Illinois Press, 1986), p. 28. Jewish Museum, Cape Town. Letter from A. M. Kaizer of the Jewish Federation of Ukrainian Jews to Isaac Ochberg of the Cape Jewish Orphanage dated 24 Februrary 1921. John Cooper, unpublished paper on "The Work of the Pinsker Orphans Relief Fund of London 1921–1936."

ingly pieced together the childhood lives of those youngsters in occupied Europe who were murdered by the Nazis and those who survived. It has been estimated that about 175,000 Jewish children remained alive in the formerly occupied areas after Hitler had been defeated; possibly more of the hidden children were girls than boys, who could be more easily detected because they were circumcised. Whereas in Belgium and Italy 20 percent of the Jews deported to the concentration camps were children, in France after the summer of 1942 a more sustained effort was made to save such children and about 13 percent of the deportees were juvenile victims. After the war, Jewish organizations tried to restore children to their families, but the result was often more pain and trauma because the children had sometimes become alienated from their heritage. In the Netherlands in 1945, there was a bitter controversy over what should be done with the three thousand Jewish war orphans, and an ill-conceived attempt was made to exclude Orthodox Jews and Zionists from the deliberations concerning their fate. In France there was a scandal in 1953, when two young Jewish orphans, Robert and Gerard Finaly, were secretly baptized by the nurse who had saved them and spirited over the frontier by priests into Spain, when surviving relatives claimed them. Jacob Kaplan (1895–1994), who was the chief rabbi of Paris, staged a national protest by ordering all Jewish households to leave two empty places at the Seder table; eventually the children were released and joined relatives in Israel in July 1953. Thus the policy of the medieval Church with regard to the enforced baptism of Jewish children was reversed in a historic decision.[5]

One final topic which we were unable to deal with at any length was the upbringing of kibbutz children, which is constantly cited as a unique method of rearing the young. Mothers spent a few hours a day with their infants but never the night, and most of the baby's stimulation came from the *metapelet*, nurse. From the time when they were infants, the kibbutz children played, ate their meals, and slept with their peer group, to whom they became very attached. Children were not pressured, and toilet train-

---

5. Deborah Dwork, *Children With a Star* (New Haven: Yale University Press, 1991). Joel S. Fishman, "The War Orphan Controversy in the Netherlands: Majority-Minority Relations," in *Dutch Jewish History,* ed. Jozeph Michman (Jerusalem: Institute for Research on Dutch Jewry, 1984), pp. 421–432. Hyam Corney, "Mission: Save Jewish Children, Story of an Unsung Heroine," *Jewish Chronicle Colour Magazine,* 26 November 1982, pp. 38–40. Obituary of Rabbi Jacob Kaplan, *Jewish Chronicle,* 16 December 1994.

ing proceeded at a slow pace, while meals were hurriedly gobbled and were not treated as training sessions for the inculcation of good manners as in middle-class families. Conflict with the parents was reduced and the kibbutz child escaped much of the emotional damage of the Oedipal relationship. Nevertheless, during adolescence the kibbutz child was subjected to strict sexual restraints. From this method of upbringing, the kibbutz child emerged anxious to please his peer group and with a relaxed, casual attitude toward others, but unable to forge ties of intimacy with individuals. Under women's influence, the traditional family bonds were revived by sometimes allowing children to sleep in their parents' houses and by the institution of the "hour of love," a session spent by parents with their offspring after work.[6]

Much work remains to be done on elucidating the history of Jewish childhood, as there are still a number of major gaps in our knowledge. We need a feminist version of these events, a history of Jewish girlhood; we need detailed histories of the youth movements in Britain and the United States and a separate survey of radical Jewish youth; we need a wide-ranging account of games and pastimes indulged in by Jewish children over the ages; we need studies of the childhoods of the Oriental Jewish communities and the Sephardim; and we now need a history of Israeli childhood.

---

6. Melford E. Spiro, *Children of the Kibbutz* (New York: Schocken Books, 1965). Bruno Bettelheim, *The Children of the Dream* (New York: Avon Books, 1970). Lionel Tiger and Joseph Shepher, *Women in the Kibbutz* (Harmondsworth: Penguin Books, 1977), pp. 225–229 and 262–263.

For Further Reading

David Aberbach, "Aggadah and Childhood Imagination in the Works of Mendele, Bialik, and Agnon," in *Jewish Education and Learning*, ed. Glenda Abramson and Tudor Parfitt (Reading: Harwood Academic, 1994), pp. 233–241.

Moses Aberbach, "The Development of the Jewish Elementary School System During the Talmudic Age," in *Studies in Jewish Education*, ed. Janet Aviad (Jerusalem: Magnes Press, 1988), Vol. 3, pp. 290–301.

Beth-Zion Abrahams, trans. and ed., *The Life of Glückel of Hameln* (London: East and West Library, 1962).

Israel Abrahams, *Hebrew Ethical Wills* (Philadelphia: Jewish Publication Society, 1948), Parts 1 and 2.

———, *Jewish Life in the Middle Ages* (London: Edward Goldston, 1932).

Hirz Abramowicz, "A Jewish Teacher in Czarist Russia," *Yivo Annual* 19 (1990): 331–363.

Nigel Allan, "A Polish Rabbi's Circumcision Manual," *Medical History* 33 (1989): 247–254.

Alexander Altmann, *Moses Mendelssohn: A Biographical Study* (Philadelphia: Jewish Publication Society, 1973).

Philippe Ariès, *Centuries of Childhood* (Harmondsworth: Penguin Books, 1979).

Simha Assaf, *Sources for the History of Jewish Education* (Hebrew) (Tel Aviv: Dvir, 1954), Vol. 1.

Jerold S. Auerbach, "From Rags to Robes: The Legal Profession, Social Mobility and the American Jewish Experience," *American Jewish Historical Quarterly* 66, no. 2 (December 1976): 249–284.

Ron Barkai, "A Medieval Hebrew Treatise on Obstetrics," *Medical History* 33 (1989): 96–119.

Lesley Beaumont, "Child's Play in Ancient Athens," *History Today* (August 1994): 30–35.

Samuel Belkin, *Philo and Oral Law: The Philonic Interpretation of Biblical Law in Relation to Palestinian Halakah* (New York: Johnson Reprint Corporation, 1968).

Steven Beller, *Vienna and the Jews 1867–1938: A Cultural History* (Cambridge: Cambridge University Press, 1990).

Issachar Ben-Ami, "Customs of Pregnancy and Childbirth among Sephardic and Oriental Jews," in *New Horizons in Sephardic Studies*, ed. Yedida Stillman and George K. Zucker (Albany: State University of New York Press, 1992), pp. 253–267.

Michael Berkowitz, *Zionist Culture and Western Jewry before the First World War* (Cambridge: Cambridge University Press, 1993).

Selma Berrol, *East Side/East End: Eastern European Jews in London and New York 1870–1920* (Westport, Conn.: Praeger, 1994).

———, "Education and Economic Mobility: The Jewish Experience in New York City, 1880–1920," *American Jewish Historical Quarterly* 65, no. 3 (March 1976): 257–271.

Sara Bershel and Allen Graubard, *Saving Remnants: Feeling Jewish in America* (New York: Free Press, 1992).

Bruno Bettelheim, *The Children of the Dream* (New York: Avon, 1970).

David Biale, "Blood Libels and Blood Vengeance," *Tikkun* (July/August 1994): 39–40 and 75.

———, "Eros and Enlightenment: Love Against Marriage in the East European Jewish Enlightenment," *Polin* 1 (1986): 49–67.

Louis Birner, "Some Speculations on the Emotional Resources of the Jewish Family," in *The Jewish Family in a Changing World*, ed. Gilbert S. Rosenthal (New York: Thomas Yoseloff, 1971), pp. 307–320.

Eugene C. Black, *The Social Politics of Anglo-Jewry 1880–1920* (Oxford: Basil Blackwell, 1988).

Gerry Black, *Living West: Jewish Life in London's West End* (London: London Museum of Jewish Life, 1994).

Zena Smith Blau, "The Strategy of the Jewish Mother," in *The Jew in American Society*, ed. Marshall Sklare (New York: Behrman House, 1974), pp. 167–187.

Gerald Blidstein, *Honor Thy Father and Mother: Filial Responsibility in Jewish Law and Ethics* (New York: Ktav, 1975).

B. Blumenkranz, *Quelques notations démographiques sur les Juifs de Rome des premiers siecles*, in *Studia Patristica*, ed. F. L. Cross (Berlin: Akademie-Verlag, 1961), Vol. 4, Part 2, pp. 341–347.

Max Bodenheimer, *Prelude to Israel: The Memoirs of M. I. Bodenheimer* (New York: Thomas Yoseloff, 1963).

Robert Bonfil, *Jewish Life in Renaissance Italy* (Berkeley and Los Angeles: University of California Press, 1994).

John Boswell, *The Kindness of Strangers: The Abandonment of Children in Western Europe from Late Antiquity to the Renaissance* (New York: Pantheon Books, 1988).

Keith R. Bradley, *Discovering the Roman Family: Studies in Roman Social History* (New York: Oxford University Press, 1991).

Erich Brauer, *The Jews of Kurdistan* (Detroit: Wayne State University Press, 1993).

A. J. Brawer, "Study and Play in the Heders of Galicia," (Hebrew) *Edoth* 2, no. 1–2 (October 1946–January 1947): 72–91.

Mordechai Breuer, *Modernity within Tradition: The Social History of Orthodox Jewry in Imperial Germany* (New York: Columbia University Press, 1992).

Herbert Chanan Brichto, "Kin, Cult, Land and Afterlife—A Biblical Complex," *HUC Annual* 44 (1973): 1–54.

Stephan A. Brumberg, *Going to America: Going to School: The Jewish Immigrant Public School Encounter in Turn-of-Century New York City* (New York: Praeger, 1986).

Sidney Bunt, *Jewish Youth Work in Britain: Past, Present and Future* (London: Bedford Square Press, 1975).

Daniel Burston, *The Legacy of Erich Fromm* (Cambridge, Mass.: Harvard University Press, 1991).

Robert Chazan, *European Jewry in the First Crusade* (Berkeley and Los Angeles: University of California Press, 1987).

David Cesarani, *Zionism in England 1917–1939*, D. Phil. Thesis, Oxford, 1986.

Gregory C. Chirichigno, *Debt-Slavery in Israel and the Ancient Near East* (Sheffield: JSOT Press, 1993).

Samuel Chotzinoff, *A Lost Paradise: Early Reminiscences* (London: Hamish Hamilton, 1956).

Hannah F. Cohen, *Changing Faces: A Memoir of Louisa Lady Cohen* (London: Martin Hopkinson, 1937).

Jeremy Cohen, *Be Fertile and Increase: Fill the Earth and Master It: The Ancient and Medieval Career of a Biblical Text* (Ithaca, N.Y.: Cornell University Press, 1989).

Lucy Cohen, *Lady De Rothschild and her Daughters 1821–1931* (London: John Murray, 1935).

Mark R. Cohen, trans. and ed., *The Autobiography of a Seventeenth-Century Venetian: Rabbi Leon Modena's Life of Judah* (Princeton, N.J.: Princeton University Press, 1988).

Gretchen A. Condran and Ellen A. Kamarow, "Child Mortality Among Jewish Immigrants to the United States," *Journal of Interdisciplinary History* 22, no. 2 (Autumn 1991): 223–254.

Neil M. Cowan and Ruth Schwartz Cowan, *Our Parents' Lives: The Americanization of Eastern European Jews* (New York: Basic Books, 1989).

Peter Cramer, *Baptism and Change in the Early Middle Ages c. 200–1150* (Cambridge: Cambridge University Press, 1993).

James L. Crenshaw, "Education in Ancient Israel," *Journal of Biblical Literature* 104, no. 4 (December 1985): 601–615.

Doris Groshen Daniels, "Colonial Jewry: Religion, Domestic and Family Relations," *American Jewish Historical Quarterly* 66, no. 3 (March 1977): 375–400.

John Day, *Molech, A God of Human Sacrifice in the Old Testament* (Cambridge: Cambridge University Press, 1989).

Luke Demaitre, "The Idea of Childhood and Child Care in the Medical Writings of the Middle Ages," *Journal of Psychohistory* 4, no. 4 (Spring 1977): 461–490.

Lloyd deMause, *The History of Childhood* (London: Souvenir Press, 1976).

Suzanne Dixon, *The Roman Mother* (London: Routledge, 1990).

Deborah Dwork, "Health Conditions of Immigrant Jews on the Lower East Side of New York City: 1880–1914," *Medical History* 25, no. 1 (1981): 1–40.

Eliezer Ebner, *Elementary Education in Ancient Israel During the Tannaitic Period (10–220 C.E.)* (New York: Bloch Publishing, 1956).

Howard Eilberg-Schwartz, *The Savage in Judaism: An Anthropology of Israelite Religion and Ancient Judaism* (Bloomington and Indianapolis: Indiana University Press, 1990).

George Eisen, *The Maccabiah Games: A History of the Jewish Olympics*, Ph.D. Thesis, University of Maryland, 1979.

Robert Étienne, "Ancient Medical Conscience and the Life of Children," *Journal of Psychohistory* 4, no. 2 (Fall 1976): 131–161.

Frank Eyck, "A Diarist in Fin-de-siecle Berlin and Her Family: Helene, Joseph and Erich Eyck," *Leo Baeck Institute Year Book* 37 (1992): 287–307.

Morris M. Faierstein, "The *Liebes Brief*: A Critique of Jewish Society in Germany (1749)," *Leo Baeck Institute Year Book* 27 (1982): 219–242.

Ze'ev W. Falk, *Introduction to Jewish Law of the Second Commonwealth* (Leiden: E. J. Brill, 1978), Part 2.

——, *Jewish Matrimonial Law in the Middle Ages* (Oxford: Oxford University Press, 1966).

William Moses Feldman, *The Child, Its Rearing, Development and Ailments* (Yiddish) (London: E. W. Rabbinowicz, 1907).

——, *The Jewish Child: Its History, Folklore, Biology & Sociology* (London: Balliere, Tindall and Cox, 1917).

——, *A Manual of Nursery Hygiene* (London: Bailliere, Tindall and Cox, 1910).

Lewis S. Feuer, *The Conflict of Generations: The Character and Significance of Student Movements* (London: Heinemann, 1969).

Valerie Fildes, *Wet Nursing: A History from Antiquity to the Present* (Oxford: Basil Blackwell, 1988).

Maurice Fishberg, *The Jews: A Study of Race and Environment* (New York: Walter Scott Publishing, 1911).

Isidore Fishman, *The History of Jewish Education in Central Europe: From the End of the Sixteenth Century to the End of the Eighteenth Century* (London: Edward Goldston, 1944).

Jean-Louis Flandrin, *Families in Former Times: Kinship, Household and Sexuality* (Cambridge: Cambridge University Press, 1979).

Joseph Fleishman, "Offences against Parents Punishable by Death," *The Jewish Law Annual* 10 (1992): 7–37.

Jonathan Frankel, *Prophecy and Politics: Socialism, Nationalism & the Russian Jews 1862–1917* (Cambridge: Cambridge University Press, 1981).

Solomon B. Freehof, "Ceremonial Creativity Among the Ashkenazim," in *The Seventy-Fifth Anniversary Volume of the Jewish Quarterly Review* (1967): 210–223.

Albert Fried, *The Rise and Fall of the Jewish Gangster in America* (New York: Columbia University Press, 1993).

Mordechai Frishtik, "Physical Violence by Parents against Their Children in Jewish History and Jewish Law," *The Jewish Law Annual* 10 (1992): 79–97.

Myrna Katz Frommer and Harvey Frommer, *It Happened in Brooklyn: An Oral History of Growing Up in the Borough in the 1940s, 1950s, and 1960s* (New York: Harcourt Brace, 1993).

Arthur Galliner, "The Philanthropin in Frankfurt: Its Educational and Cultural Significance for German Jewry," *Leo Baeck Institute Year Book* 3 (1958): 169–186.

Herbert J. Gans, *The Levittowners: Ways of Life and Politics in a New Suburban Community* (London: Allen Lane the Penguin Press, 1967).

——, "The Origin and Growth of a Jewish Community in the Suburbs: A Study of the Jews of Park Forest," in *The Jews: Social Patterns of an American Group*, ed. Marshall Sklare (New York: Free Press, 1967), pp. 205–248.

Jacques Gélis, *History of Childbirth: Fertility, Pregnancy and Birth in Early Modern Europe* (Oxford: Polity Press, 1991).

Avner Gil`adi, *Children of Islam: Concepts of Childhood in Medieval Muslim Society* (London: Macmillan, 1992).

——, "Concepts of Childhood and Attitudes towards Children in Medieval Islam . . . with Special Reference to Reactions to Infant and Child Mortality," *Journal of the Economic and Social History of the Orient*, Part 2 (June 1989): 121–152.

——, "*Sabr* (Steadfastness) of Bereaved Parents: A Motif in Medieval Muslim Consolation Treatises and Some Parallels in Jewish Writings," *Jewish Quarterly Review* 80, no. 1–2 (July–October 1989): 35–48.

Nathan Glazer, "The American Jew and the Attainment of Middle Class Rank: Some Trends and Explanations," in *The Jews: Social Patterns of an American Group*, ed. Marshall Sklare (New York: Free Press, 1967), pp. 138–146.

David L. Gohaller, "From Ritual to Science: The Medical Transformation of Circumcision in America," *Journal of Social History* 28, no. 1 (Fall 1994): 5–36.

S. D. Goitein, "Jewish Education in Yemen," in *Between Past and Future: Essays and Studies on Aspects of Immigrant Absorption in Israel*, ed. Carl Frankenstein (Jerusalem: Henrietta Szold Foundation for Child and Youth Welfare, 1953).

——, *A Mediterranean Society: The Community* (Berkeley and Los Angeles: University of California Press, 1971), Vol. 2.

——, *A Mediterranean Society: The Family* (Berkeley and Los Angeles: University of California Press, 1978), Vol. 3.

Michael Gold, *Jews Without Money* (New York: Carroll and Graff, 1984).

Mark Golden, *Children and Childhood in Classical Athens* (Baltimore: Johns Hopkins University Press, 1993).

Judah Goldin, *Studies in Midrash and Related Literature*, ed. Barry Eichler and Jeffrey H. Tigay (Philadelphia: Jewish Publication Society, 1988).

Calvin Goldscheider and Alan S. Zuckerman, *The Transformation of the Jews* (Chicago: University of Chicago Press, 1984).

Sydney Goldstein and Calvin Goldscheider, *Jewish Americans: Three Generations in a Jewish Community* (Englewood Cliffs, N.J.: Prentice-Hall, 1968).

Cary Goodman, *Choosing Sides: Playground and Street Life on the Lower East Side* (New York: Schocken Books, 1979).

Robert Gordis, "'Be Fruitful and Multiply'—A Biography of a Mitzvah," *Midstream* 28, no. 7 (Aug./Sept. 1982): 21–29.

Albert I. Gordon, *Jews in Suburbia* (Boston: Beacon Press, 1959).

——, *Jews in Transition* (Minneapolis: University of Minnesota Press, 1949).

Harvey J. Graff, *Conflicting Paths: Growing Up in America* (Cambridge, Mass.: Harvard University Press, 1995).

Michael Gray-Fow, "Pederasty, the Scantinian Law, and the Roman Army," *Journal of Psychohistory* 13, no. 4 (Spring 1986): 448–460.

Solomon Grayzel, *The Church and the Jews in the 13th Century: A Study of Their Relations During the Years 1198–1254 Based on the Papal Letters and the Conciliar Decrees of the Period* (New York: Hermon Press, 1966).

Joseph Gutmann, *The Jewish Life Cycle* (Leiden: E. J. Brill, 1987).

Zvi Halevy, *Jewish Schools Under Czarism and Communism: A Struggle for Cultural Identity* (New York: Springer, 1976).

Arthur Hanak, *Physical Education of Jews in the Middle Ages & Early Modern Times* (Tel Aviv: Maccabi World Union, 1987).

Barbara A. Hanawalt, *Growing Up in Medieval London: The Experience of Childhood History* (New York: Oxford University Press, 1993).

Andrew Handler, *From the Ghetto to the Games: Jewish Athletes in Hungary* (New York: Columbia University Press, 1985).

Oscar Handlin, *Race and Nationality in American Life* (Garden City, N.Y.: Doubleday Anchor Books, 1957).

George C. Heider, *The Cult of Molek: A Reassessment* (Sheffield: JSOT Press, 1985).

Robert W. Henderson, "Moses Provencal on Tennis," *Jewish Quarterly Review* New Series 26 (1935–1936): 1–6.

Arthur Hertzberg, *The Jews in America: Four Centuries of an Uneasy Encounter: A History* (New York: Simon and Schuster, 1989).

Patricia Hidiroglou, "*Langes De Circoncision Histories En France*," *Revue des Études Juives* 143 (Jan.–Juin 1984): 113–134.

Keith Hopkins, "Everyday Life for the Roman Schoolboy," *History Today* (October 1993).

William Horbury and David Noy, *Jewish Inscriptions of Graeco-Roman Egypt* (Cambridge: Cambridge University Press, 1992).

Elliott Horowitz, "The Eve of Circumcision: A Chapter in the History of Jewish Nightlife," *Journal of Social History* 23, no. 1 (1989): 45–69.

———, "A Jewish Youth Confraternity in Seventeenth Century Italy," *Italia* 5:1–2 (1985): 36–97.

———, "The Way We Were: Jewish Life in the Middle Ages," *Jewish History* 1, no. 1 (Spring 1986): 75–90.

Pieter W. Van Der Horst, *Ancient Jewish Epitaphs: An Introductory Survey of a Millenium of Jewish Funeral Epigraphy (300 B.C.E.–700 C.E.)* (Kampen the Netherlands: Kok Pharos Publishing House, 1991).

Irving Howe, *A Margin of Hope: An Intellectual Autobiography* (London: Secker and Warburg, 1983).

R. Po-chia Hsia, *The Myth of Ritual Murder: Jews and Magic in Reformation Germany* (New Haven: Yale University Press, 1988).

A. G. Hughes, "Jews and Gentiles, Their Intellectual and Temperamental Differences," *Eugenics Review* (July 1928): 89–94.

Gershon David Hundert, "Approaches to the History of the Jewish Family in Early Modern Poland-Lithuania," in *The Jewish Family: Myths and Reality*, ed. Steven M. Cohen and Paula E. Hyman (New York: Holmes and Meier, 1966), pp. 17–28.

Gershon David Hundert, "Jewish Children and Childhood in Early Modern East Central Europe," in *The Jewish Family: Metaphor and Memory*, ed. David Kraemer (New York: Oxford University Press, 1989), pp. 81–94.

Paula E. Hyman, "The Introduction of Bat Mitzvah in Conservative Judaism in Postwar America," *Yivo Annual* 19 (1990): 133–146.

Norbert Kampe, "Jews and Antisemites in Universities in Imperial Germany (1): Jewish Students: Social History and Social Conflict," *Leo Baeck Institute Year Book* 19 (1985): 357–394.

Ephraim Kanarfogel, "Attitudes Towards Childhood and Children in Medieval Jewish Society," in *Approaches to Judaism in Medieval Times*, ed. David R. Blumenthal (Chico, Calif.: Scholars Press, 1985), pp. 1–34.

Ephraim Kanarfogel, *Jewish Education and Society in the High Middle Ages* (Detroit: Wayne State University Press, 1992).

Marion A. Kaplan, *The Making of the Jewish Middle Class: Women, Family, and Identity in Imperial Germany* (New York: Oxford University Press, 1991).

Mordecai M. Kaplan and Bernard Cronson, "First Community Survey of Jewish Education in New York City—1909," *Jewish Education* 20, no. 3 (Summer 1949): 113–116.

Donald Katz, *Home Fires: An Intimate Portrait of One Middle-Class Family in Postwar America* (New York: HarperCollins, 1992).

Victor Keats, *Chess, Jews and History* (Oxford: Academia Publishers, 1994).

Adolf Kober, "Emancipation's Impact on the Education and Vocational Training of German Jewry," *Jewish Social Studies* 16, no. 1 (1954): 3–32 and 16, no. 2 (April 1954): 151–176.

Jacob Kohn, *Modern Problems of Jewish Parents* (New York: Women's League of the United Synagogue of America, 1932).

Samuel Kottek, "Care of Children in the Bible and Talmud," *Koroth* 7, no. 5–6 (1977): 427–436.

——, "Childhood in Medieval Jewry as Depicted in *Sefer Hasidim* (12th–13th Century): Medical, Psychological and Educational Aspects," *Koroth* 8, no. 9–10 (August 1984): 376–395.

——, "On Children and Childhood in Ancient Jewish Sources," *Koroth* 9, no. 5–6 (1987): 452–471.

David Kraemer, "Images of Childhood and Adolescence in Talmudic Literature," in *The Jewish Family: Metaphor and Memory*, ed. David Kraemer (New York: Oxford University Press, 1989).

Judith Kramer and Seymour Leventman, *Children of the Gilded Ghetto: Conflict Resolution of Three Generations of American Jews* (New Haven: Yale University Press, 1961).

Ruth Landes and Mark Zborowski, "Hypotheses Concerning the Eastern European Jewish Family," in *The Psychodynamics of the American Jewish Family: An Anthology*, ed. Norman Kiell (New York: Twayne Publishers, 1967), pp. 23–55.

Gavin I. Langmuir, *Towards a Definition of Antisemitism* (Berkeley and Los Angeles: University of California Press, 1990).

Walter Laqueur, "The German Youth Movement and the 'Jewish Question,'" *Leo Baeck Institute Year Book* 6 (1961): 193–205.

Israel Lebendiger, "The Minor in Jewish Law," in *Studies in Jewish Jurisprudence*, ed. Edward Gershfield (New York: Hermon Press, 1971), pp. 94–180.

Anita Libman Lebeson, *Jewish Pioneers in America 1492–1848* (New York: Brentano Publishers, 1931).

Jeremy Leigh, *A History of Habonim in England 1948–1950*, M.A. Thesis, University College London, 1990.

André Lemaire, "*Sagesse et Ecoles*," *Vetus Testamentum* 34, no. 3 (1984): 270–281.

Harry Joshua Leon, *The Jews of Ancient Rome* (Philadelphia: Jewish Publication Society, 1960).

Salmond S. Levin, "The Changing Pattern of Jewish Education," in *A Century of Anglo-Jewish Life 1870–1970*, ed. Salmond S. Levin (London: United Synagogue, 1970), pp. 57–73.

Shmarya Levin, *Childhood in Exile* (London: George Routledge, 1935).

——, *Youth in Revolt* (London: George Routledge, 1935).

Peter Levine, "The American Hebrew Looks at 'Our Crowd': The Jewish Country Club in the 1920s," *American Jewish History* 83, no. 1 (March 1995): 27–49.

——, *Ellis Island to Ebbets Field: Sport and the American Jewish Experience* (New York: Oxford University Press, 1992).

Saul Lieberman, *Hellenism in Jewish Palestine: Studies in the Literary Transmission Beliefs and Manners of Palestine in the 1st Century B.C.E.–4th Century C.E.* (New York: Jewish Theological Seminary of America, 1950).

——, *Texts and Studies* (New York: Ktav, 1974).

Regina Liliental, "*Das Kind bei den Juden,*" *Mitteilungen zur Judischen Volkskunde* 25, no. 1 (1908): 1–24 and 26, no. 2 (1908): 41–55.

J. M. Lilley, G. Stroud, D. R. Brothwell, and M. H. Williamson, *The Jewish Burial Ground at Jewbury York* (York: York Archaeological Trust, 1994).

Rosalyn Livshin, "The Acculturation of the Children of Immigrant Jews in Manchester 1890–1930," in *The Making of Modern Anglo-Jewry,* ed. David Cesarani (Oxford: Basil Blackwell, 1990): 79–96.

Laurence D. Loeb, *Outcaste: Jewish Life in Southern Iran* (New York: Gordon and Breach, 1977).

Leopold Löw, *Die Lebensalter in Der Jüdischen Literatur* (Szegedin, 1875).

Steven M. Lowenstein, *The Berlin Jewish Community: Enlightenment, Family and Crisis, 1770–1830* (New York: Oxford University Press, 1994).

———, *Frankfurt on the Hudson: The German-Jewish Community of Washington Heights 1933–1983* (Detroit: Wayne State University Press, 1989).

Mary Martin McLaughlin, "Survivors and Surrogates," in *The History of Childhood,* ed. Lloyd deMause (London: Souvenir Press, 1974), pp. 101–181.

Ivan G. Marcus, "Jewish Schools in Medieval Europe," *Melton Journal* 21 (Winter 1987): 4–6.

———, *Rituals of Childhood: Jewish Acculturation in Medieval Europe* (New Haven: Yale University Press, 1996).

D. Margalit, "Dr Moshe Studentsky and His Book, '*Rofe Hayeladim*' (1804–1883)," *Koroth* 4, no. 5–7 (December 1988): 363–388.

Elkana Margalit, "Social and Intellectual Origins of Hashomer Hazair Youth Movement, 1913–20," *Journal of Contemporary History* 4, no. 2 (April 1969): 25–46.

Lara V. Marks, *Model Mothers: Jewish Mothers and Maternity Provision in East London 1870–1939* (Oxford: Clarendon Press, 1994).

H. I. Marrou, *A History of Education in Antiquity* (New York: Mentor Books, 1964).

Shoshana Matzner-Bekerman, *The Jewish Child: Halakhic Perspectives* (New York: Ktav, 1984).

Paul Yogi Mayer, "Equality—Egality Jews and Sport in Germany," *Leo Baeck Institute Year Book* 25 (1980): 221–241.

Alan Mendelson, *Secular Education in Philo of Alexandria* (Cincinnati: Hebrew Union College Press, 1982).

Abraham Menes, "Patterns of Jewish Scholarship in Eastern Europe," in *The Jews: Their Religion and Culture*, ed. Louis Finkelstein (New York: Schocken Books, 1975), pp. 177–227.

Therese and Mendel Metzger, *Jewish Life in the Middle Ages* (London: Alpine Fine Arts Collection, 1985).

Carol Meyers, *Discovering Eve: Ancient Israelite Women in Context* (New York: Oxford University Press, 1991).

Michael Mitterauer, *A History of Youth* (Oxford: Blackwell, 1992).

Arnaldo Momigliano, "A Medieval Jewish Autobiography," in *History and Imagination: Essays in Honour of H. R. Trevor-Roper*, ed. Hugh Lloyd-Jones, Valerie Pearl, and Blair Worden (London: Duckworth, 1981), pp. 30–36.

Deborah Dash Moore, *At Home in America: Second Generation New York Jews* (New York: Columbia University Press, 1981).

Nathan Morris, *The Jewish School: An Introduction to the History of Jewish Education* (London: Eyre and Spottiswoode, 1937).

George L. Mosse, *Germans and Jews* (London: Orbach and Chambers, 1971).

Meir Munk, *Sparing the Rod, a Torah Perspective on Reward and Punishment in Education* (Bnei Brak: Mishor Publishing, 1989).

Sussmann Muntner, "Physical Training in the Talmud and Bible," *Koroth* 9, no. 11–12 (1991): 855–865.

J. Clark Murray, trans., *The Autobiography of Solomon Maimon* (London: East and West Library, 1954).

David Nasaw, *Children of the City: At Work and at Play* (Garden City, N.Y.: Anchor Press, 1985.

Joseph Naveh and Shaul Shaked, *Amulets and Magic Bowls: Aramaic Incantations of Late Antiquity* (Jerusalem: Magnes Press, 1987).

Irving Osborne, "Jewish Junior County Awards in East London Schools, 1893–1914," (London: Centre for East London Studies, Queen Mary College, 1988).

Steven Ozment, *When Fathers Ruled: Family Life in Reformation Europe* (Cambridge, Mass.: Harvard University Press, 1983).

Bahaya Ben Joseph Ibn Paquda, *The Book of Directions of Duties of the Heart*, trans. Menahem Mansoor (London: Routledge and Kegan Paul, 1992).

Joseph Patai, *The Middle Gate: A Hungarian Jewish Boyhood* (Philadelphia: Jewish Publication Society, 1994).

Raphael Patai, *Apprentice in Budapest* (Salt Lake City: University of Utah Press, 1988).

———, *Family, Love and the Bible* (London: MacGibbon and Kee, 1960).

———, *On Jewish Folklore* (Detroit: Wayne State University Press, 1983).

David Patterson, *The Hebrew Novel* (Edinburgh: Edinburgh University Press, 1964).

Karl Pearson and Margaret Moul, "The Problem of Alien Immigration into Great Britain, Illustrated by an Examination of Russian and Polish Jewish Children," *Annals of Eugenics* 1 (October 1925): 1–128.

Derek J. Penslar, *Zionism and Technocracy: The Engineering of Jewish Settlement in Palestine 1870–1918* (Bloomington: Indiana University Press, 1991).

Joel Perlmann, *Ethnic Differences, Schooling and Social Structure Among the Irish, Italians, Jews and Blacks in an American City, 1880–1935* (Cambridge: Cambridge University Press, 1988).

Joseph C. Pick, "Sports," in *The Jews of Czechoslovakia* (Philadelphia: Jewish Publication Society, 1971), Vol. 2, pp. 185–228.

J. H. Plumb, "The New World of Children," *The Listener* (26 February 1976).

———, "The New World of Children in Eighteenth-Century England," *Past and Present* 67 (1975): 64–95.

Herman Pollack, *Jewish Folkways in Germanic Lands 1648–1806* (Cambridge, Mass.: M.I.T. Press, 1971).

Linda A. Pollock, *Forgotten Children: Parent-Child Relations from 1500–1900* (Cambridge: Cambridge University Press, 1983).

Jeffrey Potter, *Men, Money and Magic: the Story of Dorothy Schiff* (New York: Coward, McCann and Geoghegan, 1976).

Julius Preuss, *Biblical and Talmudic Medicine*, trans. Fred Rosner (New York: Hebrew Publishing, 1983).

Louis Rabinowitz, *The Social Life of the Jews of Northern France in the 12th and 14th Centuries as Reflected in the Rabbinical Literature of the Period* (London: Edward Goldston, 1938).

Freddy Raphael, "Rites de naissance et medecine populaire dans le judaisme rural d'Alsace," *Revue de la Societe d'ethnographie francaise* 1, no. 3–4 (1971): 83–94.

Angelo S. Rappoport, *The Folklore of the Jews* (London: Soncino Press, 1937).

Beryl Rawson, "The Roman Family," in *The Family in Ancient Rome*, ed. Beryl Rawson (London: Routledge, 1992), pp. 1–57.

Jehuda Reinharz, "Hashomer Hazair in Germany (1)," *Leo Baeck Insti-*

tute Year Book 31 (1986): 173–208 and Part II, "Under the Shadow of the Swastika," *Leo Baeck Institute Year Book* 32 (1987): 183–229.

Monika Richarz ed. and trans. Stella P. Rosenfeld and Sidney Rosenfeld, *Jewish Life in Germany: Memoirs from Three Centuries* (Bloomington: Indiana University Press, 1991).

Jack Riemer and Nathaniel Stampfer, ed., *Ethical Wills: A Modern Jewish Treasury* (New York: Schocken Books, 1983).

Steven A. Riess, "A Fighting Chance: The Jewish-American Boxing Experience, 1890–1940," *American Jewish History* 74, no. 3 (March 1985): 223–254.

Chanoch Rinott, "Major Trends in Youth Movements in Germany," *Leo Baeck Institute Year Book* 19 (1974): 77–95.

Isaac Rivkind, *Le-Ot u-le-Zikkaron: Bar Mitzvah: A Study in Cultural History* (Hebrew) (New York, 1942).

Zefira Entin Rokeah, "Unnatural Child Death Among Christians and Jews in Medieval England," *Journal of Psychohistory* 18, no. 2 (Fall 1990): 201–226.

Diane Roskies, "Alphabet Instruction in the East European Heder: Some Comparative and Historical Notes," *Yivo Annual* 17 (1978): 21–53.

Cecil Roth, "Bar Mitzvah—Its History and Its Association," in *Bar Mitzvah*, ed. Abraham I. Katsh (New York: Shengold Publishers, 1955).

——, *Gleanings: Essays in Jewish History, Letters, and Art* (New York: Hermon Press, 1967).

——, *The Jews in the Rennaissance* (New York: Harper and Row, 1959).

Naftali Zvi Roth, "The Torah Education of Children at Pentecost," (Hebrew) *Yeda-'Am* 11, no. 30 (Autumn 1965): 9–12.

Norman Roth, "'Deal Gently with the Young Man': Love of Boys in Medieval Hebrew Poetry of Spain," *Speculum* 57, no. 1 (1982): 20–51.

Gladys Rothbell, "The Jewish Mother: Social Construction of a Popular Image," in *The Jewish Family: Myths and Reality*, ed. Steven M. Cohen and Paula Hyman (New York: Holmes and Meier, 1986), pp. 118–128.

Marsha L. Rozenblit, *The Jews of Vienna 1867–1914* (Albany: State University of New York Press, 1983).

Nissan Rubin, *The Beginning of Life: Rites of Birth, Circumcision and Redemption of the First-Born in the Talmud and Midrash* (Hebrew) (Israel: Hakkibutz Hameuchad, 1995).

Arthur Ruppin, *The Jews of Today* (London: G. Bell, 1913).

——, *Memoirs, Diaries, Letters* (London: Weidenfeld and Nicholson, 1971).

Miriam Russo-Katz, "Childbirth," in *Sephardi Jews in the Ottoman Empire: Aspects of Material Culture*, ed. Esther Juhasz (Jerusalem: Israel Museum, 1990), pp. 254–270.

Shmuel Safrai, "Elementary Education, Its Religious and Social Significance in the Talmudic Period," in *Jewish Society Through the Ages*, ed. H. H. Ben-Sasson and S. Ettinger (London: Vallentine Mitchell, 1971).

S. Safrai and M. Stern, ed., *The Jewish People in the First Century, Historical Geography, Political History, Social, Cultural and Religious Life and Institutions* (Assen: Van Gorcum, 1976), Vol. 2.

Ze'ev Safrai, "Family Structure During the Period of the Mishnah and Talmud," *Milet* 1 (1983): 129–156.

Victor D. Sanua, "The Contemporary Jewish Family: A Review of the Social Science Literature," in *Serving the Jewish Family*, ed. Gerald B. Bubis (New York: Ktav, 1977).

Jacob Joseph Schacter, *Rabbi Jacob Emden: Life and Major Works*, Harvard Ph.D. Thesis, 1988, Vol. 1.

Simon Schama, *The Embarrassment of Riches: An Interpretation of Dutch Culture in the Golden Age* (London: Fontana Press, 1988).

Chaim Schatzker, "The Jewish Youth Movement in Germany in the Holocaust Period (I): Youth in Confrontation with a New Reality," *Leo Baeck Institute Year Book* 32 (1987): 157–181 and Part II, "The Relations Between the Youth Movement and Hechalutz," *Leo Baeck Institute Year Book* 33 (1988): 301–325.

———, "The Jewish Youth Movements as an Historical Phenomenon," in *Sects, Religious Movements, and Political Parties*, ed. Menachem Mor (Omaha, Neb.: Creighton University Press, 1992), pp. 149–164.

———, "Martin Buber's Influence on the Jewish Youth Movement in Germany," *Leo Baeck Institute Year Book* 23 (1978): 151–171.

Hayyim Schauss, *The Lifetime of a Jew* (New York: Union of American Hebrew Congregations, 1967.

Solomon Schechter, "The Child in Jewish Literature," in *Studies in Judaism*, First Series (Philadelphia: Jewish Publication Society, 1945), pp. 282–312.

U. O. Schmelz, *Infant and Early Child Mortality Among the Jews of the Diaspora* (Jerusalem: Institute of Contemporary Jewry, 1971).

Julius H. Schoeps, "Modern Heirs of the Maccabees: The Beginning of the Vienna Kadimah, 1882–1897," *Leo Baeck Institute Year Book* 27 (1982): 159–170.

James A. Schultz, "Medieval Adolescence: The Claims of History and the Silence of German Narrative," *Speculum* 66 (1991): 519–539.

Magdalene Schultz, "The Blood Libel: A Motif in the History of Childhood,"
in *The Blood Libel Legend*, ed. Alan Dundes (Madison: University of
Wisconsin Press, 1991), pp. 273–303.

Emil Schurer, *The History of the Jewish People in the Age of Jesus
Christ*, ed. Geza Vermes, Fergus Millar, and Matthew Black (Edinburgh:
T. and T. Clark, 1986), Vol. 2.

Gwen Gibson Schwartz and Barbara Wyden, *The Jewish Wife* (New York:
Peter H. Wyden, 1969).

Leo W. Schwarz, *Memoirs of My People: Jewish Self-Portraits from
the 11th to the 20th Centuries* (New York: Schocken Books, 1963).

W. Victor Sefton, "Growing up Jewish in London 1920–1950: A Perspective from 1973," in *Studies in the Cultural Life of the Jews in
England*, ed. Dov Noy and Issachar Ben-Ami (Jerusalem: Magnes Press,
1975), pp. 311–330.

Shulamith Shahar, *Childhood in the Middle Ages* (London: Routledge,
1992).

Nissim ben Jacob Ibn Shahin, *An Elegant Composition Concerning
Relief after Adversity*, trans. William M. Brinner (New Haven: Yale
University Press, 1977).

Avraham Shapira, "Buber's Attachment to Herder and German 'Volkism,'"
Studies in Zionism 14, no. 1 (Spring 1993): 1–30.

Zohar Shavit, "From Friedlander's Lesebuch to the Jewish Campe: The
Beginnings of Hebrew Children's Literature in Germany," *Leo Baeck
Institute Year Book* 33 (1988): 385–415.

Yekhiel Shtern, "A Kheyder in Tyszowie (Tishevits)," in *East European Jews
in Two Worlds: Studies from the Yivo Annual*, ed. Deborah Dash
Moore (Evanston, Ill.: Northwestern University Press, 1990), pp. 51–70.

Helen Silman-Cheong, *Wellesley Aron: Rebel with a Cause: A Memoir*
(London: Vallentine Mitchell, 1987).

Marshall Sklare, *America's Jews* (New York: Random House, 1971).

Miriam Slater, "My Son the Doctor: Aspects of Mobility Among American Jews," *American Sociological Review* 34 (1969): 359–373.

Naomi B. Sokoloff, *The Child in Modern Jewish Fiction* (Baltimore: Johns
Hopkins University Press, 1992).

Gerald Sorin, *The Nurturing Neighbourhood: The Brownsville Boys
Club and the Jewish Community in Urban America 1940–1949*
(New York: New York University Press, 1990).

——, "Street Corner Jews: The Boys of Brownsville," *Yivo Annual* 19
(1990): 37–56.

David Sorkin, *The Transformation of German Jewry 1780–1840* (New York: Oxford University Press, 1987).

Daniel Sperber, "On the Drinking of Wine During the Circumcision," (Hebrew) *Milet* 1 (1983): 221–224.

Lawrence E. Stager, "The Archaeology of the Family in Ancient Israel," *Bulletin of the American Schools of Oriental Research* 260 (1985): 1–36.

———, "Infanticide at Ashkeleon," *Biblical Archaeology Review* 17, no. 4 (July–Aug. 1991): 35–53 and 72.

Abraham Stahl, "Children and Childhood in the View of the Traditional Jewish-Oriental Family," *Journal of Comparative Family Studies* 9 (1978): 347–354.

———, *Family and Child-rearing in Oriental Jewry: Sources, References, Comparisons* (Hebrew) (Jerusalem: Academon, 1993).

———, "Parents' Attitudes Towards the Death of Infants in the Traditional Jewish-Oriental Family," *Journal of Comparative Family Studies* 22, no. 1 (Spring 1991): 75–83.

———, "Swaddling: Its Disappearance as an Illustration of the Process of Cultural Change," *Koroth* 8, no. 1–2 (June 1981): 285–297.

Shaul Stampfer, "Gender Differentiation and Education of the Jewish Woman in Nineteenth-Century Eastern Europe," *Polin* 7 (1992): 63–87.

———, "*Heder* Study, Knowledge of Torah, and the Maintenance of Social Stratification in Traditional East European Jewish Society," in *Studies in Jewish Education*, ed. Janet Aviad (Jerusalem: Magnes Press, 1988), Vol. 3, pp. 271–289.

Michael Stanislawski, *Tsar Nicholas I and the Jews: The Transformation of Jewish Society in Russia 1825–1855* (Philadelphia: Jewish Publication Society, 1983).

Leon Stein, Abraham P. Conan, and Lynn Davison, trans., *The Education of Abraham Cahan* (Philadelphia: Jewish Publication Society, 1969).

Siegfried Stein, "Some Ashkenazi Charities in London at the End of the Eighteenth and the Beginning of the Nineteenth Centuries," *Transactions of the Jewish Historical Society of England* 20 (1964): 63–81.

Fritz Stern, *Gold and Iron: Bismarck, Bleichroder and the Building of the German Empire* (London: George Allen and Unwin, 1981).

Menachem Stern, ed., *Greek and Latin Authors on Jews and Judaism: From Herodotus to Plutarch* (Jerusalem: Israel Academy of Sciences and Humanities, 1974), Vol. 1.

S. E. Stern, "Ceremony of Induction of Children to Education by R. Efraim of Bonn and from the *Sefer Assufot*" (Hebrew), *Zefunot* 1 (1988): 15–21.

Lawrence Stone, *The Family, Sex and Marriage in England 1500–1800* (Harmondsworth: Penguin Books, 1979).

Kenneth Stow, "The Jewish Family in the High Middle Ages: Form and Function," *American Historical Review* (1987): 1085–1110.

Susan L. Tananbaum, "Making Good Little English Children: Infant Welfare and Anglicanization among Jewish Immigrants in London, 1880–1939," *Immigrants and Minorities* 12, no. 2 (July 1993): 176–196.

Stephan Thernstrom, *The Other Bostonians: Poverty and Progress in the American Metropolis, 1880–1970* (Cambridge, Mass.: Harvard University Press, 1973).

Joshua Trachtenberg, *Jewish Magic and Superstition: A Study in Folk Religion* (New York: Atheneum, 1975).

Ephraim E. Urbach, *The Laws Regarding Slavery as a Source for Social History of the Period of the Second Temple, Mishnah and Talmud* (Jerusalem, 1964).

———, "Unintentionally Caused Death and Cradle Death," (Hebrew) *Assufot: Annual for Jewish Studies* 1 (1986–1987): 319–332.

M. Vischnitzer, trans., *Memoirs of Ber of Bolechow (1732–1805)* (London: Humphrey Milford, Oxford University Press, 1922).

Joseph Walk, "The Torah va' Avodah Movement in Germany," *Leo Baeck Institute Year Book* 6 (1961): 236–256.

Sydney Stahl Weinberg, *The World of Our Mothers* (New York: Schocken Books, 1988).

Lee Shai Weissbach, "The Jewish Elite and the Children of the Poor: Jewish Apprenticeship Programs in Nineteenth Century France," *AJS Review* 20, no. 1 (Spring 1987): 123–142.

Shmuel Werses, "Jewish Education in 19th Century Russia," in *Jewish Education and Learning*, ed. Glenda Abramson and Tudor Parfitt (Reading: Harwood Academic Publishers, 1994), pp. 243–260.

Elimelech Westreich, "A Father's Obligation to Maintain His Children in Talmudic Law," *The Jewish Law Annual* 10 (1992): 177–212.

Jerry White, *Rothschild Buildings: Life in an East End Tenement Block 1887–1920* (London: Routledge and Kegan Paul, 1980).

Thomas Wiedemann, *Adults and Children in the Roman Empire* (London: Routledge, 1989).

Stephen Wilson, "The Myth of Motherhood a Myth: The Historical View of European Child-rearing," *Social History* 9, no. 2 (1984): 181–198.

Mark Wischnitzer, *A History of Jewish Crafts and Guilds* (New York: Jonathan David, 1965).

Martha Wolfenstein, "Two Types of Jewish Mothers," in *Childhood in Contemporary Cultures*, ed. Margaret Mead and Martha Wolfenstein (Chicago: University of Chicago Press, 1964), pp. 424–440.

Frances Yates, *The Art of Memory* (London: Plimlico, 1992).

Israel Jacob Yuval, "Vengeance and Damnation, Blood and Defamation: From Jewish Martyrdom to Blood Libel Accusations," *Zion* 58, no. 1 (1993): 39–90.

Mark Zborowski, "The Place of Book-Learning in Traditional Jewish Culture," in *Childhood in Contemporary Cultures*, ed. Margaret Mead and Martha Wolfenstein (Chicago: University of Chicago Press, 1964), pp. 118–141.

Mark Zborowski and Elizabeth Herzog, *Life Is With the People: The Culture of the Shtetl* (New York: Schocken Books, 1978).

Israel Zinberg, *A History of Jewish Literature* (New York: Ktav, 1965–1976), Vols. 6, 7, and 8.

Steven J. Zipperstein, "Transforming the Heder: Maskilic Politics in Imperial Russia," in *Jewish History: Essays in Honour of Chimen Abramsky*, ed. Ada Rapoport-Albert and Steven J. Zipperstein (London: Peter Halban, 1988), pp. 87–109.

Heidi Zogbaum, "Hakoah Wien: Jewish Sport Before 1938," *Australian Journal of Jewish Studies* 8, no. 2 (1994): 44–65.

Shoshana Pantel Zolty, *"And All Your Children Shall Be Learned": Women and the Study of the Torah in Jewish Law and History* (Northvale, N.J.: Jason Aronson, 1993).

Index

Credits

About the Author

John Cooper is a pioneer in the field of Jewish culinary history, and has long been fascinated with many aspects of Jewish social history. He was a lecturer at the first Oxford Symposium on Jewish Food and at the Spiro Jewish Food Conference. He is the author of *Eat and Be Satisfied: A Social History of Jewish Food* (1993) and has also contributed a paper entitled "Jewish Sexual Attitudes in Eastern Europe 1850–1920" to *Jewish Explorations of Sexuality*, edited by Jonathan Magonet (1995). Cooper studied history at Balliol College Oxford, where he received his M.A. He practices law and lives in London with his wife and two children.